Forecasting, structural time series models and the Kalman filter

Forecasting, structural time series models and the Kalman filter

ANDREW C. HARVEY
Department of Statistical and Mathematical Sciences, The London School of Economics and Political Science

CAMBRIDGE UNIVERSITY PRESS
Cambridge
New York Port Chester
Melbourne Sydney

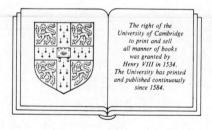

Published by the Press Syndicate of the University of Cambridge
The Pitt Building, Trumpington Street, Cambridge CB2 1RP
40 West 20th Street, New York, NY 10011–4211, USA
10 Stamford Road, Oakleigh, Victoria 3166, Australia

First published 1989
Reprinted 1990
First paperback edition 1990
Reprinted 1991

Printed in Great Britain by Redwood Press Limited,
Melksham, Wiltshire

British Library cataloguing in publication data

Harvey, Andrew C.
Forecasting, structural time series models
and the Kalman filter
1. Time series. Structural models
I. Title
519.5′5

Library of Congress cataloguing in publication data

Harvey, Andrew C.
Forecasting, structural time series models and the Kalman filter/
Andrew C. Harvey.
p. cm.
Bibliography.
Includes index.
ISBN 0-521-32196-4
1. Time-series analysis. 2. Kalman filtering. I. Title.
QA280.H38 1990
519.5′5–dc20 89-31417 CIP

ISBN 0 521 32196 4 hardback
ISBN 0 521 40573 4 paperback

Contents

Figures

Acknowledgement

Table 5.3.1 is reproduced with the permission of the *Journal of the American Statistical Association.*
Tables 5.3.2 and 5.3.3 are reproduced with the permission of the Biometrika Trustees.

Preface

Structural time series models are models which are formulated directly in terms of components of interest. They have a considerable intuitive appeal, particularly for economic and social time series. Furthermore, they provide a clear link with regression models, both in their technical formulation and in the model selection methodology which they employ. The potential of such models is only now beginning to be realised, and it seems to be an appropriate time to write a book which provides a unified view of the area and points the direction towards future research.

The Kalman filter plays a fundamental role in handling structural time series models. This technique was originally developed and exploited in control engineering. It has been increasingly used in areas such as economics, and a good deal of work has been done modifying it for use with small samples. Chapter 3 brings these methods together, and it can be read independently of the material on structural time series models. For those who are primarily interested in carrying out applied work with structural time series models, it should perhaps be stressed that the Kalman filter is simply a statistical algorithm, and it is only necessary to understand what the filter does, rather than how it does it. The same is true of the frequency-domain methods which can be used to construct the likelihood function.

The inclusion of 'forecasting' in the title of the book is perhaps a little rash. It is always very difficult to predict the future on the basis of the past. Indeed it has been likened to driving a car blindfolded while following directions given by a person looking out of the back window. Nevertheless, if this is the best we can do, it is important that it should be done properly, with an appreciation of the potential errors involved. In this way it should at least be possible to negotiate straight stretches of road without a major disaster. Too many forecasting procedures seem to attribute the person in the back seat with supernatural powers when in fact his behaviour is more consistent with that of someone who is mildly inebriated.

Structural time series models are appropriate to many subjects, including economics, sociology, management science and operational research, geography, meteorology and engineering. The emphasis in the book is primarily on economic time series, but examples will be found on such diverse topics as rainfall in Brazil, purse snatching in Chicago, telephone calls from Australia and the effect of the seat belt law in Great Britain. Most of the calculations reported can be carried out on an IBM PC using the program 'STAMP', details of which can be found at the end of chapter 1.

It is assumed that the reader is familiar with statistical theory and with the basic ideas of time series analysis and regression. Certain sections, primarily those dealing with dynamic regression and simultaneous equation systems, presuppose a knowledge of econometrics. Indeed one of the aims of the book is to provide a framework which includes behavioural econometric models as well as the simplest kinds of univariate time series models. On the time series side, it is not necessary to be an expert on what is popularly called Box-Jenkins modelling. In fact this could conceivably be a disadvantage since structural time series modelling starts from a somewhat different point and in doing so challenges some of the underlying assumptions of the Box-Jenkins approach. Nevertheless Box-Jenkins ARIMA models and univariate structural time series models do have a good deal in common in that they are both based on statistical models and are normally handled by classical procedures. As regards mathematics, I assume that the reader is familiar with linear algebra and the calculus but not with more advanced techniques such as measure theory. No attempt is made to provide rigorous proofs on topics such as the asymptotic properties of estimators. The emphasis is on the development of models which can be used in practice, and the way in which such models can be selected.

Many of my students at the LSE have helped in the development and implementation of the ideas presented in this book. I would particularly like to mention Phillipa Todd, Carla Inclan, Luiz Hotta, Lorenzo Figliuoli, Javier Fernández, Neil Shephard, Mariane Streibel, Ester Ruiz, Pablo Marshall and Christiano Fernandes. Simon Peters, who was my research assistant for three years, also played a major role in this respect. Furthermore it was he who developed the software for the STAMP program, and he must take a great deal of the credit for actually putting the methods of structural time series modelling into practice. I have also benefitted considerably from discussions with my colleagues at the LSE, and I am particularly grateful for the advice I have received from Jim Durbin and Peter Robinson. My conversations with Jim Durbin have been especially valuable in providing me with insight into the development of the subject of time series and in convincing me that the structural approach to time series modelling is indeed the best way to proceed. Outside the LSE, I have gained enormously from contacts with Piet de Jong and Jim Stock. In fact many of the ideas on multivariate models and continuous time have come from joint work carried out with Jim Stock. In addition, the section on time-varying parameters owes a good deal to discussions with Bill Brainard.

I am grateful to Alicia Kacperek, Christine Wills, Elaine Hartwell and, most notably, Lavinia Harvey for typing assistance and to the Economic and Social Research Council for financial support. Parts of the book were written during visits to IMPA, the mathematics institute in Rio de Janeiro, and to the Australian National University in Canberra. Leigh Roberts, Jim Durbin, Mark Watson, Andy Tremayne and Johannes Ledolter read through various parts of the book and made valuable comments. I am very grateful to them, but they are of course, absolved from blame for any errors and from any responsibility for the views expressed in the book.

Notation and conventions

The following conventions are adopted in the text.

(a) Matrices and vectors are printed in bold type. Vectors are denoted by lower-case letters, with a prime indicating a row vector.

(b) Greek letters are used to denote parameters or states. The nearest corresponding Latin letter denotes the linear estimator. A tilde (˜) over a Greek letter indicates a maximum likelihood estimator of a parameter or the minimum mean square estimator of a state.

(c) A single time subscript on an estimate or estimator indicates the use of information up to, and including, that time subscript. The conditional notation, for example $t|\tau$, for a subscript denotes an estimate or estimator of a quantity at time t based on information available at time τ, where τ may be less than or greater than t.

Writing $\hat{y}_{t+j|t}$ denotes an estimate of y_{t+j} made on the basis of information available at time t. A tilde rather than a hat (ˆ) indicates that the estimate is, in some sense, optimal.

(d) The notation 'log' always denotes the natural logarithm.

Abbreviations

a.c.f.	autocovariance, or autocorrelation, function
a.c.g.f.	autocovariance generating function
AIC	Akaike information criterion
AN	asymptotically normal
AR	autoregressive
ARCH	autoregressive conditional heteroscedasticity
ARE	algebraic Riccati equation
ARIMA	autoregressive integrated moving average
ASE	asymptotic standard error
BIC	Bayes information criterion
BSM	basic structural model
CSS	conditional sum of squares
CUSUM	cumulative sum
DLS	discounted least squares
D-W	Durbin-Watson
ESS	extrapolative sum of squares
EWMA	exponentially weighted moving average
FD	frequency domain
FIML	full information maximum likelihood
GLIM	general linear model
GLS	generalised least squares
IV	instrumental variable
KF	Kalman filter
LBI	locally best invariant
LIML	limited information maximum likelihood
LM	Lagrange multiplier
LR	likelihood ratio
MA	moving average
MD	mean deviation
ML	maximum likelihood
MMSE	minimum mean square estimator or estimate
MMSLE	minimum mean square linear estimator
MPI	most powerful invariant

MSE	mean square error
NID(μ, σ^2)	normally and independently distributed with mean μ and variance σ^2
OLS	ordinary least squares
p.d.f.	probability density function
p.e.v.	prediction error variance
p.(s.)d.	positive (semi-) definite
RMSE	root mean square error
SEM	simultaneous equation model
s.g.f.	spectral generating function
SSE	sum of squared errors
SSF	state space form
TD	time domain
UCARIMA	unobserved components ARIMA
VAR	vector autoregression
VARMA	vector autoregressive moving average
WLS	weighted least squares

Chapter 1

Introduction

This chapter introduces the main issues involved in modelling time series. An overview of the proposed methodology is given without going into any technical details.

1.1 The nature of time series

The time series shown in Figure 1.1.1 consists of observations on the quarterly consumption of coal in the UK by 'Other final users', a group which includes public administration, commerce and agriculture. It is typical of many economic and social time series. Its salient characteristics are a trend, which represents the long-run movements in the series, and a seasonal pattern which repeats itself more or less every year. A model of the series will need to capture these characteristics. There are many ways in which such a model may be formulated, but a useful starting point is to assume that the series may be decomposed in the following way:

$$\text{Observed series} = \text{trend} + \text{seasonal} + \text{irregular} \tag{1.1.1}$$

where the 'irregular' component reflects non-systematic movements in the series. The model is an additive one. A multiplicative form,

$$\text{Observed series} = \text{trend} \times \text{seasonal} \times \text{irregular} \tag{1.1.2}$$

may often be more appropriate, as indeed it is in the case of the series shown in Figure 1.1.1. However, a multiplicative model may be handled within the additive framework by the simple expedient of taking logarithms.

There are two reasons for wishing to model a univariate time series. The first is to provide a *description* of the series in terms of its components of interest. One may, for example, wish to examine the trend in order to see the main movements which have taken place in the series. The seasonal behaviour of the series may also be of interest and for some purposes it may be desirable to extract the seasonal component to produce a seasonally adjusted series. Traditionally such operations have been carried out without recourse to a statistical model. However, it can be shown that for many of these 'model-free' procedures there is a well-defined statistical model for which the procedure in question is optimal.

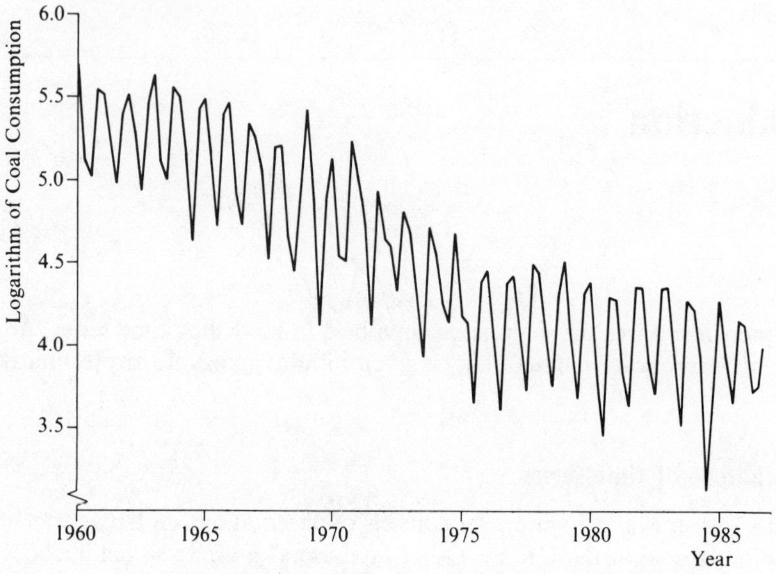

Fig. 1.1.1 UK coal consumption by 'Other final users'.

The advantage of an explicit statistical model is not only that it makes the underlying assumptions clear but that, if properly formulated, it has the flexibility to represent adequately the movements in time series which may have widely differing properties. Hence it is likely to yield a better description of the series and its components. The other motive underlying the construction of a univariate time series model is the *prediction* of future observations. As a rule, the model used for description should also be used as the basis for forecasting, and the fact that a sensible description of the series is an aim of model-building acts as a discipline for selecting models which are likely to be successful at forecasting.

Time series may contain other components. Figure 1.1.2 shows an annual series, US Real Gross National Product (GNP) over the period 1909–70. There is a clear trend, but, in addition, the earlier part of the series shows marked cyclical behaviour as the economy moves from boom to recession and back again. Indeed, we would probably have known this from the economic history of the period without even looking at the graph. Incorporating a cyclical component in a model for US Real GNP will therefore play an important role in providing a description of this series, at least in its early stages. The fact that the properties of the series appear to change shortly after the end of the Second World War illustrates another aspect of economic and social time series, namely that their properties do not necessarily remain the same over time.

A *structural time series model* is one which is set up in terms of components which have a direct interpretation. A univariate structural model is not intended

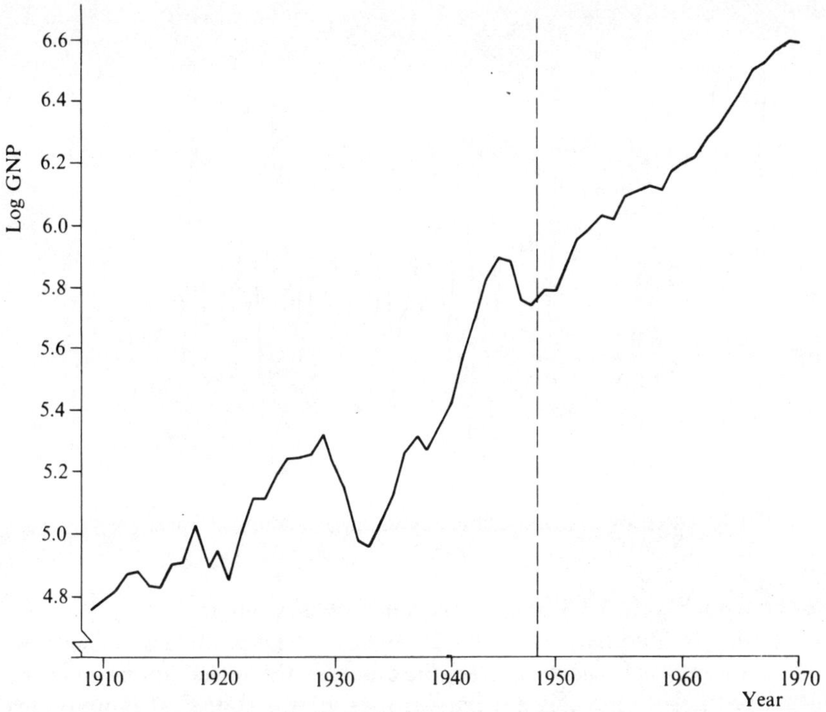

Fig. 1.1.2 US Real GNP

to represent the underlying data generation process. Rather it aims to present the 'stylised facts' of a series in terms of a decomposition into components such as trend, seasonal and cycle. These quantities are of interest in themselves. Furthermore, they highlight the features of a series which must be accounted for by a properly formulated behavioural model. Prediction from a univariate model is naive in the sense that it is just an extrapolation of past movements. Nevertheless, it is often quite effective and it provides a yardstick against which the performance of more elaborate models may be assessed.

The statistical formulation of the trend component in a structural model needs to be flexible enough to allow it to respond to general changes in the direction of the series. A trend is not seen as a deterministic function of time about which the series is constrained to move for ever more. In a similar way the seasonal component must be flexible enough to respond to changes in the seasonal pattern. A structural time series model therefore needs to be set up in such a way that its components are stochastic; in other words, they are regarded as being driven by random disturbances. The statistical framework for handling such models is outlined in section 1.4.

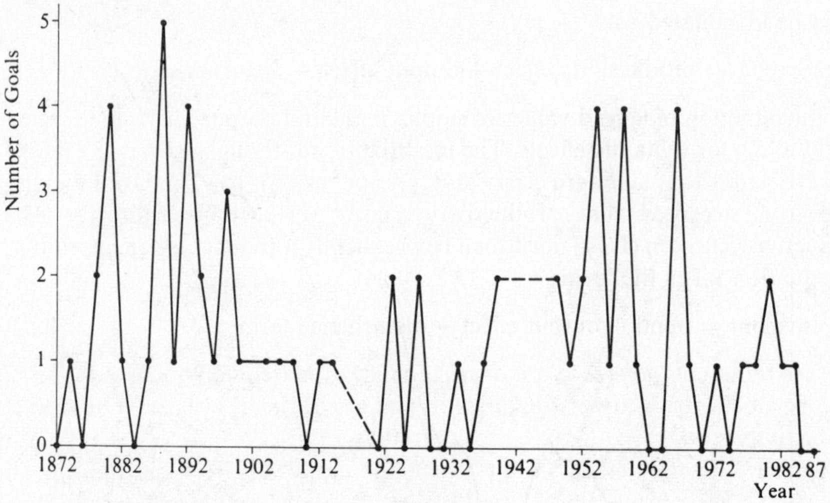

Fig. 1.1.3 Goals scored by England against Scotland at Hampden Park.

The series in Figure 1.1.3 records the number of goals scored by England against Scotland in international football matches at Hampden Park in Glasgow. This is an example of *count data*; by their nature the observations must be non-negative integers and this has implications for the statistical assumptions upon which a model should be based. The structure of the series, however, is clearly one where the underlying level moves up and down over time according to the relative strengths of the two teams. Given this level, the actual number of goals scored on the day depends on a mixture of inspiration and luck. Had the data been of the result of each match, that is a win, a loss or a draw, yet another statistical model would have been appropriate, but the underlying structure would still have been essentially the same.

1.2 Explanatory variables and intervention analysis

The employment–output equation provides a means of forecasting employment, given predictions of the future value of output. The economic theory discussed in Ball and St Cyr (1966), Nickell (1984) and Harvey *et al.* (1986), and the references therein, suggests that employment can be regarded as being dependent on firms' output expectations. This enables an equation to be constructed in which the level of employment is explained by current and past levels of output, by employment in the previous time period and by the capital stock and technical progress. These last two factors are not only difficult to measure, but are also difficult to separate conceptually. If they could be measured, their combined effect would yield a measure of productivity, and the employment–output equation could be formulated as:

Employment = productivity effect + output effect + disturbance term (1.2.1)

The introduction of lagged values of employment and output into this equation would allow for dynamic effects. The essential point, though, is that the model could be handled by standard classical regression procedures. This is not the case once it is accepted that productivity cannot be measured directly. The productivity effect in (1.2.1) must then be proxied by a trend component, so that the equation takes the form:

Employment = trend + output effect + disturbance term (1.2.2)

Like the trend component in a univariate model, the trend component in (1.2.1) must be stochastic in order to allow for changes in the extent and influence of productivity.

Figure 1.2.1(a and b) shows employment and output in UK manufacturing on a quarterly basis from 1963Q1 to 1983Q3; the data are seasonally adjusted. Employment is measured in thousands, while output is an index with 1980 = 100. Both series exhibit short-term movements which appear to be correlated. On the other hand, even without the prior knowledge that productivity changes influence employment, it is clear from Figure 1.2.1 that the level of output cannot possibly account for all the long-run movements in employment. For most of the period in question output shows a tendency to rise while employment goes down, hence the need for the introduction of a trend component into the model in order to account for the discrepancy.

Another example of a series in which the level can be only partly explained by explanatory variables is the one shown in Figure 1.2.2. The series is the number of car drivers in Great Britain killed and seriously injured (KSI) each month from January 1969 to December 1984. Explanatory variables such as the car traffic index, which measures the number of kilometres travelled by cars in a month, and the real price of petrol can be introduced into a model. However, other variables which affect road accidents, such as the quality of the roads, are difficult to quantify, and this means that some of the long-term movements in the series can only be proxied by a stochastic trend. In a similar way, the seasonal effects in the series are, to some extent, a reflection of weather conditions and the consumption of alcohol, the latter presumably having a very marked effect on the figures in December. While some attempt might be made to introduce explanatory variables into the model, it is unlikely that they could successfully account for all the seasonal movements. This being the case, there is still a role for a seasonal component in the model in the same way as there is a role for a trend.

An interesting feature of the car drivers KSI series is the sharp drop in its level in February 1983. As will be shown in section 7.5, this may be attributed to the introduction of the seat-belt law which became effective on 31 January 1983. Indeed it was this law which provided the original motivation for studying the

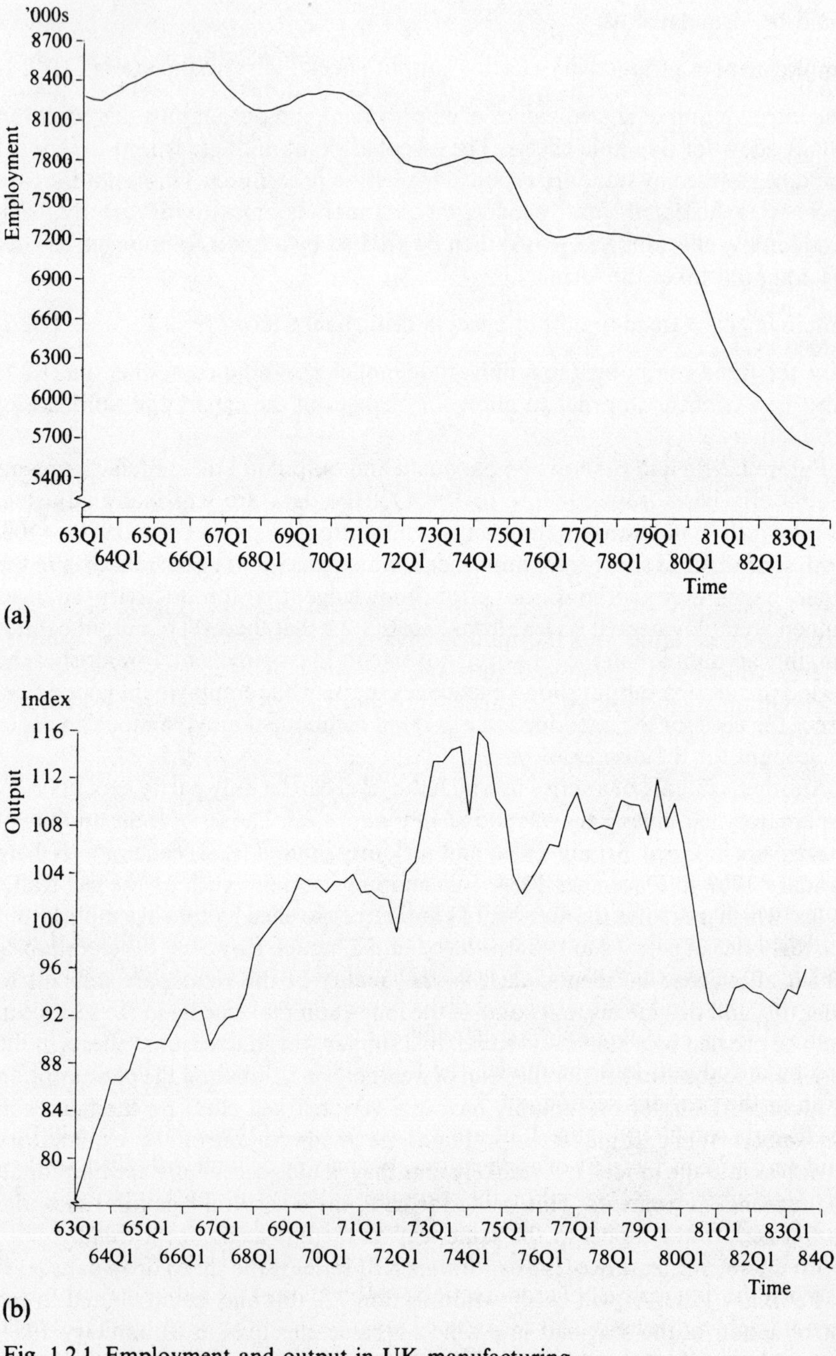

(a)

(b)

Fig. 1.2.1 Employment and output in UK manufacturing.

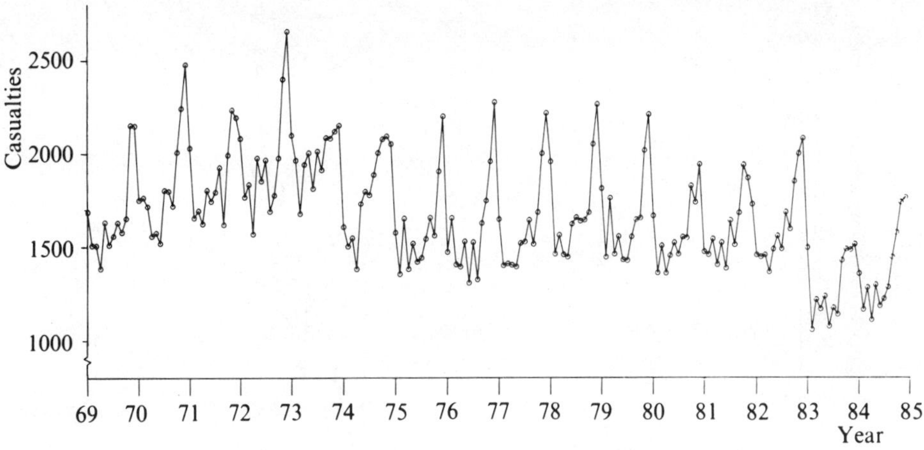

Fig. 1.2.2 Car drivers killed and seriously injured in Great Britain.

series (Durbin and Harvey, 1985; Harvey and Durbin, 1986). The effect of an event or a policy change on a series can be measured by bringing a dummy explanatory variable into the model. This is known as *intervention analysis*, a term which was introduced into the literature by Box and Tiao (1975). Intervention analysis may be carried out both with and without other explanatory variables present.

1.3 Multivariate models

The series in Figure 1.3.1 are indices showing the paid minutes of telephone calls from Australia to three other countries in the world. Each of these series could be modelled separately. However, because they are subject to similar influences, it is possible to model them jointly. When a multivariate structural model is set up to cope with this kind of situation, the disturbances in the various components are assumed to be correlated across the different series. Explanatory variables can also be introduced into the model, the rationale for doing so being exactly as given in the previous section.

The data shown in Figure 1.3.1 are a *cross-section* of time series. Data of this kind may arise in a variety of applications. We may be dealing with observations on a set countries or states, or on the sales of products of a similar type produced by a firm. The data may also be on a sample of households or individuals whose behaviour is followed over time. This is known as *panel data.*

When the data consist of cross-sections of time series, the individual elements do not interact directly with each other. This contrasts with a situation in which there are behavioural relationships between a set of variables. Such a situation

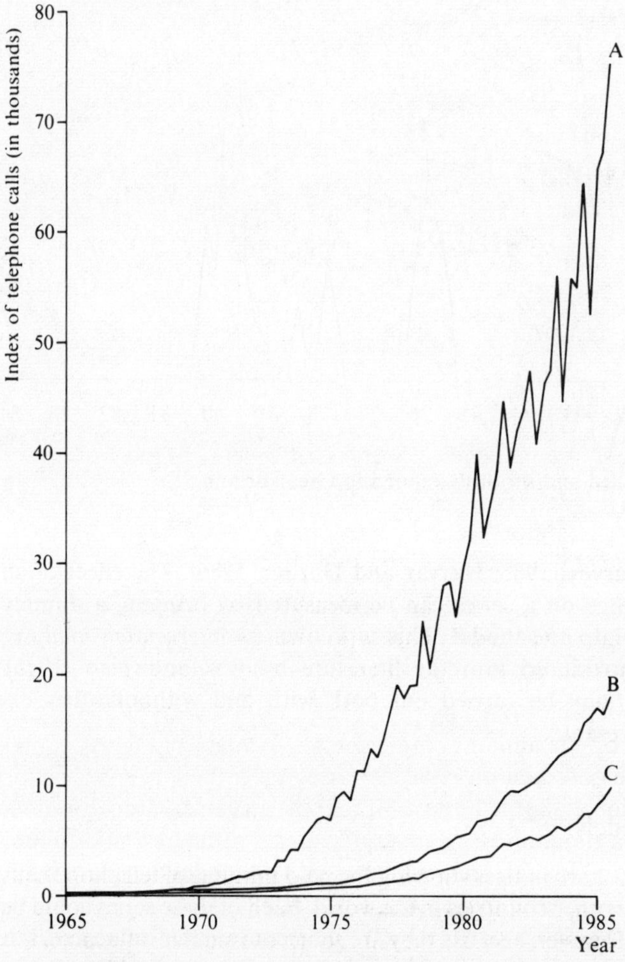

Fig. 1.3.1 Paid minutes of telephone calls from Australia to three other countries.

obtains in the two series shown in Figure 1.3.2. These series record the numbers of mink and muskrat furs traded annually by the Hudson's Bay Company in Canada from 1848 to 1909. There is known to be a prey–predator relationship between these two animals and this affects the population dynamics of both of them. Constructing a multivariate time series model for the two series reflects these dynamic interactions. Dynamic interactions are also apparent when multivariate models are constructed for economic variables, such as income, consumption and investment, which are known to affect each other. The class of models needed to handle situations of this kind is much wider than that required for cross-sections of time series. The type of model to be considered in a particular

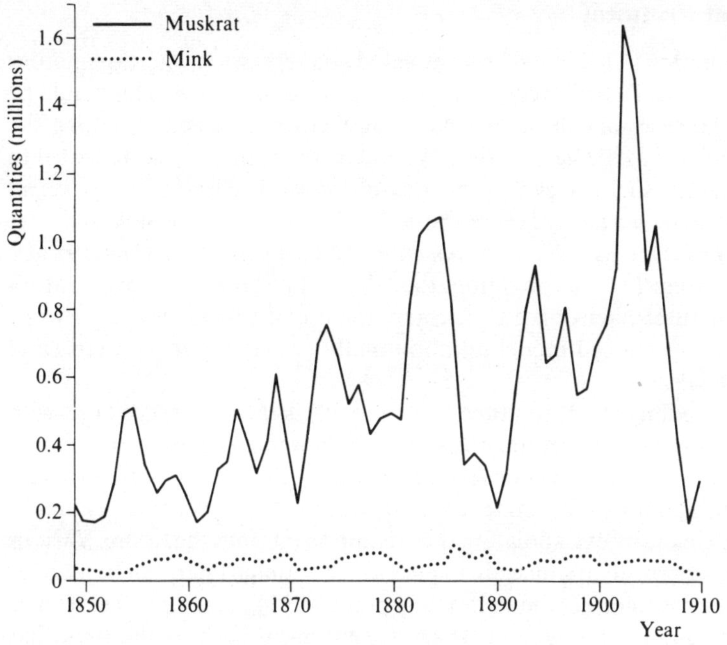

Fig. 1.3.2 Mink and muskrat furs traded by the Hudson's Bay Company.

situation will depend on the amount of information available, in terms of prior theoretical knowledge and data on relevant variables. If there is a satisfactory level of such information, it should be possible to construct an econometric model or, more specifically, a simultaneous equation model. The interest in this book, however, is on situations where a lack of information precludes the construction of a fully specified econometric model.

An interesting aspect of multivariate structural time series models concerns the possibility of components, such as the trend, being common to more than one series. This leads to a class of *dynamic factor models.* Setting up factors in terms of unobserved components produces a model which is not only tractable, but has a useful interpretation. A common trend leads to series being *co-integrated.* If two series are co-integrated, they must move together in the long term, and such a property is an important one to bear in mind, particularly when considering certain macroeconomic variables such as income and consumption.

Current practice in dealing with sets of variables which interact with each other is either to build a fully specified model, or to abandon any structure completely and set up a vector autoregression. The multivariate time series models described in this book are not only more parsimonious than vector autoregressions, but they also offer the possibility of imposing co-integrating restrictions, and taking account of explanatory variables.

1.4 Statistical treatment

A model for equation (1.1.1) could be formulated as a regression with explanatory variables consisting of a time trend and a set of seasonal dummies. This would be inadequate. The necessary flexibility may, however, be achieved by letting the regression coefficients change over time. A similar treatment may be accorded to other components, such as cycles and day-of-the-week effects. *The principal structural time series models are therefore nothing more than regression models in which the explanatory variables are functions of time and the parameters are time-varying.* Given this interpretation, the addition of observable explanatory variables is a natural extension. Furthermore the use of a regression framework opens the way to a unified model selection methodology for econometric and time series models.

The key to handling structural time series models is the *state space form*, with the state of the system representing the various unobserved components such as trends and seasonals. Once in state space form (SSF), the *Kalman filter* provides the means of updating the state as new observations become available. Predictions are made by extrapolating these components into the future. Various *smoothing* algorithms, all of which are related to the Kalman filter, can be used for obtaining the best estimate of the state at any point within the sample. This can be valuable for examining the way in which a component such as the trend has evolved in the past. Figure 1.4.1 shows the smoothed estimates of the trend for the UK coal consumption data over the period up to, and including, the last quarter of 1982. The extrapolation of the trend over the last four years is also shown. This extrapolation is roughly horizontal reflecting the halt in the decline in coal consumption, which the model estimated using the data up to 1982 has picked up. The sharp dip in the series in 1984 is due to special circumstances, namely a prolonged miners' strike.

Prediction and smoothing can only be carried out once the parameters governing the stochastic movements of the state variables have been estimated. The estimation of these parameters, which are known as *hyperparameters*, is itself based on the Kalman filter. This is because the likelihood function can be expressed in terms of one-step-ahead prediction errors, and these prediction errors emerge as a by-product of the filter. When a model is linear and time-invariant, estimation of the hyperparameters can also be carried out in the frequency domain. Again this is a maximum likelihood approach, and for many structural models it has important theoretical and computational advantages. However, the state space framework permits a much richer class of models than can be handled by frequency-domain methods. For example, it provides a vehicle for modelling non-linear effects and structural change.

Another important feature of the state space form is that it can cope with missing observations and temporal aggregation. It also permits the extension of time series models so as to make allowance for more subtle data irregularities

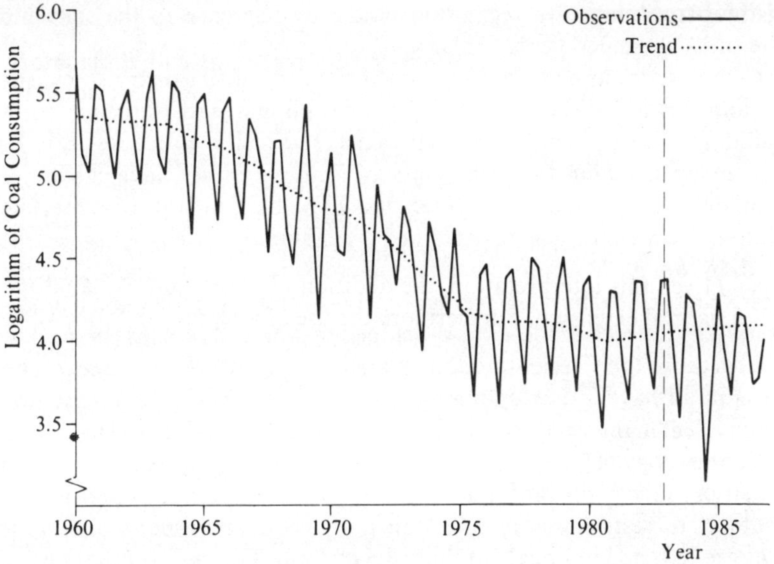

Fig. 1.4.1 UK coal consumption and estimated trend.

such as those arising from data revisions. Furthermore it is possible to modify the principal structural time series models so that they are formulated in *continuous* time. Setting up models in this way makes them independent of the time interval between observations and the flexibility of the state space form enables the Kalman filter to deal with situations in which the observations are irregularly spaced.

1.5 Modelling methodology

The most difficult aspect of working with time series data is model selection. The technical details of the Kalman filter are unimportant in this respect. The crucial point to understand is that the state space form opens up the possibility of setting up models in terms of components which have a direct interpretation. This enables the researcher to formulate, at the outset, a model which is capable of reflecting the salient characteristics of the data. Once the model has been estimated, its suitability can be assessed not only by carrying out diagnostic tests to see if the residuals have desirable properties but also by checking whether the estimated components are consistent with any prior knowledge which might be available. Thus if a cyclical component is used to model the trade cycle, a knowledge of the economic history of the period should enable one to judge whether the estimated parameters are reasonable. This is in the same spirit as assessing the plausibility of a regression model by reference to the sign and magnitude of its estimated coefficients.

Classical time series analysis is based on the theory of stationary stochastic processes, and this is the starting point for conventional statistical time series model building. It can be shown that most stationary processes can be approximated by a model from the class of autoregressive moving average (ARMA) models. However, a much wider class of models, capable of exhibiting non-stationary behaviour, can be obtained by assuming that a series can be represented by an ARMA process after differencing. This is known as the autoregressive integrated moving average (ARIMA) class of models and a model selection strategy for such models was developed by Box and Jenkins (1976). The simplest structural time series models, namely those which are linear and time-invariant, all have a corresponding *reduced form* ARIMA representation which is equivalent in the sense that it will give identical forecasts to the structural form. The terminology of reduced and structural form is used in a parallel fashion in econometrics in the context of simultaneous equation systems. The structural form is subject to restrictions imposed on it by economic theory, and these restrictions are reflected indirectly in the reduced form. The *unrestricted reduced form* has the same specification but is not subject to the restrictions. In a structural time series model the restrictions come not from economic theory but from a desire to ensure that the forecasts which emanate from it reflect features such as cycles and seasonals which are felt to be present in the data. If restrictions of this kind are not imposed, it is not difficult to select a completely inappropriate model from the ARIMA class, particularly if the sample size is small.

The fact that the simpler structural time series models can be made stationary by differencing provides an important link with classical time series analysis. However, the analysis of series which are thought to be stationary does not play a fundamental role in structural modelling methodology. This is as it should be. Few economic and social time series are stationary and there is no overwhelming reason to suppose that they can necessarily be made stationary by differencing. If a univariate structural model fails to give a good fit to a set of data, other univariate models may be considered, but there will be an increased willingness to look at more radical alternatives. For example, a search for outliers might be initiated or it may be necessary to concede that a structurally stable model can only be obtained by conditioning on an observed explanatory variable.

Introducing explanatory variables into a model requires access to a larger *information set*. Some prior knowledge of which variables should potentially enter into the model is needed, as well as data on these variables. In a structural time series model the explanatory variables enter into the model side by side with the unobserved components. In the absence of these unobserved components the model reverts to a regression, and this perhaps makes it clear why the model selection methodology which has been developed for dynamic regression is appropriate in the wider context with which we are concerned. Distributed lags can be fitted, in much the same way as in econometric modelling, and even ideas such as the error correction mechanism can be employed. The inclusion of the unobserved time series components does not affect the model selection methodology to be applied to the explanatory variables in any fundamental way. What it does is to add an extra dimension to the interpretation and specification of certain aspects of the dynamics. For example, it provides a key insight into the vexed question of whether to work with the variables in levels or first differences, and solves the problem by setting up a general framework within which the two formulations emerge as special cases.

The following criteria for a good model have been proposed in the econometrics literature; see, for example, Hendry and Richard (1983), Mizon and Richard (1986), Ericsson and Hendry (1985), Mizon (1984) and Harvey (1981a). They apply with equal force even in the more limited framework of pure time series modelling.

(a) *Parsimony* A parsimonious model is one which contains a relatively small number of parameters and, other things being equal, a simpler model is to be preferred to a complicated one. It must, however, be stressed that beginning with a simple model is not always the best way to proceed. There can be considerable advantages in starting with a general model and then simplifying it on the basis of statistical tests.

(b) *Data coherence* Diagnostic checks are performed to see if the model is consistent with the data. The essential point is that the model should provide a good fit to the data, and the residuals, as well as being relatively small, should be approximately random. A wide range of tests and graphical displays may be employed to investigate departures from randomness.

(c) *Consistency with prior knowledge* In an econometric model, economic theory may provide prior information on the size or magnitude of various parameters and the estimated model should be consistent with this information. More generally, the model should be consistent with any prior knowledge, not necessarily that which derives from economic theory. An example was given in the opening paragraph of this section when the estimation of a cycle was discussed.

(d) *Data admissibility* A model should be unable to predict values which violate definitional constraints. For example many variables cannot be negative.

(e) *Structural stability* As well as providing a good fit within the sample, a model should also give a good fit outside the sample. In order for this to be possible, the parameters should be constant within the sample period and this constancy should carry over into the post-sample period.

(f) *Encompassing* A model is said to encompass a rival formulation if it can explain the results given by the rival formulation. If this is the case, the rival model contains no information which could be used to improve the preferred model. In order to be encompassing a model does not need to be more general than its rivals. Indeed the notion of parsimonious encompassing is essential to avoid vacuous formulations.

1.6 Forecasting

A pure time series model contains no explanatory variables apart from variables which are solely functions of time. Forecasts of future observations are therefore made by extrapolating the components estimated at the end of the sample. Since these forecasts are based on a statistical model, the mean square errors (MSE) associated with them may be computed. Figure 1.6.1 shows the forecasts made for the logarithm of US Real GNP from 1948 onwards based on a model fitted using data up to 1947. The forecast function reflects the trend and cyclical movements captured by the structural time series model. The lines on either side of the forecast function are based on the estimated root mean square error (RMSE), and indicate the *prediction interval.* As the forecast horizon increases, so does the uncertainty attached to the forecasts and the prediction interval consequently becomes wider. Of course the prediction interval is only valid if the fitted model continues to be an adequate representation of the underlying data generation process and it was argued in section 1.1 that there is evidence that this changes after 1947.

When a model contains explanatory variables, forecasts can only be made conditional on future values of these variables. If lagged values of an explanatory variable enter into a model, some of the values which are needed to generate forecasts of the dependent variable are known and the explanatory variable is then referred to as a *leading indicator*. More generally, values of the explanatory variables will themselves need to be forecast. This may necessitate the construction of a model. On the other hand forecasts may be available from some outside source. For example, forecasts of key macroeconomic variables, such as national income, may be available from the Government. It is also useful, on occasions, to make forecasts conditional on a number of different *scenarios*, which are reflected in different future values of the explanatory variables.

Irrespective of the way in which explanatory variables are forecast, the use of such variables clearly requires more effort and more information than does forecasting from a pure univariate time series model. The drawback to pure univariate time series models is that they may not be stable over time and, as a consequence, the forecasts they yield may be wildly inaccurate. The introduction of certain explanatory variables may lead to a model in which the parameters remain constant over time. However, there is no guarantee that such a model can be found. Furthermore a badly misspecified model with explanatory variables may lead to worse forecasts than a naive time series model.

A multivariate time series model offers the possibility of allowing for

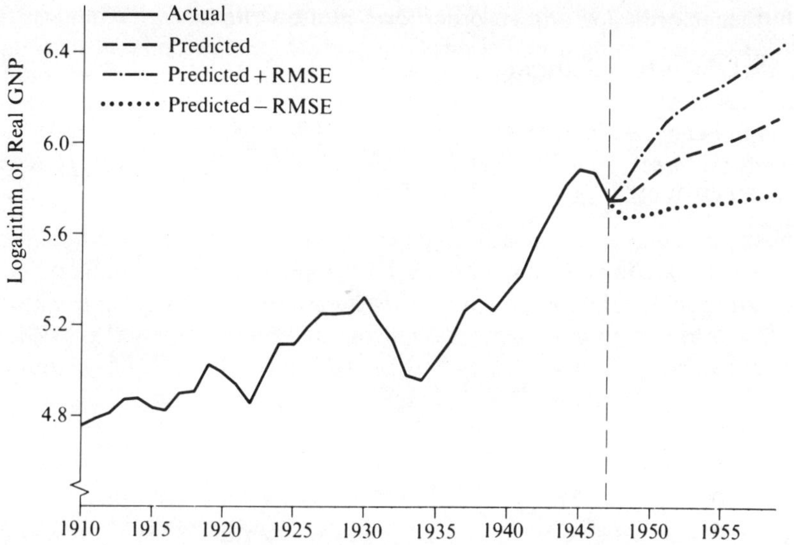

Fig. 1.6.1 Forecasts of US Real GNP.

interactions among the variables when forecasts are made. As with univariate time series modelling, the effectiveness of a multivariate model depends on the extent to which it remains stable over time. The introduction of exogenous variables may enable a structurally stable model to be constructed but a multivariate model is even more vulnerable to misspecification than a univariate one.

1.7 Computer software

A program known as STAMP (Structural Time series Analyser, Modeller and Predictor) has been developed for use on an IBM (or compatible) personal computer. STAMP is a menu-driven program which enables the user to fit univariate structural time series models, and models with intervention and explanatory variables. Estimation can be carried out either in the time domain or in the frequency domain, and a full set of diagnostics is provided. Once a model has been fitted, the Kalman filter is used to make predictions and to construct optimal estimates of trend, seasonal and cyclical components. The program has a graphics capability and there is a simulation module. At the time of writing STAMP does not handle multivariate time series or models with non-normal disturbances. It is hoped to add these facilities at a later stage.

Many of the series given at the end of the book (Appendix 2) are to be found on the diskettes provided with STAMP.

For further information and an order form please write to:

STAMP Statistical Software
Statistics Dept.
London School of Economics
Houghton Street
LONDON WC2A 2AE
England.

Chapter 2

Univariate time series models

A univariate time series consists of a set of observations on a single variable, y. If there are T observations, they may be denoted by y_t, $t=1,\ldots,T$. A univariate time series model for y_t is formulated in terms of past values of y_t and/or its position with respect to time. Forecasts from such a model are therefore nothing more than extrapolations of the observed series made at time T. These forecasts may be denoted by $\hat{y}_{T+l|T}$, where l is a positive integer denoting the *lead time*.

No univariate statistical model can be taken seriously as a mechanism describing the way in which the observations are generated. If we are to start building workable models from first principles, therefore, it is necessary to begin by asking the question of what we expect our models to do. The *ad hoc* forecasting procedures described in section 2.2 provide the starting point. These procedures make forecasts by fitting functions of time to the observations but do so by placing relatively more weight on the more recent observations. This discounting of past observations is intuitively sensible but lacks any explicit statistical foundation. The first part of section 2.3 introduces the idea of a class of statistical models known as stochastic processes. Structural time series models are then built up by formulating stochastic components which, when combined, give forecasts of the required form. It turns out that these models provide a statistical rationale for the *ad hoc* procedures introduced earlier. At the same time they expose the limitations of such procedures.

The traditional time series paradigm is one in which it is assumed that a series can be reduced to stationarity by differencing or detrending. This emphasis on stationarity at the model formulation stage is misconceived. As was argued in chapter 1, the starting point in structural time series modelling is the identification of the salient features in a series. These features are then modelled in such a way that useful predictions of future observations can be made. However, despite the fact that stationarity is not central to the formulation of structural models, nearly all the structural models described in this chapter can be reduced to a stationary form by differencing. Section 2.4 discusses the concept of stationarity and explains why it plays such an important role in the statistical handling of time series models.

Section 2.5 describes the ARIMA class of models and explores the link between these models and structural models. The ARIMA modelling strategy is set out in section 2.6. Section 2.7 provides details on a number of case studies involving structural models and contrasts the methodology with that of ARIMA modelling. The attractions of the structural approach emerge very clearly.

The present chapter deals only with linear, time-invariant structures, with normally distributed observations being assumed when a full model is formulated. Structural models of this kind are the easiest to handle from the practical point of view and they link in most easily with other approaches. However, it must be stressed that they are only a starting point. The structural framework is such as to allow modifications to handle non-linearity, time variation and non-normality. These extensions are described later in chapter 6. Interestingly enough, it transpires that certain of the *ad hoc* forecasting procedures referred to earlier can be rationalised by particular types of non-Gaussian models as well as by the more conventional models described in this chapter.

The emphasis in this chapter is on the rationale underlying the development of structural time series models, the way in which such models may be employed and the way in which the structural methodology contrasts with other approaches. The technical details of how structural models are estimated are delayed until after the Kalman filter has been described in chapter 3.

2.1 Introduction

Although the systematic development of structural time series models must await a description of *ad hoc* forecasting procedures, it is useful to present a very simple example of a structural model just to convey the essence of the approach. This is done in the first sub-section below. The second sub-section defines some of the technical aspects of time series operators. These operators are not used until the end of section 2.3 and some readers may wish to delay looking at this material until it is required. The final sub-section briefly examines the historical background to the development of structural time series models.

2.1.1 *A simple structural model*

Consider a series which moves up and down over time but without showing a tendency towards a steady upward or downward movement. An example of such a series is the one on purse snatchings in Chicago which is described later in sub-section 2.7.3 and plotted in Figure 2.7.6. The essence of the structural time series approach is conveyed by a model which regards the observations as being made up of an underlying level (or permanent) component and an irregular (or transitory) component. The simplest specification for the irregular component is that it is *white noise*, that is a sequence of serially uncorrelated random variables with constant mean, in this case zero, and constant variance. The level component can also be set up in terms of a white noise disturbance, but here the effect of these disturbances is cumulative. In other words the level in the current period is equal to the level in the previous period plus a white noise disturbance. Such a process is known as a *random walk.*

The model described above is known simply as the *random walk plus noise* or *local level* model. Its specification is completed by specifying fully the distributions of the two disturbance terms. If these are assumed to be normal, the model can be written out as:

$$y_t = \mu_t + \varepsilon_t, \quad \varepsilon_t \sim \text{NID}(0, \sigma_\varepsilon^2) \tag{2.1.1a}$$

$$\mu_t = \mu_{t-1} + \eta_t, \quad \eta_t \sim \text{NID}(0, \sigma_\eta^2) \tag{2.1.1b}$$

where the notation NID$(0, \sigma^2)$ denotes a normally distributed, serially independent, random variable with mean zero and variance σ^2. (Remember that uncorrelated random variables must also be independent if they are normally distributed.) The underlying level of the process is assumed to be generated by the random walk, μ_t, but like the irregular term, ε_t, this is not directly observable. Nevertheless it can be estimated and the forecasts for future observations will be equal to its estimate at time T. This estimate is a weighted average of the observations. The extent to which past observations are discounted depends on the relative values of the variances of the two disturbances. Basically the larger σ_η^2 is compared with σ_ε^2, the greater the discounting. In the extreme case when σ_ε^2 is zero, the observations themselves follow a random walk and the forecast of future observations is just the last observation, y_T. At the other end of the scale, if it is σ_η^2 that is zero, the level is constant and the best forecast of future observations is the sample mean.

Setting up the model in (2.1.1) immediately raises a number of questions. For example, how do we estimate the key variance parameters, σ_ε^2 and σ_η^2, and how do we estimate the unobserved level component, μ_t, and make forecasts of future observations? These questions will not be answered fully until chapter 4. Of more immediate concern is the need to provide further justification for (2.1.1) and the need to show how it can be generalised. We will start to tackle these questions in section 2.3. For the moment, though, it is worth noting two of the virtues of the random walk plus noise model. Firstly, its construction is extremely simple and, secondly, its interpretation is straightforward.

2.1.2 Time series operators

The *lag operator*, L, plays a fundamental role in the mathematics of time series analysis. It is defined by the transformation

$$\text{L}y_t = y_{t-1} \tag{2.1.2}$$

Applying L to y_{t-1} yields $\text{L}y_{t-1} = y_{t-2}$, and so, in general,

$$\text{L}^\tau y_t = y_{t-\tau} \tag*{(2.1.2)$'$}$$

It is logical to complete the definition by letting L^0 have the property $L^0 y_t = y_t$ so that (2.1.2)′ holds for any integer. As we shall see the lag operator can be manipulated in a similar way to any algebraic quantity.

A *polynomial in the lag operator* takes the form

$$\theta(L) = 1 + \theta_1 L + \cdots + \theta_q L^q \tag{2.1.3}$$

where $\theta_1, \ldots, \theta_q$ are parameters or constants. The roots of such a polynomial are defined as the q values of L which satisfy the polynomial equation

$$\theta(L) = 0 \tag{2.1.4}$$

Thus if, in (2.1.3), q is equal to one, so that

$$\theta(L) = 1 + \theta L \tag{2.1.5}$$

the root of $1 + \theta L = 0$ is $L = -1/\theta$. A root is said to lie outside the unit circle if its modulus is greater than one. Thus the condition for the root of (2.1.5) to lie outside the unit circle is that the modulus of θ should be less than one, i.e. $|\theta| < 1$.

The *first-difference operator* is defined as

$$\Delta = 1 - L \tag{2.1.6}$$

Thus $\Delta y_t = y_t - y_{t-1}$. Applying the first-difference operator twice yields a second-order polynomial in the lag operator, i.e.

$$\Delta^2 = (1 - L)^2 = 1 - 2L + L^2 \tag{2.1.7}$$

More generally $\Delta^d = (1 - L)^d$ is a d-th order polynomial. The roots of this polynomial are all equal to unity.

The τ-th *difference operator* is defined as

$$\Delta_\tau = 1 - L^\tau, \quad \tau = \cdots -1, 0, 1, 2, \ldots \tag{2.1.8}$$

and so $\Delta_\tau y_t = y_t - y_{t-\tau}$. When τ is negative, the operator induces forward differencing. For example, $\Delta_{-2} y_t = y_t - y_{t+2}$.

An important special case of (2.1.8) is the *seasonal difference operator* where τ is equal to s, the number of seasons in the data. Thus

$$\Delta_s = 1 - L^s \tag{2.1.9}$$

The *summation operator of order* τ is defined as

$$S_\tau(L) = 1 + L + L^2 + \cdots + L^{\tau-1}, \quad \tau = 1, 2, \ldots \tag{2.1.10}$$

Note that the polynomial in (2.1.10) is only of order $\tau - 1$. If it is applied in each time period, the effect of the summation operator is to create, when divided by τ, a moving average in the observations since

$$S_\tau(L) y_t = \sum_{j=0}^{\tau-1} y_{t-j}, \quad t = \tau, \tau+1, \ldots, T \tag{2.1.11}$$

When τ is equal to s, the operator in (2.1.10) is known as the *seasonal summation operator*. In this case it will simply be written as S(L), without the τ subscript.

The following important relationship holds between the difference and summation operators:

$$\Delta_\tau = \Delta . S_\tau(L) \qquad (2.1.12)$$

This relationship may be verified directly by multiplying together the two operators on the right-hand side.

The *trigonometric operator* has the form

$$\gamma(L) = 1 - (2 \cos \lambda)L + L^2 \qquad (2.1.13)$$

where λ is a pre-specified frequency in the range $0 < \lambda < \pi$ which is measured in radians. The roots of $\gamma(L)$ are a pair of complex conjugates with a modulus of one and a phase of λ, i.e. if m_1 and m_2 are the roots,

$$m_1, m_2 = \cos \lambda \pm i \sin \lambda = \exp(\pm i\lambda) \qquad (2.1.14)$$

When λ is equal to π, the appropriate trigonometric operator is $\gamma(L) = 1 + L$.

The final key relationship is between the summation operator and the trigonometric operators. Define the frequencies $\lambda_j = 2\pi j/\tau$ for $j = 1, \ldots, [\tau/2]$, where

$$[\tau/2] = \begin{cases} \tau/2 & \text{for } \tau \text{ even} \\ (\tau-1)/2 & \text{for } \tau \text{ odd} \end{cases} \qquad (2.1.15)$$

When τ is odd, the trigonometric operator corresponding to λ_j is

$$\gamma_j(L) = 1 - (2 \cos \lambda_j)L + L^2, \quad j = 1, \ldots, [\tau/2] \qquad (2.1.16)$$

When τ is even, $\gamma_j(L)$ is defined as in (2.1.16) for $j = 1, \ldots, \frac{1}{2}\tau - 1$, while for $j = \tau/2$ it is

$$\gamma_{\frac{1}{2}\tau}(L) = 1 + L \qquad (2.1.17)$$

The summation operator can be written as the product of the full complement of trigonometric operators, i.e.

$$S_\tau(L) = \prod_{j=1}^{[\tau/2]} \gamma_j(L) \qquad (2.1.18)$$

Again, it is possible to verify this relationship directly by expanding the right-hand side. Table 2.1.1 shows the six trigonometric operators which yield a factorisation of the seasonal summation operator for monthly data.

Table 2.1.1 *Factorisation of the seasonal summation operator* $S_{12}(L)$

Frequency	Period	Operator	Roots
1	12	$1-\sqrt{3}L+L^2$	$(\sqrt{3}\pm i)/2$
2	6	$1-L+L^2$	$(1\pm i\sqrt{3})/2$
3	4	$1+L^2$	$\pm i$
4	3	$1+L+L^2$	$(-1\pm i\sqrt{3})/2$
5	12/5	$1+\sqrt{3}L+L^2$	$(-\sqrt{3}\pm i)/2$
6	2	$1+L$	-1

2.1.3 Historical background

The basic *ad hoc* forecasting procedure is the exponentially weighted moving average (EWMA). This was generalised by Holt (1957) and Winters (1960). They introduced a slope component into the forecast function and allowed for seasonal effects. A somewhat different approach to generalising the EWMA was taken by Brown (1963), who set up forecasting procedures in a regression framework and adopted the method of discounted least squares. These methods became very popular with practitioners and are still widely used particularly in operational research.

Muth (1960) was the first to provide a rationale for the EWMA in terms of a properly specified statistical model, namely the random walk plus noise of (2.1.1). Later papers by Theil and Wage (1964) and Nerlove and Wage (1964) extended the model to include a slope term. As we shall see, the models proposed by Muth and by Theil and his co-authors provide some of the simplest examples of structural time series models. However, the technology of the sixties was such that further development along these lines was not pursued at the time. It was some time before statisticians became acquainted with the paper in the engineering literature by Schweppe (1965) which showed how a likelihood function could be evaluated from the Kalman filter via the prediction error decomposition. More significantly, even if this result had been known, it could not have been properly exploited because of the lack of computing power.

The most influential work on time series forecasting in the sixties was carried out by Box and Jenkins (1976). The first edition of their book appeared in 1970, but it had been preceded by a series of articles. Rather than justifying the EWMA by a structural model as Muth had done, Box and Jenkins observed that it could also be justified by a model in which the first differences of the variable followed a first-order moving average process. Similarly they noted that a rationale for the local linear trend extension proposed by Holt and Winters was given by a model in which second differences followed a second-order moving average process. A synthesis with the theory of stationary stochastic processes then led to the formulation of the class of ARIMA models, and the development of a model selection strategy. The estimation of ARIMA models proved to be a viable proposition at this time provided it was based on an approximate, rather than the exact, likelihood function.

Harrison and Stevens (1971, 1976) continued to work within the framework of structural time series models and were able to make considerable progress by exploiting the Kalman filter. However, their response to the problems posed by maximum likelihood estimation was to adopt a Bayesian approach in which knowledge of certain key parameters was assumed. This led them to consider a further class of models in which the process generating the data switches between a finite number of regimes. This line of research has proved to be somewhat tangential to the main developments in the subject, although it will be touched on again in section 6.5.

Although the ARIMA approach to time series forecasting dominated the statistical literature in the 1970s and early 1980s, the structural approach was prevalent in control engineering. This was partly because of the engineers' familiarity with the Kalman filter which has been a fundamental algorithm in control engineering since its appearance in Kalman (1960) and Kalman and Bucy (1961). However, in a typical engineering situation there are fewer parameters to estimate and there may be a very large number of observations. The work carried out in engineering therefore tended to place less emphasis on maximum likelihood estimation and the development of a model selection methodology.

The potential of the Kalman filter for dealing with econometric and statistical problems began to be exploited in the 1970s by, amongst others, Rosenberg (1973), Engle (1978), Harvey and Phillips (1979) and Garbade (1977). The subsequent development of a structural time series methodology began in the 1980s. The book by Nerlove, Grether and Carvalho (1979) was an important precursor, although the authors did not use the Kalman filter to handle the unobserved components models which they fitted to various data sets. However, they did make use of frequency-domain methods of estimation and this approach has subsequently proved to be extremely useful in structural time series modelling.

2.2 *Ad hoc* forecasting procedures

At its most basic level, time series forecasting is concerned with fitting some function of time to the data and extrapolating into the future. In fitting such a function it is intuitively sensible to place relatively more weight on the most recent observations. To quote Harrison (1967, p. 835): 'Generally, a salesman's approach to forecasting when faced with a graph of customer demand is to draw some curve, usually a straight line, through the observations and to derive forecasts by projecting the curve into the future. In drawing the curve he will make it fit the most recent observations the best.'

The notion of discounting past observations embodies the idea of a *local*, as

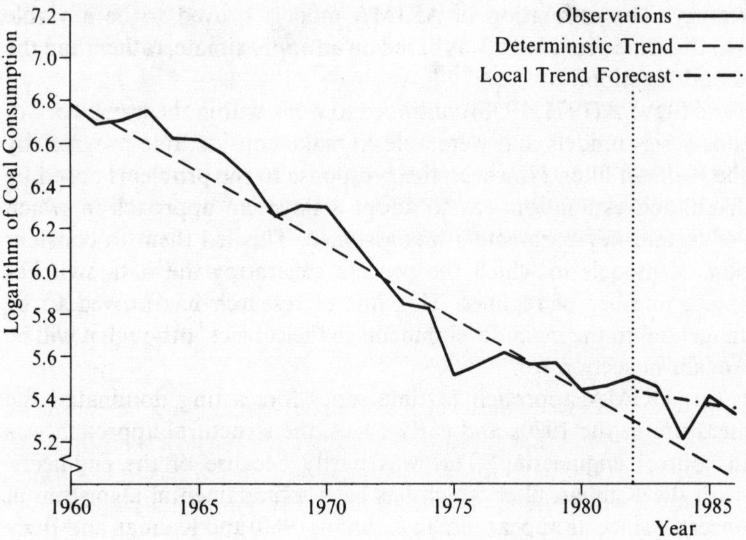

Fig. 2.2.1 Local and global trends for UK coal consumption.

opposed to a *global*, trend. A global trend may be represented by a deterministic function of time which holds at all points throughout the sample. A local trend may change direction during the sample and it is the most recent direction which we want to extrapolate into the future. A global linear trend can easily be fitted by least squares regression. The results of such an exercise are shown in Figure 2.2.1 where a linear trend has been fitted to the logarithm of annual figures of UK coal consumption over the period 1960 to 1982. The quarterly figures for this series appeared in Figure 1.1.1 and a trend was estimated and shown on Figure 1.4.1. As was noted then, the series falls rapidly in the early years but then flattens out. Forecasts made on the basis of a global trend are therefore likely to be too low. This is confirmed by comparing the forecasts for 1983 to 1986 with the actual outcome. The dotted line shows the forecast function based on a local linear trend. This forecast function was constructed using a method called discounted least squares with a discount factor of 0.80. The exact details of this method are set out in sub-section 2.2.3 below.

The construction of forecast functions based on discounted past observations is most commonly carried out by exponential smoothing procedures. These procedures have the attraction that they allow the forecast function to be updated very easily each time a new observation becomes available. This has important implications for storage since for a local linear trend forecasting procedure all that needs to be stored are the current estimates of the level and the slope.

Forecasting procedures based on exponential smoothing have become justifiably popular, particularly in operational research, since they are easy to implement and can be quite effective. However, they are *ad hoc* in that they are implemented without respect to a properly defined statistical model. Their importance in the present context is that historically they provided the starting point for the development of structural time series models. Viewed within the framework of structural time series models, certain of these exponential smoothing procedures can be seen to yield a forecast function which corresponds to the optimal forecast function for a particular model. In other instances, they merely yield an approximate solution to problems for which the exact solution is not known.

2.2.1 *Exponentially weighted moving average*

Suppose that we wish to estimate the level of a series of observations. The simplest way to do this is to use the sample mean, y. However, if the purpose of estimating the level is to use this as the basis for forecasting future observations, it is more appealing to put more weight on the most recent observations. Thus the estimate of the *current* level of the series is taken to be

$$m_T = \sum_{j=0}^{T-1} w_j y_{T-j} \tag{2.2.1}$$

where the w_j's are a set of weights which sum to unity. This estimate is then taken to be the forecast of future observations. Thus

$$\hat{y}_{T+l|T} = m_T, \quad l = 1, 2, \ldots \tag{2.2.2}$$

and the *forecast function* is a horizontal straight line.

One way of putting more weight on the most recent observations is to let the weights decline exponentially. Thus

$$m_T = \lambda \sum_{j=0}^{T-1} (1-\lambda)^j y_{T-j} \tag{2.2.3}$$

where λ is a *smoothing constant* in the range $0 < \lambda \leqslant 1$. If T is large, the condition that the weights sum to unity is approximately satisfied since

$$\lim_{T\to\infty} \sum_{j=0}^{T-1} w_j = \lambda \lim_{T\to\infty} \sum_{j=0}^{T-1} (1-\lambda)^j = 1$$

If expression (2.2.3) is defined for any value of t from $t=1$ to T, it can be split into two parts to give the recursion

$$m_t = (1-\lambda)m_{t-1} + \lambda y_t, \quad t = 1, \ldots, T \tag{2.2.4}$$

with $m_0 = 0$. This suggests that if genuine prior information is available, m_0 may be set to some value other than zero. However, such information is rarely available. Some idea of a suitable value of m_0 can usually only be obtained by looking at the data; but if this is done, m_0 is no longer based on prior information. A more satisfactory approach is to set m_1 equal to y_1 and to start the recursion in (2.2.4) at $t=2$. This gives a slightly different result from (2.2.3), since y_1 receives a weight of $(1-\lambda)^{T-1}$ rather than $\lambda(1-\lambda)^{T-1}$. However, it does have the property that the weights in (2.2.1) sum to unity, even in small samples.

Since m_t is the appropriate forecast of y_{t+1}, the recursion in (2.2.4) is often written as

$$\hat{y}_{t+1|t}=(1-\lambda)\hat{y}_{t|t-1}+\lambda y_t \tag{2.2.5}$$

Thus next period's forecast is a weighted average of the current observation and the forecast of the current observation made in the previous time period. Alternatively

$$\hat{y}_{t+1|t}=\hat{y}_{t|t-1}+\lambda(y_t-\hat{y}_{t|t-1}) \tag{2.2.6}$$

so that forecasts are modified according to the size of the forecast error in the current period. If a value of λ equal to zero were admissible, it would mean that no updating would take place. A value of unity for λ means that all the information needed for forecasting is contained in the current observation.

The recursion in (2.2.4), or (2.2.5), is known as an *exponentially weighted moving average* (EWMA). The procedure of forming a forecast function, (2.2.2), from (2.2.4) is known as *simple exponential smoothing*. The extent to which past observations are discounted in forming (2.2.2) depends on the value of λ. This may be set on *a priori* grounds, in which case it is usually somewhere between 0.05 and 0.30. However, if a reasonable number of observations are available, λ can be chosen as that value which minimises the sum of squares of the one-step-ahead forecast errors, i.e.

$$S(\lambda)=\sum \tilde{v}_t^2 \tag{2.2.7}$$

where

$$\tilde{v}_t=y_t-\hat{y}_{t|t-1} \tag{2.2.8}$$

If the recursion in (2.2.5) is started off with $\hat{y}_{2|1}$ equal to y_1, which is equivalent to setting m_1 equal to y_1 in (2.2.4), the forecast errors are defined for $t=2,\ldots,T$.

Simple exponential smoothing leaves open a number of issues. Firstly, the sample mean cannot be obtained as a special case by setting λ equal to zero. Secondly, there appears to be no ideal solution to finding starting values for the EWMA recursion. As we shall see, both these problems are solved by setting up a model which encapsulates the notion that the observations are randomly distributed about a level which drifts slowly up and down. For the moment, however, we concentrate on how the EWMA can be generalised.

2.2.2 *Holt-Winters forecasting procedure for a local linear trend*

The forecast function for the EWMA procedure is a horizontal straight line. Bringing a slope, b_T, into the forecast function gives

$$\hat{y}_{T+l|T} = m_T + b_T l, \quad l = 1, 2, \ldots \tag{2.2.9}$$

Holt (1957) and Winters (1960) introduced an updating scheme for calculating m_T and b_T in which past observations are discounted by means of two smoothing constants, λ_0 and λ_1, in the range $0 < \lambda_0, \lambda_1 < 1$. Let m_{t-1} and b_{t-1} denote the estimates of the level and slope at time $t-1$. The one-step-ahead forecast is then

$$\hat{y}_{t|t-1} = m_{t-1} + b_{t-1} \tag{2.2.10}$$

As in the EWMA, the updated estimate of the level, m_t, is a linear combination of $\hat{y}_{t|t-1}$ and y_t. Thus

$$m_t = \lambda_0 y_t + (1-\lambda_0)(m_{t-1} + b_{t-1}) \tag{2.2.11a}$$

From this new estimate of m_t, an estimate of the slope can be constructed as $m_t - m_{t-1}$. This suggests that an updated estimate, b_t, be formed by a linear combination of $m_t - m_{t-1}$ and the previous estimate and so

$$b_t = \lambda_1 (m_t - m_{t-1}) + (1-\lambda_1) b_{t-1} \tag{2.2.11b}$$

Together (2.2.11a) and (2.2.11b) form Holt's recursions. Following the argument given for the EWMA, starting values may be constructed from the initial observations as $m_2 = y_2$ and $b_2 = y_2 - y_1$. Hence the recursions run from $t = 3$ to $t = T$ whereupon the forecast function (2.2.9) is set up.

The recursions in (2.2.11) can be re-arranged so as to be in terms of the one-step-ahead forecast error, $\hat{v}_t$, defined in (2.2.8). Thus

$$m_t = m_{t-1} + b_{t-1} + \lambda_0 \hat{v}_t \tag{2.2.12a}$$

$$b_t = \qquad b_{t-1} + \lambda_0 \lambda_1 \hat{v}_t \tag{2.2.12b}$$

The closer λ_0 is to zero, the less past observations are discounted in forming a current estimate of the level. Similarly, the closer λ_1 is to zero, the less they are discounted in estimating the slope. As with the EWMA, these smoothing constants can be fixed *a priori* or estimated by minimising the sum of squares function analogous to (2.2.7).

2.2.3 *Discounted least squares*

A global trend can be fitted by ordinary least squares. Thus a global linear trend is obtained by regressing the observations on a constant and time. A global level is simply the sample mean, $\bar{y}$, though, of course, this is also an OLS estimator. Simple exponential smoothing, on the other hand, can be obtained by introducing a *discount factor*, ω, into the sum of squares function. This is the simplest example of the technique known as *discounted least squares* (DLS).

Estimation of a local level is based on finding the value of m which minimises

$$S(m;\omega)=\sum_{j=0}^{T-1}\omega^j(y_{T-j}-m)^2 \tag{2.2.13}$$

where $0\leqslant\omega\leqslant 1$. Differentiating (2.2.13) with respect to m gives the discounted least squares estimate

$$m_T=\left[\sum_{j=0}^{T-1}\omega^j\right]^{-1}\sum_{j=0}^{T-1}\omega^j y_{T-j} \tag{2.2.14}$$

This reduces to the sample mean if ω equals one. For ω strictly less than one,

$$m_T=[(1-\omega)/(1-\omega^T)]\sum_{j=0}^{T-1}\omega^j y_{T-j} \tag{2.2.15}$$

On setting $\omega=1-\lambda$, expression (2.2.15) is seen to be the same as (2.2.3) apart from the divisor $1-(1-\lambda)^T$.

If a slope term is to be introduced into a forecast function, discounted least squares amounts to finding values of the level, m, and the slope, b, which minimise

$$S(m,b;\omega)=\sum_{j=0}^{T-1}\omega^j(y_{T-j}-m+bj)^2 \tag{2.2.16}$$

These values are

$$\begin{bmatrix} m_T \\ b_T \end{bmatrix}=\begin{bmatrix} \sum\omega^j & -\sum j\omega^j \\ -\sum j\omega^j & \sum j^2\omega^j \end{bmatrix}^{-1}\begin{bmatrix} \sum\omega^j y_{T-j} \\ -\sum j\omega^j y_{T-j} \end{bmatrix} \tag{2.2.17}$$

If T is large it can be shown that

$$m_T=(1-\omega^2)\sum\omega^j y_{T-j}-(1-\omega)^2\sum j\omega^j y_{T-j} \tag{2.2.18a}$$

$$b_T=(1-\omega)^2\sum\omega^j y_{T-j}-\omega^{-1}(1-\omega)^3\sum j\omega^j y_{T-j}; \tag{2.2.18b}$$

see Abraham and Ledolter (1983, p.105) or Montgomery and Johnson (1976, pp. 85–6). Further manipulation indicates that these quantities may be obtained from the recursions

$$m_t=m_{t-1}+b_{t-1}+(1-\omega^2)\hat{v}_t \tag{2.2.19a}$$

$$b_t=\qquad b_{t-1}+(1-\omega)^2\hat{v}_t \tag{2.2.19b}$$

where $\hat{v}_t$ is the one-step-ahead forecast error.

The use of the recursions in (2.2.19) coupled with the linear forecast function (2.2.9) is known as *double exponential smoothing*. It is usually suggested that the discount factor be set fairly close to one. For example, Brown (1963) suggests a value between $\sqrt{0.70}=0.84$ and $\sqrt{0.95}=0.97$. A comparison of (2.2.19) with

(2.2.12) shows double exponential smoothing to be a special case of Holt's procedure in which $\lambda_0 = 1 - \omega^2$ and $\lambda_1 = (1-\omega)/(1+\omega)$.

The discounted least squares principle may be extended further so as to cover a wide range of functions of time, including higher-order polynomials and sinusoids. The general form of the forecast function is

$$\hat{y}_{T+l|T} = \mathbf{f}'(l)\mathbf{a}_T, \quad l = 1, 2, \ldots \tag{2.2.20}$$

where $\mathbf{f}(l)$ is a known $d \times 1$ vector and $\mathbf{a}_T$ is an $d \times 1$ vector obtained from the data. Thus for a linear trend, $\mathbf{f}'(l) = [1 \quad l]$ and $\mathbf{a}'_T = [m_T \quad b_T]$. The origin of the forecast function is always taken to be $t = T$ and so $\mathbf{a}_T$ is always chosen as that value of $\mathbf{a}$ which minimises

$$S(\mathbf{a}; \omega) = \sum_{j=0}^{T-1} \omega^j (y_{T-j} - \mathbf{f}'(-j)\mathbf{a})^2 \tag{2.2.21}$$

The associated recursions are based on finding a $d \times d$ transition matrix, $\mathbf{A}$, such that

$$\mathbf{f}(j) = \mathbf{A}\mathbf{f}(j-1) \tag{2.2.22}$$

Thus for a linear trend

$$\mathbf{A} = \begin{bmatrix} 1 & 0 \\ 1 & 1 \end{bmatrix} \tag{2.2.23}$$

while for a sinusoid

$$\mathbf{f}'(j) = [\cos \lambda j \quad \sin \lambda j] \tag{2.2.24}$$

and

$$\mathbf{A} = \begin{bmatrix} \cos \lambda & \sin \lambda \\ -\sin \lambda & \cos \lambda \end{bmatrix} \tag{2.2.25}$$

The pioneering work on DLS and the corresponding exponential smoothing procedures was carried out by Brown (1963). A full description can be found there and in the texts by Abraham and Ledolter (1983), Montgomery and Johnson (1976) and Granger and Newbold (1977). As will be seen in section 4.1, the various special cases of (2.2.22) are not unlike the transition equations which are set up when a structural time series model is put in state space form.

2.2.4 *Seasonality*

Seasonal effects may be handled in two ways. The first is to seasonally adjust the data, construct a suitable forecast function for the trend and then add the seasonal effects back on to the forecast function. The second is to build the seasonal effects directly into the forecasting procedure.

Seasonal adjustment The simplest way to seasonally adjust a series is to smooth it first by means of a moving average. If there are s seasons in the year and s is even, the smoothed series is given by

$$y_t^* = \sum_{j=-s/2}^{s/2} w_j y_{t-j}, \quad t=(s/2)+1, \ldots, T-(s/2)-1 \tag{2.2.26}$$

where $w_j = 1/s$ for $j=0, \pm 1, \ldots, \pm(\frac{1}{2}s-1)$ and $w_{-j}=w_j=1/(2s)$ for $j=\pm s/2$. The residuals $y_t - y_t^*$ are then averaged over each season to give a set of seasonal factors, c_h^*, $h=1, \ldots, s$. Subtracting these factors from the original series gives the seasonally adjusted series, y_t^a, $t=1, \ldots, T$. More elaborate procedures such as the Bureau of the Census X-11 are essentially modifications of this basic procedure.

A forecast function for the trend in the seasonally adjusted series can be constructed in the way described in the previous two sub-sections. Forecasts for the series, including seasonal factors, can be obtained simply by adding the appropriate seasonal factor, c_j, at each lead time in the forecast function.

Discounted least squares Seasonal effects can be incorporated into a forecast function by a set of cosine and sine terms defined at the frequencies $\lambda_j = 2\pi j/s$, $j=1, \ldots, [s/2]$, where $[s/2]$ is defined in the same way as in (2.1.15). The seasonal effect at lead time l is

$$c_{T+l|T} = \sum_{j=1}^{[s/2]} (d_{j,T} \cos \lambda_j l + d_{j,T}^* \sin \lambda_j l), \quad l=1, 2, \ldots \tag{2.2.27}$$

where $d_{j,T}$ and $d_{j,T}^*$ are estimated coefficients. The seasonal forecast function has two important properties. Firstly, it repeats itself every year, i.e.

$$c_{T+s+h|T} = c_{T+h|T}, \quad h=1, 2, \ldots \tag{2.2.28}$$

Secondly, the seasonal effects sum to zero over any s consecutive time periods, i.e.

$$\sum_{h=k+1}^{k+s} c_{T+h|T} = 0, \quad k=0, 1, 2, \ldots \tag{2.2.29}$$

If the forecast function consists of a linear trend and a seasonal effect, it may be written as:

$$\hat{y}_{T+l|T} = m_T + b_T l + c_{T+l|T}, \quad l=1, 2, \ldots \tag{2.2.30}$$

The coefficients m_T, b_T, and $d_{j,T}$ and $d_{j,T}^*$, $j=1, \ldots, [s/2]$ may be determined by discounted least squares. In terms of the general formulation in (2.2.20), $\mathbf{f}'(l) = [1 \quad l \quad \cos \lambda_1 l \quad \sin \lambda_1 l \quad \cos \lambda_2 l \quad \ldots]$ and $\mathbf{a}_T' = [m_T \quad b_T \quad d_{1,T} \quad d_{1,T^*} \quad d_{2,T} \quad \ldots]$. The transition matrix in (2.2.22) is block diagonal, the first block being given by (2.2.23) with the remaining $[s/2]$ of the form (2.2.25).

The disadvantage of using DLS in this context is that the same discount factor is applied to both the trend and the seasonal components. Practical experience suggests that this arrangement is unsatisfactory since the seasonal pattern will typically change much more slowly than the trend. Harrison and Akram (1983) have recently suggested a way in which different discount factors can be applied to the trend and seasonal components.

Holt-Winters The Holt-Winters local linear trend forecasting procedure may be extended to allow for seasonality. There are two versions, depending on whether the trend and seasonal components are thought to combine in an additive or multiplicative fashion. Only the additive version will be described here. The reader may refer to one of the texts cited earlier, such as Montgomery and Johnson (1976, ch.5) or Abraham and Ledolter (1983), for a description of the multiplicative procedure.

The Holt-Winters procedure uses three smoothing constants, λ_0, λ_1 and λ_s, all of which lie between zero and one. The first two play a similar role to the smoothing constants in the local linear trend forecasting procedure. The recursions for the level, slope and seasonal components, m_t, b_t and c_t respectively are as follows:

$$m_t = \lambda_0(y_t - c_{t-s}) + (1-\lambda_0)(m_{t-1} + b_{t-1}) \tag{2.2.31a}$$

$$b_t = \lambda_1(m_t - m_{t-1}) + (1-\lambda_1)b_{t-1} \tag{2.2.31b}$$

$$c_t = \lambda_s(y_t - m_t) + (1-\lambda_s)c_{t-s} \tag{2.2.31c}$$

The forecast function is of the form (2.2.30) but with $c_{T+l|T}$ taken to be the appropriate seasonal factor obtained from (2.2.31c).

The Holt-Winters procedure has an intuitive appeal. The first two recursions (2.2.31a) and (2.2.31b), are the same as those in (2.2.11) but with y_t corrected for the seasonal effect. Similarly, (2.2.31c) is a weighted average of the seasonal effect s periods ago and the current detrended observations. An obvious weakness is that each seasonal component is only updated every s periods and the deseasonalising in (2.2.31a) is carried out using an estimate of the seasonal component which is s periods out of date. Nevertheless, as Chatfield (1978) and others have argued, the method seems to work well in practice.

2.3 The structure of time series models

A statistical model is based on certain probabilistic assumptions, which attempt to capture the essential characteristics of the data generation process. Given such a model, it becomes possible to do several things: (a) the parameters can be estimated by a statistical procedure, such as maximum likelihood, which has known properties; (b) prediction (confidence) intervals can be constructed for forecasts made from the model; (c) the model can be expanded or generalised in a systematic way; and (d) statistical tests can be carried out to see if the model can be simplified or whether it is necessary for it to be generalised.

The starting point for the development of time series models is a regression model in which the explanatory variables are functions of time. Thus, for example, a model with trend and seasonal components may be formulated as

$$y_t = \alpha + \beta t + \sum_j \gamma_j z_{jt} + \varepsilon_t \tag{2.3.1}$$

where α and β are the coefficients associated with the trend and the γ_j's are seasonal coefficients constrained to sum to zero. This constraint is effected by setting up the z_{jt}'s as dummy variables defined such that for $j=1,\ldots,s-1$,

$$z_{jt} = \begin{cases} 1, & t=j, j+s, j+2s, \ldots \\ 0, & t \neq j, j+s, j+2s, \ldots \\ -1, & t=s, 2s, 3s, \ldots \end{cases} \tag{2.3.2}$$

The trend could be modified by adding a term in, say, t^2, while other components, representing features such as cycles could also be added. The key feature of (2.3.1), though, is that the only stochastic part of the model is the irregular component, ε_t. This is assumed to be a normally distributed random disturbance term with mean zero and variance σ^2, that is $\varepsilon_t \sim \text{NID}(0, \sigma^2)$.

The consequences of the formulation in (2.3.1) are that the coefficients can be estimated by ordinary least squares (OLS) and forecasts made by a forecast function similar in form to the one given in (2.2.30). Prediction intervals for these forecasts can also be constructed, something which is not possible with the *ad hoc* techniques described in the previous section. For example, if the model simply contains a linear trend, i.e.

$$y_t = \alpha + \beta t + \varepsilon_t \tag{2.3.3}$$

the l-step-ahead prediction is given by

$$\tilde{y}_{T+l|T} = a + b(T+l) \tag{2.3.4}$$

where a and b are the OLS estimators of α and β. The prediction mean square error is

$$\text{MSE}(\tilde{y}_{T+l|T}) = \sigma^2 \left\{ 1 + \frac{2[(2T-1)(T-1) + 6l(T+l-1)]}{T(T^2-1)} \right\} \tag{2.3.5}$$

and this may be estimated by replacing σ^2 by its unbiased estimator, i.e. the residual sum of squares divided by $T-2$. Lower case letters will be used to denote the estimated mean square error and the corresponding root mean square error (RMSE). The $100(1-\alpha)\%$ prediction interval for y_{T+l} is therefore

$$\tilde{y}_{T+l|T} \pm t_{T-2}^{(\alpha/2)} \cdot \text{RMSE}\ (\tilde{y}_{T+l|T})$$

where $t_{T-2}^{(\alpha/2)}$ is the point on the t distribution with $T-2$ degrees of freedom such that the probability to the right of it is $\alpha/2$.

The drawback with models like (2.3.1) is that they are rarely appropriate. The trend and seasonal components are deterministic functions of time and so all observations receive the same weight when predictions are made. It was argued in the previous section that this is unreasonable. It is therefore necessary to formulate models which lead to the discounting of past observations. In the case of (2.3.1) this may be accomplished by letting α, β and the γ_j's evolve over time. A time series model may therefore be regarded as a regression model with time-varying parameters.

The essentially static formulation of (2.3.1) is converted into a dynamic time series model by incorporating certain stochastic processes within it. These stochastic processes not only provide models which allow the parameters to evolve over time but also lead to the consideration of other dynamic effects which would not necessarily be suggested by a static regression model. The first sub-section below describes the nature of stochastic processes, while the remaining sub-sections show how these processes can be used in the formulation of structural time series models. A more formal discussion of the statistical properties of stochastic processes is delayed until section 2.4. The present section focusses on the way in which these processes can provide models for prediction.

2.3.1 Stochastic processes

It will be recalled from sub-section 2.1.1 that a white-noise process is a sequence of serially uncorrelated random variables with constant mean and variance. A stochastic process in which the current value, y_t, depends on the previous value, y_{t-1}, and a white noise disturbance term, ξ_t, is known as an *autoregressive* process. It may be written

$$y_t = \varphi y_{t-1} + \xi_t, \quad t = 1, \ldots, T \tag{2.3.6}$$

where ξ_t has mean zero and variance σ^2, and φ is a parameter. Although the series is first observed at time $t=1$, the process is regarded as having started at some time in the remote past.

The value of φ plays the key role in determining the way in which the observations behave and the form which the forecast function takes. If $|\varphi| < 1$, the process hovers around a constant mean of zero, and is said to be *stationary.* The concept of stationarity is defined formally in section 2.4. The point to note at the moment is that a stationary process is a short memory one in that the current position is more dependent on the recent shocks than on those which occurred some time ago. When $|\varphi| \geqslant 1$, on the other hand, the influence of past shocks does not diminish over time. In order to see these points explicitly, consider substituting repeatedly for lagged values of y_t. This gives

$$y_t = \sum_{j=0}^{J-1} \varphi^j \xi_{t-j} + \varphi^J y_{t-J}, \quad J = 1, 2, 3, \ldots \tag{2.3.7}$$

The right-hand side of (2.3.7) consists of two parts, the first of which contains lagged values of the disturbances driving the process. If $|\varphi|<1$ the weights attached to past disturbances die away exponentially. Furthermore, if y_{t-J} is the starting value for the process, its influence will be smaller, the larger is J. In fact as $J\rightarrow\infty$, the influence of y_{t-J} effectively disappears, and if the process is regarded as having started off at some time in the remote past, it is quite legitimate to write it as

$$y_t=\sum_{j=0}^{\infty}\varphi^j\xi_{t-j} \tag{2.3.8}$$

The only autoregressive process with $|\varphi|\geqslant 1$ which features prominently in structural time series modelling is the one in which $\varphi=1$. This model,

$$y_t=y_{t-1}+\xi_t \tag{2.3.9}$$

is the random walk. The process is an evolutionary one with the current level shifting each time there is a shock to the system. The contrast between stationary autoregressive processes and the random walk shows up clearly when predictions are made.

Given the availability of a set of observations up to, and including, y_T, the *optimal predictor* l steps ahead is the expected value of y_{T+l} conditional on the information at time T. This may be written as

$$\tilde{y}_{T+l|T}=\mathrm{E}(y_{T+l}|Y_T)=\underset{T}{\mathrm{E}}(y_{T+l}) \tag{2.3.10}$$

where Y_T denotes the information set $\{y_T, y_{T-1},\ldots\}$ and the 'T' below the expectation conveys the same message as explicitly conditioning on Y_T. This predictor is optimal in the sense that it has minimum mean square error. This is easily seen by observing that for any predictor, $\hat{y}_{T+l|T}$, constructed on the basis of the information available at time T, the estimation error can be split into two parts:

$$y_{T+l}-\hat{y}_{T+l|T}=[y_{T+l}-\mathrm{E}(y_{T+l}|Y_T)]+[\mathrm{E}(y_{T+l}|Y_T)-\hat{y}_{T+l|T}]$$

Since the second term on the right-hand side is fixed at time T, it follows that, on squaring the whole expression and taking conditional expectations, the cross-product term disappears leaving

$$\mathrm{MSE}\,(\hat{y}_{T+l|T})=\mathrm{Var}\,(y_{T+l}|Y_T)+[\hat{y}_{T+l|T}-\mathrm{E}(y_{T+l}|Y_T)]^2 \tag{2.3.11}$$

The first term on the right-hand side of (2.3.11), the conditional variance of y_{T+l}, does not depend on $\hat{y}_{T+l|T}$. Hence the *minimum mean square estimate* (MMSE) of y_{T+l} is given by the conditional mean, (2.3.10), and it is unique. When (2.3.10) is viewed as a rule, rather than a number, it is an estimator, rather than an estimate of y_{T+l}. It can be shown that it is the *minimum mean square estimator* (also abbreviated as MMSE) since it minimises the MSE when the expectation is taken over all the observations in the information set; see the discussion and references in sub-section 3.2.3. When the observations are normally distributed, the expression corresponding to $\mathrm{Var}(y_{T+l}|Y_T)$ in (2.3.11) does not depend on the observations and so can be interpreted as the MSE of the estimator. However, as we shall see shortly, normality of the observations is not always needed for the MSE to have this property.

If the disturbances in an autoregressive process are independent, rather than just uncorrelated, the predictor in (2.3.10) can be built up recursively by the *chain rule*. If independence does not hold, the predictor given by the chain rule is only optimal within the class of *linear* predictors. The predictive recursion is obtained by writing down (2.3.6) at time $T+l$ and taking expectations conditional on the information at time T to yield

$$\tilde{y}_{T+l|T}=\varphi\tilde{y}_{T+l-1|T}, \quad l=1,2,\ldots \tag{2.3.12}$$

with $\tilde{y}_{T|T}=y_T$. Hence $\tilde{y}_{T+1|T}=\varphi y_T$, $\tilde{y}_{T+2|T}=\varphi\tilde{y}_{T+1|T}=\varphi^2 y_T$ and so on. As an alternative to building up the predictions in this way, we may simply solve the difference equation in (2.3.12) to obtain

$$\tilde{y}_{T+l|T}=\varphi^l y_T, \quad l=1,2,\ldots \tag{2.3.13}$$

This expression is known as the *forecast function*. When $|\varphi|<1$, the forecasts decay exponentially towards zero. In the case of the random walk, however, the current value provides the best forecast of y_t any number of steps ahead and the forecast function is horizontal.

The process defined in (2.3.6) is a *first-order* autoregressive process. This is often denoted by writing $y_t \sim \mathrm{AR}(1)$. It is straightforward to extend the model so that y_t depends on more lagged values. Thus the second-order, AR(2), process is

$$y_t=\varphi_1 y_{t-1}+\varphi_2 y_{t-2}+\xi_t, \quad t=1,\ldots,T \tag{2.3.14}$$

The conditions for stationarity are somewhat more complex than in the AR(1) case, but they translate into three linear inequalities for φ_1 and φ_2 with the admissible region for values of φ_1 and φ_2 being a triangle; see, for example, Harvey (1981b, p. 32) or Box and Jenkins (1976, p. 59). Predictions can be built up recursively by means of the equation

$$\tilde{y}_{T+l|T}=\varphi_1\tilde{y}_{T+l-1|T}+\varphi_2\tilde{y}_{T+l-2|T}, \quad l=1,2,\ldots \tag{2.3.15}$$

with $\tilde{y}_{T|T}=y_T$ and $\tilde{y}_{T-1|T}=y_{T-1}$. The form of the forecast function depends on φ_1 and φ_2. For certain values of these parameters within the stationarity region the forecast function takes the form of a damped cosine wave. This reflects the fact that the process exhibits some kind of cyclical behaviour. On the other hand, for the non-stationary model in which $\varphi_1=2$ and $\varphi_2=-1$ the forecast function is a straight line passing through y_T and y_{T-1} with slope y_T-y_{T-1}.

Multivariate stochastic processes are formulated when $\mathbf{y}_t$ is an $N\times 1$ vector of observations. The multivariate generalisation of (2.3.6), known as a first-order vector autoregressive process, is

$$\mathbf{y}_t=\mathbf{\Phi}\mathbf{y}_{t-1}+\boldsymbol{\xi}_t, \quad t=1,\ldots,T \tag{2.3.16}$$

where $\mathbf{\Phi}$ is an $N \times N$ matrix of autoregressive parameters and $\boldsymbol{\xi}_t$ is an $N \times 1$ vector of serially uncorrelated random variables with mean vector zero and covariance matrix $\mathbf{\Sigma}$. Predictions are built up in the same way as in the univariate case. Under the stronger assumption that the disturbances are independent, these predictors are optimal; otherwise they are only optimal within the class of linear predictors. The multivariate difference equation corresponding to (2.3.12) is

$$\tilde{\mathbf{y}}_{T+l|T} = \mathbf{\Phi}\tilde{\mathbf{y}}_{T+l-1|T}, \quad l=1,2,\ldots \tag{2.3.17}$$

with solution

$$\tilde{\mathbf{y}}_{T+l|T} = \mathbf{\Phi}^l \mathbf{y}_T, \quad l=1,2,\ldots \tag{2.3.18}$$

One of the attractions of (2.3.16) is that it provides a general method of handling higher-order lags. Thus the univariate AR(2) model, (2.3.14), can be expressed in the form (2.3.16) by defining $\mathbf{y}_t = [y_t \quad y_{t-1}]'$ and writing

$$\begin{bmatrix} y_t \\ y_{t-1} \end{bmatrix} = \begin{bmatrix} \varphi_1 & \varphi_2 \\ 1 & 0 \end{bmatrix} \begin{bmatrix} y_{t-1} \\ y_{t-2} \end{bmatrix} + \begin{bmatrix} \xi_t \\ 0 \end{bmatrix} \tag{2.3.19}$$

The predictions built up via (2.3.17) are exactly the same as those obtained from (2.3.15). As will be seen in chapter 3, it is the first-order vector autoregressive representation which plays the key role in setting up models in state space form.

Stochastic processes are able to characterise some of the main features of observed time series and to provide the basis upon which predictions of future observations can be made. Furthermore, mean square errors can be computed for these predictions. In the case of the univariate AR(1) process, (2.3.6), writing out the equation for y_{T+l} in the form (2.3.7) with $J = l$ gives

$$y_{T+l} = \sum_{j=0}^{l-1} \varphi^j \xi_{T+l-j} + \varphi^l y_T \tag{2.3.20}$$

The MSE of the forecast is

$$\text{MSE}(\tilde{y}_{T+l|T}) = \underset{T}{\text{E}}[(y_{T+l} - \tilde{y}_{T+l|T})^2], \quad l = 1,2,\ldots \tag{2.3.21}$$

Substituting from (2.3.13) and (2.3.20) yields

$$\begin{aligned} \text{MSE}(\tilde{y}_{T+l|T}) &= \underset{T}{\text{E}}\left[\left(\sum_{j=0}^{l-1} \varphi^j \xi_{T+l-j}\right)^2\right] \\ &= \sigma^2(1 + \varphi^2 + \cdots + \varphi^{2(l-1)}) \end{aligned} \tag{2.3.22}$$

For the multivariate process, (2.3.16), a similar argument gives the MSE matrix

$$\text{MSE}(\tilde{\mathbf{y}}_{T+l|T}) = \sum_{j=0}^{l-1} \mathbf{\Phi}^j \mathbf{\Sigma} \mathbf{\Phi}'^j \tag{2.3.23}$$

Of course if prediction intervals are to be set up, it must further be assumed that the disturbances have a particular distribution. This almost invariably means an assumption of normality.

2.3.2 *Trend*

The trend represents the long-term movements in a series which can be extrapolated into the future. The simplest structural time series models consist of a trend component plus a random disturbance term. The random disturbance term may be interpreted as an irregular component in the time series or as a measurement error. Either way the model may be written as

$$y_t = \mu_t + \varepsilon_t, \quad t = 1, \ldots, T \tag{2.3.24}$$

where μ_t is the trend and ε_t is a white-noise disturbance term which is assumed to be uncorrelated with any stochastic elements in μ_t.

The trend may take a variety of forms. This section concentrates on the case when it is linear. The deterministic linear trend is

$$\mu_t = \alpha + \beta t, \quad t = 1, \ldots, T \tag{2.3.25}$$

and on substituting in (2.3.24), model (2.3.3) is obtained. The deterministic trend in (2.3.25) could be made stochastic by letting α and β follow random walks. However, this would lead to a somewhat discontinuous pattern for μ_t; see the discussion in section 2.2. A more satisfactory model is obtained by working directly with the current level, μ_t, rather than with the intercept, α. Since μ_t may be obtained recursively from

$$\mu_t = \mu_{t-1} + \beta, \quad t = 1, \ldots, T \tag{2.3.26}$$

with $\mu_0 = \alpha$, stochastic terms may be introduced as follows:

$$\mu_t = \mu_{t-1} + \beta_{t-1} + \eta_t \tag{2.3.27a}$$

$$\beta_t = \qquad \beta_{t-1} + \zeta_t, \quad t = \ldots, -1, 0, 1, \ldots \tag{2.3.27b}$$

where η_t and ζ_t are mutually uncorrelated white-noise disturbances with zero means and variances σ_η^2 and σ_ζ^2 respectively. The effect of η_t is to allow the level of the trend to shift up and down, while ζ_t allows the slope to change. The larger the variances, the greater the stochastic movements in the trend. If $\sigma_\eta^2 = \sigma_\zeta^2 = 0$, (2.3.27) collapses to (2.3.26) showing that the deterministic trend is a limiting case.

Although the effect of (2.3.27) is to allow the parameters in the trend to change over time, the further assumption that all three disturbances are mutually and serially independent means that the forecast function still has the linear form of (2.3.4). The process generating μ_t and β_t is a first-order vector autoregression

$$\begin{bmatrix} \mu_t \\ \beta_t \end{bmatrix} = \begin{bmatrix} 1 & 1 \\ 0 & 1 \end{bmatrix} \begin{bmatrix} \mu_{t-1} \\ \beta_{t-1} \end{bmatrix} + \begin{bmatrix} \eta_t \\ \zeta_t \end{bmatrix} \tag{2.3.28}$$

and taking conditional expectations at lead times $l = 1, 2, \ldots$ and solving the resulting difference equation as in (2.3.18) gives

$$\tilde{\mu}_{T+l|T}=\tilde{\mu}_T+\tilde{\beta}_T l \tag{2.3.29}$$

where $\tilde{\mu}_T$ and $\tilde{\beta}_T$ are the conditional expectations of μ_T and β_T at time T. Since model (2.3.24) specifies that the observations are equal to a trend plus a white-noise disturbance term, (2.3.29) is also the forecast function for the series itself, i.e.

$$\tilde{y}_{T+l|T}=\tilde{\mu}_T+\tilde{\beta}_T l, \quad l=1,2,\ldots \tag{2.3.30}$$

When the disturbances ε_t, η_t and ζ_t are normally distributed, the computation of $\tilde{\mu}_T$ and $\tilde{\beta}_T$ can be carried out by putting the model in state space form and applying the Kalman filter. Without the assumption of normality, uncorrelatedness of the disturbances is sufficient for the Kalman filter to yield optimal linear forecasts. It will be shown in Chapter 4 that, provided σ_ζ^2 is strictly positive, the Kalman filter forecasts are approximately the same as would be obtained by applying the Holt-Winters local linear trend recursions (2.2.11) with suitably defined smoothing constants. The actual relationship is

$$q_\eta=(\lambda_0^2+\lambda_0^2\lambda_1-2\lambda_0\lambda_1)/(1-\lambda_0) \tag{2.3.31a}$$

$$q_\zeta=\lambda_0^2\lambda_1^2/(1-\lambda_0) \tag{2.3.31b}$$

where q_η and q_ζ are the relative variances $\sigma_\eta^2/\sigma_\varepsilon^2$ and $\sigma_\zeta^2/\sigma_\varepsilon^2$ respectively.

Expressions linking λ_0 and λ_1 to the discount factor, ω, in discounted least squares were given below equation (2.2.19b). It therefore follows from (2.3.31) that forecasts corresponding to those obtained by double exponential smoothing are given by setting

$$q_\zeta=(q_\eta/2)^2$$

Since $q_\zeta=(1-\omega)^4/\omega^2$, a discount factor of $\omega=0.9$ gives $q_\zeta=0.000123$ and $q_\eta=0.0222$.

If $\sigma_\zeta^2=0$, so that the slope, β, is constant, the process generating the trend reduces to a random walk plus drift,

$$\mu_t=\mu_{t-1}+\beta+\eta_t \tag{2.3.32}$$

If, furthermore, β is equal to zero, the model collapses to the simple random walk plus noise introduced in sub-section 2.1.1. The forecast functions in (2.3.29) and (2.3.30) then have $\tilde{\beta}_T$ equal to zero, and $\tilde{\mu}_T$ is given approximately by the EWMA of (2.2.4).

2.3.3 Cycles

Let ψ_t be a cyclical function of time with frequency λ_c, which is measured in radians. The period of the cycle, which is the time taken to go through its complete sequence of values, is $2\pi/\lambda_c$. A cycle can be expressed either as a sine wave or a cosine wave with additional parameters representing the amplitude and the phase. Thus, if a cosine wave is used,

$$\psi_t = A\cos(\lambda_c t - \theta), \quad t = 1, \ldots, T \tag{2.3.33}$$

where A is amplitude and θ is phase. A more convenient formulation is obtained by writing the cycle as a mixture of sine and cosine waves. The amplitude and phase are replaced by two new parameters, α and β, and

$$\psi_t = \alpha\cos\lambda_c t + \beta\sin\lambda_c t \tag{2.3.34}$$

where $(\alpha^2 + \beta^2)^{\frac{1}{2}}$ is the amplitude and $\tan^{-1}(\beta/\alpha)$ is the phase.

If the observations were given by

$$y_t = \psi_t + \varepsilon_t, \quad t = 1, \ldots, T \tag{2.3.35}$$

where ε_t is a white-noise disturbance term and ψ_t is as defined in (2.3.34) with λ_c known, OLS would be an appropriate estimation technique. However, in order to introduce some discounting into the system, the cycle needs to be made stochastic by allowing the parameters α and β to evolve over time. As with the linear trend, continuity is preserved by writing down a recursion for constructing ψ_t before introducing the stochastic components into the model. This recursion is

$$\begin{bmatrix}\psi_t \\ \psi_t^*\end{bmatrix} = \begin{bmatrix}\cos\lambda_c & \sin\lambda_c \\ -\sin\lambda_c & \cos\lambda_c\end{bmatrix}\begin{bmatrix}\psi_{t-1} \\ \psi_{t-1}^*\end{bmatrix}, \quad t = 1, \ldots, T \tag{2.3.36}$$

with $\psi_0 = \alpha$ and $\psi_0^* = \beta$; note the use of the standard trigonometric identities given in Harvey (1981b, p. 95). The new parameters are ψ_t, the current value of the cycle, and ψ_t^*, which appears by construction in order to form ψ_t.

Introducing two white-noise disturbances, κ_t and κ_t^*, into (2.3.36) yields

$$\begin{bmatrix}\psi_t \\ \psi_t^*\end{bmatrix} = \begin{bmatrix}\cos\lambda_c & \sin\lambda_c \\ -\sin\lambda_c & \cos\lambda_c\end{bmatrix}\begin{bmatrix}\psi_{t-1} \\ \psi_{t-1}^*\end{bmatrix} + \begin{bmatrix}\kappa_t \\ \kappa_t^*\end{bmatrix} \tag{2.3.37}$$

For the model to be identifiable it must be assumed either that the two disturbances have the same variance or that they are uncorrelated. In practice both of these assumptions are usually imposed for reasons of parsimony.

Further flexibility can be introduced into (2.3.37) by bringing in a damping factor, ρ, to give

$$\begin{bmatrix}\psi_t \\ \psi_t^*\end{bmatrix} = \rho\begin{bmatrix}\cos\lambda_c & \sin\lambda_c \\ -\sin\lambda_c & \cos\lambda_c\end{bmatrix}\begin{bmatrix}\psi_{t-1} \\ \psi_{t-1}^*\end{bmatrix} + \begin{bmatrix}\kappa_t \\ \kappa_t^*\end{bmatrix} \tag{2.3.38}$$

where $0 \leqslant \rho \leqslant 1$. Model (2.3.38) is a vector AR(1) process.

If $\tilde{\psi}_T$ and $\tilde{\psi}_T^*$ denote the expected values of ψ_T and ψ_T^* at time T, the l-step-ahead prediction of ψ_t under the assumption of independent disturbances is

$$\tilde{\psi}_{T+l|T} = \rho^l(\tilde{\psi}_T\cos\lambda_c l + \tilde{\psi}_T^*\sin\lambda_c l), \quad l = 1, 2, \ldots \tag{2.3.39}$$

If $0<\rho<1$, the forecast function is a damped sine, or cosine, wave. If $\rho=1$ the forecast function is again a sine or cosine wave but no damping is present. The situation is therefore analogous to that of the AR(1) forecast function in (2.3.13), and indeed the condition that ρ be strictly less than unity is the one which is needed for stationarity.

A final point to note about the stochastic cycle in (2.3.38) is that it collapses to an AR(1) process when $\lambda_c=0$ or π. This arises because sin λ_c is zero when $\lambda_c=0$ or π and so the equation generating ψ_t^* is redundant. The first equation in (2.3.38) is therefore

$$\psi_t=\rho\psi_{t-1}+\kappa_t \tag{2.3.40a}$$

when $\lambda_c=0$ and

$$\psi_t=-\rho\psi_{t-1}+\kappa_t \tag{2.3.40b}$$

when $\lambda_c=\pi$. Thus although ρ is non-negative the autoregressive parameter in the AR(1) model can be either positive or negative.

2.3.4 Seasonality

In formulating a deterministic seasonal component in (2.3.1), the requirement that the seasonal effects sum to zero was made. This is reflected in (2.3.2) since for $t=s$, $2s$, $3s\ldots$ the seasonal effect is

$$\sum_{j=1}^{s-1} z_{jt}\gamma_j=-\sum_{j=1}^{s-1}\gamma_j$$

and denoting this effect by γ_s means that

$$\sum_{j=1}^{s}\gamma_j=0 \tag{2.3.41}$$

Now consider a slight change in notation whereby we let γ_t denote the seasonal effect at time t. Consistency with (2.3.41) requires that

$$\sum_{j=0}^{s-1}\gamma_{t-j}=0 \tag{2.3.42}$$

By introducing a disturbance term into the right-hand side of this equation, the seasonal effects can be allowed to change over time. Since the disturbance term has zero expectation these effects will still sum to zero in the forecast function. Formally the model is

$$\sum_{j=0}^{s-1}\gamma_{t-j}=\omega_t \quad \text{or} \quad \gamma_t=-\sum_{j=1}^{s-1}\gamma_{t-j}+\omega_t \tag{2.3.43}$$

where ω_t is white noise with mean zero and variance σ_ω^2. The bigger the value of the variance σ_ω^2 relative to σ_ε^2, the more are past observations discounted in constructing a seasonal pattern for the forecast function. For independent disturbances the optimal forecasts satisfy the recursion

$$\tilde{\gamma}_{T+l|T} = -\sum_{j=1}^{s-1} \tilde{\gamma}_{T+l-j|T}, \quad l=1,2,\ldots \tag{2.3.44}$$

where the starting values are given by the conditional expectations of the seasonal effects, $\gamma_T, \ldots \gamma_{T-s+2}$, at time T. Thus the seasonal pattern projected into the future is fixed, and its components sum to zero over any period of s consecutive months.

An alternative way of allowing the seasonal dummy variables to change over time is to suppose that the effect of each season evolves as a random walk. This model was introduced by Harrison and Stevens (1976, pp. 217–18). Let γ_{jt} denote the effect of season j at time t. Then

$$\gamma_{jt} = \gamma_{j,t-1} + \omega_{jt}, \quad j=1,\ldots,s \tag{2.3.45}$$

where ω_{jt} is a white-noise disturbance term with mean zero and variance σ_ω^2. Although all s seasonal components are continually evolving, only one affects the observations at any particular point in time, i.e.

$$\gamma_t = \gamma_{jt}, \quad t=1,\ldots,T \tag{2.3.46}$$

when season j is prevailing at time t. The requirement that the seasonal components in the forecast function sum to zero over s consecutive time periods is enforced by the restriction that, at any particular point in time, the seasonal components, and hence the disturbances, sum to zero, that is

$$\sum_{j=1}^{s} \gamma_{jt} = 0 = \sum_{j=1}^{s} \omega_{jt} \tag{2.3.47}$$

As we shall see in the discussion of daily effects, this restriction is implemented by an appropriate correlation structure between the ω_{jt}'s.

The stochastic formulation in (2.3.43) follows from the standard dummy variable methods of modelling a fixed seasonal pattern in regression. An alternative way of modelling such a pattern is by a set of trigonometric terms at the seasonal frequencies, $\lambda_j = 2\pi j/s$, $j=1,\ldots,[s/2]$; see Hannan, Terrell and Tuckwell (1970). The seasonal effect at time t is then

$$\gamma_t = \sum_{j=1}^{[s/2]} (\gamma_j \cos \lambda_j t + \gamma_j^* \sin \lambda_j t) \tag{2.3.48}$$

When s is even, the sine term disappears for $j=s/2$ and so the number of trigonometric parameters, the γ_j's and γ_j^*'s, is always $s-1$, which is the same as the number of coefficients in the seasonal dummy formulation. It is straightforward to show that (2.3.42) holds by using standard trigonometric identities.

If the trigonometric seasonal components of (2.3.48) are incorporated into a linear trend plus error model, in a similar way to (2.3.1), the parameters γ_j and γ_j^*, $j=1,\ldots,[s/2]$, can be estimated by OLS. Provided that the full set of trigonometric terms is included, (2.3.48) is equivalent to the dummy variable specifications of (2.3.43) and (2.3.45) and the estimated seasonal patterns will be identical. However, because seasonal patterns change relatively smoothly over the year, it may sometimes be reasonable to drop some of the higher-order frequencies. Abraham and Box (1978) give an example of the temperature recorded every month in Montana in which only the first frequency, $\lambda_1=2\pi/12$, is necessary. This first frequency, which corresponds to a period of twelve months, is known as the *fundamental frequency* while the remaining frequencies are *harmonics.* A second example given by Anderson (1971, pp. 106–7) concerns monthly sales of butter over a three-year period. Here the first two frequencies, corresponding to twelve and six months respectively, accounted for a high proportion of the seasonal variation. In some cases it may not simply be the higher frequencies which are dropped. Suppose, for example, that the data are collected *weekly* and that there is a pattern within each four-week period. This is an *intra-month* effect; an example of such an effect is given in Pierce *et al.* (1984). Since $s=52$, a full seasonal model would require trigonometric components at the 26 frequencies $\lambda_j=2\pi j/52$, $j=1,\ldots,26$. However, it might be possible to model the seasonal pattern using the frequencies for $j=1,\ldots,6$, while the intra-month effect is captured using the frequencies λ_{13} and λ_{26} corresponding to periods of 4 and 2 weeks respectively.

A seasonal pattern based on (2.3.48) is the sum of $[s/2]$ cyclical components and it may be allowed to evolve over time in exactly the same way as a cycle was allowed to evolve over time in sub-section 2.3.3. Thus

$$\gamma_t=\sum_{j=1}^{[s/2]}\gamma_{jt} \tag{2.3.49}$$

and following (2.3.37)

$$\left.\begin{aligned}\gamma_{jt}&=\gamma_{j,t-1}\cos\lambda_j+\gamma_{j,t-1}^*\sin\lambda_j+\omega_{jt}\\ \gamma_{jt}^*&=-\gamma_{j,t-1}\sin\lambda_j+\gamma_{j,t-1}^*\cos\lambda_j+\omega_{jt}^*\end{aligned}\right\}\quad j=1,\ldots,[s/2] \tag{2.3.50}$$

where ω_{jt} and ω_{jt}^* are zero mean white-noise processes which are uncorrelated with each other, with a common variance σ_j^2 for $j=1,\ldots,[s/2]$. The larger these variances, the more past observations are discounted in estimating the seasonal pattern. As in the cycle (2.3.30), γ_{jt}^* appears as a matter of construction, and its interpretation is not particularly important. Note that when s is even, the component at $j=s/2$ collapses to

$$\gamma_{jt}=\gamma_{j,t-1}\cos\lambda_j+\omega_{jt},\quad j=s/2 \tag{2.3.51}$$

Assigning different variances to each harmonic allows them to evolve at varying rates. However, from a practical point of view it is usually desirable to let these variances be the same. Thus

$$\mathrm{Var}(\omega_{jt}) = \mathrm{Var}(\omega_{jt}^*) = \sigma_j^2 = \sigma_\omega^2, \quad j = 1, \ldots, [s/2] \tag{2.3.52}$$

As a rule, very little is lost in terms of goodness of fit by having a common variance for the disturbances and a good deal of computer time is saved.

By setting up the model as in (2.3.48), a current estimate of the seasonal component is obtained just as it is in the dummy variable formulations of (2.3.43) and (2.3.45). At time T, the estimators of the γ_{jt}'s and γ_{jt}^*'s form starting values for a projection of a seasonal pattern into the future in a similar way to (2.3.39).

2.3.5 *Daily effects*

Let w be the number of different types of day in a week and let k_j be the number of days of the j-th type for $j = 1, \ldots, w$. Thus, for example, if all weekdays are alike but both Saturdays and Sundays are different, $w = 3$, $k_1 = 5$, and $k_2 = k_3 = 1$. If daily observations are available, a model is needed for the component in the series, θ_t, attributable to the type of day prevailing at time t. The model to be presented is not confined to daily effects. In fact it can be regarded as a generalisation of the seasonality model of (2.3.45); in that case $w = s$ and $k_j = 1$ for $j = 1, \ldots, s$ since all the seasons are assumed to be different.

The effect associated with the j-th type of day is θ_{jt}, where

$$\theta_{jt} = \theta_{j,t-1} + \chi_{jt}, \quad j = 1, \ldots, w-1 \tag{2.3.53}$$

the disturbance term χ_{jt} having zero mean and variance

$$\mathrm{Var}(\chi_{jt}) = \sigma_\chi^2 (1 - k_j^2/K), \quad j = 1, \ldots, w-1 \tag{2.3.54a}$$

where

$$K = \sum_{j=1}^{w} k_j^2$$

The covariances between the disturbances are

$$E(\chi_{jt}\chi_{ht}) = -\sigma_\chi^2 k_j k_h / K, \quad j \neq h, \quad j, h = 1, \ldots, w-1 \tag{2.3.54b}$$

Although all w daily effects are changing every day, only one of them affects the observations at any particular point in time. Thus the daily component in the model as a whole is

$$\theta_t = \theta_{jt}, \quad t = 1, \ldots, T$$

when the j-th type of day is prevailing at time t.

The reason for the specification of the variances and covariances of the disturbances in (2.3.54) is as follows. Suppose that the model in (2.3.53) is only formulated for the first $w-1$ daily effects. The effect for the w-th type of day is then defined by the requirement that, at any particular point in time, the sum of the daily effects over a week should be zero. Thus

$$\theta_{wt} = -k_w^{-1} \sum_{j=1}^{w-1} k_j \theta_{jt} \tag{2.3.55}$$

Substituting for the θ_{jt}'s in (2.3.55) from (2.3.53) shows that θ_{wt} follows a random walk with a disturbance term

$$\chi_{wt} = -k_w^{-1} \sum_{j=1}^{w-1} k_j \chi_{jt}$$

This can be written as

$$\chi_{wt} = -k_w^{-1} \mathbf{k}' \boldsymbol{\chi}_t$$

where $\mathbf{k}$ and $\boldsymbol{\chi}_t$ are $(w-1) \times 1$ vectors with j-th elements k_j and χ_{jt} respectively. Thus

$$\begin{aligned}
\mathrm{Var}(\chi_{wt}) &= k_w^{-2} \mathbf{k}' \, \mathrm{Var}(\boldsymbol{\chi}_t) \mathbf{k} = k_w^{-2} \mathbf{k}'(\mathrm{I} - K^{-1} \mathbf{k}\mathbf{k}')\mathbf{k}\sigma_\chi^2 \\
&= k_w^{-2} \left[\mathbf{k}'\mathbf{k} - \frac{1}{K} \mathbf{k}'\mathbf{k}.\mathbf{k}'\mathbf{k} \right] \sigma_\chi^2 = \sigma_\chi^2 k_w^{-2} [\mathbf{k}'\mathbf{k}(\mathbf{k}'\mathbf{k} + k_w^2) - (\mathbf{k}'\mathbf{k})^2]/K \\
&= \sigma_\chi^2 \mathbf{k}'\mathbf{k}/K = \sigma_\chi^2 (K - k_w^2)/K = \sigma_\chi^2 (1 - k_w^2/K)
\end{aligned}$$

This is the same expression as (2.3.54a). Furthermore,

$$\begin{aligned}
\mathrm{E}(\chi_{wt}\chi_{jt}) &= -k_w^{-1} \sum_{h=1}^{w-1} k_h \mathrm{E}(\chi_{jt}\chi_{ht}) \\
&= \frac{-\sigma_\chi^2}{k_w} \left[k_j - \frac{k_j \Sigma k_h^2}{K} \right] = -\sigma_x^2 \frac{k_j}{k_w} \left[1 - \frac{(K - k_w^2)}{K} \right] = -\sigma_x^2 \frac{k_w k_j}{K}
\end{aligned}$$

which corresponds to (2.3.54b). Therefore θ_{wt} has exactly the same properties as the other daily effects.

2.3.6 Structural models

A univariate structural time series model is one which is formulated in terms of components which, although unobservable, have a direct interpretation. Thus the model fulfils two roles. It not only provides the basis for making predictions of future observations, but it also provides a description of the salient features of a time series. The previous sub-sections described how components like trends and seasonals could be allowed to evolve over time in such a way that they satisfied certain desirable properties. The present sub-section discusses how these components are brought together in the main structural models. It is also shown how each of the models can be expressed in terms of a single equation.

All the models described below are such that the various components enter into the model in an additive fashion. However, if y_t is in logarithms the formulation is effectively a multiplicative one for the original observations.

The specification of a model is completed by making assumptions about the distributions of the various disturbance terms. The usual assumption is that these distributions are all normal. The consequences of non-normality are discussed in the introduction to section 6.6.

Local level/random walk plus noise The local level model was originally introduced in sub-section 2.1.1. The first equation is

$$y_t = \mu_t + \varepsilon_t, \quad t = 1, \ldots, T \tag{2.3.56a}$$

where the trend component, μ_t, is simply a level which fluctuates up and down according to a random walk,

$$\mu_t = \mu_{t-1} + \eta_t, \quad t = \ldots, -1, 0, 1, \ldots \tag{2.3.56b}$$

No starting value needs to be specified for μ_t since it is assumed to have started at some point in the remote past.

The single equation form of the model is obtained by adopting the convention that a non-stationary process like that in (2.3.56b) can be written as $\mu_t = \eta_t/\Delta$, where Δ is the first-difference operator defined in (2.1.6). Substituting in (2.3.56a) then gives

$$y_t = \frac{\eta_t}{\Delta} + \varepsilon_t, \quad t = 1, \ldots, T \tag{2.3.57}$$

When a drift term is added to the level as in (2.3.32), the single equation form of the model is

$$y_t = \frac{\eta_t}{\Delta} + \beta t + \varepsilon_t, \quad t = 1, \ldots, T \tag{2.3.58}$$

Local linear trend The local linear trend model consists of (2.3.56a) with the trend generated by (2.3.27). Substituting for $\beta_{t-1} = \zeta_{t-1}/\Delta$ in (2.3.27a) and then substituting for μ_t in (2.3.56a) gives

$$y_t = \frac{\eta_t}{\Delta} + \frac{\zeta_{t-1}}{\Delta^2} + \varepsilon_t, \quad t = 1, \ldots, T \tag{2.3.59}$$

The first component on the right-hand side of (2.3.59) is that part of the trend which derives from movements in the level. The second component is the contribution of the slope. Note that when σ_ζ^2 is zero, (2.3.59) reduces to (2.3.58).

Cyclical models The cycle plus noise model is

$$y_t = \mu + \psi_t + \varepsilon_t, \quad t = 1, \ldots, T \tag{2.3.60}$$

with ψ_t generated by the stochastic process (2.3.38). The irregular term ε_t is assumed to be uncorrelated with the disturbances κ_t and κ_t^* in (2.3.38), while μ is a constant term.

A single equation expression for ψ_t, and therefore y_t, can be obtained by noting that $[\psi_t \quad \psi_t^*]'$ is a vector AR(1) process and writing

$$\begin{bmatrix} \psi_t \\ \psi_t^* \end{bmatrix} = \begin{bmatrix} 1-\rho\cos\lambda_c.\mathrm{L} & -\rho\sin\lambda_c.\mathrm{L} \\ \rho\sin\lambda_c.\mathrm{L} & 1-\rho\cos\lambda_c.\mathrm{L} \end{bmatrix}^{-1} \begin{bmatrix} \kappa_t \\ \kappa_t^* \end{bmatrix} \tag{2.3.61}$$

where L is the lag operator, (2.1.2). Substituting the resulting expression for ψ_t in (2.3.60) gives

$$y_t = \mu + \frac{(1-\rho\cos\lambda_c\mathrm{L})\kappa_t + (\rho\sin\lambda_c\mathrm{L})\kappa_t^*}{1-2\rho\cos\lambda_c\mathrm{L}+\rho^2\mathrm{L}^2} + \varepsilon_t, \quad t=1,\ldots,T \tag{2.3.62}$$

A cycle may be combined with a trend in several ways. The two most important formulations seem to be the *trend plus cycle* model and the *cyclical trend* model. In the former the trend and cycle are simply added to each other so that

$$y_t = \mu_t + \psi_t + \varepsilon_t, \quad t=1,\ldots,T \tag{2.3.63}$$

when μ_t is given by (2.3.27). In the cyclical trend model, on the other hand, the cycle is actually incorporated within the trend. Thus the model consists of equations (2.3.56a) and (2.3.27b) with (2.3.27a) modified to

$$\mu_t = \mu_{t-1} + \psi_{t-1} + \beta_{t-1} + \eta_t \tag{2.3.64}$$

In both cases the cyclical component is assumed to be stationary so that ρ is strictly less than one.

The single equation form of the trend plus cycle follows immediately from (2.3.59) and (2.3.62). Similarly it is not difficult to show that for the cyclical trend,

$$y_t = \frac{\eta_t}{\Delta} + \frac{(1-\rho\cos\lambda_c\mathrm{L})\kappa_{t-1} + (\rho\sin\lambda_c\mathrm{L})\kappa_{t-1}^*}{\Delta(1-2\rho\cos\lambda_c\mathrm{L}+\rho^2\mathrm{L}^2)} + \frac{\zeta_{t-1}}{\Delta^2} + \varepsilon_t \tag{2.3.65}$$

Damped trend The local linear trend model may be modified by introducing a damping factor into the slope component. Thus

$$\beta_t = \rho\beta_{t-1} + \zeta_t, \quad 0 \leqslant \rho \leqslant 1 \tag{2.3.66}$$

This model may be formulated within the cyclical trend framework by setting $\lambda_c = 0$ and letting ψ_t play the role of β_t. The damped trend model differs from the local linear trend model in that the eventual forecast function is horizontal.

The single equation form of the damped trend model is

$$y_t = \frac{\eta_t}{\Delta} + \frac{\zeta_{t-1}}{\Delta(1-\rho\mathrm{L})} + \varepsilon_t$$

Basic structural model The basic structural model (BSM) is the stochastic generalisation of (2.3.1), namely

$$y_t = \mu_t + \gamma_t + \varepsilon_t \tag{2.3.67}$$

where μ_t is the local linear trend of (2.3.27) and γ_t is either the *dummy variable* seasonal component of (2.3.43) or the *trigonometric* seasonal component of (2.3.48). The Harrison-Stevens dummy variable seasonal model, (2.3.46), will not usually be used in this context. The irregular component, ε_t, is assumed to be random, and the disturbances in all three components are taken to be mutually uncorrelated.

The single equation form for the dummy variable seasonal component is easily seen to be

$$y_t = \frac{\eta_t}{\Delta} + \frac{\zeta_{t-1}}{\Delta^2} + \frac{\omega_t}{S(L)} + \varepsilon_t, \tag{2.3.68}$$

where S(L) is the seasonal summation operator defined in sub-section 2.1.2. This expression follows almost immediately once it has been noted that (2.3.43) can be written as

$$S(L)\gamma_t = \omega_t \tag{2.3.69}$$

As regards trigonometric seasonality, it follows from (2.3.61) and (2.3.62) that for each harmonic

$$\gamma_{jt} = \frac{(1-\cos\lambda_j L)\omega_{jt} + (\sin\lambda_j L)\omega_{jt}^*}{1-2\cos\lambda_j L + L^2}, \quad j=1,\ldots,[s/2] \tag{2.3.70a}$$

where, for s even, the last component collapses to

$$\gamma_{\frac{1}{2}s,t} = \omega_{\frac{1}{2}s,t}/(1+L) \tag{2.3.70b}$$

The seasonal component consists of the sum of the γ_{jt}'s, as given by (2.3.49), and so for s even

$$\gamma_t = \sum_{j=1}^{\frac{1}{2}s-1} \frac{(1-\cos\lambda_j L)\omega_{jt} + (\sin\lambda_j L)\omega_{jt}^*}{\mathrm{Y}_j(L)} + \frac{\omega_{\frac{1}{2}s,t}}{\mathrm{Y}_{\frac{1}{2}s}(L)} \tag{2.3.71}$$

where $\mathrm{Y}_j(L)$ and $\mathrm{Y}_{\frac{1}{2}s}(L)$ are the trigonometric operators, (2.1.16) and (2.1.17). If s is odd, the summation in (2.3.71) runs from $j=1$ to $(s-1)/2$ and the last term on the right-hand side does not appear.

Autoregressive models Autoregressive components may be quite properly included within structural models since the autoregressive mechanism often has a natural interpretation within the context of particular problems. Thus, for example, the irregular term in (2.3.56a) may be generalised to a stationary autoregressive process in which case the first equation in the model becomes

$$y_t = \mu_t + \upsilon_t \tag{2.3.72a}$$

$$\upsilon_t = \varphi_1 \upsilon_{t-1} + \cdots + \varphi_p \upsilon_{t-p} + \varepsilon_t \tag{2.3.72b}$$

where p is the order of the autoregression. This may be written more compactly as

$$y_t = \mu_t + \varphi^{-1}(L)\varepsilon_t \tag{2.3.73}$$

where $\varphi(L)$ is a p-th order polynomial in the lag operator

$$\varphi(L) = 1 - \varphi_1 L - \cdots - \varphi_p L^p \tag{2.3.74}$$

An alternative way of bringing an autoregressive mechanism into a model is by putting lags directly on y_t. Thus instead of (2.3.72) we may have

$$y_t = \varphi_1 y_{t-1} + \cdots + \varphi_p y_{t-p} + \mu_t + \varepsilon_t \tag{2.3.75}$$

In this case the trend may be re-defined as

$$\mu_t^\dagger = \varphi^{-1}(L)\mu_t \tag{2.3.76a}$$

so that

$$y_t = \mu_t^\dagger + \varphi^{-1}(L)\,\varepsilon_t \tag{2.3.76b}$$

Hence the trend and irregular components are both subject to similar autoregressive effects.

Weekly and daily data In sub-section 2.3.4, it was suggested that with weekly data it may sometimes be appropriate to split the full complement of trigonometric components into two sets representing seasonal and intra-month effects. Thus

$$y_t = \mu_t + \gamma_t + \gamma_t^* + \varepsilon_t, \tag{2.3.77}$$

where γ_t contains the frequencies $2\pi j/52$, $j = 1, \ldots, 6$ and γ_t^* contains the frequencies $\frac{1}{2}\pi$ and π. If the intra-month effects are within calendar, rather than lunar, months, it is necessary to let the intra-month frequencies vary according to the number of days in each month.

With daily observations, daily effects will normally need to be incorporated in the model as well. The specification of a daily effects component was discussed in sub-section 2.3.5.

A summary of the main structural models and their properties may be found in Appendix 1. Many more structural models may be constructed. Additional components may be introduced and the components defined above may be modified. For example, quadratic trends may replace linear ones, and the irregular component may be formulated so as to reflect the sampling scheme used to collect the data as in Hausman and Watson (1985). For most models it will be necessary to assume that the disturbances in the different components are uncorrelated with each other. This is for reasons of identifiability and will be discussed in section 4.4.

2.4 Stochastic properties

In a structural model components such as trend and seasonality reduce to deterministic functions of time when their stochastic parts are removed. The final forecast function for a particular component is of the same form as this deterministic function of time. Thus in the local linear trend model, setting η_t and ζ_t equal to zero for all t in (2.3.27) leads to $\mu_t = \alpha + \beta t$ and the forecast function is a straight line.

For a given component, the role of the stochastic disturbance term or terms is to allow what would have been a deterministic function to evolve over time. The stochastic properties of the model as a whole depend on the full set of disturbances. The ability to characterise the properties of these disturbances is essential, not only to an understanding of the way in which a model works, but also to the analysis and estimation of models. The first step in such a characterisation is to transform the model to a stationary process. This is normally carried out by differencing and related operations. The stochastic properties of the model can then be examined in both the time and frequency domains.

2.4.1 Stationary stochastic processes

A stochastic process is a mechanism which generates observations, y_t, over a period of time, $t = 1, \ldots, T$. In principle, the stochastic process could generate an infinite set of time series over the period in question. Each of these individual sets of observations is known as a realisation. For the process to be (*weakly*) *stationary* the following conditions must be satisfied for all values of t:

$$E(y_t) = \mu \tag{2.4.1}$$

$$E[(y_t - \mu)^2] = \text{Var}(y_t) = \gamma(0) \tag{2.4.2}$$

and

$$E[(y_t - \mu)(y_{t-\tau} - \mu)] = \gamma(\tau), \quad \tau = 1, 2, \ldots \tag{2.4.3}$$

The expectation is taken over all possible realisations of the process.

The essential feature of a stationary process is that its properties do not change over time. Thus the mean remains at a constant level, μ, and is independent of t. In a similar way the variance, $\gamma(0)$, and *autocovariances*, $\gamma(\tau)$, do not depend on t. The practical consequence of this property is that the mean, variance and autocovariances can be estimated from a single realisation. Thus

$$\hat{\mu}=\bar{y}=T^{-1}\sum_{t=1}^{T} y_t \tag{2.4.4}$$

$$\hat{\gamma}(0)=c(0)=T^{-1}\sum_{t=1}^{T}(y_t-\bar{y})^2 \tag{2.4.5}$$

and

$$\hat{\gamma}(\tau)=c(\tau)=T^{-1}\sum_{t=\tau+1}^{T}(y_t-\bar{y})(y_{t-\tau}-\bar{y}), \quad \tau=1,2,3,\ldots \tag{2.4.6}$$

The above quantities are known as the sample mean, sample variance and sample autocovariances respectively.

The dynamic properties of a stationary stochastic process can be summarised by plotting $\gamma(\tau)$ against τ. The full set of $\gamma(\tau)$'s is known as the autocovariance function. Since $\gamma(\tau)=\gamma(-\tau)$ for real series, it is unnecessary to extend the plot over negative values of τ. The autocovariances may be standardised by dividing through by the variance of the process. This yields the *autocorrelations*:

$$\rho(\tau)=\gamma(\tau)/\gamma(0), \quad \tau=0,1,2,\ldots \tag{2.4.7}$$

A plot of $\rho(\tau)$ against τ shows the autocorrelation function. Note that $\rho(0)$ is always equal to unity by definition.

The sample autocorrelations are defined by

$$r(\tau)=c(\tau)/c(0), \quad \tau=0,1,2,\ldots \tag{2.4.8}$$

A plot of the sample autocorrelations against τ is known as the *correlogram*. The sample autocorrelations are, of course, subject to sampling variability and so although the correlogram will tend to mirror the properties of the theoretical autocorrelation function it will not reproduce them exactly. Note that if the mean of the process μ, is known to be zero, the sample mean need not be used in the calculation of $c(0)$ and $c(\tau)$ in (2.4.5) and (2.4.6).

There is a stronger definition of stationarity than the one given above. A process is said to be *strictly stationary* if the joint probability distribution of a set of r observations at times $t_1, t_2, \ldots, t_r$ is identical to the joint probability distribution of the observations at times $t_1+k, t_2+k, \ldots, t_r+k$ for any k. If a process is strictly stationary, then it must be weakly stationary. The converse is not true. However if a series is weakly stationary and normally distributed, then it must be stationary in the strict sense.

2.4.2 Time domain properties of stationary stochastic processes

Since a white noise process is a sequence of uncorrelated random variables with constant mean and variance, $\gamma(\tau)=\rho(\tau)=0$ for $\tau\neq 0$. Although such a process is weakly stationary, it is not necessarily strictly stationary; this requires that the variables be independently and identically distributed. The distinction can be important in certain respects. For example, it is possible to construct non-linear models which are white noise, but for which non-trivial predictions of future observations can be made; see the discussion at the beginning of section 6.5. Of course, for normally distributed or *Gaussian* white noise, uncorrelatedness implies independence.

The next three sections are concerned only with the second-order properties of stochastic processes. Thus it is only necessary to invoke weak stationarity and so any disturbances appearing in a model need only be assumed to be white noise. No assumption regarding, say, normality needs to be made. The relevance of higher-order properties is not discussed until section 6.5 when the properties of non-linear models are examined.

The autocorrelation function characterises the second order properties of a stationary stochastic process in the time domain. In many cases it can be evaluated very easily.

Example 2.4.1 For the stationary AR(1) process, (2.3.6), taking expectations in (2.3.8) shows that y_t has zero mean. The variance is

$$\gamma(0)=\sigma^2(1+\varphi^2+\varphi^4+\cdots)=\sigma^2/(1-\varphi^2) \tag{2.4.9a}$$

Multiplying (2.3.6) through by $y_{t-\tau}$ and taking expectations gives

$$\gamma(\tau)=\varphi\gamma(\tau-1), \quad \tau=1,2,\ldots \tag{2.4.9b}$$

since $E(\xi_t y_{t-\tau})=0$ for $\tau\geqslant 1$. Dividing by $\gamma(0)$ and solving the resulting first-order difference equation gives

$$\rho(\tau)=\varphi^\tau, \quad \tau=0,1,2,\ldots \tag{2.4.10}$$

Since $|\varphi|<1$ for a stationary process, the autocorrelation function exhibits exponential decay.

Example 2.4.2 A first-order moving average, MA(1), process is defined as

$$y_t=\xi_t+\theta\xi_{t-1}, \quad t=1,\ldots,T \tag{2.4.11}$$

where θ is a parameter and ξ_t is white noise with mean zero and variance σ^2. No restrictions need to be imposed on θ for the model for it to be stationary. The mean of y_t is equal to zero while the variance is

$$E(y_t^2)=\sigma^2(1+\theta^2) \tag{2.4.12a}$$

The first-order autocovariance is

$$\gamma(1)=E(y_t y_{t-1})=E[(\xi_t+\theta\xi_{t-1})(\xi_{t-1}+\theta\xi_{t-2})]=\theta\sigma^2 \tag{2.4.12b}$$

while higher-order autocovariances are zero. The autocorrelation function is therefore

$$\rho(\tau)=\begin{cases}\theta/(1+\theta^2), & \tau=1\\ 0 & , \quad \tau\geqslant 2\end{cases} \tag{2.4.13}$$

Example 2.4.3 Suppose that a stationary AR(1) process is observed with error. The resulting model may be written as

$$y_t=y_t^{\dagger}+\varepsilon_t, \quad t=1,\dots,T \tag{2.4.14a}$$

$$y_t^{\dagger}=\varphi y_{t-1}^{\dagger}+\eta_t \tag{2.4.14b}$$

where $|\varphi|<1$ and η_t and ε_t are mutually uncorrelated white noise disturbances with variances σ_η^2 and σ_ε^2 respectively. The observed series y_t, has zero mean as each of the components has zero mean. Since the two components are uncorrelated with each other, the autocovariance of the observed series is equal to the sum of the autocovariances of the individual series. Thus

$$\gamma(\tau)=\gamma^{\dagger}(\tau)+\gamma_\varepsilon(\tau), \quad \tau=0,1,2,\dots \tag{2.4.15}$$

where $\gamma^{\dagger}(\tau)$ is the τ-th autocovariance of $y_t^{\dagger}$. From (2.4.10)

$$\gamma^{\dagger}(\tau)=\varphi^{\tau}\gamma^{\dagger}(0)=\varphi^{\tau}\sigma_\eta^2/(1-\varphi^2)$$

and so the autocorrelation function of the observations is:

$$\rho(\tau)=\frac{\varphi^{\tau}\sigma_\eta^2(1-\varphi^2)^{-1}}{\sigma_\eta^2(1-\varphi^2)^{-1}+\sigma_\varepsilon^2}, \quad \tau=1,2,3,\dots \tag{2.4.16}$$

The AR(1) and MA(1) processes are special cases of a class known as *autoregressive-moving average* processes. The importance of such processes for modelling stationary series is discussed at some length in sub-section 2.5.1. For the moment we note that an autoregressive-moving average process is defined as

$$y_t=\varphi_1 y_{t-1}+\cdots+\varphi_p y_{t-p}+\xi_t+\theta_1\xi_{t-1}+\cdots+\theta_q\xi_{t-q} \tag{2.4.17}$$

where $\varphi_1,\dots,\varphi_p$ are the autoregressive parameters, $\theta_1,\dots,\theta_q$ are the moving average parameters and the variance of the white-noise process, ξ_t, is σ^2. Such a process is normally referred to as ARMA(p, q). Thus the MA(1) process (2.4.11) can also be described as ARMA(0, 1).

By defining polynomials in the lag operator,

$$\varphi(\mathrm{L})=1-\varphi_1\mathrm{L}-\cdots-\varphi_p\mathrm{L}^p \tag{2.4.18a}$$

and

$$\theta(\mathrm{L})=1+\theta_1\mathrm{L}+\cdots+\theta_q\mathrm{L}^q \tag{2.4.18b}$$

the ARMA model can be written more compactly as

$$\varphi(L)y_t=\theta(L)\xi_t$$

or

$$y_t=\frac{\theta(L)}{\varphi(L)}\xi_t=\varphi^{-1}(L)\theta(L)\xi_t \tag{2.4.19}$$

The conditions for stationarity can be expressed in terms of the autoregressive polynomial, $\varphi(L)$, by the requirement that its roots should lie outside the unit circle; see the discussion below (2.1.3). No restrictions are needed on $\theta(L)$ for the process to be stationary.

The *autocovariance generating function* (a.c.g.f.) of a stationary process is defined as a polynomial in the lag operator, $g(L)$, such that

$$g(L)=\sum_{\tau=-\infty}^{\infty}\gamma(\tau)L^{\tau} \tag{2.4.20}$$

For an ARMA process, the a.c.g.f. is

$$g(L)=\sigma^2\frac{\theta(L)\theta(L^{-1})}{\varphi(L)\varphi(L^{-1})} \tag{2.4.21}$$

and the autocovariances can be obtained as the coefficients of powers of L.

Example 2.4.4 In the MA(1) model, (2.4.11),

$$\begin{aligned}g(L)&=(1+\theta L)(1+\theta L^{-1})\sigma^2\\&=(1+\theta^2)\sigma^2+\sigma^2\theta L+\sigma^2\theta L^{-1}\\&=\gamma(0)+\gamma(1)L+\gamma(-1)L^{-1}\end{aligned}$$

as $L^0=1$. The resulting autocorrelation function is as given in (2.4.13).

Suppose that a process is made up of a set of $n+1$ uncorrelated unobserved ARMA components, so that

$$y_t=\sum_{j=0}^{n}\theta_j(L)\varphi_j^{-1}(L)\xi_{jt} \tag{2.4.22}$$

where

$$E(\xi_{jt}\xi_{ht})=\begin{cases}0 & \text{for } j,h=0,\dots,n \text{ and } j\neq h\\ \sigma_j^2 & \text{for } h=j=1,\dots,n\end{cases}$$

The a.c.g.f. of the observed process is then the sum of the individual a.c.g.f.'s, that is

$$g(L)=\sum_{j=0}^{n}g_j(L) \tag{2.4.23}$$

2.4.3 Stationary form of structural models

The single equation form of the local linear trend model was given in (2.3.59). Applying the first-difference operator twice yields the stationary process

$$\Delta^2 y_t = \Delta\eta_t + \zeta_{t-1} + \Delta^2\varepsilon_t \tag{2.4.24}$$

For the BSM, the stationarity is achieved by multiplying through by the first and seasonal difference operators and taking note of the identity $\Delta_s = \Delta . S(L)$. For the seasonal dummy formulation, (2.3.43), this gives

$$\Delta\Delta_s y_t = \Delta_s\eta_t + S(L)\zeta_{t-1} + \Delta^2\omega_t + \Delta\Delta_s\varepsilon_t \tag{2.4.25a}$$

The trigonometric seasonal component, (2.3.71), is also reduced to stationarity by the seasonal summation operator. This is easily verified using the result given in (2.1.18) which yields

$$S(L)\gamma_t = \left\{ \sum_{j=1}^{\frac{1}{2}s-1} \bar{\gamma}_j(L)[(1-\cos\lambda_j L)\omega_{jt} + (\sin\lambda_j L)\omega_{jt}^*] \right\} + \bar{\gamma}_{\frac{1}{2}s}(L)\omega_{\frac{1}{2}s,t} \tag{2.4.25b}$$

where

$$\begin{aligned}\bar{\gamma}_j(L) &= S(L)/\gamma_j(L)\\ &= \prod_{i\neq j} \gamma_i(L)\end{aligned}$$

The third component on the right-hand side of (2.4.25a) is therefore replaced by Δ^2 multiplied by the right-hand side of (2.4.25b).

In general a linear, time-invariant structural model with components driven by $g+1$ white-noise disturbances ε_{kt}, $k=0,\ldots,g$ may be written in single equation form as

$$y_t = \sum_{k=0}^{g} \frac{\theta_k(L)}{\Delta_k(L)\varphi_k(L)}\varepsilon_{kt} \tag{2.4.26}$$

where $\theta_k(L)$ is an MA polynomial in the lag operator of order q_k, $\varphi_k(L)$ is a stationary AR polynomial of order p_k and $\Delta_k(L)$ is a non-stationary polynomial of order d_k. If the k-th component is stationary, $d_k=0$ and $\Delta_k(L)$ is equal to unity. As a rule, the roots of non-stationary $\Delta_k(L)$'s will be on the unit circle. This is the case with the difference operator, Δ, the seasonal difference operator, Δ_s, and the seasonal summation operator, S(L). However, it should be noted that it is possible to conceive of models, as in Parzen (1982), in which some of the roots of the non-stationary operators lie inside the unit circle.

The *stationary form* of (2.4.26) is obtained by finding a non-stationary operator $\Delta(L)$ which is of the minimum order necessary to contain all the roots of each of the individual non-stationary operators. If the individual non-stationary operators contain common factors then the order of $\Delta(L)$, d^*, will be less than the sum of the d_k's. Thus

$$d^* \leqslant d_0 + d_1 + \cdots + d_g \qquad (2.4.27)$$

Multiplying y_t by $\Delta(L)$ gives

$$\Delta(L)y_t = \sum_{k=0}^{g} \Delta_k^\dagger(L)\theta_k(L)\varphi_k^{-1}(L)\varepsilon_{kt} \qquad (2.4.28)$$

where

$$\Delta_k^\dagger(L) = \Delta(L)/\Delta_k(L), \quad k=0,\ldots,g$$

and the $\Delta_k^\dagger(L)$'s are of order $d^* - d_k$ for $k=0,\ldots,g$.

In the case of the local linear trend model, the first two components in (2.3.59) have the non-stationary operators Δ and Δ^2. Hence there is a common factor of Δ and so $\Delta(L)$ is set to Δ^2. Similarly in the BSM, $\Delta(L)$ is set equal to $\Delta^2 S(L)$, which is $\Delta\Delta_s$, rather than to $\Delta\Delta^2 S(L) = \Delta^3 S(L)$.

2.4.4 *Time domain properties of structural models*

It follows from (2.4.23) that the a.c.g.f. of the stationary series, $\Delta(L)y_t$ of (2.4.28), is given by

$$g(L) = \sum_{k=0}^{g} \frac{\Delta_k^\dagger(L)\Delta_k^\dagger(L^{-1})\theta_k(L)\theta_k(L^{-1})}{\varphi_k(L)\varphi_k(L^{-1})}\sigma_k^2. \qquad (2.4.29)$$

The a.c.g.f. could, in principle, be used to evaluate the autocorrelation function of $\Delta(L)y_t$. However, for the simpler structural models it is not necessary to resort to the a.c.g.f. for the evaluation of the autocorrelation function.

Random walk plus noise Taking first differences in (2.3.57) yields

$$\Delta y_t = \eta_t + \Delta\varepsilon_t \qquad (2.4.30)$$

from which it is easy to see that

$$E(\Delta y_t) = E(\eta_t) + E(\varepsilon_t) - E(\varepsilon_{t-1}) = 0$$

and

$$\gamma(0) = E[(\eta_t + \Delta\varepsilon_t)^2] = \sigma_\eta^2 + 2\sigma_\varepsilon^2$$
$$\gamma(1) = E[(\eta_t + \Delta\varepsilon_t)(\eta_{t-1} + \Delta\varepsilon_{t-1})] = -\sigma_\varepsilon^2$$
$$\gamma(\tau) = 0, \quad \tau \geqslant 2 \qquad (2.4.31)$$

Hence

$$\rho(\tau) = \begin{cases} -\sigma_\varepsilon^2/(\sigma_\eta^2 + 2\sigma_\varepsilon^2), & \tau = 1 \\ 0 & , \tau \geqslant 2 \end{cases} \qquad (2.4.32)$$

The only non-zero autocorrelation is therefore confined to the range $-0.5 \leqslant \rho(1) \leqslant 0$.

Local linear trend Evaluating the autocovariance function of (2.4.24) gives

$$\left.\begin{aligned} \gamma(0) &= 2\sigma_\eta^2 + \sigma_\zeta^2 + 6\sigma_\varepsilon^2 \\ \gamma(1) &= -\sigma_\eta^2 \quad\quad -4\sigma_\varepsilon^2 \\ \gamma(2) &= \quad\quad\quad\quad \sigma_\varepsilon^2 \\ \gamma(\tau) &= 0, \quad\quad\quad\quad \tau \geqslant 3 \end{aligned}\right\} \tag{2.4.33}$$

Dividing the $\gamma(\tau)$'s by $\gamma(0)$ gives the autocorrelation function. The first two autocorrelations satisfy the restrictions

$-0.667 \leqslant \rho(1) \leqslant 0$ and $0 \leqslant \rho(2) \leqslant 0.167$.

Basic structural model The BSM based on seasonal dummies, (2.3.43), is such that the autocovariance function for $\Delta\Delta_s y_t$ is

$$\left.\begin{aligned} \gamma(0) &= 2\sigma_\eta^2 + s\sigma_\zeta^2 + 6\sigma_\omega^2 + 4\sigma_\varepsilon^2 \\ \gamma(1) &= (s-1)\sigma_\zeta^2 - 4\sigma_\omega^2 - 2\sigma_\varepsilon^2 \\ \gamma(2) &= (s-2)\sigma_\zeta^2 + \sigma_\omega^2 \\ \gamma(\tau) &= (s-\tau)\sigma_\zeta^2, \quad\quad \tau = 3, \ldots, s-2 \\ \gamma(s-1) &= \sigma_\zeta^2 \quad\quad + \sigma_\omega^2 \\ \gamma(s) &= -\sigma_\eta^2 \quad\quad -2\sigma_\varepsilon^2 \\ \gamma(s+1) &= \quad\quad\quad \sigma_\varepsilon^2 \\ \gamma(\tau) &= 0, \quad\quad \tau \geqslant s+2 \end{aligned}\right\} \tag{2.4.34}$$

Some examples of typical autocorrelation functions for the BSM are given later in Table 2.5.1. Assuming that all the variances in the model are strictly positive, the equations in (2.4.34) imply the following constraints on the autocorrelations:

$$\left.\begin{aligned} &\rho(\tau)/\rho(\tau+1) = (s-\tau)/(s-1-\tau), \quad \tau = 3, \ldots, s-3 \\ &\rho(\tau) > 0 \\ &\rho(s) < 0 \\ &\rho(\tau-1) > \rho(\tau+1) > 0 \\ &|\rho(s)| > \rho(s+1) \end{aligned}\right\} \tag{2.4.35}$$

With trigonometric seasonality the autocovariance function is somewhat more complicated. However, it is not difficult to evaluate for quarterly data. The stationary form is

$$\begin{aligned} \Delta\Delta_4 y_t = \Delta_4\eta_t + (1 + L + L^2 + L^3)\zeta_{t-1} + \Delta^2(1+L)(\omega_{1t} + \omega_{1t}^*) \\ + \Delta^2(1+L^2)\omega_{2t} + \Delta\Delta_4\varepsilon_t \end{aligned} \tag{2.4.36}$$

with the simplifications arising because $\cos\frac{1}{2}\pi=0$ and $\sin\frac{1}{2}\pi=1$. The autocovariance function is therefore

$$\left.\begin{aligned}
\gamma(0) &= 2\sigma_\eta^2+4\sigma_\zeta^2+8\sigma_1^2+14\sigma_2^2+4\sigma_\varepsilon^2\\
\gamma(1) &= 3\sigma_\zeta^2-2\sigma_1^2-12\sigma_2^2-2\sigma_\varepsilon^2\\
\gamma(2) &= 2\sigma_\zeta^2-4\sigma_1^2+8\sigma_2^2\\
\gamma(3) &= \sigma_\zeta^2+2\sigma_1^2-4\sigma_2^2+\sigma_\varepsilon^2\\
\gamma(4) &= -\sigma_\eta^2+\sigma_2^2-2\sigma_\varepsilon^2\\
\gamma(5) &= \sigma_\varepsilon^2\\
\gamma(\tau) &= 0, \qquad \tau\geqslant 6
\end{aligned}\right\} \tag{2.4.37}$$

The fact that the seasonal component now depends on two parameters rather than one leads to a wider variety of patterns in the autocorrelation function. Even imposing the constraint that $\sigma_1^2=\sigma_2^2$ leads to fewer definite constraints on the signs and relative sizes of the autocorrelations than in the dummy variable formulation. In fact it appears that we can say that $\rho(5)$ is positive but little else.

Cycle The autocovariance function of the cycle, ψ_t of (2.3.38), is most easily derived by working with the model as a vector autoregression; see Exercise 8.1. Proceeding this way, it is found that

$$\text{Var}(\psi_t)=\sigma_\kappa^2/(1-\rho^2) \tag{2.4.38}$$

for $0\leqslant\rho<1$, and that

$$\rho(\tau)=\rho^\tau\cos\lambda_c\tau, \quad \tau=0,1,2,\ldots \tag{2.4.39}$$

Note that when $\lambda_c=0$ or π, these expressions reduce to the corresponding formulae for an AR(1) process, namely (2.4.9a) and (2.4.10).

For the cycle plus noise model, (2.3.60), it follows that

$$\rho(\tau)=\frac{\rho^\tau\cos\lambda_c\tau}{1+[(1-\rho^2)\sigma_\varepsilon^2/\sigma_\kappa^2]} \tag{2.4.40}$$

2.4.5 Frequency domain

The properties of a stationary stochastic process are captured in the frequency domain by taking a Fourier transform of the autocovariances. This yields the *power spectrum*

$$f(\lambda)=(2\pi)^{-1}\sum_{\tau=-\infty}^{\infty}\gamma(\tau)e^{-i\lambda\tau} \tag{2.4.41}$$

where λ is a frequency, in radians, in the range $[-\pi,\pi]$ and $i=\sqrt{-1}$. Since in the applications considered in this book y_t will always be real, $f(\lambda)$ will always be symmetric around zero and so the range of λ can be taken as $[0,\pi]$. Furthermore,

(2.4.41) may be written as

$$f(\lambda)=(2\pi)^{-1}[\gamma(0)+2\sum_{\tau=1}^{\infty}\gamma(\tau)\cos\lambda\tau] \qquad (2.4.42)$$

The power spectrum contains the same information as the autocovariances but presents it in a different way. Thus, for example, the spectrum of a white-noise process with variance σ^2 is

$$f(\lambda)=\sigma^2/2\pi \qquad (2.4.43)$$

The spectrum is therefore flat, and the process may be regarded as consisting of an infinite number of cyclical components all of which have equal weight.

Looking at (2.4.43) it will be seen that the area under the power spectrum over the range $[-\pi,\pi]$ is equal to the variance of the process. More generally

$$\int_{-\pi}^{\pi} f(\lambda)d\lambda=\gamma(0) \qquad (2.4.44)$$

Thus the power spectrum may be viewed as a decomposition of the variance of the process in terms of frequency. Sometimes the power spectrum is standardised by dividing by $\gamma(0)$. The same effect is achieved by replacing the autocovariances in (2.4.41) and (2.4.42) by the corresponding autocorrelations. This standardised function is known as the spectral density.

The *sample spectrum*, $I^{\#}(\lambda)$, is obtained by replacing the autocovariances in (2.4.42) by their estimators, (2.4.6). Thus

$$I^{\#}(\lambda_j)=(2\pi)^{-1}\left[c(0)+2\sum_{\tau=1}^{T-1}c(\tau)\cos\lambda_j\tau\right] \qquad (2.4.45)$$

Although $I^{\#}(\lambda)$ could, in principle, be calculated for any value of λ in the range $[0,\pi]$, it is normally only evaluated at the points $\lambda_j=2\pi j/T$, $j=0,\ldots,[T/2]$. When complex notation is used, the sample spectrum can be written as

$$I^{\#}(\lambda_j)=\frac{1}{2\pi}\sum_{\tau=-(T-1)}^{T-1}c(\tau)e^{-i\lambda_j\tau} \qquad (2.4.46)$$

$$=\frac{1}{2\pi T}\left|\sum_{t=1}^{T}(y_t-\bar{y})e^{-i\lambda_j t}\right|^2 \qquad (2.4.47)$$

Although λ_j is normally defined as in (2.4.45), it is sometimes useful, for theoretical purposes, to double its range to $[-\pi,\pi]$ or $[0,2\pi]$. Thus in the latter case $\lambda_j=2\pi j/T$, $j=0,\ldots,T-1$. As will be seen in section 4.3, this avoids certain complexities associated with odd and even numbers of observations and factors of two.

Subtracting the sample mean from the observations in (2.4.47) or in the sample autocovariances only affects the frequency $\lambda=0$. If the mean is not subtracted, the sample spectrum is

$$I(\lambda_j) = \frac{1}{2\pi T}\left|\sum_{t=1}^{T} y_t e^{-i\lambda_j t}\right|^2 \tag{2.4.48}$$

It is not difficult to show that $I(\lambda) = I^*(\lambda)$ except at $\lambda = 0$ where $I^*(0) = 0$ and $I(0) = (T/2\pi)\bar{y}^2$.

The sample spectrum is proportional to a quantity known as the periodogram. It is often referred to in this way in the literature, and this usage will sometimes be adopted here when the distinction is unimportant.

The sample spectrum is of direct use in estimating and testing time series models in the frequency domain; see sections 4.3 and 5.2. However, it is not a suitable estimator of the power spectrum. Although it can be shown to be unbiased in large samples, its variance does not decrease as the sample size increases. Hence it is inconsistent. The solution is to average over neighbouring frequencies. There are a number of ways in which this may be carried out and details may be found in any book which deals with spectral analysis, for example, Anderson (1971), Priestley (1981), Harvey (1981b) or Fishman (1969).

A brief review of the main trigonometric identities needed to cope with spectral analysis can be found in Harvey (1981b, ch. 3, appendix).

2.4.6 Frequency domain properties of stationary stochastic processes

The power spectrum of a stationary stochastic process may be obtained by evaluating the autocovariances and then substituting in (2.4.41) or (2.4.42). However, it is usually easier to proceed by working with the *spectral generating function* (s.g.f.). The s.g.f. is obtained from the a.c.g.f. by replacing the lag operator by $\exp(-i\lambda)$. Thus $g(L)$ becomes $g[\exp(-i\lambda)]$. For real series the minus sign can be dropped. The power spectrum is then given by

$$f(\lambda) = (2\pi)^{-1} g(e^{i\lambda}) \tag{2.4.49}$$

For an ARMA(p, q) model, defined in terms of the lag operator as in (2.4.19),

$$f(\lambda) = \frac{\sigma^2}{2\pi}\frac{|\theta(e^{i\lambda})|^2}{|\varphi(e^{i\lambda})|^2}; \tag{2.4.50}$$

see, for example, Harvey (1981b, pp. 70–4). Given the a.c.g.f., (2.4.21), the correspondence between (2.4.49) and (2.4.50) is immediate.

Example 2.4.5 For the AR(1) model, (2.3.6), $\varphi(L) = 1 - \varphi L$ and so

$$g(e^{i\lambda}) = \sigma^2/|1 - \varphi e^{i\lambda}|^2 = \sigma^2/[1 + \varphi^2 - 2\varphi \cos \lambda] \tag{2.4.51}$$

Corresponding to the result already noted for the a.c.g.f., the s.g.f. of a sum of uncorrelated stationary ARMA processes is given by the sum of the individual s.g.f.'s. Thus for the unobserved component ARMA model defined in (2.4.22)

$$g(e^{i\lambda}) = \sum_{j=0}^{n} g_j(e^{i\lambda}) = \sum_{j=0}^{n} \frac{|\theta_j(e^{i\lambda})|^2}{|\varphi_j(e^{i\lambda})|^2} \sigma_j^2 \tag{2.4.52}$$

Example 2.4.6 For the model, (2.4.14), the AR(1) process observed with error,

$$g(e^{i\lambda}) = \frac{\sigma_\eta^2}{1+\varphi^2-2\varphi\cos\lambda} + \sigma_\varepsilon^2 \tag{2.4.53}$$

The models for which the power spectrum conveys the most useful information are, not surprisingly, those which exhibit some kind of cyclical behaviour. The best illustration is provided by the cycle process defined in (2.3.38). When written in single equation form, the cycle is seen to be the sum of two uncorrelated components; see the formulation of the cyclical component in (2.3.62). Applying (2.4.52) the s.g.f. is

$$\begin{aligned} g_\psi(e^{i\lambda}) &= \frac{|1-\rho\cos\lambda_c e^{i\lambda}|^2 + |\rho\sin\lambda_c e^{i\lambda}|^2}{|1-2\rho\cos\lambda_c e^{i\lambda} + \rho^2 e^{i2\lambda}|^2} \sigma_\kappa^2 \\ &= \frac{(1-2\rho\cos\lambda_c\cos\lambda+\rho^2)}{(1-2\rho\cos(\lambda_c-\lambda)+\rho^2)(1-2\rho\cos(\lambda_c+\lambda)+\rho^2)} \sigma_\kappa^2 \\ &= \frac{1+\rho^2-2\rho\cos\lambda_c\cos\lambda}{1+\rho^4+4\rho^2\cos^2\lambda_c - 4\rho(1+\rho^2)\cos\lambda_c\cos\lambda + 2\rho^2\cos 2\lambda} \sigma_\kappa^2 \end{aligned} \tag{2.4.54}$$

As can be seen from the formula, the shape of the spectrum depends on λ_c and ρ, while σ_κ^2 is simply a scale parameter.

Figure 2.4.1 shows the power spectrum of a cycle with λ_c equal to $\pi/4$ and ρ taking the values 0.7, 0.9 and 0.99 respectively. As can be seen, the peak in the spectrum becomes sharper as ρ tends towards unity. The last panel in the figure shows the spectrum of the sum of two cyclical components, with frequencies $\pi/2$ and $\pi/10$, the former with ρ equal to 0.9 and the latter with ρ equal to 0.8. In both cases the variance, σ_κ^2, is unity.

When ρ is unity the cyclical process is non-stationary. The spectrum is no longer defined although a pseudo-spectrum, in which the frequency at λ_c is infinity, can be defined; see sub-section 2.4.8 below. If, on the other hand, σ_κ^2 is zero when ρ is unity, it is possible to regard ψ_t as being a stationary process provided that ψ_0 and ψ_0^* are taken to be mutually uncorrelated random variables with zero mean and common variance. The frequency domain properties of such a process can be handled by working with the spectral distribution function, which has a jump at frequency λ_c. Wold (1938) referred to a process of this kind as being deterministic, since once ψ_0 and ψ_0^*, or indeed any two observations, are given, its path is predetermined for evermore. From the practical point of view, ψ_0 and ψ_0^* can just as easily be regarded as fixed parameters; all that is lost is the spectral representation.

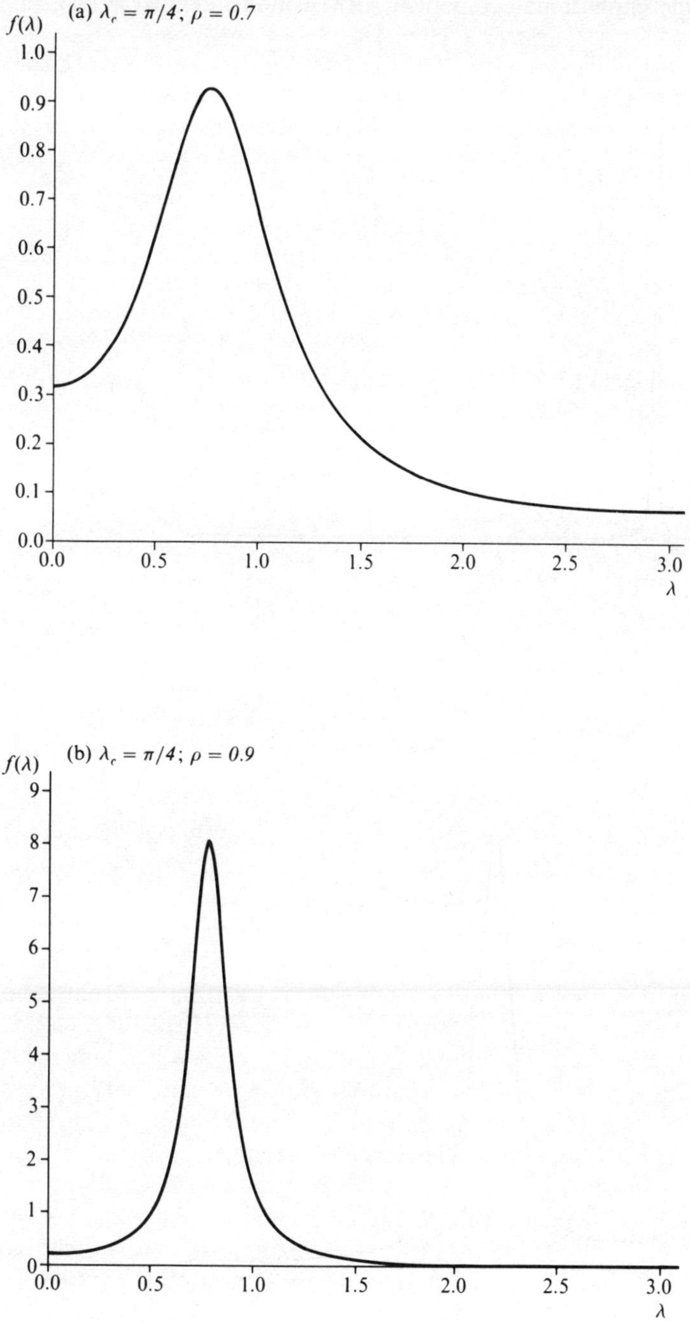

Fig. 2.4.1 Power spectra for stochastic cycles.

(*continued overleaf*)

(c) $\lambda_c = \pi/4;\ \rho = 0.99$

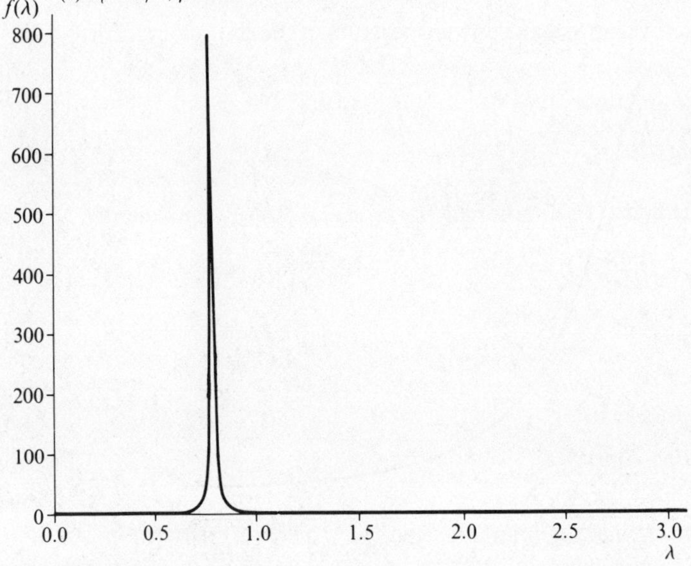

(d) $\lambda_c = \pi/10;\ \rho = 0.8$ *and* $\lambda_c = \pi/2;\ \rho = 0.9$

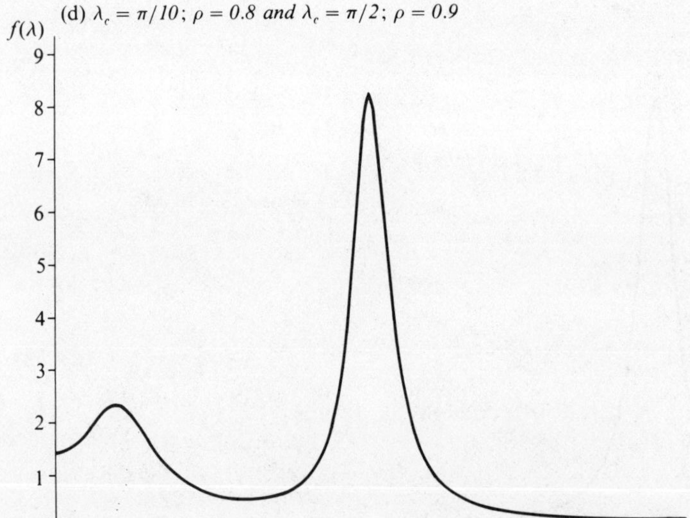

Fig. 2.4.1 (*continued*)

2.4.7 *Frequency domain properties of structural models*

For a general structural model, the power spectrum of the stationary form (2.4.28) is

$$f(\lambda)=\frac{1}{2\pi}\sum_{k=0}^{g}\frac{|\Delta_k^{\dagger}(e^{i\lambda})\theta_k(e^{i\lambda})|^2}{|\varphi_k(e^{i\lambda})|^2}\sigma_k^2 \tag{2.4.55}$$

Random walk plus noise The stationary form is (2.4.30) or, equivalently,

$$\Delta y_t=\eta_t+(1-\mathrm{L})\varepsilon_t$$

Hence

$$\begin{aligned} g(e^{i\lambda}) &= \sigma_\eta^2+|1-e^{i\lambda}|^2\sigma_\varepsilon^2 \\ &= \sigma_\eta^2+[2-(e^{i\lambda}+e^{-i\lambda})]\,\sigma_\varepsilon^2 \\ &= \sigma_\eta^2+2(1-\cos\lambda)\,\sigma_\varepsilon^2 \end{aligned} \tag{2.4.56}$$

Local linear trend The stationary form for the local linear trend model is

$$\Delta^2 y_t=(1-\mathrm{L})\eta_t+\zeta_{t-1}+(1-\mathrm{L})^2\varepsilon_t$$

Hence

$$g(e^{i\lambda})=2(1-\cos\lambda)\sigma_\eta^2+\sigma_\zeta^2+4(1-\cos\lambda)^2\sigma_\varepsilon^2 \tag{2.4.57}$$

Basic structural model The a.c.g.f. for the stationary form of the BSM with seasonal dummies is

$$\begin{aligned} g(\mathrm{L}) &= (1-\mathrm{L}^s)(1-\mathrm{L}^{-s})\sigma_\eta^2+\mathrm{S}(\mathrm{L})\mathrm{S}(\mathrm{L}^{-1})\sigma_\zeta^2+(1-\mathrm{L})^2(1-\mathrm{L}^{-1})^2\sigma_\omega^2\cdot \\ &\quad +(1-\mathrm{L})(1-\mathrm{L}^{-1})(1-\mathrm{L}^s)(1-\mathrm{L}^{-s})\sigma_\varepsilon^2 \end{aligned}$$

The s.g.f. is therefore

$$\begin{aligned} g(e^{i\lambda}) &= 2(1-\cos\lambda s)\sigma_\eta^2+\left[s+2\sum_{h=1}^{s-1}(s-h)\cos\lambda h\right]\sigma_\zeta^2+(6-8\cos\lambda+2\cos 2\lambda)\sigma_\omega^2 \\ &\quad +4(1-\cos\lambda)(1-\cos\lambda s)\sigma_\varepsilon^2 \end{aligned} \tag{2.4.58}$$

The term involving σ_ζ^2 can also be written as

$$|\mathrm{S}(e^{i\lambda})|^2=\frac{|1-e^{i\lambda s}|^2}{|1-e^{i\lambda}|^2}=\frac{(1-\cos\lambda s)}{(1-\cos\lambda)} \tag{2.4.59}$$

This expression can be used to evaluate the coefficient of σ_ζ^2 but it should be noted that it is indeterminate at $\lambda=0$. However, in this case it is easy to see that $\mathrm{S}(e^{i\lambda})=s$.

As regards trigonometric seasonality, it follows from (2.4.25b) that the term in the s.g.f. associated with the common variance, σ_ω^2, is

$$4(3-4\cos\lambda+\cos 2\lambda)\left\{\sum_{j=1}^{\frac{1}{2}s-1}[|\bar{\gamma}_j(e^{i\lambda})|^2(1-\cos\lambda_j\cos\lambda)]+|\gamma_{\frac{1}{2}s}(e^{i\lambda})|^2\right\}$$

Cyclical models Having determined the form of $g_\psi(e^{i\lambda})$ in (2.4.54), the power spectrum of any model involving a cyclical component can be obtained very easily. For example, the cyclical trend model has

$$g(e^{i\lambda})=g_\mu(e^{i\lambda})+2(1-\cos\lambda)\,g_\psi(e^{i\lambda}) \tag{2.4.60}$$

where $g_\mu(e^{i\lambda})$ is the power spectrum for the stationary form of a local linear trend model given in (2.4.57). The trend plus cycle model has a similar spectrum but with $2(1-\cos\lambda)$ replaced by $4(1-\cos\lambda)^2$. Adding a cycle to a BSM trend simply means replacing the last term by

$$4(1-\cos\lambda)(1-\cos\lambda s)[\sigma_\varepsilon^2+g_\psi(e^{i\lambda})] \tag{2.4.61}$$

2.4.8 *Pseudo-spectrum*

The frequency domain properties of a process, as manifested in the power spectrum, apply to the stationary form. However, as in the time domain, the transformations needed to make a process stationary have a distorting effect. While working with non-stationary processes in the time domain is of limited value as far as analysing their properties via the correlogram goes, the frequency domain offers somewhat greater scope in this respect.

For a non-stationary structural model in the component form of (2.4.26), the *pseudo-spectrum* is defined as

$$f^\dagger(\lambda)=\frac{1}{2\pi}\sum_{k=0}^{g}\frac{|\theta_k(e^{i\lambda})|^2}{|\Delta_k(e^{i\lambda})\,\varphi_k(e^{i\lambda})|^2}\sigma_k^2 \tag{2.4.62}$$

The pseudo-spectrum is finite for all values of λ in the range $[-\pi,\pi]$ except those associated with (unit) roots of the non-stationary operators. Specifically,

(i) if the non-stationary operator contains real roots then $f^\dagger(\lambda)$ is infinite at $\lambda=0$;
(ii) if the non-stationary operator contains complex roots then $f^\dagger(\lambda)$ is infinite when λ is equal to the phase of a pair of complex conjugates.

The difference operator has a real root of unity. As regards the S(L) operator, it was shown in (2.1.18) that this may be expressed as the product of the trigonometric polynomials at the seasonal frequencies. It therefore follows from (2.1.14) that the roots of S(L) are in pairs of complex conjugates with the phase of each pair equal to the seasonal frequency for $j=1,\ldots,(s/2)-1$ when s is even and $j=1,\ldots,(s-1)/2$ when s is odd. When s is even the component at frequency $\lambda=\pi$ has a real root of minus one. Bearing these results in mind, the pseudo-spectrum of the BSM will always be infinite at $\lambda_j=2\pi j/s$, $j=0,\ldots,[s/2]$. When a pseudo-spectrum is estimated, however, the infinite values are estimated as finite. How useful an estimated pseudo-spectrum is as a data analytic tool depends on the extent to which the ordinates which should theoretically be infinity dominate the other points.

2.5 ARIMA models and the reduced form

The class of autoregressive-moving average process was introduced in subsection 2.4.2, with an ARMA(p, q) model being defined in (2.4.17). If the roots of the autoregressive polynomial, $\varphi(L)$, lie outside the unit circle, the model is stationary. However, a much wider class of models, capable of exhibiting non-stationary behaviour, is obtained by supposing that series follow stationary ARMA processes after they have been differenced. These models are known as ARIMA processes.

This section explores the links between structural and ARIMA models. It is shown that the reduced forms of the principal structural time series models are ARIMA processes, and that linear structural models can be formulated as what are known as unobserved component ARIMA processes. Section 2.6 discusses the statistical treatment of ARIMA models when they are viewed, not as a reduced form, but as a class of models in their own right.

2.5.1 Stationarity and invertibility of ARMA models

If an ARMA process is stationary, it may be expressed as an MA(∞) process,

$$y_t = \sum_{j=0}^{\infty} \psi_j \xi_{t-j} \tag{2.5.1}$$

in which the MA coefficients satisfy the condition that

$$\sum_{j=0}^{\infty} \psi_j^2 < \infty \tag{2.5.2}$$

Since it is assumed that the white-noise disturbances, ξ_t, have finite variance, condition (2.5.2) ensures that the variance of y_t is also finite.

The condition that an ARMA model be *invertible* is, in a sense, the dual of the stationarity condition since it means that the model may be expressed as an AR(∞) process. Stated formally, invertibility requires that the roots of the MA polynomial, (2.4.18b), lie outside the unit circle. Thus for the MA(1) model, (2.4.11), the invertibility condition is $|\theta| < 1$. Repeated substitution for lagged values of ξ_t or, more elegantly, the inversion of the MA polynomial operator, $\theta(L) = 1 + \theta L$, gives the AR(∞) model

$$y_t = -\sum_{j=1}^{\infty} (-\theta)^j y_{t-j} + \xi_t \tag{2.5.3}$$

Compare the conversion of the AR(1) model to an MA(∞) process in (2.3.8).

An important reason for imposing the invertibility condition is to ensure identifiability. If the invertibility condition is not imposed on a model with an MA component, different sets of MA parameter values give rise to the same autocorrelation function. Thus suppose that an MA(1) model has a parameter θ with modulus greater than one. Its autocorrelation function can be reproduced exactly by an invertible process with parameter $1/\theta$. This can be seen by substituting in (2.4.13) to give

$$\rho(1) = \frac{1/\theta}{1+(1/\theta)^2} = \frac{\theta}{1+\theta^2}$$

An MA(1) model with $|\theta|$ equal to unity is something of an anomaly since it is not possible to find another parameter value which gives the same autocorrelation function. However, a model with $|\theta|$ equal to unity is *strictly non-invertible.* More generally an ARMA(p, q) model is strictly non-invertible if one or more of the roots of $\theta(L)$ lies on the unit circle while the others lie outside. As we shall see later, the concept of strict non-invertibility is quite an important one in time series modelling.

2.5.2 *ARIMA class of models*

Suppose that a series is stationary after it has been first-differenced d times. Such a series is said to be *integrated* of order d and this may be expressed by writing $y_t \sim I(d)$. A model in which the observations are taken to follow a stationary and invertible ARMA(p, q) process after they have been differenced d times is known as an *autoregressive-integrated-moving average* process of order (p, d, q). Adopting the notation used to write an ARMA model in (2.4.19) gives

$$\varphi(L)\Delta^d y_t = \theta(L)\xi_t \tag{2.5.4}$$

where ξ_t is a white-noise process with mean zero and variance σ^2. In more concise notation, $y_t \sim \text{ARIMA}(p, d, q)$.

A slight extension is to include a constant term θ_0 in (2.5.4). Thus

$$\varphi(L)\Delta^d y_t = \theta_0 + \theta(L)\xi_t \tag{2.5.5}$$

More fundamentally, perhaps, the class of models may be extended so as to include summation and higher order differencing operators. Thus Δ^d may be replaced by the general non-stationary operator, $\Delta(L)$, introduced at the end of sub-section 2.4.3 to give

$$\varphi(L)\Delta(L)y_t = \theta_0 + \theta(L)\xi_t \tag{2.5.6}$$

The order of $\Delta(L)$ is d^*, the highest power of L and the model may be referred to as ARIMA(p, d^*, q)+constant. In the special case when the seasonal difference operator is applied D times in conjunction with the Δ^d operator, the model becomes

$$\varphi(L)\Delta_s^D \Delta^d y_t = \theta_0 + \theta(L)\xi_t \tag{2.5.7}$$

The order of the non-stationary operator in this case is $d^* = d + sD$. Note that since $\Delta_s = \Delta S(L)$, a series generated by (2.5.7) is integrated of order $d + D$. The presence of the constant term does not affect the order of integration although, as will be seen in sub-section 2.6.1, it does affect the form of the forecast function.

A final point to note about an ARIMA model is that it can be regarded as an ARMA model in which some of the roots of the AR polynomial lie on the unit circle. Thus the ARIMA(p, d, q) model (2.5.4) is also an ARMA $(p + d, q)$ model with AR polynomial $(1 - L)^d \varphi_p(L)$.

2.5.3 Reduced form

A structural time series model normally contains several disturbance terms. Provided the model is linear, the components driven by these disturbances can be combined to give a model with a single disturbance. This is known as the *reduced form* or sometimes, as in Nerlove *et al.* (1979), the canonical form. The reduced form is an ARIMA model, and the fact that it is derived from a structural form will typically imply restrictions on the parameter space. If these restrictions are not imposed when an ARIMA model of the implied order is fitted, we are dealing with the *unrestricted* reduced form.

The order of the ARIMA reduced form is given in the general case by noting that the stationary form of a structural model, (2.4.28), can be written as

$$\varphi(L)\Delta(L)y_t = \sum_{k=0}^{g} \Delta_k^\dagger(L)\varphi_k^\dagger(L)\theta_k(L)\varepsilon_{kt} \tag{2.5.8a}$$

where

$$\varphi(L) = \prod_{k=0}^{g} \varphi_k(L) \tag{2.5.8b}$$

and

$$\varphi_k^\dagger(L) = \prod_{i \neq k} \varphi_i(L), \quad k = 0, \ldots, g \tag{2.5.8c}$$

Assuming that the autoregressive polynomials, $\varphi_k(L)$, $k = 0, \ldots, g$, contain no common factors, equation (2.5.8) may be compared with equation (2.5.6) in order to determine p and q; the constant term θ_0 is irrelevant to this comparison and can be ignored. As regards p it follows from (2.5.8b) that

$$p = p_0 + p_1 + \cdots + p_g \tag{2.5.9}$$

In order to determine q, first note that the right-hand side of (2.5.8a) consists of $g + 1$ moving average components, the k-th of which is of order $d - d_k + p - p_k + q_k$, $k = 0, \ldots, g$. Since the autocorrelation function of an MA(q) process has a cut-off at lag q, it follows that the cut-off in the autocorrelation function of the right-hand side of (2.5.8a) is at

$$q = \max_k (d - d_k + p - p_k + q_k) \tag{2.5.10}$$

The reduced form ARIMA(p, d^*, q) model therefore has p and q given by (2.5.9) and (2.5.10) respectively.

The actual values of the reduced form parameters may, in principle, be determined by equating the autocovariances in the structural and reduced forms. In practice this is rather complicated except in the simplest cases. A general algorithm is given in Nerlove *et al.* (1979, pp. 70–78).

The reduced forms of the principal structural models are set out below, and the restrictions on the ARIMA parameter space are explored. Most of the reduced forms may be derived without recourse to the general results derived above. As regards the restrictions, it will be argued later that they are an advantage rather than a disadvantage.

Local level/random walk plus noise models The autocorrelation function of first differences in the random walk plus noise model, (2.4.32), exhibits the cut-off at lag one characteristic of the MA(1) process. The reduced form is therefore ARIMA(0, 1, 1). Equating the autocorrelations at lag one in (2.4.13) and (2.4.32) gives

$$\theta = [(q^2 + 4q)^{\frac{1}{2}} - 2 - q]/2 \tag{2.5.11}$$

where q is the signal–noise ratio $q = \sigma_\eta^2/\sigma_\varepsilon^2$. Furthermore $\sigma^2 = -\sigma_\varepsilon^2/\theta$.

In solving the quadratic equation to get (2.5.11) the negative of the square root is dropped as it implies a non-invertible MA parameter. With θ as defined in (2.5.11), $0 \leqslant q \leqslant \infty$ corresponds to $-1 \leqslant \theta \leqslant 0$. Thus the MA parameter in the ARIMA(0, 1, 1) reduced form covers only half the usual parameter space for this model. Positive values of θ cannot be obtained from the random walk plus noise structural form.

Finally note that the reduced form ARIMA(0, 1, 1) model is strictly non-invertible when $\sigma_\eta^2 = 0$ since this corresponds to $\theta = -1$.

Local linear trend It can be seen from the autocovariance function in (2.4.33) that the reduced form of the local linear trend is an ARIMA(0, 2, 2) process. The restrictions on the parameter space are even more severe than in the case of the random walk plus noise model. Figure 2.5.1, adapted from Godolphin and Stone (1980), shows the admissible region.

The reduced form is strictly non-invertible if $\sigma_\zeta^2 = 0$. In this case the model has effectively collapsed to (2.3.32) and so taking first differences yields

$$\Delta y_t = \beta + \eta_t + \Delta\varepsilon_{t-1} \tag{2.5.12}$$

which is an ARIMA(0, 1, 1) model plus constant. Taking second differences gives

$$\Delta^2 y_t = (1 - \mathrm{L})(\eta_t + \varepsilon_t - \varepsilon_{t-1}) \tag{2.5.13}$$

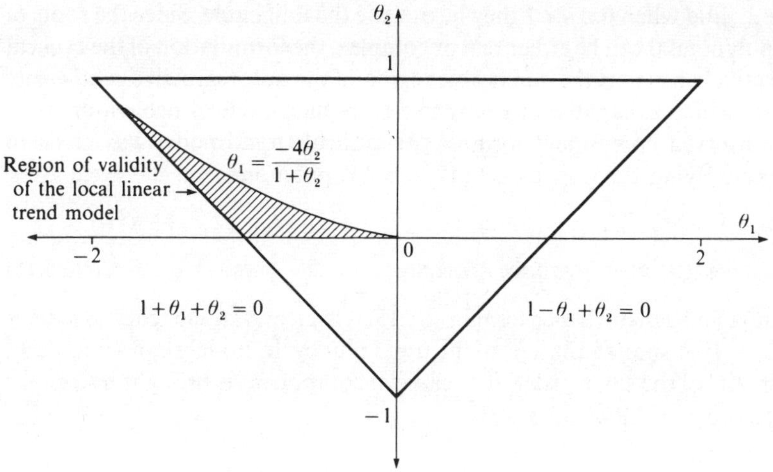

Fig. 2.5.1 Admissibility region of reduced form parameters of a local linear trend model.

and so the MA(2) process on the right-hand side must contain a unit root. Note that if σ_ζ^2 is positive, the model is invertible irrespective of whether σ_η^2 is zero.

Basic structural model The autocovariance function, (2.4.34), immediately indicates that the reduced form is such that $\Delta\Delta_s y_t \sim \text{MA}(s+1)$. The unrestricted reduced form therefore contains more parameters than the structural form, namely $s+2$ as opposed to four.

The discussion of the properties of the daily component below shows that the alternative dummy variable formulation of (2.3.45) also leads to $\Delta\Delta_s y_t$ being $\text{MA}(s+1)$. The same result follows for trigonometric seasonality since, as shown in sub-section 2.5.6, $\text{S(L)}\gamma_t \sim \text{MA}(s-2)$.

Cyclical models Writing the cycle plus noise model, (2.3.35), in the form

$$\begin{aligned} & y_t-(2\rho \cos \lambda_c)y_{t-1}+\rho^2 y_{t-2} \\ & \quad =\kappa_t-(\rho \cos \lambda_c)\kappa_{t-1}+(\rho \sin \lambda_c)\kappa_{t-1}^*+\varepsilon_t-(2\rho \cos \lambda_c)\varepsilon_{t-1}+\rho^2\varepsilon_{t-2} \end{aligned}$$

shows it to be an ARMA(2, 2) process. The cycle by itself is ARMA(2, 1). The MA part is subject to restrictions but the more interesting constraints are on the AR parameters. The AR polynomial, $\varphi(\text{L})=1-\varphi_1\text{L}-\varphi_2\text{L}^2$ has $\varphi_1=2\rho \cos \lambda_c$ and $\varphi_2=-\rho^2$ and so its roots are

$$m_1, m_2=\left(2\rho\cos\lambda_c \pm\sqrt{4\rho^2\cos^2\lambda_c-4\rho^2}\right)/2\rho^2=\rho^{-1}\exp(\pm i\lambda_c) \qquad (2.5.14)$$

Thus, for $0<\lambda_c<\pi$, the roots are a pair of complex conjugates with modulus ρ^{-1}

and phase λ_c, and when $0 \leqslant \rho < 1$ they lie outside the unit circle. Since the roots of an AR(2) polynomial can be either real or complex, the formulation of the cyclical model effectively restricts the admissible region of the autoregressive coefficients to that part which is capable of giving rise to pseudo-cyclical behaviour.

The unobserved component form of the cyclical trend model was given in (2.3.65). Multiplying through by Δ^2 and the AR polynomial in the cycle gives

$$(1-2\rho \cos \lambda_c L+\rho^2 L^2)\Delta^2 y_t=(1-2\rho \cos \lambda_c L+\rho^2 L^2)(\Delta\eta_t+\zeta_{t-1}+\Delta^2\varepsilon_t)$$
$$+\Delta(1-\rho \cos \lambda_c L)\kappa_{t-1}+\Delta(\rho \sin \lambda_c L)\kappa^*_{t-1} \qquad (2.5.15)$$

The largest lag on a disturbance term in (2.5.15) is four, and so the reduced form is ARIMA(2, 2, 4). A similar analysis of the trend plus cycle model shows it to be an ARIMA model of the same order. If a seasonal component is brought into either model then $\Delta\Delta_s y_t \sim$ ARMA$(2, s+3)$.

Daily component The reduced form of a daily component model, (2.3.53), with $k_j=1$ for $j=1,\ldots, w$ is such that $S_w(L)\theta_t$ is an MA$(w-2)$ process. This can be shown as follows. For any given t, only one of the θ_{jt}'s represents the daily effect, θ_t, at that time. Suppose, without any loss in generality, that the value of t is such that $\theta_t=\theta_{wt}$. Then $\theta_{t-1}=\theta_{w-1,t-1}$ and so

$$\theta_{w-1,t}=\theta_{w-1,t-1}+\chi_{w-1,t}=\theta_{t-1}+\chi_{w-1,t}$$

More generally, since $\theta_{t-i}=\theta_{w-i,t-i}$,

$$\theta_{w-i,t}=\theta_{t-i}+\sum_{h=0}^{i-1}\chi_{w-i,t-h}, \quad i=1,\ldots, w-1$$

From (2.3.55),

$$\theta_t=-\sum_{j=1}^{w-1}\theta_{jt}=-\sum_{i=1}^{w-1}\theta_{w-i,t}$$

and so summing over the $\theta_{w-i,t}$'s and rearranging gives

$$\sum_{j=0}^{w-1}\theta_{t-j}=-\sum_{i=1}^{w-1}\sum_{h=0}^{i-1}\chi_{w-i,t-h}$$

The right-hand side of the above expression is the sum of a white-noise process, an MA(1) process, an MA(2) process, and so on up to an MA$(w-2)$ process. This sum is an MA$(w-2)$ process. Hence $S_w(L)\theta_t \sim$ MA$(w-2)$.

2.5.4 *Multiplicative seasonal ARIMA models*

For modelling seasonal data, Box and Jenkins (1976, ch. 9) proposed a class of multiplicative ARIMA models. The most important model within this class has subsequently become known as the 'airline model' since it was originally fitted to a monthly series on UK airline passenger totals. The model is written as

$$\Delta\Delta_s y_t = (1+\theta L)(1+\Theta L^s)\xi_t \tag{2.5.16}$$

where θ and Θ are MA parameters which, if the model is to be invertible, must have modulus less than one. Setting $\theta = \Theta = -1$ yields a model which is equivalent to the deterministic trend and seasonal of (2.3.1). This may be seen by observing that the $\Delta\Delta_s$ operator removes both deterministic components to give

$$\Delta\Delta_s y_t = (1-L)(1-L^s)\varepsilon_t \tag{2.5.17}$$

Since $\Delta\Delta_s$ is equal to $\Delta^2 S(L)$, the trend can be thought of as being annihilated by Δ^2, while the seasonal is averaged out by the summation operator, S(L).

Box and Jenkins (1976, pp. 305–6) gave the following rationale for the airline model. They first noted that the forecasts from an ARIMA(0, 1, 1) model take the form of an EWMA. This may be shown directly, as in Example 2.6.1, although it also follows indirectly from the discussion in the previous sub-section where it was shown that the random walk plus noise model is equivalent to ARIMA(0, 1, 1). Bearing in mind the ARIMA(0, 1, 1) rationalisation for the EWMA, the following model may be put forward for linking observations one year apart:

$$\Delta_s y_t = (1+\Theta L^s)\alpha_t \tag{2.5.18a}$$

where α_t is a stochastic disturbance. A similar process may be postulated for linking the α_t's one month (or one quarter) apart, i.e.

$$\Delta\alpha_t = (1+\theta L)\xi_t \tag{2.5.18b}$$

Combining (2.5.18a) and (2.5.18b) gives (2.5.16). If the ξ_t's are independent, the optimal forecasts for the model may be constructed in terms of EWMAs in the following way. Let $\mathrm{EWMA}_\lambda(x_t)$ denote the standard EWMA of (2.2.3) applied to a variable x_t, that is

$$\mathrm{EWMA}_\lambda(x_t) = \lambda x_t + \lambda(1-\lambda)x_{t-1} + \lambda(1-\lambda)^2 x_{t-2} + \cdots$$

Similarly, let

$$\mathrm{EWMA}_\Lambda(x_t) = \Lambda x_t + \Lambda(1-\Lambda)x_{t-s} + \Lambda(1-\Lambda)^2 x_{t-2s} + \cdots$$

If $\lambda = 1+\theta$ and $\Lambda = 1+\Theta$, Box and Jenkins (1976, p. 312) show that the one-step-ahead forecast for (2.5.16) is given by

$$\tilde{y}_{t+1|t} = \mathrm{EWMA}_\lambda(y_t) + \mathrm{EWMA}_\Lambda[y_{t-s+1} - \mathrm{EWMA}_\lambda(y_{t-s})]$$

Thus the forecast is the EWMA taken over previous months, modified by a second EWMA of discrepancies found between similar monthly EWMAs and actual values in previous years.

The success of the airline model led Box and Jenkins to propose a class of multiplicative seasonal ARIMA models. Let $\Phi(L^s)$ and $\Theta(L^s)$ denote seasonal polynomials in the lag operator of orders P and Q respectively defined by

$$\Phi(L^s) = 1 - \Phi_1 L^s - \cdots - \Phi_P L^{Ps} \tag{2.5.19a}$$

$$\Theta(L^s) = 1 + \Theta_1 L^s + \cdots + \Theta_Q L^{Qs} \tag{2.5.19b}$$

A multiplicative seasonal ARIMA process of order $(p, d, q) \times (P, D, Q)_s$ is

$$\Phi(L^s)\varphi(L)\Delta^d \Delta_s^D y_t = \theta_0 + \Theta(L^s)\theta(L)\xi_t \tag{2.5.20}$$

where ξ_t is a white-noise process with mean zero and variance σ^2, $\varphi(L)$ and $\theta(L)$ are defined as in (2.4.18) and Δ_s^D denotes the seasonal difference operator applied D times. The airline model is of order $(0, 1, 1) \times (0, 1, 1)_s$ with no constant.

2.5.5 *Airline and basic structural models*

It was shown in sub-section 2.5.3 that both the trigonometric and dummy variable forms of the BSM are such that $\Delta\Delta_s y_t \sim \text{MA}(s+1)$. The non-stationary operator in the reduced form is therefore the same as the non-stationary operator in the airline model, (2.5.16). However, the MA$(s+1)$ process is not of the multiplicative form. This then raises the question as to the relationship between the BSM and the airline model. Both appear to be relatively successful at modelling time series which exhibit trend and seasonal movements and so one would expect them to be fairly close.

The autocovariance function for the airline model is:

$$\begin{aligned}
\gamma(0) &= (1+\theta^2)(1+\Theta^2)\sigma^2 \\
\gamma(1) &= \theta(1+\Theta^2)\sigma^2 \\
\gamma(\tau) &= 0 \qquad , \quad \tau = 2, \ldots, s-2 \\
\gamma(s-1) &= \theta\Theta\sigma^2 \\
\gamma(s) &= \Theta(1+\theta^2)\sigma^2 \\
\gamma(s+1) &= \theta\Theta\sigma^2 \\
\gamma(\tau) &= 0 \qquad , \quad \tau \geqslant s+2
\end{aligned} \tag{2.5.21}$$

As it stands, this autocovariance function of the BSM with dummy variable seasonality, (2.4.34), is rather different to that of (2.5.21) because of the 'gaps' in the latter. However, if, as often happens in practice, the structural model has $\sigma_\zeta^2 = 0$ the properties of its autocovariance function become

$$\begin{aligned}
&\rho(1) < 0 \\
&\rho(2) > 0 \\
&\rho(\tau) = 0 \qquad , \quad \tau = 3, \ldots, s-2 \\
&\rho(s) < 0 \\
&|\rho(s)| > \rho(s-1) > 0 \\
&\rho(s-1) = \rho(s+1)
\end{aligned} \tag{2.5.22}$$

This is in contrast to the earlier properties given in (2.4.35). In the airline model there are good reasons for requiring θ and Θ to be negative; see sub-section 2.5.6.

Table 2.5.1 *Autocorrelation functions of BSM and airline models*

Model	$\rho(1)$	$\rho(2)$	$\rho(11)$	$\rho(12)$	$\rho(13)$
Airline					
$\theta=-0.8,\quad \Theta=-0.8$	-0.488	—	0.238	-0.488	0.238
$\theta=-0.8,\quad \Theta=-0.4$	-0.488	—	0.168	-0.345	0.168
$\theta=-0.4,\quad \Theta=-0.8$	-0.345	—	0.168	-0.488	0.168
$\theta=-0.4,\quad \Theta=-0.4$	-0.345	—	0.119	-0.345	0.199
BSM					
$\sigma_\eta^2=1,\quad \sigma_\omega^2=0.25,\quad \sigma_\varepsilon^2=20$	-0.490	0.003	0.239	-0.490	0.239
$\sigma_\eta^2=1,\quad \sigma_\omega^2=0.75,\quad \sigma_\varepsilon^2=3$	-0.486	0.040	0.162	-0.378	0.162
$\sigma_\eta^2=1,\quad \sigma_\omega^2=0.01,\quad \sigma_\varepsilon^2=1.13$	-0.350	0.001	0.172	-0.495	0.172
$\sigma_\eta^2=1,\quad \sigma_\omega^2=0.25,\quad \sigma_\varepsilon^2=0.70$	-0.380	0.039	0.111	-0.380	0.111

When this is true (2.5.21) satisfies all the constraints in (2.5.22). The only difference is that $\rho(2)$ is positive in the structural model while in the airline model it is zero. However, since $\gamma(2)=\sigma_\omega^2$, $\rho(2)$ will typically be rather small. Table 2.5.1, taken from Maravall (1985), compares the autocorrelation functions of the two models for some typical values of the parameters. As can be seen, they are quite similar, particularly when the seasonal MA parameter, Θ, is close to minus one. In fact in the limiting case when Θ is equal to minus one, the airline model is equivalent to a BSM in which σ_ζ^2 and σ_ω^2 are both zero. It is straightforward to see that this is true from the stationary form of the BSM given in (2.4.25): removing the terms in ω_t and ζ_t gives

$$\begin{aligned}\Delta\Delta_s y_t &= \Delta_s \eta_t + \Delta\Delta_s \varepsilon_t \\ &= \Delta_s(\eta_t + \varepsilon_t - \varepsilon_{t-1}) \\ &= (1+\theta \mathrm{L})(1-\mathrm{L}^s)\xi_t \end{aligned} \tag{2.5.23}$$

with θ given by (2.5.11).

In terms of the BSM, therefore, the airline model provides a close approximation to the reduced form when σ_ω^2 and σ_ζ^2 are close to zero. In relatively short time series, consisting of only a few years, it is difficult to detect a change in the seasonal pattern which suggests that σ_ω^2 will be zero or close to zero. Changes in the slope may also be difficult to detect in a short time series. For longer stretches of data, non-negligible values for either σ_ω^2 or σ_ζ^2 may lead to the airline model being relatively less good as an approximation to the reduced form since there is effectively only one parameter to pick up changes in the slope and the seasonal pattern.

The above comparison has been confined to the airline model and the BSM with dummy variable seasonality. With trigonometric seasonality the autocorrelation function of $\Delta\Delta_s y_t$ is somewhat more complicated and, as noted below (2.3.37), it leads to fewer definite restrictions. When σ_ζ^2 is set equal to zero, there are correspondingly fewer restrictions than in (2.5.22), though for quarterly data it can be shown that

$$\rho(1)<0, \quad \rho(2)>0 \quad \text{and} \quad \rho(4)>0$$

as well as $\rho(\tau)=0$ for $\tau \geqslant 6$. Of course when σ_ω^2 is zero as well, the model is equivalent to the dummy variable seasonal BSM and there is exact equivalence with the airline model.

2.5.6 *UCARIMA form*

In the single equation form of a structural model, the component associated with each disturbance term is written separately. Thus the single equation form the trend plus cycle model is:

$$y_t = \frac{\eta_t}{\Delta} + \frac{\zeta_{t-1}}{\Delta^2} + \frac{(1-\rho\cos\lambda_c \mathrm{L})}{1-2\rho\cos\lambda_c \mathrm{L}+\rho^2\mathrm{L}^2}\kappa_t$$

$$+\frac{\rho\sin\lambda_c \mathrm{L}}{1-2\rho\cos\lambda_c \mathrm{L}+\rho^2\mathrm{L}^2}\kappa_t^* + \varepsilon_t \qquad (2.5.24)$$

The first two components make up the trend, μ_t, while the second two form the cycle. Amalgamating these components allows the model to be written in the form

$$y_t = \frac{(1+\theta_1 \mathrm{L})}{\Delta^2}\xi_{1t} + \frac{(1+\theta_2 \mathrm{L})}{1-2\rho\cos\lambda_c \mathrm{L}+\rho^2\mathrm{L}^2}\xi_{2t} + \xi_{0t} \qquad (2.5.25)$$

where ξ_{1t} is a composite of η_t and ζ_{t-1}, ξ_{2t} is a composite of κ_t and κ_t^* and ξ_{0t} is the same as ε_t. Since $(1+\theta_1 \mathrm{L})\xi_{1t}=\Delta\eta_t+\zeta_{t-1}$, it follows by similar reasoning to that employed in obtaining the reduced form of a local level model that θ_1 must be negative, lying in the range $-1 \leqslant \theta_1 \leqslant 0$. In fact θ_1 is given by (2.5.11) with q replaced by $\sigma_\eta^2/\sigma_\zeta^2$. As regards the cycle, a consideration of the special cases arising when $\lambda_c=0$ or π shows that $|\theta_2|<1$ provided that $|\rho|<1$.

Viewed as (2.5.25) the model is seen as the sum of an ARIMA (0, 2, 1) process for the trend, a stationary ARMA(2, 1) process for the cycle and a white-noise disturbance term for the irregular. Since each component is a member of the ARIMA class, the representation in (2.5.25) is known as the *unobserved components autoregressive-integrated-moving average* form or, more simply, as the UCARIMA form. This terminology was introduced by Engle (1978).

The BSM can also be expressed in UCARIMA form. In the case when the seasonal component is derived from the dummy variable formulation, (2.3.43), this is straightforward. All that is required is the amalgamation of the first two terms in (2.3.67). As in the previous model, these two terms make up the trend and they follow an ARIMA (0, 2, 1) model. The seasonal component, $\gamma_t=\omega_t/\mathrm{S(L)}$, falls within the definition of an ARIMA model given in (2.5.6) with $\Delta(L)$ equal to $S(L)$ and d^* equal to $s-1$. As regards the BSM with trigonometric seasonality, an examination of (2.4.25b) shows that the right-hand side contains no powers of L higher than $s-2$ and hence is an MA($s-2$) process. It is invertible provided that the σ_j^2's are strictly positive for all $j=1,\ldots,[s/2]$.

The UCARIMA form provides an intermediate step between the structural form and the reduced form and provides a further link with the ARIMA framework. In particular, Burman (1980) and Hillmer and Tiao (1982) have argued that an ARIMA model such as the airline model may be decomposed into a trend plus seasonal plus irregular model of the UCARIMA form. A comparison of such decompositions with the BSM is undertaken in section 6.2.

In general, the UCARIMA form of the model will be defined as a component form of the model in which $M+1 \leqslant g+1$ components are of direct interest. Thus, for example, in the trigonometric seasonal model the individual trigonometric components, the γ_{jt}'s, are not normally of direct interest. Hence the UCARIMA form only includes the composite seasonal component, γ_t. Furthermore, if a non-stationary operator in the component form is included in the non-stationary operator of another component, the two components will normally be merged in the UCARIMA form. The merging of the level and slope components into a single trend component in (2.5.25) provides an illustration.

The general UCARIMA form can be written as

$$y_t = \sum_{m=0}^{M} \frac{\theta_m(L)}{\varphi_m(L)\Delta_m(L)} \xi_{mt} \tag{2.5.27}$$

where the ξ_{mt}'s are white-noise disturbances, $\theta_m(L)$ is an MA polynomial in the lag operator and so on. If the non-stationary polynomials $\Delta_m(L)$ have no roots in common, the operator which reduces the whole model to stationarity is

$$\Delta(L) = \prod_{m=0}^{M} \Delta_m(L) \tag{2.5.28}$$

and this operator is the same as the $\Delta(L)$ of (2.4.28). It is worth noting that distinct roots for the individual non-stationary operators, the $\Delta_m(L)$'s, combined with strictly positive variances for the ξ_{mt}'s guarantee that the reduced form is invertible; see also Pierce (1979, p. 1306).

2.6 ARIMA modelling

The previous section introduced the class of ARIMA models and showed how such models could arise as the reduced forms of structural time series models. However, we may wish to work directly with the class of ARIMA models without reference to any underlying structural models. If this approach is taken, it is necessary to have some method of determining the order of the model. This requires a model selection strategy. The actual estimation of a model in the ARIMA class is carried out without placing any restrictions on the parameter space, apart from those implied by stationarity and invertibility.

The logic underlying the choice of the ARIMA class as the basic class of models for time series forecasting is as follows. Firstly, it follows from the Wold decomposition theorem that any indeterministic stationary process can be written as an infinite moving average as in (2.5.1). Such a process can be approximated, to any level of accuracy, by a model within the ARMA class. As a rule it should be possible to find an ARMA model which is parsimonious in the sense that p and q are relatively small. The next step is to argue that while most time series are non-stationary, they can be made stationary by operations such as differencing. The practical appeal of this argument is backed up by the observation that the forecasts obtained from some of the models constructed in this way correspond to the forecasts obtained by the basic *ad hoc* procedures. Thus the ARIMA (0, 1, 1) model leads to forecasts produced by an EWMA while ARIMA (0, 2, 2) corresponds to the more elaborate discounting of Holt's method; see Box and Jenkins (1976, pp. 105–8, 146–9) and Harrison (1967). As was noted in sub-section 2.5.4 a further extension of this line of argument leads to the class of multiplicative seasonal ARIMA models.

A viable model selection strategy plays a central role in ARIMA modelling. Such a strategy was originally developed by Box and Jenkins in a series of papers in the 1960s, and is set out in detail in Box and Jenkins (1976). Although subsequent developments have led to some changes in the details of this strategy, the main features, namely specification ('identification'), estimation and diagnostic checking still remain. Before setting out the details of the model selection strategy, we describe the mechanics by which prediction and estimation are made. Since ARIMA models contain only one disturbance term these methods are relatively simple to apply if certain simplifying assumptions are made. Indeed this was part of the initial appeal of ARIMA models.

2.6.1 Prediction

The mechanics of making predictions are described here for the basic ARIMA (p, d, q) model of (2.5.5). The same principles apply in dealing with the more general non-stationarity embodied in (2.5.6) and with the multiplicative seasonal models of (2.5.20). It will be assumed that the AR and MA parameters are known. If it is assumed that the disturbances are independently distributed, rather than just being uncorrelated, this ensures that the predictors obtained are MMSEs rather than simply being optimal within the class of linear estimators; see Priestley (1981, pp. 738–40, 762–5).

The AR and difference polynomials in (2.5.5) are first expanded to give a non-stationary AR polynomial of order $p+d$, i.e.

$$\varphi(L)\Delta^d = \varphi^\dagger(L) = 1 - \varphi_1^\dagger L - \cdots - \varphi_{p+d}^\dagger L^{p+d} \tag{2.6.1}$$

Predictions are then made from the recursion

$$\tilde{y}_{T+l|T} = \varphi_1^\dagger \tilde{y}_{T+l-1|T} + \cdots + \varphi_{p+d}^\dagger \tilde{y}_{T+l-p-d|T}$$
$$+\theta_0 + \xi_{T+l|T} + \cdots + \theta_q \xi_{T+l-q|T}, \quad l=1, 2, \ldots \tag{2.6.2a}$$

where $\tilde{y}_{T+j|T} = y_{T+j}$ for $j \leqslant 0$, and

$$\xi_{T+j|T} = \begin{cases} 0 \quad , & j>0 \\ \xi_{T+j}, & j \leqslant 0 \end{cases} \tag{2.6.2b}$$

The ξ_t's are calculated recursively from an equation similar in form to (2.6.2a) applied to the sample. This is an application of the chain rule. In order to start off this recursion some assumption is needed about the initial values of the ξ_t's and the usual one is to assume that $\xi_{p+d} = \cdots \xi_{p+d-q} = 0$ and to let the recursion run from $t=p+d+1$ to $t=T$. Thus

$$\xi_t = y_t - \varphi_1^\dagger y_{t-1} - \cdots - \varphi_{p+d}^\dagger y_{t-p-d} - \theta_0 - \theta_1 \xi_{t-1} - \cdots - \theta_q \xi_{t-q},$$
$$t = p+d+1, \ldots, T \tag{2.6.3}$$

The forecast function will tend towards a polynomial which is of order d if the model contains a constant and $d-1$ if it does not. This limiting polynomial is known as the final forecast function.

Example 2.6.1 The ARIMA(0, 1, 1) model may be written as

$$y_t = y_{t-1} + \xi_t + \theta \xi_{t-1}, \quad t=2, \ldots, T \tag{2.6.4}$$

and so

$$\tilde{y}_{t+1|t} = \underset{t}{\mathrm{E}}(y_{t+1}) = y_t + \theta \xi_t \tag{2.6.5}$$

If $\xi_1 = 0$, subsequent ξ_t's are computed from the recursion

$$\xi_t = y_t - y_{t-1} - \theta \xi_{t-1}, \quad t=2, \ldots, T \tag{2.6.6}$$

and each represents the one-step-ahead prediction error at time t, i.e.

$$\xi_t = y_t - \tilde{y}_{t|t-1}, \quad t=2, \ldots, T \tag{2.6.7}$$

Substituting from (2.6.7) into (2.6.5) and re-arranging gives

$$\tilde{y}_{t+1|t} = (1+\theta) y_t - \theta \tilde{y}_{t|t-1}, \quad t=2, \ldots, T \tag{2.6.8}$$

with $\tilde{y}_{2|1} = y_1$. Setting $1+\theta$ equal to λ gives an identical recursion to the EWMA, (2.2.5). Note that the range $0<\lambda\leqslant 1$ corresponds to $-1<\theta\leqslant 0$.

The probabilistic nature of ARIMA models allows MSEs to be calculated for the predictions. This can be carried out relatively straightforwardly since

$$\mathrm{MSE}(\tilde{y}_{T+l|T}) = \sigma^2(1 + \psi_1^2 + \cdots + \psi_{l-1}^2)$$

where the ψ's are the coefficients obtained when the process is expressed in terms of current and past independent disturbances. Prediction intervals can be constructed on making the further assumption that the disturbances are normally distributed.

2.6.2 *Estimation*

Since the AR and MA parameters of an ARIMA model will, in general, be unknown, they must be estimated. Under the normality assumption, approximate maximum likelihood (ML) estimators can be obtained by minimising, with respect to φ and θ, the residual sum of squares function

$$S(\varphi, \theta) = \sum_{t=p+d+1}^{T} \xi_t^2 \tag{2.6.9}$$

where the ξ_t's are not the true disturbances but are residuals obtained from a recursion of the form (2.6.3). The approximation arises because of the assumptions made about the initial values of the y_t's and ξ_t's. Hence the estimator obtained by maximising $S(\varphi, \theta)$ is often referred to as the *conditional sum of squares* (CSS) estimator.

There are a number of ways in which an *exact* ML estimator may be computed. However, one of the most efficient methods is based on the Kalman filter and this approach is particularly attractive in cases where there are missing observations; see Gardner *et al.* (1980), Harvey (1981b, ch. 5), Jones (1980), Kohn and Ansley (1983), Harvey and Pierse (1984), and section 3.4.

The exact ML estimator and the CSS estimator are asymptotically equivalent in the sense that they have the same distribution in large samples. It can be shown that both sets of estimators are asymptotically normally distributed with a mean equal to the vector of true parameter values and a covariance matrix equal to the inverse of the information matrix; see Box and Jenkins (1976, pp. 274–84) or Harvey (1981b, ch. 5).

Finally when $q=0$, so that $\Delta^d y_t$ follows a pure AR(p) process, estimation is particularly easy. If the first $p+d$ observations are regarded as being fixed, the CSS estimator is linear and can be computed by OLS. When $q>0$, the estimator is non-linear and some kind of iterative optimisation procedure is needed.

2.6.3 *Model selection strategy*

The model selection strategy advocated by Box and Jenkins consists of three stages: identification, estimation and diagnostic checking. It is almost always assumed that the disturbances are normally distributed.

At the first stage, identification, an attempt is made to find an initial specification for the model, that is, to determine suitable values of p, d and q. For reasons which will become clear shortly, this initial specification should be reasonably parsimonious in terms of the number of AR and MA parameters.

Note that the term 'identification' when used in this way is not to be confused with 'identification' or 'identifiability' in the econometric sense, as discussed in section 4.4.

The main tool used in finding an initial specification is the correlogram. Differencing is carried out until the correlogram shows a tendency to die away towards zero as τ increases. The pattern of the correlogram is then matched up with the patterns of autocorrelation functions known to be produced by certain ARMA(p, q) processes. Other identification techniques based on the sample partial autocorrelation function or the inverse autocorrelation function can also be used.

Once a tentative specification has been obtained, the model may be estimated and the residuals examined to see if they indicate a departure from randomness. This last stage is known as diagnostic checking, and the main tool used is the portmanteau or Box–Pierce Q-test. A more satisfactory version of this statistic is the Box–Ljung statistic defined by

$$Q^* = T(T+2) \sum_{\tau=1}^{P} (T-\tau)^{-1} r^2(\tau) \tag{2.6.10}$$

where $r(\tau)$ is the sample autocorrelation at lag τ computed from the residuals. Under the null hypothesis that the model is correctly specified, Q^* is asymptotically distributed as a χ^2 with P-p-q degrees of freedom. Test statistics can also be constructed using the Lagrange multiplier (LM) principle; see Harvey (1981b, pp. 134, 149–50, 156–7). If these tests indicate that the model is inadequate, the complete cycle of identification, estimation and diagnostic checking is repeated.

An alternative strategy would be to fit a fairly general, high-order ARMA model initially and then to 'test down' to see if the model could be simplified. Unfortunately, moving from a general to a specific model is difficult in this case since if both the AR and MA polynomials are of too high an order, the model will not be identifiable, because different values of the parameters will yield the same likelihood function. It is therefore preferable to attempt to find a parsimonious model at the outset.

A way out of the above difficulty would be to restrict attention to models which, after differencing, were pure AR processes. One obvious disadvantage of doing this is that it will require at least the same number of parameters as a mixed ARMA model which approximates the underlying stochastic process with the same degree of accuracy. However, the pure AR has two compensating advantages. First of all, it is easier to estimate and secondly, and more significantly, it is easier to specify because no identifiability problems arise in a procedure of 'testing down'. Apart from being easy to implement, such a procedure has the methodological attraction of being endowed with certain optimal properties; see Anderson (1971, pp. 270–76). These arguments explain why pure AR models have been advocated by a number of time series analysts; see, for example, Granger and Newbold (1977). The main problem arises because, in general, time series only tend to become stationary after differencing, and differencing may result in an MA component in which the parameters are very close to the boundary of the invertibility region. A large number of AR parameters will then be needed. In the extreme case when the underlying data-generating process is a linear trend plus noise, taking first differences leads to a stationary process, but the fact that the MA component is strictly non-invertible means that an AR representation does not exist. An alternative strategy is to avoid differencing at the initial stage by working with an unrestricted AR polynomial and then testing for the presence of unit roots; this approach is discussed in sub-section 6.1.4.

Finally, a completely different approach to model selection may be based on a goodness-of-fit criterion such as the Akaike information criterion (AIC) or the Bayes information criterion (BIC). If log $L(\tilde{\psi})$ denotes the logarithm of the likelihood function evaluated at the ML estimator $\tilde{\psi}$ and n denotes the number of parameters then

$$\text{AIC} = -2 \log L(\tilde{\psi}) + 2n \tag{2.6.11}$$

while

$$\text{BIC} = -2 \log L(\tilde{\psi}) + n \log T \tag{2.6.12}$$

A number of ARIMA models are fitted and the one which maximises AIC or BIC is selected. Hannan (1980) has generalised these goodness-of-fit criteria and determined conditions under which they are consistent in choosing the 'correct' model. The evidence presented in Sneek (1984) suggests that there is a tendency for the AIC to choose a model which is overparameterised.

2.6.4 Problems with ARIMA modelling

The attraction of the ARIMA class of models is that they provide a general framework for forecasting time series in which the specification of a model within the class is determined by the data. This may be quite advantageous in certain situations, particularly when it is difficult to identify the main components in a series and to construct suitable models for them. Unfortunately the very flexibility of ARIMA modelling is also its main disadvantage. The decision to view all the models within this class as potential candidates for yielding good forecasts is an arbitrary one. Although a lot of useful forecasting models are found within the ARIMA class, it also contains many which have undesirable properties. The practical problem is that unless one has some experience in time series analysis – which effectively means *a priori* knowledge of the models which tend to be most useful – it is easy to select an inappropriate model. Such a model may pass the diagnostics, particularly if it is overparameterised, but may not yield sensible forecasts. Some examples can be found in Harvey and Todd (1983). Tied in with this is the point that ARIMA modelling is based on the assumption that a time series can be reduced to stationarity by differencing. This is quite an heroic assumption, and the surprising thing is perhaps that so many economic and social time series can be made stationary, or approximately so, by differencing. Non-stationarity can arise in a variety of ways, for example because of a changing structure. While this may lead to the rejection of simple models, there is always the danger that an elaborate ARIMA model will be accepted instead. Such a model is likely to break down when it is used for forecasting.

As indicated in the previous sub-section, model selection may proceed in a variety of ways. One way is to use the correlogram and the partial and inverse sample autocorrelation functions to select a model. However, in small or moderate samples the message in these statistics may become quite distorted due to sampling error; see, for example, Kendall (1973, ch. 7). Even the theoretical a.c.f.'s and partial a.c.f.'s tend to become complicated for mixed processes and these complexities are compounded further when differencing takes place. One way out of these difficulties is to select a model by an automatic procedure such as minimising a criterion such as the AIC or BIC. However, as Jenkins (1982) showed, abandoning judgement altogether in model selection can lead to the potential for selecting even more inappropriate models.

Once the ARIMA class is extended to handle seasonality, many of the difficulties described above are compounded. The class of multiplicative seasonal models derives from the airline model which, for the reasons given in sub-section 2.5.4, has considerable practical appeal. However, the class as a whole is not a particularly natural one, and the problems of selecting a suitable model from this class after first and seasonal differencing has taken place is far from easy. For weekly and daily data the ARIMA approach starts to become unworkable.

2.7 Applications

The essence of a structural time series model is that it attempts to represent the main features of a time series. Components such as trends and cycles are formulated in the way already described and combined together so as to produce a plausible model at the outset. Differencing transformations aimed at achieving stationarity play a less prominent role than in ARIMA modelling. The main reason for inspecting the correlogram or estimated spectrum is to ensure that the data are not inconsistent with a model which has already been specified. There is also a recognition that it may not be possible to transform to stationarity. If this appears to be the case, the possibility of allowing for, say, structural change or including explanatory variables in the model may need to be seriously considered. An example is provided by the series for car drivers KSI graphed in Figure 1.2.2. Because of the fall in the level of the series at the time of the introduction of the seat belt law at the beginning of 1983, stationarity of the series over its full length cannot be achieved by differencing. A stable model requires the introduction of an intervention variable.

Once a tentative model has been estimated, it is subject to diagnostic tests and checks. In what follows below only the Q-statistic, (2.6.10), is reported, together with s, the square root of $\tilde{\sigma}^2$, the estimator of the prediction error variance. A more exhaustive set of diagnostics and goodness-of-fit measures is given in chapter 5. If, in the face of these checks, the model appears to be inadequate, its specification is changed and the process repeated. If the model survives the diagnostics, it is either accepted or an attempt is made to simplify it. Simplification may involve imposing restrictions, for example by setting parameters with small values equal to zero, or even by dropping a component completely.

While diagnostic checking is common to both structural and ARIMA model building, the way in which models are initially specified is quite different. The model selection methodology for structural models is more akin to that adopted in, say, econometrics where a tentative model is formulated on the basis of a knowledge of the nature of the variables and the relationship between them. Theoretical considerations may point to certain restrictions on the parameters, while the fact that the model has a direct interpretation is helpful in suggesting simplifications or amendments once it has been estimated.

The applications set out below illustrate various aspects of structural time series modelling. They also highlight some of the differences and similarities between structural and ARIMA models.

2.7.1 Road accidents in Great Britain

Figure 1.2.2 showed the monthly figures for car drivers killed and seriously injured in Great Britain. In this sub-section we consider the construction of a univariate time series model for the period prior to the introduction of the seat belt law at the beginning of 1983. A model is first fitted to the observations over the period January 1968 to December 1981. This leaves 1982 as a post-sample period which can be used to validate the model. A full discussion of the methodology of post-sample predictive testing is given later in section 5.6.

The observations in Figure 1.2.2 show a clear seasonal pattern and although it could be argued that the inclusion of a slope component in the trend is unnecessary, it is preferable to include one in the initial specification. Little is lost by proceeding in this way whereas incorrectly constraining a slope to be zero could have serious consequences. Fitting the BSM to the logarithms of the data gives the following estimates when estimation is carried out by exact ML:

$$\underset{(0.582\times 10^{-3})}{\tilde{\sigma}_\varepsilon^2 = 3.871\times 10^{-3}}, \quad \underset{(0.252\times 10^{-3})}{\tilde{\sigma}_\eta^2 = 0.609\times 10^{-3}}, \quad \tilde{\sigma}_\zeta^2 = 0, \quad \tilde{\sigma}_\omega^2 = 0$$

with

$$s = \tilde{\sigma} = 0.076 \qquad Q(15) = 16.80$$

The figures in parentheses under the parameter estimates are asymptotic standard errors. According to the argument presented in section 5.4, the Box–Ljung Q-statistic should be tested against a chi-square distribution with 14 degrees of freedom. Since the 5% point on such a distribution is 23.68, this particular diagnostic appears to be satisfactory.

The parameter estimates indicate that both the slope and the seasonal pattern are constant. The estimated value of the slope itself is -0.0005. Since this is very small and its standard deviation is 0.0020, the specification of the trend could be reduced to a random walk without a drift.

Estimating in logarithms means that the model is a multiplicative one. Exponentiating the estimated seasonal effects therefore gives the following set of multiplicative seasonal factors:

J	F	M	A	M	J	J	A	S	O	N	D
1.020	0.908	0.934	0.866	0.946	0.916	0.967	0.969	0.993	1.073	1.204	1.281

The current level of the trend, μ_T, is estimated to be 7.337. With the slope taken to be zero, the forecasts from January 1982 onwards are produced by extrapolating $\exp(7.337) = 1536$, and multiplying this figure by the appropriate seasonal factor as given in the table above. As can be seen, the main adverse seasonal effects occur in November and December.

Post-sample predictive testing consists of comparing the one-step-ahead predictions from the fitted model with the actual values obtained in 1982. The post-sample predictive test statistic, which is similar to the Chow statistic in regression, takes the value 0.450. If the model is correctly specified, this statistic is approximately distributed as $F(12, 143)$ and so the value obtained is clearly not significant. In fact it indicates rather better predictions than in the sample period. Overall, therefore, the initial choice of the BSM seems eminently reasonable, although it turns out that some simplification in the trend is possible. Re-estimating the model using data up to December 1982 changes the parameter estimates very little:

$$\underset{(0.532\times 10^{-3})}{\tilde{\sigma}_\varepsilon^2 = 3.703\times 10^{-3}}, \quad \underset{(0.223\times 10^{-3})}{\tilde{\sigma}_\eta^2 = 0.585\times 10^{-3}}, \quad \tilde{\sigma}_\zeta^2 = 0, \quad \tilde{\sigma}_\omega^2 = 0$$

with

$$s = \tilde{\sigma} = 0.074 \qquad Q(15) = 18.81$$

Figure 2.7.1(a) shows the correlogram of $\Delta\Delta_{12} y_t$, where y_t is the logarithm of car drivers KSI from January 1969 until December 1982. The first point to note is that although this correlogram was not used in the selection of a structural model, it is nevertheless consistent with the theoretical a.c.f. implied by the fitted BSM.

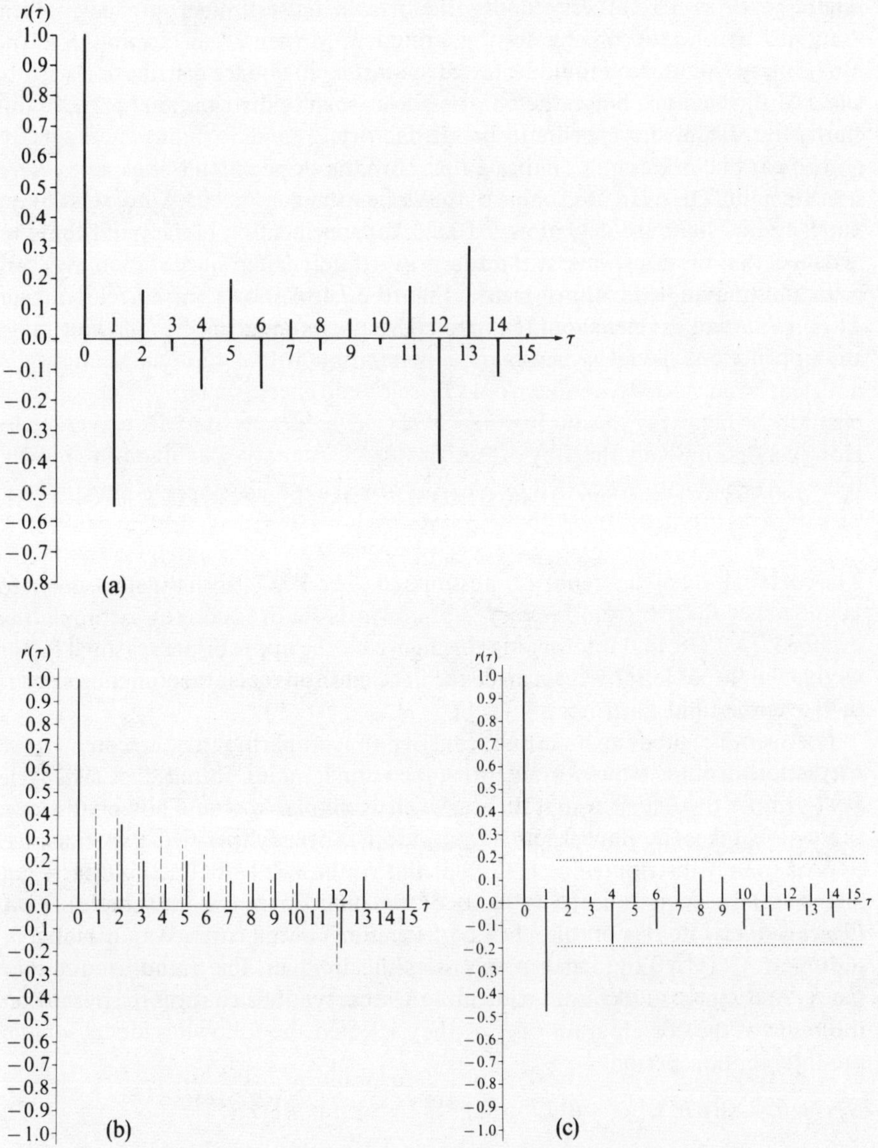

Fig. 2.7.1 Correlograms for logarithms of car drivers killed and seriously injured in Great Britain.

As regards ARIMA model selection, the correlogram in Figure 2.7.1(a) would almost certainly lead an experienced analyst to choose the airline model, (2.5.16). Estimating such a model by exact ML using the SAS package gave $\theta = -0.684$ and $\Theta = -0.995$ with $\tilde{\sigma} = 0.075$. Since Θ is effectively equal to minus one, the model is compatible with the reduced form of a BSM with $\sigma_\zeta^2 = \sigma_\omega^2 = 0$; see (2.5.23). The value of θ implied by the fitted BSM is -0.682.

The series on car drivers KSI therefore provides an illustration of a situation in which the airline and basic structural models are not only close, but are actually equivalent. However, since the airline model with Θ equal to minus one is strictly non-invertible, it is not clear that an ARIMA model builder would necessarily select it in this case. (In fact if he did not have a program to carry out exact finite sample prediction, the choice would be inappropriate; see Harvey, 1981c.) The reason is that the $\Delta\Delta_{12}$ operator leads to overdifferencing, since stationarity can be achieved using the Δ_{12} operator. Figure 2.7.1(b) shows the correlogram of $\Delta_{12}y_t$. (The broken lines should be ignored for the moment.) Although the sample autocorrelations die away in a manner compatible with a stationary series, it is not clear what ARIMA model would be selected. There is a fairly wide range of possibilities involving various mixtures of AR, MA and seasonal MA polynomials. However, it is unlikely that any of these would be a suitable parsimonious model. If the data really are generated by an airline model with $\Theta = -1$, or equivalently by a BSM with $\sigma_\zeta^2 = \sigma_\omega^2 = 0$, then

$$\Delta_{12}y_t = (1+\theta\mathrm{L})\mathrm{S}(\mathrm{L})\xi_t \qquad (2.7.1a)$$

$$= \mathrm{S}(\mathrm{L})\eta_t + \Delta_{12}\varepsilon_t \qquad (2.7.1b)$$

Setting $\theta = -0.684$ in (2.7.1a) leads to the implied autocorrelation function shown by the broken lines in Figure 2.7.1(b).

The use of the seasonal difference operator by itself is not uncommon in ARIMA modelling. However, an autocorrelation function such as that displayed in Figure 2.7.1(b) suggests that seasonal differencing only would potentially lead to a wide range of inappropriate ARIMA models being chosen. As a specific case consider the study by Bhattacharyya and Layton (1979). Their work is an investigation, using quarterly data, of the effects of the seat belt law in Queensland on deaths of car drivers. It represents a well carried out example of the use of ARIMA and intervention analysis techniques. The authors found that the Δ_4 operator was sufficient to reduce the observations to stationarity and on the basis of the correlogram of $\Delta_4 y_t$ they selected the following model for the pre-intervention period:

$$\Delta_4 y_t = \theta_0 + (1+\theta_4\mathrm{L}^4)(1+\theta_3\mathrm{L}^3+\theta_5\mathrm{L}^5)\xi_t \qquad (2.7.2)$$

The properties of this model are not particularly appealing and the fact that Bhattacharyya and Layton report that it failed the Chow test (albeit marginally) could well be an indication of its overparameterisation and inappropriateness.

Actually the appropriate stationarity transformation for this time series is to take first differences and then to remove the seasonal means. This is because, as can be seen from (2.7.1), both sides of the equation still contain a common operator, namely S(L). Applying this transformation to the car drivers KSI series gives the correlogram shown in Figure 2.7.1(c). The dotted horizontal lines show ± 2 s.d. on the assumption that the first-order autocorrelation is the only non-zero one and its theoretical value is equal to the sample value of $r(1) = -0.475$. In contrast to the correlogram of $\Delta_{12} y_t$, the message in Figure 2.7.1(c) is clear. It indicates an MA(1) process and this is consistent with the fitted basic structural and airline models.

2.7.2 Rainfall in north-east Brazil

Figure 2.7.2 shows a series of 131 annual observations on rainfall taken at Fortaleza, Ceará State, Brazil over the period from 1849 to 1979. The unit of measurement is centimetres, with the data being recorded to the nearest millimetre. As this series is probably the longest available one on rainfall in a region which has frequently suffered from severe drought, it has been subject to a great deal of study; see Markham (1974), Morettin *et al.* (1985) and Kane and Trivedi (1986). Most researchers argue that the series contains two distinct cycles; one corresponding to a period of 13 years and the other to 26 years. The cycles were detected by direct application of conventional significance tests to the estimated periodogram of the series, and on this basis, Morettin *et al.* (1985) were led to estimate the model:

$$\hat{y}_t = 142.5 + 20.3 \cos(0.240t + 1.99) + 25.6 \cos(0.480t + 2.20), \quad t = 1, \dots, T \tag{2.7.3}$$

The cycles in model (2.7.3) are deterministic. The cyclical component defined in sub-section 2.3.3 is stochastic, but a deterministic cycle emerges as a limiting case. Setting up a model with stochastic cycles is therefore more general. While two stochastic cycles could, in principle, be included in the model, we first consider including only one. Thus the model is

$$y_t = \mu + \psi_t + \varepsilon_t \tag{2.7.4}$$

where μ is a constant term and ψ_t is given by (2.3.38). Estimating model (2.7.4) by exact maximum likelihood gives the following results:

$$\tilde{\mu} = 142.2, \quad \tilde{\sigma}_\varepsilon^2 = 1593, \quad \tilde{\sigma}_\kappa^2 = 214, \quad \tilde{\rho} = 0.84, \quad \tilde{\lambda}_c = 0.41$$
$$(4.7) \qquad (304) \qquad (193) \qquad (0.11) \qquad (0.09)$$

where the figures in parentheses denote asymptotic standard errors and the estimated value of the frequency, λ_c, corresponds to a period of 15.3 years; see Harvey and Souza (1987). The diagnostic and goodness-of-fit statistics, which are presented in sub-section 5.7.3, suggest that the model is an appropriate one for the data. Furthermore an examination of the estimated power spectrum for the residuals shows no indication of any significant peaks. A similar message is conveyed by Figure 2.7.3 which shows the theoretical power spectrum,

$$f(\lambda) = [g_\psi(e^{i\lambda}) + \sigma_\varepsilon^2]/2\pi$$

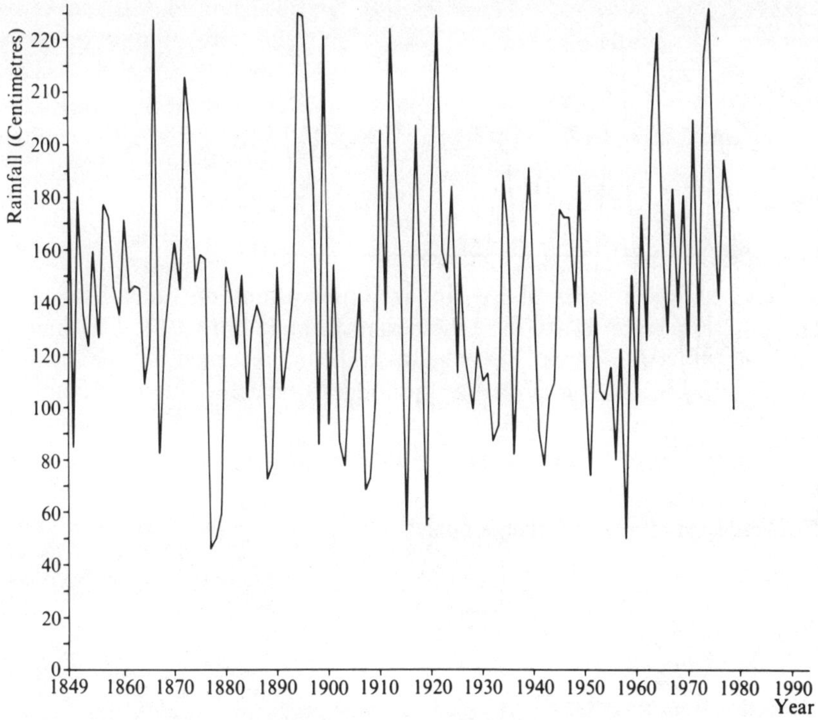

Fig. 2.7.2 Rainfall in Fortaleza, north-east Brazil.

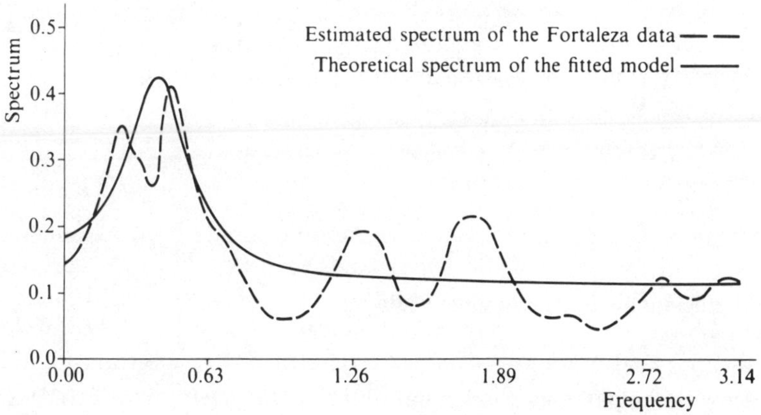

Fig. 2.7.3 Estimated spectrum and theoretical spectrum for the model fitted to Fortaleza rainfall data.

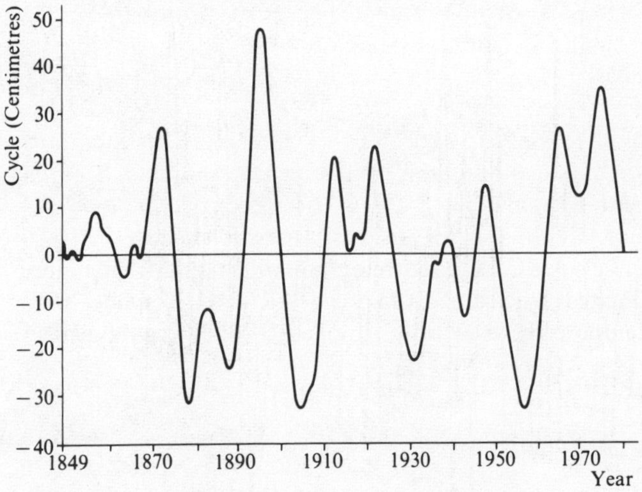

Fig. 2.7.4 Estimated cycle for Fortaleza rainfall data.

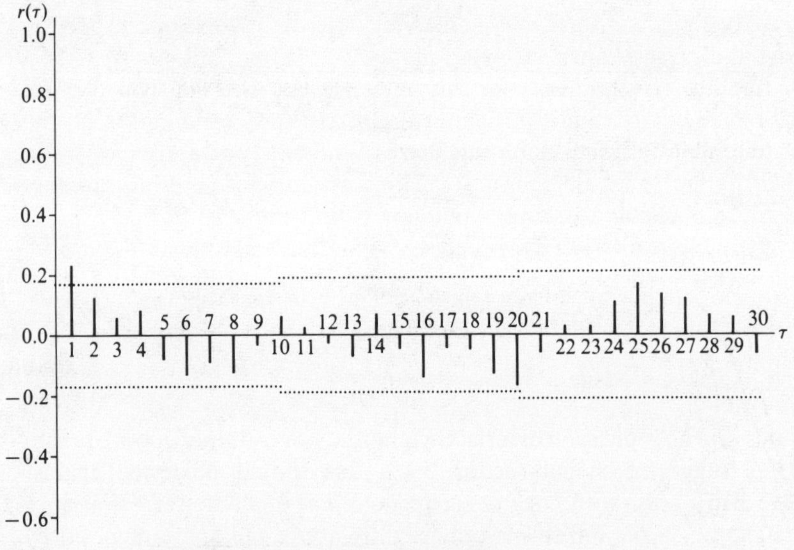

Fig. 2.7.5 Correlogram for Fortaleza rainfall data.

for the model with the parameters set equal to the values given above; $g_\psi(e^{i\lambda})$ is defined as in (2.4.48). The broken line shows the estimated spectrum based on a Parzen window with M, the maximum lag at which raw autocovariances are estimated, set equal to 43; see Nerlove *et al.* (1979, p. 66). As can be seen the shape of the theoretical spectrum is close to the estimated spectrum. Furthermore, the peak in the estimated spectrum corresponding to a 26-year cycle appears considerably less impressive when viewed in the context of a stochastic cycle centred around a 13- to 15-year period.

Figure 2.7.4 shows the estimated cycle, ψ_t, calculated by a smoothing algorithm. As can be seen the stochastic nature of the cycle means that it does not take the form of a smooth cosine wave.

The reduced form of model (2.7.4) is ARMA(2, 2). It seems unlikely that such a model would have been selected from the correlogram, which is shown in Figure 2.7.5, or from the estimated spectrum. Even if an ARMA(2, 2) model were selected, the failure to impose the constraints implied by (2.7.4) could lead to estimation problems.

2.7.3 Purse snatching in Chicago

Figure 2.7.6 shows a time series of reported purse snatchings in the Hyde Park neighbourhood of Chicago. The observations are 28 days apart and run from January 1968 to September 1973. The data were collected by Reed (1978) and are reproduced in the textbook of McCleary and Hay (1980). McCleary and Hay decided that the series was stationary and on the basis of the correlogram and the sample partial a.c.f. they fitted an AR(2) model.

The assumption of stationarity for this series implies that the level of purse snatchings remained constant throughout the period in question and that the variations observed were simply fluctuations around this constant level. This in turn implies that purse snatching is in some kind of equilibrium. While this may be true, a more plausible working hypothesis is that the level of this crime is gradually changing over time. This suggests a random walk plus noise model. Estimating such a model in the time domain gives:

$$\underset{(2.973)}{\tilde{\sigma}_\eta^2 = 5.149} \quad , \quad \underset{(5.58)}{\tilde{\sigma}_\varepsilon^2 = 24.79}$$

The residuals give no indication of serial correlation. For example $Q(8)$ is equal to 7.88 and, as suggested in sub-section 5.4.2, this should be tested against a chi-square distribution with 7 degrees of freedom. The prediction error variance is estimated to be 38.94, and this is only slightly above the figure reported by McCleary and Hay for their AR(2) model which, of course, contains one more parameter. The practical implications for forecasting become apparent when it is noted that the forecasted level of future observations is 7.39 while the mean of the series is 13.92.

In summary, basic *a priori* considerations give rise to a structural time series model which not only has a clearer interpretation than the ARIMA model fitted by McCleary and Hay but is more parsimonious as well. What could be simpler?

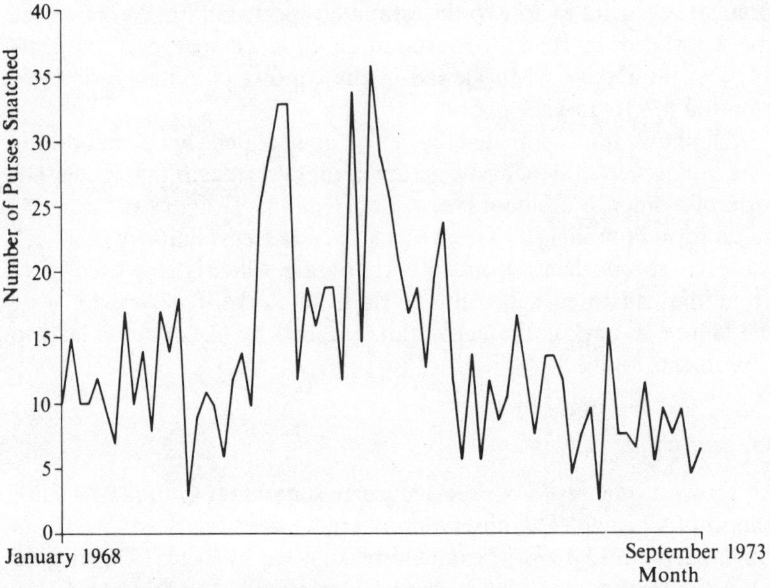

Fig. 2.7.6 Purse snatchings in Hyde Park, Chicago.

Actually, this is not quite the end of the Chicago purse snatchers. While the idea of a local level model is quite reasonable, the nature of the data leaves the normality assumption open to question. The story is taken up again in sub-section 6.6.4.

2.7.4 Trends and cycles in US macroeconomic time series

An article by Nelson and Plosser (1982) is concerned with the properties of US macroeconomic time series. In it they examine the evidence for supposing that such series can be regarded as the sum of a deterministic time trend and a cyclical component which exhibits transitory movements around the trend. An article by Harvey (1985) studies five of these series, but here we just concentrate on what is arguably the most important one, namely Real GNP.

The natural logarithm of Real GNP was plotted in Figure 1.1.2. It was observed then that there is a fairly dramatic change in the series after about 1947. As might be expected, the movements in post-war GNP are much smoother. (The years 1946 and 1947 represent a settling down period after the war.) The break shows up even more clearly in the plot of first differences in Figure 2.7.7, and the contrasting properties of the two parts of the series are apparent from the correlograms of first differences shown in Figure 2.7.8. The analysis in Nelson and Plosser (1982) is based on the full series from 1909 to 1970 and the fact that there

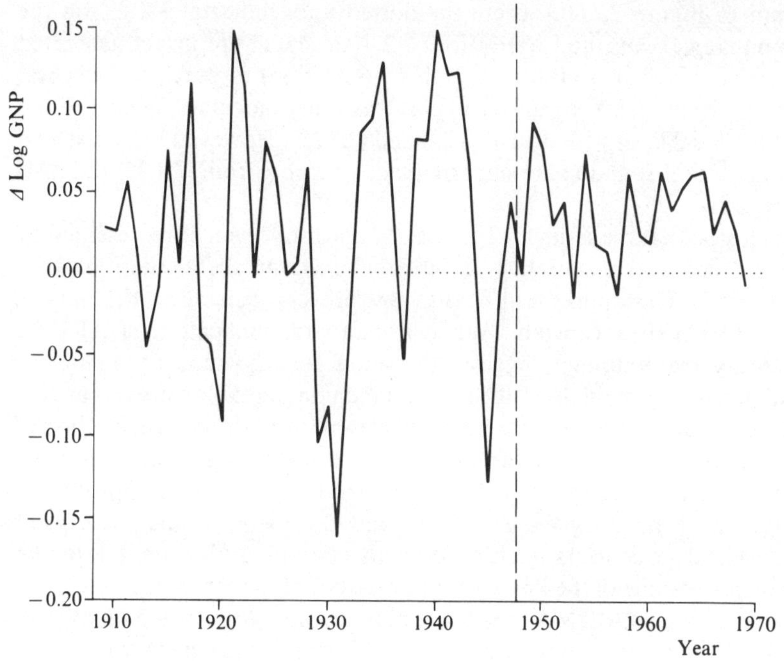

Fig. 2.7.7 First differences of logarithms of US Real GNP.

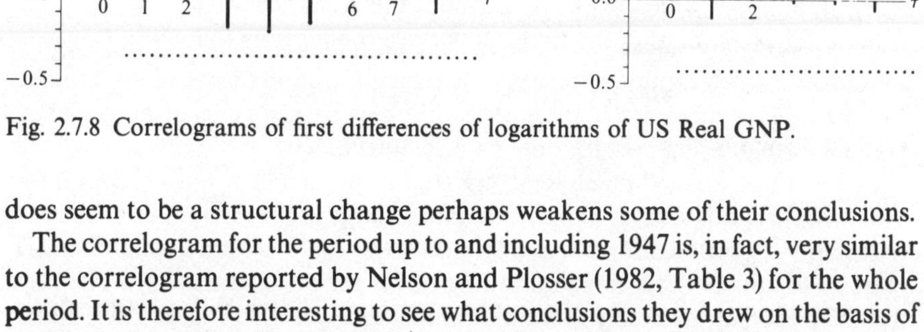

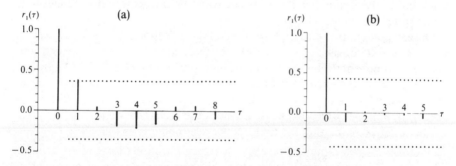

Fig. 2.7.8 Correlograms of first differences of logarithms of US Real GNP.

does seem to be a structural change perhaps weakens some of their conclusions.

The correlogram for the period up to and including 1947 is, in fact, very similar to the correlogram reported by Nelson and Plosser (1982, Table 3) for the whole period. It is therefore interesting to see what conclusions they drew on the basis of such a correlogram. They essentially argued as follows. The first-order autocorrelation, $r(1)$, is quite strongly positive and most of the remaining autocorrelations are statistically insignificant at the 5% level. This is illustrated by the correlogram in Figure 2.7.8(a) where the dotted lines indicate ± 2 s.e. on the assumption that $\rho(1)=r(1)$ and $\rho(\tau)=0$ for $\tau \geqslant 2$. If the data were, in fact, generated by a process in which $\rho(\tau)=0$ for $\tau \geqslant 2$, this would seem to preclude a cyclical component in the model. The only trend plus transitory model which has $\rho(\tau)=0$ for $\tau \geqslant 2$ is the local level with drift, (2.3.24) and (2.3.32). However, this must also be ruled out since if ε_t and η_t are uncorrelated, we know from (2.4.32) that $\rho(1)$ must be negative.

The conclusion that the series for US Real GNP cannot even be represented by a stochastic trend and a stationary component rests on the assumption that $\rho(\tau)=0$ for $\tau \geqslant 2$. The implication is that the process generating the data is ARIMA (0, 1, 1) with a constant. While a standard application of ARIMA model-building methodology suggests this model as a prime candidate on grounds of parsimony, it might well be considered unacceptable since it is unable to generate cyclical behaviour of the kind which is plausible from an inspection of Figure 1.1.2. (Notwithstanding the insignificance of the higher-order sample autocorrelations it could be argued that an ARIMA (2, 1, 0) model is appropriate. Estimating such a model gives $\tilde{\varphi}_1=0.417$ and $\tilde{\varphi}_2=-0.115$ and these yield a damped cyclical autocorrelation function with a period of 7.0 years. The model therefore displays some of the known characteristics of the series. However, it is not clear that standard ARIMA model selection methodology would select such a model. Since the t-statistic for $\tilde{\varphi}_2$ is only -0.65, many researchers would have dropped this term and estimated an ARIMA (1, 1, 0) model. On re-examining the correlogram they would then have been led back to the choice of ARIMA (0, 1, 1) since the correlogram is not consistent with the autocorrelation function of a first-order AR process.)

Once the assumption that $\rho(\tau)=0$ for $\tau \geqslant 2$ is dropped, the fact that $\rho(1)$ is positive is still consistent with a wide range of models containing trend and cyclical components. This includes the trend plus cycle model, (2.3.63). In fact since the aim of the exercise is to examine the nature of the trend and cyclical movements which are known to exist in real GNP, it is sensible to start off by specifying a model which explicitly includes these characteristics.

The result of estimating the trend plus cycle model is as follows:

$$\tilde{\sigma}_\eta^2=23.7\times 10^{-4}, \qquad \tilde{\sigma}_\zeta^2=6.1\times 10^{-4}, \qquad \tilde{\sigma}_\varepsilon^2=0$$

$$\tilde{\sigma}_\kappa^2=3.3\times 10^{-4}, \qquad \tilde{\rho}=0.97, \qquad \tilde{\lambda}=0.90$$

with

$$s=0.0767, \qquad Q(10)=5.10$$

The frequency of $\lambda=0.90$ corresponds to a period of 7.0, which is not unrealistic for the period 1909–47. The Q-statistic is asymptotically χ_6^2 if the model is correctly specified.

Although prior knowledge tells us that there is cyclical behaviour in GNP, it does not tell us precisely how to model it. An alternative possibility is the cyclical trend model, in which the cycle is incorporated in the trend as in (2.3.64). While the trend plus cycle model passes the diagnostics, it turns out to be inferior to the cyclical trend model in terms of goodness of fit. Estimation of the latter yields:

$$\tilde{\sigma}_\eta^2 = 0, \qquad \tilde{\sigma}_\zeta^2 = 0, \qquad \tilde{\sigma}_\varepsilon^2 = \underset{(3.7\times 10^{-4})}{4.9\times 10^{-4}}$$

$$\tilde{\sigma}_\kappa^2 = \underset{(12.9\times 10^{-4})}{24.3\times 10^{-4}}, \qquad \tilde{\rho} = \underset{(0.13)}{0.73}, \qquad \tilde{\lambda} = \underset{(0.04)}{0.72}$$

with

$$s = 0.0706, \qquad Q(10) = 5.90$$

This model is effectively more parsimonious than the trend plus cycle as both σ_η^2 and σ_ζ^2 are zero. The Q-statistic test should therefore be based on seven degrees of freedom and it is clearly insignificant. It is also easy to see from (2.4.40) how the implied autocorrelation function mirrors that of Figure 2.7.8(a). The period of the stochastic cycle is 8.7 years with a 95% confidence interval of 6.0 to 15.7 years.

Overall the cyclical trend model seems to provide a very useful summary of the 'stylised facts' associated with the behaviour of Real GNP over the period 1909 to 1947. The stylised facts associated with the post-1947 period are quite different, at least if annual data up to 1970 are used. The behaviour of the series is effectively captured by a random walk plus drift; see sub-section 5.7.2. However, it should be noted that the use of quarterly observations up to the mid-1980s leads to the re-appearance of a cyclical trend with a period of about three years and ρ equal to approximately 0.7.

2.7.5 Airline passengers

The airline passenger data is one of the classic time series testbeds; see, in particular, the books by Brown (1963) and Box and Jenkins (1976). Needless to say, the ARIMA 'airline' model gives a rather good fit to this series. The selection of a structural model is completely straightforward, since a glance at a plot of the series shows immediately that its salient features are trend and seasonality; see Figure 5.7.2. Hence the BSM is appropriate.

As might be expected from sub-section 2.5.5, the fit of the BSM and airline models is similar. The goodness of fit of the two models can be compared on the basis of their respective prediction error variances (p.e.v.). The p.e.v. is the variance of the one-step-ahead prediction error and for an ARIMA model the estimated p.e.v. is given directly by the estimator of σ^2. For a structural model, the p.e.v. is not normally given directly and has to be computed by one of the methods outlined in section 5.5.

Table 2.7.1 shows the results of fitting various models to the airline passenger

Table 2.7.1 *Models fitted to the quarterly airline passenger series*

Model	Number of hyper-parameters	Estimates of hyper-parameters	Estimated p.e.v.	AIC†	BIC†
(a) Deterministic	1	$\tilde{\sigma}_\varepsilon^2 = 302$	302	388	490
(b) Partially deterministic	1	$\tilde{\sigma}_\eta^2 = 205$	205	263	333
(c) Basic structural model	4	$\tilde{\sigma}_\eta^2 = 53.2$, $\tilde{\sigma}_\zeta^2 = 0.108$ $\sigma_\omega^2 = 13.2$, $\tilde{\sigma}_\varepsilon^2 = 0$	140	204	289
(d) BSM with $q_\zeta = (q_\eta/2)^2$	3	$\tilde{\sigma}_\eta^2 = 22.6$, $\tilde{\sigma}_\zeta^2 = 13.1$ $\tilde{\sigma}_\omega^2 = 10.4$, $\tilde{\sigma}_\varepsilon^2 = 9.7$	172	240	328
(e) BSM with $\sigma_\eta^2 = 0$	3	$\tilde{\sigma}_\zeta^2 = 21.3$, $\tilde{\sigma}_\omega^2 = 10.4$ $\tilde{\sigma}_\varepsilon^2 = 14.7$	174	243	332
(f) ARIMA (0, 1, 1) $\times (0, 1, 1)_4$	3	$\tilde{\theta} = -0.052$, $\tilde{\Theta} = -0.451$ $\tilde{\sigma}^2 = 158$	158	221	301

data after it has been aggregated to produce a quarterly series of 48 observations and logarithms have been taken. The models estimated are as follows:

(a) the deterministic trend and seasonal model of (2.3.1);
(b) a partially deterministic model in which the first differences of the observations are equal to a constant term, a deterministic seasonal component and a random disturbance term;
(c) the BSM;
(d) the BSM with the variances in the trend component constrained to satisfy the double exponential smoothing condition $q_\zeta = (q_\eta/2)^2$;
(e) the BSM with σ_η^2 constrained to be zero;
(f) the airline model.

Models (a) and (b) are both special cases of the BSM, the former with $\sigma_\eta^2 = \sigma_\zeta^2 = \sigma_\omega^2 = 0$ and the latter with $\sigma_\varepsilon^2 = \sigma_\zeta^2 = \sigma_\omega^2 = 0$ but σ_η^2 positive. Both can be fitted by OLS, although in the case of (b) this simplifies to the removal of seasonal means from first differences. The importance of model (b) as a yardstick in modelling series of this kind is discussed in sub-section 5.5.5.

The BSM was estimated by exact ML in the time domain as described in section 4.2. The two variants of the BSM, (d) and (e), were also estimated by exact ML. The suggestion that the double exponential smoothing constraint be imposed on a BSM is made by Harrison and Akram (1983), although they do not suggest that the model be estimated by ML. The rationale for setting σ_η^2 equal to zero is based on an argument relating to the smoothness of the trend. It is this formulation which is adopted by Kitagawa (1981) and Gersch and Kitagawa

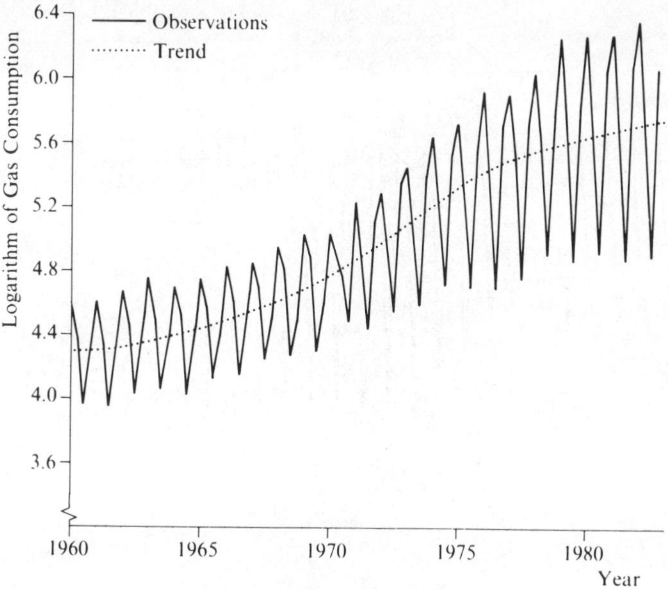

Fig. 2.7.9 UK gas consumption by 'Other final users' and estimated trend.

(1983). Further details on the smoothness argument can be found in sub-section 6.1.1.

The estimated parameters for the various models are set out in Table 2.7.1, together with the estimated p.e.v.'s. All estimates of variances, together with AIC† and BIC†, have been multiplied by 10^5. As might be expected, the models with more hyperparameters tend to give a better fit. The criteria AIC† and BIC† make an allowance for the number of parameters in the model. These criteria were introduced in (2.6.11) and (2.6.12), but they are reported here in the modified form indicated by expression (5.5.18). A discussion of their significance in the present context is given later in sub-section 5.5.6.

2.7.6 Energy consumption

Figure 1.4.1 showed the trend for the logarithm of coal consumption based on a model fitted using the observations from 1960 to 1982. On the basis of the clear trend and seasonal movements in the original plot of Figure 1.1.1, a BSM had been selected. The estimated parameters, multiplied by 10^4, are:

$$\tilde{\sigma}_\eta^2 = \underset{(11.26)}{6.42}, \quad \tilde{\sigma}_\zeta^2 = \underset{(0.25)}{0.29}, \quad \tilde{\sigma}_\omega^2 = \underset{(0.58)}{0.84}, \quad \tilde{\sigma}_\varepsilon^2 = \underset{(25)}{114}$$

with

$$s = 0.045, \qquad Q(10) = 9.11$$

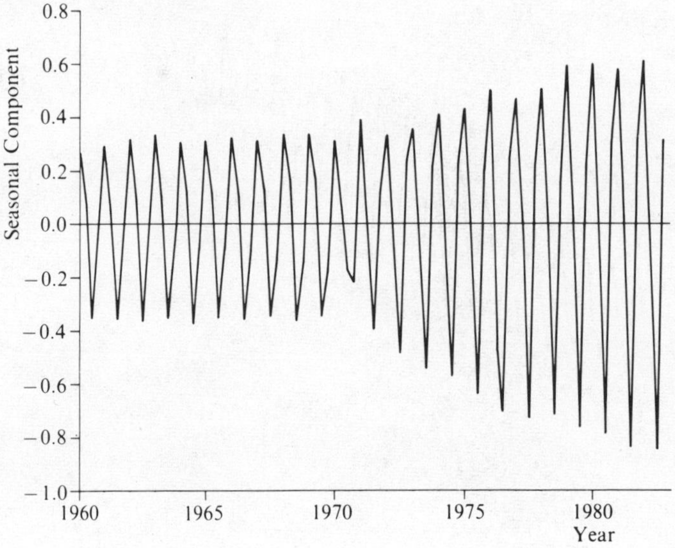

(a)

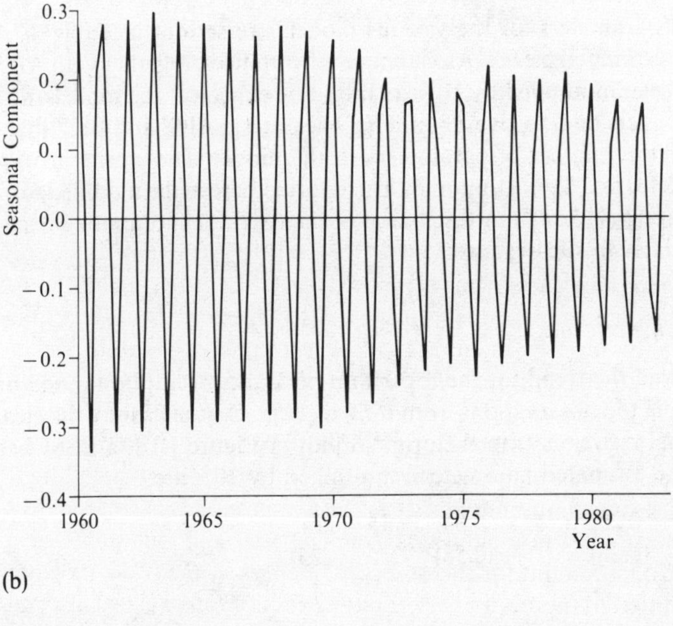

(b)

Fig. 2.7.10 Seasonal components in (a) gas and (b) electricity consumption.

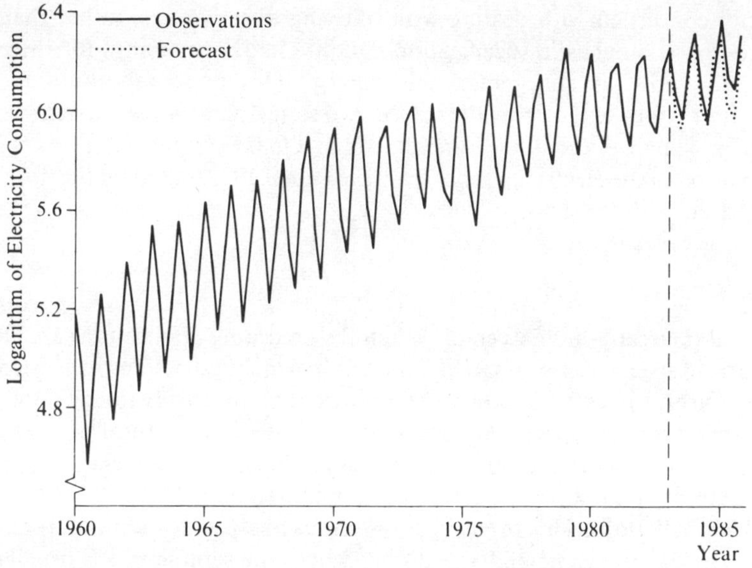

Fig. 2.7.11 Forecasts of electricity consumption from 1982 to 1985 and actual values.

The slope of the trend is 0.0022 with a RMSE of 0.0152, indicating a growth rate very close to zero. This is reflected in the extrapolation of the trend in Figure 1.4.1.

The BSM gives a reasonably good fit to the coal consumption data although it could be made more elaborate by making allowances for various industrial disputes. Similarly, the BSM performs reasonably well on other energy series. Figure 2.7.9 shows gas consumption for UK 'Other final users' together with the estimated trend based on the observations up to 1982. Unlike coal, the trend is upwards, with some increase in the rate of growth in the years following the introduction of cheaper natural gas from the North Sea at the end of the 1960s. A corresponding dampening of the rate of growth of electricity consumption can be observed in this period. A more subtle effect concerns the change in the seasonal pattern in the gas and electricity series. Figure 2.7.10(a) shows the seasonal effects in gas consumption becoming more marked after the introduction of natural gas. Figure 2.7.10(b) shows exactly the opposite happening for electricity. The reason lies in the use of gas in place of electricity for heating. This, of course, affects consumption primarily in the winter months. Other uses of gas and electricity have a less pronounced seasonal pattern, and such a change in the mix of usage would account for the observed changes in the seasonal patterns.

The models fitted to the gas and electricity series do not, in fact, satisfy all the diagnostics, and some modifications are required. However, these modifications are primarily concerned with dealing with outlying observations, rather than changing the basic stochastic specification. Despite its shortcomings for these two series, the BSM is still remarkably robust. This applies both to the description it provides of the properties of the two series, namely the movements in trend and seasonality, and to the forecasts which it makes. Figure 2.7.11 shows the extrapolation of the electricity series from the end of 1982, based on the fitted BSM, compared with the actual values.

2.7.7 Conclusions

The structural time series models employed in the preceding applications are all linear and are all special cases of ARIMA models in which restrictions have been imposed. As the examples have shown, these restrictions are an advantage rather than a disadvantage. The ARIMA class is not a particularly natural one. The components in a structural model, on the other hand, are associated with particular features of the series, and therefore the chosen model is more likely to yield sensible predictions. This robustness to serious misspecification is particularly important for economic and social data where the sample size is usually small and the assumption that the (differenced) series is stationary is, at best, an approximation.

The implicit restrictions on the structural model are also important for estimation. Consider the local linear trend model. This has an ARIMA (0, 2, 2) reduced form with an admissible region shown in Figure 2.5.1. In small samples the chances of unrestricted reduced form estimates of the MA parameters lying in the admissible region may be quite small and it is not clear that the forecasting properties of models with MA parameters lying outside the region are necessarily sensible. In a more complex situation, such as the cyclical trend model of sub-section 2.7.4, the chances of an unrestricted reduced form ARIMA model of the appropriate order giving admissible estimates may be even more remote. Indeed, an attempt to estimate an ARIMA (2, 2, 4), or even the ARIMA (2, 1, 3) implied by having σ_ξ^2 zero, would be quite likely to run into practical problems of convergence when estimation was attempted.

In assessing the preceding applications it must be remembered that the full model selection methodology has yet to be described. This is done in section 5.7. It must also be remembered that the models described have not exhausted the full range of structural models. The specifications of the trend and seasonal components could be modified in various ways and other components may be added if there is some rationale for them. In particular, daily and weekly effects may be included if the data is available on this level, while for monthly data it will often be necessary to allow for calendar and trading-day effects. More fundamentally the range of models may be extended to include time-variation, non-linearity and non-normality; this is done in sections 6.5 and 6.6.

EXERCISES

2.1 Consider the model (2.3.24) and (2.3.32). Find a modification of the EWMA for making predictions. Write down an expression for the forecast function.

2.2 If, in the model of Exercise 2.1, ε_t and η_t are correlated, show that the first-order autocorrelation of the first differences can be positive.

2.3 Derive (2.3.5), the MSE of the l-step-ahead predictor for a deterministic linear trend model.

2.4 Express (2.2.26) in terms of the L and S(L) operators.

2.5 Write down expressions for the a.c.f. and for the s.g.f. of the stationary form of the damped trend model of (2.3.66).

Chapter 3

State space models and the Kalman filter

The state space form is an enormously powerful tool which opens the way to handling a wide range of time series models. Once a model has been put in state space form, the Kalman filter may be applied and this in turn leads to algorithms for prediction and smoothing. The state space form is described in the first section of this chapter, while the second section develops the Kalman filter. Prediction and smoothing are described in sections 3.5 and 3.6 respectively. The Kalman filter also opens the way to the maximum likelihood estimation of the unknown parameters in a model. This is done via the prediction error decomposition and a full account can be found in section 3.4.

The present chapter can be read independently of the rest of the book, and taken as a guide to the uses of the state space models in areas outside engineering. On the other hand, those interested primarily in the practical aspects of structural time series modelling will be reassured to know that they do not have to master all the technical details of the Kalman filter set out here. The most important parts of the chapter with which to become familiar are sections 3.1 and 3.5, the earlier parts of sections 3.2, 3.4 and 3.6, and, for those interested in non-linear models, sub-section 3.7.1. The reader will also benefit by at least skimming through the remaining sections, since there is some reference back to the various algorithms in later chapters and it is useful to have some idea of what these algorithms do and how they fit into the overall picture.

3.1 The state space form

The general state space form (SSF) applies to a multivariate time series, $\mathbf{y}_t$, containing N elements. These observable variables are related to an $m \times 1$ vector, $\boldsymbol{\alpha}_t$, known as the *state vector*, via a *measurement equation*

$$\mathbf{y}_t = \mathbf{Z}_t \boldsymbol{\alpha}_t + \mathbf{d}_t + \boldsymbol{\varepsilon}_t, \quad t = 1, \ldots, T \tag{3.1.1a}$$

where Z_t is an $N \times m$ matrix, $\mathbf{d}_t$ is an $N \times 1$ vector and $\boldsymbol{\varepsilon}_t$ is an $N \times 1$ vector of serially uncorrelated disturbances with mean zero and covariance matrix $\mathbf{H}_t$, that is

$$\mathrm{E}(\boldsymbol{\varepsilon}_t) = \mathbf{0} \quad \text{and} \quad \mathrm{Var}(\boldsymbol{\varepsilon}_t) = \mathbf{H}_t \tag{3.1.1b}$$

In a univariate model, $N=1$ and the measurement equation is written as

$$y_t = \mathbf{z}_t'\boldsymbol{\alpha}_t + d_t + \varepsilon_t, \quad \text{Var}(\varepsilon_t) = h_t, \quad t = 1, \ldots, T \tag{3.1.2}$$

In general the elements of $\boldsymbol{\alpha}_t$ are not observable. However, they are known to be generated by a first-order Markov process,

$$\boldsymbol{\alpha}_t = \mathbf{T}_t\boldsymbol{\alpha}_{t-1} + \mathbf{c}_t + \mathbf{R}_t\boldsymbol{\eta}_t, \quad t = 1, \ldots, T \tag{3.1.3a}$$

where $\mathbf{T}_t$ is an $m \times m$ matrix, $\mathbf{c}_t$ is an $m \times 1$ vector, $\mathbf{R}_t$ is an $m \times g$ matrix and $\boldsymbol{\eta}_t$ is a $g \times 1$ vector of serially uncorrelated disturbances with mean zero and covariance matrix, $\mathbf{Q}_t$, that is

$$\text{E}(\boldsymbol{\eta}_t) = \mathbf{0} \quad \text{and} \quad \text{Var}(\boldsymbol{\eta}_t) = \mathbf{Q}_t \tag{3.1.3b}$$

Equation (3.1.3a) is the *transition equation.* The inclusion of the matrix $\mathbf{R}_t$ in front of the disturbance term is, to some extent, arbitrary. The disturbance term could always be redefined so as to have a covariance matrix $\mathbf{R}_t\mathbf{Q}_t\mathbf{R}_t'$. Nevertheless the representation in (3.1.3a) is often more natural when $\boldsymbol{\eta}_t$ is identified with a particular set of disturbances in the model.

The specification of the state space system is completed by two further assumptions:

(a) the initial state vector, $\boldsymbol{\alpha}_0$, has a mean of $\mathbf{a}_0$ and a covariance matrix $\mathbf{P}_0$, that is

$$\text{E}(\boldsymbol{\alpha}_0) = \mathbf{a}_0 \quad \text{and} \quad \text{Var}(\boldsymbol{\alpha}_0) = \mathbf{P}_0 \tag{3.1.4}$$

(b) the disturbances $\boldsymbol{\varepsilon}_t$ and $\boldsymbol{\eta}_t$ are uncorrelated with each other in all time periods, and uncorrelated with the initial state, that is

$$\text{E}(\boldsymbol{\varepsilon}_t\boldsymbol{\eta}_s') = 0 \quad \text{for all } s, t = 1, \ldots, T \tag{3.1.5a}$$

and

$$\text{E}(\boldsymbol{\varepsilon}_t\boldsymbol{\alpha}_0') = 0, \quad \text{E}(\boldsymbol{\eta}_t\boldsymbol{\alpha}_0') = \mathbf{0} \quad \text{for } t = 1, \ldots, T \tag{3.1.5b}$$

The assumption in (3.1.5a) may be relaxed, and is done so in sub-section 3.2.5.

The matrices $\mathbf{Z}_t$, $\mathbf{d}_t$ and $\mathbf{H}_t$ in the measurement equation and the matrices $\mathbf{T}_t$, $\mathbf{c}_t$, $\mathbf{R}_t$ and $\mathbf{Q}_t$ in the transition equation will be referrred to as the *system matrices.* Unless otherwise stated, it will be assumed that they are non-stochastic. Thus although they may change with time they do so in a way which is predetermined. As a result the system is *linear* and for any value of t, $\mathbf{y}_t$ can be expressed as a linear combination of present and past $\boldsymbol{\varepsilon}_t$'s and $\boldsymbol{\eta}_t$'s and the initial state vector, $\boldsymbol{\alpha}_0$. The consequences of allowing the system matrices to depend on past observations is explored in section 3.7.

If the system matrices $\mathbf{Z}_t$, $\mathbf{d}_t$, $\mathbf{H}_t$, $\mathbf{T}_t$, $\mathbf{c}_t$, $\mathbf{R}_t$ and $\mathbf{Q}_t$ do not change over time, the model is said to be *time-invariant* or *time-homogeneous.* Stationary models are a special case. However, although the class of time-invariant models is much broader than the class of stationary models, many time-invariant models have a stationary form which can be obtained by applying a transformation such as differencing.

Example 3.1.1 The random walk plus noise model

$$y_t = \mu_t + \varepsilon_t, \quad \mathrm{Var}(\varepsilon_t) = \sigma_\varepsilon^2 \tag{3.1.6a}$$

$$\mu_t = \mu_{t-1} + \eta_t, \quad \mathrm{Var}(\eta_t) = \sigma_\eta^2 \tag{3.1.6b}$$

is a time-invariant state space model with μ_t the state. As was shown in sub-section 2.4.4, Δy_t is stationary.

The definition of $\boldsymbol{\alpha}_t$ for any particular statistical model is determined by construction. Its elements may or may not be identifiable with components which have a substantive interpretation, for example as a trend or a seasonal. From the technical point of view, the aim of the state space formulation is to set up $\boldsymbol{\alpha}_t$ in such a way that it contains all the relevant information on the system at time t and that it does so by having as small a number of elements as possible. A state space form which minimises the length of the state vector is said to be a *minimal realisation*. Other things being equal, a minimal realisation is a basic criterion for a good state space representation. However, it does not imply that there is necessarily a unique representation for any particular problem. In fact a unique representation is the exception rather than the rule. This can be seen very easily by defining an arbitrary non-singular $m \times m$ matrix, $\mathbf{B}$, and considering a new state vector, $\boldsymbol{\alpha}_t^* = \mathbf{B}\boldsymbol{\alpha}_t$. Premultiplying the original transition equation through by $\mathbf{B}$ yields

$$\boldsymbol{\alpha}_t^* = \mathbf{T}_t^* \boldsymbol{\alpha}_{t-1}^* + \mathbf{c}_t^* + \mathbf{R}_t^* \boldsymbol{\eta}_t \tag{3.1.7a}$$

where $\mathbf{T}_t^* = \mathbf{B}\mathbf{T}_t\mathbf{B}^{-1}$, $\mathbf{c}_t^* = \mathbf{B}\mathbf{c}_t$ and $\mathbf{R}_t^* = \mathbf{B}\mathbf{R}_t$. The corresponding measurement equation is

$$\mathbf{y}_t = \mathbf{Z}_t^* \boldsymbol{\alpha}_t^* + \mathbf{d}_t + \boldsymbol{\varepsilon}_t \tag{3.1.7b}$$

where $\mathbf{Z}_t^* = \mathbf{Z}_t\mathbf{B}^{-1}$.

Example 3.1.2 Two possible state space representations for the second-order autoregressive process, (2.3.14), are

$$y_t = [1 \quad 0]\boldsymbol{\alpha}_t \tag{3.1.8a}$$

$$\boldsymbol{\alpha}_t = \begin{bmatrix} y_t \\ \varphi_2 y_{t-1} \end{bmatrix} = \begin{bmatrix} \varphi_1 & 1 \\ \varphi_2 & 0 \end{bmatrix} \boldsymbol{\alpha}_{t-1} + \begin{bmatrix} 1 \\ 0 \end{bmatrix} \xi_t \tag{3.1.8b}$$

and

$$y_t = [1 \quad 0]\boldsymbol{\alpha}_t^* \tag{3.1.9a}$$

$$\boldsymbol{\alpha}_t^* = \begin{bmatrix} y_t \\ y_{t-1} \end{bmatrix} = \begin{bmatrix} \varphi_1 & \varphi_2 \\ 1 & 0 \end{bmatrix} \boldsymbol{\alpha}_{t-1}^* + \begin{bmatrix} 1 \\ 0 \end{bmatrix} \xi_t \tag{3.1.9b}$$

The transition equation in (3.1.3a) is sometimes shifted forward one period so as to become

$$\boldsymbol{\alpha}_{t+1} = \mathbf{T}_t \boldsymbol{\alpha}_t + \mathbf{c}_t + \mathbf{R}_t \boldsymbol{\eta}_t \tag{3.1.10}$$

From the practical point of view it makes very little difference whether (3.1.3a) or (3.1.10) is used in conjunction with (3.1.1a). However, it is necessary to be careful in certain circumstances, for example when dealing with correlated measurement and transition equation noise; see sub-section 3.2.4. Throughout this book the emphasis will be on (3.1.3a). Jazwinski (1970) also uses this formulation, though Anderson and Moore (1979) prefer (3.1.10).

Example 3.1.3 The MA(1) model

$$y_t = \xi_t + \theta \xi_{t-1}, \quad t = 1, \ldots, T \tag{3.1.11}$$

can be put in state space form by defining the state vector $\boldsymbol{\alpha}_t = [y_t \quad \theta\xi_t]'$ and writing

$$y_t = [1 \quad 0]\boldsymbol{\alpha}_t, \quad t = 1, \ldots, T \tag{3.1.12a}$$

$$\boldsymbol{\alpha}_t = \begin{bmatrix} 0 & 1 \\ 0 & 0 \end{bmatrix} \boldsymbol{\alpha}_{t-1} + \begin{bmatrix} 1 \\ \theta \end{bmatrix} \xi_t \tag{3.1.12b}$$

A feature of this representation is that there is no measurement equation noise. The alternative state space representation, based on (3.1.10), is able to reduce the dimension of the state vector to one by defining α_{t+1} to be ξ_t and writing

$$y_t = \theta \alpha_t + \xi_t \tag{3.1.13a}$$

$$\alpha_{t+1} = \xi_t \tag{3.1.13b}$$

The price paid for reducing the dimension of the state vector is that the measurement and transition equation disturbances are now correlated.

The system matrices $\mathbf{Z}_t, \mathbf{H}_t, \mathbf{T}_t, \mathbf{R}_t$ and $\mathbf{Q}_t$ may depend on a set of unknown parameters, and one of the main statistical tasks will often be the estimation of these parameters. Thus in the random walk plus noise model, (3.1.6), the parameters σ_η^2 and σ_ε^2 will, in general, be unknown, while in the AR(2) and MA(1) models of Examples 3.1.2 and 3.1.3 the AR and MA parameters will be unknown. These parameters will be denoted by an $n \times 1$ vector $\boldsymbol{\psi}$ and referred to as *hyperparameters* in order to distinguish them from parameters which may enter into the model via $\mathbf{c}_t$ or $\mathbf{d}_t$. The hyperparameters determine the stochastic properties of the model, whereas the parameters appearing in $\mathbf{c}_t$ and $\mathbf{d}_t$ only affect the expected value of the state and the observations in a deterministic way. It should, however, be noted that this distinction can become blurred, for example if $\mathbf{d}_t$ is a function of a lagged value of $\mathbf{y}_t$.

If $\mathbf{c}_t$ or $\mathbf{d}_t$ is a linear function of unknown parameters, these parameters can be treated as state variables.

Example 3.1.4 If μ_t in (3.1.6a) is generated by a random walk plus drift,

$$\mu_t = \mu_{t-1} + \beta + \eta_t \tag{3.1.14}$$

the parameter β can be treated as part of the state, even though it is a constant, by defining the state vector as $\boldsymbol{\alpha}_t = [\mu_t \quad \beta_t]'$ and letting the model be written in SSF as

$$y_t = [1 \quad 0]\boldsymbol{\alpha}_t + \varepsilon_t \quad t = 1, \ldots, T \tag{3.1.15a}$$

$$\boldsymbol{\alpha}_t = \begin{bmatrix} \mu_t \\ \beta_t \end{bmatrix} = \begin{bmatrix} 1 & 1 \\ 0 & 1 \end{bmatrix} \begin{bmatrix} \mu_{t-1} \\ \beta_{t-1} \end{bmatrix} + \begin{bmatrix} \eta_t \\ 0 \end{bmatrix} \tag{3.1.15b}$$

For some purposes it is useful to transfer $\mathbf{c}_t$ to the measurement equation. By repeated substitution, we find that

$$\boldsymbol{\alpha}_t = \boldsymbol{\alpha}_t^* + \mathbf{c}_t^* \tag{3.1.16}$$

where $\boldsymbol{\alpha}_t^*$ satisfies the transition equation without $\mathbf{c}_i$ present, $\boldsymbol{\alpha}_0^* = \boldsymbol{\alpha}_0$, and

$$\mathbf{c}_t^* = \mathbf{c}_t + \sum_{i=1}^{t-1} \left(\prod_{j=1}^{t-i} \mathbf{T}_{i+j} \right) \mathbf{c}_i \tag{3.1.17}$$

Substituting from (3.1.16) into the measurement equation then gives the system

$$\mathbf{y}_t = \mathbf{Z}_t \boldsymbol{\alpha}_t^* + (\mathbf{d}_t + \mathbf{Z}_t \mathbf{c}_t^*) + \varepsilon_t \tag{3.1.18a}$$

$$\boldsymbol{\alpha}_t^* = \mathbf{T}_t \boldsymbol{\alpha}_{t-1}^* + \mathbf{R}_t \boldsymbol{\eta}_t \tag{3.1.18b}$$

This formulation makes it clear how $\mathbf{c}_t$, and the parameters which it may contain, influences the mean path of $\mathbf{y}_t$. It is straightforward to carry out this exercise for the model in Example 3.1.4. This is done explicitly later in the book in (4.1.8).

3.2 The Kalman filter

Once a model has been put in a state space form, the way is opened for the application of a number of important algorithms. At the centre of these is the Kalman filter. The Kalman filter is a recursive procedure for computing the optimal estimator of the state vector at time t, based on the information available at time t. This information consists of the observations up to and including $\mathbf{y}_t$. The system matrices together with $\mathbf{a}_0$ and $\mathbf{P}_0$ are assumed to be known in all time periods and so do not need to be explicitly included in the information set.

In certain engineering applications the Kalman filter is important because of on-line estimation. The current value of the state vector is of prime interest (for example, it may represent the co-ordinates of a rocket in space) and the Kalman filter enables the estimate of the state vector to be continually updated as new observations become available. At first sight, the value of such a procedure in economic applications would appear to be limited. New observations tend to appear at rather less frequent intervals and the emphasis is on making predictions of future observations based on a given sample. The state vector does not always have an economic interpretation and, in cases where it does, it is more appropriate to estimate its value at a particular point in time using all the information in the sample, not just a part of it. These two problems are known as prediction and smoothing respectively. It turns out that the Kalman filter provides the basis for the solution of both of them.

Another reason for the central role of the Kalman filter is that when the disturbances and the initial state vector are normally distributed, it enables the likelihood function to be calculated via what is known as the prediction error decomposition. This opens the way for the estimation of any unknown parameters in the model. It also provides the basis for statistical testing and model specification.

The derivation of the Kalman filter given below rests on the assumption that the disturbances and initial state vector are normally distributed. A standard result on the multivariate normal distribution is then used to show how it is possible to calculate recursively the distribution of $\boldsymbol{\alpha}_t$, conditional on the information set at time t, for all t from 1 to T. These conditional distributions are themselves normal and hence are completely specified by their means and covariance matrices. It is these quantities which the Kalman filter computes. After having derived the Kalman filter, it is shown that the mean of the conditional distribution of $\boldsymbol{\alpha}_t$ is an optimal estimator of $\boldsymbol{\alpha}_t$ in the sense that it minimises the mean square error (MSE). When the normality assumption is dropped, there is no longer any guarantee that the Kalman filter will give the conditional mean of the state vector. However, it is still an optimal estimator in the sense that it minimises the mean square error within the class of all linear estimators.

3.2.1 General form of the Kalman filter

Consider the state space model of (3.1.1) and (3.1.3). Let $\mathbf{a}_{t-1}$ denote the optimal estimator of $\boldsymbol{\alpha}_{t-1}$ based on the observations up to and including $\mathbf{y}_{t-1}$. Let $\mathbf{P}_{t-1}$ denote the $m \times m$ covariance matrix of the estimation error, i.e.

$$\mathbf{P}_{t-1} = \mathrm{E}[(\boldsymbol{\alpha}_{t-1} - \mathbf{a}_{t-1})(\boldsymbol{\alpha}_{t-1} - \mathbf{a}_{t-1})'] \tag{3.2.1}$$

Given $\mathbf{a}_{t-1}$ and $\mathbf{P}_{t-1}$, the optimal estimator of $\boldsymbol{\alpha}_t$ is given by

$$\mathbf{a}_{t|t-1} = \mathbf{T}_t \mathbf{a}_{t-1} + \mathbf{c}_t \tag{3.2.2a}$$

while the covariance matrix of the estimation error is

$$\mathbf{P}_{t|t-1} = \mathbf{T}_t \mathbf{P}_{t-1} \mathbf{T}_t' + \mathbf{R}_t \mathbf{Q}_t \mathbf{R}_t', \quad t = 1, \ldots, T \tag{3.2.2b}$$

These two equations are known as the *prediction equations.*

Once the new observation, $\mathbf{y}_t$, becomes available, the estimator of $\boldsymbol{\alpha}_t$, $\mathbf{a}_{t|t-1}$, can be updated. The *updating equations* are

$$\mathbf{a}_t = \mathbf{a}_{t|t-1} + \mathbf{P}_{t|t-1} \mathbf{Z}_t' \mathbf{F}_t^{-1} (\mathbf{y}_t - \mathbf{Z}_t \mathbf{a}_{t|t-1} - \mathbf{d}_t) \tag{3.2.3a}$$

and

$$\mathbf{P}_t = \mathbf{P}_{t|t-1} - \mathbf{P}_{t|t-1} \mathbf{Z}_t' \mathbf{F}_t^{-1} \mathbf{Z}_t \mathbf{P}_{t|t-1} \tag{3.2.3b}$$

where[1]

$$\mathbf{F}_t = \mathbf{Z}_t \mathbf{P}_{t|t-1} \mathbf{Z}_t' + \mathbf{H}_t, \quad t = 1, \ldots, T \tag{3.2.3c}$$

Taken together (3.2.2) and (3.2.3) make up the Kalman filter. If desired they can be written as a single set of recursions going directly from $\mathbf{a}_{t-1}$ to $\mathbf{a}_t$ or, alternatively, from $\mathbf{a}_{t|t-1}$. In the latter case

$$\mathbf{a}_{t+1|t} = (\mathbf{T}_{t+1} - \mathbf{K}_t \mathbf{Z}_t) \mathbf{a}_{t|t-1} + \mathbf{K}_t \mathbf{y}_t + (\mathbf{c}_{t+1} - \mathbf{K}_t \mathbf{d}_t) \tag{3.2.4a}$$

where the gain matrix, $\mathbf{K}_t$, is given by

$$\mathbf{K}_t = \mathbf{T}_{t+1} \mathbf{P}_{t|t-1} \mathbf{Z}_t' \mathbf{F}_t^{-1}, \quad t = 1, \ldots, T \tag{3.2.4b}$$

The recursion for the error covariance matrix is

$$\mathbf{P}_{t+1|t} = \mathbf{T}_{t+1} (\mathbf{P}_{t|t-1} - \mathbf{P}_{t|t-1} \mathbf{Z}_t' \mathbf{F}_t^{-1} \mathbf{Z}_t \mathbf{P}_{t|t-1}) \mathbf{T}_{t+1}' + \mathbf{R}_{t+1} \mathbf{Q}_{t+1} \mathbf{R}_{t+1}', \quad t = 1, \ldots, T \tag{3.2.4c}$$

This is known as a *Riccati equation.*

The starting values for the Kalman filter may be specified in terms of $\mathbf{a}_0$ and $\mathbf{P}_0$ or $\mathbf{a}_{1|0}$ and $\mathbf{P}_{1|0}$. Given these initial conditions, the Kalman filter delivers the optimal estimator of the state vector as each new observation becomes available. When all T observations have been processed, the filter yields the optimal estimator of the current state vector, and/or the state vector in the next time period, based on the full information set. This estimator contains all the information needed to make optimal predictions of future values of both the state and the observations.

When the Kalman filter is applied to a univariate series, writing the measurement equation as in (3.1.2) implies a slight change in notation for the filtering equations, with the $N \times N$ matrix $\mathbf{F}_t$ being replaced by the scalar

$$f_t = \mathbf{z}_t' \mathbf{P}_{t|t-1} \mathbf{z}_t + h_t \tag{3.2.5}$$

[1]It is assumed that the inverse of $\mathbf{F}_t$ exists. It can be replaced by a pseudo-inverse. However, in the models presented in this book, $\mathbf{F}_t$ is always p.d.

Another aspect of filtering a univariate series is that it is often convenient to set up the state space model by letting the variance of the disturbances be proportional to a positive scalar, σ_*^2. Thus

$$\text{Var}(\varepsilon_t)=\sigma_*^2 h_t \quad \text{and} \quad \text{Var}(\boldsymbol{\eta}_t)=\sigma_*^2 \mathbf{Q}_t \tag{3.2.6}$$

If the initial covariance matrix is also specified up to the factor of proportionality, σ_*^2, the Kalman filter can be run independently of σ_*^2 with the starred quantities defined by

$$\mathbf{P}_{t+1|t}=\sigma_*^2 \mathbf{P}_{t+1|t}^* \quad \text{and} \quad f_t=\sigma_*^2 f_t^* \tag{3.2.7}$$

appearing in the recursions. One of the reasons for proceeding in this way is that if σ_*^2 is one of the unknown parameters in $\boldsymbol{\psi}$ it can be concentrated out of the likelihood function. In what follows the variances will frequently be specified as in (3.2.6.), but the asterisks will be omitted from $\mathbf{P}_{t+1|t}$ and f_t except where there is danger of ambiguity or a specific point is to be stressed.

Example 3.2.1 The random walk plus noise model, (3.1.6), provides a simple, but important, illustration of the Kalman filter. By letting σ_ε^2 play the role of σ_*^2, the model can be parameterised in terms of σ_ε^2 and the signal–noise ratio, q. Thus

$$\text{Var}(\varepsilon_t)=\sigma_\varepsilon^2 \quad \text{and} \quad \text{Var}(\eta_t)=\sigma_\varepsilon^2 q$$

Using $m_{t+1|t}$ to denote the estimator of the scalar state, μ_{t+1}, at time t and letting its MSE up to a factor of proportionality of σ_ε^2 be denoted by $p_{t+1|t}$, the Kalman filter (3.2.4) becomes

$$m_{t+1|t}=(1-k_t)m_{t|t-1}+k_t y_t \tag{3.2.8}$$

where the gain is

$$k_t=p_{t|t-1}/(p_{t|t-1}+1) \tag{3.2.9a}$$

and

$$p_{t+1|t}=p_{t|t-1}-[p_{t|t-1}^2/(1+p_{t|t-1})]+q, \quad t=1,\ldots,T \tag{3.2.9b}$$

As it stands the model does not explicitly specify initial conditions. However, if the random walk process started at some point in the remote past then $p_{1|0}$ is infinity. Setting $p_{1|0}=\kappa$ where κ is a positive number gives the first set of recursions as

$$m_{2|1}=[1-(\kappa/(1+\kappa))]m_{1|0}+[\kappa/(1+\kappa)]y_t$$

$$p_{2|1}=\kappa-[\kappa^2/(1+\kappa)]+q$$

As $\kappa\rightarrow\infty$,

$$m_{2|1}=y_1$$

irrespective of the value of $m_{1|0}$, while

$$p_{2|1}=1+q$$

These are exactly the starting values which would have been obtained if one had decided to use y_1 as an initial estimator of μ_1 and had noted that its MSE was σ_ε^2, implying that $p_1=1$.

The Kalman filter remains valid even if the variance of ε_t or η_t is zero. The latter case corresponds to a model in which the mean is fixed, so the estimation problem is a very basic one. Setting $q=0$ in (3.2.9b) gives

$$p_{t+1|t}=p_{t|t-1}/(1+p_{t|t-1}), \quad t=1,\ldots,T \tag{3.2.10}$$

and since $p_{2|1}=1$, it follows that $p_{3|2}=1/2$, $p_{4|3}=1/3$ and so on. Thus in general

$$p_{t+1|t}=1/t, \quad t=1,\ldots,T \tag{3.2.11}$$

The recursion for the estimator of the mean is therefore

$$m_{t+1|t}=\left(\frac{t-1}{t}\right)m_{t|t-1}+\frac{1}{t}y_t, \quad t=1,\ldots,T \tag{3.2.12}$$

Thus the MMSE of μ is the sample mean based on the first t observations, and its MSE or variance is σ^2/t.

From the computational point of view, using the Kalman filter equations directly as written in (3.2.2) and (3.2.3) is not necessarily the best way to proceed; see Anderson and Moore (1979, ch. 6). An alternative algorithm is the *information filter*. Rather than yielding a set of recursions for the MSE matrix, $\mathbf{P}_t$, the information filter gives a set for its inverse, $\mathbf{P}_t^{-1}$, which is known as the information matrix. It proves awkward to find appropriate recursions for the state vector, and, instead, the information filter gives recursions for the vector $\mathbf{b}_t=\mathbf{P}_t^{-1}\mathbf{a}_t$. Of course, given $\mathbf{b}_t$, $\mathbf{a}_t$ can always be recovered. The information filter is quite convenient when the initial covariance matrix, $\mathbf{P}_0$, is infinite, since then $\mathbf{P}_0^{-1}=\mathbf{0}$; see Example 3.2.1 and sub-section 3.3.4. Overall it appears to be more attractive than the conventional Kalman filter when the number of series, N, is significantly greater than the dimension of the state, m. This is because the information filter does not require the inversion of the $N\times N$ matrix $\mathbf{F}_t$. However, it should be noted that a standard matrix inversion lemma gives

$$\mathbf{F}_t^{-1}=\mathbf{H}_t^{-1}-\mathbf{H}_t^{-1}\mathbf{Z}_t(\mathbf{P}_{t|t-1}^{-1}+\mathbf{Z}_t'\mathbf{H}_t^{-1}\mathbf{Z}_t)^{-1}\mathbf{Z}_t'\mathbf{H}_t^{-1}$$

This is easily evaluated if $\mathbf{H}_t$ is time-invariant, since then it only needs to be inverted once, or if it is diagonal. The associated expression for the determinant, which appears explicitly in the likelihood function developed in section 3.4, is

$$|\mathbf{F}_t|=|\mathbf{H}_t|.|\mathbf{P}_{t|t-1}|.|\mathbf{P}_{t|t-1}^{-1}+\mathbf{Z}_t'\mathbf{H}_t^{-1}\mathbf{Z}_t|$$

The *square root* filter operates on a matrix $\mathbf{P}_t^\dagger$, such that $\mathbf{P}_t=\mathbf{P}_t^\dagger\mathbf{P}_t^{\dagger\prime}$, and by doing so avoids the problem that the Kalman filter may fail due to $\mathbf{P}_t$ not being non-negative definite. Similar techniques are often used in regression programs in order to avoid numerical instabilities due to ill-conditioning. The use of a square root algorithm in the filter is generally regarded as being the most numerically stable algorithm. Despite this attraction square root filters have not been used a great deal outside engineering, although an exception is Kitagawa (1981). Square root algorithms require more programming and involve a higher computational burden. The use of double precision and the fact that economic and social time series are typically much shorter than engineering series perhaps makes them less necessary.

3.2.2 Derivation of the Kalman filter

Under the normality assumption, the initial state vector, $\boldsymbol{\alpha}_0$, has a multivariate normal distribution with mean $\mathbf{a}_0$ and covariance matrix $\mathbf{P}_0$. The disturbances $\boldsymbol{\eta}_t$ and $\boldsymbol{\varepsilon}_t$ also have multivariate normal distributions for $t=1,\ldots,T$ and are distributed independently of each other and of $\boldsymbol{\alpha}_0$.

The state vector at $t=1$ is given by

$$\boldsymbol{\alpha}_1=\mathbf{T}_1\boldsymbol{\alpha}_0+\mathbf{c}_1+\mathbf{R}_1\boldsymbol{\eta}_1$$

Thus $\boldsymbol{\alpha}_1$ is a linear combination of two vectors of random variables, both with multivariate normal distributions, and a vector of constants. Hence it is itself multivariate normal with a mean of

$$\mathbf{a}_{1|0}=\mathbf{T}_1\mathbf{a}_0+\mathbf{c}_1 \tag{3.2.13a}$$

and a covariance matrix

$$\mathbf{P}_{1|0}=\mathbf{T}_1\mathbf{P}_0\mathbf{T}_1'+\mathbf{R}_1\mathbf{Q}_1\mathbf{R}_1' \tag{3.2.13b}$$

The notation $\mathbf{a}_{1|0}$ indicates the mean of the distribution of $\boldsymbol{\alpha}_1$ conditional on the information at time $t=0$. If the prior distribution is specified as the distribution of $\boldsymbol{\alpha}_1$ at $t=0$, (3.2.13a) and (3.2.13b) are redundant while $\mathbf{a}_{1|0}$ and $\mathbf{P}_{1|0}$ are specified as initial conditions.

In order to obtain the distribution of $\boldsymbol{\alpha}_1$ conditional on $\mathbf{y}_1$, write

$$\boldsymbol{\alpha}_1=\quad \mathbf{a}_{1|0}\qquad +(\boldsymbol{\alpha}_1-\mathbf{a}_{1|0}) \tag{3.2.14a}$$

$$\mathbf{y}_1=\mathbf{Z}_1\mathbf{a}_{1|0}+\mathbf{d}_1+\mathbf{Z}_1(\boldsymbol{\alpha}_1-\mathbf{a}_{1|0})+\boldsymbol{\varepsilon}_1 \tag{3.2.14b}$$

The second of these equations, (3.2.14b), is simply a rearrangement of the measurement equation. From (3.2.14) it can be seen that the vector $[\boldsymbol{\alpha}_1' \quad \mathbf{y}_1']'$ has a multivariate normal distribution with a mean of $[\mathbf{a}_{1|0}' \quad (\mathbf{Z}_1\mathbf{a}_{1|0}+\mathbf{d}_1)']'$ and a covariance matrix

$$\begin{bmatrix} \mathbf{P}_{1|0} & \mathbf{P}_{1|0}\mathbf{Z}_1' \\ \mathbf{Z}_1\mathbf{P}_{1|0} & \mathbf{Z}_1\mathbf{P}_{1|0}\mathbf{Z}_1'+\mathbf{H}_1 \end{bmatrix}$$

Applying the lemma in the appendix to this chapter gives the result that the distribution of $\boldsymbol{\alpha}_1$, conditional on a particular value of $\mathbf{y}_1$, is multivariate normal with mean

$$\mathbf{a}_1 = \mathbf{a}_{1|0} + \mathbf{P}_{1|0}\mathbf{Z}_1'\mathbf{F}_1^{-1}(\mathbf{y}_1 - \mathbf{Z}_1\mathbf{a}_{1|0} - \mathbf{d}_1) \tag{3.2.15a}$$

and covariance matrix

$$\mathbf{P}_1 = \mathbf{P}_{1|0} - \mathbf{P}_{1|0}\mathbf{Z}_1'\mathbf{F}_1^{-1}\mathbf{Z}_1\mathbf{P}_{1|0} \tag{3.2.15b}$$

where

$$\mathbf{F}_1 = \mathbf{Z}_1\mathbf{P}_{1|0}\mathbf{Z}_1' + \mathbf{H}_1 \tag{3.2.15c}$$

Repeating the steps used to get (3.2.14) and (3.2.15) for $t = 2, \ldots, T$ yields a set of equations which have exactly the same form as the Kalman filter recursions, (3.2.2) and (3.2.3). However, the derivation given so far only enables us to interpret $\mathbf{a}_t$ and $\mathbf{P}_t$ as the mean and covariance matrix of the conditional distribution of $\boldsymbol{\alpha}_t$. In setting out the Kalman filter in the previous sub-section, $\mathbf{a}_t$ was described as an optimal estimator of $\boldsymbol{\alpha}_t$, based on the information available at time t, while $\mathbf{P}_t$ was described as the covariance matrix of the estimation error. The following sub-section provides the link.

3.2.3 Interpretation and properties

In the Gaussian model, the Kalman filter yields the mean and covariance matrix of the distribution of $\boldsymbol{\alpha}_t$ conditional on the information available at time t. Thus

$$\mathbf{a}_t = \underset{t}{\mathrm{E}}(\boldsymbol{\alpha}_t) = \mathrm{E}(\boldsymbol{\alpha}_t \mid \mathbf{Y}_t) \tag{3.2.16}$$

and

$$\mathbf{P}_t = \underset{t}{\mathrm{E}}\{[\boldsymbol{\alpha}_t - \underset{t}{\mathrm{E}}(\boldsymbol{\alpha}_t)][\boldsymbol{\alpha}_t - \underset{t}{\mathrm{E}}(\boldsymbol{\alpha}_t)]'\} \tag{3.2.17}$$

where the subscript below the expectation operator indicates that the expectation is taken with respect to the conditional distribution of $\boldsymbol{\alpha}_t$ at time t. The conditional mean is a *minimum mean square estimate* of $\boldsymbol{\alpha}_t$. The argument used to show that the conditional mean of y_{T+l}, (2.3.10), is the minimum mean square estimate of y_{T+l} can be applied directly to a single element of (3.2.16). Furthermore, it can be generalised to show that the full conditional mean vector is the minimum mean square estimate of $\boldsymbol{\alpha}_t$ in the sense that the MSE matrix of any other estimate can be expressed as the conditional covariance matrix of $\boldsymbol{\alpha}_t$ plus a matrix which is p.s.d.

The conditional mean can also be regarded as an *estimator* of $\boldsymbol{\alpha}_t$. As noted in sub-section 2.3.1, the difference between an estimate and an estimator is that the former is a number while the latter is a rule. In the present context this means that when viewed as an estimate, the conditional mean is a vector of numbers associated with a particular realisation of observations, but when viewed as an estimator, it is an expression which applies to any set of observations. With this change in interpretation, the expression for the conditional mean becomes a vector of random variables. Now it can be shown that this estimator minimises the MSE when the expectation is taken over all the variables in the information set rather than being conditional on a particular set of values; see Anderson and Moore (1979, pp. 29–32) for a detailed discussion. Thus the conditional mean estimator is the *minimum mean square estimator* (MMSE) of $\boldsymbol{\alpha}_t$. The estimator is unbiased in the sense that the expectation of the estimation error is zero. Since this expectation can be taken over all variables in the information set, this property is sometimes referred to as unconditional unbiasedness.

Since, as a general rule, the quantity to be estimated, namely the state vector, is itself random, it is not legitimate to speak of the conditional mean estimator as having a covariance matrix. However, just as it is possible to define bias in terms of the estimation error, so it is legitimate to define a covariance matrix for the estimation error. This same matrix can be referred to, quite properly, as the *mean square error* (MSE) matrix of the estimator. In the Gaussian model, the covariance matrix defined in (3.2.17) is given by the Kalman filter. However, it will be seen from (3.2.2b) and (3.2.3b) that in a linear model this matrix is independent of the observations. Thus it is also the *unconditional* error covariance matrix associated with the conditional mean estimator. This means that (3.2.17) can be written without the expectation being conditioned on t.

When the disturbances in the state space model are not normally distributed, it is no longer true, in general, that the Kalman filter yields the conditional mean of the state vector. In other words (3.2.16) does not hold. The way in which the conditional mean can be computed in this situation is discussed in sub-section 3.7.3. But what of the Kalman filter estimator, $\mathbf{a}_t$? If attention is restricted to estimators which are *linear* combinations of the observations, then $\mathbf{a}_t$ is the one which minimises the MSE. Thus $\mathbf{a}_t$ is the *minimum mean square linear estimator* (MMSLE) of $\boldsymbol{\alpha}_t$ based on observations up to and including time t. This estimator is unconditionally unbiased and the unconditional covariance matrix of the estimation error is the $\mathbf{P}_t$ matrix given by the Kalman filter. Proofs of these results can be found in Anderson and Moore (1979), Duncan and Horn (1972) or Harvey (1981b, ch. 4).

The above points apply in exactly the same way to $\mathbf{a}_{t|t-1}$ and $\mathbf{P}_{t|t-1}$. Furthermore, the conditional mean of $\mathbf{y}_t$ at time $t-1$, namely

$$\tilde{\mathbf{y}}_{t|t-1} = \mathbf{Z}_t \mathbf{a}_{t|t-1} + \mathbf{d}_t \tag{3.2.18}$$

can be interpreted as the MMSE of $\mathbf{y}_t$ in a Gaussian model, and as the MMSLE otherwise.

The prediction errors

$$\mathbf{v}_t = \mathbf{y}_t - \tilde{\mathbf{y}}_{t|t-1} = \mathbf{Z}_t(\boldsymbol{\alpha}_t - \mathbf{a}_{t|t-1}) + \boldsymbol{\varepsilon}_t, \quad t = 1, \ldots, T \tag{3.2.19}$$

are known as *innovations*, since they represent the new information in the latest observation. As can be seen from (3.2.3), they play a key role in updating the estimator of the state vector. The further $\mathbf{v}_t$ is from a null vector, the greater the 'correction' in the estimator of $\boldsymbol{\alpha}_t$.

In a Gaussian model, it follows from the definition of $\tilde{\mathbf{y}}_{t|t-1}$ that the mean of $\mathbf{v}_t$ is a vector of zeros. Furthermore, it is easy to see from (3.2.19) that

$$\text{Var}(\mathbf{v}_t) = \mathbf{F}_t$$

where $\mathbf{F}_t$ is given by (3.2.3c). In (3.4.5) it is shown that the joint density of the observations can be decomposed in terms of the innovations, which are independently and normally distributed. Hence,

$$\mathbf{v}_t \sim \text{NID}(\mathbf{0}, \mathbf{F}_t)$$

In the absence of the normality assumption the mean of the innovation vector is still a zero vector, while its covariance matrix at time t is $\mathbf{F}_t$. In addition the innovations in different time periods can be shown to be uncorrelated, that is

$$\text{E}(\mathbf{v}_t \mathbf{v}_s') = 0 \quad \text{for } t \neq s, \quad \text{and} \quad t, s = 1, \ldots, T$$

It should perhaps be stressed that these results on the distribution of the innovations only hold exactly if the system matrices are fixed and known. They are not generally true if these matrices contain unknown hyperparameters which are replaced by estimators.

3.2.4 Correlated measurement and transition equation disturbances

When the measurement and transition equation disturbances are correlated, the Kalman filter needs to be modified. In this case it makes a difference whether the transition equation is as in (3.1.1) or as in (3.1.10). The results below are given without proof. Derivations can be found in Jazwinski (1970, pp. 209–11).

Consider the state space form with measurement equation (3.1.1) and transition equation (3.1.3) and suppose that

$$\text{E}(\boldsymbol{\eta}_t \boldsymbol{\varepsilon}_s') = \begin{Bmatrix} \mathbf{G}_t, & t = s \\ \mathbf{0}, & t \neq s \end{Bmatrix} \tag{3.2.20}$$

where $\mathbf{G}_t$ is a known $g \times N$ matrix. Note that while the measurement and transition equation disturbances are contemporaneously correlated they remain uncorrelated at non-zero lags. The prediction equations (3.2.2) remain unaltered in the face of contemporaneous correlation. The updating equations are modified as follows: in (3.2.3a) and (3.2.3b) the matrix $\mathbf{P}_{t|t-1}\mathbf{Z}_t'$ becomes $\mathbf{P}_{t|t-1}\mathbf{Z}_t' + \mathbf{R}_t\mathbf{G}_t$ while

$$\mathbf{F}_t = \mathbf{Z}_t\mathbf{P}_{t|t-1}\mathbf{Z}_t' + \mathbf{Z}_t\mathbf{R}_t\mathbf{G}_t + \mathbf{G}_t'\mathbf{R}_t'\mathbf{Z}_t' + \mathbf{H}_t \tag{3.2.21}$$

The alternative state space form consists of the measurement equation (3.1.1a) together with the transition equation (3.1.10). The correlation between the disturbances may again be written as in (3.2.20) but, because of the forward shift in the time subscripts on the state vector, the model is a different one. The Kalman filter is most conveniently expressed by merging the updating and prediction equations as in (3.2.4). The recursion for the state vector, (3.2.4a), is modified by redefining the gain matrix, (3.2.4b), as

$$\mathbf{K}_t=(\mathbf{T}_{t+1}\mathbf{P}_{t|t-1}\mathbf{Z}_t'+\mathbf{R}_t\mathbf{G}_t)\mathbf{F}_t^{-1} \tag{3.2.22}$$

The definition of the innovation covariance matrix, $\mathbf{F}_t$, is not (3.2.21) but remains as in (3.2.3c). As regards the error covariance matrix, the recursion in (3.2.4c) becomes

$$\mathbf{P}_{t+1|t}=\mathbf{T}_{t+1}\mathbf{P}_{t|t-1}\mathbf{T}_{t+1}'-(\mathbf{T}_{t+1}\mathbf{P}_{t|t-1}\mathbf{Z}_t'+\mathbf{R}_t\mathbf{G}_t)\mathbf{F}_t^{-1}(\mathbf{T}_{t+1}\mathbf{P}_{t|t-1}\mathbf{Z}_t'+\mathbf{R}_t\mathbf{G}_t)' \\ +\mathbf{R}_t\mathbf{Q}_t\mathbf{R}_t' \tag{3.2.23}$$

A somewhat different approach to the problem of correlated measurement and transition equation disturbances in the alternative SSF is to transform to a new system in which these disturbances are uncorrelated. Following Chan *et al.* (1984), taking the transition equation, (3.1.10), and adding the measurement equation to it gives

$$\begin{aligned}\boldsymbol{\alpha}_{t+1}&=\mathbf{T}_t\boldsymbol{\alpha}_t+\mathbf{R}_t\boldsymbol{\eta}_t-\mathbf{R}_t\mathbf{G}_t\mathbf{H}_t^{-1}(\mathbf{Z}_t\boldsymbol{\alpha}_t+\boldsymbol{\varepsilon}_t-\mathbf{y}_t)\\ &=\mathbf{T}_t^*\boldsymbol{\alpha}_t+\mathbf{R}_t\mathbf{G}_t\mathbf{H}_t^{-1}\mathbf{y}_t+\mathbf{R}_t\boldsymbol{\eta}_t^*\end{aligned} \tag{3.2.24}$$

where

$$\mathbf{T}_t^*=\mathbf{T}_t-\mathbf{R}_t\mathbf{G}_t\mathbf{H}_t^{-1}\mathbf{Z}_t$$
$$\boldsymbol{\eta}_t^*=\boldsymbol{\eta}_t-\mathbf{G}_t\mathbf{H}_t^{-1}\boldsymbol{\varepsilon}_t$$

The new system consists of the original measurement equation, together with the transition equation defined by (3.2.24). The inclusion of $\mathbf{y}_t$ in (3.2.24) does not affect the Kalman filter, as $\mathbf{y}_t$ is known at time t; see the discussion on conditionally Gaussian models in sub-section 3.7.1. By construction $\mathrm{E}(\boldsymbol{\eta}_t^*\boldsymbol{\varepsilon}_s')=\mathbf{0}$ for all t, s, while

$$\mathrm{Var}(\boldsymbol{\eta}_t^*)=\mathbf{Q}_t^*=\mathbf{Q}_t-\mathbf{G}_t\mathbf{H}_t^{-1}\mathbf{G}_t' \tag{3.2.25}$$

3.3 Properties of time-invariant models

In many applications the state space model is time-invariant. In other words the system matrices $\mathbf{Z}_t$, $\mathbf{d}_t$, $\mathbf{H}_t$, $\mathbf{T}_t$, $\mathbf{c}_t$, $\mathbf{R}_t$ and $\mathbf{Q}_t$ are all independent of time and so can be written without a subscript. This section examines the properties of such models. In fact all the properties in which we are interested apply to a system in which $\mathbf{c}_t$ and $\mathbf{d}_t$ are allowed to change over time and so the class of models under discussion is effectively

$$\mathbf{y}_t = \mathbf{Z}\boldsymbol{\alpha}_t + \mathbf{d}_t + \boldsymbol{\varepsilon}_t, \quad \text{Var}(\boldsymbol{\varepsilon}_t) = \mathbf{H} \tag{3.3.1a}$$

and

$$\boldsymbol{\alpha}_t = \mathbf{T}\boldsymbol{\alpha}_{t-1} + \mathbf{c}_t + \mathbf{R}\boldsymbol{\eta}_t, \quad \text{Var}(\boldsymbol{\eta}_t) = \mathbf{Q} \tag{3.3.1b}$$

with $\text{E}(\boldsymbol{\varepsilon}_t \boldsymbol{\eta}_s') = \mathbf{0}$ for all s, t. Since the disturbances in the measurement and transition equations are uncorrelated, the discussion applies equally well to a model in which the transition equation is for $\boldsymbol{\alpha}_{t+1}$ rather than $\boldsymbol{\alpha}_t$, as in (3.1.10).

Certain properties of models of the form (3.3.1) can be characterised in terms of the properties of an analogous system in control engineering. This system has no disturbance term on the measurement equation, while in the transition equation the disturbance term is replaced by a vector of control variables. Thus

$$\mathbf{y}_t = \mathbf{Z}\boldsymbol{\alpha}_t \tag{3.3.2a}$$

and

$$\boldsymbol{\alpha}_t = \mathbf{T}\boldsymbol{\alpha}_{t-1} + \mathbf{G}\mathbf{u}_t \tag{3.3.2b}$$

where $\mathbf{u}_t$ is the $n \times 1$ vector of control variables and $\mathbf{G}$ is a fixed $m \times n$ matrix. The system in (3.3.2) is stable if, for any initial state, $\boldsymbol{\alpha}_0$, the state vector converges to an equilibrium solution, $\bar{\boldsymbol{\alpha}}$, when $\mathbf{u}_t$ is constant. *The necessary and sufficient condition for stability is that the characteristic roots of the transition matrix*, **T**, *should have modulus less than one*, that is

$$|\lambda_i(\mathbf{T})| < 1, \quad i = 1, \ldots, m \tag{3.3.3}$$

More generally, the key properties of (3.3.2) are those of observability and controllability and the related, but slightly weaker, properties of detectability and stabilisability. These properties have a definite physical meaning in control engineering. When applied to the system (3.3.1) they provide the basis for assessing certain statistical properties.

The properties of observability, controllability, detectability and stabilisability are defined in the first sub-section. The sub-section which follows then shows how these concepts can be applied to the statistical model, (3.3.1). This is important for both theoretical and practical reasons. In particular, it becomes possible to determine whether the Kalman filter goes to a steady state in the sense that the error covariance matrices $\mathbf{P}_{t|t-1}$ and $\mathbf{P}_t$ are time-invariant. These matrices are independent of $\mathbf{c}_t$ and $\mathbf{d}_t$ in (3.3.1) and the question is whether the time invariance of the remaining system matrices is sufficient for the filter to settle into a steady state. It is also important to know whether the initial conditions have any bearing on this question. The results given in sub-section 3.3.3 provide the answer. The appropriate initial conditions for both stationary and non-stationary models are discussed in sub-section 3.3.4.

3.3.1 *Controllability, observability, stabilisability and detectability*

Whether or not (3.3.2) is controllable depends on the properties of the two matrices $\mathbf{T}$ and $\mathbf{G}$. Whether or not it is observable depends on $\mathbf{T}$ and $\mathbf{Z}$.

The meaning of controllability is as follows. Suppose that at some point in time, t, the state vector has a particular value and that at time $t+m$ it is required that it takes an arbitrary prescribed value $\boldsymbol{\alpha}^*$. If the system is controllable, the control vectors, $\mathbf{u}_{t+1}, \ldots, \mathbf{u}_{t+m}$, can be chosen in such a way that $\boldsymbol{\alpha}^*_{t+m}$ is attained.

Definition of controllability The system (3.3.2) is controllable if

$$\text{Rank}[\mathbf{G}, \mathbf{TG}, \ldots, \mathbf{T}^{m-1}\mathbf{G}] = m \tag{3.3.4}$$

If $\mathbf{G}$ is of rank m, the controllability condition is clearly satisfied. In fact it can be seen directly that the system can be brought to the desired state; rearranging the transition equation (3.3.2b) gives

$$\mathbf{u}_{t+1} = \mathbf{G}^{-1}(\boldsymbol{\alpha}^* - \mathbf{T}\boldsymbol{\alpha}_t)$$

and this control vector converts $\boldsymbol{\alpha}_t$ into $\boldsymbol{\alpha}^*$ in one time period. There are, however, many cases when $\mathbf{G}$ is not of rank m. In these cases certain elements in the state vector can only be manipulated indirectly via other elements.

Example 3.3.1 Consider the transition equation

$$\begin{bmatrix} \alpha_{1t} \\ \alpha_{2t} \end{bmatrix} = \begin{bmatrix} a & 0 \\ b & c \end{bmatrix} \begin{bmatrix} \alpha_{1,t-1} \\ \alpha_{2,t-1} \end{bmatrix} + \begin{bmatrix} 1 \\ 0 \end{bmatrix} u_t$$

where u_t is a single control variable. The matrix

$$[\mathbf{G}, \mathbf{TG}] = \begin{bmatrix} 1 & \vdots & a \\ 0 & \vdots & b \end{bmatrix}$$

is of rank $m=2$ if and only if $b \neq 0$.

The state vector, $\boldsymbol{\alpha}_t$, is said to be observable if it can be determined exactly, given the observations $\mathbf{y}_t, \ldots, \mathbf{y}_{t+m-1}$. (The values of the control vector $\mathbf{u}_{t+1}, \ldots, \mathbf{u}_{t+m-1}$ are also needed to determine $\boldsymbol{\alpha}_t$ and these are assumed to be known.)

Definition of observability The system (3.3.2) is observable if

$$\text{Rank}\,[\mathbf{Z}', \mathbf{T}'\mathbf{Z}', \ldots, (\mathbf{T}')^{m-1}\mathbf{Z}'] = m \tag{3.3.5}$$

A number of variations of the above definitions can be found in the literature. For example, in Anderson and Moore (1979, pp. 341–2), (3.3.4) and (3.3.5) actually define two closely related properties called reachability and constructability respectively. The definitions of controllability and observability are slightly different but for our purposes the distinction is unimportant.

Stabilisability and detectability are properties which are closely related to controllability and observability. However, the conditions under which a system possesses these properties are slightly weaker than the conditions under which it is controllable and observable. Thus controllability (observability) implies stabilisability (detectability) but not vice versa.

Definition of stabilisability The system (3.3.2) is stabilisable if there exists an $m \times n$ matrix, $\mathbf{S}$, such that

$$|\lambda_i(\mathbf{T}+\mathbf{G}\mathbf{S}')|<1 \quad \text{for } i=1,\ldots,m \tag{3.3.6}$$

where, as in (3.3.3), $\lambda_i(.)$ denotes the i-th characteristic root of a square matrix.

Definition of detectability The system (3.3.2) is detectable if there exists an $m \times N$ matrix, $\mathbf{D}$, such that

$$|\lambda_i(\mathbf{T}-\mathbf{D}\mathbf{Z})|<1 \quad \text{for } i=1,\ldots,m \tag{3.3.7}$$

3.3.2 *Properties of state space representations of statistical models*

The properties of controllability, observability, stabilisability and detectability have all been defined in terms of the state space system (3.3.2). However, they also apply to the statistical state space model (3.3.1). All that is needed is a slight amendment to the transition equation so that the covariance matrix of the disturbance term is an identity matrix. Let $\mathbf{R}^\dagger$ be an $n \times n$ matrix such that $\mathbf{R}^\dagger\mathbf{R}^{\dagger\prime}=\mathbf{Q}$. Then the transition equation can be written as

$$\boldsymbol{\alpha}_t=\mathbf{T}\boldsymbol{\alpha}_{t-1}+\mathbf{c}_t+\mathbf{G}\boldsymbol{\eta}_t^\dagger \tag{3.3.8}$$

where $\mathbf{G}=\mathbf{R}\mathbf{R}^\dagger$ and $\boldsymbol{\eta}_t^\dagger$ is a redefined disturbance term with the property that $\mathrm{E}(\boldsymbol{\eta}_t^\dagger)=0$ and $\mathrm{Var}(\boldsymbol{\eta}_t^\dagger)=\mathbf{I}$. The matrices $\mathbf{T}$ and $\mathbf{G}$ in (3.3.8) together with $\mathbf{Z}$ in (3.3.1a) can now be used to determine the properties of the model.

Example 3.3.2 Consider the local linear trend model defined by (2.3.24) and (2.3.27). This can be written

$$y_t=[1 \quad 0]\boldsymbol{\alpha}_t+\varepsilon_t \tag{3.3.9a}$$

and

$$\boldsymbol{\alpha}_t=\begin{bmatrix}\mu_t\\ \beta_t\end{bmatrix}=\begin{bmatrix}1 & 1\\ 0 & 1\end{bmatrix}\begin{bmatrix}\mu_{t-1}\\ \beta_{t-1}\end{bmatrix}+\begin{bmatrix}\sigma_\eta & 0\\ 0 & \sigma_\zeta\end{bmatrix}\begin{bmatrix}\eta_t^*\\ \zeta_t^*\end{bmatrix} \tag{3.3.9b}$$

making it clear that

$$\mathbf{Z}=[1 \quad 0], \quad \mathbf{T}=\begin{bmatrix}1 & 1\\ 0 & 1\end{bmatrix} \quad \text{and } \mathbf{G}=\begin{bmatrix}\sigma_\eta & 0\\ 0 & \sigma_\zeta\end{bmatrix}$$

The model is controllable if the matrix

$$[\mathbf{G}, \mathbf{TG}] = \begin{bmatrix} \sigma_\eta & 0 & \vdots & \sigma_\eta & \sigma_\zeta \\ 0 & \sigma_\zeta & \vdots & 0 & \sigma_\zeta \end{bmatrix}$$

is of full rank. A necessary and sufficient condition for this to hold is that σ_ζ^2 should be strictly positive, i.e. $\sigma_\zeta^2 > 0$. No conditions need be placed on σ_η^2 and so the system may still be controllable even if it is zero.

Conditions which are sufficient for controllability must also be sufficient for stabilisability. In order to determine whether the condition $\sigma_\zeta^2 > 0$ is necessary for stabilisability we form the matrix

$$\mathbf{T} + \mathbf{GS}' = \begin{bmatrix} 1 + s_{11}\sigma_\eta & 1 + s_{21}\sigma_\eta \\ s_{12}\sigma_\zeta & 1 + s_{22}\sigma_\zeta \end{bmatrix}$$

The characteristic roots of this matrix are obtained as the solution to the determinantal equation

$$|\mathbf{T} + \mathbf{GS}' - \lambda\mathbf{I}| = 0$$

When $\sigma_\zeta^2 = 0$, this yields

$$(1 + s_{11}\sigma_\eta - \lambda)(1 - \lambda) = 0$$

Thus at least one of the roots must be equal to unity and so the condition $\sigma_\zeta^2 > 0$ is necessary for stabilisability as well as controllability.

The system is observable if the matrix

$$[\mathbf{Z}' \quad \mathbf{T}'\mathbf{Z}'] = \begin{bmatrix} 1 & 1 \\ 0 & 1 \end{bmatrix}$$

is of full rank. Clearly this is the case, without even placing restrictions on the parameters of the model. The system must also therefore be detectable in all cases. On the other hand, consider a modification of (3.3.9) in which the level equation is replaced by

$$\mu_t = \mu_{t-1} + \eta_t$$

Unlike the original equation, this new equation does not contain the lagged value of the slope parameter, β_{t-1}. Hence β_t never influences y_t and so cannot ever be observed. This is confirmed by the fact that the observability matrix $[\mathbf{Z}' \quad \mathbf{T}'\mathbf{Z}']$ is of rank one rather than rank two.

Example 3.3.3 In order to determine the properties of the MA(1) model, (3.1.11), it is necessary to consider the minimal realisation given in (3.1.13). However, since the measurement and transition equation disturbances are correlated, it is necessary to follow Chan *et al.* (1984) and transform the system so that the disturbances are uncorrelated. Applying the results at the end of sub-section 3.2.4, it will be seen that the MA(1) model can be written in the form

$$y_t = \theta\alpha_t + \xi_t \tag{3.3.10a}$$

$$\alpha_{t+1} = -\theta\alpha_t + y_t + \eta_t^* \tag{3.3.10b}$$

where $\alpha_t = \xi_{t-1}$ and $\eta_t^* = 0$. The appearance of y_t in (3.3.10b) is not important in the present context and (3.3.10b) can be written in the form (3.3.8) with an artificial disturbance term, $\eta_t^\dagger$, defined such that $\text{Var}(\eta_t^\dagger) = 1$, while $G = 0$. Once expressed in this way, the model is seen to be always observable, but it is never controllable and is only stabilisable if $|\theta| < 1$.

3.3.3 Time-invariant filters

The Kalman filter applied to the model in (3.3.1) is in a steady state if the error covariance matrix is time-invariant, that is

$$\mathbf{P}_{t+1|t} = \bar{\mathbf{P}} \tag{3.3.11}$$

The recursion for the error covariance matrix is redundant in the steady state, while the recursion for the state becomes

$$\mathbf{a}_{t+1|t} = \bar{\mathbf{T}}\mathbf{a}_{t|t-1} + \bar{\mathbf{K}}\mathbf{y}_t + (\mathbf{c}_{t+1} - \bar{\mathbf{K}}\mathbf{d}_t) \tag{3.3.12a}$$

where the transition and gain matrices are defined by

$$\bar{\mathbf{T}} = \mathbf{T} - \bar{\mathbf{K}}\mathbf{Z} \tag{3.3.12b}$$

and

$$\bar{\mathbf{K}} = \mathbf{T}\bar{\mathbf{P}}\mathbf{Z}'(\mathbf{Z}\bar{\mathbf{P}}\mathbf{Z}' + \mathbf{H})^{-1} \tag{3.3.12c}$$

respectively. The steady-state filter is said to be stable if the roots of $\bar{\mathbf{T}}$ are less than one in absolute value. The Kalman filter has a steady-state solution if there exists a time-invariant error covariance matrix which satisfies the Riccati equation obtained in (3.2.4c), namely

$$\mathbf{P}_{t+1|t} = \mathbf{T}_{t+1}[\mathbf{P}_{t|t-1} - \mathbf{P}_{t|t-1}\mathbf{Z}_t'(\mathbf{Z}_t\mathbf{P}_{t|t-1}\mathbf{Z}_t' + \mathbf{H}_t)^{-1}\mathbf{Z}_t\mathbf{P}_{t|t-1}]\mathbf{T}_{t+1}' + \mathbf{R}_{t+1}\mathbf{Q}_{t+1}\mathbf{R}_{t+1}' \tag{3.3.13}$$

If such a solution exists, we can set

$$\mathbf{P}_{t+1|t} = \mathbf{P}_{t|t-1} = \bar{\mathbf{P}}$$

thereby obtaining the *algebraic Riccati equation* (ARE),

$$\bar{\mathbf{P}} - \mathbf{T}\bar{\mathbf{P}}\mathbf{T}' + \mathbf{T}\bar{\mathbf{P}}\mathbf{Z}'(\mathbf{Z}\bar{\mathbf{P}}\mathbf{Z}' + \mathbf{H})^{-1}\mathbf{Z}\bar{\mathbf{P}}\mathbf{T}' - \mathbf{R}\mathbf{Q}\mathbf{R}' = \mathbf{0} \tag{3.3.14}$$

Unfortunately it is usually difficult to obtain an explicit solution to the ARE. Furthermore even if it is known that a solution exists, it is not immediately apparent whether the $\bar{\mathbf{P}}$ matrix will be unique or whether it will be p.s.d. The results below, taken primarily from Anderson and Moore (1979, section 4.4), Caines and Mayne (1970) and Chan *et al.* (1984) throw some light on these issues and on the question of convergence to a steady state.

Result 3.3.1 If the model is stable, that is $|\lambda_i(\mathbf{T})|<1, i=1,\ldots,m$ and if the initial covariance matrix, $\mathbf{P}_{1|0}$, is p.s.d., then

$$\lim_{t\to\infty} \mathbf{P}_{t+1|t}=\bar{\mathbf{P}} \tag{3.3.15}$$

with $\bar{\mathbf{P}}$ independent of $\mathbf{P}_{1|0}$. Convergence to $\bar{\mathbf{P}}$ is exponentially fast provided that $\bar{\mathbf{P}}$ is the only p.s.d. matrix satisfying the algebraic Riccati equation.

Result 3.3.2 If the system is detectable and stabilisable, but not necessarily stable, and if $\mathbf{P}_{1|0}$ is p.s.d., then the above results continue to hold.

Result 3.3.1 is a special case of Result 3.3.2 since if a system is stable it is automatically detectable and stabilisable. It is interesting that on p. 78 of their book, Anderson and Moore (1979) dismiss Result 3.3.2 as being 'of limited utility'. This is an indication of the different kinds of applications which arise in engineering and economics. When structural time series models are used to model economic and social time series, non-stationarity is the rule rather than the exception.

The properties of state space models which are not stabilisable have been examined by Chan *et al.* (1984) with particular reference to cases where some of the roots of the transition matrix lie on the unit circle. Their theorem 4.3 can be summarised as follows:

Result 3.3.3 If the system is observable and if $\mathbf{P}_{1|0}-\bar{\mathbf{P}}$ is p.d. or $\mathbf{P}_{1|0}=\bar{\mathbf{P}}$, then (3.3.15) holds.

The conditions in Result 3.3.3 are not sufficient for covergence to the steady state to take place exponentially fast.

Example 3.3.4 In the random walk plus noise model of Example 3.2.1, the algebraic Riccati equation obtained from (3.2.9b) is

$$\bar{p}-\bar{p}+[\bar{p}^2/(\bar{p}+1)]-q=0$$

Solving the resulting quadratic equation,

$$\bar{p}^2-\bar{p}q-q=0$$

yields

$$\bar{p}=(q+\sqrt{q^2+4q})/2 \tag{3.3.16}$$

The other solution to the quadratic is not applicable since for $q>0$ it yields a negative value of $\bar{p}$.

The model is always observable but it is not stabilisable when $q=0$. In Example 3.2.1 it was shown that in this case the Riccati equation becomes $p_{t+1|t}=1/t$. Thus $p_{t+1|t}$ converges to the steady-state solution of $\bar{p}=0$ but does not do so exponentially fast.

Example 3.3.5 The canonical decomposition of a random walk is

$$y_t=\mu_t+\varepsilon_t^*$$
$$\mu_t=\mu_{t-1}+\eta_t^*+\eta_{t-1}^*$$

with $\text{Var}(\varepsilon_t^*)=\text{Var}(\eta_t^*)=\sigma_*^2$; see the derivation in sub-section 6.1.2. The state space representation has

$$\mathbf{T}=\begin{bmatrix}1 & 1\\ 0 & 0\end{bmatrix}, \mathbf{R}=\begin{bmatrix}1\\ 1\end{bmatrix} \quad \text{and} \quad \mathbf{Z}=\mathbf{z}'=[1 \quad 0]$$

It is straightforward to verify that the model is controllable and observable and so, even though it is non-stationary, it converges to a steady state exponentially fast. Writing out the algebraic Riccati equation for the model gives $\bar{p}_{22}=\bar{p}_{12}=\bar{p}_{21}=1$. It follows almost immediately that $\bar{p}_{11}=3$, and so

$$\bar{\mathbf{P}}=\sigma_*^2\begin{bmatrix}3 & 1\\ 1 & 1\end{bmatrix}$$

Example 3.3.6 The application of the above results to an MA(1) model requires that it be in the form (3.3.10). Stability requires that $|\theta|<1$, and so Result 3.3.1 does not apply to non-invertible models. Nor does Result 3.3.2 apply since the model is only stabilisable if $|\theta|<1$. However, the model is always observable if $\theta\neq 0$ and so Result 3.3.3 applies if the initial conditions are appropriate. This question is taken up in the next sub-section.

A final point to note is that if the covariance matrix, $\mathbf{P}_{t+1|t}$, has a steady state solution, then $\mathbf{F}_t$, the covariance matrix of the innovations, also converges to a steady state, that is

$$\lim_{t\to\infty} \mathbf{F}_t=\mathbf{\Sigma}=\mathbf{Z}\bar{\mathbf{P}}\mathbf{Z}'+\mathbf{H} \tag{3.3.17}$$

3.3.4 Initial conditions and convergence

In this sub-section, we consider the initial conditions for a time-invariant model. Attention will be restricted to univariate series, with the SSF being

$$y_t=\mathbf{z}'\boldsymbol{\alpha}_t+d_t+\varepsilon_t, \quad \text{Var}(\varepsilon_t)=h$$

$$\boldsymbol{\alpha}_t=\mathbf{T}\boldsymbol{\alpha}_{t-1}+\mathbf{c}_t+\mathbf{R}\boldsymbol{\eta}_t, \quad \text{Var}(\boldsymbol{\eta}_t)=\mathbf{Q}$$

In principle, the starting values for the Kalman filter are given by the mean and covariance matrix of the unconditional distribution of the state vector. The state vector in (3.3.1b) is stationary if $|\lambda_i(\mathbf{T})| < 1$ and $\mathbf{c}_t$ is time-invariant. This being the case, it has mean $(\mathbf{I}-\mathbf{T})^{-1}\mathbf{c}$ and a covariance matrix, $\mathbf{P}$, which is the unique solution to the equation

$$\mathbf{P} = \mathbf{TPT}' + \mathbf{RQR}' \tag{3.3.18}$$

A derivation of this equation can be found later in (8.1.20).

Example 3.3.7 In the stochastic cycle model, (2.3.60), with $\text{Var}(\kappa_t) = \text{Var}(\kappa_t^*) = \sigma_\kappa^2$, the scalar 2×2 matrix

$$\mathbf{P} = [\sigma_\kappa^2/(1-\rho^2)]\mathbf{I} \tag{3.3.19}$$

satisfies (3.3.18).

Example 3.3.8 If the MA(1) model is put in SSF as in (3.1.12), the state vector is $\boldsymbol{\alpha}_t = [y_t \quad \theta\xi_t]'$. Its unconditional mean is clearly a null vector while its unconditional covariance matrix may be evaluated directly as

$$\mathbf{P} = \text{E}(\boldsymbol{\alpha}_t\boldsymbol{\alpha}_t') = \sigma^2\begin{bmatrix} 1+\theta^2 & \theta \\ \theta & \theta^2 \end{bmatrix} \tag{3.3.20}$$

There are a number of ways in which $\mathbf{P}$ may be evaluated in more complex models. One possibility is based on the observation that

$$\text{vec}(\mathbf{P}) = [\mathbf{I} - \mathbf{T} \otimes \mathbf{T}]^{-1} \text{vec}(\mathbf{RQR}') \tag{3.3.21}$$

where $\otimes$ is the Kronecker product, while the vec(.) operator indicates that the columns of the matrix are being stacked one upon the other; see Gardner *et al.* (1980). Note that, since the unconditional distribution of $\boldsymbol{\alpha}_1$ is the same as the unconditional distribution of $\boldsymbol{\alpha}_0$, the Kalman filter can be initialised as $\mathbf{a}_0 = \mathbf{0}$, $\mathbf{P}_0 = \mathbf{P}$ or $\mathbf{a}_{1|0} = \mathbf{0}$, $\mathbf{P}_{1|0} = \mathbf{P}$. The covariance matrices $\mathbf{P}_0$ and $\mathbf{P}_{1|0}$ are consistent with each other, as can be seen by comparing (3.3.18) with the prediction equation (3.2.2b).

When the transition equation is non-stationary, the unconditional distribution of the state vector is not defined. Unless genuine prior information is available, therefore, the initial distribution of $\boldsymbol{\alpha}_0$ must be specified in terms of a diffuse or non-informative prior. If we write

$$\mathbf{P}_0 = \kappa\mathbf{I} \tag{3.3.22a}$$

where κ is a positive scalar, the diffuse prior is obtained as $\kappa \rightarrow \infty$. This corresponds to $\mathbf{P}_0^{-1} = \mathbf{0}$. The distribution is an improper one since it does not integrate to one. Note that it is also possible to regard the diffuse prior as applying to $\boldsymbol{\alpha}_1$ in which case

$$\mathbf{P}_{1|0} = \kappa\mathbf{I} \tag{3.3.22b}$$

As was shown earlier, in Example 3.2.1, the Kalman filter cannot be run with κ set equal to infinity, but by setting it equal to a large but finite number a good approximation can be obtained. Furthermore it is possible to use κ as an analytic device which enables the $\mathbf{a}_t$ and $\mathbf{P}_t$ corresponding to $\kappa=\infty$ to be evaluated exactly once t is sufficiently large. In Example 3.2.1 this device was used to show that a diffuse prior implies the construction of a proper prior using the first observation.

For univariate models, the result in Example 3.2.1 generalises as follows. *The use of a diffuse prior is equivalent to the construction of a proper prior from the first* m *sets of observations provided that the model is observable.* This result emerges as a special case of a more general proposition given in sub-section 3.4.3. The proof sketched out below assumes that the transition matrix, $\mathbf{T}$, is non-singular for $m>1$, although the result also holds without this assumption.

The first $m-1$ measurement equations in (3.3.1) can be written out in terms of $\boldsymbol{\alpha}_m$ by repeated substitution for $\boldsymbol{\alpha}_t$ from the transition equation. This yields

$$y_t=\mathbf{z}'\mathbf{T}^{t-m}\boldsymbol{\alpha}_m+\left(-\mathbf{z}'\sum_{j=0}^{m-1-t}\mathbf{T}^{t-m+j}\mathbf{R}\boldsymbol{\eta}_{m-j}+\varepsilon_t\right),\quad t=1,\ldots,m-1 \tag{3.3.23}$$

These $m-1$ equations, together with the equation for y_m, can be written in matrix form as

$$\mathbf{y}=\mathbf{X}\boldsymbol{\alpha}_m+\mathbf{u} \tag{3.3.24}$$

where $\mathbf{y}=[y_1 \ldots y_m]'$, $\mathbf{u}$ is the $m\times 1$ vector of disturbances defined in brackets and $\mathbf{X}$ is the $m\times m$ matrix such that

$$\mathbf{X}'=[\mathbf{T}^{1-m},\ldots,\mathbf{T}^{-1},\mathbf{I}]'\mathbf{z} \tag{3.3.25}$$

The model is observable if

$$\text{Rank}[\mathbf{z},\mathbf{T}'\mathbf{z},\ldots,(\mathbf{T}')^{m-1}\mathbf{z}]=m \tag{3.3.26}$$

Pre-multiplying this matrix by the $m\times m$ matrix $(\mathbf{T}')^{-m}$ gives the transpose of the matrix $\mathbf{X}$ defined in (3.3.25). If $\mathbf{T}$ is non-singular, it follows that the rank of $\mathbf{X}$ is the same as the rank of the observability matrix in (3.3.26). Hence if the model is observable, $\mathbf{X}$ is of full rank. This being the case, (3.3.24) can be rearranged to give

$$\boldsymbol{\alpha}_m=\mathbf{X}^{-1}\mathbf{y}+\mathbf{X}^{-1}\mathbf{u}$$

If the disturbances in the model are normally distributed, then conditional on $y_1,\ldots,y_m$, the vector $\boldsymbol{\alpha}_m$ is normally distributed with mean

$$\mathbf{a}_m=\mathbf{X}^{-1}\mathbf{y} \tag{3.3.27a}$$

and covariance matrix

$$\mathbf{P}_m=\mathbf{X}^{-1}\mathbf{V}\mathbf{X}^{-1\prime} \tag{3.3.27b}$$

where $\mathbf{V}$ is the covariance matrix of the disturbance vector in (3.3.24). Without the normality assumption $\mathbf{a}_m$ is the MMSLE of $\boldsymbol{\alpha}_m$. Either way, $\mathbf{a}_m$ corresponds to the estimator obtained from the Kalman filter with a diffuse prior since the information set is the same and the MMSLE is unique.

It is not unusual for some of the elements in the state vector to be stationary and some non-stationary. If, without any loss in generality the non-stationary elements are taken to be the first d, where $d \leqslant m$, the transition matrix must be of the form

$$\mathbf{T}=\left[\begin{array}{c:c}\mathbf{T}_1 & \mathbf{T}_2 \\ \hdashline \mathbf{0} & \mathbf{T}_4\end{array}\right] \tag{3.3.28}$$

where $\mathbf{T}_1$ is $d \times d$, $\mathbf{T}_2$ is $d \times (m-d)$ and $\mathbf{T}_4$ is $(m-d)\times(m-d)$ with $|\lambda(\mathbf{T}_4)|<1$. If $\mathbf{P}_{1|0}$ is partitioned conformably with (3.3.28), the initial conditions are

$$\mathbf{P}_{1|0}=\begin{bmatrix}\kappa\mathbf{I} & \mathbf{0} \\ \mathbf{0} & \mathbf{P}\end{bmatrix} \tag{3.3.29}$$

If $\mathbf{z}$ is partitioned conformably with $\mathbf{T}$, i.e. $\mathbf{z}'=[\mathbf{z}_1' \quad \mathbf{z}_2']$, then by generalising the argument above, it can be shown that a proper prior can be constructed from the first d observations provided that $\mathbf{T}_1$ is non-singular and the first d elements of $\boldsymbol{\alpha}_t$, namely the non-stationary ones, are observable, that is

$$\text{Rank } [\mathbf{z}_1, \mathbf{T}_1'\mathbf{z}_1, \ldots, (\mathbf{T}_1')^{d-1}\mathbf{z}_1]=d \tag{3.3.30}$$

We now turn to consider various aspects of convergence given that the stationary part of a model is initialised in the Kalman filter by its unconditional mean and covariance matrix, while the non-stationary part is initialised with a diffuse prior. Following the discussion in the previous paragraph, assume that $\mathbf{T}_1$ in (3.3.28) is non-singular and that (3.3.30) holds. Convergence to the steady state is monotonic in the sense that the MSE matrix of $\mathbf{a}_{t|t-1}$ exceeds the MSE matrix of $\mathbf{a}_{t+1|t}$ by a p.s.d. matrix, that is

$$\mathbf{P}_{t|t-1} \geqslant \mathbf{P}_{t+1|t}, \quad t=d+1, d+2, \ldots \tag{3.3.31}$$

This follows because there is no information at time 0 and so the estimator at t is based on more information than the estimator at $t-1$, and its precision, $\mathbf{P}_{t|t-1}$, does not depend on the actual observations. By a similar argument

$$\mathbf{F}_t \geqslant \mathbf{F}_{t+1}, \quad t=d+1, d+2, \ldots \tag{3.3.32}$$

In fact, this is a consequence of (3.3.31) since

$$\mathbf{F}_t=\mathbf{Z}\mathbf{P}_{t|t-1}\mathbf{Z}'+\mathbf{H}$$

and $\mathbf{Z}$ is of rank N, while $\mathbf{H}$ is p.s.d. Given (3.3.32), it follows that

$$|\mathbf{F}_t| \geqslant |\mathbf{F}_{t+1}| \geqslant |\boldsymbol{\Sigma}| \geqslant 0 \tag{3.3.33}$$

where $\boldsymbol{\Sigma}$ is the steady state of $\mathbf{F}_t$, defined earlier in (3.3.17).

Example 3.3.9 For the random walk plus noise model, Figure 3.3.1 shows the

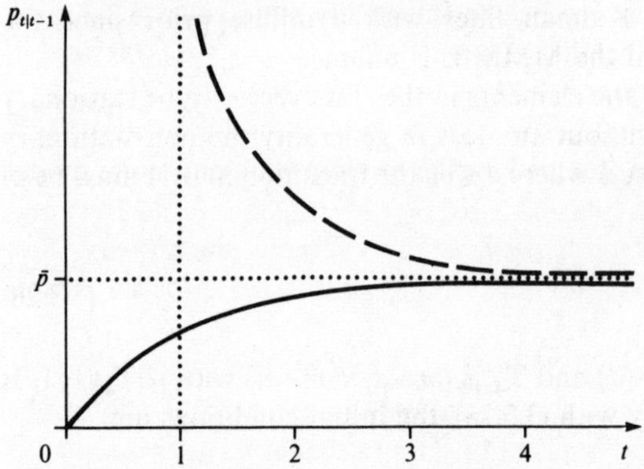

Fig. 3.3.1 Convergence of Kalman filter for a random walk plus noise model.

behaviour of $p_{t|t-1}$, computed from (3.2.9b) for $q=1$ as t increases. Note that $f_t = p_{t|t-1}+1$ so a plot of f_t would simply involve changing the scale on the vertical axis.

The broken line in Figure 3.3.1 shows $p_{t|t-1}$ for a diffuse prior, i.e. $p_{1|0}=p_0=\infty$. The solid line shows $p_{t|t-1}$ for $p_0=p_{0|-1}=0$. The relevance of a starting value of $p_0=0$ will become apparent in sub-section 3.4.4. The only point to note is that it leads to $p_{t+1|t}$ monotonically increasing with t; see Anderson and Moore (1979, pp. 79–80) for a general proof.

The knowledge that a state space model has a steady-state Kalman filter can be exploited in computational algorithms. The most time-consuming part of the filter is the updating of the error covariance matrix in the Riccati equation (3.2.4c). Thus once it is known that $\mathbf{P}_{t+1|t}$ has converged to $\bar{\mathbf{P}}$, (3.2.4c) becomes redundant, as the gain matrix in the state equation, (3.2.4b), is time-invariant. In practice it is necessary to monitor the progress of the filter in order to determine when $\mathbf{P}_{t+1|t}$ is sufficiently close to $\bar{\mathbf{P}}$ to deem it to have converged. This may be carried out indirectly by examining the sequence of prediction error covariance matrix determinants as in (3.3.33). An example of the application of such a device can be found in the ARMA model estimation algorithm of Gardner *et al.* (1980).

Example 3.3.10 In the MA(1) model considered in Example 3.3.8 it can be verified that the matrix

$$\bar{\mathbf{P}} = \begin{bmatrix} 1 & \theta \\ \theta & \theta^2 \end{bmatrix} \tag{3.3.34}$$

satisfies the algebraic Riccati equation (3.3.14). Hence $P_{1|0}=P \geqslant \bar{P}$. Furthermore it can be shown that

$$f_t = 1+\theta^{2t}/(1+\theta^2+\cdots+\theta^{2(t-1)}) \tag{3.3.35}$$

see Harvey (1981b, p. 112). Convergence to the steady state value of unity is exponentially fast for $|\theta| < 1$. When $|\theta| = 1$,

$$f_t = (t+1)/t, \quad t = 1, 2, \ldots \tag{3.3.36}$$

This is exactly the same solution obtained for the random walk plus noise model in Example 3.2.1 when $q=0$; in that case $p_{t+1|t} = 1/t$ in equation (3.2.11) and $f_{t+1} = p_{t+1|t} + 1$. Such a correspondence is to be expected since taking first differences in the random walk plus noise model with $q=0$ gives an MA(1) process with $\theta = -1$.

As a final point the fact that a steady-state error covariance matrix, $\bar{\mathbf{P}}$, may not be p.d. has some important practical implications. In particular if $\mathbf{P}_{t|t-1}$ is replaced by $\bar{\mathbf{P}}$, the Kalman filter will be partially, or even completely, closed to new information. Thus, in the random walk plus noise model with $q=0$, replacing $p_{t|t-1}$ by $\bar{p}=0$ leads to $k_t = 0$ in (3.2.8) and results in no updating whatsoever.

3.4 Maximum likelihood estimation and the prediction error decomposition

The classical theory of maximum likelihood is based on a situation in which the T sets of observations, $\mathbf{y}_1, \ldots, \mathbf{y}_T$, are independently and identically distributed. The joint density function is therefore given by

$$L(\mathbf{y};\boldsymbol{\psi}) = \prod_{t=1}^{T} p(\mathbf{y}_t) \tag{3.4.1}$$

where $p(\mathbf{y}_t)$ is the (joint) probability density function (p.d.f.) of the t-th set of observations. Once the observations have been made, $L(\mathbf{y};\boldsymbol{\psi})$ is reinterpreted as a likelihood function and the ML estimator is found by maximising this function with respect to $\boldsymbol{\psi}$.

The principal characteristic of a time series model is that the observations are not independent. Hence (3.4.1) is not applicable. Instead the definition of a conditional probability density function is used to write the joint density function as

$$L(\mathbf{y};\boldsymbol{\psi}) = \prod_{t=1}^{T} p(\mathbf{y}_t | \mathbf{Y}_{t-1}) \tag{3.4.2}$$

where $p(\mathbf{y}_t|\mathbf{Y}_{t-1})$ denotes the distribution of $\mathbf{y}_t$ conditional on the information set at time $t-1$, that is $\mathbf{Y}_{t-1} = \{\mathbf{y}_{t-1}, \mathbf{y}_{t-2}, \ldots, \mathbf{y}_1\}$.

If the disturbances and initial state vector in model (3.1.1) have proper multivariate normal distributions, the distribution of $\mathbf{y}_t$, conditional on $\mathbf{Y}_{t-1}$, is itself normal. Furthermore, the mean and covariance matrix of this conditional distribution are given directly by the Kalman filter. From the derivation of the Kalman filter in section 3.2, it will be recalled that conditional on $\mathbf{Y}_{t-1}$, $\boldsymbol{\alpha}_t$ is normally distributed with a mean of $\mathbf{a}_{t|t-1}$ and a covariance matrix of $\mathbf{P}_{t|t-1}$. If the measurement equation is written as

$$\mathbf{y}_t = \mathbf{Z}_t\mathbf{a}_{t|t-1} + \mathbf{Z}_t(\boldsymbol{\alpha}_t - \mathbf{a}_{t|t-1}) + \mathbf{d}_t + \boldsymbol{\varepsilon}_t \tag{3.4.3}$$

it can be seen immediately that the conditional distribution of $\mathbf{y}_t$ is normal with mean

$$\underset{t-1}{\mathrm{E}}(\mathbf{y}_t) = \tilde{\mathbf{y}}_{t|t-1} = \mathbf{Z}_t\mathbf{a}_{t|t-1} + \mathbf{d}_t \tag{3.4.4}$$

and a covariance matrix, $\mathbf{F}_t$, given by (3.2.3c). For a Gaussian model, therefore, the likelihood function of (3.4.2) can be written immediately as

$$\log L = -\frac{NT}{2}\log 2\pi - \frac{1}{2}\sum_{t=1}^{T}\log|\mathbf{F}_t| - \frac{1}{2}\sum_{t=1}^{T}\mathbf{v}_t'\mathbf{F}_t^{-1}\mathbf{v}_t \tag{3.4.5}$$

where

$$\mathbf{v}_t = \mathbf{y}_t - \tilde{\mathbf{y}}_{t|t-1}, \quad t = 1, \ldots, T \tag{3.4.6}$$

Since the conditional mean, $\tilde{\mathbf{y}}_{t|t-1}$, is also the MMSE of $\mathbf{y}_t$, the $N \times 1$ vector $\mathbf{v}_t$ can be interpreted as a vector of prediction errors. Hence (3.4.5) is sometimes known as the *prediction error decomposition* form of the likelihood. Note that although $\mathbf{v}_t$ and $\mathbf{F}_t$ can always be obtained from the Kalman filter, it is not always necessary, or indeed desirable, to compute them in this way. For example, in a univariate AR(1) model, the likelihood function can be written down directly in the form (3.4.5) since $v_1 = y_1$ and $v_t = y_t - \varphi y_{t-1}$, $t = 2, \ldots, T$, while $f_1 = \sigma^2/(1-\varphi^2)$ and $f_t = \sigma^2$ for $t = 2, \ldots, T$.

Once an algorithm for computing the likelihood function has been found, it must be maximised with respect to the unknown parameters $\boldsymbol{\psi}$. This will normally be carried out by some kind of numerical optimisation procedure; see, for example, Harvey (1981a, ch. 4). However, in maximising the likelihood function it is usually advantageous to exploit any linearities in order to reduce the dimension of the search. Techniques for concentrating out of the likelihood function parameters which enter linearly into $\mathbf{c}_t$ and $\mathbf{d}_t$ are described in sub-section 3.4.2.

A univariate model can usually be reparameterised so that $\boldsymbol{\psi} = [\boldsymbol{\psi}_*' \quad \sigma_*^2]'$ where $\boldsymbol{\psi}_*$ is a vector containing $n-1$ parameters and σ_*^2 is one of the disturbance variances in the model. The variances of the disturbances can then be expressed as in (3.2.6), that is $\mathrm{Var}(\varepsilon_t) = \sigma_*^2 h_t$ and $\mathrm{Var}(\boldsymbol{\eta}_t) = \sigma_*^2\mathbf{Q}_t$, where h_t and $\mathbf{Q}_t$ depend on $\boldsymbol{\psi}_*$ but not on σ_*^2. As a rule, h_t or one of the diagonal elements in $\mathbf{Q}_t$ will be set equal to unity. The reparameterisation of the model enables σ_*^2 to be concentrated out of the likelihood function. The prediction error decomposition yields

$$\log L = -\frac{T}{2}\log 2\pi - \frac{T}{2}\log\sigma_*^2 - \frac{1}{2}\sum_{t=1}^{T}\log f_t - \frac{1}{2\sigma_*^2}\sum_{t=1}^{T}v_t^2/f_t \tag{3.4.7}$$

and since v_t and f_t do not depend on σ_*^2, differentiating (3.4.7) with respect to σ_*^2 gives

$$\tilde{\sigma}_*^2(\psi_*) = \frac{1}{T}\sum_{t=1}^{T}\frac{v_t^2}{f_t} \tag{3.4.8}$$

The notation $\tilde{\sigma}_*^2(\psi_*)$ indicates that (3.4.8) is the ML estimator of σ_*^2 conditional on a given value of ψ_*. Substituting in (3.4.7) gives the concentrated log-likelihood function

$$\log L_c(\psi_*) = -\frac{T}{2}(\log 2\pi + 1) - \frac{1}{2}\sum_{t=1}^{T}\log f_t - \frac{T}{2}\log \tilde{\sigma}_*^2(\psi_*) \tag{3.4.9a}$$

which must be maximised with respect to the elements of ψ_*. Alternatively

$$\log L_c^*(\psi_*) = \sum_{t=1}^{T}\log f_t + T\log \tilde{\sigma}_*^2(\psi_*) \tag{3.4.9b}$$

may be minimised.

If prior information is available on all the elements of $\boldsymbol{\alpha}_0$, then $\boldsymbol{\alpha}_0$ has a proper prior distribution with known mean, $\mathbf{a}_0$, and bounded covariance matrix, $\mathbf{P}_0$. The Kalman filter then yields the *exact* likelihood function of the observations, y, via the prediction error decomposition. Unfortunately, genuine prior information is rarely available. This has led some statisticians to conclude that Kalman filter techniques are only appropriate if (a) one is able to adopt a Bayesian approach in which a proper prior distribution for $\boldsymbol{\alpha}_0$ is always specified, or (b) the sample size is so large that the specification of initial conditions is unimportant. Such a conclusion is unwarranted. From the discussion in sub-section 3.3.4, we know that for a univariate series the Kalman filter can always be initialised with the mean and covariance matrix of the unconditional distribution of $\boldsymbol{\alpha}_t$ when $\boldsymbol{\alpha}_t$ is stationary. This is valid even if the matrices $\mathbf{z}_t$, $\mathbf{H}_t$ and $\mathbf{d}_t$ in the measurement equation are not time-invariant. For non-stationary state vectors, the results of sub-section 3.3.4 indicated that, in a time-invariant model, observability of the *d* non-stationary components according to the criterion in (3.3.30) is sufficient for the construction of a proper distribution for $\boldsymbol{\alpha}_d$. When this is the case, the joint density function of $y_{d+1}, \ldots, y_T$, conditional on $y_1, \ldots, y_d$ is given by the prediction error decomposition (3.4.7), with the summations running from $t = d + 1$ instead of $t = 1$. If $y_1, \ldots, y_d$ are regarded as being fixed, the joint density function is an unconditional one. The way in which this result generalises to multivariate, time-varying systems is discussed in sub-section 3.4.3. The knowledge that a certain number of observations are needed to form a proper prior is helpful conceptually in defining a likelihood function and practically in computing that likelihood function. From the computational point of view, we know not to include the first *d* innovations and their associated variances in the prediction error decomposition likelihood function for a univariate model when the Kalman filter is started off at $t=0$ with a diffuse prior.

Some care is needed if the Kalman filter is initialised with a diffuse prior using the 'large κ' approximation of (3.3.22), since numerical problems can arise due to rounding errors. One way of overcoming this problem is to compute starting values explicitly from the initial observations as in (3.3.27). However in more complex multivariate models it is not always clear how to compute the appropriate starting values. A more general algorithm has recently been provided by Ansley and Kohn (1985). They propose a transformation which eliminates the dependence on the initial conditions. A modified form of the Kalman filter is then constructed and this enables the likelihood function to be constructed via the prediction error decomposition. More recently, de Jong (1989) has proposed an algorithm which is based on an extension of the Kalman filter and does not require any transformations of the data. This algorithm is easier to implement and is described in sub-section 3.4.3.

An alternative way of handling the initialisation problem in non-stationary models is to treat $\boldsymbol{\alpha}_0$ as a vector of fixed elements. Its distribution is then degenerate as $\mathbf{P}_0=\mathbf{0}$. However, since $\boldsymbol{\alpha}_0$ is unknown, its elements must be estimated by treating them as extra parameters in the model. For such a procedure to be viable, it must be possible to concentrate $\boldsymbol{\alpha}_0$ out of the likelihood function. Two methods of achieving this are described in sub-section 3.4.4.

3.4.1 Asymptotic properties

Let $\tilde{\boldsymbol{\psi}}$ denote the maximum likelihood (ML) estimator of the $n\times 1$ vector $\boldsymbol{\psi}$, obtained by maximising (3.4.5) and suppose that the information matrix, $\mathbf{I}(\boldsymbol{\psi})$, converges to a p.d. matrix, $\mathbf{IA}(\boldsymbol{\psi})$, when divided by T, that is:

$$\mathbf{IA}(\boldsymbol{\psi})=\lim T^{-1}\mathbf{I}(\boldsymbol{\psi}) \tag{3.4.10}$$

Subject to certain regularity conditions $\sqrt{T}(\tilde{\boldsymbol{\psi}}-\boldsymbol{\psi})$ has a limiting multivariate normal distribution with mean vector zero and covariance matrix $\mathbf{IA}^{-1}(\boldsymbol{\psi})$. The same result is implied by the statement that $\tilde{\boldsymbol{\psi}}$ is *asymptotically normal* with mean $\boldsymbol{\psi}$ and covariance matrix

$$\text{Avar}\,(\tilde{\boldsymbol{\psi}})=T^{-1}\mathbf{IA}^{-1}(\boldsymbol{\psi}) \tag{3.4.11}$$

The above result is subject to the following conditions:

(i) $\boldsymbol{\psi}$ is an interior point of the parameter space;

(ii) derivatives of $\log L$ up to order three with respect to $\boldsymbol{\psi}$ exist and are continuous in the neighbourhood of the true parameter value;

(iii) $\boldsymbol{\psi}$ is identifiable.

The difficulty lies in pinning down the remaining conditions, given the generality of the state space model. Ljung and Caines (1979) consider a fairly general model but they impose a condition on the memory of the process which effectively rules out the type of non-stationarity implied by stochastic trend components. This kind of non-stationarity is allowed in the univariate time series model examined by Pagan (1980), but there the transition equation is time-invariant. The conditions imposed by Pagan are that the model should be observable and controllable and that, if the transition matrix contains unknown parameters, its roots should be less than one in absolute value. Since the measurement equation can be time-varying, conditions must also be placed on $\mathbf{z}_t$; specifically the elements of $\mathbf{z}_t$ must be bounded from above and non-stochastic. If both the measurement and transition equations are time-invariant, Pagan's observability and controllability conditions can be weakened to detectability and stabilisability. As we know from Result 3.3.2 these conditions are necessary and sufficient for the Kalman filter to converge to a steady state exponentially fast. The condition that the roots of $\mathbf{T}$ should all lie inside the unit circle when $\mathbf{T}$ contains unknown parameters can also be relaxed. Details are given in section 4.5.

When the Kalman filter converges to a steady state exponentially fast, the properties of the ML estimator do not depend on the way in which the filter is started off. Furthermore, for a univariate model in which the likelihood can be expressed in the form (3.4.7), an estimator with the same asymptotic distribution as the ML estimator may be obtained by minimising the sum of squares function

$$S(\psi)=\sum v_t^2 \tag{3.4.12}$$

In contrast to the likelihood function, the criterion function in (3.4.12) depends solely on the prediction errors. To see that minimising this criterion function is asymptotically equivalent to maximising the likelihood function, first note that in large samples the expressions in (3.4.8) and (3.4.9b) remain approximately the same if the f_t's are replaced by their steady state value, $\bar{f}$. On substituting (3.4.8) into (3.4.9b), the $\bar{f}$'s cancel, leaving (3.4.12) as the function to be minimised.

Criterion functions depending only on the prediction errors may be set up for multivariate models. Examples include the minimands

$$S(\psi)=\sum_t \mathbf{v}_t'\mathbf{W}\mathbf{v}_t \tag{3.4.13}$$

where $\mathbf{W}$ is a fixed $N\times N$ weighting matrix, and

$$S(\psi)=\left|\sum_t \mathbf{v}_t\mathbf{v}_t'\right| \tag{3.4.14}$$

For certain models, minimising the second of these functions is asymptotically equivalent to maximising the likelihood of (3.4.5). This is the case if the unknown parameters in the $\mathbf{\Sigma}$'s, the steady state $\mathbf{F}_t$'s of (3.3.17), are independent of the unknown parameters determining the $\tilde{\mathbf{y}}_{t|t-1}$'s, as in a multivariate ARIMA model. Minimising (3.4.14) is also asymptotically equivalent to maximising the likelihood function in a homogeneous structural time series model; see (8.3.20).

The results in Ljung and Caines (1979) apply to a wider class of estimators than those obtained by maximising the likelihood function of a correctly specified model. They consider an estimator of $\boldsymbol{\psi}$, $\tilde{\boldsymbol{\psi}}_l$, obtained by minimising a general function of the prediction errors

$$S_l(\boldsymbol{\psi}) = \sum_{t=1}^{T} l(\mathbf{v}_t) \tag{3.4.15}$$

and so (3.4.13) and (3.4.14) are special cases. Minimising a criterion function of this form is known in the engineering literature as *prediction error 'identification'*. The asymptotic properties of $\tilde{\boldsymbol{\psi}}_l$ can be obtained even though the model may not be correctly specified. The results are similar to those given by White (1982) for the quasi-ML estimator obtained when a likelihood function for a model which is not necessarily the correct one is maximised.

3.4.2 Generalised least squares

Consider the univariate state space model

$$y_t = \mathbf{z}_t'\boldsymbol{\alpha}_t + \mathbf{x}_t'\boldsymbol{\delta} + \varepsilon_t \tag{3.4.16a}$$

$$\boldsymbol{\alpha}_t = \mathbf{T}_t\boldsymbol{\alpha}_{t-1} + \mathbf{R}_t\boldsymbol{\eta}_t \tag{3.4.16b}$$

where $\mathbf{x}_t$ is a non-stochastic $k \times 1$ vector and $\boldsymbol{\delta}$ is a $k \times 1$ vector of unknown parameters. The remaining parameters are included in the vector $\boldsymbol{\psi}$. It will be assumed initially that $\boldsymbol{\alpha}_0$ has a mean of zero and a bounded covariance matrix, $\mathbf{P}_0$. Both of these assumptions will be relaxed in due course. The transition equation could be extended so as to contain a vector $\mathbf{c}_t$ such that

$$\mathbf{c}_t = \mathbf{w}_t'\boldsymbol{\gamma}$$

where $\mathbf{w}_t$ is a matrix of observable variables and $\boldsymbol{\gamma}$ is a vector of unknown parameters. However, this model can always be written in the form (3.4.16) by making use of the result in (3.1.17). In dealing with the estimation of $\boldsymbol{\delta}$ in (3.4.16), therefore, the estimation of $\boldsymbol{\gamma}$ is dealt with implicitly.

The state space model may be rewritten in regression form as

$$y_t = \mathbf{x}_t'\boldsymbol{\delta} + u_t, \quad t = 1, \ldots, T \tag{3.4.17a}$$

$$u_t = \mathbf{z}_t'\boldsymbol{\alpha}_t + \varepsilon_t \tag{3.4.17b}$$

In view of the assumptions on $\boldsymbol{\alpha}_0$, the expected value of u_t is zero for all t but it is, in general, serially correlated and heteroscedastic. Writing the model in matrix terms yields

$$\mathbf{y} = \mathbf{X}\boldsymbol{\delta} + \mathbf{u}, \qquad \mathrm{E}(\mathbf{u}) = \mathbf{0}, \qquad \mathrm{Var}(\mathbf{u}) = \mathbf{V} \tag{3.4.18}$$

where $\mathbf{y}$ is $T \times 1$, $\mathbf{X}$ is $T \times k$ and $\mathbf{V}$ is a $T \times T$ covariance matrix which depends on $\boldsymbol{\psi}$ and which is assumed to be p.d. The generalised least squares (GLS) estimator of $\boldsymbol{\delta}$ is given by

$$\tilde{\boldsymbol{\delta}} = (\mathbf{X}'\mathbf{V}^{-1}\mathbf{X})^{-1}\mathbf{X}'\mathbf{V}^{-1}\mathbf{y} \tag{3.4.19}$$

Since $\mathbf{V}$ is p.d. there exists a p.d. lower triangular matrix, $\mathbf{L}$, with ones on the leading diagonal, and a p.d. diagonal matrix, $\mathbf{F}$, such that

$$\mathbf{V}^{-1} = \mathbf{L}'\mathbf{F}^{-1}\mathbf{L} \tag{3.4.20}$$

Pre-multiplying (3.4.18) through by $\mathbf{L}$ and defining $\mathbf{y}^*$, $\mathbf{X}^*$ and $\mathbf{u}^*$ as $\mathbf{Ly}$, $\mathbf{LX}$ and $\mathbf{Lu}$ respectively gives the heteroscedastic regression model

$$\mathbf{y}^* = \mathbf{X}^*\boldsymbol{\delta} + \mathbf{u}^*, \quad \text{Var}(\mathbf{u}^*) = \mathbf{F} \tag{3.4.21a}$$

or

$$y_t^* = \mathbf{x}_t^{*\prime}\boldsymbol{\delta} + u_t^*, \quad t = 1, \ldots, T, \quad \text{Var}(u_t^*) = f_t \tag{3.4.21b}$$

where $f_t > 0$ is the t-th diagonal element of $\mathbf{F}$. The GLS estimator of $\boldsymbol{\delta}$ is then obtained by WLS regression:

$$\tilde{\boldsymbol{\delta}} = \left[\sum_{t=1}^{T} \mathbf{x}_t^*\mathbf{x}_t^{*\prime}/f_t\right]^{-1} \sum_{t=1}^{T} \mathbf{x}_t^* y_t^*/f_t \tag{3.4.22}$$

In order to compute $\tilde{\boldsymbol{\delta}}$ there is no need to evaluate $\mathbf{V}$. The Kalman filter effectively performs the Cholesky decomposition (3.4.20). Suppose for a moment, that $\boldsymbol{\delta}$ were known. In this case the 'observations', $y_t - \mathbf{x}_t'\boldsymbol{\delta}$ could be regarded as being generated by a state space model in which the measurement equation

$$y_t - \mathbf{x}_t'\boldsymbol{\delta} = \mathbf{z}_t'\boldsymbol{\alpha}_t + \varepsilon_t, \quad t = 1, \ldots, T \tag{3.4.23}$$

was coupled with the transition equation (3.4.16b). Applying the Kalman filter to these 'observations' would then give a set of innovations, v_t. Conditional on $\boldsymbol{\psi}$ these innovations would be uncorrelated with mean zero and variance f_t. But this is exactly the property possessed by the disturbances in the transformed equation, (3.4.21b), and since the Kalman filter is a linear operation and the Cholesky decomposition is unique, it follows that, for a given $\boldsymbol{\psi}$,

$$v_t = y_t^* - \mathbf{x}_t^{*\prime}\boldsymbol{\delta}, \quad t = 1, \ldots, T \tag{3.4.24}$$

In matrix terms, therefore, the effect of the Kalman filter is to produce the innovation vector, $\mathbf{v} = [v_1 \quad \ldots \quad v_T]'$ by pre-multiplying the vector $\mathbf{y} - \mathbf{X}\boldsymbol{\delta}$ by the $T \times T$ matrix $\mathbf{L}$ defined in (3.4.20). However, since

$$\mathbf{L}(\mathbf{y} - \mathbf{X}\boldsymbol{\delta}) = \mathbf{Ly} - \mathbf{LX}\boldsymbol{\delta} = \mathbf{y}^* - \mathbf{X}^*\boldsymbol{\delta}$$

the *same* Kalman filter can be applied separately to the observations, y_t, and each of the explanatory variables in the vector, $\mathbf{x}_t$. The GLS estimator, $\tilde{\boldsymbol{\delta}}(\boldsymbol{\psi})$, is then computed by regressing the 'innovations' from y_t, that is, the y_t^*'s, on the 'innovations' from $\mathbf{x}_t$, the $\mathbf{x}_t^*$'s. The fact that these 'innovations' do not possess the usual properties of innovations is irrelevant.

An alternative way of calculating $\tilde{\boldsymbol{\delta}}$ is by letting $\boldsymbol{\delta}$ become part of the state vector. The state space model is then

$$y_t = [\mathbf{z}_t' \quad \mathbf{x}_t']\boldsymbol{\alpha}_t^\dagger + \varepsilon_t, \quad t=1,\ldots,T \tag{3.4.25a}$$

$$\boldsymbol{\alpha}_t^\dagger = \begin{bmatrix} \boldsymbol{\alpha}_t \\ \boldsymbol{\delta}_t \end{bmatrix} = \begin{bmatrix} \mathbf{T}_t & \mathbf{0} \\ \mathbf{0} & \mathbf{I} \end{bmatrix} \begin{bmatrix} \boldsymbol{\alpha}_{t-1} \\ \boldsymbol{\delta}_{t-1} \end{bmatrix} + \begin{bmatrix} \boldsymbol{\eta}_t \\ \mathbf{0} \end{bmatrix} \tag{3.4.25b}$$

and $\boldsymbol{\delta}_t$ is initialised with a diffuse prior. The prediction errors from applying the Kalman filter to (3.4.25) may be denoted by $v_t^\dagger, t=k+1,\ldots,T$; they have variance $f_t^\dagger$ and so may be standardised by dividing by $\sqrt{f_t^\dagger}$. By generalising an argument in Harvey and Phillips (1979), it can be shown that

$$\sum_{t=1}^{T} v_t^2/f_t = \sum_{t=k+1}^{T} v_t^{\dagger 2}/f_t^\dagger \tag{3.4.26}$$

where v_t is the GLS residual

$$v_t = y_t^* - \mathbf{x}_t^{*\prime}\tilde{\boldsymbol{\delta}} \tag{3.4.27}$$

Now consider the ML estimation of the full set of parameters $(\boldsymbol{\psi}, \boldsymbol{\delta})$, when the disturbances and the initial state in (3.4.16) are normally distributed. Since, in (3.4.18), $\mathbf{y}$ has a multivariate normal distribution with mean $\mathbf{X}\boldsymbol{\delta}$ and covariance matrix $\mathbf{V}$, the likelihood function for $(\boldsymbol{\psi}, \boldsymbol{\delta})$ is

$$\log L(\boldsymbol{\psi}, \boldsymbol{\delta}) = -\frac{T}{2}\log 2\pi - \tfrac{1}{2}\log|\mathbf{V}| - \tfrac{1}{2}(\mathbf{y}-\mathbf{X}\boldsymbol{\delta})'\mathbf{V}^{-1}(\mathbf{y}-\mathbf{X}\boldsymbol{\delta}) \tag{3.4.28}$$

However, substituting V from (3.4.20) and noting that

$$\begin{aligned} \log|\mathbf{V}| &= -\log|\mathbf{V}^{-1}| = -\log|\mathbf{L}\mathbf{F}^{-1}\mathbf{L}'| \\ &= \log|\mathbf{L}||\mathbf{F}||\mathbf{L}'| = \log|\mathbf{F}| = \sum_{t=1}^{T}\log f_t \end{aligned} \tag{3.4.29}$$

enables the likelihood function to be written as

$$\log L(\boldsymbol{\psi}, \boldsymbol{\delta}) = -\frac{T}{2}\log 2\pi - \frac{1}{2}\sum_{t=1}^{T}\log f_t - \frac{1}{2}\sum_{t=1}^{T}\frac{(y_t^* - \mathbf{x}_t^{*\prime}\boldsymbol{\delta})^2}{f_t} \tag{3.4.30}$$

Maximising the likelihood function with respect to $\boldsymbol{\delta}$, for a given value of $\boldsymbol{\psi}$, yields the GLS estimator, $\boldsymbol{\delta}(\boldsymbol{\psi})$, given earlier in (3.4.22). The concentrated likelihood function is therefore

$$\log L(\boldsymbol{\psi}) = -\frac{T}{2}\log 2\pi - \frac{1}{2}\sum_{t=1}^{T}\log f_t - \frac{1}{2}\sum_{t=1}^{T} v_t^2/f_t \tag{3.4.31}$$

where v_t is as defined in (3.4.27). This concentrated likelihood function must be maximised with respect to $\boldsymbol{\psi}$. If σ_*^2 is concentrated out of the likelihood function as in (3.4.8), a function analogous to (3.4.9) is minimised with respect to $\boldsymbol{\psi}_*$.

The likelihood function for the state space model given in (3.4.25) is of the form (3.4.7) with the summations running from $t=k+1$ to T. As noted in (3.4.26) above, the sum of squares term in this likelihood function will be the same as the sum of squares term in (3.4.31) for a given value of $\boldsymbol{\psi}$. However, the determinantal terms make the two likelihood functions different. This is because in one case, $\boldsymbol{\delta}$ is treated as fixed, while in the other it is regarded as a vector of random variables.

The assumption that $\boldsymbol{\alpha}_0$ has a bounded variance may be relaxed. If some or all of the elements in $\boldsymbol{\alpha}_0$ have a diffuse prior distribution the GLS estimator of $\boldsymbol{\delta}$ is formed from the transformed observations y_t^* and x_t^* for $t=d+1, \ldots, T$. The summations in the likelihood function are correspondingly amended. The case where $\mathbf{a}_0$ is not zero, but $\mathbf{P}_0$ is bounded, is handled in the manner described in sub-section 3.4.3.

The results on GLS estimation generalise to a multivariate model in which the measurement equation is

$$\mathbf{y}_t = \mathbf{Z}_t \boldsymbol{\alpha}_t + \mathbf{X}_t \boldsymbol{\delta} + \boldsymbol{\varepsilon}_t \tag{3.4.32}$$

where $\mathbf{X}_t$ is an $N \times K$ matrix of observed values and $\boldsymbol{\delta}$ is a $K \times 1$ vector of unknown parameters. Applying the Kalman filter to $\mathbf{y}_t$ and each of the columns of $\mathbf{X}_t$ yields an $N \times 1$ vector of 'innovations', $\mathbf{y}_t^*$, and an $N \times K$ matrix of 'innovations', $\mathbf{X}_t^*$, respectively. The GLS estimator of $\boldsymbol{\delta}$ is then

$$\tilde{\boldsymbol{\delta}} = \left[\sum_{t=1}^{T} \mathbf{X}_t^{*\prime} \mathbf{F}_t^{-1} \mathbf{X}_t^* \right]^{-1} \sum_{t=1}^{T} \mathbf{X}_t^{*\prime} \mathbf{F}_t^{-1} \mathbf{y}_t^* \tag{3.4.33}$$

where $\mathbf{F}_t$ is the $N \times N$ covariance matrix, (3.2.3c), produced by the Kalman filter. As in the univariate model the fact that the same Kalman filter is being used for the $\mathbf{y}_t$'s and $\mathbf{X}_t$'s means that for a given value of $\boldsymbol{\psi}$, the recursion for $\mathbf{P}_{t|t-1}$ is run only once rather than $K+1$ times. Under the normality assumption, the residuals from (3.4.33)

$$\mathbf{v}_t = \mathbf{y}_t^* - \mathbf{X}_t^* \tilde{\boldsymbol{\delta}}, \quad t=1, \ldots, T \tag{3.4.34}$$

are used to construct the concentrated likelihood function

$$\log L_c(\boldsymbol{\psi}) = -\frac{TN}{2} \log 2\pi - \frac{1}{2} \sum_{t=1}^{T} \log |\mathbf{F}_t| - \frac{1}{2} \sum_{t=1}^{T} \mathbf{v}_t' \mathbf{F}_t^{-1} \mathbf{v}_t \tag{3.4.35}$$

3.4.3 General algorithm for a diffuse prior

The algorithm devised by de Jong (1988, 1989) provides a means of calculating the likelihood function without resorting to the 'large κ' approximation of (3.3.22). The algorithm applies to the general state space model (3.1.1a) and (3.1.3a), but without any loss in generality $\mathbf{c}_t$ and $\mathbf{d}_t$ may be omitted in what follows. The dimension of the observation vector may vary over time as would be the case if some observations were missing; see sub-section 3.4.7. It is assumed that $\text{Var}(\mathbf{y}_t|\mathbf{Y}_{t-1})$ is non-singular; in other words, no linear combination of the observations can be predicted perfectly from the past. However, this is a fairly innocuous requirement.

It is supposed that the initial state vector can be expressed as

$$\boldsymbol{\alpha}_1 = \mathbf{C}_1\boldsymbol{\gamma}_1 + \mathbf{C}_2\boldsymbol{\gamma}_2 \tag{3.4.36}$$

where $\boldsymbol{\gamma}_1$ is a $D \times 1$ vector with a diffuse prior, that is $\text{Var}(\boldsymbol{\gamma}_1) = \infty\mathbf{I}$ or $[\text{Var}(\boldsymbol{\gamma}_1)]^{-1} = \mathbf{0}$, while $\boldsymbol{\gamma}_2$ has a proper prior, that is

$$\text{E}(\boldsymbol{\gamma}_2) = \mathbf{m} \quad \text{and} \quad \text{Var}(\boldsymbol{\gamma}_2) = \mathbf{V} \tag{3.4.37}$$

The matrices $\mathbf{C}_1$ and $\mathbf{C}_2$ are fixed, but may depend on the hyperparameters, $\boldsymbol{\psi}$, as may $\mathbf{m}$ and $\mathbf{V}$. The matrix $\mathbf{C}_1$ is assumed to be of full column rank. This set-up is very general, but it includes the important special case in which $\boldsymbol{\gamma}_1$ contains the non-stationary elements which actually appear in the state vector and $\boldsymbol{\gamma}_2$ is the stationary component in the state vector. This being the case, $\mathbf{C}_1 = [\mathbf{I}_D \quad \mathbf{0}]'$ and $\mathbf{C}_2 = [\mathbf{0} \quad \mathbf{I}_{m-D}]'$.

The use of a 'large κ' approximation for γ_1 is avoided by extending the Kalman filter algorithm as follows. The order of these extensions is D, but no additional matrix inversions are required. Define

$$\mathbf{Y}_t^\dagger = [\mathbf{y}_t \quad \mathbf{0}] \tag{3.4.38}$$

where $\mathbf{0}$ is a null matrix with D columns. The standard Kalman filter recursions for the MSE matrix, (3.2.2b) and (3.2.3b), are initiated with

$$\mathbf{P}_{1|0}^0 = \mathbf{C}_2\mathbf{V}\mathbf{C}_2' \tag{3.4.39}$$

This follows from (3.4.36) by setting $\text{Var}(\boldsymbol{\gamma}_1) = \mathbf{0}$; hence the zero superscript on $\mathbf{P}_{1|0}^0$. The recursion for the state vector is augmented so as to become a recursion for the $m \times (D+1)$ matrices $\mathbf{A}_{t|t-1}^\dagger$ and $\mathbf{A}_t^\dagger$. Thus

$$\mathbf{A}_t^\dagger = \mathbf{A}_{t|t-1}^\dagger + \mathbf{P}_{t|t-1}^0\mathbf{Z}_t'(\mathbf{F}_t^0)^{-1}\mathbf{N}_t^\dagger, \quad t = 1, \ldots, T \tag{3.4.40}$$

where

$$\mathbf{N}_t^\dagger = \mathbf{Y}_t - \mathbf{Z}_t\mathbf{A}_{t|t-1}^\dagger \tag{3.4.41}$$

and

$$\mathbf{A}_{t|t-1}^\dagger = \mathbf{T}_t\mathbf{A}_{t-1}^\dagger, \quad t = 2, \ldots, T \tag{3.4.42}$$

The starting value is $\mathbf{A}_{1|0}^\dagger = [\mathbf{C}_2\mathbf{m} \quad \mathbf{C}_1]$. The first column of $\mathbf{A}_t^\dagger$ is the standard Kalman filter recursion for the estimated state vector, $\mathbf{a}_t^0$, obtained by setting $\text{E}(\boldsymbol{\gamma}_1) = \mathbf{0}$ and $\text{Var}(\boldsymbol{\gamma}_1) = \mathbf{0}$. Similarly the first column of $\mathbf{N}_t^\dagger$ is the corresponding vector of innovations, $\mathbf{v}_t^0$. The other columns of $\mathbf{A}_t^\dagger$ are obtained by applying the same Kalman filter to the zero observations which make up the last D columns of $\mathbf{Y}_t^\dagger$.

The final recursion is for a $(D+1)\times(D+1)$ matrix $\mathbf{S}_t^\dagger$:

$$\mathbf{S}_t^\dagger=\mathbf{S}_{t-1}^\dagger+\mathbf{N}_t^{\dagger\prime}(\mathbf{F}_t^0)^{-1}\mathbf{N}_t^\dagger,\quad t=1,\ldots,T \tag{3.4.43}$$

with $\mathbf{S}_0^\dagger=\mathbf{0}$.

The output from the above recursions is used to construct the required statistics from the diffuse prior model as follows. First let $\mathbf{N}_t^\dagger$, $\mathbf{A}_t^\dagger$ and $\mathbf{S}_t^\dagger$ be partitioned conformably as

$$\mathbf{N}_t^\dagger=[\mathbf{v}_t^0\quad \mathbf{N}_t],\quad \mathbf{A}_t^\dagger=[\mathbf{a}_t^0\quad \mathbf{A}_t]\quad\text{and}\quad \mathbf{S}_t^\dagger=\begin{bmatrix} S_t^0 & \mathbf{s}_t' \\ \mathbf{s}_t & \mathbf{S}_t\end{bmatrix} \tag{3.4.44}$$

where $\mathbf{N}_t$ and $\mathbf{A}_t$ both have D columns, S_t^0 is a scalar, $\mathbf{s}_t$ is a $D\times 1$ vector and $\mathbf{S}_t$ is $D\times D$. Then, as shown by de Jong (1989), the estimator of the state vector for the diffuse prior starting values is

$$\mathbf{a}_t=\mathbf{a}_t^0-\mathbf{A}_t\mathbf{S}_t^-\mathbf{s}_t=\mathbf{A}_t^\dagger[1\quad -\mathbf{s}_t'\mathbf{S}_t^-]' \tag{3.4.45a}$$

with MSE matrix

$$\mathbf{P}_t=\mathbf{P}_t^0+\mathbf{A}_t\mathbf{S}_t^-\mathbf{A}_t' \tag{3.4.45b}$$

where $\mathbf{S}_t^-$ is the generalised inverse of $\mathbf{S}_t$.

The likelihood function, ignoring the constant term, is given by

$$\log L=-\frac{1}{2}\sum_{t=1}^{T}\log|\mathbf{F}_t^0|-\tfrac{1}{2}S_T^0-\tfrac{1}{2}\log|\mathbf{S}_T|+\tfrac{1}{2}\mathbf{s}_T'\mathbf{S}_T^{-1}\mathbf{s}_T \tag{3.4.46}$$

The first two terms are the likelihood for the state space model in which $\text{Var}(\boldsymbol{\gamma}_1)=\mathbf{0}$. The second two terms are a correction factor which converts this likelihood into the likelihood for $\boldsymbol{\gamma}_1$ having a diffuse prior.

The expression in (3.4.46) assumes that the augmented Kalman filter recursions are carried on until the end of the sample. However, once $\mathbf{S}_t$ becomes non-singular, the extended filter can be collapsed to the usual filter. If $\mathbf{S}_t$ is non-singular at some point, $t=\tau$, then the usual Kalman filter can be employed starting from values obtained using (3.4.45), namely

$$\mathbf{a}_\tau=\mathbf{a}_\tau^0-\mathbf{A}_\tau\mathbf{S}_\tau^{-1}\mathbf{s}_\tau \tag{3.4.47a}$$

and

$$\mathbf{P}_\tau=\mathbf{P}_\tau^0+\mathbf{A}_\tau\mathbf{S}_\tau^{-1}\mathbf{A}_\tau' \tag{3.4.47b}$$

It can be shown that $\mathbf{S}_\tau$ is non-singular if

$$\text{Rank}[\mathbf{C}_1'\mathbf{Z}_1',\mathbf{C}_1'\mathbf{T}_2'\mathbf{Z}_2',\mathbf{C}_1'\mathbf{T}_3'\mathbf{T}_2'\mathbf{Z}_3',\ldots,\mathbf{C}_1'\mathbf{T}_\tau'\ldots\mathbf{T}_2'\mathbf{Z}_\tau]=D \tag{3.4.48}$$

This can be regarded as a generalisation of the observability condition to time-varying models; compare a related criterion in Jazwinski (1970, p. 231).

As regards the likelihood function, if $\log L_\tau$ denotes (3.4.46) computed for the first τ observations, the likelihood for all T observations is

$$\log L = \log L_\tau - \frac{1}{2}\sum_{t=\tau+1}^{T} \log|\mathbf{F}_t| - \frac{1}{2}\sum_{t=\tau+1}^{T} \mathbf{v}_t'\mathbf{F}_t^{-1}\mathbf{v}_t \tag{3.4.49}$$

In a univariate model with d non-stationary elements in the state vector, $D=d$ and it is normally the case that $\mathbf{S}_t$ is non-singular at $t=d$ and $\log L_d=0$. For a time-invariant univariate model the observability condition in (3.3.30) is equivalent to the one given above in (3.4.48).

Random walk plus noise Consider the random walk plus noise model set up as in Example 3.2.1 with $\sigma_\varepsilon^2=1$. The augmented observations are given by the 1×2 row vector $\mathbf{Y}_t^\dagger=[y_t \quad 0]$, while $\mathbf{C}_1=1$, $\mathbf{C}_2=0$ and $\mathbf{A}_{1|0}^\dagger=[0 \quad 1]$. As regards the MSE matrix, or scalar as it is in this case, we have $p_{1|0}^0=0$ and so

$$p_1^0=0$$

and

$$f_1^0=1$$

For the augmented state

$$\mathbf{A}_{1|0}^\dagger=[0 \quad 1]$$

and so

$$\mathbf{N}_1^\dagger=[y_1 \quad 0]-[0 \quad 1]=[y_1 \quad -1]$$

while

$$\mathbf{A}_1^\dagger=[0 \quad 1]$$

Finally $\mathbf{S}_0^\dagger=0$ and so

$$\mathbf{S}_1^\dagger=\begin{bmatrix} y_1^2 & -y_1 \\ -y_1 & 1 \end{bmatrix}$$

Now $\mathbf{S}_1=1$ and is clearly non-singular. Thus from (3.4.47)

$$\mathbf{a}_1=\mathbf{m}_1=0-(-y_1)=y_1 \tag{3.4.50a}$$

and

$$p_1=1 \tag{3.4.50b}$$

These values are exactly the same as the values obtained in Example 3.2.1. As regards the likelihood function, the argument in the introductory part of this section is that it cannot be defined for a single observation in this case, since one observation is needed to compute a proper prior. Evaluating (3.4.46) for $T=1$

yields

$\log L_1 = -\frac{1}{2}[(\log 1) + y_1^{*2} + (\log 1) - y_1^{*2}] = 0$

which is obviously consistent with the likelihood function not being defined. Running the usual Kalman filter starting with m_1 and p_1 of (3.4.50) enables the likelihood to be evaluated in terms of the prediction errors for $t=2,\ldots,T$; compare (3.4.49).

Starting the Kalman filter with a null MSE matrix for the initial state of γ_1 avoids the rounding errors which can arise when the 'large κ' approximation is used. Further numerical stability can be introduced into the algorithm by using a square root filter for the recursion for $\mathbf{P}_t^0$; see Anderson and Moore (1979, pp. 147–50). The square root filter is more accurate than the standard filter and it ensures that $\mathbf{P}_t^0$ and $\mathbf{P}_{t|t-1}^0$ are always p.s.d.

3.4.4 Fixed elements in the initial state vector

Up to now it has been assumed that the (unknown) elements of $\boldsymbol{\alpha}_0$ are all stochastic. However, it is sometimes more appropriate to assume that they are fixed. They can then be treated as extra parameters which need to be estimated as part of the maximum likelihood procedure. This could be done by treating the elements of $\boldsymbol{\alpha}_0$ in the same way as the parameters in $\boldsymbol{\psi}$, and maximising the likelihood function non-linearly with respect to the set $[\boldsymbol{\alpha}_0 \quad \boldsymbol{\psi}]$. However, treating $\boldsymbol{\alpha}_0$ in this way complicates the numerical optimisation considerably. A more practical solution is to recognise that, conditional on $\boldsymbol{\psi}$, the ML estimator of $\boldsymbol{\alpha}_0$ is a linear function of the observations. It can therefore be concentrated out of the likelihood function, which then only needs to be maximised non-linearly with respect to the elements of $\boldsymbol{\psi}$. There are two ways in which this may be done. One is to use the GLS procedure described in sub-section 3.4.2. The other is to use an algorithm due to Rosenberg (1973).

For simplicity the discussion will be based on the state space model

$$\mathbf{y}_t = \mathbf{Z}_t\boldsymbol{\alpha}_t + \boldsymbol{\varepsilon}_t, \quad t=1,\ldots,T \tag{3.4.51a}$$

$$\boldsymbol{\alpha}_t = \mathbf{T}_t\boldsymbol{\alpha}_{t-1} + \mathbf{R}_t\boldsymbol{\eta}_t, \quad t=1,\ldots,T \tag{3.4.51b}$$

with $\boldsymbol{\varepsilon}_t \sim \text{NID}(\mathbf{0}, \mathbf{H}_t)$, $\boldsymbol{\eta}_t \sim \text{NID}(\mathbf{0}, \mathbf{Q}_t)$ and $\boldsymbol{\eta}_t$ and $\boldsymbol{\varepsilon}_t$ independent of each other. The assumption that all the elements of $\boldsymbol{\alpha}_0$ are fixed means that $\mathbf{a} = \boldsymbol{\alpha}_0$ and $\mathbf{P}_0 = \mathbf{0}$. Thus there is no starting-value problem with the initial covariance matrix, $\mathbf{P}_0$. The difficulty arises with $\boldsymbol{\alpha}_0$, which is unknown.

Rosenberg's algorithm Rosenberg sets up a Kalman filter in which the starting values are $\boldsymbol{\alpha}_0^* = \mathbf{0}$ and $\mathbf{P}_0^* = \mathbf{0}$ and a set of prediction error vectors, $\mathbf{v}_1^*$, $\mathbf{v}_2^*, \ldots,$ $\mathbf{v}_T^*$ are produced. For a given value of $\boldsymbol{\alpha}_0$, the Kalman filter initialised with $\mathbf{a}_0 = \boldsymbol{\alpha}_0$ and $\mathbf{P}_0 = \mathbf{0}$ would yield $\mathbf{v}_1, \mathbf{v}_2, \ldots, \mathbf{v}_T$. It is this second set of prediction errors which is needed to form the likelihood function. Bearing in mind that the $\mathbf{P}_{t|t-1}$ matrices in the two filters are the same, the idea behind Rosenberg's algorithm is to obtain $\mathbf{v}_1, \ldots, \mathbf{v}_T$ from the output from the first filter.

Since $\mathbf{a}_0^* = \mathbf{0}$, the initial state vector can be written as

$$\boldsymbol{\alpha}_0 = \mathbf{a}_0^* + \boldsymbol{\alpha}_0 \tag{3.4.52}$$

and so

$$\mathbf{a}_{1|0} = \mathbf{T}_1 \mathbf{a}_0 = \mathbf{T}_1 \mathbf{a}_0^* + \mathbf{T}_1 \boldsymbol{\alpha}_0 \tag{3.4.53}$$

The state vector recursion for $\mathbf{a}_{t+1|t}$, (3.2.4a), requires an initial value of $\boldsymbol{\alpha}_0$. However, it can be split up into two parts and written as

$$\mathbf{a}_{t+1|t} = \mathbf{a}_{t+1|t}^* + \mathbf{G}_t \boldsymbol{\alpha}_0, \quad t = 1, \ldots, T-1 \tag{3.4.54}$$

where $\mathbf{a}_{t+1|t}^*$ is output from the first filter and $\mathbf{G}_t$ is computed recursively from

$$\mathbf{G}_t = (\mathbf{T}_{t+1} - \mathbf{K}_t \mathbf{Z}_t)\mathbf{G}_{t-1}, \quad t = 1, \ldots, T-1 \tag{3.4.55}$$

with $\mathbf{G}_0 = \mathbf{T}_1$.

The prediction error vector can similarly be split into two parts:

$$\begin{aligned} \mathbf{v}_t &= \mathbf{y}_t - \mathbf{Z}_t \mathbf{a}_{t|t-1} = \mathbf{y}_t - \mathbf{Z}_t \mathbf{a}_{t|t-1}^* - \mathbf{Z}_t \mathbf{G}_{t-1} \boldsymbol{\alpha}_0 \\ &= \mathbf{v}_t^* - \mathbf{Z}_t \mathbf{G}_{t-1} \boldsymbol{\alpha}_0, \quad t = 1, \ldots, T \end{aligned} \tag{3.4.56}$$

Substituting (3.4.56) into the likelihood in (3.4.5) and differentiating with respect to $\boldsymbol{\alpha}_0$ gives

$$\tilde{\boldsymbol{\alpha}}_0 = \left[\sum_{t=1}^{T} \mathbf{G}_{t-1}' \mathbf{Z}_t' \mathbf{F}_t^{-1} \mathbf{Z}_t \mathbf{G}_{t-1}\right]^{-1} \sum_{t=1}^{T} \mathbf{G}_{t-1}' \mathbf{Z}_t' \mathbf{F}_t^{-1} \mathbf{v}_t^* \tag{3.4.57}$$

This expression is the ML estimator of $\boldsymbol{\alpha}_0$, conditional on any other parameters in the model. It can therefore be used to concentrate $\boldsymbol{\alpha}_0$ out of the likelihood function. This gives

$$\begin{aligned} \log L &= -\frac{1}{2}\sum_{t=1}^{T} \log|\mathbf{F}_t| - \frac{1}{2}\sum_{t=1}^{T} [\mathbf{v}_t^* - \mathbf{Z}_t \mathbf{G}_{t-1} \tilde{\boldsymbol{\alpha}}_0]' \mathbf{F}_t^{-1} [\mathbf{v}_t^* - \mathbf{Z}_t \mathbf{G}_{t-1} \tilde{\boldsymbol{\alpha}}_0] \\ &= -\frac{1}{2}\sum_{t=1}^{T} \log|\mathbf{F}_t| - \frac{1}{2}\sum_{t=1}^{T} \mathbf{v}_t^{*\prime} \mathbf{F}_t^{-1} \mathbf{v}_t^* + \tfrac{1}{2}\tilde{\boldsymbol{\alpha}}_0' \sum_{t=1}^{T} \mathbf{G}_{t-1}' \mathbf{Z}_t' \mathbf{F}_t^{-1} \mathbf{v}_t^* \end{aligned} \tag{3.4.58}$$

In order to estimate $\boldsymbol{\alpha}_0$ in (3.4.57) it is necessary for the matrix in brackets to be of full rank. A sufficient condition for this to hold in a time-invariant model is that the observability condition is satisfied.

Example 3.4.1 Suppose that μ_0 is the random walk plus noise model is taken to be fixed. The Riccati equation follows the path shown as the lower curve in Figure 3.3.1, with $p_{t+1|t}$ gradually converging to the steady state, $\bar{p}$. The recursion in

(3.4.55) is simply

$$g_t = (1 + p_{t|t+1})^{-1} g_{t-1}, \quad t = 1, \ldots, T-1 \tag{3.4.59}$$

with $g_0 = 1$, while $\tilde{\boldsymbol{\alpha}}_0$ is computed in (3.4.57) by a weighted least squares regression of v_t^* on g_t in which the weights are $f_t = 1 + p_{t|t-1}$.

GLS transformation An alternative approach to estimating a model with a fixed initial state vector is to formulate the problem in terms of a GLS regression and to follow the procedure described in sub-section 3.4.2. This approach was originally suggested by Wecker and Ansley (1983).

By substituting repeatedly from the transition equation, the state vector at time t can be written as the sum of two parts, namely,

$$\boldsymbol{\alpha}_t = \left[\prod_{j=1}^{t} \mathbf{T}_j\right] \boldsymbol{\alpha}_0 + \boldsymbol{\alpha}_t^*, \quad t = 1, \ldots, T \tag{3.4.60}$$

where $\boldsymbol{\alpha}_t^*$ satisfies a transition equation of the form (3.4.51b), that is

$$\boldsymbol{\alpha}_t^* = \mathbf{T}_t \boldsymbol{\alpha}_{t-1}^* + \mathbf{R}_t \boldsymbol{\eta}_t, \quad t = 1, \ldots, T \tag{3.4.61}$$

but has a known starting value of $\boldsymbol{\alpha}_0^* = \mathbf{0}$.

Substituting for $\boldsymbol{\alpha}_t$ in the measurement equation allows it to be written as

$$\mathbf{y}_t = \mathbf{X}_t \boldsymbol{\alpha}_0 + \mathbf{Z}_t \boldsymbol{\alpha}_t^* + \boldsymbol{\varepsilon}_t \tag{3.4.62a}$$

where

$$\mathbf{X}_t = \mathbf{Z}_t \prod_{j=1}^{t} \mathbf{T}_j \tag{3.4.62b}$$

The model therefore consists of (3.4.62) together with (3.4.61), and the initial conditions that $\mathbf{a}_0^* = \mathbf{0}$ and $\mathbf{P}_0^* = \mathbf{0}$. Thus $\boldsymbol{\alpha}_0$ plays the role of $\boldsymbol{\delta}$ in (3.4.32) and it may be estimated accordingly by the right-hand side of (3.4.33). The likelihood function is as in (3.4.35).

The GLS algorithm and Rosenberg's algorithm will yield identical numerical results. Thus, for a given value of $\boldsymbol{\psi}$, the estimators of $\boldsymbol{\alpha}_0$ are the same, and Rosenberg's concentrated likelihood function, (3.4.58), is the same as the concentrated likelihood function in (3.4.35).

As regards the contrast between the diffuse prior and fixed initial state vector likelihood functions, a result similar to (3.4.26) holds, and the only difference in the likelihood function is in the determinantal term. This is shown in Harvey and Peters (1984, appendix) for univariate models following the line of argument in Harvey and Phillips (1979). A much more general proof is given by de Jong (1988). He presents a general algorithm which applies to the complete range of starting value assumptions and which includes Rosenberg's algorithm as a special case. In de Jong (1989) he shows that the diffuse prior likelihood of

(3.4.46) differs from the likelihood obtained with fixed initial conditions by the presence of the term $(-\frac{1}{2}\log|\mathbf{S}_T|)$.

3.4.5 *Information matrix*

The information matrix plays an important role in ML estimation. Not only does it provide an estimate of the covariance matrix of ML estimates but it may also feature in algorithms used to compute these estimates. The prediction error decomposition likelihood function, (3.4.5), has the important property that it yields an information matrix which depends on first derivatives only. The next sub-section shows how these derivatives may be obtained either numerically or analytically when the model is in state space form.

Expressions for the score vector and the information matrix for (3.4.5) are obtained as follows. First write the log-likelihood function in the form

$$\log L = \sum_{t=1}^{T} l_t$$

where l_t is the logarithm of $p(\mathbf{y}_t|\mathbf{Y}_{t-1})$, i.e.

$$l_t = -\tfrac{1}{2}\log 2\pi - \tfrac{1}{2}\log|\mathbf{F}_t| - \tfrac{1}{2}\mathbf{v}_t'\mathbf{F}_t^{-1}\mathbf{v}_t$$

For any symmetric matrix $\mathbf{A}$, the derivatives of the determinant and the inverse with respect to a variable, $\mathbf{x}$, are

$$\frac{\partial|\mathbf{A}|}{\partial\mathbf{x}} = |\mathbf{A}|\,\mathrm{tr}\left[\mathbf{A}^{-1}\frac{\partial\mathbf{A}}{\partial\mathbf{x}}\right] \tag{3.4.63a}$$

and

$$\frac{\partial\mathbf{A}^{-1}}{\partial\mathbf{x}} = -\mathbf{A}^{-1}\frac{\partial\mathbf{A}}{\partial\mathbf{x}}\mathbf{A}^{-1} \tag{3.4.63b}$$

Differentiating l_t with respect to the i-th element of $\boldsymbol{\psi}$, therefore gives

$$-\frac{1}{2}\mathrm{tr}\left[\mathbf{F}_t^{-1}\frac{\partial\mathbf{F}_t}{\partial\psi_i}\right] - \frac{1}{2}\left[\frac{\partial\mathbf{v}_t'}{\partial\psi_i}\mathbf{F}_t^{-1}\mathbf{v}_t - \mathbf{v}_t'\mathbf{F}_t^{-1}\frac{\partial\mathbf{F}_t}{\partial\psi_i}\mathbf{F}_t^{-1}\mathbf{v}_t + \mathbf{v}_t'\mathbf{F}_t^{-1}\frac{\partial\mathbf{v}_t}{\partial\psi_i}\right] \tag{3.4.64}$$

Taking the trace of the last term allows this expression to be re-written as

$$\frac{\partial l_t}{\partial\psi_i} = -\frac{1}{2}\mathrm{tr}\left[\left[\mathbf{F}_t^{-1}\frac{\partial\mathbf{F}_t}{\partial\psi_i}\right][\mathbf{I} - \mathbf{F}_t^{-1}\mathbf{v}_t\mathbf{v}_t']\right] - \left(\frac{\partial\mathbf{v}_t}{\partial\psi_i}\right)'\mathbf{F}_t^{-1}\mathbf{v}_t \tag{3.4.65}$$

Differentiating (3.4.65) with respect to the j-th element of $\boldsymbol{\psi}$ gives

$$\frac{\partial^2 l_t}{\partial\psi_i \partial\psi_j} = -\frac{1}{2}\mathrm{tr}\left[\partial\left[\mathbf{F}_t^{-1}\frac{\partial \mathbf{F}_t}{\partial\psi_i}\right] \Big/ \partial\psi_j \right]\left[\mathbf{I}-\mathbf{F}_t^{-1}\mathbf{v}_t\mathbf{v}_t'\right]$$

$$-\frac{1}{2}\mathrm{tr}\left[\mathbf{F}_t^{-1}\frac{\partial \mathbf{F}_t}{\partial\psi_i}\mathbf{F}_t^{-1}\frac{\partial \mathbf{F}_t}{\partial\psi_j}\mathbf{F}_t^{-1}\mathbf{v}_t\mathbf{v}_t'\right]$$

$$+\frac{1}{2}\mathrm{tr}\left[\mathbf{F}_t^{-1}\frac{\partial \mathbf{F}_t}{\partial\psi_i}\mathbf{F}_t^{-1}\left[\frac{\partial \mathbf{v}_t}{\partial\psi_j}\mathbf{v}_t' + \mathbf{v}_t\frac{\partial \mathbf{v}_t'}{\partial\psi_j}\right]\right]$$

$$-\frac{\partial^2 \mathbf{v}_t'}{\partial\psi_i\partial\psi_j}\mathbf{F}_t^{-1}\mathbf{v}_t - \frac{\partial \mathbf{v}_t'}{\partial\psi_i}\frac{\partial \mathbf{F}_t^{-1}}{\partial\psi_j}\mathbf{v}_t - \frac{\partial \mathbf{v}_t'}{\partial\psi_i}\mathbf{F}_t^{-1}\frac{\partial \mathbf{v}_t}{\partial\psi_j} \tag{3.4.66}$$

The ij-th element of the information matrix is by definition

$$-\mathrm{E}\left[\frac{\partial^2 \log L}{\partial\psi_i\partial\psi_j}\right] = -\mathrm{E}\left[\sum_{t=1}^{T}\frac{\partial^2 l_t}{\partial\psi_i\partial\psi_j}\right]$$

but its evaluation in the present context is simplified considerably by noticing that

$$\mathrm{E}(l_t) = \mathrm{E}\left[\underset{t-1}{\mathrm{E}}(l_t)\right] \tag{3.4.67}$$

Now consider taking expectations of the terms in (3.4.66) conditional on the information at time $t-1$. The only random variables are the elements of the innovation vector, $\mathbf{v}_t$, and their first and second derivatives. However, the derivatives are fixed with respect to the expectation operator at time $t-1$. This follows because

$$\mathbf{v}_t = \mathbf{y}_t - \underset{t-1}{\mathrm{E}}(\mathbf{y}_t)$$

and so

$$\frac{\partial \mathbf{v}_t}{\partial\psi_i} = -\frac{\partial}{\partial\psi_i}\underset{t-1}{\mathrm{E}}(\mathbf{y}_t)$$

The conditional expectation of $\mathbf{v}_t$ is zero and therefore

$$\underset{t-1}{\mathrm{E}}\left[\frac{\partial \mathbf{v}_t'}{\partial\psi_i}\mathbf{v}_t\right] = \frac{\partial \mathbf{v}_t'}{\partial\psi_i}\underset{t-1}{\mathrm{E}}(\mathbf{v}_t) = \mathbf{0} \tag{3.4.68}$$

A similar result holds for terms involving $\mathbf{v}_t$ and its second derivatives. The net effect on the conditional expectation of (3.4.66) is that the third, fourth and fifth terms disappear. In addition the first term disappears because the conditional expectation of $\mathbf{v}_t\mathbf{v}_t'$ is $\mathbf{F}_t$ and for the same reason the second term simplifies. This leaves the following expression for the ij-th element of the information matrix

$$I_{ij}(\psi)=\frac{1}{2}\sum_t\left[\operatorname{tr}\left[\mathbf{F}_t^{-1}\frac{\partial\mathbf{F}_t}{\partial\psi_i}\mathbf{F}_t^{-1}\frac{\partial\mathbf{F}_t}{\partial\psi_j}\right]\right]$$

$$+\mathrm{E}\left[\sum_t\left(\frac{\partial\mathbf{v}_t}{\partial\psi_i}\right)'\mathbf{F}_t^{-1}\frac{\partial\mathbf{v}_t}{\partial\psi_j}\right],\quad i,j=1,\ldots,n \qquad (3.4.69)$$

Dropping the expectation operator from the second term gives an expression which is asymptotically equivalent to (3.4.69) and which may, in some cases be easier to evaluate.

3.4.6 *Derivatives of the likelihood function*

As was shown in the previous sub-section the i-th element in the score vector for (3.4.5) is

$$\frac{\partial\log L}{\partial\psi_i}=-\frac{1}{2}\sum_t\left\{\operatorname{tr}\left[\left[\mathbf{F}_t^{-1}\frac{\partial\mathbf{F}_t}{\partial\psi_i}\right](\mathbf{I}-\mathbf{F}_t^{-1}\mathbf{v}_t\mathbf{v}_t')\right]-\frac{\partial\mathbf{v}_t'}{\partial\psi_i}\mathbf{F}_t^{-1}\mathbf{v}_t\right\},\quad i=1,\ldots,n \qquad (3.4.70)$$

Evaluating the score vector therefore requires the evaluation of the $N\times N$ matrices of derivatives, $\partial\mathbf{F}_t/\partial\psi_i$, and the $N\times 1$ vectors of derivatives $\partial\mathbf{v}_t/\partial\psi_i$ for $t=1,\ldots,T$ and $i=1,\ldots,n$. These same derivatives may then be used to compute the information matrix via (3.4.69).

The derivatives of $\mathbf{F}_t$ and $\mathbf{v}_t$ for the state space form (3.1.1) and (3.1.3) may be evaluated numerically or analytically. Computing them numerically requires n additional passes of the Kalman filter. For $i=1,\ldots,n$ a small amount, δ_i, is added to ψ_i, and the Kalman filter is run with this new value but with all the other elements in $\boldsymbol{\psi}$ remaining at their original values. This yields a new set of innovations and their covariance matrices, $\mathbf{v}_t^{(i)}$ and $\mathbf{F}_t^{(i)}$. The expressions $\delta_i^{-1}[\mathbf{v}_t^{(i)}-\mathbf{v}_t]$ and $\delta_i^{-1}[\mathbf{F}_t^{(i)}-\mathbf{F}_t]$ are then numerical approximations to the required derivatives. Of course, numerically evaluating the derivatives is only useful if they are to be used in computing the information matrix. If all that is required is the score vector, the numerical derivatives of the log-likelihood function can be evaluated directly.

The derivatives of $\mathbf{F}_t$ and $\mathbf{v}_t$ may be evaluated analytically by programming n sets of recursions to run in parallel with the Kalman filter. These recursions all have a common form, which is set out below. The i-th set of recursions yields the quantities needed to calculate the derivatives of $\mathbf{F}_t$ and $\mathbf{v}_t$ with respect to the i-th element of $\boldsymbol{\psi}$. Since

$$\mathbf{v}_t=\mathbf{y}_t-\mathbf{Z}_t\mathbf{a}_{t|t-1}-\mathbf{d}_t,\quad t=1,\ldots,T \qquad (3.4.71a)$$

the vector of derivatives with respect to ψ_i is

$$\frac{\partial \mathbf{v}_t}{\partial \psi_t} = -\mathbf{Z}_t \frac{\partial \mathbf{a}_{t|t-1}}{\partial \psi_i} - \frac{\partial \mathbf{Z}_t}{\partial \psi_i} \mathbf{a}_{t|t-1} - \frac{\partial \mathbf{d}_t}{\partial \psi_i} \tag{3.4.71b}$$

and so a recursion is needed to provide $\partial \mathbf{a}_{t|t-1}/\partial \psi_i$. Similarly

$$\frac{\partial \mathbf{F}_t}{\partial \psi_i} = \frac{\partial \mathbf{Z}_t}{\partial \psi_i} \mathbf{P}_{t|t-1} \mathbf{Z}_t' + \mathbf{Z}_t \frac{\partial \mathbf{P}_{t|t-1}}{\partial \psi_i} \mathbf{Z}_t' + \mathbf{Z}_t \mathbf{P}_{t|t-1} \frac{\partial \mathbf{Z}_t'}{\partial \psi_i} + \frac{\partial \mathbf{H}_t}{\partial \psi_i} \tag{3.4.72}$$

and so a recursion is also needed for the derivatives of $\mathbf{P}_{t|t-1}$.

The recursions for the derivatives of $\mathbf{a}_{t|t-1}$ and $\mathbf{P}_{t|t-1}$ are obtained by differentiating the Kalman filter prediction and updating equations (3.2.2) and (3.2.3). With $\mathbf{R}_t = \mathbf{I}$, differentiating the prediction equations yields

$$\frac{\partial \mathbf{a}_{t|t-1}}{\partial \psi_i} = \frac{\partial \mathbf{T}_t}{\partial \psi_i} \mathbf{a}_{t-1} + \mathbf{T}_t \frac{\partial \mathbf{a}_{t-1}}{\partial \psi_i} + \frac{\partial \mathbf{c}_t}{\partial \psi_i} \tag{3.4.73a}$$

and

$$\frac{\partial \mathbf{P}_{t|t-1}}{\partial \psi_i} = \frac{\partial \mathbf{T}_t}{\partial \psi_i} \mathbf{P}_{t-1} \mathbf{T}_t' + \mathbf{T}_t \frac{\partial \mathbf{P}_{t-1}}{\partial \psi_i} \mathbf{T}_t' + \mathbf{T}_t \mathbf{P}_{t-1} \frac{\partial \mathbf{T}_t'}{\partial \psi_i} + \frac{\partial \mathbf{Q}_t}{\partial \psi_i} \tag{3.4.73b}$$

while for the updating equations

$$\begin{aligned} \frac{\partial \mathbf{a}_t}{\partial \psi_i} = {} & \frac{\partial \mathbf{a}_{t|t-1}}{\partial \psi_i} + \frac{\partial \mathbf{P}_{t|t-1}}{\partial \psi_i} \mathbf{Z}_t' \mathbf{F}_t^{-1} \mathbf{v}_t + \mathbf{P}_{t|t-1} \frac{\partial \mathbf{Z}_t'}{\partial \psi_i} \mathbf{F}_t^{-1} \mathbf{v}_t \\ & - \mathbf{P}_{t|t-1} \mathbf{Z}_t' \mathbf{F}_t^{-1} \frac{\partial \mathbf{F}_t}{\partial \psi_i} \mathbf{F}_t^{-1} \mathbf{v}_t + \mathbf{P}_{t|t-1} \mathbf{Z}_t' \mathbf{F}_t^{-1} \frac{\partial \mathbf{v}_t}{\partial \psi_i} \end{aligned} \tag{3.4.74a}$$

and

$$\begin{aligned} \frac{\partial \mathbf{P}_t}{\partial \psi_i} = {} & \frac{\partial \mathbf{P}_{t|t-1}}{\partial \psi_i} - \frac{\partial \mathbf{P}_{t|t-1}}{\partial \psi_i} \mathbf{Z}_t' \mathbf{F}_t^{-1} \mathbf{Z}_t \mathbf{P}_{t|t-1} - \mathbf{P}_{t|t-1} \frac{\partial \mathbf{Z}_t'}{\partial \psi_i} \mathbf{F}_t^{-1} \mathbf{Z}_t \mathbf{P}_{t|t-1} \\ & + \mathbf{P}_{t|t-1} \mathbf{Z}_t' \mathbf{F}_t^{-1} \frac{\partial \mathbf{F}_t}{\partial \psi_i} \mathbf{F}_t^{-1} \mathbf{Z}_t \mathbf{P}_{t|t-1} - \mathbf{P}_{t|t-1} \mathbf{Z}_t' \mathbf{F}_t^{-1} \frac{\partial \mathbf{Z}_t}{\partial \psi_i} \mathbf{P}_{t|t-1} \\ & - \mathbf{P}_{t|t-1} \mathbf{Z}_t' \mathbf{F}_t^{-1} \mathbf{Z}_t \frac{\partial \mathbf{P}_{t|t-1}}{\partial \psi_i} \end{aligned} \tag{3.4.74b}$$

for $t = 1, \ldots, T$. Equations (3.4.73) and (3.4.74) together with (3.4.71) and (3.4.72) provide the required derivatives. The starting values depend on the starting values for the Kalman filter proper. If $\mathbf{a}_0$ and $\mathbf{P}_0$ are independent of $\boldsymbol{\psi}$, as in the case of a diffuse prior, then $\partial \mathbf{a}_0/\partial \psi_i = \mathbf{0}$ and $\partial \mathbf{P}_0/\partial \psi_i = \mathbf{0}$.

3.4.7 *Missing observations*

The discussion so far has assumed that N observations are available in each time period. This may not always be the case. Some of the observations may be missing or they may be subject to contemporaneous aggregation. In order to set up this kind of problem, let $\mathbf{y}_t^\dagger$ denote the full $N \times 1$ vector which is produced as an output from the system, and let $\mathbf{y}_t$ denote the $N_t \times 1$ vector of observations. These are related by the identity

$$\mathbf{y}_t = \mathbf{W}_t \mathbf{y}_t^\dagger, \quad t = 1, \ldots, T \tag{3.4.75}$$

where $\mathbf{W}_t$ is an $N_t \times N$ matrix of fixed weights. Thus if $N = 3$ and only $y_{1t}^\dagger$ is observed, $\mathbf{W}_t = [1 \quad 0 \quad 0]$; if all three variables are *contemporaneously aggregated* then $\mathbf{W}_t = [1 \quad 1 \quad 1]$ giving

$$y_t = y_{1t}^\dagger + y_{2t}^\dagger + y_{3t}^\dagger$$

The full model therefore consists of (3.4.75) together with the transition equation (3.1.3a) and an equation which takes the form of a measurement equation but is set up in terms of $\mathbf{y}_t^\dagger$, that is

$$\mathbf{y}_t^\dagger = \mathbf{Z}_t \boldsymbol{\alpha}_t + \mathbf{d}_t + \boldsymbol{\varepsilon}_t \tag{3.4.76}$$

However, if $N_t \geqslant 1$, (3.4.75) and (3.4.76) can be combined to give a measurement equation written in terms of $\mathbf{y}_t$. The only difference is that the dimension of $\mathbf{y}_t$ is N_t, the subscript indicating that the number of elements in $\mathbf{y}_t$ may vary with t. This does not affect the Kalman filter once a proper prior for the state vector has been obtained. Nor does it affect the form of the prediction error decomposition except insofar as the dimensions of $\mathbf{v}_t$ and $\mathbf{F}_t$ are now subject to change over time.

Now suppose that no observations are available for certain values of t. For these values (3.4.75) is no longer defined. In order to cope with this situation we will assume that observations are available at the points t_τ, $\tau = 1, \ldots, T$ where the t_τ's are integers such that $0 < t_1 < t_2 < \cdots < t_T$. Equation (3.4.75) is then replaced by

$$\mathbf{y}_\tau = \mathbf{W}_\tau \mathbf{y}_{t_\tau}^\dagger, \quad \tau = 1, \ldots, T \tag{3.4.77}$$

Thus the system generates t_T values of $\mathbf{y}_t^\dagger$ at unit intervals, but observations on this vector are only made in T time periods. The fact that these time periods may not be evenly spaced does not affect the validity of the prediction error decomposition. Furthermore the information matrix and first derivatives can be computed as before. The joint density function of the observations may be written as

$$L(\mathbf{y}; \boldsymbol{\psi}) = \prod_{\tau=1}^{T} p(\mathbf{y}_\tau | \mathbf{Y}_{\tau-1}) \tag{3.4.78}$$

the only difference between this expression and (3.4.2) being the use of the subscript τ rather than t.

Example 3.4.2 Consider an AR(1) process

$$y_t^\dagger = \varphi y_{t-1}^\dagger + \xi_t, \quad |\varphi| < 1 \tag{3.4.79}$$

which is observed at times $t=1,\ldots,m-1, m+1,\ldots,T+1$. There is a missing value at time $t=m$ and so the T observations are defined by

$$y_\tau = y^\dagger_{t_\tau}, \quad \tau=1,\ldots,T \tag{3.4.80a}$$

where

$$t_\tau = \begin{cases} \tau, & \tau=1,\ldots,m-1 \\ \tau+1, & \tau=m,\ldots,T \end{cases} \tag{3.4.80b}$$

Since $y^\dagger_{m+1}$ can be written as

$$y^\dagger_{m+1} = \varphi(\varphi y_{m-1}+\xi_m)+\xi_{m+1} = \varphi^2 y_{m-1}+\xi_{m+1}+\varphi\xi_m \tag{3.4.81}$$

and since $y^\dagger_{m+1}=y_m$ by definition, it follows that

$$E(y_m|\mathbf{Y}_{m-1})=\varphi^2 y_{m-1}$$

and

$$\text{Var}(y_m|\mathbf{Y}_{m-1})=\sigma^2(1+\varphi^2) \tag{3.4.82}$$

Thus if $\xi_t \sim \text{NID}(0,\sigma^2)$, the log-likelihood function of the observations is:

$$\log L = -\frac{T}{2}\log 2\pi + \tfrac{1}{2}\log(1-\varphi^2) - \tfrac{1}{2}\log(1+\varphi^2) - \frac{T}{2}\log\sigma^2 - \frac{1}{2\sigma^2}y_1^2(1-\varphi)^2$$

$$-\frac{1}{2\sigma^2}\frac{(y_m-\varphi^2 y_{m-1})^2}{1+\varphi^2} - \frac{1}{2\sigma^2}\sum_{\tau\neq m}(y_\tau-\varphi y_{\tau-1})^2 \tag{3.4.83}$$

The third and sixth terms are the ones which arise because of the missing value. The second and fifth would not have appeared if y_1 had been assumed to be fixed.

In more general cases where the model is in state space form, and the disturbances are normal, the prediction errors associated with the observations $\mathbf{y}_\tau$, $\tau=1,\ldots,T$ can be obtained simply by skipping the Kalman filter updating equations for the SSF of $\mathbf{y}^\dagger_t$ at the points where there are no observations; see (3.5.7). Thus, if there is no observation at $t=m$,

$$\mathbf{a}_m = \mathbf{a}_{m|m-1} \quad \text{and} \quad \mathbf{P}_m = \mathbf{P}_{m|m-1} \tag{3.4.84}$$

An alternative way of proceeding is to construct a state space model on the time scale $\tau=1,\ldots,T$ and to apply the Kalman filter to this model directly; see section 6.3. Both approaches can be used to compute derivatives and the information matrix. The attraction of working with the SSF for $\mathbf{y}^\dagger_t$ is that the missing observations can be estimated by a smoothing algorithm as described in section 3.6. The question of estimating structural models with missing observations is discussed in sub-section 6.4.1, as is the problem of dealing with temporal aggregation. Algorithms for handling ARIMA models can be found in Harvey and Pierse (1984) and Kohn and Ansley (1986).

A different way of handling a missing observation is to give it a value of zero, and to introduce a dummy variable into the model. The dummy variable takes a value of unity at the point where the observation is missing and zero elsewhere. The likelihood function is then constructed as though no observations were missing but it now needs to be maximised with respect to the coefficient of the dummy variable as well as the other parameters in the model. When several observations are missing, a dummy variable has to be introduced for each one. This may start to become cumbersome, even though the likelihood function is usually linear in the dummy variable coefficients. Furthermore, as shown in Sargan and Drettakis (1974, pp. 40–41), a correction has to be applied to the determinantal term in the likelihood function and this is not straightforward to compute. The effect of this correction factor may be negligible if only a very small number of observations are missing, and can probably be safely ignored. This suggests that dummy variables are only a viable proposition for handling a small number of missing observations.

Example 3.4.3 The missing observation in Example 3.4.2 may be handled by defining the dummy variable

$$w_t = \begin{cases} 1, & t=m \\ 0, & t \neq m \end{cases} \tag{3.4.85}$$

The model then becomes

$$y_t = y_t^\dagger + \lambda w_t, \quad t=1,\ldots,T+1 \tag{3.4.86}$$

where $y_t^\dagger$ is generated by (3.4.79), λ is an unknown parameter and $y_t = 0$ at $t=m$. In Sargan and Drettakis (1974) no dummy variable is included and the missing observation itself is treated as an unknown parameter. It is straightforward to see that the effect is the same and that the estimator of the missing value of $y_t^\dagger$ is the ML estimator of λ multiplied by minus one.

The likelihood function for (3.4.86) is

$$\log L(y) = -\frac{(T+1)}{2}\log 2\pi - \tfrac{1}{2}\log(1-\varphi^2)$$

$$-\frac{(T+1)}{2}\log\sigma^2 - \frac{1}{2\sigma^2}y_1^2(1-\varphi^2)$$

$$-\frac{1}{2\sigma^2}\sum_{t=2}^{T+1}[y_t - \lambda w_t - \varphi(y_{t-1} - \lambda w_{t-1})]^2 \tag{3.4.87}$$

Differentiating with respect to λ and rearranging gives

$$\frac{\partial \log L}{\partial \lambda} = \sigma^{-2}[(-\lambda - \varphi y_{m-1}) - \varphi(y_{m+1} + \varphi\lambda)]$$

and so

$$\tilde{\lambda} = -\varphi(y_{m+1} + y_{m-1})/(1+\varphi^2) \tag{3.4.88}$$

Substituting $\tilde{\lambda}$ in the last term in (3.4.87) and rearranging gives the last two terms in (3.4.83). The correction factor involves replacing $T+1$ by T, the number of actual observations, and bringing in the third term in (3.4.83), $-\frac{1}{2}\log(1+\varphi^2)$.

3.5 Prediction

In the Gaussian model, (3.1.1) and (3.1.3), the Kalman filter yields $\mathbf{a}_T$, the MMSE of $\boldsymbol{\alpha}_T$ based on all the observations. In addition it gives

$$\mathbf{a}_{T+1|T} = \mathbf{T}_{T+1}\mathbf{a}_T + \mathbf{c}_{T+1} \tag{3.5.1}$$

together with the one-step-ahead prediction

$$\tilde{\mathbf{y}}_{T+1|T} = \mathbf{Z}_{T+1}\mathbf{a}_{T+1|T} + \mathbf{d}_{T+1} \tag{3.5.2}$$

Now consider the problem of multi-step prediction, that is, making predictions of future observations at times $T+2$, $T+3$ and so on. Substituting repeatedly in the transition equation at time $T+l$ yields

$$\boldsymbol{\alpha}_{T+l} = \left[\prod_{j=1}^{l} \mathbf{T}_{T+j}\right]\boldsymbol{\alpha}_T + \sum_{j=1}^{l-1}\left[\prod_{i=j+1}^{l} \mathbf{T}_{T+i}\right][\mathbf{R}_{T+j}\boldsymbol{\eta}_{T+j} + \mathbf{c}_{T+j}]$$
$$+\mathbf{R}_{T+l}\boldsymbol{\eta}_{T+l} + \mathbf{c}_{T+l}, \quad l=2,3,\ldots \tag{3.5.3}$$

From the discussion in section 3.2, we know that the MMSE of $\boldsymbol{\alpha}_{T+l}$ at time T is the conditional mean of $\boldsymbol{\alpha}_{T+l}$. Taking conditional expectations at time T in (3.5.3) gives

$$\underset{T}{\mathrm{E}}(\boldsymbol{\alpha}_{T+l}) = \mathbf{a}_{T+l|T} = \left[\prod_{j=1}^{l} \mathbf{T}_{T+j}\right]\mathbf{a}_T + \sum_{j=1}^{l-1}\left[\prod_{i=j+1}^{l} \mathbf{T}_{T+i}\right]\mathbf{c}_{T+j} + \mathbf{c}_{T+l} \tag{3.5.4}$$

The conditional distribution of $\boldsymbol{\alpha}_{T+l}$ is normal and its covariance matrix, $\mathbf{P}_{T+l|T}$, can be obtained from (3.5.3) and (3.5.4). In the time-invariant case the appropriate expression is

$$\mathbf{P}_{T+l|T} = \mathbf{T}^l\mathbf{P}_T\mathbf{T}^{l\prime} + \sum_{j=0}^{l-1} \mathbf{T}^j\mathbf{R}\mathbf{Q}\mathbf{R}'\mathbf{T}^{j\prime}, \quad l=1,2,\ldots \tag{3.5.5}$$

The MMSE of $\mathbf{y}_{T+l}$ can be obtained directly from $\mathbf{a}_{T+l|T}$. Taking conditional expectations in the measurement equation at time $T+l$ gives

$$\underset{T}{\mathrm{E}}(\mathbf{y}_{T+l}) = \tilde{\mathbf{y}}_{T+l|T} = \mathbf{Z}_{T+l}\mathbf{a}_{T+l|T} + \mathbf{d}_{T+l}, \quad l=1,2,\ldots \tag{3.5.6a}$$

The MSE matrix is

$$\mathrm{MSE}(\tilde{\mathbf{y}}_{T+l|T}) = \mathbf{Z}_{T+l}\mathbf{P}_{T+l|T}\mathbf{Z}'_{T+l} + \mathbf{H}_{T+l}, \quad l=1,2,\ldots \tag{3.5.6b}$$

The easiest way to evaluate $\mathbf{a}_{T+l|T}$ and $\mathbf{P}_{T+l|T}$ is by repeatedly applying the Kalman filter prediction equations, (3.2.2). This is an example of the chain rule; see (2.3.12). The transition equation at $T+2$ is

$$\boldsymbol{\alpha}_{T+2}=\mathbf{T}_{T+2}\boldsymbol{\alpha}_{T+1}+\mathbf{c}_{T+2}+\mathbf{R}_{T+2}\boldsymbol{\eta}_{T+2}$$

and taking conditional expectations yields

$$\underset{T}{\mathrm{E}}(\boldsymbol{\alpha}_{T+2})=\mathbf{T}_{T+2}\,\underset{T}{\mathrm{E}}(\boldsymbol{\alpha}_{T+1})+\mathbf{c}_{T+2}$$

which can also be written as

$$\mathbf{a}_{T+2|T}=\mathbf{T}_{T+2}\mathbf{a}_{T+1|T}+\mathbf{c}_{T+2}$$

However $\mathbf{a}_{T+1|T}$ is given by (3.5.1). Repeating this argument for all lead times gives the multi-step prediction equations

$$\mathbf{a}_{T+l|T}=\mathbf{T}_{T+l}\mathbf{a}_{T+l-1|T}+\mathbf{c}_{T+l} \tag{3.5.7a}$$

and

$$\mathbf{P}_{T+l|T}=\mathbf{T}_{T+l}\mathbf{P}_{T+l-1|T}\mathbf{T}'_{T+l}+\mathbf{R}_{T+l}\mathbf{Q}_{T+l}\mathbf{R}'_{T+l}, \quad l=1,2,3,\ldots \tag{3.5.7b}$$

Before proceeding to some examples three points need to be made. Firstly, the MSE matrices, the $\mathbf{P}_{T+l|T}$'s, do not take account of the errors which arise from estimating any unknown parameters in the system matrices $\mathbf{T}_t$, $\mathbf{c}_t$ and so on. Secondly, when the normality assumption is relaxed, $\mathbf{a}_{T+l|T}$ and $\tilde{\mathbf{y}}_{T+l|T}$ are still minimum mean square *linear* estimators. Thirdly, if the assumption of uncorrelatedness is replaced by the stronger assumption of independence, (3.5.4) and (3.5.6b) are still valid, though without normality $\mathbf{a}_T$ is not, in general, a linear function of the observations, $\mathbf{Y}_T$; see (3.7.29).

Example 3.5.1 In the random walk plus noise model of Example 3.2.1,

$$\tilde{y}_{T+l|T}=m_T, \quad l=1,2,\ldots \tag{3.5.8a}$$

Thus the forecast function is a horizontal straight line which passes through the final estimator of the level of the process. Since the model is time-invariant, expression (3.5.5) can be evaluated and substituted into (3.5.6b). The forecast MSE, conditional on q, is

$$\mathrm{MSE}(\tilde{y}_{T+l|T})=(p_T+lq+1)\sigma_\varepsilon^2, \quad l=1,2,\ldots \tag{3.5.8b}$$

The MSE increases with the forecast horizon.

Example 3.5.2 Consider the damped trend model set up in (2.3.66). The state space form is:

$$y_t=[1 \quad 0]\boldsymbol{\alpha}_t+\varepsilon_t \tag{3.5.9a}$$

$$\boldsymbol{\alpha}_t = \begin{bmatrix} \mu_t \\ \beta_t \end{bmatrix} = \begin{bmatrix} 1 & 1 \\ 0 & \rho \end{bmatrix} \begin{bmatrix} \mu_{t-1} \\ \beta_{t-1} \end{bmatrix} + \begin{bmatrix} \eta_t \\ \zeta_t \end{bmatrix} \tag{3.5.9b}$$

If b_T denotes the estimate of β_T obtained from the Kalman filter, then from the prediction equations, (3.5.1),

$$m_{T+1|T} = m_T + b_T \tag{3.5.10a}$$

$$b_{T+1|T} = \rho b_T \tag{3.5.10b}$$

and $\tilde{y}_{T+1|T} = m_{T+1|T}$. Repeating this process yields

$$\tilde{y}_{T+l|T} = m_{T+l|T} = m_T + b_T + \rho b_T + \rho^2 b_T + \dots + \rho^{l-1} b_T$$
$$= m_T + [(1-\rho^l)/(1-\rho)] b_T$$

The final forecast function is a horizontal straight line at a height of

$$\lim_{l \to \infty} \tilde{y}_{T+l|T} = m_T + b_T/(1-\rho) \tag{3.5.11}$$

The discussion so far has assumed that there are no unknown parameters in the model. If, as is usually the case, the model contains a set of unknown parameters, $\boldsymbol{\psi}$, the formula for MSE $(\tilde{\mathbf{y}}_{T+l|T})$ will underestimate the true MSE because it does not take into account the extra variation due to estimating $\boldsymbol{\psi}$. An expression for approximating this additional variation $\mathbf{a}_{T+l|T}$ has been obtained by Ansley and Kohn (1986). They show that under certain regularity conditions, it is appropriate to take the following expression as an approximation to the MSE matrix of $\mathbf{a}_{T+l|T}$:

$$\mathbf{P}_{T+l|T} + \frac{\partial \mathbf{a}_{T+l|T}}{\partial \boldsymbol{\psi}'} \mathbf{I}^{-1}(\tilde{\boldsymbol{\psi}}) \frac{\partial \mathbf{a}'_{T+l|T}}{\partial \boldsymbol{\psi}} \tag{3.5.12}$$

where $\mathbf{a}_{T+l|T}$, like the information matrix, is evaluated at the ML estimator $\tilde{\boldsymbol{\psi}}$. The derivatives of $\mathbf{a}_{T+l|T}$ can be evaluated numerically or analytically by extending the recursions of sub-section 3.4.6. If $\mathbf{y}_t$ does not appear directly in the state vector, the previous theory can be applied by augmenting the state vector by $\mathbf{y}_t$.

If the only unknown parameters enter into the model linearly in $\mathbf{c}_t$ and $\mathbf{d}_t$, they can be estimated by being included in an augmented state vector as in (3.4.25). The Kalman filter prediction equations then give an exact expression for the MSE of the predictions via (3.6.6b).

3.6 Smoothing

The aim of filtering is to find the expected value of the state vector, $\boldsymbol{\alpha}_t$, conditional on the information available at time t, that is $E(\boldsymbol{\alpha}_t | \mathbf{Y}_t)$. The aim of smoothing is to take account of the information made available after time t. The mean of the distribution of $\boldsymbol{\alpha}_t$, conditional on all the sample, may be written as $E(\boldsymbol{\alpha}_t|\mathbf{Y}_T)$ and is known as a *smoothed estimate*. The corresponding estimator is called a *smoother*. Since the smoother is based on more information than the filtered estimator, it will have a MSE which, in general, is smaller than that of the filtered estimator; it cannot be greater.

In a linear Gaussian model, the smoothed estimator is denoted by $\mathbf{a}_{t|T}$. Thus

$$\mathbf{a}_{t|T} = \underset{T}{E}(\boldsymbol{\alpha}_t) = E(\boldsymbol{\alpha}_t|\mathbf{Y}_T) \tag{3.6.1}$$

As with the filtered estimator, $\mathbf{a}_{t|T}$ is the MMSE of $\boldsymbol{\alpha}_t$ based on the available information set. If the Gaussian assumption is dropped, it is the MMSLE of $\boldsymbol{\alpha}_t$; see the discussion in sub-section 3.2.3.

There are basically three smoothing algorithms in a linear model. *Fixed-point* smoothing is concerned with computing smoothed estimates of the state vector at some fixed point in time. Thus it gives $\mathbf{a}_{\tau|t}$ for particular values of τ at all time periods $t>\tau$. *Fixed-lag* smoothing computes smoothed estimates for a fixed delay, that is $\mathbf{a}_{t-j|t}$ for $j=1,\ldots,M$ where M is some maximum lag. Both of these algorithms can be applied in an *on-line* situation. *Fixed-interval* smoothing, on the other hand, is concerned with computing the full set of smoothed estimates for a fixed span of data. Hence it is an *off-line* technique which yields $\mathbf{a}_{t|T}$, $t=1,\ldots,T$. It therefore tends to be the most widely used algorithm for economic and social data. However, fixed-point smoothing can be attractive in an off-line situation where the state vector only needs to be estimated at a limited number of points in time.

All three smoothing algorithms are recursive and are linked closely to the Kalman filter. The fixed-point algorithm runs in parallel with the Kalman filter, while the fixed-interval algorithm is a backward recursion which starts at time T, and produces the smoothed estimates in the order $T,\ldots,1$. Fixed-lag smoothing also runs in parallel with the Kalman filter, but since it is less important than the other two algorithms for our purposes, it will not be described here. Full details can be found in Anderson and Moore (1979, ch. 7).

The covariance matrix of $\boldsymbol{\alpha}_t$ conditional on all T observations is denoted by

$$\mathbf{P}_{t|T} = \underset{T}{E}[(\boldsymbol{\alpha}_t - \mathbf{a}_{t|T})(\boldsymbol{\alpha}_t - \mathbf{a}_{t|T})'] \tag{3.6.2}$$

When $\mathbf{a}_{t|T}$ is viewed as an estimator, $\mathbf{P}_{t|T}$ is its MSE matrix. As with the MSE matrix of the filtered estimator, $\mathbf{P}_{t|T}$ is independent of the observations for a linear filter and so is unconditional. The three smoothing algorithms all yield MSE matrices corresponding to the estimators which they compute. Since a smoothed estimator is based on at least as much information as the corresponding filtered estimator, it follows that the MSE matrix of the filtered estimator exceeds the MSE matrix of the smoothed estimator by a p.s.d. matrix, that is

$$\mathbf{P}_{t|T} \leqslant \mathbf{P}_t, \quad t=1,\ldots,T \tag{3.6.3}$$

The smoothed estimator exists if its elements can be estimated with finite MSE, that is if $\mathbf{P}_{t|T}$ is bounded. Thus if $\mathbf{a}_t$ exists so must $\mathbf{a}_{t|T}$. The converse is not true. For example in a time-invariant model, the smoothed estimators will exist for all $t=1,\ldots,T$ if the model is observable, even though the filtered estimators have unbounded MSE matrices for some, or all, of the first m time periods.

The gain from smoothing is reflected in the difference between $\mathbf{P}_{t|T}$ and $\mathbf{P}_t$. As a rule, the gain in a time-invariant model will be greater the larger is $\mathbf{H}$ relative to $\mathbf{Q}$. As an illustration consider the random walk plus noise model. When the signal–noise ratio, q, is infinity, there is no gain to be had from smoothing since the state, μ_t, is equal to y_t, and so is known exactly at time t. On the other hand when q is zero, so that the state is fixed, $\text{MSE}(m_t)/\text{MSE}(m_{t|T})=t/T$. When parameters in the model have to be estimated, $\mathbf{P}_{t|T}$ will underestimate the true MSE matrix. An approximation to the true MSE may be made by using the techniques suggested by Ansley and Kohn (1986), which were described briefly at the end of section 3.5.

Finally it is worth noting that a linear state space model may be expressed as a generalised regression model in which the regression coefficients are the state vector at time τ. Thus

$$\mathbf{y}=\mathbf{X}_\tau\boldsymbol{\alpha}_\tau+\mathbf{u}_\tau \tag{3.6.4}$$

where $\mathbf{X}_\tau$ is a $T\times m$ matrix depending on the $\mathbf{z}_t$'s and $\mathbf{T}_t$'s throughout the sample, and $\mathbf{u}_\tau$ is a $T\times 1$ vector of disturbances. Writing the model in this way is a generalization of the conditioning on $\boldsymbol{\alpha}_0$ which was carried out in equations (3.4.60) to (3.4.62). The mean of the $\mathbf{u}_\tau$ vector is zero and its covariance matrix can be derived in principle. Applying GLS to (3.6.4) yields $\mathbf{a}_{\tau|T}$, the smoothed estimator of $\boldsymbol{\alpha}_\tau$.

3.6.1 *Fixed-point smoothing*

From the theoretical point of view, the fixed-point smoother is the most straightforward of the smoothing algorithms. Suppose that we wish to estimate $\boldsymbol{\alpha}_\tau$, the state vector at time $t=\tau<T$. Adding $\boldsymbol{\alpha}_\tau$ to the state vector at times $t\geqslant\tau$ yields an augmented state space model and applying the Kalman filter to this augmented model yields $\mathbf{a}_{\tau|T}$ when all the observations have been processed. In practice the smoothed estimator does not have to be computed by running this particular Kalman filter, since it is possible to break it down into the filter for the original state space model and a filter for $\boldsymbol{\alpha}_\tau$. It is this second set of recursions which is known as the fixed-point smoother.

The derivation of the fixed-point smoother is as follows. When $\boldsymbol{\alpha}_\tau$ is added to the state vector it remains constant throughout the remaining time periods. Thus if $\boldsymbol{\alpha}_\tau$ is renamed as $\boldsymbol{\alpha}_\tau^*$ it obeys the transition equation

$$\boldsymbol{\alpha}_t^*=\boldsymbol{\alpha}_{t-1}^*,\quad t=\tau+1,\ldots,T \tag{3.6.5}$$

with $\boldsymbol{\alpha}_\tau^* = \boldsymbol{\alpha}_\tau$ as the initial condition. The augmented state space model is therefore

$$\mathbf{y}_t = [\mathbf{Z}_t \quad \mathbf{0}]\boldsymbol{\alpha}_t^\dagger + \mathbf{d}_t + \boldsymbol{\varepsilon}_t, \quad t=\tau, \tau+1, \ldots, T \tag{3.6.6a}$$

$$\boldsymbol{\alpha}_t^\dagger = \begin{bmatrix} \boldsymbol{\alpha}_t \\ \boldsymbol{\alpha}_t^* \end{bmatrix} = \begin{bmatrix} \mathbf{T}_t & \mathbf{0} \\ \mathbf{0} & \mathbf{I} \end{bmatrix} \begin{bmatrix} \boldsymbol{\alpha}_{t-1} \\ \boldsymbol{\alpha}_{t-1}^* \end{bmatrix} + \begin{bmatrix} \mathbf{c}_t \\ \mathbf{0} \end{bmatrix} + \begin{bmatrix} \mathbf{R}_t \\ \mathbf{0} \end{bmatrix} \boldsymbol{\eta}_t \tag{3.6.6b}$$

The corresponding augmented Kalman filter, in the form (3.2.4), is

$$\mathbf{a}_{t+1|t}^\dagger = \begin{bmatrix} \mathbf{a}_{t+1|t} \\ \mathbf{a}_{t+1|t}^* \end{bmatrix} = \left[\begin{bmatrix} \mathbf{T}_{t+1} & \mathbf{0} \\ \mathbf{0} & \mathbf{I} \end{bmatrix} - \begin{bmatrix} \mathbf{K}_t \\ \mathbf{K}_t^* \end{bmatrix} [\mathbf{Z}_t \quad \mathbf{0}] \right] \begin{bmatrix} \mathbf{a}_{t|t-1} \\ \mathbf{a}_{t|t-1}^* \end{bmatrix} + \begin{bmatrix} \mathbf{K}_t \\ \mathbf{K}_t^* \end{bmatrix} \mathbf{y}_t$$

$$+ \left[\begin{bmatrix} \mathbf{c}_{t+1} \\ \mathbf{0} \end{bmatrix} - \begin{bmatrix} \mathbf{K}_t \\ \mathbf{K}_t^* \end{bmatrix} \mathbf{d}_t \right] \tag{3.6.7a}$$

and

$$\mathbf{P}_{t+1|t}^\dagger = \begin{bmatrix} \mathbf{P}_{t+1|t} & \mathbf{P}_{t+1|t}^{*\prime} \\ \mathbf{P}_{t+1|t}^* & \mathbf{P}_{t+1|t}^{**} \end{bmatrix} = \begin{bmatrix} \mathbf{T}_{t+1} & \mathbf{0} \\ \mathbf{0} & \mathbf{I} \end{bmatrix} \begin{bmatrix} \mathbf{P}_{t|t-1} & \mathbf{P}_{t|t-1}^{*\prime} \\ \mathbf{P}_{t|t-1}^* & \mathbf{P}_{t|t-1}^{**} \end{bmatrix} \left[\begin{bmatrix} \mathbf{T}_{t+1}' & \mathbf{0} \\ \mathbf{0} & \mathbf{I} \end{bmatrix} \right.$$

$$\left. - \begin{bmatrix} \mathbf{Z}_t' \\ \mathbf{0} \end{bmatrix} [\mathbf{K}_t' \quad \mathbf{K}_t^{*\prime}] \right] + \begin{bmatrix} \mathbf{R}_{t+1} \\ \mathbf{0} \end{bmatrix} \mathbf{Q}_{t+1} [\mathbf{R}_{t+1}' \quad \mathbf{0}], \quad t=\tau, \ldots, T \tag{3.6.7b}$$

In view of the initial condition attached to (3.6.1), it follows that the starting values for (3.6.7) are

$$\mathbf{a}_{\tau|\tau-1}^\dagger = \begin{bmatrix} \mathbf{a}_{\tau|\tau-1} \\ \mathbf{a}_{\tau|\tau-1} \end{bmatrix} \quad \text{and} \quad \mathbf{P}_{\tau|\tau-1}^\dagger = \begin{bmatrix} \mathbf{P}_{\tau|\tau-1} & \mathbf{P}_{\tau|\tau-1} \\ \mathbf{P}_{\tau|\tau-1} & \mathbf{P}_{\tau|\tau-1} \end{bmatrix} \tag{3.6.8}$$

where $\mathbf{a}_{\tau|\tau-1}$ and $\mathbf{P}_{\tau|\tau-1}$ are obtained from the original Kalman filter applied to the model for the first $\tau-1$ observations.

Running the augmented Kalman filter with starting values (3.6.8) produces the smoothed estimator of $\boldsymbol{\alpha}_\tau$ as $\mathbf{a}_{T+1|T}^*$. Its MSE matrix, $\mathbf{P}_{\tau|T}$, is $\mathbf{P}_{T+1|T}^{**}$. The need to run the augmented filter can be avoided by first noting that the gain matrix can be written as

$$\begin{bmatrix} \mathbf{K}_t \\ \mathbf{K}_t^* \end{bmatrix} = \begin{bmatrix} \mathbf{T}_{t+1} & \mathbf{0} \\ \mathbf{0} & \mathbf{I} \end{bmatrix} \begin{bmatrix} \mathbf{P}_{t|t-1} & \mathbf{P}_{t|t-1}^{*\prime} \\ \mathbf{P}_{t|t-1}^* & \mathbf{P}_{t|t-1}^{**} \end{bmatrix} \begin{bmatrix} \mathbf{Z}_t' \\ \mathbf{0} \end{bmatrix} \mathbf{F}_t^{-1} = \begin{bmatrix} \mathbf{T}_{t+1}\mathbf{P}_{t|t-1}\mathbf{Z}_t'\mathbf{F}_t^{-1} \\ \mathbf{P}_{t|t-1}^*\mathbf{Z}_t'\mathbf{F}_t^{-1} \end{bmatrix} \tag{3.6.9}$$

where $\mathbf{F}_t = \mathbf{Z}_t\mathbf{P}_{t|t-1}\mathbf{Z}_t' + \mathbf{H}_t$ as in (3.2.3c). Substituting from (3.6.9) into (3.6.7) gives two separate recursions, the first being (3.2.4a) and the second

$$\mathbf{a}_{t+1|t}^* = \mathbf{a}_{t|t-1}^* + \mathbf{K}_t^* \mathbf{v}_t, \quad t=\tau, \ldots, T \tag{3.6.10}$$

The recursion for $\mathbf{a}_{t+1|t}$ is just the Kalman filter as applied to the original model, while the innovations, $\mathbf{v}_t$, in (3.6.10) are the innovations produced from this same filter. Similarly, (3.6.7b) may be decomposed into the original recursion

$\mathbf{P}_{t+1|t}$ together with

$$\mathbf{P}^*_{t+1|t} = \mathbf{P}^*_{t|t-1}[\mathbf{T}_{t+1} - \mathbf{K}_t\mathbf{Z}_t]' \tag{3.6.11a}$$

and

$$\mathbf{P}^{**}_{t+1|t} = \mathbf{P}^{**}_{t|t-1} - \mathbf{P}^*_{t|t-1}\mathbf{Z}_t'\mathbf{K}_t^{*\prime}, \quad t=\tau,\ldots,T \tag{3.6.11b}$$

The second of these recursions yields the MSE matrix of the smoothed estimator.

To summarise, the fixed-point smoother is run in conjunction with the usual Kalman filter for the model (3.1.1) and (3.1.3). The smoother recursions consist of (3.6.10) with $\mathbf{a}^*_{t+1|t}$ set equal to $\mathbf{a}_{\tau|t}$, and (3.6.11) with $\mathbf{P}^{**}_{t+1|t}$ set equal to $\mathbf{P}_{\tau|t}$, together with the identity

$$\mathbf{K}_t^* = \mathbf{P}^*_{t|t-1}\mathbf{Z}_t'\mathbf{F}_t^{-1}, \quad t=\tau,\ldots,T \tag{3.6.12}$$

The initial vector for (3.6.10) is $\mathbf{a}^*_{t|t-1} = \mathbf{a}_{t|t-1}$, while the initial matrix for both parts of (3.6.11) is $\mathbf{P}^*_{t|t-1} = \mathbf{P}^{**}_{t|t-1} = \mathbf{P}_{t|t-1}$.

Example 3.6.1 Consider the problem of estimating the level of the trend, μ_t, at time $t=\tau$ in the random walk plus noise model of Example 3.2.1. By substituting for k_t from (3.2.9a) it can be seen that (3.6.11a) is

$$p^*_{t+1|t} = p^*_{t|t-1}\left[1 - \frac{p_{t|t-1}}{1+p_{t|t-1}}\right]$$

If the Kalman filter is in a steady state this recursion becomes

$$p^*_{t+1|t} = p^*_{t|t-1}(1-\lambda), \quad t=\tau,\ldots,T \tag{3.6.13}$$

where $\lambda = \bar{p}/(1+\bar{p})$ and $\bar{p}$ is defined by (3.3.16). Noting that $p^*_{t|\tau-1} = \bar{p}$ and that $f_t = \bar{p}+1$, gives

$$k_t^* = (p^*_{t|t-1})/f_t = \lambda(1-\lambda)^{t-\tau}, \quad t=\tau,\ldots,T$$

Hence the fixed-point recursion for the smoothed estimator of μ_τ is:

$$m_{\tau|t} = m_{\tau|t-1} + \lambda(1-\lambda)^{t-\tau}v_t, \quad t=\tau,\ldots,T \tag{3.6.14}$$

Solving this difference equation for $t=T$ gives

$$m_{\tau|T} = m_{\tau|\tau-1} + \lambda\sum_{j=0}^{T-\tau}(1-\lambda)^j v_{\tau+j} \tag{3.6.15}$$

This expression shows how the smoothed estimator depends on the innovations produced by the Kalman filter. The weights attached to these innovations decline exponentially over time. The higher the signal–noise ratio, q, the closer is λ to unity, and the more rapidly the bulk of the gain from smoothing is achieved.

The application of the fixed-point smoother to other structural models prompts the question as to whether it is always necessary to set up recursions for the complete state vector. For example, suppose that we wish to remove the irregular component from a basic structural model. The quantity to be estimated is then the linear combination $\mathbf{z}_t'\boldsymbol{\alpha}_t = \mu_t + \gamma_t$. More generally suppose that $\mathbf{W}_\tau$ is an $M \times m$ matrix and that the M linear combinations $\mathbf{W}_\tau\boldsymbol{\alpha}_\tau$ are to be estimated. The fixed-point smoother can easily be amended by multiplying (3.6.10) through by $\mathbf{W}_\tau$ and making corresponding amendments to (3.6.11). The resulting smoother is then of dimension M and the smoothed estimator of $\mathbf{W}_\tau\boldsymbol{\alpha}_\tau$, together with its MSE matrix, is produced directly. The same considerations apply when estimating missing observations, or observations which have been subject to temporal aggregation; see Harvey and Pierse (1984). In terms of (3.4.76) the required estimator is

$$\underset{T}{\mathrm{E}}(\mathbf{y}_t^\dagger) = \underset{T}{\mathrm{E}}(\mathbf{Z}_t\boldsymbol{\alpha}_t) + \underset{T}{\mathrm{E}}(\mathbf{d}_t) + \underset{T}{\mathrm{E}}(\boldsymbol{\varepsilon}_t) = \mathbf{Z}_t\mathbf{a}_{t|T} + \mathbf{d}_t$$

3.6.2 Fixed-interval smoothing

The fixed-interval smoothing algorithm consists of a set of recursions which start with the final quantities, $\mathbf{a}_T$ and $\mathbf{P}_T$, given by the Kalman filter and work backwards. The equations are

$$\mathbf{a}_{t|T} = \mathbf{a}_t + \mathbf{P}_t^*(\mathbf{a}_{t+1|T} - \mathbf{T}_{t+1}\mathbf{a}_t) \tag{3.6.16a}$$

and

$$\mathbf{P}_{t|T} = \mathbf{P}_t + \mathbf{P}_t^*(\mathbf{P}_{t+1|T} - \mathbf{P}_{t+1|t})\mathbf{P}_t^{*\prime} \tag{3.6.16b}$$

where

$$\mathbf{P}_t^* = \mathbf{P}_t\mathbf{T}_{t+1}'\mathbf{P}_{t+1|t}^{-1}, \quad t = T-1, \ldots, 1 \tag{3.6.16c}$$

with $\mathbf{a}_{T|T} = \mathbf{a}_T$ and $\mathbf{P}_{T|T} = \mathbf{P}_T$. The algorithm therefore requires that $\mathbf{a}_t$ and $\mathbf{P}_t$ be stored for all t so that they can be combined with $\mathbf{a}_{t+1|T}$ and $\mathbf{P}_{t+1|T}$. Derivations of these equations can be found in Anderson and Moore (1979, ch. 7), Jazwinski (1970, pp. 216–17) and Ansley and Kohn (1982). If $\mathbf{P}_{t+1|T}$ is singular for some t, it may be replaced by a generalised inverse as suggested by Kohn and Ansley (1983).

Example 3.6.2 In the random walk plus noise model,

$$p_t^* = p_t/(p_t + q)$$

and so

$$m_{t|T} = (1 - p_t^*)m_t + p_t^* m_{t+1|T}, \quad t = T-1, \ldots, 1 \tag{3.6.17}$$

Thus the smoothed estimator at time t is a simple weighted average of the smoothed estimator at time $t+1$ and the filtered estimator at time t. In a steady-state filter, p_t^* is constant and (3.6.17) is similar in form to the EWMA.

Example 3.6.3 Consider an AR(1) model with a missing observation at time $t=m$, as in Example 3.4.2, and suppose that we wish to estimate this observation for a given value of φ. Since y_t itself is the state, we know that at time $t=m-1$, $a_{m-1}=y_{m-1}$ and so $p_{m-1}=0$. As was observed in (3.4.84), a_m and p_m are equal to $a_{m|m-1}$ and $p_{m|m-1}$ respectively. Thus in this case

$$a_m=\varphi y_{m-1} \quad \text{and} \quad p_m=1$$

Applying the Kalman filter prediction equations yields

$$a_{m+1|m}=\varphi^2 y_{m-1} \quad \text{and} \quad p_{m+1|m}=1+\varphi^2$$

but since $y^{\dagger}_{m+1}$ is observed, $a_{m+1}=a_{m+1|T}=y_{m+1}$ and $p_{m+1}=p_{m+1|T}=0$.

Starting the smoothing recursion, (3.6.16a), at $t=m+1$, then gives

$$a_{m|T}=\varphi y_{m-1}+\varphi(y_{m+1}-\varphi^2 y_{m-1})/(1+\varphi^2)$$

This is the optimal estimator of the missing observation $y^{\dagger}_m$, which on rearrangement becomes

$$\tilde{y}^{\dagger}_{m|T}=\varphi(y_{m+1}+y_{m-1})/(1+\varphi^2) \tag{3.6.18}$$

The fixed-interval smoother can also be adapted for use with the diffuse prior algorithm of sub-section 3.4.3. The smoothing recursion in (3.6.16a) is modified to

$$\mathbf{a}_{t|T}=\mathbf{a}^0_t-\mathbf{A}_t\mathbf{S}^-_t\mathbf{s}_t+\mathbf{P}^{*0}_t[\mathbf{a}_{t+1|T}-\mathbf{T}_{t+1}(\mathbf{a}^0_t-\mathbf{A}_t\mathbf{S}^-_t\mathbf{s}_t)] \tag{3.6.19}$$

where

$$\mathbf{P}^{*0}_t=\mathbf{P}^0_t\mathbf{T}'_{t+1}(\mathbf{P}^0_{t+1|t})^{-1};$$

see de Jong (1989). If the criterion in (3.4.48) is satisfied, then $\mathbf{a}_{1|T}$ must exist and hence all subsequent smoothed values must exist. Note that if a switch back to the conventional Kalman filter is made at some point in time, τ, the implied existence of $\mathbf{a}_\tau$ means that smoothed estimates at time τ and beyond can be made by the conventional smoother (3.6.16).

Finally it is worth noting that information filter forms of the fixed-interval smoother are available; see Kitagawa (1981) and Cooley *et al.* (1977).

3.7 Non-linearity and non-normality

Non-linearities can be introduced into state space models in a variety of ways. One of the most important classes of models has Gaussian disturbances but allows the system matrices to be stochastic in that they depend on information, that is observations, available at time $t-1$. These models are known as *conditionally Gaussian* models and they have the attractive property of still being susceptible to treatment by the Kalman filter. They are described in sub-section 3.7.1.

A somewhat different kind of non-linearity is obtained when the observations in the measurement equation are no longer a linear function of the state vector and, in the transition equation, the state vector itself is no longer a linear function of the state vector in the previous time period and the matrix $\mathbf{R}_t$ may also depend on the lagged state vector. We will refer to such models as being *functionally non-linear*. They are not, in general, conditionally Gaussian. In the absence of this property, it is necessary to resort to approximate filters and the most basic of these, the extended Kalman filter, is described in sub-section 3.7.2.

Applying the Kalman filter to a model with a linear SSF yields MMSEs of the state vector under the normality assumption. This is not generally true once the normality assumption is dropped, although it is still possible to make the statement that the Kalman filter yields MMSEs within the class of linear estimators. However, given alternative distributional assumptions, the theoretical solution to the problem of finding minimum mean square estimates of the state vector may be obtained. This is set out in sub-section 3.7.3.

3.7.1 Conditionally Gaussian models

A conditionally Gaussian model may be written explicitly as

$$\mathbf{y}_t = \mathbf{Z}_t(\mathbf{Y}_{t-1})\boldsymbol{\alpha}_t + \mathbf{d}_t(\mathbf{Y}_{t-1}) + \boldsymbol{\varepsilon}_t, \tag{3.7.1a}$$

$$\boldsymbol{\alpha}_t = \mathbf{T}_t(\mathbf{Y}_{t-1})\boldsymbol{\alpha}_{t-1} + \mathbf{c}_t(\mathbf{Y}_{t-1}) + \mathbf{R}_t(\mathbf{Y}_{t-1})\boldsymbol{\eta}_t \tag{3.7.1b}$$

where

$$\boldsymbol{\varepsilon}_t|\mathbf{Y}_{t-1} \sim \mathrm{N}(\mathbf{0}, \mathbf{H}_t(\mathbf{Y}_{t-1})), \quad \boldsymbol{\eta}_t|\mathbf{Y}_{t-1} \sim \mathrm{N}(\mathbf{0}, \mathbf{Q}_t(\mathbf{Y}_{t-1})) \text{ and } \boldsymbol{\alpha}_0 \sim \mathrm{N}(\mathbf{a}_0, \mathbf{P}_0)$$

Even though the system matrices may depend on observations up to and including $\mathbf{y}_{t-1}$, they may be regarded as being fixed once we are at time $t-1$. Hence the derivation of the Kalman filter goes through exactly as in section 3.2 with $\mathbf{a}_{t|t-1}$ and $\mathbf{P}_{t|t-1}$ now interpreted as the mean and covariance matrix of the distribution of $\boldsymbol{\alpha}_t$ conditional on the information at time $t-1$. However, since the conditional mean of $\boldsymbol{\alpha}_t$ will no longer be a linear function of the observations, it will be denoted by $\tilde{\boldsymbol{\alpha}}_{t|t-1}$ rather than by $\mathbf{a}_{t|t-1}$. When $\tilde{\boldsymbol{\alpha}}_{t|t-1}$ is viewed as an estimator of $\boldsymbol{\alpha}_t$, then $\mathbf{P}_{t|t-1}$ can be regarded as its conditional error covariance, or MSE, matrix. Since $\mathbf{P}_{t|t-1}$ will now depend on the particular realisation of observations in the sample, it is no longer an unconditional error covariance matrix as it was in the linear case.

The system matrices will usually contain unknown parameters, $\boldsymbol{\psi}$. However, since the distribution of $\mathbf{y}_t$, conditional on $\mathbf{Y}_{t-1}$, is normal for all $t = 1, \ldots, T$, the likelihood function can be written down in the prediction error decomposition form (3.4.5). Furthermore the information matrix and the derivatives can be obtained using the formulae given in sub-sections 3.4.5 and 3.4.6. This opens the way for setting up scoring algorithms, and for calculating various Wald and Lagrange multiplier test statistics analytically; see sub-section 5.2.1. The only point to note is that expression (3.4.69) is no longer, strictly speaking, the information matrix since it is only the sum of the conditional expectations of the matrices of second derivatives; the subsequent taking of unconditional expectations is not necessarily the trivial operation it is for linear models. Hence (3.4.69) must be regarded as an approximation to the information matrix, although, like the Hessian, it will still be asymptotically equivalent to it under fairly general conditions.

Further details on the statistical theory associated with conditionally Gaussian models can be found in Liptser and Shiryayev (1978).

Example 3.7.1 Granger and Andersen (1978) describe the properties of a number of classes of non-linear time series models. Some importance is attached to bilinear models, the simplest of which is

$$y_t = \varphi y_{t-1} + \theta \varepsilon_{t-1} + \beta \varepsilon_{t-1} y_{t-1} + \varepsilon_t, \quad t=1,\ldots,T \tag{3.7.2}$$

where $\varepsilon_t \sim \text{NID}(0, \sigma^2)$ and φ, θ and β are unknown parameters. This model could be put in SSF, for example as

$$y_t = [1 \quad 0]\boldsymbol{\alpha}_t \tag{3.7.3a}$$

$$\boldsymbol{\alpha}_t = \begin{bmatrix} y_t \\ \varepsilon_t \end{bmatrix} = \begin{bmatrix} \varphi & \theta + \beta y_{t-1} \\ 0 & 0 \end{bmatrix} \begin{bmatrix} y_{t-1} \\ \varepsilon_{t-1} \end{bmatrix} + \begin{bmatrix} 1 \\ 1 \end{bmatrix} \varepsilon_t \tag{3.7.3b}$$

However, if y_0 is a given fixed number and ε_0 is zero, the one-step-ahead prediction errors, v_t, are equal to the disturbances, ε_t, and may be obtained directly from the recursion

$$v_t = y_t - \varphi y_{t-1} - \beta v_{t-1} y_{t-1} - \theta v_{t-1}, \quad t=1,\ldots T$$

The ML estimators of φ, θ and β are then obtained by minimising the sum of squares function

$$S(\varphi, \theta, \beta) = \sum_{t=1}^{T} v_t^2$$

Example 3.7.2 In the *autoregressive conditional heteroscedasticity* model introduced by Engle (1982a), there is a single disturbance term, ε_t. The non-linearity stems from the variance of this disturbance term. As a simple example, suppose that

$$y_t = \varphi y_{t-1} + \varepsilon_t, \quad \varepsilon_t | Y_{t-1} \sim \text{N}(0, \sigma_t^2) \tag{3.7.4a}$$

$$\sigma_t^2 = \alpha_0 + \alpha_1 \varepsilon_{t-1}^2 \tag{3.7.4b}$$

where α_0 and α_1 are unknown parameters, as is φ. If α_1 were equal to zero, the model would be the conventional AR(1) model, but the effect of (3.7.4b) is to make the variance of the disturbance terms at time t dependent on the realised value of the disturbance term in the previous period. If y_0 is fixed and known and ε_0 is zero, the likelihood function for this conditionally Gaussian model is again obtained by noting that $v_t = \varepsilon_t$ and writing

$$\log L = -\frac{T}{2}\log 2\pi - \frac{1}{2}\sum_{t=1}^{T}\log(\alpha_0 + \alpha_1 v_{t-1}^2) - \frac{1}{2}\sum_{t=1}^{T}\frac{(y_t - \varphi y_{t-1})^2}{\alpha_0 + \alpha_1 v_{t-1}^2} \tag{3.7.5}$$

where $v_t = y_t - \varphi y_{t-1}, t = 1, \ldots, T$.

Example 3.7.3 Allowing the system matrices to depend on past observations enables expectations of unobservables to be introduced into a model. Consider the model

$$y_t = \alpha_t + \varepsilon_t, \quad \varepsilon_t \sim \text{NID}(0, \sigma_\varepsilon^2) \tag{3.7.6a}$$

$$\alpha_t = \varphi\alpha_{t-1} + \gamma \underset{t-1}{\text{E}}(\alpha_t) + \eta_t, \quad \eta_t \sim \text{NID}(0, \sigma_\eta^2) \tag{3.7.6b}$$

where α_t is an unobservable variable, φ and γ are unknown parameters such that $0 < \varphi, \gamma < 1$ and ε_t and η_t are mutually independent. The expectational term in (3.7.6b) is the conditional expectation implied by the model itself. Terms of this kind are of some importance in econometrics, particularly in the context of models involving rational expectations. Applying the conditional expectation operator to both sides of (3.7.6b) gives

$$\underset{t-1}{\text{E}}(\alpha_t) = \varphi \underset{t-1}{\text{E}}(\alpha_{t-1}) + \gamma \underset{t-1}{\text{E}}(\alpha_t)$$

and so

$$\underset{t-1}{\text{E}}(\alpha_t) = \tilde{\alpha}_{t|t-1} = \frac{\varphi}{1-\gamma}\tilde{\alpha}_{t-1}$$

Thus (3.7.6b) is

$$\alpha_t = \varphi\alpha_{t-1} + \frac{\gamma\varphi}{1-\gamma}\tilde{\alpha}_{t-1} + \eta_t$$

Therefore, past information on the observations enters into the model via α_{t-1}. The model is conditionally Gaussian and the likelihood function can be obtained from the prediction error decomposition.

Example 3.7.4 An AR(1) model with a parameter which also follows an AR(1) process may be written as

$$y_t = \varphi_t y_{t-1} + \varepsilon_t, \quad \varepsilon_t \sim \text{NID}(0, \sigma_\varepsilon^2) \tag{3.7.7a}$$

$$\varphi_t = \alpha\varphi_{t-1} + \eta_t, \quad \eta_t \sim \text{NID}(0, \sigma_\eta^2) \tag{3.7.7b}$$

where α is a fixed parameter. The properties of this model are examined in Weiss (1985), where conditions under which y_t has a finite variance are derived. If φ_t is regarded as the state, the model is conditionally Gaussian with $z_t = y_{t-1}$.

The fixed point smoothing algorithm can be applied as described in sub-section 3.6.1 for a conditionally Gaussian model. As regards multi-step prediction, the *predictive* distribution of y_{T+l} for $l>1$ is given by

$$p(y_{T+l}|Y_T) = \int \cdots \int \prod_{j=1}^{l} p(y_{T+j}|Y_{T+j-1}) dy_{T+1} \ldots dy_{T+l-1} \tag{3.7.8}$$

This expression follows by observing that the joint distribution of the future observations may be written in terms of conditional distributions, in a similar way to (3.4.2), that is

$$p(y_{T+l}, y_{T+l-1}, \ldots, y_{T+1}|Y_T) = \prod_{j=1}^{l} p(y_{T+j}|Y_{T+j-1})$$

The predictive distribution of y_{T+l} is then obtained as a marginal distribution by integrating out y_{T+1} to y_{T+l-1}.

The predictive distribution of y_{T+l} will not usually be normal for $l>1$. Furthermore it is not, in general, straightforward to determine the form of the distribution from (3.7.8). Evaluating conditional moments tends to be easier, though whether it is a feasible proposition depends on the way in which past observations enter into the system matrices. At the least one would hope to be able to evaluate the conditional expectations of future observations thereby obtaining the MMSEs of these observations.

Evaluation of the conditional moments of the predictive distribution of y_{T+l} is effected by repeated application of the conditional expectation operator. Consider the expectation of some function $g(y_{T+l})$ and suppose, for simplicity, that $l=2$. Using (3.7.8) and interchanging the order of integration, the required quantity is

$$\begin{aligned}
\underset{T}{\mathrm{E}}[g(y_{T+2})] = \mathrm{E}[g(y_{T+2}|Y_T)] &= \int g(y_{T+2}) p(y_{T+2}|Y_T) dy_{T+2} \\
&= \int \left[\int g(y_{T+2}) p(y_{T+2}|y_{T+1}, Y_T) dy_{T+2} \right] p(y_{T+1}|Y_T) dy_{T+1} \\
&= \int \underset{T+1}{\mathrm{E}} [g(y_{T+2})]\, p(y_{T+1}|Y_T) dy_{T+1} = \underset{T}{\mathrm{E}} \left\{ \underset{T+1}{\mathrm{E}} [g(y_{T+2})] \right\}
\end{aligned}$$

This argument may be repeated for any lead time, so that in the case of the mean, for example, we have the important result that the MMSE of y_{T+l} is

$$\underset{T}{\mathrm{E}}(y_{T+l}) = \underset{T}{\mathrm{E}}\ \underset{T+1}{\mathrm{E}} \cdots \underset{T+l-1}{\mathrm{E}} (y_{T+l}) \tag{3.7.9}$$

where the expectation operators are applied sequentially starting with the one at $t=T+l-1$. The corresponding prediction MSE is obtained by evaluating the conditional expectation of y_{T+l}^2 in the formula

$$\text{MSE}[\underset{T}{\text{E}}(y_{T+l})]=\text{Var}(y_{T+l}|Y_T)=\underset{T}{\text{E}}(y_{T+l}^2)-[\underset{T}{\text{E}}(y_{T+l})]^2$$

Example 3.7.2 (continued) In the ARCH model of (3.7.4), repeatedly applying the conditional expectation operator gives

$$\underset{T+l-1}{\text{E}}(y_{T+l})=\varphi y_{T+l-1}$$

$$\underset{T+l-2}{\text{E}}\;\underset{T+l-1}{\text{E}}(y_{T+l})=\varphi^2 y_{T+l-2}$$

and so on to yield

$$\underset{T}{\text{E}}(y_{T+l})=\varphi^l y_T \tag{3.7.10}$$

This is exactly the same as the predictor (2.3.12) in the linear Gaussian AR(1) model. Evaluating the MSE is a little more complicated. Only the case in which $\varphi=0$ is considered here; the more general model is left to the reader in Exercise 3.9. With $\varphi=0$, $y_t=\varepsilon_t$, and so

$$\underset{T+l-1}{\text{E}}(y_{T+l}^2)=\alpha_0+\alpha_1 y_{T+l-1}^2$$

On repeating this process and noting that the conditional expectation of y_{T+l} is zero, one obtains

$$\text{MSE}(\tilde{y}_{T+l|T})=\alpha_0(1+\alpha_1+\cdots+\alpha_1^{l-1})+\alpha_1^l y_T^2$$

If the conditional mean cannot be evaluated it may be reasonable to build up predictions recursively from one-step-ahead predictions as in the chain rule (3.5.7). In the case of the ARCH model above, the chain rule predictor is (2.3.12) and this gives the same result as (3.7.9). However, in general, predictors obtained in this way will be sub-optimal.

3.7.2 Extended Kalman filter

Consider the *functionally* non-linear state space model:

$$\mathbf{y}_t=\mathbf{z}_t(\boldsymbol{\alpha}_t)+\boldsymbol{\varepsilon}_t, \tag{3.7.11a}$$

$$\boldsymbol{\alpha}_t=\mathbf{t}_t(\boldsymbol{\alpha}_{t-1})+\mathbf{R}_t(\boldsymbol{\alpha}_{t-1})\boldsymbol{\eta}_t \tag{3.7.11b}$$

where $\mathbf{z}_t(\boldsymbol{\alpha}_t)$ and $\mathbf{t}_t(\boldsymbol{\alpha}_{t-1})$ denote $N\times 1$ and $m\times 1$ vectors respectively, and $\mathbf{R}_t(\boldsymbol{\alpha}_{t-1})$ is an $m\times g$ matrix. The elements of $\mathbf{z}_t(\boldsymbol{\alpha}_t)$ and $\mathbf{t}_t(\boldsymbol{\alpha}_{t-1})$ are no longer necessarily linear functions of the elements of the state vector, as in (3.1.1a). Furthermore

$\mathbf{R}_t(\boldsymbol{\alpha}_{t-1})$ may depend on the state vector whereas $\mathbf{R}_t$ in (3.1.3a) does not.

Even under the assumption that $\boldsymbol{\varepsilon}_t$ and $\boldsymbol{\eta}_t$ are normally distributed, obtaining an optimal filter for a model of this kind is not, in general, possible. However, an approximate filter can be obtained by linearising the model and then applying a modification of the usual Kalman filter. If the non-linear functions $\mathbf{z}_t(\boldsymbol{\alpha}_t)$, $\mathbf{t}_t(\boldsymbol{\alpha}_{t-1})$ and $\mathbf{R}_t(\boldsymbol{\alpha}_{t-1})$ are sufficiently smooth, they can be expanded in Taylor series around conditional means, $\hat{\mathbf{a}}_{t|t-1}$ and $\hat{\mathbf{a}}_{t-1}$, to give

$$\mathbf{z}_t(\boldsymbol{\alpha}_t) \simeq \mathbf{z}_t(\hat{\mathbf{a}}_{t|t-1}) + \hat{\mathbf{Z}}_t(\boldsymbol{\alpha}_t - \hat{\mathbf{a}}_{t|t-1}) \tag{3.7.12a}$$

$$\mathbf{t}_t(\mathbf{a}_{t-1}) \simeq \mathbf{t}_t(\hat{\mathbf{a}}_{t-1}) + \hat{\mathbf{T}}_t(\boldsymbol{\alpha}_{t-1} - \hat{\mathbf{a}}_{t-1}) \tag{3.7.13a}$$

and

$$\mathbf{R}_t(\boldsymbol{\alpha}_{t-1}) \simeq \hat{\mathbf{R}}_t \tag{3.7.14a}$$

where

$$\hat{\mathbf{Z}}_t = \left. \frac{\partial \mathbf{z}_t(\boldsymbol{\alpha}_t)}{\partial \boldsymbol{\alpha}'_{t-1}} \right|_{\boldsymbol{\alpha}_t = \hat{\mathbf{a}}_{t|t-1}} \tag{3.7.12b}$$

$$\hat{\mathbf{T}}_t = \left. \frac{\partial \mathbf{t}_t(\boldsymbol{\alpha}_{t-1})}{\partial \boldsymbol{\alpha}'_{t-1}} \right|_{\boldsymbol{\alpha}_{t-1} = \hat{\mathbf{a}}_{t-1}} \tag{3.7.13b}$$

and

$$\hat{\mathbf{R}}_t = \mathbf{R}_t(\hat{\mathbf{a}}_{t-1}) \tag{3.7.14b}$$

Substituting (3.7.12) to (3.7.14) in (3.2.3) and assuming knowledge of $\hat{\mathbf{a}}_{t|t-1}$ and $\hat{\mathbf{a}}_{t-1}$ leads us to approximate the original non-linear model by

$$\mathbf{y}_t \simeq \hat{\mathbf{Z}}_t \boldsymbol{\alpha}_t + \hat{\mathbf{d}}_t + \boldsymbol{\varepsilon}_t \tag{3.7.15a}$$

$$\boldsymbol{\alpha}_t \simeq \hat{\mathbf{T}}_t \boldsymbol{\alpha}_{t-1} + \hat{\mathbf{c}}_t + \hat{\mathbf{R}}_t \boldsymbol{\eta}_t \tag{3.7.15b}$$

where $\hat{\mathbf{d}}_t$ and $\hat{\mathbf{c}}_t$ are defined by

$$\hat{\mathbf{d}}_t = \mathbf{z}_t(\hat{\mathbf{a}}_{t|t-1}) - \hat{\mathbf{Z}}_t \hat{\mathbf{a}}_{t|t-1} \tag{3.7.15c}$$

and

$$\hat{\mathbf{c}}_t = \mathbf{t}_t(\hat{\mathbf{a}}_{t-1}) - \hat{\mathbf{T}}_t \hat{\mathbf{a}}_{t-1} \tag{3.7.15d}$$

respectively. The quantities $\hat{\mathbf{a}}_t$ and $\hat{\mathbf{a}}_{t|t-1}$ are calculated by applying the Kalman filter to (3.7.15) with the modification that the state prediction equation (3.2.2a) becomes

$$\hat{\mathbf{a}}_{t|t-1} = \mathbf{t}_t(\hat{\mathbf{a}}_{t-1}) \tag{3.7.16}$$

while the state updating equation (3.2.3a) is

$$\hat{\mathbf{a}}_t = \hat{\mathbf{a}}_{t|t-1} + \mathbf{P}_{t|t-1}\mathbf{Z}'_t\mathbf{F}_t^{-1}[\mathbf{y}_t - \mathbf{z}_t(\hat{\mathbf{a}}_{t|t-1})] \tag{3.7.17}$$

These recursions are known as the extended Kalman filter. Note that $\hat{\mathbf{c}}_t$ and $\hat{\mathbf{d}}_t$ are never actually computed.

Example 3.7.5 The linear approximation to the non-linear model,

$$y_t = \log \alpha_t + \varepsilon_t \tag{3.7.18a}$$

$$\alpha_t = \alpha_{t-1}^2 + \eta_t \tag{3.7.18b}$$

in which α_t is a scalar is

$$y_t \simeq \hat{a}_{t|t-1}^{-1} \alpha_t + [\log \hat{a}_{t|t-1} - 1] + \varepsilon_t \tag{3.7.19a}$$

$$\alpha_t \simeq 2\hat{a}_{t-1}\alpha_{t-1} + [\hat{a}_{t-1}^2 - 2\hat{a}_{t-1}] + \eta_t \tag{3.7.19b}$$

Example 3.7.6 Suppose that the level component in a model is known to lie between zero and one. One way of incorporating a constraint of this kind into a model is by means of a logistic transformation. Thus

$$y_t = 1/[1 + \exp(-\mu_t)] + \varepsilon_t \tag{3.7.20a}$$

$$\mu_t = \mu_{t-1} + \eta_t \tag{3.7.20b}$$

The range $[-\infty, \infty]$ for μ_t translates into a range of $[0, 1]$ for the component

$$z_t(\mu_t) = 1/[1 + \exp(-\mu_t)] \tag{3.7.21}$$

The extended Kalman filter for this problem takes the form of the usual Kalman filter with

$$\hat{Z}_t = \left.\frac{\partial z_t(\mu_t)}{\partial \mu_t}\right|_{\mu_t = \hat{\mu}_{t|t-1}} = \frac{\exp(-\hat{\mu}_{t|t-1})}{[1 + \exp(-\mu_{t|t-1})]^2}$$

and $v_t = y_t - [1 + \exp(-\hat{\mu}_{t|t-1})]^{-1}$.

The above methods can be extended to handle other kinds of non-linearity in the state space model. The quality of the approximations will depend on the degree of non-linearity and the accuracy of $\hat{\mathbf{a}}_{t|t-1}$ and $\mathbf{a}_{t-1}$ as estimators of $\boldsymbol{\alpha}_t$ and $\boldsymbol{\alpha}_{t-1}$ respectively.

Further discussion on the extended Kalman filter and other non-linear filtering techniques, such as Gaussian sum filters, can be found in Anderson and Moore (1979, ch. 8) and Jazwinski (1970).

3.7.3 Non-Gaussian disturbances

The Kalman filter can be generalised so as to provide optimal updating for a system in which the disturbances are no longer normally distributed. Following the derivation of the Kalman filter in section 3.2, the aim is to derive a recursion for $p(\boldsymbol{\alpha}_t|\mathbf{Y}_t)$, the distribution of the state vector conditional on the information at time t. If this can be done, the conditional distribution of $\mathbf{y}_t$ can also be obtained, and so the likelihood function may be constructed via the prediction error decomposition. Minimum mean square estimates of the state and future observations can be obtained by computing the means of the appropriate conditional distributions.

The system is as written in (3.1.1a) and (3.1.3a) with the disturbances $\boldsymbol{\varepsilon}_t$ and $\boldsymbol{\eta}_t$ being mutually and serially independent with p.d.f.'s of known form. The initial state vector has a p.d.f. $p(\boldsymbol{\alpha}_0)$. It will be assumed that the series is univariate, although the same general principles apply in the multivariate case.

The distribution of $\boldsymbol{\alpha}_t$ conditional on Y_{t-1} is given by

$$p(\boldsymbol{\alpha}_t|Y_{t-1})=\int_{-\infty}^{\infty} p(\boldsymbol{\alpha}_t, \boldsymbol{\alpha}_{t-1}|Y_{t-1})\, d\boldsymbol{\alpha}_{t-1}$$

but by the definition of a conditional p.d.f. the right-hand side may be rearranged to give

$$p(\boldsymbol{\alpha}_t|Y_{t-1})=\int_{-\infty}^{\infty} p(\boldsymbol{\alpha}_t|\boldsymbol{\alpha}_{t-1})p(\boldsymbol{\alpha}_{t-1}|Y_{t-1})\, d\boldsymbol{\alpha}_{t-1} \qquad (3.7.22)$$

The conditional distribution $p(\boldsymbol{\alpha}_t|\boldsymbol{\alpha}_{t-1})$ can be obtained directly from the assumed distribution of $\boldsymbol{\eta}_t$. Therefore $p(\boldsymbol{\alpha}_t|Y_{t-1})$ may, in principle, be obtained from $p(\boldsymbol{\alpha}_{t-1}|Y_{t-1})$. In the case of a Gaussian model these conditional distributions are characterised by their first two moments and the operation implied by (3.7.22) may be carried out by means of the prediction equations (3.2.2).

As regards updating, we have, by definition,

$$p(\boldsymbol{\alpha}_t|Y_t)=p(\boldsymbol{\alpha}_t|y_t, Y_{t-1}) \qquad (3.7.23)$$

By manipulations similar to those involved in deriving Bayes' theorem,

$$\begin{aligned} p(\boldsymbol{\alpha}_t|Y_t)&=p(\boldsymbol{\alpha}_t, y_t|Y_{t-1})/p(y_t|Y_{t-1}) \\ &=p(y_t|\boldsymbol{\alpha}_t)p(\boldsymbol{\alpha}_t|Y_{t-1})/p(y_t|Y_{t-1}) \qquad (3.7.24a)\end{aligned}$$

where

$$p(y_t|Y_{t-1})=\int_{-\infty}^{\infty} p(y_t|\boldsymbol{\alpha}_t)p(\boldsymbol{\alpha}_t|Y_{t-1})d\boldsymbol{\alpha}_t \qquad (3.7.24b)$$

and $p(y_t|\boldsymbol{\alpha}_t)$ is given from the assumed distribution of the measurement equation disturbance term, ε_t. In the Gaussian case, (3.7.24) implies the Kalman filter updating equations (3.2.3).

The likelihood function is given directly by the prediction error decomposition (3.4.2), the p.d.f.'s of the one-step-ahead prediction errors being obtained from (3.7.24b). As regards prediction and smoothing, the former is effected by repeated application of (3.7.22) to give $p(\boldsymbol{\alpha}_{T+l}|Y_T)$. The conditional distribution of y_{T+l} is then obtained by evaluating an expression similar to (3.7.24b), namely

$$p(y_{T+l}|Y_T)=\int_{-\infty}^{\infty} p(y_{T+l}|\boldsymbol{\alpha}_{T+l})p(\boldsymbol{\alpha}_{T+l}|Y_T)\,d\boldsymbol{\alpha}_{T+l} \tag{3.7.25}$$

Alternatively, this distribution may be obtained from (3.7.8); which is the easier route depends on the nature of the particular problem.

Smoothing is carried out by first noting that

$$\begin{aligned}p(\boldsymbol{\alpha}_t,\boldsymbol{\alpha}_{t+1}|Y_T)&=p(\boldsymbol{\alpha}_{t+1}|Y_T)p(\boldsymbol{\alpha}_t|\boldsymbol{\alpha}_{t+1},Y_T)\\&=p(\boldsymbol{\alpha}_{t+1}|Y_T)p(\boldsymbol{\alpha}_t|\boldsymbol{\alpha}_{t+1},Y_t)\\&=p(\boldsymbol{\alpha}_{t+1}|Y_T)p(\boldsymbol{\alpha}_t,\boldsymbol{\alpha}_{t+1}|Y_t)/p(\boldsymbol{\alpha}_{t+1}|Y_t)\\&=p(\boldsymbol{\alpha}_{t+1}|Y_T)p(\boldsymbol{\alpha}_{t+1}|\boldsymbol{\alpha}_t)p(\boldsymbol{\alpha}_t|Y_t)/p(\boldsymbol{\alpha}_{t+1}|Y_t)\end{aligned}$$

The formula for smoothing is therefore

$$\begin{aligned}p(\boldsymbol{\alpha}_t|Y_T)&=\int_{-\infty}^{\infty} p(\boldsymbol{\alpha}_t,\boldsymbol{\alpha}_{t+1}|Y_T)\,d\boldsymbol{\alpha}_{t+1}\\&=p(\boldsymbol{\alpha}_t|Y_t)\int_{-\infty}^{\infty}[p(\boldsymbol{\alpha}_{t+1}|Y_T)p(\boldsymbol{\alpha}_{t+1}|\boldsymbol{\alpha}_t)/p(\boldsymbol{\alpha}_{t+1}|Y_t)]\,d\boldsymbol{\alpha}_{t+1}\end{aligned} \tag{3.7.26}$$

In the Gaussian case, this is equivalent to the fixed-interval smoothing algorithm.

Point estimates may be obtained from the relevant conditional distributions. The conditional means obtained in this way are minimum mean square estimates. Thus the conditional mean of the future observation y_{T+l} is given by

$$\mathrm{E}(y_{T+l}|Y_T)=\underset{t}{\mathrm{E}}(y_{T+l})=\int_{-\infty}^{\infty} y_{T+l}\,p(y_{T+l}|Y_T)\,dy_{T+l} \tag{3.7.27}$$

where $p(y_{T+l})$ is given by (3.7.25). Alternatively, we can proceed as in section 3.5 to obtain

$$\mathrm{E}(y_{T+l}|Y_T)=\mathbf{z}'_{T+l}\mathrm{E}(\boldsymbol{\alpha}_{T+l}|Y_T)=\mathbf{z}'_{T+l}\mathbf{T}^l\mathrm{E}(\boldsymbol{\alpha}_T|Y_T) \tag{3.7.28}$$

This formula requires that $\mathrm{E}(\boldsymbol{\alpha}_T|Y_T)$ be evaluated; compare (3.7.27). Once this has been done, computation of the MMSE of y_{T+l} can be carried out for any value of l just as in the Gaussian case. The covariance matrices associated with conditional mean estimates may, in principle, be computed in a similar way.

Other point estimates may be constructed. In particular the maximum *a posteriori* estimate is the mode of the relevant conditional distribution. However, once we move away from normality, there is a case for expressing forecasts in terms of the whole of the predictive distribution.

The problem with the above filtering and smoothing expressions is that they may be difficult to solve analytically. The Gaussian case is an obvious exception and tractable solutions are possible in a number of other cases. Some examples are given in section 6.6 when methods for *Poisson* and *binomially* distributed observations are developed. However, in these cases a slightly different set-up is used insofar as $p(\boldsymbol{\alpha}_t|\boldsymbol{\alpha}_{t-1})$ is defined implicitly rather than explicitly. Furthermore the models are limited to those which are essentially of the local level variety.

Where an analytic solution is not available, Kitagawa (1987) has suggested using numerical methods to evaluate the various densities. The main drawback with this approach is the computational requirement. This is considerable if a reasonable degree of accuracy is to be achieved.

Appendix. Properties of the multivariate normal distribution

Lemma *Let the pair of vectors* **x** *and* **y** *be jointly multivariate normal such that* $(\mathbf{x}', \mathbf{y}')'$ *has mean and covariance matrix given by*

$$\boldsymbol{\mu} = \begin{bmatrix} \boldsymbol{\mu}_x \\ \boldsymbol{\mu}_y \end{bmatrix} \quad \text{and} \quad \boldsymbol{\Sigma} = \begin{bmatrix} \boldsymbol{\Sigma}_{xx} & \boldsymbol{\Sigma}_{xy} \\ \boldsymbol{\Sigma}_{yx} & \boldsymbol{\Sigma}_{yy} \end{bmatrix}$$

respectively. Then the distribution of **x** *conditional on* **y** *is also multivariate normal with mean*

$$\boldsymbol{\mu}_{x|y} = \boldsymbol{\mu}_x + \boldsymbol{\Sigma}_{xy}\boldsymbol{\Sigma}_{yy}^{-1}(\mathbf{y} - \boldsymbol{\mu}_y) \tag{3.A.1}$$

and covariance matrix

$$\boldsymbol{\Sigma}_{xx|y} = \boldsymbol{\Sigma}_{xx} - \boldsymbol{\Sigma}_{xy}\boldsymbol{\Sigma}_{yy}^{-1}\boldsymbol{\Sigma}_{yx} \tag{3.A.2}$$

Note that (3.A.2) *does not depend on* **y**. *Note also that* $\boldsymbol{\Sigma}$ *and* $\boldsymbol{\Sigma}_{yy}$ *are assumed to be non-singular, although in fact* $\boldsymbol{\Sigma}_{yy}^{-1}$ *can be replaced by a pseudo inverse.*

The proof of the above lemma is as follows. The joint density of $(\mathbf{x}', \mathbf{y}')'$ is

$$p(\mathbf{x}, \mathbf{y}) = \frac{1}{(2\pi)^{(M+N)/2}|\boldsymbol{\Sigma}|^{\frac{1}{2}}} \exp[-\tfrac{1}{2}(\mathbf{x}' - \boldsymbol{\mu}_x', \mathbf{y}' - \boldsymbol{\mu}_y')\boldsymbol{\Sigma}^{-1}(\mathbf{x} - \boldsymbol{\mu}_x, \mathbf{y} - \boldsymbol{\mu}_y)] \tag{3.A.3}$$

where M and N are the lengths of **x** and **y** respectively. The density of **x** conditional on **y** is therefore

$$\begin{aligned} p(\mathbf{x}|\mathbf{y}) &= \frac{p(\mathbf{x}, \mathbf{y})}{p(\mathbf{y})} \\ &= \frac{1}{(2\pi)^{N/2}} \frac{|\boldsymbol{\Sigma}_{yy}|^{\frac{1}{2}}}{|\boldsymbol{\Sigma}|^{\frac{1}{2}}} \frac{\exp[-\frac{1}{2}(\mathbf{x}' - \boldsymbol{\mu}_x', \mathbf{y}' - \boldsymbol{\mu}_y')\boldsymbol{\Sigma}^{-1}(\mathbf{x} - \boldsymbol{\mu}_x, \mathbf{y} - \boldsymbol{\mu}_y)]}{\exp[-\frac{1}{2}(\mathbf{y}' - \boldsymbol{\mu}_y')\boldsymbol{\Sigma}_{yy}^{-1}(\mathbf{y} - \boldsymbol{\mu}_y)]} \end{aligned}$$

The following formula, which can be easily checked, is used to rewrite $p(\mathbf{x}|\mathbf{y})$:

$$\begin{bmatrix} \mathbf{I} & -\boldsymbol{\Sigma}_{xy}\boldsymbol{\Sigma}_{yy}^{-1} \\ \mathbf{0} & \mathbf{I} \end{bmatrix} \boldsymbol{\Sigma} \begin{bmatrix} \mathbf{I} & \mathbf{0} \\ -\boldsymbol{\Sigma}_{yy}^{-1}\boldsymbol{\Sigma}_{xy}' & \mathbf{I} \end{bmatrix} = \begin{bmatrix} \boldsymbol{\Sigma}_{xx} - \boldsymbol{\Sigma}_{xy}\boldsymbol{\Sigma}_{yy}^{-1}\boldsymbol{\Sigma}_{yx} & \mathbf{0} \\ \mathbf{0} & \boldsymbol{\Sigma}_{yy} \end{bmatrix}$$

First, on taking determinants and recalling that the determinant of the product of two non-singular matrices is the product of the determinants, we have

$$|\boldsymbol{\Sigma}| = |\boldsymbol{\Sigma}_{xx} - \boldsymbol{\Sigma}_{xy}\boldsymbol{\Sigma}_{yy}^{-1}\boldsymbol{\Sigma}_{yx}||\boldsymbol{\Sigma}_{yy}| \tag{3.A.4}$$

Secondly,

$$\boldsymbol{\Sigma}^{-1} = \begin{bmatrix} \mathbf{I} & \mathbf{0} \\ -\boldsymbol{\Sigma}_{yy}^{-1}\boldsymbol{\Sigma}_{xy}' & \mathbf{I} \end{bmatrix} \begin{bmatrix} (\boldsymbol{\Sigma}_{xx} - \boldsymbol{\Sigma}_{xy}\boldsymbol{\Sigma}_{yy}^{-1}\boldsymbol{\Sigma}_{yx})^{-1} & \mathbf{0} \\ \mathbf{0} & \boldsymbol{\Sigma}_{yy}^{-1} \end{bmatrix} \begin{bmatrix} \mathbf{I} & -\boldsymbol{\Sigma}_{xy}\boldsymbol{\Sigma}_{yy}^{-1} \\ \mathbf{0} & \mathbf{I} \end{bmatrix}$$

and substituting for $\boldsymbol{\Sigma}^{-1}$ in

$$(\mathbf{x}' - \boldsymbol{\mu}_x', \mathbf{y}' - \boldsymbol{\mu}_y')\boldsymbol{\Sigma}^{-1}(\mathbf{x} - \boldsymbol{\mu}_x, \mathbf{y} - \boldsymbol{\mu}_y)$$

yields

$$(\mathbf{x}' - \boldsymbol{\mu}_{x|y}')(\boldsymbol{\Sigma}_{xx} - \boldsymbol{\Sigma}_{xy}\boldsymbol{\Sigma}_{yy}^{-1}\boldsymbol{\Sigma}_{yx})^{-1}(\mathbf{x} - \boldsymbol{\mu}_{x|y}) + (\mathbf{y}' - \boldsymbol{\mu}_y')\boldsymbol{\Sigma}_{yy}^{-1}(\mathbf{y} - \boldsymbol{\mu}_y)$$

where $\boldsymbol{\mu}_{x|y}$ is defined as in (3.A.1). Thus

$$p(\mathbf{x}|\mathbf{y}) = \frac{1}{(2\pi)^{M/2}|\boldsymbol{\Sigma}_{xx} - \boldsymbol{\Sigma}_{xy}\boldsymbol{\Sigma}_{yy}^{-1}\boldsymbol{\Sigma}_{yx}|} \exp[-\tfrac{1}{2}(\mathbf{x} - \boldsymbol{\mu}_{x|y})' \times (\boldsymbol{\Sigma}_{xx} - \boldsymbol{\Sigma}_{xy}\boldsymbol{\Sigma}_{yy}^{-1}\boldsymbol{\Sigma}_{yx})^{-1}(\mathbf{x} - \boldsymbol{\mu}_{x|y})]$$

EXERCISES

3.1 Consider the following state space model

$$y_t = [1 \quad 1]\boldsymbol{\alpha}_t + \varepsilon_t, \quad \mathrm{Var}(\varepsilon_t) = \sigma_\varepsilon^2$$

$$\boldsymbol{\alpha}_t = \begin{bmatrix} \varphi_1 & 0 \\ 0 & \varphi_2 \end{bmatrix} \boldsymbol{\alpha}_{t-1} + \begin{bmatrix} 1 \\ 0 \end{bmatrix} \eta_t, \quad \mathrm{Var}(\eta_t) = \sigma_\eta^2$$

where $\sigma_\varepsilon^2 > 0, \sigma_\eta^2 > 0$ and the 2×1 state vector $\boldsymbol{\alpha}_t$ is stationary. Is the model (a) controllable; (b) stabilisable; (c) observable and (d) detectable?

What do your answers to these questions imply about the existence of a steady-state solution to the Kalman filter?

3.2 Repeat Exercise 3.1 with (i) $\varphi_1 = 1$ and $|\varphi_2| < 1$; and (ii) $\varphi_1 = \varphi_2 = 1$.

3.3 Consider the random walk plus noise model as set out in Example 3.1.1. If q is known, show that the ML estimator of σ_ε^2 is unbiased if μ_0 is taken to be random with a diffuse prior, but biased if it is taken to be fixed. Comment briefly on the implications of this result in the case of $q = 0$.

3.4 Consider a stationary AR(1) process

$$y_t = \varphi y_{t-1} + \varepsilon_t, \quad |\varphi| < 1$$

with $\varepsilon_t \sim \mathrm{NID}(0, \sigma^2)$ which is observed from $t = 1$ to T. Write down the exact likelihood function. Compare this with the likelihood function obtained if (i) a diffuse prior is adopted for y_0; (ii) y_0 is taken to be fixed; (iii) y_1 is taken to be fixed.

3.5 Suppose that T observations are made on an AR(1) process every other time period, i.e. at $t=2, 4, 6, \ldots, 2T$. Write down the likelihood function on the assumption that the first observation is fixed and evaluate the covariance matrix of the ML estimators of φ and σ^2. Compare the form of this covariance matrix with that of the covariance matrix of the ML estimator of φ and σ^2 obtained from T consecutive observations.

3.6 Write down the likelihood functions of $y_2, \ldots, y_T$ for the following non-linear time series models, assuming, in all cases, that y_1 is fixed and $\varepsilon_t \sim \text{NID}(0, \sigma^2)$:

(i) $y_t = \varphi y_{t-1}^2 + \varepsilon_t$
(ii) $\log y_t = \varphi y_{t-1} + \varepsilon_t$
(iii) $y_t = \varphi y_{t-1} + \upsilon_t$

where $\upsilon_t = \varepsilon_t h_t^{\frac{1}{2}}$ and $h_t = \alpha_0 + \alpha_1 y_{t-1}^2 + \gamma \upsilon_{t-1}^2$.

3.7 Consider the AR(1) model with a missing observation at $t=m$ introduced in Example 3.4.2. Show that, for a given value of φ, the fixed point smoother gives the estimator (3.6.18).

3.8 Show that an MA(q) model is observable provided that $\theta_q \neq 0$. Show that it is stabilisable if the roots of the polynomial $\theta(L)$ of (2.4.18b) lie outside the unit circle. What can be said about convergence to a steady state for a model which is strictly non-invertible?

3.9 For the ARCH model (3.7.4), evaluate the MSE of the MMSE estimator of y_{T+l} given in (3.7.10) for $l=2$.

Chapter 4

Estimation, prediction and smoothing for univariate structural time series models

The general properties of state space models were set out in chapter 3. The opening section of this chapter shows how the structural models introduced in section 2.3 can be put in state space form. The state space form provides the key to the statistical treatment of structural models. It enables ML estimators of the unknown parameters in a Gaussian model to be computed via the Kalman filter and the prediction error decomposition. Once estimates of these parameters have been obtained, it provides algorithms for prediction of future observations and estimation of the unobserved components.

Section 4.2 describes various ways in which the unknown parameters in structural models can be estimated in the time domain. Estimation can also be carried out in the frequency domain. This latter approach has a number of attractions and is described in detail in section 4.3. (Note that even if frequency-domain methods are used for ML estimation, the state space form is still needed for prediction and estimation of the unobserved components.) Frequency-domain methods are also important in determining the asymptotic properties of ML estimators. Both asymptotic and small sample properties of estimators for structural models are considered in section 4.5. The preceding material, in section 4.4, is primarily to assure the reader that the models under consideration are identifiable. Finally, sections 4.6 and 4.7 discuss various aspects of prediction and the estimation of unobserved components.

4.1 Application of the Kalman filter

4.1.1 State space form

All linear univariate structural models have a state space representation of the form

$$y_t = \mathbf{z}_t'\boldsymbol{\alpha}_t + \varepsilon_t, \quad \text{Var}(\varepsilon_t) = h_t \tag{4.1.1a}$$

$$\boldsymbol{\alpha}_t = \mathbf{T}_t\boldsymbol{\alpha}_{t-1} + \mathbf{R}_t\boldsymbol{\eta}_t, \quad \text{Var}(\boldsymbol{\eta}_t) = \mathbf{Q}_t \tag{4.1.1b}$$

When the model contains M distinct components, the state vector can be partitioned as $\boldsymbol{\alpha}_t = [\boldsymbol{\alpha}_{1t}' \quad \boldsymbol{\alpha}_{2t}' \ \dots \ \boldsymbol{\alpha}_{Mt}']'$; compare the UCARIMA form of (2.5.27). As a rule the matrices $\mathbf{T}_t$ and $\mathbf{R}_t\mathbf{Q}_t\mathbf{R}_t'$ in the transition equation will have a corresponding block diagonal structure, and so

$$y_t = \sum_{m=1}^{M} \mathbf{z}'_{mt}\boldsymbol{\alpha}_{mt} + \varepsilon_t, \quad \text{Var}(\varepsilon_t) = h_t \tag{4.1.2a}$$

$$\boldsymbol{\alpha}_{mt} = \mathbf{T}_{mt}\boldsymbol{\alpha}_{m,t-1} + \mathbf{R}_{mt}\boldsymbol{\eta}_{mt}, \quad \text{Var}(\boldsymbol{\eta}_{mt}) = \mathbf{Q}_{mt}, \quad m = 1, \ldots, M \tag{4.1.2b}$$

with $\text{E}(\boldsymbol{\eta}_{mt}\boldsymbol{\eta}'_{ht}) = \mathbf{0}$ for $m \neq h, \quad m, h = 1, \ldots, M$.

The model is *time-invariant* (or *time-homogeneous*) if the subscripts on $\mathbf{z}_t, \mathbf{T}_t, \mathbf{R}_t, \mathbf{h}_t$ and $\mathbf{Q}_t$ can be dropped. Then (4.1.1) becomes

$$y_t = \mathbf{z}'\boldsymbol{\alpha}_t + \varepsilon_t, \quad \text{Var}(\varepsilon_t) = h \tag{4.1.3a}$$

$$\boldsymbol{\alpha}_t = \mathbf{T}\boldsymbol{\alpha}_{t-1} + \mathbf{R}\boldsymbol{\eta}_t, \quad \text{Var}(\boldsymbol{\eta}_t) = \mathbf{Q} \tag{4.1.3b}$$

The corresponding matrices in (4.1.2) are also without subscripts. A necessary and sufficient condition for the model as a whole to be observable and controllable (and detectable and stabilisable) is that each of the M time-invariant sub-models

$$y_t = \mathbf{z}'_m\boldsymbol{\alpha}_{mt} + \varepsilon_t, \quad \text{Var}(\varepsilon_t) = h \tag{4.1.4a}$$

$$\boldsymbol{\alpha}_{mt} = \mathbf{T}_m\boldsymbol{\alpha}_{m,t-1} + \mathbf{R}_m\boldsymbol{\eta}_{mt}, \quad \text{Var}(\boldsymbol{\eta}_{mt}) = \mathbf{Q}_m \tag{4.1.4b}$$

should have these properties.

All the principal structural models have a time-invariant state space form. The exceptions are models containing a daily component; such a component requires $\mathbf{z}_t$ to change with time.

Once a model has been put in state space form, the Kalman filter can be applied. In the absence of any genuine prior information on non-stationary components, such as trends and seasonals, the initial conditions for such components are normally given by a diffuse prior; see sub-section 3.3.4. The initial conditions for stationary components are taken to be the mean and covariance matrix of the unconditional distribution. The question regarding the convergence of the filter to a steady state can be answered by relating the properties of the SSF to the results given in section 3.3.

Under the normality assumption, the Kalman filter gives the mean and covariance matrix of the state vector, conditional on the information available at that particular point in time. This could be regarded as Bayesian. However, since the state vector is stochastic, this is also quite legitimate as a classical interpretation. The classical framework also enables the conditional mean of the state vector to be interpreted as the MMSE of the state; recall the discussion in sub-section 3.2.3. If there are no unknown hyperparameters in the model, there is no conflict between a classical and a Bayesian approach except insofar as the Bayesian might insist on a proper prior for the initial state vector.

It was pointed out in section 3.1 that the state space form is not unique. However, in a structural time series model, components such as the trend have a direct interpretation and we therefore want them to appear in the state vector.

Because the model is formulated in terms of unobserved components with a direct interpretation, non-uniqueness of the state space form is not an issue.

Local linear trend The local linear trend model is

$$y_t = \mu_t + \varepsilon_t, \quad t=1,\dots,T \tag{4.1.5}$$

$$\mu_t = \mu_{t-1} + \beta_{t-1} + \eta_t \tag{4.1.6a}$$

$$\beta_t = \beta_{t-1} + \zeta_t \tag{4.1.6b}$$

where ε_t, η_t and ζ_t are mutually uncorrelated white-noise disturbances with variances $\sigma_\varepsilon^2, \sigma_\eta^2$ and σ_ζ^2 respectively. It is effectively in state space form as it stands with $\boldsymbol{\alpha}_t = [\mu_t \quad \beta_t]'$. In Example 3.3.2 it was shown that the model is always observable, but is only controllable and stabilisable if σ_ζ^2 is strictly positive. Thus if $\sigma_\zeta^2 > 0$ it follows from Result 3.3.2 that the Kalman filter converges to a steady state and does so exponentially fast. The question of whether or not σ_η^2 is zero is irrelevant. The steady-state solution is derived in the next sub-section.

When $\sigma_\zeta^2 = 0$, convergence to the steady state does not take place exponentially fast, and $\bar{\mathbf{P}}$ is not p.d. The slope component in this case is *deterministic*. One of the attractions of the Kalman filter is that it can handle deterministic components. However, since $\bar{\mathbf{P}}$ is not p.d. a switch to the steady-state filter should not be made. An alternative way of handling the deterministic slope is to drop it from the state vector and to write the model as

$$y_t = \mu_t + \varepsilon_t \tag{4.1.7a}$$

$$\mu_t = \mu_{t-1} + \beta + \eta_t \tag{4.1.7b}$$

in which case the trend is seen as a random walk plus drift or, following (3.1.18), as

$$y_t = \mu_t^* + \beta t + \varepsilon_t \tag{4.1.8a}$$

$$\mu_t^* = \mu_{t-1}^* + \eta_t \tag{4.1.8b}$$

where μ_t^* is interpreted as a stochastic level. Either way, the Kalman filter is basically the one appropriate for the local level model, and σ_η^2 must be strictly positive if it is to converge to a steady state exponentially fast.

The local linear trend model preferred by Harrison and Stevens (1976) is slightly different to (4.1.6) in that it is the current value of the slope which appears in the level equation. Thus equation (4.1.6a) is replaced by

$$\mu_t = \mu_{t-1} + \beta_t + \eta_t^* \tag*{(4.1.6a)$'$}$$

where η_t^* is a white-noise disturbance term with mean zero and variance $\sigma_{\eta^*}^2$ which is uncorrelated with ζ_t. In order to put the model in state space form it is necessary to first substitute from (4.1.6b) to give

$$\mu_t = \mu_{t-1} + \beta_{t-1} + (\eta_t^* + \zeta_t)$$

The transition equations are now exactly as in (4.1.6) except that η_t is equal to

$\eta_t^* + \zeta_t$ and so is correlated with the disturbance in the slope equation, that is

$$\mathrm{Var}\begin{bmatrix}\eta_t\\ \zeta_t\end{bmatrix}=\begin{bmatrix}\sigma_{\eta^*}^2+\sigma_\zeta^2 & \sigma_\zeta^2\\ \sigma_\zeta^2 & \sigma_\zeta^2\end{bmatrix} \tag{4.1.9}$$

Is the difference between (4.1.6a) and (4.1.6a)′ important? In order to answer this question, consider the unobserved component form of the model containing (4.1.6a)′. This is

$$y_t=\frac{\eta_t^*}{\Delta}+\frac{\zeta_t}{\Delta^2}+\varepsilon_t \tag{4.1.10}$$

The only formal difference between (4.1.10) and (2.3.59) is that the latter contains ζ_{t-1} whereas the former contains ζ_t. Thus the reduced forms of the two models are identical, with the parameters σ_η^2 and $\sigma_{\eta^*}^2$ playing exactly the same role. Furthermore since the forecast functions for the two models are identical, the estimators of the level and the slope are the same. The only difference that arises is in the MSE matrices, $\mathbf{P}_t$ and $\mathbf{P}_{t|t-1}$, where the MSEs of b_t and $b_{t|t-1}$ from (4.1.6a) each exceed the corresponding MSEs from (4.1.6a)′ by σ_ζ^2. This is because in (4.1.6a), β_t takes an extra time period to work its way into the μ_t compared with (4.1.6a)′. In terms of (4.1.6a), b_t is the current estimator of the slope looking forward from time t. In contrast, b_{t-1} is the current estimator of the slope looking back and it plays exactly the same role as b_t in (4.1.6a)′. Whether it is more appropriate to measure the MSE of the slope looking forward or backwards is really a matter of taste. A possible compromise is to adopt a continuous time model as described in section 9.2.

Trend plus cycle model The stochastic trend plus cycle model was introduced in (2.3.63). The state space formulation is straightforward. The measurement equation is

$$y_t=[1\quad 0\quad 1\quad 0]\boldsymbol{\alpha}_t+\varepsilon_t,\quad t=1,\ldots,T \tag{4.1.11a}$$

while the transition equation is

$$\boldsymbol{\alpha}_t=\begin{bmatrix}\mu_t\\ \beta_t\\ \cdots\\ \psi_t\\ \psi_t^*\end{bmatrix}=\left[\begin{array}{cc:cc}1 & 1 & \multicolumn{2}{c}{\mathbf{0}}\\ 0 & 1 & & \\ \hline \multicolumn{2}{c:}{\mathbf{0}} & \rho\cos\lambda_c & \rho\sin\lambda_c\\ & & -\rho\sin\lambda_c & \rho\cos\lambda_c\end{array}\right]\begin{bmatrix}\mu_{t-1}\\ \beta_{t-1}\\ \cdots\\ \psi_{t-1}\\ \psi_{t-1}^*\end{bmatrix}+\begin{bmatrix}\eta_t\\ \zeta_t\\ \cdots\\ \kappa_t\\ \kappa_t^*\end{bmatrix} \tag{4.1.11b}$$

The covariance matrix of the vector of disturbances in (4.1.11b) is a diagonal matrix with diagonal elements $\{\sigma_\eta^2, \sigma_\zeta^2, \sigma_\kappa^2, \sigma_\kappa^2\}$.

The model is observable unless ρ is zero or λ_c is zero or π. However, it is always detectable. The condition that σ_κ^2, as well as σ_ζ^2, be strictly positive is necessary for controllability and stabilisability. The implications for steady-state behaviour can be deduced from the discussion surrounding the local linear trend model above.

As regards starting values for the Kalman filter, the stationarity of the cyclical component when ρ is strictly less than unity can be exploited. The initial estimator of the state vector, $\mathbf{a}_{1|0}$, can be set equal to a vector of zeros, with covariance matrix

$$\mathbf{P}_{1|0}=\begin{bmatrix} \kappa\mathbf{I} & \mathbf{0} \\ \mathbf{0} & \mathbf{P}^{*}_{1|0} \end{bmatrix} \tag{4.1.12}$$

where $\mathbf{P}^{*}_{1|0}$ is a covariance matrix of order two given by (3.3.19). Thus a diffuse prior is only needed for the level and slope components and a proper prior for the whole state vector can be constructed from the first two observations.

Cyclical trend The cyclical trend model can be put in state space form in a similar way to the trend plus cycle model. Only a minor amendment is needed to the measurement equation and the first row of the transition equation. The stationarity of the cyclical component can again be exploited in setting up starting values for the Kalman filter. The conditions required for the resulting filter to have a steady-state solution may be derived by the reader.

Basic structural model The basic structural model consists of trend, seasonal and irregular components combined in an additive form, i.e.

$$y_t=\mu_t+\gamma_t+\varepsilon_t, \quad t=1,\ldots, T \tag{4.1.13}$$

The trend component is taken to be a local linear trend of the form (4.1.6) while the irregular component is white noise. In the dummy variable form of seasonality

$$\sum_{j=0}^{s-1} \gamma_{t-j}=\omega_t$$

where ω_t is a white-noise disturbance with mean zero and variance σ^2_ω. For $s=4$ the state space form is:

$$y_t=[1 \quad 0 \quad 1 \quad 0 \quad 0]\boldsymbol{\alpha}_t+\varepsilon_t \tag{4.1.14a}$$

$$\boldsymbol{\alpha}_t=\begin{bmatrix} \mu_t \\ \beta_t \\ \cdots\cdots \\ \gamma_t \\ \gamma_{t-1} \\ \gamma_{t-2} \end{bmatrix}=\left[\begin{array}{cc:ccc} 1 & 1 & & \mathbf{0} & \\ 0 & 1 & & & \\ \cdots & \cdots & \cdots & \cdots & \cdots \\ & & -1 & -1 & -1 \\ & \mathbf{0} & 1 & 0 & 0 \\ & & 0 & 1 & 0 \end{array}\right]\begin{bmatrix} \mu_{t-1} \\ \beta_{t-1} \\ \cdots\cdots \\ \gamma_{t-1} \\ \gamma_{t-2} \\ \gamma_{t-3} \end{bmatrix}+\begin{bmatrix} \eta_t \\ \zeta_t \\ \cdots \\ \omega_t \\ 0 \\ 0 \end{bmatrix} \tag{4.1.14b}$$

The third element in the state vector therefore represents the current seasonal effect. The model is always observable, but is only controllable and stabilisable if both σ_ξ^2 and σ_ω^2 are strictly positive.

Trigonometric seasonality was defined in (2.3.49) and (2.3.50). For quarterly data the state space form is:

$$y_t = [1 \quad 0 \quad 1 \quad 0 \quad 1]\boldsymbol{\alpha}_t + \varepsilon_t \tag{4.1.15a}$$

$$\boldsymbol{\alpha}_t = \begin{bmatrix} \mu_t \\ \beta_t \\ \cdots\cdots \\ \gamma_{1t} \\ \gamma_{1t}^* \\ \cdots\cdots \\ \gamma_{2t} \end{bmatrix} = \begin{bmatrix} \begin{matrix} 1 & 1 \\ 0 & 1 \end{matrix} & \vdots & \mathbf{0} & \vdots & \mathbf{0} \\ \cdots\cdots & \cdots & \cdots & \cdots & \cdots \\ \mathbf{0} & \vdots & \mathbf{C}_1 & \vdots & \mathbf{0} \\ \cdots\cdots & \cdots & \cdots & \cdots & \cdots \\ \mathbf{0}' & \vdots & \mathbf{0}' & \vdots & (-1) \end{bmatrix} \begin{bmatrix} \mu_{t-1} \\ \beta_{t-1} \\ \cdots\cdots \\ \gamma_{1,t-1} \\ \gamma_{1,t-1}^* \\ \cdots\cdots \\ \gamma_{2,t-1} \end{bmatrix} + \begin{bmatrix} \eta_t \\ \zeta_t \\ \cdots\cdots \\ \omega_{1t} \\ \omega_{1t}^* \\ \cdots\cdots \\ \omega_{2t} \end{bmatrix} \tag{4.1.15b}$$

where

$$\mathbf{C}_1 = \begin{bmatrix} \cos(\pi/2) & \sin(\pi/2) \\ -\sin(\pi/2) & \cos(\pi/2) \end{bmatrix} = \begin{bmatrix} 0 & 1 \\ -1 & 0 \end{bmatrix} \tag{4.1.15c}$$

For monthly data the block diagonal structure of the transition matrix is still present with the seasonal blocks now being $\mathbf{C}_j$, $j=1,\ldots,5$, with the j-th such block corresponding to the frequency $\lambda_j = 2\pi j/12$. Stabilisability requires that the variance of each harmonic be strictly positive, i.e. $\sigma_j^2 > 0, j=1,\ldots,[s/2]$.

Daily effects The model for a daily component was described in sub-section 2.3.5. In view of the identity of (2.3.55), the state vector need only contain $w-1$ daily effect variables, θ_{jt}; it is immaterial which one is left out. The transition equation can be written in matrix terms as

$$\boldsymbol{\theta}_t = \boldsymbol{\theta}_{t-1} + \boldsymbol{\chi}_t \tag{4.1.16}$$

where $\boldsymbol{\theta}_t$ is a $(w-1)\times 1$ vector containing the daily effects and $\boldsymbol{\chi}_t$ is the corresponding $(w-1)\times 1$ vector of disturbances. If $\mathbf{k}$ is defined as the $(w-1)\times 1$ vector $[k_1 \quad \cdots \quad k_{w-1}]'$ then

$$\text{Var}(\boldsymbol{\chi}_t) = \sigma_\chi^2[\mathbf{I} - K^{-1}\mathbf{kk}'] \tag{4.1.17}$$

Unlike the components considered so far, the $\mathbf{z}_t$ vector in the measurement equation changes over time so that each day it picks out the appropriate daily effect from $\boldsymbol{\theta}_t$. Thus the first $w-1$ elements of $\mathbf{z}_t$ are such that for a day of type j, there is a one in the j-th position and zeros elsewhere. The exception is for the w-th type of day in which case (2.3.55) leads to the requirement that the j-th element be equal to $-k_j/k_w$ for $j=1,\ldots,w-1$.

Mixed multiplicative-additive model The models considered so far have all been additive, and hence linear, perhaps after an appropriate transformation such as taking logarithms. It is, however, possible to conceive of models which cannot be put in this additive form. Durbin and Murphy (1975) argued that in some situations the trend and seasonal components might combine multiplicatively, while the irregular component was additive. A structural formulation of a model with these characteristics might be:

$$y_t = \mu_t \exp(\gamma_t) + \varepsilon_t \tag{4.1.18}$$

where μ_t and γ_t are specified as in the seasonal dummy form of the BSM. A model of this kind has a *non-linear* state space form, as in (3.7.11). Hence the Kalman filter cannot be applied, but it is possible to consider handling the model by the extended Kalman filter.

In terms of the notation of (3.7.11),

$$z_t(\boldsymbol{\alpha}_t) = \mu_t \exp(\gamma_t) \tag{4.1.19}$$

For quarterly data

$$\mathbf{Z}_t = \frac{\partial z_t(\boldsymbol{\alpha}_t)}{\partial \boldsymbol{\alpha}_t'} = [\exp(\gamma_t) \quad 0 \quad \mu_t \exp(\gamma_t) \quad 0 \quad 0]$$

and so the measurement equation in (3.7.15a) is

$$y_t \simeq \hat{\mathbf{Z}}_t' \boldsymbol{\alpha}_t + \hat{d}_t + \varepsilon_t \tag{4.1.20a}$$

where the 'hat' over $\mathbf{Z}_t$ indicates that μ_t and γ_t are replaced by $m_{t|t-1}$ and $c_{t|t-1}$ respectively, and

$$\hat{d}_t = -m_{t|t-1} c_{t|t-1} \exp(c_{t|t-1}) \tag{4.1.20b}$$

The transition equation is linear, taking the form indicated by (4.1.14b), and so no further amendments need to be considered.

Another way of formulating a mixed multiplicative-additive model is

$$y_t = \mu_t + \mu_t \gamma_t + \varepsilon_t \tag{4.1.21}$$

where μ_t and γ_t are again set up as in the BSM. The application of the extended Kalman filter follows along similar lines to the previous model.

4.1.2 The steady state and exponential smoothing

The conditions under which structural models have a steady-state Kalman filter were discussed in the previous sub-section. For the simpler models, the steady-state recursions are equivalent to the recursions used in the *ad hoc* forecasting procedures based on exponential smoothing. These methods were described in section 2.2.

Local level The fact that the optimal forecasts in the random walk plus noise model are given by an EWMA was first pointed out by Muth (1960). The result can be demonstrated by showing that the EWMA is the steady-state solution of the model. From Example 3.3.4,

$$\bar{p} = \lim_{t \to \infty} p_{t|t-1} = (q + \sqrt{q^2 + 4q})/2 \tag{4.1.22}$$

where q is the signal–noise ratio $\sigma_\eta^2/\sigma_\varepsilon^2$. Since the transition matrix is a scalar equal to unity, the optimal estimator of μ_t, m_t, satisfies the steady-state recursion

$$m_t = (1-\lambda)m_{t-1} + \lambda y_t \tag{4.1.23}$$

where

$$\lambda = \frac{\bar{p}}{1+\bar{p}} = \frac{q + \sqrt{q^2+4q}}{2+q+\sqrt{q^2+4q}} \tag{4.1.24}$$

Equation (4.1.23) is the EWMA and since the forecast function for the random walk plus noise model is $\hat{y}_{T+l|T} = m_T$, the EWMA forecasting procedure is seen to be justified by such a model.

Since q is non-negative, the smoothing constant λ must lie in the range $0 \leqslant \lambda \leqslant 1$. However, when q is equal to zero, the steady-state solution has $\bar{p}$ equal to zero. In this case λ is equal to zero and the EWMA recursions would never be applied. The Kalman filter applied with a diffuse prior is valid for q equal to zero and the filter is just the updating formula for the sample mean. Thus by constructing a model underlying the EWMA, the problem of reconciling OLS and DLS is resolved, and an optimal solution for the starting value is obtained. A more general form of the EWMA, corresponding to the Kalman filter for the state, would be:

$$m_t = (1-\lambda_t)m_{t-1} + \lambda_t y_t, \quad t = 2, \ldots, T \tag{4.1.25}$$

with

$$\lambda_t = p_{t|t-1}/(1 + p_{t|t-1})$$

and $m_1 = y_1$ and $p_{2|1} = 1 + q$.

Local linear trend The steady-state Kalman filter for the local linear trend model, (4.1.6), takes the form of Holt's recursions, (2.2.11). The equivalence may be shown as follows. Let p_{ij} denote the ij-th element in the steady-state covariance matrix, $\bar{\mathbf{P}}$, defined in (3.3.11). In the steady state, the Kalman filter for $\mathbf{a}_t = [m_t \quad b_t]'$ is:

$$m_t = m_{t-1} + b_{t-1} + [p_{11}/(1+p_{11})]v_t \tag{4.1.26a}$$

$$b_t = b_{t-1} + [p_{12}/(1+p_{11})]v_t \tag{4.1.26b}$$

where $v_t = y_t - \hat{y}_{t|t-1} = y_t - m_{t-1} - b_{t-1}$. The form of these equations is exactly the same as (2.2.11) with smoothing constants given by:

$$\lambda_0 = p_{11}/(1+p_{11}) \tag{4.1.27a}$$

and since

$$\lambda_0\lambda_1 = p_{12}/(1+p_{11})$$

$$\lambda_1 = p_{12}/p_{11} \tag{4.1.27b}$$

The relationship between the smoothing constants and the relative variances q_η and q_ζ may be found from the algebraic Riccati equation, (3.3.14). This is:

$$\bar{\mathbf{P}} = \begin{bmatrix} p_{11} & p_{12} \\ p_{21} & p_{22} \end{bmatrix} = \begin{bmatrix} p_{11}+p_{22}+2p_{12} & p_{12}+p_{22} \\ p_{12}+p_{22} & p_{22} \end{bmatrix}$$

$$-\frac{1}{1+p_{11}}\begin{bmatrix} (p_{11}+p_{12})^2 & p_{12}(p_{11}+p_{12}) \\ p_{12}(p_{11}+p_{12}) & p_{12}^2 \end{bmatrix} + \begin{bmatrix} q_\eta & 0 \\ 0 & q_\zeta \end{bmatrix} \tag{4.1.28}$$

since $p_{21} = p_{12}$. Three equations are obtained from (4.1.28), namely

$$p_{11} = q_\eta + p_{11} + p_{22} + 2p_{12} - (1+p_{11})^{-1}(p_{11}+p_{12})^2 \tag{4.1.29a}$$

$$p_{22} = q_\zeta + p_{22} - (1+p_{11})^{-1}p_{12}^2 \tag{4.1.29b}$$

$$p_{12} = p_{12} + p_{22} - (1+p_{11})^{-1}p_{12}(p_{11}+p_{12}) \tag{4.1.29c}$$

Rearranging gives

$$\begin{aligned} q_\eta &= -p_{22} - 2p_{12} + (1+p_{11})^{-1}(p_{11}+p_{12})^2 \\ &= -2p_{12} + (1+p_{11})^{-1}(p_{11}+p_{12})^2 - (1+p_{11})^{-1}p_{12}(p_{11}+p_{12}) \\ &= (1+p_{11})^{-1}(p_{11}^2 - p_{12}) - p_{12} \end{aligned} \tag{4.1.30a}$$

and

$$q_\zeta = (1+p_{11})^{-1}p_{12}^2 \tag{4.1.30b}$$

From equations (4.1.27),

$$p_{11} = \lambda_0/(1-\lambda_0) \text{ and } p_{12} = \lambda_0\lambda_1/(1-\lambda_0) \tag{4.1.31}$$

Substituting for p_{11} and p_{12} in (4.1.30) gives

$$q_\zeta = \frac{1}{1+p_{11}}p_{12}^2 = \frac{\lambda_0^2\lambda_1^2}{(1-\lambda_0)^2}(1-\lambda_0) = \frac{\lambda_0^2\lambda_1^2}{1-\lambda_0} \tag{4.1.32a}$$

and

$$q_\eta = (1-\lambda_0)\left[\frac{\lambda_0^2}{(1-\lambda_0)^2} - \frac{\lambda_0\lambda_1}{1-\lambda_0}\right] - \frac{\lambda_0\lambda_1}{1-\lambda_0}$$

$$= \frac{1}{1-\lambda_0}[\lambda_0^2 + \lambda_0^2\lambda_1 - 2\lambda_0\lambda_1] \tag{4.1.32b}$$

which are the equations presented earlier in (2.3.31).

It was shown in sub-section 2.2.3 that double exponential smoothing is a special case of Holt's procedure. The discount factor, ω, is related to λ_0 and λ_1 by the equations $\lambda_0 = 1-\omega^2$ and $\lambda_1 = (1-\omega)/(1+\omega)$. Substituting for λ_0 and λ_1 in (2.3.31) and rearranging gives

$$q_\eta = 2(1-\omega)^2/\omega$$

$$q_\zeta = (1-\omega)^4/\omega^2 = [(1-\omega)^2/\omega]^2$$

This in turn implies that double exponential smoothing is obtained when the parameters in the model satisfy the restriction

$$q_\zeta = (q_\eta/2)^2 \tag{4.1.33}$$

The admissibility region for the smoothing constants corresponding to a local linear trend is such that $0 < \lambda_0, \lambda_1 \leqslant 1$ and

$$\lambda_1 \leqslant \lambda_0/(2-\lambda_0)$$

This last inequality is needed for σ^2 to be non-negative since, from (4.1.32b), $\lambda_0 + \lambda_0\lambda_1 - 2\lambda_0\lambda_1 \geqslant 0$. As regards the other constraints, both λ_0 and λ_1 must be strictly positive for a steady-state solution. On the other hand, both λ_0 and λ_1 can be equal to the upper limit of unity, with $\lambda_0 = 1$ corresponding to the case $\sigma_\varepsilon^2 = 0$. Since estimation of local linear trend models is sometimes carried out in terms of λ_0 and λ_1, or in terms of λ_0 and $\lambda_1^\dagger = \lambda_0\lambda_1$, it is important to be aware of the implications of the above constraints, particularly for testing.

Basic structural model In the BSM the state vector is of length $s+1$, and it is not easy to work out the steady-state form of the filtering equations. On the other hand, the extension of the Holt-Winters local linear trend recursions to cope with seasonality involves only a single extra equation. When the Holt-Winters recursions were introduced in (2.2.31), it was observed that the component for each season is only updated every s periods. Thus there is a price to be paid for having only three equations because when the Kalman filter is applied to the BSM, the seasonal components are updated in every period. The Holt-Winters procedure may be regarded as an approximation to the Kalman filter applied to the BSM. As McKenzie (1976) observes, it is possible to derive an ARIMA model which gives the same forecast function as Holt-Winters, and this model is such that $\Delta\Delta_s y_t \sim \text{MA}(s+1)$. This corresponds to the specification of the reduced form of the BSM, and it is possible to find parameters in the BSM such that the a.c.f. of the stationary form is very close to the a.c.f. of the ARIMA model corresponding to a particular choice of parameters in the Holt-Winters procedure.

The multiplicative form of the Holt-Winters procedure is also widely used. Part of the motivation for the multiplicative-additive structural model of (4.1.18) is the need to provide a statistical framework for making forecasts similar to multiplicative Holt-Winters.

4.1.3 UCARIMA and reduced forms

The UCARIMA and reduced forms of time-invariant structural models can be obtained from their state space forms.

Substituting for $\boldsymbol{\alpha}_t$ in the measurement equation of (4.1.3) gives

$$y_t = \mathbf{z}'(\mathbf{I}-\mathbf{T}\text{L})^{-1}\,\mathbf{R}\boldsymbol{\eta}_t + \varepsilon_t \tag{4.1.34}$$

and if $(\mathbf{I}-\mathbf{T}\text{L})^{\dagger}$ denotes the adjoint matrix of $\mathbf{I}-\mathbf{T}\text{L}$, then

$$|\mathbf{I}-\mathbf{T}\text{L}|\,y_t = \mathbf{z}'(\mathbf{I}-\mathbf{T}\text{L})^{\dagger}\,\mathbf{R}\boldsymbol{\eta}_t + |\mathbf{I}-\mathbf{T}\text{L}|\varepsilon_t \tag{4.1.35}$$

When there are several distinct components in the state vector, the model can be expressed as in (4.1.3), but without the time subscripts. The $M+1$ components in (4.1.3) correspond to the components in the UCARIMA formulation of (2.5.27). Thus if $(\mathbf{I}-\mathbf{T}_m\text{L})^{\dagger}$ is the adjoint matrix of $\mathbf{I}-\mathbf{T}_m\text{L}$ for $m=1,\ldots,M$, then

$$y_t = \sum_{m=1}^{M} |\mathbf{I}-\mathbf{T}_m\text{L}|^{-1}\,\mathbf{z}_m'(\mathbf{I}-\mathbf{T}_m\text{L})^{\dagger}\mathbf{R}_m\boldsymbol{\eta}_{mt} + \varepsilon_t \tag{4.1.36}$$

In terms of the notation of (2.5.27), $|\mathbf{I}-\mathbf{T}_m\text{L}| = \varphi_m(\text{L})\Delta_m(\text{L})$ while $\mathbf{z}_m'(\mathbf{I}-\mathbf{T}_m\text{L})^{\dagger}\mathbf{R}_m\boldsymbol{\eta}_{mt}$ is equivalent to an MA process the order of which is one less than the order of $\varphi_m(\text{L})\Delta_m(\text{L})$. The product of the determinants $|\mathbf{I}-\mathbf{T}_m\text{L}|, m=1,\ldots,M$ is equal to the overall determinantal term $|\mathbf{I}-\mathbf{T}\text{L}|$ and if the polynomials $\varphi_m(\text{L})\Delta_m(\text{L})$, $m=1,\ldots,M$ have no roots in common, we can write

$$|\mathbf{I}-\mathbf{T}\text{L}| = \Delta(\text{L})\varphi(\text{L}) \tag{4.1.37}$$

where $\Delta(\text{L})$ is the product of the non-stationary polynomials, as given in (2.5.28), and $\varphi(\text{L})$ is a stationary autoregressive polynomial, equal to the product of the $\varphi_m(\text{L})$'s.

The components on the right-hand side of (4.1.35) combine to make an MA process, the order of which cannot exceed the length of the state vector. The coefficients in the MA process can be related to the elements of the steady-state covariance matrix, $\bar{\mathbf{P}}$, in the following way. From the definition of an innovation, the observations in a time-invariant model can be expressed as

$$y_t = \mathbf{z}'\mathbf{a}_{t|t-1} + v_t \tag{4.1.38a}$$

Rearranging the Kalman filter equation (3.2.4a) without the term $(\mathbf{c}_{t+1}-\mathbf{K}_t\mathbf{d}_t)$, gives

$$\mathbf{a}_{t+1|t}=\mathbf{T}\mathbf{a}_{t|t-1}+\bar{\mathbf{K}}v_t \tag{4.1.38b}$$

when the Kalman filter is in the steady state, where $\bar{\mathbf{K}}$ is the steady-state gain matrix

$$\bar{\mathbf{K}}=\mathbf{T}\bar{\mathbf{P}}\mathbf{z}(\mathbf{z}'\bar{\mathbf{P}}\mathbf{z}+1)^{-1} \tag{4.1.39}$$

Lagging (4.1.38b) one time period and substituting in (4.1.38a) gives

$$y_t=\mathbf{z}'(\mathbf{I}-\mathbf{T}\mathrm{L})^{-1}\mathbf{T}\bar{\mathbf{P}}\mathbf{z}(\mathbf{z}'\bar{\mathbf{P}}\mathbf{z}+h)^{-1}v_{t-1}+v_t \tag{4.1.40}$$

Thus

$$|\mathbf{I}-\mathbf{T}\mathrm{L}|\,y_t=[|\mathbf{I}-\mathbf{T}\mathrm{L}|+\mathbf{z}'(\mathbf{I}-\mathbf{T}\mathrm{L})^{\dagger}\mathbf{T}\bar{\mathbf{P}}\mathbf{z}(\mathbf{z}'\bar{\mathbf{P}}\mathbf{z}+h)^{-1}\mathrm{L}]v_t \tag{4.1.41}$$

This model corresponds to the reduced form

$$\varphi(\mathrm{L})\Delta(\mathrm{L})y_t=\theta(\mathrm{L})\xi_t \tag{4.1.42}$$

with $\theta(\mathrm{L})$ equal to the polynomial in square brackets. The variance of the steady-state innovations in (4.1.41) is equal to $\mathrm{Var}(\xi_t)$ while $\Delta(\mathrm{L})$ and $\varphi(\mathrm{L})$ are as defined below (4.1.37). Again, it can be seen directly from (4.1.41) that the order of $\theta(\mathrm{L})$ cannot exceed the length of the state vector, m. If the roots of $\Delta(\mathrm{L})$ are all equal to unity, then the reduced form is an ARIMA (p, d, q) model with $p+d\leqslant m$. It can be shown that if $\bar{\mathbf{P}}$ is p.d., then the MA part of the model is invertible.

If the Riccati equation can be solved in terms of the parameters in $\boldsymbol{\psi}$, then expressions for the MA parameters can be obtained directly in terms of $\boldsymbol{\psi}$. Unfortunately, it is not easy to do this except in certain special cases such as those given in the previous sub-section. However, given particular numerical values of the $\boldsymbol{\psi}$ parameters in a structural model, $\bar{\mathbf{P}}$ can always be evaluated and substituted into (4.1.41) to give the corresponding values of the reduced form parameters.

Local level The reduced form of the local level model follows immediately from (4.1.41):

$$\Delta y_t=(1-\mathrm{L}+\bar{p}(1+\bar{p})^{-1}\mathrm{L})v_t=v_t-(1+\bar{p})^{-1}v_{t-1} \tag{4.1.43}$$

This model is ARIMA(0,1,1) with MA coefficient

$$\theta=-1/(1+\bar{p})=[(q^2+4q)^{\frac{1}{2}}-2-q]/2 \tag{4.1.44}$$

the final term having been obtained by substituting for $\bar{p}$ from (4.1.22) and multiplying numerator and denominator by $[-2-q+\sqrt{(q^2+4q)}]$. This checks with the result obtained earlier, as (2.5.11), by equating the autocorrelations at lag one for the random walk plus noise and ARIMA(0, 1, 1) models. Note that θ is only invertible if q is strictly positive. If q is zero, then $\bar{p}$ is zero and $\theta=-1$.

On combining equation (4.1.44) with equation (4.1.24), it can be seen that $\theta=\lambda-1$ where λ is the EWMA smoothing constant. This relationship between θ and λ was also obtained in Example 2.6.1.

Local linear trend In the local linear trend model, (4.1.6),

$$|\mathbf{I}-\mathbf{T}\mathrm{L}|=(1-\mathrm{L})^2 \quad \text{and} \quad (\mathbf{I}-\mathbf{T}\mathrm{L})^{\dagger}=\begin{bmatrix} 1-\mathrm{L} & \mathrm{L} \\ 0 & 1-\mathrm{L} \end{bmatrix}$$

Thus (4.1.35) gives

$$(1-\mathrm{L})^2 y_t=(1-\mathrm{L})\eta_t+\zeta_{t-1}+(1-\mathrm{L})^2\varepsilon_t \tag{4.1.45}$$

This corresponds to the equation obtained in (2.4.24). Evaluating the MA(2) process on the right-hand side of (4.1.45) via (4.1.41) yields

$$\begin{aligned}\Delta^2 y_t&=\left\{(1-\mathrm{L})^2+[1-\mathrm{L}, \quad \mathrm{L}]\begin{bmatrix}(p_{11}+p_{21})/(1+p_{11}) \\ p_{21}/(1+p_{11})\end{bmatrix}\mathrm{L}\right\}v_t \\ &=v_t+\{[(p_{11}+p_{12})/(1+p_{11})]-2\}v_{t-1}+\{1-[p_{11}/(1+p_{11})]\}v_{t-2}\end{aligned}$$

Thus the reduced form is ARIMA(0, 2, 2), a result which was established earlier in sub-section 2.5.3. On substituting from (4.1.31)

$$\Delta^2 y_t=v_t+(\lambda_0\lambda_1+\lambda_0-2)v_{t-1}+(1-\lambda_0)v_{t-2} \tag{4.1.46}$$

and so the MA parameters, θ_1 and θ_2, are related to the smoothing constants, λ_0 and λ_1, by

$$\theta_1=\lambda_0\lambda_1+\lambda_0-2 \quad \text{and} \quad \theta_2=1-\lambda_0 \tag{4.1.47}$$

The relationship between θ_1 and θ_2 and thc structural parameters q_η and q_ζ can be obtained using (4.1.32). Note that the inequality $\theta_1\leqslant-4\theta_2/(1+\theta_2)$ in Figure 2.5.1 is equivalent to the constraint $\lambda_1\leqslant\lambda_0/(2-\lambda_0)$ obtained in the previous sub-section.

4.2 Estimation in the time domain

We now turn to the question of estimating the vector of hyperparameters, $\boldsymbol{\psi}$, in a structural time series model under the assumption that the disturbances are all normally distributed. The discussion will be framed in terms of the general time-invariant model, (4.1.3). *The number of non-stationary elements in the state vector of* (4.1.3) *is* $d\leqslant m$. (In terms of the notation of Chapter 2, d is equal to d^*, the order of the operator, $\Delta(\mathrm{L})$, needed to make y_t stationary; it is not the number of times the first-difference operator is applied except in cases where no other operator is applied.)

If a parameter is to be concentrated out of the likelihood function, the variance term, h, and the covariance matrix, $\mathbf{Q}$, may be redefined by writing

$$\text{Var}(\varepsilon_t)=\sigma_*^2 h \quad \text{and} \quad \text{Var}(\boldsymbol{\eta}_t)=\sigma_*^2 \mathbf{Q}$$

where σ_*^2 is a positive scalar. As a rule, σ_*^2 is set equal to either σ_ε^2, the variance of the measurement equation disturbance, or to σ_η^2. This means that when ML estimation is carried out, it is done so with respect to a vector of hyperparameters, $\boldsymbol{\psi}_*$, in which the variances are expressed relative to σ_*^2. Thus, for example, in the trend plus cycle model, (4.1.11), the full parameter vector is $\boldsymbol{\psi}=(\sigma_\varepsilon^2, \sigma_\eta^2, \sigma_\zeta^2, \lambda_c, \rho)'$, and setting σ_*^2 equal to σ_η^2 would give $\boldsymbol{\psi}_*=(h, q_\zeta, \lambda_c, \rho)'$ where $q_\zeta=\sigma_\zeta^2/\sigma_\eta^2$.

This section deals with estimation of structural models in the time domain. The emphasis is on the computation of maximum likelihood estimators via the prediction error decomposition and the key sub-section is 4.2.2. Before this approach is described, a brief consideration is given as to how estimators might be obtained from the correlogram. The later sub-sections on computation via the reduced form and using the EM algorithm can be omitted at first reading.

4.2.1 Correlogram

The autocovariance and autocorrelation functions of the principal structural time series models were derived in sub-section 2.4.3. This suggests that estimators of the hyperparameters might be obtained directly from the correlogram of the series after the appropriate differencing transformations have been carried out.

For the local level model, replacing the non-zero theoretical autocovariances of first differences, given in expression (2.4.31), by the corresponding sample autocovariances implies that σ_η^2 and σ_ε^2 may be estimated by

$$\hat{\sigma}_\eta^2=c(0)+2c(1) \qquad (4.2.1a)$$

$$\hat{\sigma}_\varepsilon^2=-c(1) \qquad (4.2.1b)$$

Alternatively the relative variance, $q=\sigma_\eta^2/\sigma_\varepsilon^2$, may be estimated from the first-order sample autocorrelation of first differences as

$$\hat{q}=-2-r^{-1}(1) \qquad (4.2.2)$$

As was shown in (2.4.32), the theoretical first-order correlation from the random walk plus noise model is confined to the range $-0.5\leqslant\rho(1)\leqslant 0$. The estimator of q obtained from (4.2.2) is similarly only admissible if $r(1)$ lies in the same range. If this is not the case, a negative estimator is obtained.

For the local linear trend model, the equations for the non-zero autocovariances in (2.4.33) may be rearranged to give estimators of σ_η^2, σ_ζ^2 and σ_ε^2. Estimators of the relative variances, $\sigma_\eta^2/\sigma_\varepsilon^2$ and $\sigma_\zeta^2/\sigma_\varepsilon^2$, can be obtained from the first two sample autocorrelations. Again the estimators will only be admissible if the sample autocorrelations satisfy the restrictions implied for the theoretical autocorrelations.

The estimators obtained above for the local level and local linear trend models are consistent but not asymptotically efficient. This can be shown by working in the frequency domain; see expression (4.5.3). The fact that the estimators are inefficient is perhaps not surprising in view of the known inefficiency of estimators of MA parameters obtained directly from the correlogram. For example, the reduced form of the local level model is an ARIMA(0, 1, 1) process and the inefficiency of the estimator of θ obtained by solving (2.4.13) is well known.

The properties of estimators obtained from the correlogram suggest that they may be useful as preliminary estimators or as starting values for iterative procedures. However, although the construction of suitable estimators for the local level and local linear trend models is unambiguous, this is not the case with more complex models such as the BSM. The seasonal dummy formulation of the BSM has a theoretical autocovariance function, (2.4.34), in which the autocovariances are only zero for lags greater than $s+1$. This leads to a set of $s+2$ equations to be solved for four unknown parameters. Bearing in mind that $s+2$ is fourteen for monthly data, the solution is not at all obvious. In fact it turns out, somewhat paradoxically, that the estimator can be obtained almost immediately by working in the frequency domain. Sub-section 4.3.4 provides the details.

4.2.2 Prediction error decompositon

The likelihood function may be obtained from the state space form via the prediction error decomposition. It may then be maximised with respect to the hyperparameters by a suitable numerical optimisation procedure. Analytic derivatives can be calculated using the recursions given in sub-section 3.4.6. However, numerical derivatives are given by many numerical optimisation routines. A quasi-Newton method such as the Gill-Murray-Pitfield algorithm, E04JBF in the NAG library, seems to work well in practice. A brief discussion on this kind of algorithm may be found in Harvey (1981a, ch. 4). Note that the algorithm used should be able to handle constraints, since estimates of variances must be non-negative while in the cycle model ρ and λ_c must lie in the ranges [0, 1] and [0, π] respectively. If the algorithm does not handle constraints, some kind of transformation needs to be made. An alternative approach to a quasi-Newton algorithm is to maximise the likelihood function using the EM algorithm. This method is described separately in sub-section 4.2.4.

There are a number of different ways of defining the likelihood function depending on the assumptions made about the initial conditions. All are equivalent asymptotically, although they may have very different small sample properties. After describing the various definitions of the likelihood function, the relationship between the various methods is discussed and a parallel drawn with ML procedures for ARIMA models.

Exact ML In the absence of any prior information on the initial state vector, the

d non-stationary elements are taken to have a diffuse prior, while the initial conditions for the $m-d$ stationary elements are the mean and covariance matrix of the unconditional distribution; see (3.3.29) or (4.1.2). Following the discussion at the beginning of section 3.4, the likelihood function for $y_{d+1}, \ldots, y_T$ conditional on $y_1, \ldots, y_d$, is

$$\log L = -\frac{(T-d)}{2}\log 2\pi - \frac{1}{2}\sum_{t=d+1}^{T}\log f_t - \frac{1}{2}\sum_{t=d+1}^{T} v_t^2/f_t \tag{4.2.3}$$

Kohn and Ansley (1986) point out that this likelihood function can also be regarded as a marginal likelihood in the sense of Kalbfleisch and Sprott (1970).

If σ_*^2 is concentrated out of the likelihood function, as in (3.4.9), the following quantity may be minimised:

$$S^{\dagger}(\boldsymbol{\psi}_*) = S(\boldsymbol{\psi}_*)\left(\prod_{t=d+1}^{T} f_t\right)^{1/(T-d)} \tag{4.2.4a}$$

where

$$S(\boldsymbol{\psi}_*) = \sum_{t=d+1}^{T} v_t^2/f_t \tag{4.2.4b}$$

The ML estimator of σ_*^2 is

$$\sigma_*^2(\boldsymbol{\psi}_*) = S(\boldsymbol{\psi}_*)/(T-d) \tag{4.2.5}$$

Concentrating out a parameter reduces the dimension of the search involved in the numerical optimisation procedure. There is no doubt that concentrating a parameter out of the likelihood is not only computationally efficient but is also likely to give more reliable results. The only practical question is the choice of σ_*^2. If σ_*^2 is equated with a parameter which is zero, or close to zero, numerical problems may arise as the relative variances will tend to become very large.

The easiest way of computing the likelihood function in either its concentrated or unconcentrated form is to initialise the Kalman filter at $t=0$ with $\mathbf{a}_0=0$ and κ set equal to a large but finite number. Alternatively $\mathbf{a}_d$ and $\mathbf{P}_d$ may be computed explicitly from the first d observations as in (3.3.27). The method described in sub-section 3.4.3 may also be used to avoid the 'large κ' approximation as may an information filter. If the Kalman filter is monitored, it is possible to switch to steady-state recursions at a suitable point.

Fixed initial state vector If the non-stationary components in the initial state vector, $\boldsymbol{\alpha}_0$, are taken to be fixed, the observations may be expressed in terms of $\boldsymbol{\alpha}_0$ by repeated substitution. The general procedure was outlined in sub-section 3.4.4. In the case of model (4.1.3), we obtain

$$y_t = \mathbf{x}'_{0t}\boldsymbol{\alpha}_0 + u_t, \quad t=1,\ldots,T \tag{4.2.6a}$$

where $\mathbf{x}_{0t} = \mathbf{T}'\mathbf{z}_t$ and

$$u_t = \mathbf{z}_t' \sum_{j=1}^{t} \mathbf{T}^{t-j}\mathbf{R}\boldsymbol{\eta}_j + \varepsilon_t \tag{4.2.6b}$$

The disturbance term has mean zero and covariance matrix $\sigma_*^2\boldsymbol{\Omega}_0$, where the element (s, t) of the $T \times T$ matrix $\boldsymbol{\Omega}_0$ is

$$\omega_{st} = \delta_{st} h + \mathbf{z}_t'\left[\sum_{j=1}^{min(s,t)} \mathbf{T}^{t-j}\mathbf{RQR}'\mathbf{T}'^{s-j}\right]\mathbf{z}_s$$
$$= \delta_{st} h + \sum_{j=1}^{min(s,t)} \mathbf{x}_{0,t-j}'\mathbf{RQR}'\mathbf{x}_{0,s-j} \tag{4.2.7}$$

where δ_{st} is the Kronecker delta, taking a value of one if $s=t$ and zero otherwise.

The ML estimator of $\boldsymbol{\alpha}_0$, conditional on the relative hyperparameters in the model, is

$$\tilde{\mathbf{a}}_0 = [\mathbf{X}_0'\boldsymbol{\Omega}_0^{-1}\mathbf{X}_0]^{-1}\mathbf{X}_0'\boldsymbol{\Omega}_0^{-1}\mathbf{y} \tag{4.2.8}$$

where the notation follows from writing (4.2.6) in matrix form

$$\mathbf{y} = \mathbf{X}_0\boldsymbol{\alpha}_0 + \mathbf{u}, \quad \mathrm{Var}(\mathbf{u}) = \sigma_*^2\boldsymbol{\Omega}_0 \tag{4.2.9}$$

Concentrating both $\boldsymbol{\alpha}_0$ and σ_*^2 out of the likelihood function leads to ML estimators of the hyperparameters being obtained by minimising

$$S_0(\boldsymbol{\psi}_*) = S(\boldsymbol{\psi}_*)[|\boldsymbol{\Omega}_0|^{1/T}] \tag{4.2.10a}$$

where $S(\boldsymbol{\psi})$ is the generalised residual sum of squares

$$S(\boldsymbol{\psi}) = (\mathbf{y} - \mathbf{X}_0\tilde{\boldsymbol{\alpha}}_0)'\boldsymbol{\Omega}_0^{-1}(\mathbf{y} - \mathbf{X}_0\tilde{\boldsymbol{\alpha}}_0) \tag{4.2.10b}$$

As regards computation, the repeated construction and inversion of the $T \times T$ matrix $\boldsymbol{\Omega}_0$ is avoided by using the GLS transformation or Rosenberg algorithms as described in sub-section 3.4.4. If the GLS transformation is used, the SSF is

$$y_t = \mathbf{x}_{0t}'\boldsymbol{\alpha}_0 + \mathbf{z}'\boldsymbol{\alpha}_t^* + \varepsilon_t$$
$$\boldsymbol{\alpha}_t^* = \mathbf{T}\boldsymbol{\alpha}_{t-1}^* + \mathbf{R}\boldsymbol{\eta}_t$$

where the first equation corresponds to (4.2.6a); compare (3.4.62). By applying the Kalman filter to this model, $S_0(\boldsymbol{\psi}_*)$ of (4.2.10) can be constructed as

$$S_0(\boldsymbol{\psi}_*) = S(\boldsymbol{\psi}_*)\left[\prod_{t=1}^{T} f_t\right]^{1/T} \tag{4.2.11a}$$

with

$$S(\boldsymbol{\psi}_*) = \sum_{t=1}^{T} v_t^2/f_t \tag{4.2.11b}$$

Note that the f_t in (4.2.11) is different from the f_t in (4.2.4) because of the way the Kalman filter is initiated.

Steady-state filter A third possibility for a time-invariant model is to compute $\mathbf{a}_{d+1|d}$ from the first d observations as in exact ML, either directly or indirectly from a diffuse prior. The covariance matrix $\mathbf{P}_{d+1|d}$ is then set equal to the steady-state matrix $\bar{\mathbf{P}}$. The steady-state Kalman filter is used to give a set of prediction errors and the likelihood function is expressed in prediction error decomposition form analogous to (4.2.3). However, since f_t is time-invariant in a steady-state model, concentrating σ_*^2 out of the likelihood function leads to the hyperparameters being computed by minimising the sum of squares function,

$$\bar{S}(\psi_*) = \sum_{t=d+1}^{T} v_t^2 \tag{4.2.12}$$

where v_t now denotes the one-step-ahead prediction error obtained from the steady-state filter. This approach would be attractive if it were possible to calculate $\mathbf{P}$ easily. A number of algorithms for explicitly solving the algebraic Riccati equation (3.3.14) are given in Anderson and Moore (1979, pp. 155–62). Unfortunately, these methods possess no dramatic advantages over calculating $\bar{\mathbf{P}}$ by running the Riccati difference equation (3.3.13) until it converges. Hence the computational burden is likely to be much the same as in exact ML.

As regards the relationship between the various methods, the argument used to obtain (3.4.26) can be developed to show that, for a given value of ψ_*, the sum-of-squares functions, $S(\psi_*)$, in (4.2.4b) and (4.2.11b) are identical. Thus the only difference between the criterion functions, (4.2.4) and (4.2.11), derived from the respective likelihood functions, is in the corrections for the determinantal terms and these will become the same asymptotically. Although minimising (4.2.10) yields exact ML estimators if $\boldsymbol{\alpha}_0$ is indeed fixed, this assumption seems to be a less natural one than initialisation using a diffuse prior; see also Ansley and Kohn (1985). Furthermore, if one considers the reduced form ARIMA model corresponding to a structural model, the usual definition of the exact likelihood function is equivalent to the exact likelihood function based on a diffuse prior. This is shown in the next sub-section which also shows that the sum-of-squares function, (4.2.12), obtained from the steady-state Kalman filter is identical to the conditional sum-of-squares function from the reduced form ARIMA process. As is well known from studies of ARIMA models, the small sample properties of, say, the CSS and exact ML procedures may differ considerably; see, *inter alia*, Harvey (1981b, ch. 6) and Ansley and Newbold (1980).

Example 4.2.1 The Kalman filter for μ_t in the random walk plus noise model is given by (4.1.23). Subtracting both the right- and left-hand sides of (4.1.25) from

y_{t+1} gives

$$y_{t+1}-m_t=y_{t+1}-(1-\lambda_t)m_{t-1}-\lambda_t y_t \tag{4.2.13}$$

The left-hand side of (4.2.13) is equal to the innovation, v_{t+1}, and on rearranging the right-hand side one obtains the recursion

$$v_{t+1}=\Delta y_{t+1}+(1-\lambda_t)v_t \tag{4.2.14}$$

or

$$v_{t+1}=\Delta y_{t+1}+v_t/f_t, \quad t=2,\ldots,T-1 \tag{4.2.15a}$$

Since $f_t=p_{t|t-1}+1$, it follows from (3.2.9b) that f_t can be updated directly by the recursion

$$f_{t+1}=f_t-(f_t-1)^2/f_t+q, \quad t=2,\ldots,T-1 \tag{4.2.15b}$$

The starting values $v_2=y_2-y_1$ and $f_2=1+p_{2|1}=2+q$ generate the v_t's and f_t's which go in the exact likelihood function (4.2.3).

If μ_0 is regarded as fixed, the computation of the likelihood function is based on recursions similar to (4.2.15) with t running from 1 to $T-1$ and the initial value, f_1, in (4.2.15b) being unity. At each evaluation of the likelihood function two sets of innovations, y_t^* and x_t^*, $t=1,\ldots,T$ are produced by

$$y_{t+1}^*=\Delta y_{t+1}+y_t^*/f_t \tag{4.2.16a}$$

$$x_{t+1}^*=x_t^*/f_t, \quad t=1,\ldots,T-1 \tag{4.2.16b}$$

with $y_1^*=y_1$ and $x_1^*=1$. The ML estimator of μ_0, conditional on a given value of ψ_* is then given by the WLS regression

$$\tilde{\mu}_0=\left[\sum_{t=1}^{T} x_t^* y_t^*/f_t\right]\Bigg/\left[\sum_{t=1}^{T} x_t^{*2}/f_t\right] \tag{4.2.17}$$

The criterion function (4.2.11) has $\upsilon_t=y_t-\tilde{\mu}_0$ for $t=1\ldots,T$.

In the steady state, $\bar{f}=\bar{p}+1$ where $\bar{p}$ is given by (3.3.16) when σ_*^2 is taken to be σ_ε^2. The starting value for the recursion (4.2.14), with t from 1 to $T-1$ is $v_1=0$. As should be clear from the discussion in sub-section 4.1.2, the υ_t's obtained in this way are the residuals given by the standard EWMA.

4.2.3 Reduced form

The reduced form ARIMA models for the principal structural time series models were set out in sub-section 2.5.3. A good deal of work has been done to construct algorithms for estimating ARIMA models and this suggests the possibility of estimating the structural parameters via the reduced form. Before considering the merits of such an approach, it is worth considering why the exact likelihood function described in the previous sub-section is equivalent to the exact likelihood function for the corresponding ARIMA model and why the steady-state criterion function is the same as the conditional sum of squares.

The exact likelihood function for a stationary ARMA model is defined unambiguously. In an ARIMA model, the exact likelihood function of $\Delta^d y_t$ can be defined in the same way, and it can be shown that this likelihood function is the same as the likelihood function of $y_{d+1}, \ldots, y_T$, conditional on $y_1, \ldots, y_d$; see Harvey (1981c). For a structural time series model, the use of a diffuse prior for the d non-stationary elements in the state vector also yields a likelihood function for $y_{d+1}, \ldots, y_T$ conditional on $y_1, \ldots, y_d$; see (4.2.3). As regards the CSS estimator, it is clear that this must correspond to a steady-state Kalman filter, initiated at $t=d+1$ with $\mathbf{P}_{d+1}=\bar{\mathbf{P}}$.

Example 4.2.2 The reduced form of the random walk plus noise model is an ARIMA(0,1,1) model, for which the CSS recursion is

$$\xi_t = \Delta y_t - \theta \xi_{t-1}, \quad t=2, \ldots, T \tag{4.2.18}$$

with $\xi_1 = 0$. This is the equivalent to the recursion for v_t in (4.2.15a) when f_t is set equal to its steady-state value of $\bar{p}+1$, which from (4.1.44) is $-1/\theta$, and the starting value is $v_2 = y_2 - y_1$.

Estimation via the reduced form could proceed in two ways. The first would be to estimate the unrestricted reduced form and then to construct estimators of the structural parameters from the AR and MA parameters. Thus for a local linear trend model an ARIMA(0, 2, 2) model is estimated, and estimators of q_η and q_ζ are obtained from (2.3.31). There are two problems with this approach. The first is that the estimators of the structural parameters may not be admissible. The restrictions on the MA parameter space implied by the local linear trend model are quite severe, as shown in Figure 2.5.1. It is quite possible for these restrictions not to be met even though the data really are generated by a local linear trend model. The second problem is more serious, and relates to the fact that in more elaborate structural models there is no one-to-one relationship between the structural and reduced form parameters. Thus in the BSM, the reduced form is such that $\Delta\Delta_s y_t$ follows an MA($s+1$) process and the implied constraints on the $s+1$ MA parameters will virtually never be satisfied in practice.

The second way of estimating via the reduced form is to maximise the likelihood function with respect to the structural parameters. This ensures that the admissibility constraints are all satisfied. In order to apply the method, a general procedure for computing the reduced form AR and MA parameters from the structural parameters is needed. Nerlove *et al.* (1979, pp. 125–31) give such a procedure but show that it can be quite complex and time consuming.

Is there any practical advantage to estimation via the reduced form? If exact ML estimators are required, the answer must be no, since it is as time consuming to compute exact ML estimators for an ARIMA model as it is for the corresponding structural model. Computing the CSS estimator for an ARIMA model, on the other hand, is relatively easy and if it is this estimator which is required, working with the reduced form may have some advantages over working with the steady-state Kalman filter. However, as Nerlove *et al.* (1979) point out, approximate ML estimators of the structural parameters can be computed more easily in the frequency domain.

4.2.4 EM algorithm

Watson and Engle (1983) have used the EM algorithm to estimate the unknown parameters in an unobserved components model and the method may be adopted here. Consider the general time-invariant model (4.1.3) with σ_*^2 set equal to one and suppose, initially, that $\mathbf{Q}$ is unrestricted and that $\mathbf{a}_0$ and $\mathbf{P}_0$ are known. If the elements in the state vector were observed for $t=0,\ldots,T$, the log-likelihood function for the y_t's and $\boldsymbol{\alpha}_t$'s would be

$$\log L(\mathbf{y},\boldsymbol{\alpha}) = -\frac{T}{2}\log 2\pi - \frac{T}{2}\log h - \frac{1}{2h}\sum_{t=1}^{T}(y_t - \mathbf{z}'\boldsymbol{\alpha}_t)^2$$
$$-\frac{Tn}{2}\log 2\pi - \frac{T}{2}\log|\mathbf{Q}| - \frac{1}{2}\sum_{t=1}^{T}(\boldsymbol{\alpha}_t - \mathbf{T}\boldsymbol{\alpha}_{t-1})'\mathbf{Q}^{-1}(\boldsymbol{\alpha}_t - \mathbf{T}\boldsymbol{\alpha}_{t-1})$$
$$-\frac{n}{2}\log 2\pi - \tfrac{1}{2}\log|\mathbf{P}_0| - \tfrac{1}{2}(\boldsymbol{\alpha}_0 - \mathbf{a}_0)'\mathbf{P}_0^{-1}(\boldsymbol{\alpha}_0 - \mathbf{a}_0) \tag{4.2.19}$$

The last three terms disappear if a proper prior distribution for $\boldsymbol{\alpha}_0$ is not available and $\mathbf{P}_0^{-1} = \mathbf{0}$. The EM algorithm proceeds iteratively by evaluating

$$\mathrm{E}\left[\frac{\partial \log L}{\partial \boldsymbol{\psi}}\bigg|\, Y_T\right] \tag{4.2.20}$$

conditional on the latest estimate of $\boldsymbol{\psi}$. The expression is then set equal to a vector of zeros and solved to yield a new set of estimates of $\boldsymbol{\psi}$. The procedure is repeated until convergence. It can be shown that, under suitable conditions, the likelihood will remain the same or increase at each iteration and it will converge to a local maximum; see Dempster *et al.* (1977), Wu (1983) and Boyles (1983).

Applying (4.2.20) to the likelihood function in (4.2.19) gives the following expression for the estimator of h:

$$\tilde{h} = T^{-1}\sum_{t=1}^{T}[e_{t|T}^2 + \mathbf{z}'\mathbf{P}_{t|T}\mathbf{z}] \tag{4.2.21}$$

where

$$e_{t|T} = y_t - \mathbf{z}'\mathbf{a}_{t|T}, \quad t=1,\ldots,T \tag{4.2.22}$$

and $\mathbf{a}_{t|T}$ is the smoothed estimator of $\boldsymbol{\alpha}_t$ and $\mathbf{P}_{t|T}$ is its MSE matrix; it will be recalled from (3.6.1) that this is the expectation of $\boldsymbol{\alpha}_t$ conditional on $\mathbf{Y}_T$. The estimator of $\mathbf{Q}$ is

$$\hat{\mathbf{Q}}=T^{-1}\sum_{t=1}^{T}[\mathbf{n}_{t|T}\mathbf{n}'_{t|T}+\mathbf{P}_{t|T}+\mathbf{TP}_{t-1|T}\mathbf{T}'-\mathbf{TP}_{t,t-1|T}-\mathbf{P}'_{t,t-1|T}\mathbf{T}'] \tag{4.2.23}$$

where

$$\mathbf{n}_{t|T}=\mathbf{a}_{t|T}-\mathbf{Ta}_{t-1|T},\quad t=1,\ldots,T \tag{4.2.24}$$

and

$$\mathbf{P}_{t,t-1|T}=\mathrm{E}[(\mathbf{a}_{t|T}-\boldsymbol{\alpha}_t)(\mathbf{a}_{t-1|T}-\boldsymbol{\alpha}_{t-1})'],\quad t=1,\ldots T \tag{4.2.25}$$

As Watson and Engle (1983) point out, a relatively straightforward way of computing $\mathbf{P}_{t,t-1|T}$ is to augment the state vector by the vector of lagged values, $\boldsymbol{\alpha}_{t-1}$. The matrix $\mathbf{P}_{t,t-1|T}$ then appears as the off-diagonal block of the $\mathbf{P}_{t|T}$ matrix of the augmented state vector.

The application of the EM algorithm to structural models may sometimes require modifications. Consider the BSM with seasonal dummies. All but the first three equations in the transition equation are identities and the only unknown elements in $\mathbf{Q}$ are σ_η^2, σ_ζ^2 and σ_ω^2. Thus in (4.2.19) n is three and $\mathbf{Q}$ is diagonal. Furthermore, because the only elements in $\boldsymbol{\alpha}_{t-1}$ which do not appear in $\boldsymbol{\alpha}_t$ are μ_{t-1}, β_{t-1} and γ_{t-s}, it is only necessary to augment $\boldsymbol{\alpha}_t$ by these three elements. Thus, the augmented state vector is an $(s+4)\times 1$ vector defined by $\boldsymbol{\alpha}_t^\dagger=[\boldsymbol{\alpha}_t' \quad \gamma_{t-s} \quad \mu_{t-1} \quad \beta_{t-1}]'$. Let $n_{i,t|T}$ denote the i-th element of $\mathbf{n}_{t|T}$ and define three vectors, $\mathbf{d}_1, \mathbf{d}_2$ and $\mathbf{d}_3$ such that the first element of $\mathbf{d}_1$ is unity, the last two are both minus one and the remainder are zero, the second element of $\mathbf{d}_2$ is one, the last is minus one and the remainder are zero, and all the elements in $\mathbf{d}_3$ are unity apart from the first two and the last two. Then

$$n_{i,t|T}=\mathbf{d}_i'\mathbf{a}_{t|T}^\dagger,\quad i=1,2,3,\quad t=1,\ldots,T \tag{4.2.26}$$

and

$$\hat{\sigma}_i^2=T^{-1}\left\{\sum_{t=1}^{T}n_{i,t|T}^2+\mathbf{d}_i'\left[\sum_{t=1}^{T}\mathbf{P}_{t|T}^\dagger\right]\mathbf{d}_i\right\},\quad i=1,2,3 \tag{4.2.27}$$

where $\sigma_1^2=\sigma_\eta^2, \sigma_2^2=\sigma_\zeta^2$ and $\sigma_3^2=\sigma_\omega^2$. Equation (4.2.21) gives the estimator of $\sigma_\varepsilon^2(=h)$.

Three minor points may be made concerning the implementation of the algorithm. Firstly, since $\mathbf{n}_{1|T}=0$, (4.2.27) can be written with a divisor of $T-1$ and a summation running from $t=2$ to T. Secondly, if the Kalman filter reaches a steady state in the sense that $\mathbf{P}_t$ is effectively time-invariant, considerable computational savings can be effected in the smoothing algorithm. Thirdly, if the variances of η_t, ζ_t and ω_t are expressed relative to σ_ε^2, the latter may be concentrated out of the likelihood function as in the prediction error decompositon methods.

Finally note that the form of (4.2.21) and (4.2.27) is such that the estimates of the variances will always satisfy the non-negativity constraints. This is a reflection of the self-consistency property of the EM algorithm; see Efron (1982, remark H).

4.2.5 Deterministic components

The notion that some components may be deterministic was mentioned in the discussion of the local linear trend model in sub-section 4.1.1. Models containing a deterministic component are not stabilisable. Nevertheless, the Kalman filter may still be applied provided that non-stationary and deterministic elements in the state vector are initiated with a diffuse prior or are treated as fixed at time $t=0$. The model may then be estimated by ML. Procedures based on the steady-state filter are inappropriate since in a non-stabilisable model $\bar{\mathbf{P}}$ is not p.d.

An alternative approach is to construct a modified state space model in which the deterministic components are removed from the state vector and placed in the measurement equation. The modified model is stabilisable and may be written as

$$y_t = \mathbf{z}^{\#\prime}\boldsymbol{\alpha}_t^{\#} + \mathbf{x}_t^{\#\prime}\boldsymbol{\delta}^{\#} + \varepsilon_t \tag{4.2.28a}$$

$$\boldsymbol{\alpha}_t^{\#} = \mathbf{T}^{\#}\boldsymbol{\alpha}_{t-1} + \mathbf{R}^{\#}\boldsymbol{\eta}_t^{\#} \tag{4.2.28b}$$

where $\boldsymbol{\alpha}_t^{\#}$ is a state vector of length $m^{\#} < m$, $\mathbf{x}_t^{\#}$ is an $(m-m^{\#})\times 1$ vector consisting of known functions of time and $\boldsymbol{\delta}^{\#}$ is an $(m-m^{\#})\times 1$ vector consisting of parameters which in the original formulation were treated as state variables. Thus in the local linear trend model $\mathbf{x}_{1t}^{\#}=t$, $\boldsymbol{\delta}^{\#}=\beta$ and the SSF is as in (4.1.8). In this case $\boldsymbol{\delta}^{\#}$ corresponds to an element which originally appeared in the state, but in other cases, a fixed seasonal component for example, $\boldsymbol{\delta}^{\#}$ may be a linear transformation of elements which originally appeared in the state. In the framework of (4.2.28), $\boldsymbol{\delta}^{\#}$ is treated as a vector of fixed parameters. ML estimation of $\boldsymbol{\delta}^{\#}$ and the hyperparameters, $\boldsymbol{\psi}$, can proceed via the GLS algorithm of sub-section 3.4.2. This is a special case of the procedure for handling exogenous explanatory variables, which are introduced into structural time series models in chapter 7.

When non-stationary elements in the state vector are initiated with a diffuse prior, the likelihood functions obtained from the modified SSF, (4.2.28), and the original SSF will be different. However, the difference lies only in the determinantal term and is asymptotically negligible. Nevertheless, the estimates of $\boldsymbol{\psi}$ may be different in small samples. The case for using the original SSF is that it yields a likelihood function which is consistent with the likelihood function obtained when the constraint that certain components be deterministic is not imposed. If all non-stationary elements are treated as fixed at $t=0$, the conflict between different definitions of the likelihood function does not arise. This is because $\boldsymbol{\alpha}_0$ is treated as a vector of parameters irrespective of whether or not it forms the starting point for a state vector which evolves stochastically over time. The likelihood function is the same irrespective of the SSF upon which it is based; if $\boldsymbol{\delta}^{\#}$

is defined as $\boldsymbol{\alpha}_0^{\#}$, the fixed elements in the state vector at $t=0$, (4.2.28) is part way towards the SSF given immediately below (4.2.10).

Within the diffuse prior framework, the likelihood function obtained from (4.2.28) is at odds with the likelihood function obtained from the original SSF because the elements of $\boldsymbol{\delta}^{\#}$ are treated as parameters. In the original SSF, the corresponding components are handled by state variables which are regarded as being random even though they do not change stochastically over time. The attraction of regarding them as random is that in more general models they may change over time. This not only yields the consistent definition of likelihood alluded to in the previous paragraph but also permits a consistent interpretation of the fitted model.

4.3. Estimation in the frequency domain

The frequency-domain approach to the ML estimation of unknown parameters in stationary Gaussian processes is based on a Fourier transform which converts serial correlation into heteroscedasticity. This enables the likelihood function to be written in the form

$$\log \mathrm{L} = -\tfrac{1}{2}T\log 2\pi - \frac{1}{2}\sum_{j=0}^{T-1}\log g_j - \pi\sum_{j=0}^{T-1}\frac{I(\lambda_j)}{g_j} \tag{4.3.1}$$

where $I(\lambda_j)$ and g_j are, respectively, the sample spectrum (or periodogram)

$$I(\lambda_j) = \frac{1}{2\pi T}\left|\sum_{t=1}^{T} y_t e^{-i\lambda_j t}\right|^2 \tag{4.3.2}$$

and the spectral generating function,

$$g_j = g[\exp(i\lambda_j)] \tag{4.3.3}$$

defined at the points $\lambda_j = 2\pi j/T$, $j=0,\ldots,T-1$. The unknown parameters, $\boldsymbol{\psi}$, appear in the spectral generating function and so ML estimation involves iterating with different values of $\boldsymbol{\psi}$, and hence g_j, until (4.3.1) is maximised. The periodogram ordinates are independent of $\boldsymbol{\psi}$ and so are only calculated once. For a structural model it will normally be necessary to apply a transformation, $\Delta(\mathrm{L})$, to the observations before computing (4.3.2). Hence T is redefined as $T-d$, where d is the order of the non-stationary operator $\Delta(\mathrm{L})$.

The attraction of frequency-domain methods for structural time series models is that the spectral generating function is usually very easy to evaluate. Since the s.g.f. is the only part of the likelihood function which changes when a new estimate of $\boldsymbol{\psi}$ is produced in an iterative optimisation procedure, the calculations involved in such a procedure can be carried out quite rapidly. For the BSM the s.g.f. was given in (2.4.58). This can be written as

$$g_j = z_{\mu j}\sigma_\eta^2 + z_{\beta j}\sigma_\zeta^2 + z_{\gamma j}\sigma_\omega^2 + z_{\varepsilon j}\sigma_\varepsilon^2 \tag{4.3.4}$$

where

$$z_{\mu j} = 2(1 - \cos \lambda_j s) \tag{4.3.5a}$$

$$z_{\beta j} = (1 - \cos \lambda_j s)/(1 - \cos \lambda_j) = s + 2 \sum_{h=1}^{s-1} (s-h) \cos \lambda_j h \tag{4.3.5b}$$

$$z_{\gamma j} = 6 - 8 \cos \lambda_j + 2 \cos 2\lambda_j \tag{4.3.5c}$$

and

$$z_{\varepsilon j} = 4(1 - \cos \lambda_j)(1 - \cos \lambda_j s) \tag{4.3.5d}$$

The quantities in (4.3.5) are independent of the unknown parameters in the model. This is characteristic of a *pure variance component model* and it has important implications for estimation and testing.

Strictly speaking, the expression in (4.3.1) is only equal to the likelihood function if the stationary process in question has the characteristics of a *circular* process. This assumption is unrealistic. Nevertheless (4.3.1) is approximately equal to the likelihood function for any stationary, invertible process and any results which can be shown to hold exactly under the circularity assumption will, in general, hold asymptotically when it is relaxed. The first sub-section below provides more details. Sub-section 4.3.2 shows that the information matrix can be obtained very easily in the frequency domain. The form of the information matrix is exploited in the scoring algorithm developed in sub-section 4.3.3 and it plays an important role when the properties of estimators are discussed in section 4.5.

4.3.1 Derivation of the spectral likelihood function

Consider a stationary stochastic process with mean zero and a strictly positive spectral density. The log-likelihood function for T normally distributed observations, denoted by the $T \times 1$ vector $\mathbf{y}$, is

$$\log L(\mathbf{y}) = -\tfrac{1}{2} T \log 2\pi - \tfrac{1}{2} \log |\mathbf{V}| - \tfrac{1}{2} \mathbf{y}' \mathbf{V}^{-1} \mathbf{y} \tag{4.3.6}$$

where $\mathbf{V}$ is the $T \times T$ covariance matrix of the observations, i.e. $E(\mathbf{yy}') = \mathbf{V}$.

The complex $T \times T$ Fourier matrix, $\mathbf{W}$, has as its jt-th element

$$w_{jt} = (2\pi T)^{-\frac{1}{2}} [\exp(i\lambda_{j-1} t)], \quad j, t = 1, \ldots, T \tag{4.3.7}$$

This matrix has the property that it diagonalises what is known as a Toeplitz matrix. If the stationary stochastic process is such that $\mathbf{V}$ has the form of a *circulant*, then its covariance matrix has the Toeplitz form and

$$\mathbf{WVW}^\dagger = \mathbf{F} \tag{4.3.8}$$

where $\mathbf{W}^\dagger$ is the complex conjugate transpose of $\mathbf{W}$ and $\mathbf{F}$ is a $T \times T$ diagonal matrix with j-th diagonal element $f(\lambda_{j-1})$, $j = 1, \ldots, T$. A covariance matrix has the form of a circulant if $\gamma(\tau)=\gamma(T-\tau)$ for $\tau=1,\ldots,T-1$, and if this condition is satisfied the process is said to be circular.

Since the Fourier matrix is proportional to a unitary matrix with

$$\mathbf{W}^{\dagger}\mathbf{W}=(1/2\pi)\mathbf{I} \tag{4.3.9}$$

it follows from (4.3.8) firstly that:

$$\mathbf{V}=(2\pi)^2\mathbf{W}^{\dagger}\mathbf{F}\mathbf{W} \tag{4.3.10}$$

and so

$$|\mathbf{V}|=(2\pi)^{2T}|\mathbf{W}^{\dagger}|\,|\mathbf{F}|\,|\mathbf{W}|=(2\pi)^{2T}|\mathbf{F}|\,|\mathbf{W}^{\dagger}\mathbf{W}|=(2\pi)^{T}|\mathbf{F}|$$

from which

$$-\tfrac{1}{2}\log|\mathbf{V}|=-\tfrac{1}{2}T\log 2\pi-\frac{1}{2}\sum_{j=0}^{T-1}\log f(\lambda_j)$$

and, secondly that:

$$\mathbf{V}^{-1}=\mathbf{W}^{\dagger}\mathbf{F}^{-1}\mathbf{W} \tag{4.3.11}$$

The likelihood function is therefore

$$\log L(\mathbf{y})=-T\log 2\pi-\frac{1}{2}\sum_{j=0}^{T-1}\log f(\lambda_j)-\tfrac{1}{2}\mathbf{y}'\mathbf{W}^{\dagger}\mathbf{F}^{-1}\mathbf{W}\mathbf{y} \tag{4.3.12}$$

However, bearing in mind the definition of the sample spectral density, (4.3.2), the last term can be written as

$$\mathbf{y}'\mathbf{W}^{\dagger}\mathbf{F}^{-1}\mathbf{W}\mathbf{y}=\sum_{j=0}^{T-1}\frac{I(\lambda_j)}{f(\lambda_j)} \tag{4.3.13}$$

since the j-th element of $\mathbf{Wy}$ is

$$\frac{1}{\sqrt{2\pi T}}\sum_{t=1}^{T}y_t e^{i\lambda_{j-1}t}$$

Therefore

$$\log L(\mathbf{y})=-T\log 2\pi-\frac{1}{2}\sum_{j=0}^{T-1}\log f(\lambda_j)-\frac{1}{2}\sum_{j=0}^{T-1}\frac{I(\lambda_j)}{f(\lambda_j)} \tag{4.3.14}$$

Replacing $f(\lambda_j)$ by $g_j/2\pi$ gives the likelihood function as written in (4.3.1). If the process does not satisfy the circularity assumption, the diagonalisation in (4.3.8) only holds asymptotically and (4.3.1) has to be regarded as an approximation to the likelihood function.

Some technical points concerned with the spectral likelihood are as follows.

(i) For a white-noise process, the diagonalisation in (4.3.8) follows trivially from the unitary property of **W**. Indeed, since $\mathbf{V}=\mathbf{I}$ for white noise, it obviously satisfies the circularity condition. The s.g.f. is $g(\lambda)=\sigma^2$ for all λ, and since

$$2\pi \sum_{j=0}^{T-1} I(\lambda_j)=\sum_{t=1}^{T} y_t^2 \tag{4.3.15}$$

is a consequence of Parseval's theorem, the log-likelihood function for Gaussian white noise, as given in (4.3.1), collapses to the familiar form

$$\log L=-\tfrac{1}{2}T\log 2\pi-\tfrac{1}{2}T\log\sigma^2-\frac{1}{2\sigma^2}\sum_{t=1}^{T} y_t^2 \tag{4.3.16}$$

(ii) For a model in canonical form, the estimation criterion function can be based solely on the last term in (4.3.1). Such a simplification is not possible for structural models containing more than one stochastic component. The reasoning is set out below.

It follows from a classical result of Kolmogorov, given in (5.5.4), that, in large samples,

$$\log\sigma^2\simeq\frac{1}{T}\sum_{j=0}^{T-1}\log 2\pi f(\lambda_j) \tag{4.3.17}$$

where σ^2 is the prediction error variance. Rearranging this expression gives

$$\frac{1}{2}\sum\log f(\lambda_j)=-\frac{T}{2}\log\sigma^2-\frac{T}{2}\log 2\pi$$

and substituting in (4.3.14) yields:

$$\log L(y)=-\frac{T}{2}\log 2\pi-\frac{T}{2}\log\sigma^2-\frac{1}{2}\sum_{j=0}^{T-1}\frac{I(\lambda_j)}{f(\lambda_j)} \tag{4.3.18}$$

For the corresponding reduced form ARMA process

$$f(\lambda_j)=g_j/2\pi=\sigma^2 g_j(\varphi,\theta)/2\pi \tag{4.3.19a}$$

where $g_j(\varphi,\theta)$, which is defined by

$$g_j(\varphi,\theta)=|\theta(e^{i\lambda j})|^2/|\varphi(e^{i\lambda j})|^2 \tag{4.3.19b}$$

is independent of σ^2. The likelihood function is therefore

$$\log L=-\frac{T}{2}\log 2\pi-\frac{T}{2}\log\sigma^2-\frac{\pi}{\sigma^2}\sum_{j=0}^{T-1}\frac{I(\lambda_j)}{g_j(\varphi,\theta)} \tag{4.3.20}$$

Maximising $\log L$ with respect to σ^2 gives

$$\tilde{\sigma}^2(\varphi,\theta)=\frac{2\pi}{T}\sum_{j=0}^{T-1}\frac{I(\lambda_j)}{g_j(\varphi,\theta)} \tag{4.3.21}$$

The prediction error variance may therefore be concentrated out of the likelihood function, with the result that maximising $\log L$ in (4.3.20) is equivalent to minimising

$$S(\boldsymbol{\varphi}, \boldsymbol{\theta}) = \sum_{j=0}^{T-1} \frac{I(\lambda_j)}{g_j(\varphi, \theta)} \tag{4.3.22}$$

with respect to $\boldsymbol{\varphi}$ and $\boldsymbol{\theta}$.

(iii) The reason for defining $I(\lambda_j)$ over the range $[0, 2\pi]$ is for convenience of presentation. However, since $I(\pi+\lambda)=I(\pi-\lambda)$ there is no point in computing almost twice as many periodogram ordinates as are necessary. Indeed an alternative expression to (4.3.1) is

$$\log L = -\frac{T}{2}\log 2\pi - \sum_{j=0}^{[T/2]} \delta_j \log g_j - 2\pi \sum_{j=0}^{[T/2]} \delta_j \frac{I(\lambda_j)}{g_j} \tag{4.3.23}$$

where $[T/2]$ is as defined in (2.1.15) and δ_j is the Kronecker delta defined as

$$\delta_j = \begin{cases} 1/2, & j=0, \tfrac{1}{2}T \text{ (when } T \text{ is even)} \\ 1, & \text{elsewhere} \end{cases} \tag{4.3.24}$$

(iv) If the process is postulated to have a non-zero mean, this will usually be estimated by the sample mean. The sample spectral density ordinates will then be computed from the mean corrected expression (2.4.46). The only consequence is that the ordinate at λ_0 is identically equal to zero. If the process is assumed to have a zero mean, it is preferable, other things being equal, not to correct for the mean; in other words (4.3.2) should be used. Asymptotically there is no difference. Note that if (4.3.2) is used when the mean, μ, is non-zero, then $I(\lambda_0)$ must be divided by $g_0 + \mu^2 T^2$.

(v) A further consequence of the diagonalisation of the covariance matrix is that for Gaussian observations

$$\left.\begin{aligned} 4\pi I(\lambda_j)/g_j &\sim \chi_2^2 \quad \text{for } j \neq 0, \tfrac{1}{2}T \text{ (for } T \text{ even)} \\ 2\pi I(\lambda_j)/g_j &\sim \chi_1^2 \quad \text{for } j = 0, \tfrac{1}{2}T \text{ (for } T \text{ even)} \end{aligned}\right\} \tag{4.3.25}$$

Furthermore the $I(\lambda_j)$'s are mutually independent for $j=0,\ldots,[T/2]$. An immediate corollary to (4.3.25) is that, since the mean and variance of a χ_k^2 distribution are k and $2k$ respectively, $I(\lambda_j)$ has a mean of $g_j/2\pi$ and a variance of $g_j^2/4\pi^2$ for $j=0,\ldots,[T/2]$. If the circularity assumption does not hold, then these results still hold asymptotically; see Anderson (1971).

4.3.2 *Derivatives and the information matrix*

Differentiating the log-likelihood function in (4.3.1) with respect to the $n \times 1$

vector of hyperparameters, $\boldsymbol{\psi}$ gives

$$\frac{\partial \log L}{\partial \boldsymbol{\psi}} = -\frac{1}{2}\sum_{j=0}^{T-1}\frac{1}{g_j}\frac{\partial g_j}{\partial \boldsymbol{\psi}} + \pi \sum_{j=0}^{T-1}\frac{I(\lambda_j)}{g_j^2}\frac{\partial g_j}{\partial \boldsymbol{\psi}}$$

$$= \frac{1}{2}\sum_{j=0}^{T-1}\left(\frac{2\pi I(\lambda_j)}{g_j} - 1\right)\frac{1}{g_j}\frac{\partial g_j}{\partial \boldsymbol{\psi}} \tag{4.3.26}$$

Differentiating a second time gives

$$\frac{\partial^2 \log L}{\partial \boldsymbol{\psi}\partial \boldsymbol{\psi}'} = \sum_{j=0}^{T-1}\left(\frac{2\pi I(\lambda_j)}{g_j} - 1\right)\frac{1}{2g_j}\frac{\partial^2 g_j}{\partial \boldsymbol{\psi}\partial \boldsymbol{\psi}'}$$

$$-2\sum_{j=0}^{T-1}\left(\frac{4\pi I(\lambda_j)}{g_j} - 1\right)\left(\frac{1}{2g_j}\right)^2\frac{\partial g_j}{\partial \boldsymbol{\psi}}\frac{\partial g_j}{\partial \boldsymbol{\psi}'} \tag{4.3.27}$$

The derivatives of g_j will normally be quite easy to obtain. Second derivatives may be more complicated, although in a pure variance component model such as the BSM they are, in fact, all zero. However, if expectations are taken in (4.3.27) the first term disappears in any case since, as noted in point (v) at the end of the previous sub-section,

$$\mathrm{E}[I(\lambda_j)] = g_j/2\pi, \quad j = 0, \ldots, T-1 \tag{4.3.28}$$

The information matrix is therefore

$$\mathbf{I}(\boldsymbol{\psi}) = \frac{1}{2}\sum_{j=0}^{T-1}\frac{1}{g_j^2}\frac{\partial g_j}{\partial \boldsymbol{\psi}}\frac{\partial g_j}{\partial \boldsymbol{\psi}'} \tag{4.3.29a}$$

$$= \sum_{j=0}^{[T/2]}\frac{\delta_j}{g_j^2}\frac{\partial g_j}{\partial \boldsymbol{\psi}}\frac{\partial g_j}{\partial \boldsymbol{\psi}'} \tag{4.3.29b}$$

This expression may be regarded as a large sample approximation to the information matrix if the process is not circular.

Example 4.3.1 For the random walk plus noise model it was shown in (2.4.56) that

$$g_j = \sigma_\eta^2 + 2(1 - \cos \lambda_j)\sigma_\varepsilon^2 \tag{4.3.30}$$

Differentiating g_j with respect to σ_η^2 and σ_ε^2 respectively and substituting in (4.3.29a) gives:

$$\mathbf{I}(\psi) = \frac{1}{2}\sum_{j=0}^{T-1}\frac{1}{[\sigma_\eta^2 + 2(1-\cos\lambda_j)\sigma_\varepsilon^2]^2}\begin{bmatrix} 1 & 2(1-\cos\lambda_j) \\ 2(1-\cos\lambda_j) & 4(1-\cos\lambda_j)^2 \end{bmatrix} \tag{4.3.31}$$

4.3.3 *Method of scoring*

The method of scoring is an iterative optimisation procedure of the form

$$\boldsymbol{\psi}^* = \hat{\boldsymbol{\psi}} + [\mathbf{I}(\hat{\boldsymbol{\psi}})]^{-1}(\partial \log L/\partial \boldsymbol{\psi}) \tag{4.3.32}$$

where $\hat{\boldsymbol{\psi}}$ is the current estimate of $\boldsymbol{\psi}$ and $\boldsymbol{\psi}^*$ is the updated estimate. Both the information matrix $\mathbf{I}(\boldsymbol{\psi})$ and the score vector $\partial \log L/\partial \boldsymbol{\psi}$ are evaluated at $\boldsymbol{\psi} = \hat{\boldsymbol{\psi}}$.

Setting $\mathbf{I}(\boldsymbol{\psi})$ equal to the information matrix of (4.3.29) and substituting for the score vector from (4.3.26) yields the following algorithm

$$\boldsymbol{\psi}^* = \hat{\boldsymbol{\psi}} + \left(\sum_{j=0}^{T-1} \frac{1}{g_j^2} \frac{\partial g_j}{\partial \boldsymbol{\psi}} \frac{\partial g_j}{\partial \boldsymbol{\psi}'}\right)^{-1} \sum_{j=0}^{T-1} \frac{1}{g_j^2} \frac{\partial g_j}{\partial \boldsymbol{\psi}} [2\pi I(\lambda_j) - g_j] \tag{4.3.33}$$

where g_j and its derivatives are evaluated at $\boldsymbol{\psi} = \hat{\boldsymbol{\psi}}$. The scoring algorithm therefore takes the form of a weighted Gauss-Newton algorithm as described, for example, in Harvey (1981a, ch. 4). At each iteration the estimate of $\boldsymbol{\psi}$ is updated by a weighted regression of $[2\pi I(\lambda_j) - g_j]$ on the elements of $\partial g_j/\partial \boldsymbol{\psi}$.

In a pure variance components model g_j is a linear function of the unknown parameters of $\boldsymbol{\psi}$. Thus it may be written in the form

$$g_j = \mathbf{z}_j' \boldsymbol{\psi} \tag{4.3.34}$$

where $\mathbf{z}_j$ is the vector of derivatives, $\partial g_j/\partial \boldsymbol{\psi}$, but all its elements are independent of $\boldsymbol{\psi}$. Expression (4.3.4) shows the s.g.f. of the BSM to be of the form (4.3.34) since $\boldsymbol{\psi} = [\sigma_\eta^2 \quad \sigma_\zeta^2 \quad \sigma_\omega^2 \quad \sigma_\varepsilon^2]'$ and the elements of $\mathbf{z}_j$ are as given in (4.3.5).

Substituting (4.3.34) in (4.3.33) and replacing $\partial g_j/\partial \boldsymbol{\psi}$ by $\mathbf{z}_j$ gives

$$\begin{aligned}\boldsymbol{\psi}^* &= \hat{\boldsymbol{\psi}} + \left[\sum g_j^{-2} \mathbf{z}_j \mathbf{z}_j'\right]^{-1} \sum g_j^{-2} \mathbf{z}_j 2\pi I(\lambda_j) \\ &\quad - \left[\sum g_j^{-2} \mathbf{z}_j \mathbf{z}_j'\right]^{-1} \sum g_j^{-2} \mathbf{z}_j \mathbf{z}_j' \hat{\boldsymbol{\psi}} \\ &= \left[\sum g_j^{-2} \mathbf{z}_j \mathbf{z}_j'\right]^{-1} \sum g_j^{-2} \mathbf{z}_j 2\pi I(\lambda_j) \end{aligned} \tag{4.3.35}$$

Further insight into the nature of this WLS regression can be obtained by observing that since, from (4.3.25), $2\pi I(\lambda_j)$ has a mean of g_j and a variance of g_j^2 in large samples, we can write

$$2\pi I(\lambda_j) \simeq \mathbf{z}_j' \boldsymbol{\psi} + \nu_j, \quad j = 0, \ldots, [T/2] \tag{4.3.36}$$

The disturbances, ν_j, are independently distributed in large samples with mean zero and variance $(\mathbf{z}_j' \boldsymbol{\psi})^2$. When $j = 0$ or $\frac{1}{2}T$ (for T even), ν_j/g_j has a centred χ_1^2 distribution. For all other values of j it follows a centred χ_2^2 distribution. The structure of (4.3.36) is the same as that of the dependent variable heteroscedasticity model which arises in econometrics; see Amemiya (1973). The only difference is that dependent variable heteroscedasticity models normally contain an unknown scale factor.

The introduction of a cyclical component into a model means that it cannot be a pure variance component model. Thus the scoring algorithm must be applied in the form (4.3.31). The contribution of the cycle to the s.g.f. is a term of the form $z_j^* g_{\psi j}$ where $g_{\psi j}$ is as defined in (2.4.54) for $\lambda = \lambda_j$, and z_j^* is an appropriate operator such as $z_{\mu j}$ or $z_{\varepsilon j}$, the expressions for which are defined in (4.3.5a) and (4.3.5d) respectively. The scoring algorithm thus involves the addition of three derivatives, with respect to the parameters σ_κ^2, ρ and λ_c respectively. Unlike the derivatives in a pure variance component model, these depend on the unknown parameters which the scoring algorithm is estimating: hence they must be updated at each iteration.

If we write $g_{\psi j} = (g_{jN}/g_{jD})\sigma_\kappa^2$, then

$$\frac{\partial g_{\psi j}}{\partial \sigma_\kappa^2} = g_{jN}/g_{jD}$$

$$\frac{\partial g_{\psi j}}{\partial \rho} =$$

$$\frac{g_{jD}[2\rho - 2\cos\lambda_c \cos\lambda_j] - g_{jN}[4\rho^3 + 8\rho\cos\lambda_c - 4(1+3\rho^2)\cos\lambda_c\cos\lambda_j + 4\rho\cos 2\lambda_j]\sigma_\kappa^2}{[g_{jD}]^2}$$

$$\frac{\partial g_{\psi j}}{\partial \lambda_c} = \frac{g_{jD}[2\rho\sin\lambda_c\cos\lambda_j] - g_{jN}[-4\rho^2\sin\lambda_c + 4\rho(1+\rho^2)\sin\lambda_c\cos\lambda_j]\sigma_\kappa^2}{[g_{jD}]^2}$$

Certain practical issues arise in implementing the algorithm in this case. Firstly, if $\rho = 0$ the algorithm breaks down since

$$\left.\frac{\partial g_{\psi j}}{\partial \lambda_c}\right|_{\rho=0} = 0$$

The reason for the failure is that λ_c is not identifiable when $\rho = 0$. It is therefore inappropriate to take $\rho = 0$ as a starting value. Secondly, the value of ρ must be kept in the range $0 < \rho < 1$ by resetting its value inside this range if it strays onto or outside the boundary during iterations. The alternative is to reparameterise ρ. This can be done by maximising with respect to a transformed parameter $\bar{\rho}$, say, where $\rho = \exp(-\bar{\rho}^2)$, or $\rho = \exp(-\bar{\rho})/[1 + \exp(-\bar{\rho})]$. Transformations may also be applied to keep λ_c in the range $0 \leqslant \lambda \leqslant \pi$.

Example 4.3.2. The scoring algorithm was applied to the data on rainfall in north-east Brazil described in sub-section 2.7.2. Using starting values of $\hat{\sigma}_\varepsilon^2 = \hat{\sigma}_\kappa^2 = 1$, $\hat{\rho} = 0.5$ and $\hat{\lambda}_c = 0.78$, convergence to the following solution was obtained in 16 iterations:

$$\begin{array}{cccc} \tilde{\sigma}_\varepsilon^2 = 1612, & \tilde{\sigma}_\kappa^2 = 200, & \tilde{\rho} = 0.84, & \tilde{\lambda}_c = 0.41 \\ (309) & (187) & (0.11) & (0.09) \end{array}$$

The period of the cycle was 15.3 years. These estimates are close to the time-domain estimates reported in sub-section 2.7.2.

4.3.4 *An asymptotically efficient two-step estimator*

Given an initial consistent estimator of $\boldsymbol{\psi}$, a single iteration of an algorithm such as scoring, Gauss-Newton or Newton-Raphson will yield an asymptotically efficient estimator of $\boldsymbol{\psi}$; see, for example, Harvey (1981a, p. 138). If the model is of a form in which (4.3.34) holds, an initial consistent estimator of $\boldsymbol{\psi}$ can be computed by setting $g_j = 1$ in the WLS formula, (4.3.35). This yields the OLS estimator:

$$\hat{\boldsymbol{\psi}} = \left[\sum_{j=0}^{T-1} \mathbf{z}_j \mathbf{z}_j'\right]^{-1} \sum_{j=0}^{T-1} \mathbf{z}_j 2\pi I(\lambda_j) \tag{4.3.37}$$

Evaluating g_j as $\mathbf{z}_j'\hat{\boldsymbol{\psi}}$ in (4.3.35) then gives an asymptotically efficient two-step estimator of $\boldsymbol{\psi}$ in the form of a WLS regression:

$$\hat{\boldsymbol{\psi}}^* = \left[\sum_{j=0}^{T-1} g_j^{-2} \mathbf{z}_j \mathbf{z}_j'\right]^{-1} \sum_{j=0}^{T-1} g_j^{-2} \mathbf{z}_j 2\pi I(\lambda_j) \tag{4.3.38}$$

An alternative way of constructing an asymptotically efficient two-step estimator is to replace g_j by a consistent smoothed estimator of the power spectrum. Such an estimator may be obtained by using a standard lag window or spectral window; see the discussion in section 2.4. An explicit initial estimator of $\boldsymbol{\psi}$ is not therefore computed. This estimator, like (4.3.37), was originally suggested by de Jong (1985).

Given that no prior information on $\boldsymbol{\psi}$ or $f(\lambda)$ is available, (4.3.37) is the most efficient estimator that can be computed directly from the sample autocorrelations without using an iterative procedure. As noted in sub-section 4.2.1, it is not easy to derive the form of this estimator in the time domain except in certain special cases. The following example serves to confirm that (4.3.37) does indeed correspond to the estimator, which can be worked out directly for one of these special cases.

Example 4.3.3. In the random walk plus noise model the s.g.f. and information matrix are as given in (4.3.30) and (4.3.31). The initial estimators of σ_η^2 and σ_ε^2 are obtained by regressing $2\pi I(\lambda_j)$ on a constant term and $2(1 - \cos \lambda_j)$, i.e.

$$\begin{bmatrix} \hat{\sigma}_\eta^2 \\ \hat{\sigma}_\varepsilon^2 \end{bmatrix} = \begin{bmatrix} T & 2\sum(1-\cos\lambda_j) \\ 2\sum(1-\cos\lambda_j) & 4\sum(1-\cos\lambda_j)^2 \end{bmatrix}^{-1} \begin{bmatrix} 2\pi\sum I(\lambda_j) \\ 4\pi\sum(1-\cos\lambda_j)I(\lambda_j) \end{bmatrix} \tag{4.3.39}$$

where all the summations are from $j=0$ to $T-1$. As in (4.3.15),

$$2\pi \sum I(\lambda_j) = \sum y_t^2 \simeq Tc(0) \tag{4.3.40}$$

where $c(0)$ is defined as in (2.4.5), except that it is the estimator of the variance of first differences. The approximation sign rather than an equality is needed because $c(0)$ involves the sample mean. However, this makes no difference asymptotically and if a mean were subtracted from the observations before computing the sample spectral density the equality would hold in any case. Using other trigonometric identities gives

$$\begin{aligned} 4\pi\sum(1-\cos\lambda_j)I(\lambda_j) &= 4\pi\sum I(\lambda_j) - 4\pi\sum I(\lambda_j)\cos\lambda_j \\ &= 2Tc(0) - 2Tc(1) \end{aligned}$$

$$\sum(1-\cos\lambda_j) = T$$

$$\sum(1-\cos\lambda_j)^2 = T - 0 + \tfrac{1}{2}T = 3T/2$$

Substituting in (4.3.39) gives

$$\begin{bmatrix} \hat{\sigma}_\eta^2 \\ \hat{\sigma}_\varepsilon^2 \end{bmatrix} = \begin{bmatrix} T & 2T \\ 2T & 6T \end{bmatrix}^{-1} \begin{bmatrix} Tc(0) \\ 2Tc(0) - 2Tc(1) \end{bmatrix} = \begin{bmatrix} c(0) + 2c(1) \\ -c(1) \end{bmatrix} \tag{4.3.41}$$

These estimators are the same as those which were obtained in the time domain in sub-section 4.2.1.

One minor problem which arises with the initial estimator, (4.3.37), is that it does not necessarily produce estimates of the variances which are positive. As a result the estimated g_j's used in the two-step estimator may be zero or negative and the procedure breaks down. One way of overcoming this difficulty is to amend any negative or zero estimates as follows: if $\hat{\sigma}_1^2 \leqslant 0$, then it is redefined as

$$\hat{\sigma}_1^2 = (a/T)\hat{\sigma}_2^2 \tag{4.3.42}$$

where a is a positive number and $\hat{\sigma}_2^2$ is the smallest positive estimate of a variance in the model. This modification does not affect the consistency of the estimator. In practice a value of $a = 10$ seems to work well.

Irrespective of the way in which the initial estimator of g_j is computed, the two-step estimator itself may yield negative estimates of the variances in small samples. When this happens it is suggested that they be set equal to zero.

4.3.5. Concentrating the likelihood function

One of the variances in a structural model can always be concentrated out of the likelihood function. For generality denote this parameter by σ_*^2 and define g_j^* such that

$$g_j = \sigma_*^2 g_j^* \tag{4.3.43}$$

where g_j^* is independent of σ_*^2 and depends on a set of parameters denoted by $\boldsymbol{\psi}_*$. In a BSM, σ_*^2 will usually be σ_ε^2 or σ_η^2. If it is the former, g_j^* is simply the s.g.f. defined in (4.3.4) with $\sigma_\eta^2, \sigma_\zeta^2$ and σ_ω^2 replaced by their relative variances q_η, q_ζ and q_ω, and σ_ε^2 set equal to unity. The parameter vector $\boldsymbol{\psi}_*$ is $\boldsymbol{\psi}_* = [q_\eta \quad q_\zeta \quad q_\omega]'$.

Substituting (4.3.43) into the likelihood function (4.3.1) yields

$$\log L = -\frac{T}{2}\log 2\pi - \frac{T}{2}\log \sigma_*^2 - \frac{1}{2}\sum_{j=0}^{T-1} \log g_j^* - \frac{\pi}{\sigma_*^2}\sum_{j=0}^{T-1} \frac{I(\lambda_j)}{g_j^*} \tag{4.3.44}$$

Note that the determinantal term involving the sum of the $\log g_j^*$'s will not, in general, be asymptotically negligible unless σ_*^2 is the prediction error variance. This is normally only the case if the model is in canonical form; compare the likelihood function (4.3.20). Bearing in mind that g_j^* is independent of σ_*^2, maximising (4.3.44) with respect to σ_*^2 gives

$$\sigma_*^2(\psi_*) = \frac{2\pi}{T}\sum_{j=0}^{T-1} \frac{I(\lambda_j)}{g_j^*} \tag{4.3.45}$$

Thus the concentrated log-likelihood function is:

$$\log L_c(\psi_*) = -\frac{T}{2}(\log 2\pi + 1) - \frac{T}{2}\log \sigma_*^2 - \frac{1}{2}\sum_{j=0}^{T-1} \log g_j^* \tag{4.3.46}$$

When the model is in canonical form, so that σ_*^2 is the prediction error variance,

$$\frac{\partial^2 \log L}{\partial \sigma_*^2 \partial \psi_*} \simeq \mathbf{0} \tag{4.3.47}$$

because the penultimate term in (4.3.44) is asymptotically negligible. Thus the Hessian matrix and the information matrix are block diagonal with respect to σ_*^2 and ψ_* in large samples. However, this result does not hold in general. This point should be borne in mind when devising a scoring algorithm or constructing a two-step estimator since some of the simplicity associated with the unconcentrated likelihood function is lost.

4.3.6 Deterministic components

Time-domain estimation of models containing deterministic components was discussed in sub-section 4.2.5. If such models are to be estimated in the frequency domain, the deterministic component must be handled by introducing an exogenous variable into the model. The estimation of models with exogenous variables is treated in detail in chapter 7, but since the variables in question are functions of time, it turns out that in many cases of interest they can be estimated independently of the stochastic part of the model.

Fixed level Consider a stationary and invertible series with a non-zero, unknown mean, μ. It is well known that the sample mean is an asymptotically efficient estimator of μ. This result is easy to demonstrate in the frequency domain, and, in fact, it is the case that if the circularity condition holds, the sample mean is the ML estimator of μ.

Let the model be

$$y_t = \mu + w_t \tag{4.3.48}$$

where w_t is a stationary indeterministic stochastic process with s.g.f. g(.) which is continuous and strictly positive everywhere in the range $[-\pi, \pi]$. The likelihood function is of the form (4.3.1) with

$$I(\lambda_j) = \frac{1}{2\pi T}\left|\sum_{t=1}^{T}(y_t-\mu)e^{-i\lambda_j t}\right|^2 \tag{4.3.49}$$

but since

$$\sum_{t=1}^{T} e^{-i\lambda_j t} = \begin{cases} T, & \lambda_j = 0 \\ 0, & \text{otherwise} \end{cases} \tag{4.3.50}$$

it follows that μ can be omitted from the expression for $I(\lambda_j)$ except in the case of $\lambda_j = 0$ when

$$I(\lambda_0) = \frac{1}{2\pi T}\left(\sum_{t=1}^{T} y_t - T\mu\right)^2 \tag{4.3.51}$$

Since $g(.)$ does not depend on μ, differentiating the log-likelihood function with respect to μ yields

$$\frac{\partial \log L}{\partial \mu} = \left(\sum_{t=1}^{T} y_t - T\mu\right)\bigg/ g_0 \tag{4.3.52}$$

and so the ML estimator of μ is

$$\tilde{\mu} = \bar{y} \tag{4.3.53}$$

Substituting $\bar{y}$ for μ in the likelihood function gives a concentrated likelihood function which takes the form of (4.3.1) but with $I(\lambda_j)$ replaced by $I^{\#}(\lambda_j)$ as defined in (2.4.47). Note, though, that $I(\lambda_j)$ and $I^{\#}(\lambda_j)$ are identical, except at λ_0, when $I^{\#}(\lambda_0)$ is zero. Hence ML estimators of the hyperparameters, $\boldsymbol{\psi}$, can be computed without actually computing $\bar{y}$.

Fixed slope Suppose that σ_ζ^2 is zero in the local linear trend model, (4.3.1) and (4.3.2). The model is now (2.3.58) and only first differences are required to give the stationary form:

$$\Delta y_t = \beta + \eta_t + \Delta\varepsilon_t \tag{4.3.54}$$

Provided that σ_η^2 is positive, the s.g.f. of $\Delta y_t - \beta$ is everywhere positive, and the frequency-domain likelihood is as in (4.3.1). It follows immediately from the argument leading to (4.3.53), that the ML estimator of β is

$$\tilde{\beta} = \sum_{t=2}^{T} \Delta y_t/(T-1) = (y_T - y_1)/(T-1) \tag{4.3.55}$$

In fact this is the ML estimator of β for any model in which Δy_t is a stationary and invertible stochastic process.

If second differences are taken in the local linear trend model and σ_ζ^2 is set equal to zero, g_0 is zero and so the likelihood function cannot be defined.

Fixed slope in a seasonal model If a model contains a seasonal component, as well as a trend with a fixed slope, the stationary form is obtained by taking seasonal differences. Thus for the BSM, (2.3.68), with $\sigma_\zeta^2=0$,

$$\Delta_s y_t = s\beta + S(L)\eta_t + \Lambda\omega_t + \Delta_s\varepsilon_t \tag{4.3.56}$$

Again it follows from the argument leading to (4.3.53) that for $\Delta_s y_t$ following any stationary, invertible process, the ML estimator of β is

$$\begin{aligned}\tilde{\beta} &= \frac{1}{s(T-s)}\sum_{t=s+1}^{T}\Delta_s y_t\\ &= \left(\frac{1}{s}\sum_{j=0}^{s-1} y_{T-j} - \frac{1}{s}\sum_{t=1}^{s} y_t\right)\Big/(T-s)\end{aligned} \tag{4.3.57}$$

This expression can be interpreted as the average in the last year minus the average in the first year, divided by the total number of periods minus the number of seasons

Fixed slope and seasonals If in the BSM, σ_ζ^2 and σ_ω^2 are both zero, taking first differences gives

$$\Delta y_t = \beta + \Delta\gamma_t + \eta_t + \Delta\varepsilon_t, \quad t=2,\ldots,T \tag{4.3.58}$$

where, from (2.3.42), summing any consecutive run of s $\Delta\gamma_t$'s gives zero. Let

$$\gamma_t^* = \beta + \Delta\gamma_t, \quad t=2,\ldots,T \tag{4.3.59}$$

and note that

$$\gamma_t^* = \gamma_{t-s}^*, \quad t=s+2,\ldots,T \tag{4.3.60}$$

Define the spectral likelihood function (4.3.1) for the process $\Delta y_t - \gamma_t^*$. After some manipulation, it can be shown that if $(T-1)/s$ is an integer, the ML estimators of the s distinct values of γ_t^* are given by

$$\tilde{\gamma}_t^* = \frac{s}{T-1}\sum_{p=0}^{[(T-1)/s]-1}\Delta y_{ps+t}, \quad t=2,\ldots,s+1; \tag{4.3.61}$$

see Fernández (1986, pp. 152–7). In other words, the ML estimator of γ_t^* is the seasonal mean of the first differences for month t.

The ML estimator of β is simply the average of the γ_t^*'s, that is

$$\tilde{\beta} = \frac{1}{s}\sum_{t=2}^{s+1}\gamma_t^* = \frac{1}{T-1}\sum_{t=2}^{T}\Delta y_t = (y_T - y_1)/(T-1) \tag{4.3.62}$$

This is identical to the estimator derived for a non-seasonal model in (4.3.55).

The estimators of the original seasonal effects, the γ_t's, are obtained as follows. First subtract $\tilde{\beta}$ from the γ_t^*'s to yield estimators of the differences of the γ_t's, that is

$$\tilde{\gamma}_t^\dagger = \tilde{\gamma}_t^* - \tilde{\beta}, \quad t = 2, \ldots, s+1 \tag{4.3.63}$$

where $\gamma_t^\dagger = \Delta\gamma_t$. Then, following Pierce (1978, p. 248),

$$\tilde{\gamma}_t = \sum_{i=2}^{t} \tilde{\gamma}_i^\dagger + \frac{1}{s}\sum_{i=2}^{s+1} (i-1)\tilde{\gamma}_i^\dagger, \quad t = 2, \ldots, s \tag{4.3.64a}$$

and

$$\tilde{\gamma}_1 = \frac{1}{s}\sum_{i=2}^{s+1} (i-1)\tilde{\gamma}_i^\dagger \tag{4.3.64b}$$

Since

$$\tilde{\gamma}_t = \tilde{\gamma}_{t-s}, \quad t = s+1, \ldots, T \tag{4.3.65}$$

the series may be seasonally adjusted by subtracting the estimate of the seasonal effect for the current month.

4.3.7 Further computational issues

Two main computational issues arise in carrying out ML estimation in the frequency domain. The first concerns the nature of the iterative procedure used to maximise the likelihood function. The second concerns the way in which the periodogram is computed.

The scoring algorithm provides one iterative procedure. In practice it will be implemented by incorporating a variable step-length into (4.3.33); see the discussion in Harvey (1981a, ch. 4). One point to note about the algorithm, though, is that it does not guarantee that the estimated variances will be positive. The same problem was noted in the case of the two-step estimator and a possible remedy was suggested. The same remedy can be used here. An alternative solution is to treat the standard deviations rather than the variances as the unknown parameters. A negative estimate of a standard deviation then becomes a positive variance when it is squared.

An alternative to the scoring algorithm is to use a general numerical optimisation procedure. The latest version of the quasi-Newton Gill-Murray-Pitfield algorithm, EO4JBF in the NAG library, is designed to handle constraints such as those which arise in estimating variances. When using a numerical optimisation procedure of this kind it always pays to concentrate one of the parameters out of the likelihood function. In a pure variance component model the scoring algorithm, or even the two-step estimator, not only gives suitable starting values but also indicates which parameter is a suitable candidate for being concentrated out. The important point to watch is that one does not attempt to concentrate out, σ_ε^2, say, when its 'true value' is actually zero.

For long time series, the *fast Fourier transform* (FFT) provides a very efficient method of calculating the periodogram; see Priestley (1981, pp. 575–7). For the shorter time series which are more typical in economic and social applications, there is less need for the FFT. However, the direct calculation of the periodogram ordinates can be speeded up considerably by calculating the required sines and cosines recursively as advocated in Pukkila (1977, p. 32).

4.4 Identifiability

The question of identifiability is a fundamental one in statistical modelling. It is particularly important in the context of unobserved components models since it is very easy to set up models which are not identifiable. This section does not attempt to give a definitive treatment of identifiability conditions in unobserved components models. What it does is to prove that the main structural models considered in this book are identifiable and to indicate why certain other models are not.

4.4.1 The concept of identifiability

In order to discuss identifiability it is important to distinguish between a *model* and a *structure*. A model specifies a distribution for the variable in question while a structure specifies the parameters of that distribution. Given this background, the following concepts may be defined.

(a) If two structures have the same joint density function they are said to be *observationally equivalent*.
(b) A structure is identifiable if there exists no other observationally equivalent structure.
(c) A model is *identifiable* if all its possible structures are identifiable. If no structure is identifiable, the model is said to be *underidentified*.

This is the standard definition of identifiability (or identification) in the econometric and statistical literature. It should not be confused with the concept of identification as it is used in Box and Jenkins (1976) to denote specification or with the engineering usage where it means estimation.

Identifiability has an immediate bearing on estimation. If two structures have the same joint density function, the probability of generating a particular set of observations is the same for both structures. Thus there is no way of differentiating between them on the basis of the data. Furthermore, it will often be the case that attempts to estimate models which are not identifiable will run into practical difficulties.

4.4.2 Identifiability of structural time series models

A time-invariant structural model can be made stationary by multiplying through by the operator $\Delta(L)$. The transformed observations have a multivariate distribution with zero mean vector and a covariance matrix which depends on the parameters in the model. Under the normality assumption the identifiability of the model depends on the form of this covariance matrix. However, since the process is stationary, the covariance matrix can be expressed in terms of the autocovariances. *Two Gaussian structures can therefore be defined as being observationally equivalent if their stationary forms have the same autocovariance function or, alternatively, the same power spectrum.* Furthermore, since a unique autocovariance function is associated with any invertible ARMA process, it follows that when two structures are observationally equivalent, they will have the same reduced form. When this situation arises, the solution, as in econometrics, is to place restrictions on the structural form. A model-admissible structure is one which satisfies these *a priori* restrictions.

A time-invariant structural model can be written in the UCARIMA form (2.5.27). Hotta (1983) has shown that the identifiability of such a model can be assessed in terms of a very simple order condition. The following assumptions on (2.5.27) are made, the asterisks on the AR and MA parameters being dropped for notational convenience.

(i) Each of the $\varphi_m(L)$ polynomials is stationary and of order p_m. Thus the p_m-th coefficient is non-zero for $m=0, 1, \ldots, M$. Similarly each $\theta_m(L)$ is invertible, though not necessarily strictly invertible, and of order q_m for $m=0, \ldots, M$.
(ii) Each pair, $\varphi_m(L)$ and $\theta_m(L), m=0, \ldots, M$, contains no common factors.
(iii) The polynomials $\varphi_m(L)$ and $\varphi_h(L)$ contain no common factors for $m \neq h$, $m, h=0, \ldots, M$.
(iv) The non-stationary polynomials, $\Delta_m(L)$, have no common factors.
(v) The disturbances, ξ_{mt}, $m=0, \ldots, M$ are mutually uncorrelated.
(vi) The disturbances are normally distributed.

Assumptions (iii), (iv) and (v) can be relaxed in certain cases. Thus the above conditions are best regarded as being sufficient rather than necessary.

Order condition for identifiability A sufficient condition for the identifiability of (2.5.27) is that at least M of the components should have $p_m + d_m \geqslant q_m + 1$. If there are no constraints on any of the $\varphi_m(L)$ or $\theta_m(L)$ polynomials then this condition is both necessary and sufficient.

The proof, which is due to Hotta (1983), is sketched at the end of this sub-section.

The only remaining problem in determining the identifiability of a structural model lies in the fact that the AR and MA parameters in (2.5.27) may not correspond to the stuctural parameters themselves. A one-to-one mapping between the UCARIMA parameters and the stuctural parameters must therefore be established in each case.

Example 4.4.1 Consider the local linear trend model (4.1.6). The UCARIMA form is

$$y_t = \frac{\xi_t + \theta\xi_{t-1}}{\Delta^2} + \varepsilon_t \tag{4.4.1}$$

and there is a one-to-one mapping between the structural parameters, σ_η^2 and σ_ζ^2, and the UCARIMA parameters, θ and σ_ξ^2. The structural model is therefore identified because the order condition for the trend component is satisfied. No conditions are needed on the irregular component. A white-noise specification is perfectly acceptable.

It is instructive to verify the identifiability of the model directly without invoking the general result. The autocovariance function of $\Delta^2 y_t$ is:

$$\gamma(0) = 6\sigma_\varepsilon^2 + 2\sigma_\eta^2 + \sigma_\zeta^2 \tag{4.4.2a}$$

$$\gamma(1) = -4\sigma_\varepsilon^2 - \sigma_\eta^2 \tag{4.4.2b}$$

$$\gamma(2) = \sigma_\varepsilon^2 \tag{4.4.2c}$$

Identifiability therefore follows immediately because the three equations are linearly independent and so can be solved to yield unique values of $\sigma_\varepsilon^2, \sigma_\eta^2$ and σ_ζ^2 given the autocovariance function.

Example 4.4.2 Adding a stochastic cycle to the moel in the previous example gives the UCARIMA form shown in (2.5.25). Since $\psi_t \sim \text{ARMA}(2, 1)$, the order condition is satisfied provided that ρ is strictly positive. If ρ is zero, ψ_t reduces to white noise and cannot be separated from the irregular term. Furthermore, λ_c is not identifiable when ρ is zero, irrespective of whether or not the irregular term is present.

When $\lambda_c = 0$, the numerator and denominator of ψ_t contain a common factor, $(1-\rho\text{L})$, and ψ_t reduces to an AR(1) process. However, because the parameter, ρ, in the common factor is the same as the parameter of the AR(1) process, the full cyclical component itself remains identifiable. Since the cycle is equivalent to an AR(1) process, the order condition is still satisified in the full model.

The conditions $\rho > 0, 0 \leqslant \lambda_c \leqslant \pi$, and $\text{E}(\kappa_t \kappa_t^*) = 0$ are sufficient to guarantee a unique mapping from the UCARIMA parameters to the structural parameters. Given these conditions, it is not necessary to assume that $\text{Var}(\kappa_t) = \text{Var}(\kappa_t^*)$.

Example 4.4.3 The basic structural model with seasonal dummies clearly satisfies the order condition. If the seasonal component is modelled in the trigonometric form, then, as noted in sub-section 2.5.6, the denominator in the seasonal component is S(L) while the numerator is an MA$(s-2)$ process. Since the order of S(L) is $s-1$, the order condition again holds.

Proof of the order condition The essential part of the proof of the order condition is to show that it holds for a two-component model. To do this, one component is taken to be ARMA(p, q) while the other is ARMA(r, s). Having shown that a sufficient condition for identifiability is that $p \geqslant q + 1$, a third component can be added to the model. Amalgamating the first two components then gives an ARMA(p^*, q^*) process in which $p^* = p + r$ and $q^* = \max(q + r, s + p)$. If in addition to $p \geqslant q + 1$ it is also the case that $r \geqslant q + 1$, then $p^* \geqslant q^* + 1$ and so the new two-component model is identifiable irrespective of the form of the new component. However, letting the second of the original components have $r \geqslant s + 1$ does not affect the identifiability of the original model and so the complete three-component model is identifiable. This argument can then be repeated to give the general result for an M-component UCARIMA model.

The principal result is based on the following stationary model

$$y_t = \varphi_p^{-1}(\mathrm{L})\theta_q(\mathrm{L})\eta_t + \beta_s(\mathrm{L})\varepsilon_t \tag{4.4.3}$$

where η_t and ε_t are independent white-noise processes with variances σ_η^2 and σ_ε^2 respectively. Contrary to the usual practice for an AR polynomial, $\varphi(\mathrm{L})$ will be defined with positive signs on the coefficients, i.e.

$$\varphi(\mathrm{L}) = \varphi_0 + \varphi_1 \mathrm{L} + \ldots + \varphi_p \mathrm{L}^p \quad \text{with } \varphi_0 = 1$$

The model can be written as

$$\varphi_p(\mathrm{L})y_t = \theta_q(\mathrm{L})\eta_t + \varphi_p(\mathrm{L})\beta_s(\mathrm{L})\varepsilon_t \tag{4.4.4}$$

The right-hand side is an MA process of order $q^* = \max(p + s, q)$. Thus the reduced form is an ARMA(p, q^*) process. It contains $p + q^* + 1$ parameters, including the variance of the disturbance term, while the structural model contains $p + q + s + 2$ parameters. The identifiability of the reduced form is guaranteed by the fact that since $\varphi(\mathrm{L})$ and $\theta(\mathrm{L})$ have no roots in common, neither do its own polynomials. It would therefore seem that identifiability of the structural model requires

$$p + q + s + 2 \geqslant p + q^* + 1$$

i.e.

$$p \geqslant q + 1 \tag{4.4.5}$$

The proof that this condition is both necessary and sufficient is as follows.

Since the φ_m's in the structural model are the same as the φ_i's in the reduced form, it follows from the identifiability of the reduced form that the φ_m's are identifiable. (It will be recalled that in an ARMA(p, q) model, the autoregressive parameters can be estimated from the autocorrelations at lag $q + m$, $m = 1, \ldots, p$, while the MA parameters can be estimated from the first q autocorrelations.)

Write the model in the form (4.4.3). Since the φ's are identifiable, the identifiability of the remaining structural parameters depends on the autocovariances up to order q^*. Now the autocovariance generating function of $\varphi(L)y_t$ is given by

$$\gamma(L)=\theta(L)\theta(L^{-1})\sigma_\eta^2+\varphi(L)\varphi(L^{-1})\beta(L)\beta(L^{-1})\sigma_\varepsilon^2 \tag{4.4.6}$$

If $p=q+1$, the autocovariances at lags $\tau=p,\ldots,p+s$ provide $s+1$ equations for estimating the $s+1$ parameters $\beta_1,\ldots,\beta_s$ and σ_ε^2. This can be seen as follows. In (4.4.6)

$$\varphi(L)\varphi(L^{-1})=\sum_{\tau=-\infty}^{\infty}\varphi_\tau^\dagger L^\tau \tag{4.4.7}$$

where

$$\varphi_\tau^\dagger=\sum_{j=0}^{\infty}\varphi_j\varphi_{j+\tau},\quad \tau=0,\ldots,p$$

The symbol $\beta_\tau^\dagger$ is defined in a similar way. It then follows from the second term of the right-hand side of (4.4.6) that the autocovariances of $\varphi(L)y_t$ for $\tau=p,\ldots,p+s$ are given by

$$\gamma(\tau)=\sigma^2\sum_{k=0}^{p+s-\tau}\varphi_{p-k}^\dagger\beta_k^\dagger,\quad \tau=p,\ldots,p+s \tag{4.4.8}$$

(The above expression assumes $s<p$ but it can easily be verified that the argument still holds if $s\geqslant p$.) Given the φ's, the s equations for $\tau=p+1,\ldots,p+s$ form a triangular system which has a unique solution for the $\beta^\dagger$'s and hence for the β's. The equation for $\tau=p$ can then be used to obtain a unique solution for σ_ε^2.

Given that the φ's, the β's and σ_ε^2 are identified, the $q+1$ equations involving $\gamma(0),\ldots,\gamma(q)$ can be used to estimate the θ's. Hence the order condition is necessary and sufficient for identifiability for the model as a whole.

The argument in Hotta (1983) is more detailed and is carried out in the frequency domain.

4.5 Properties of estimators

The first sub-section below sets out the asymptotic properties of ML estimators of linear time-invariant models. Equivalent regularity conditions may be formulated in either the time domain or the frequency domain. The behaviour of ML estimators of parameters which lie on the boundary of the parameter space is examined in sub-section 4.5.2. This is important for structural models because of the key role played by variance parameters. When certain variance parameters are equal to zero, the model contains deterministic components and sub-section 4.5.3 examines the asymptotic properties of the estimators of such components. The next sub-section discusses practical experience in small samples and concludes by illustrating, with the results from two applications, some of the points made. Sub-section 4.5.5 looks at the effect of non-normality.

4.5.1 Asymptotic properties

The regularity conditions needed for the ML estimator, $\tilde{\psi}$, to be asymptotically normal with mean ψ and covariance matrix Avar($\tilde{\psi}$) defined in (3.4.11) are as follows for a linear time-invariant model of the form (4.1.3):

(i) ψ is an interior point of the parameter space;
(ii) ψ is identifiable;
(iii) derivatives of log L up to order three exist and are continuous in the neighbourhood of the true parameter value ψ;
(iv) the state space model is detectable and stabilisable;
(v) $|\mathbf{I}-\mathbf{T}\mathrm{L}|$ can be factorised as $\Delta(\mathrm{L})\varphi(\mathrm{L})$ where $\Delta(\mathrm{L})$ contains no unknown parameters and $\varphi(\mathrm{L})$ has all its roots outside the unit circle.

The first three of the above conditions are standard and were given in sub-section 3.4.1. The reason for the last two is most easily demonstrated by showing their equivalence with certain conditions in the frequency domain.

In the frequency domain it can be shown that when the observations are generated by a stationary Gaussian stochastic process, $T^{\frac{1}{2}}(\tilde{\psi}-\psi)$ has a limiting normal distribution with mean vector zero and covariance matrix $\mathbf{IA}^{-1}(\psi)$, where $\mathbf{IA}(\psi)$ is given by

$$\mathbf{IA}(\psi)=\frac{1}{4\pi}\int_{-\pi}^{\pi}\frac{\partial \log g(e^{i\lambda})}{\partial\psi}\frac{\partial \log g(e^{i\lambda})}{\partial\psi'}\,\mathrm{d}\lambda \tag{4.5.1}$$

The conditions under which this result is valid are summarised in Hannan (1970, pp. 395–8) and Walker (1964). The first two conditions are the same as conditions (i) and (ii) listed above, that is ψ is an interior point of the parameter space and it is identifiable. The remaining conditions are as follows:

(iii) the derivatives of $1/g(.)$ up to order three exist and are continuous in the neighbourhood of the true parameter value;
(iv) the spectral density, and hence the s.g.f. $g(e^{i\lambda})$, is nowhere zero in the range $[-\pi,\pi]$;
(v) the parameters, θ_h, in the MA representation of the model are such that

$$\sum_{h=0}^{\infty} h|\theta_h| < \infty$$

Condition (iii) is effectively the same as condition (iii) in the time domain, while condition (v) in the time domain is implicitly invoked in the frequency domain since the results are being applied to a model which has first been made stationary by the known transformation, $\Delta(\mathrm{L})$. This leaves the two condition (iv)'s which, in fact, are equivalent. It was pointed out in sub-section 4.1.3, that a detectable and stabilisable model has an invertible reduced form, (4.1.42). If this is so, then the spectral density is strictly positive. As expected, therefore, the time- and frequency-domain regularity conditions are equivalent. Note that the question of whether or not the process is circular is not important in this context.

In finite samples, Avar($\tilde{\psi}$) is taken to be the inverse of the information matrix. It was shown in sub-section 3.4.5 that, in the time domain, the information matrix (3.4.69) depends only on first derivatives and so can be computed analytically or numerically as described in sub-section 3.4.6. In the frequency domain, Avar ($\tilde{\psi}$) can be set equal to the expression for the inverse of the information matrix given in (4.3.29a), that is

$$\text{Avar}(\tilde{\psi})=2\left[\sum_{j=0}^{T-1}\frac{1}{g_j^2}\frac{\partial g_j}{\partial\psi}\frac{\partial g_j}{\partial\psi'}\right]^{-1}$$

$$=2\left[\sum_{j=0}^{T-1}\frac{\partial\log g_j}{\partial\psi}\frac{\partial\log g_j}{\partial\psi'}\right]^{-1} \tag{4.5.2}$$

In moving from an infinite to a finite sample, integration over the range $[-\pi, \pi]$ is replaced by summation over T points and the divisor of 2π becomes a divisor of T. (The T does not appear in (4.5.2) because Avar ($\tilde{\psi}$) relates to the distribution of $\tilde{\psi}$, not $T^{\frac{1}{2}}\tilde{\psi}$.) As a rule it is much easier to evaluate the asymptotic covariance matrix from the finite summation in (4.5.2) than it is by working out the integrals in (4.5.1). Furthermore, for models which are not in canonical form, evaluating (4.5.2) analytically is normally considerably easier than evaluating the corresponding expression in the time domain.

Example 4.5.1 The information matrix for the variance parameters σ_η^2 and σ_ε^2 was given in (4.3.31). Inverting this matrix gives the finite sample approximation to the asymptotic covariance matrix of (4.5.2). If the model is reparameterised as $\psi=[q \quad \sigma_\varepsilon^2]'$, the corresponding expression, derived from (4.3.44) with $\sigma_*^2=\sigma_\varepsilon^2$ and $g_j^*=g_{\varepsilon j}=q+2(1-\cos\lambda_j)$ is

$$\text{Avar}\begin{bmatrix}\tilde{q}\\ \tilde{\sigma}_\varepsilon^2\end{bmatrix}=\frac{2}{v}\begin{bmatrix}1 & -\dfrac{\sigma_\varepsilon^2}{T}\displaystyle\sum_{j=0}^{T-1}\frac{1}{g_{\varepsilon j}}\\ -\dfrac{\sigma_\varepsilon^2}{T}\displaystyle\sum_{j=0}^{T-1}\frac{1}{g_{\varepsilon j}} & \dfrac{\sigma_\varepsilon^4}{T}\displaystyle\sum_{j=0}^{T-1}\frac{1}{g_{\varepsilon j}^2}\end{bmatrix} \tag{4.5.3}$$

where

$$v=\sum_{j=0}^{T-1}1/(g_{\varepsilon j})^2-\frac{1}{T}\left(\sum_{j=0}^{T-1}1/g_{\varepsilon j}\right)^2$$

The expression for the asymptotic variance of $\tilde{q}$ depends only on q.

The canonical form of the model is an MA(1) process. Unlike $\tilde{q}$ and $\tilde{\sigma}_\varepsilon^2$, the ML estimators of the parameters θ and σ_ε^2 are asymptotically independent.

Even if a structural time series model has been parameterised as $\boldsymbol{\psi}=(\boldsymbol{\psi}_*, \sigma_*^2)$, the information matrix is not, in general, block diagonal. This contrasts with a model with a single disturbance term where the information matrix is block diagonal with respect to the disturbance term variance and the other parameters.

The regularity conditions set out above also need to be invoked when certain estimators other than ML are employed. In a pure variance component model the frequency-domain OLS estimator (4.3.37) provides an initial estimator of $\boldsymbol{\psi}$. This estimator can also be interpreted as a moment estimator computed from the correlogram. Although it is consistent, the preliminary estimator will not, in general, be efficient. The asymptotic distribution of $\hat{\boldsymbol{\psi}}$ can be deduced from the regression formulation, (4.3.36). Although the disturbances are asymptotically independent of each other, they are heteroscedastic, with variances equal to the square of the expectation of the random variable. The finite sample approximation to the asymptotic covariance matrix of the OLS estimator is therefore

$$\text{Avar}(\hat{\boldsymbol{\psi}})=\frac{1}{2}\left(\sum_{j=0}^{T-1}\mathbf{z}_j\mathbf{z}_j'\right)^{-1}\left(\sum_{j=0}^{T-1}g_j^2\,\mathbf{z}_j\mathbf{z}_j'\right)\left(\sum_{j=}^{T-1}\mathbf{z}_j\mathbf{z}_j'\right)^{-1};$$

compare Amemiya (1973). The one-half disappears if the summations are taken over $j = 0, \ldots, [T/2]$ rather than over $j = 0, \ldots, T-1$.

4.5.2 *Boundary of the parameter space*

For all the structural models considered in chapter 2, the regularity conditions of the previous sub-section are satisfied if $\boldsymbol{\psi}$ is an interior point of the parameter space. If this is the case there is always a SSF which is detectable and stabilisable, and a transformation, $\Delta(L)$, which is independent of $\boldsymbol{\psi}$ and will reduce the model to stationarity. The question posed in this sub-section is what happens if one or more of the elements of $\boldsymbol{\psi}$ lies on the boundary of the parameter space. The answer depends partly on whether the remaining conditions (ii) to (v) are still satisfied. If they are, and only a single parameter lies on the boundary, the asymptotic distribution of its ML estimator is still related to a normal distribution, but is modified so as to take account of the boundary. Thus it may have a half-normal distribution, with a variance given by the information matrix, and a mass of one-half on the boundary. The distribution of the other parameters is unaffected though, of course, their joint distribution with the parameter whose true value lies on the boundary is affected. Such results may be generalised to cases where several parameters lie on the boundary of the parameter space.

Random walk plus noise Condition (iv) is satisfied if σ_η^2 is strictly positive. The stabilisability and detectability conditions are easy to verify – see Example 3.3.4

– while in the frequency domain the s.g.f.

$$g(e^{i\lambda}) = \sigma_\eta^2 + 2(1 - \cos\lambda)\sigma_\varepsilon^2 \tag{4.5.4}$$

is zero at $\lambda = 0$ unless $\sigma_\eta^2 > 0$. Note that when σ_η^2 is zero, the reduced form MA(1) process,

$$\Delta y_t = \xi_t + \theta\xi_{t-1} \tag{4.5.5}$$

is strictly non-invertible since $\theta = -1$.

It can be seen immediately from (4.5.4) that it is not necessary to have σ_ε^2 strictly positive in order to satisfy condition (iv). Thus provided that σ_η^2 is strictly positive, the ML estimator of σ_ε^2 will be such that, in large samples, it will have a half-normal distribution with probability equal to one-half, and a value of zero with probability equal to one-half. In terms of the reduced form, having σ_ε^2 equal to zero is equivalent to θ being zero in (4.5.5) and the unrestricted ML estimator of θ has an asymptotic normal distribution in these circumstances because it can take both positive and negative values; positive estimates of θ correspond to boundary estimates of σ_ε^2. The presence of a deterministic drift component makes no difference to the above results as the model can always be put in the SSF of (4.1.8).

The breakdown of the regularity condition (iv) makes it difficult to determine the sampling distribution of the ML estimator of σ_η^2 when the true value is equal to zero. However, the finite sample properties of the ML estimator of the MA parameter θ have been studied by Sargan and Bhargava (1983) and Anderson and Takemura (1986). They show that there is a non-zero probability that the ML estimator of θ is exactly equal to ± 1 and this probability may be calculated for all values of θ including $\theta = \pm 1$. Since (4.5.5) is the reduced form of the random walk plus noise model and it is strictly non-invertible when $\sigma_\eta^2 = 0$, these results have implications for the distribution of the ML estimator of σ_η^2. Indeed it is possible to analyse the random walk plus noise model directly and to evaluate the probability that the ML estimator of σ_η^2 is exactly equal to zero for different initial conditions. For a diffuse prior, this probability is equal to 0.657 when the sample size is large and the true value of σ_η^2 is zero; see Shephard and Harvey (1989).

Local linear trend As noted in sub-section 4.1.1, detectability and stabilisability of the local linear trend model hold if and only if $\sigma_\zeta^2 > 0$. The same condition can be verified quite easily in the frequency domain. With $\sigma_\zeta^2 > 0$, condition (iv) is satisfied irrespective of whether σ_η^2 and σ_ε^2 are zero.

Basic structural model The BSM is detectable and stabilisable if and only if σ_ζ^2 and σ_ω^2 are strictly positive. In a trigonometric seasonality model with different variances for each frequency, it is necessary to have all these variances strictly positive. The s.g.f. is given in (4.3.4). At $\lambda_j = 0$, $z_{\mu j}$, $z_{\beta j}$ and $z_{\gamma j}$ are all zero and so $\sigma_\zeta^2 > 0$ is necessary for the s.g.f. to be positive at this point. Similarly at the seasonal frequencies, $\lambda_j = 2\pi j/s, j = 1, \ldots, [s/2]$, all the terms disappear except for the one involving σ_ω^2.

Cycles Models containing a cyclical component, such as the trend plus cycle and cyclical trend models, are such that

$$|\mathbf{I} - \mathbf{T}\mathrm{L}| = \Delta(\mathrm{L})\varphi(\mathrm{L})$$

where the autoregressive polynomial, $\varphi(\mathrm{L}) = 1 - 2\rho \cos \lambda_c \mathrm{L} + \rho^2 \mathrm{L}^2$, is stationary if ρ is strictly less than one. A value of ρ equal to one leads to the standard asymptotic distribution theory breaking down. This is the *unit root* problem, which has been studied at some length in the context of autoregressive models which can be estimated by OLS; see sub-section 6.1.3. At the other extreme, a value of ρ equal to zero means that λ_c is no longer identifiable; see Example 4.4.2. If λ_c is known, the requirement that ρ be non-negative gives its ML estimator a half-normal distribution.

4.5.3 Deterministic components

The properties of deterministic components depend on whether they are regarded as being fixed or stochastic; see the discussion in sub-section 4.2.5. If they are stochastic, it is appropriate to retain them in the state vector, and to report their estimated RMSEs at the end of the sample period. These RMSEs will, in general, be affected by the variability of the other elements in the state vector. If the components are regarded as fixed, they are treated as unknown parameters. In this case it is appropriate to report their asymptotic standard errors as computed from the information matrix.

It can be shown, as a special case of a result given in section 7.3, that the asymptotic information matrix is block diagonal with respect to the parameters associated with the deterministic components and the hyperparameters, $\boldsymbol{\psi}$. Thus the two sets of ML estimators are asymptotically independent. The asymptotic covariance matrix of $\tilde{\boldsymbol{\psi}}$ is estimated in finite samples by an expression of the form (4.5.2). We now proceed to obtain the asymptotic covariance matrix of the ML estimator of the parameters associated with the deterministic components. Again this is most easily done in the frequency domain. The stochastic part of the model is assumed to satisfy the regularity conditions of sub-section 4.5.1.

Fixed level Differentiating (4.3.52) yields

$$\frac{\partial^2 L}{\partial \mu^2} = -\frac{T}{g_0}$$

Hence

$$\mathrm{Avar}(\bar{y}) = g_0/T \tag{4.5.6}$$

This expression is very easy to evaluate. As an example, consider the cycle plus irregular model used in sub-section 2.7.4. It follows from (2.4.54) that

$$\text{Avar}(\bar{y}) = [\sigma_\kappa^2/(1-\rho)^2 + \sigma_\varepsilon^2]/T \tag{4.5.7}$$

If y_t is the sum of $n+1$ ARMA components, that is

$$y_t = \mu + \sum_{j=0}^{n} \varphi_j^{-1}(L)\,\theta_j(L)\xi_{jt} \tag{4.5.8}$$

then

$$\text{Avar}(\bar{y}) = \sum_{j=0}^{n} \varphi_j^{-2}(1)\,\theta_j^2(1)\,\sigma_j^2 \tag{4.5.9}$$

Fixed slope For the fixed slope local linear trend model, (4.3.54), it follows immediately from (4.5.6) that

$$\text{Var}(\tilde{\beta}) = \sigma_\eta^2/(T\text{-}1) \tag{4.5.10}$$

More generally, if η_t in (4.3.54) is a process other than white noise, the s.g.f. of η_t at $\lambda=0$ appears in (4.5.10) in place of σ_η^2. The irregular component, ε_t, makes no contribution to this expression even if it follows a more general process than white noise. The reason is that the s.g.f. of $\Delta\varepsilon_t$ is always zero at $\lambda=0$. When a seasonal component is present, the asymptotic variance of the slope estimator in (4.3.57) is

$$\text{Avar}(\tilde{\beta}) = g_0/(T-s) \tag{4.5.11}$$

where g_0 is the s.g.f. of $\Delta_s y_t$ at $\lambda=0$.

Fixed slope and seasonals Following Fernández (1986, pp. 152–7), the asymptotic covariance matrix of $\tilde{\gamma}^* = (\tilde{\gamma}_2^*, \ldots, \tilde{\gamma}_{s+1}^*)'$ is

$$\text{Avar}(\tilde{\gamma}^*) = \frac{s^2}{T-1}\left[\sum_{r=0}^{s-1} g_r \mathbf{C}_r\right]^{-1} \tag{4.5.12}$$

where $g_r = g\{\exp[-i2\pi r(T-1)/s]\}$, $g\{\,.\,\}$ being the s.g.f. of the indeterministic part of Δy_t, and $\mathbf{C}_r$ is an $s \times s$ matrix the jk-th element of which is $\cos 2\pi r(j-k)/s$, $r=0, \ldots, s-1$. A seasonality test may be carried out by testing the hypothesis that all s elements of $\tilde{\gamma}^*$ are identical.

4.5.4 Small samples

Experience with computing ML estimators for small and moderate sample sizes, smaller than 200 on the whole, leads to the following conclusions. First of all, frequency-domain procedures are considerably faster than time-domain procedures, with the method of scoring performing very well in most cases. After computing estimates via the method of scoring, a switch to a general numerical optimisation procedure, such as the quasi-Newton method of Gill-Murray-Pitfield, rarely produces any significant changes. In the time domain, the performance of the EM algorithm seems to be disappointingly slow. For it to be viable at all, it must be modified by incorporating a line-search procedure into it. However, even if this is done, it appears to be hardly faster than maximising the likelihood function directly by numerical optimisation; see Harvey and Peters (1984).

As regards the values of the estimators, the major differences occur when certain of the variance parameters are close to, or equal to their boundary values of zero. Thus in a local linear trend model, the frequency domain always yields positive values of $\tilde{\sigma}_\zeta^2$. This is because the frequency-domain likelihood is zero when $\tilde{\sigma}_\zeta^2$ is zero. Similarly when the model contains a seasonal component, σ_ω^2 must be positive if the frequency-domain likelihood function is not to become zero. On the other hand, it is not unusual, for the reasons suggested in sub-section 4.5.2, for exact ML in the time domain to yield zero estimates for σ_ζ^2 and σ_ω^2.

Although the frequency-domain procedures are relatively fast and work well in most cases, there are occasions when the time-domain and frequency-domain estimates are not close to each other. When there is some conflict, experience suggests that the exact ML estimators computed in the time domain are more reliable. This is presumably because the criterion function in the time domain is based on prediction errors. Therefore, if in doubt, the rule is to use the time-domain estimates. However, it should be borne in mind that a wide discrepancy between estimates computed from different procedures can be an indication of model misspecification. The same is true when problems of convergence are encountered.

Asymptotic standard errors are almost invariably easier to compute in the frequency domain using (4.5.2), even if estimation has been carried out in the time domain. Some care must be taken if estimates of parameters such as σ_ζ^2 and σ_ω^2 are close to, or equal to, zero. In these circumstances it is necessary to recognise that the model contains a deterministic component and to compute the asymptotic standard errors of the hyperparameters with respect to models for which the stationary form has a positive s.g.f. everywhere in the range $[-\pi, \pi]$. Thus, if in a local linear trend model, σ_ζ^2 is estimated to be zero, or very close to zero, the asymptotic standard errors of the estimates of σ_ε^2 and σ_η^2 are computed using expression (4.5.3).

The limited Monte Carlo evidence available suggests that the use of asymptotic standard errors is not unreasonable in small samples. Table 4.5.1 shows the results of a study carried out as part of an MSc project at the LSE by P. Gonzalez. The model is a random walk plus noise with $\sigma_\varepsilon^2 = \sigma_\eta^2 = 1$ and estimation was carried out by the method of scoring on 200 artificially generated series for each of the sample sizes $T = 50$, 200 and 1000. The standard deviation of the estimates estimated over the 200 series is close to the asymptotic standard error computed

Table 4.5.1 *Estimates for random walk plus noise models based on 200 artificially generated observations*

Sample size	Parameter	Mean	Standard deviation	Asymptotic standard error	Kolmogorov-Smirnov statistic
50	σ_η^2	0.980	0.473	0.473	0.060
	σ_ε^2	1.015	0.408	0.400	0.055
200	σ_η^2	0.985	0.236	0.235	0.061
	σ_ε^2	1.018	0.188	0.199	0.061
1000	σ_η^2	0.999	0.102	0.105	0.033
	σ_ε^2	0.991	0.094	0.089	0.049[a]

[a] Statistically significant at 5% level.

using the true values of the parameters for each sample size. Furthermore, the Kolmogorov-Smirnov statistic shows that only for σ_ε^2 for $T=1000$ can the null hypothesis of normality be rejected at the 5% level of significance. However, one would presumably expect estimates to be relatively less normal in finite samples, the closer the signal–noise ratio, q, is to zero.

Some of the points made above are illustrated by the applications reported below. The estimates labelled 'TD' were computed by exact ML in the time domain using the Gill-Murray-Pitfield numerical optimisation algorithm. Starting values were obtained by using the frequency-domain method of scoring. The frequency-domain results themselves are reported as 'FD*', while 'FD' denotes the estimates obtained by running through the Kalman filter with the relative variances given by 'FD*', computing the time-domain estimate of σ_*^2 by (4.3.5) and then multiplying the relative variances by this estimate. This 'fine tuning' of the frequency-domain estimates by time-domain methods seems, in general, to be desirable.

Purse snatching in Chicago The time series on purse snatching in Chicago was introduced in sub-section 2.7.3 where it was argued that a local level model was appropriate. The results of fitting the more general local linear trend model are compared with the estimates obtained from the local level model in Table 4.5.2.

The TD estimates obtained for the local linear trend model are quite close to the estimates for the local level model, with $\tilde{\sigma}_\zeta^2$ being equal to zero. As expected from the discussion earlier, the FD estimate of σ_ζ^2 is not equal to zero. However, it is not far from zero, and the estimates of the other two parameters are not very different to the estimates obtained in the time domain. The FD estimates were

Table 4.5.2 *Estimation of local trend models for purse-snatching data*

		σ_η^2	σ_ζ^2	σ_ε^2
Local linear trend	TD	6.174	0	23.93
	Est. SE	(3.175)	—	(5.57)
	FD*	7.855	0.074	23.28
	FD	7.404	0.070	21.95
	Est. SE	(4.994)	(0.082)	(5.76)
Local level	TD	5.149	n.a.	24.79
	Est. SE	(2.973)	n.a.	(5.58)
	FD*	4.726	n.a.	25.37
	FD	4.725	n.a.	25.37
	Est. SE	(2.586)	n.a.	(5.55)

computed by the method of scoring. This converged in 32 iterations, and numerical optimisation in the frequency domain did not lead to any change. The asymptotic standard errors reported for the TD estimates were computed in the FD by treating the slope as though it were known to be deterministic. In other words, they were based on the s.g.f. of Δy_t rather than $\Delta^2 y_t$; attempting to use the latter would have been inappropriate as the spectrum is zero at $\lambda=0$.

When the model was estimated with β treated as a fixed parameter, the TD estimates were, as might be expected, virtually identical to those reported for the more general model. However, the method of scoring, although it converged in two iterations, did so to a result in which the estimate σ_η^2 was zero. The inadequacy of this solution showed up in the diagnostics. Dropping the deterministic slope component from the model gave the perfectly acceptable estimates reported in Table 4.5.2 in 12 iterations of the scoring algorithm.

Returning to the model with the slope treated as a deterministic component, the estimated standard error of $\tilde{\beta}$, computed in the time domain by treating t like any other exogenous variable, is 0.304. The corresponding estimate, obtained directly from (4.5.10) is very similar:

$$\text{ASE}(\tilde{\beta})=\sqrt{6.174/70}=0.297$$

(The estimate of β itself is 0.075.) When β is treated as stochastic and included in the state vector, its estimated RMSE is 0.367. The reason this is greater than the estimated asymptotic SE is that the MSE matrix $\mathbf{P}_T$ is not block diagonal. In other words the estimation errors $m_T-\mu_T$ and $b_T-\beta$ are correlated with each other.

Airline passengers Various estimates of the quarterly airline passenger series

Table 4.5.3 *Estimation of BSM for monthly airline data: January 1949 to December 1958*[a]

		σ_η^2	σ_ζ^2	σ_ω^2	σ_ε^2
Scoring iterations	1	36.0	-0.0489^b	0.32	22.3
	2	33.3	0.0036	0.60	12.7
	3	33.4	0.0034	0.55	16.0
	⋮	⋮	⋮	⋮	⋮
	7	33.1	0.0034	0.55	16.0
	FD	31.9	0.0033	0.53	15.4
	Est. SE	(11.2)	(0.0046)	(0.17)	(11.8)
	Exact ML	40.3	0	0.35	18.7
	Est. SE	(13.0)	—	(0.13)	(11.6)

[a] All estimates have been multiplied by 10^5.
[b] As negative, this was re-set to a positive value.

were presented in sub-section 2.7.5. The results of estimating the monthly series in the time and frequency domains are shown in Table 4.5.3. The frequency-domain estimates were computed by the method of scoring. Convergence was achieved in seven iterations. Transferring these estimates to a numerical optimisation procedure failed to produce any change. The frequency-domain estimates are reasonably close to the time-domain estimates, based on the exact likelihood function, although the latter took considerably longer to compute. The TD estimate of σ_ζ^2 is zero. The FD estimate is very close to zero.

The preliminary estimator, labelled as the first iteration of scoring in Table 4.5.3, yields an inadmissible estimate of σ_ζ^2. However, since this estimate was finally deemed to be zero, this is not too serious. The remaining estimates are not too far removed from the final estimates. The two-step estimates, obtained by setting σ_ζ^2 to a small positive number, are even closer while the estimates obtained at the third step are very close.

The estimates in Table 4.5.3 are based on the observations from January 1949 to December 1958. In sub-section 5.7.4, the results of making predictions over the next two years are reported. The differences in the time- and frequency-domain estimates of the parameters make virtually no difference to the predictions. Because σ_ζ^2 is effectively zero, the SEs were estimated using the s.g.f. for $\Delta_{12}y_t$ rather than $\Delta\Delta_{12}y_t$. It could also be argued that since σ_ω^2 is small it might be appropriate to treat the seasonal component as deterministic also. As it is, the estimated standard error reported for both the TD and FD estimates is very small, and it must be remembered that if the seasonal component is, in fact, deterministic, the ML estimator of σ_ω^2 will not be asymptotically normal.

A final issue which deserves investigation is the modification of the FD estimator by means of tapering. Tapering consists of introducing a weighting function into the sample spectrum, (4.3.2), which becomes

$$I(\lambda_j)=\frac{1}{2\pi H}\left|\sum_{t=1}^{T} y_t h_t e^{-i\lambda_j t}\right|^2 \tag{4.5.13}$$

where

$$H=\sum_{t=1}^{T} h_t^2$$

The taper, h_t, normally decreases as t goes to one or T. Pukkila (1979) suggested that tapering might improve the properties of FD estimators of parameters of ARMA models. More recently Dahlhaus (1988) has provided a theoretical justification for the technique and argued that it is likely to be particularly effective when some of the roots of the AR or MA polynomial lie close to the unit circle. In the context of a structural model, therefore, tapering may be of value in estimating a cyclical component in which the damping factor, ρ, is close to one. More fundamentally, it may give better estimators when the stationary form of the model is close to being non-invertible, for example because either σ_ζ^2 or σ_ω^2 is close to zero in a BSM. Indeed Dahlhaus (1988) goes further than this and presents results which suggest that a suitably tapered FD procedure would be consistent even if the true values of σ_ζ^2 and/or σ_ω^2 were zero.

4.5.5 *Non-normality*

When the observations are not necessarily normally distributed, the estimators computed by maximising the Gaussian likelihood function are known as *quasi-maximum likelihood* estimators. The asymptotic properties of quasi-ML estimators may be derived provided that the following condition is added to those set out in sub-section 4.5.1:

(vi) the moments of the disturbance term in the reduced form exist up to order four.

In an ARMA model, the parameters in $\boldsymbol{\varphi}$ and $\boldsymbol{\theta}$ vary independently of σ^2, and with normal disturbances the information matrix is block diagonal with respect to $(\boldsymbol{\varphi}, \boldsymbol{\theta})$ and σ^2. As a result, the asymptotic distribution of the estimators of $\boldsymbol{\varphi}$ and $\boldsymbol{\theta}$ is not affected by non-normality of ML observations. Thus inference concerning $\boldsymbol{\varphi}$ and $\boldsymbol{\theta}$, but not σ^2, remains valid even if the Gaussianity assumption is incorrect, although, of course, there will usually be a loss in efficiency. In structural models on the other hand, the information matrix for the parameters associated with the stochastic part of the model is not, in general, block diagonal; see (4.5.3). Dropping the normality assumption tends to affect the asymptotic distribution of all the parameters, except those which are associated with deterministic components and hence are independent of $g(e^{i\lambda})$. Using $\boldsymbol{\psi}^*$ to denote the quasi-ML estimator of ψ, the general result, as proved in Dunsmuir (1979), is that $T^{\frac{1}{2}}(\tilde{\psi}-\psi)$ has a limiting normal distribution with mean vector zero and covariance matrix

$$\mathbf{C}(\psi)=\mathbf{A}^{-1}(2\mathbf{A}+\mathbf{B})\mathbf{A}^{-1}=2\mathbf{A}^{-1}+\mathbf{A}^{-1}\mathbf{B}\mathbf{A}^{-1} \tag{4.5.14}$$

where

$$\mathbf{A}=2\mathbf{IA}(\psi)$$

with $\mathbf{IA}(\psi)$ defined as in (4.5.1) and

$$\mathbf{B}=\kappa\left[\frac{1}{2\pi}\int_{-\pi}^{\pi}\frac{\partial\log g(e^{i\lambda})}{\partial\psi}\right]\left[\frac{1}{2\pi}\int_{-\pi}^{\pi}\frac{\partial\log g(e^{i\lambda})}{\partial\psi'}\right] \tag{4.5.15}$$

where κ is the measure of excess kurtosis of the reduced-form disturbance term, that is

$$\kappa=\mathrm{E}(\xi_t^4)/\sigma^4-3 \tag{4.5.16}$$

Thus if $\kappa=0$, as it is under normality, the asymptotic covariance matrix reduces to $\mathbf{IA}^{-1}(\psi)$ evaluated at $\psi=\tilde{\psi}^*$. Excess kurtosis, on the other hand, will result in $\mathbf{IA}^{-1}(\psi)$ being an underestimate of $\mathbf{C}(\psi)$ since $\mathbf{A}^{-1}\mathbf{B}\mathbf{A}^{-1}$ is p.s.d.

The finite sample expression for the asymptotic covariance of $\tilde{\psi}$, corresponding to (4.5.2) in the Gaussian case, is

$$\mathrm{Avar}(\tilde{\psi}^*)=\mathbf{A}_T^{-1}(2\mathbf{A}_T+\mathbf{B}_T)\mathbf{A}_T^{-1} \tag{4.5.17a}$$

where

$$\mathbf{A}_T=\left[\sum_{j=0}^{T-1}\frac{1}{g_j^2}\frac{\partial g_j}{\partial\psi}\frac{\partial g_j}{\partial\psi'}\right] \tag{4.5.17b}$$

and

$$\mathbf{B}_T=\kappa\left[\sum_{j=0}^{T-1}\frac{1}{g_j}\frac{\partial g_j}{\partial\psi}\right]\left[\sum_{j=0}^{T-1}\frac{1}{g_j}\frac{\partial g_j}{\partial\psi'}\right] \tag{4.5.17c}$$

Thus an estimator of the asymptotic covariance matrix of $\tilde{\psi}^*$ may be computed by evaluating (4.5.17) at $\psi=\tilde{\psi}^*$ and estimating κ from the Kalman filter innovations, that is $\hat{\kappa}=b_2-3$, where b_2 is given in (5.4.11). The problem with this estimator of the asymptotic covariance matrix is that being based on an estimator of a fourth moment, it is likely to be subject to considerable sampling variability itself. Tests for normality were given at the end of sub-section 5.4.2, and one would not recommend the use of the estimator based on (4.5.17) unless these tests showed a clear rejection of normality. It is also important to bear in mind that rejection of normality could be an indication of the presence of outliers and it would be wise to investigate this possibility; see sub-section 6.4.2.

4.6 Prediction

Once a structural model has been put in state space form, running the Kalman filter up to time T gives the current estimate of the state vector. This contains the starting values for the forecast functions of the various components and the series itself. For a time-invariant model of the form (4.1.3), the expression for the *multi-step predictor*, (3.5.4), reduces to

$$\tilde{y}_{T+l|T} = \mathbf{z}'\mathbf{a}_{T+l|T} = \mathbf{z}'\mathbf{T}^l\mathbf{a}_T, \quad l = 1, 2, \ldots \tag{4.6.1}$$

This is the MMSLE of y_{T+l}, and in a Gaussian model it is the MMSE. If (4.1.3) can be broken down into components, as in (4.1.2), the forecast function for the series can be expressed as the sum of the forecast functions for the individual components, that is

$$\tilde{y}_{T+l|T} = \sum_{m=1}^{M} \mathbf{T}_m^l \mathbf{a}_{mT} \tag{4.6.2}$$

The forecast functions of the various stochastic components typically found in structural models were given when these components were introduced in section 2.3.

The forecasts of the series and its components can be obtained recursively, as can the MSE matrix of the predicted state vector, $\mathbf{a}_{T+l|T}$. However, for a time-invariant model it is straightforward to write down an expression for this MSE matrix in terms of the MSE matrix of $\mathbf{a}_T$. This was done in (3.5.5). Note that although the forecast functions for the various components in a model of the form (4.1.13) can be written down separately, as in (4.6.2), they are not uncorrelated because the $\mathbf{P}_T$ matrix is not block diagonal. Using (3.5.5) and (3.5.6b), the MSE of $\tilde{y}_{T+l|T}$ for (4.1.3) is seen to be

$$\text{MSE}(\tilde{y}_{T+l|T}) = \left[\mathbf{z}'\mathbf{T}^l\mathbf{P}_T\mathbf{T}^{l'}\mathbf{z} + \mathbf{z}'\left(\sum_{j=0}^{l-1} \mathbf{T}^j\mathbf{R}\mathbf{Q}\mathbf{R}'\mathbf{T}^{j'}\right)\mathbf{z} + 1\right]\sigma_*^2 \tag{4.6.3}$$

This formula gives the MSE of the forecast conditional on the unknown hyperparameters, $\boldsymbol{\psi}_*$. If these are estimated, an approximation to the MSE can be obtained by adding another term to (4.6.3) as suggested by formula (3.5.12). This term is of $O(T^{-1})$, whereas (4.6.3) is of $O(1)$. The discussion here will be carried out on the assumption that $\boldsymbol{\psi}_*$ is known, so that (4.6.3) is correct.

The expression for the MSE of predictions in a random walk plus noise model was given in (3.5.8b). It was noted that the MSE increases linearly with the lead time. For other models the increase can be more rapid. In the local linear trend model

$$\begin{aligned}\text{MSE}(\tilde{y}_{T+l|T}) = [&(p_T^{(1,1)} + 2lp_T^{(1,2)} + l^2p_T^{(2,2)}) \\ &+ lq_\eta + \tfrac{1}{6}l(l-1)(2l-1)q_\zeta + 1]\,\sigma_\varepsilon^2, \quad l = 1, 2, \ldots\end{aligned} \tag{4.6.4}$$

where $p_T^{(i,j)}$ is the ij-th element of the matrix $\mathbf{P}_T = \sigma_\varepsilon^{-2}\text{MSE}(\mathbf{a}_T)$. The third term, which is the contribution arising from changes in the slope, leads to the most dramatic increases as l increases. If the trend model was completely deterministic both the second and third terms would disappear from (4.6.4) which would collapse to (2.3.5). In a model where some components are deterministic, including them in the state vector ensures that their contribution to the MSE of predictions is accounted for via the first term in (4.6.3).

It is perhaps important to stress that a rapid deterioration in the prediction MSE as the lead time increases does not mean that the model is misspecified. What it does indicate is that the behaviour of the series is such that it is a difficult one to forecast accurately several steps ahead. It may be that the only way in which more accurate medium-term predictions may be achieved is by constructing a model which uses information on several series rather than on just one.

In a Gaussian model, the prediction error is normally distributed. Hence, given ψ_*, a $100(1-\alpha)\%$ prediction interval for y_{T+l} is

$$\tilde{y}_{T+l|T} \pm t_{T-d}^{(\alpha/2)} . \mathrm{RMSE}(\tilde{y}_{T+l|T}) \tag{4.6.5}$$

where $t_{T-d}^{(\alpha/2)}$ is the $\alpha/2$ significance point on a t-distribution, as defined below (2.3.5), and $\mathrm{RMSE}(\tilde{y}_{T+l|T})$ is the square root of (4.6.3) with σ_*^2 replaced by its unbiased estimator, (4.2.5). For a reasonably large value of T, $\tilde{y}_{T+l|T} \pm \mathrm{RMSE}(\tilde{y}_{T+l|T})$ is a 68% prediction interval. In a Gaussian model $\tilde{y}_{T+l|T}$ can be interpreted as the mean of the distribution of y_{T+l}, conditional on the observations up to and including y_T. This interpretation will be used in the first two sub-sections below. When referring to the conditional distribution of y_{T+l}, (4.6.3) will be denoted by $\sigma_{T+l|T}^2$.

4.6.1 *Instantaneous data transformations*

Suppose that a series has been transformed so as to better satisfy the normality and time-homogeneity conditions. The most common transformation is to take logarithms although a more general transformation such as the Box-Cox may sometimes be appropriate. Transformations of this kind give rise to a minor problem since what is usually required is a predictor for the original rather than the transformed series.

Consider taking logarithms. Let y_t be the transformed series and suppose that the conditional distribution of y_{T+l} is $N(\tilde{y}_{T+l|T}, \sigma_{T+l|T}^2)$. Let $y_t^\dagger$ denote the original series. It then follows from the properties of the log-normal distribution that

$$\underset{T}{\mathrm{E}}(y_{T+l}^\dagger) = \exp(\tilde{y}_{T+l|T} + \tfrac{1}{2}\tilde{\sigma}_{T+l|T}^2), \quad l=1,2,\ldots \tag{4.6.6}$$

In other words, the naive forecast, obtained by simply exponentiating $\tilde{y}_{T+l|T}$, is not an unbiased forecast of $y_{T+l}^\dagger$. Fortunately there is usually very little difference between the two. In any case, prediction intervals are obtained without recourse to corrections of the kind embodied in (4.6.6). Thus a 95% prediction interval for $y^{\dagger}_{T+l}$ is

$$\exp(\tilde{y}_{T+l|T} - 1.96\ \sigma^2_{T+l|T}) \leqslant y^{\dagger}_{T+l} \leqslant \exp(\tilde{y}_{T+l|T} + 1.96\ \sigma^2_{T+l|T}) \tag{4.6.7}$$

A more general treatment of instantaneous data transformations can be found in Granger and Newbold (1977, ch. 9).

4.6.2 Loss functions

In making forecasts of y_{T+l}, the appropriate predictor has been taken to be $\tilde{y}_{T+l|T}$. This estimator, which is the mean of the conditional distribution of y_{T+l}, has the attraction of being the MMSE of y_{T+l} under the normality assumption.

Suppose that there is a loss, or cost, function associated with the error in predicting y_{T+l}. This function will be zero when the predictor is exactly equal to the actual value and will be monotonically non-decreasing as the absolute value of the prediction error increases. Given such a function we seek a predictor, $\tilde{y}^*_{T+l|T}$, which minimises the expected loss, where the expectation is taken with respect to the conditional distribution of y_{T+l}.

Let the loss function be denoted by $L(y, \tilde{y}^*)$, where the subscripts have been dropped to avoid notational complexity. Under the normality assumption, the conditional distribution of y is $N(\tilde{y}, \sigma^2)$. If the loss function is symmetric with respect to the error, $y - \tilde{y}^*$, the optimal predictor of y, namely the one which minimises $E[L(y, \tilde{y}^*)]$, is $\tilde{y}^* = \tilde{y}$; see Granger and Newbold (1977, pp. 116–17). A special case is the quadratic loss function, which has an expected loss of σ^2.

The assumption of a symmetric loss function is often not a reasonable one. Two asymmetric loss functions for which the optimal predictor can be found are as follows.

Linear The linear loss function is defined as

$$L(y, \tilde{y}^*) = \begin{Bmatrix} a(y - \tilde{y}^*), & y > \tilde{y}^* \\ 0 \quad , & y = \tilde{y}^* \\ b(y - \tilde{y}^*), & y < \tilde{y}^* \end{Bmatrix} \tag{4.6.8}$$

with $a > 0$ and $b < 0$. In this case Granger and Newbold (1977, pp. 118–19) show that

$$\tilde{y}^* = \tilde{y} + \sigma . \Phi(a/(a-b)) \tag{4.6.9}$$

where $\Phi(\,.\,)$ denotes a cumulative standard normal distribution. In the symmetric case $a = -b$, and $\tilde{y}^*$ reduces to $\tilde{y}$ since $\Phi(\frac{1}{2}) = 0$.

Linex A more elaborate loss function, suggested by Varian (1975) and developed further by Zellner (1986), is

$$L(y, \tilde{y}^*) = b\{\exp[a(\tilde{y}^* - y)] - (\tilde{y}^* - y) - 1\}, \quad a \neq 0, b > 0 \tag{4.6.10}$$

There are two parameters, a and b, in (4.6.10) with b serving to scale the loss function and a determining its shape. As can be seen directly there is a minimum loss of zero at $y = \tilde{y}^*$. The shape of the loss function is shown in the figures presented in Varian (1975, p. 197) and Zellner (1986, p. 447). It combines linear and exponential features, hence the name 'linex'.

The estimator which minimises the expected loss can be found by noting that, since $-ay \sim N(-ay, a^2\sigma^2)$, it follows from (4.6.6) that

$$E[\exp(-ay)] = \exp(-a\tilde{y} + \tfrac{1}{2}a^2\sigma^2)$$

Therefore, taking expectations of (4.6.10) gives

$$E[L(y, \tilde{y}^*)] = b[\exp(a\tilde{y}^*)\exp(-a\tilde{y} + \tfrac{1}{2}a^2\sigma^2) + \tilde{y}^* - \tilde{y} + 1]$$

Differentiating with respect to $\tilde{y}^*$, setting the result equal to zero and rearranging, gives the loss-minimising estimator of y as

$$\tilde{y}^* = \tilde{y} - \tfrac{1}{2}a\sigma^2 \tag{4.6.11}$$

As with the linear loss function, the optimal predictor is equal to the conditional expectation of y plus a correction factor.

When a series has been subject to an instantaneous data transformation, the conditional distribution of a future value of the original series, $y^{\dagger}_{T+l}$, will no longer be normal. Furthermore it will usually be asymmetric. However, if the loss function is quadratic, the expected loss is minimised by the mean of the conditional distribution of $y^{\dagger}_{T+l}$. Thus, if logarithms have been taken, (4.6.6) is the appropriate predictor. On the other hand, for a symmetric linear loss function, that is (4.6.8) with $a = b$, the predictor which minimises the expected loss is the median of the conditional distribution of $y^{\dagger}_{T+l}$. If the conditional distribution of the predictor of a future value of the transformed series is normal with a mean of $\tilde{y}_{T+l|T}$, the median of $y^{\dagger}_{T+l|T}$ is obtained simply by applying the reverse transformation to $\tilde{y}_{T+l|T}$. Thus in the case of the logarithmic transformation, the optimal predictor of $y^{\dagger}_{T+l}$ is the naive predictor

$$\tilde{y}^{\dagger *}_{T+l|T} = \exp(\tilde{y}_{T+l|T})$$

rather than (4.6.6).

4.6.3 Cumulative predictions

When dealing with flow variables, such as income and expenditure, it is sometimes necessary to make predictions of the cumulative effect of the variable up to lead time l. This kind of application arises in assessing cumulative demand for the purpose of stock control or production control in operational research.

The cumulative prediction, $\tilde{y}^c_{T+l|T}$, is simply

$$\tilde{y}^c_{T+l|T} = \sum_{j=1}^{l} y_{T+j|T} \tag{4.6.12}$$

However, as pointed out in Johnston and Harrison (1986), some care is needed in working out its MSE,

$$\text{MSE}(\tilde{y}^c_{T+l|T}) = \text{E}\left[\left(\sum_{j=1}^{l}(y_{T+j} - \tilde{y}_{T+j|T})\right)^2\right] \tag{4.6.13}$$

Consider first the random walk plus noise model. In this case

$$y_{T+j} - \tilde{y}_{T+j|T} = \mu_T - m_T + \sum_{h=1}^{j} \eta_{T+h} + \varepsilon_{T+j}, \quad j = 1, \ldots, l \tag{4.6.14}$$

and so

$$\sum_{j=1}^{l}(y_{T+j} - \tilde{y}_{T+j|T}) = l(\mu_T - m_T) + \sum_{j=1}^{l}\sum_{h=1}^{j} \eta_{T+h} + \sum_{j=1}^{l} \varepsilon_j$$

The MSE of the cumulative forecast is therefore

$$\text{MSE}(\tilde{y}^c_{T+l|T}) = [l^2 p_T + \tfrac{1}{6}l(l+1)(2l+1)q + l]\sigma^2_\varepsilon, \quad l = 1, 2, \ldots \tag{4.6.15}$$

More generally for any model of the form (4.1.3),

$$y_{T+j} - \tilde{y}_{T+j|T} = \mathbf{z}'\mathbf{T}^j(\boldsymbol{\alpha}_T - \mathbf{a}_T) + \mathbf{z}'\mathbf{R}\sum_{r=1}^{j} \boldsymbol{\eta}_{T+r} + \varepsilon_j \tag{4.6.16}$$

and so

$$\text{MSE}(\tilde{y}^c_{T+l|T}) = \left[\mathbf{z}'(\mathbf{W}_l - \mathbf{I})\mathbf{P}_T(\mathbf{W}_l - \mathbf{I})'\mathbf{z} + \mathbf{z}'\left(\sum_{j=0}^{l-1} \mathbf{W}_j\mathbf{RQR}'\mathbf{W}_j'\right)\mathbf{z} + lh\right]\sigma^2_* \tag{4.6.17}$$

where the matrices $\mathbf{W}_l$ and $\mathbf{W}_j$ are defined by the expression

$$\mathbf{W}_r = \sum_{s=0}^{r} \mathbf{T}^s \tag{4.6.18}$$

This expression can be evaluated by augmenting the state vector by a cumulator variable and making predictions from the Kalman filter in the usual way; see sub-section 6.3.3 for details.

4.7 Estimation of components

The estimation of the unobserved components in a structural time series model at all points throughout the sample is often of some interest. Linear estimates may be obtained by applying one of the smoothing algorithms described in section 3.6.

An example of smoothed trend and seasonal components was given in section 1.4, while the smoothed cycle fitted to data on rainfall in north-east Brazil was shown in sub-section 2.7.2. The important general application of seasonal adjustment will be discussed in section 6.2.

The smoothing algorithms based on the state space form are very general. For given values of the hyperparameters they yield the optimal estimators of the various components at any point in the sample. The sample may be finite and the components and their MSEs may be estimated at any point between $t=1$ and $t=T$. Unfortunately, it is rather difficult, in general, to obtain expressions from the state space smoothing algorithms showing the weights being applied to the observations in estimating various components. Such expressions can be derived much more easily within the classical framework. This section is concerned primarily with exploring the relationship between the classical and state space approaches to the estimation of unobserved components or, as it is often known, signal extraction.

4.7.1 Classical formulae for signal extraction

The classical Kolmogorov–Wiener approach to signal extraction is set out in the book by Whittle (1983), the first edition of which appeared in 1963. The formulae developed are applicable to the optimal estimation of a stationary component embedded in a stationary observed process. However, Bell (1984) has recently established that the results extend to non-stationary unobserved components models of the form (2.5.27), that is

$$y_t = \sum_{m=0}^{M} \frac{\theta_m(L)}{\Delta_m(L)\varphi_m(L)} \xi_{mt} \tag{4.7.1}$$

where the ξ_{mt}'s are mutually uncorrelated white-noise processes, and $\varphi_m(L)$, $\theta_m(L)$ and $\Delta_m(L)$ are polynomials in the lag operator for $m=0$ to M. The non-stationary operators, $\Delta_m(L)$, have all their roots on the unit circle but, for the reasons discussed in the next sub-section, they are assumed to have no roots in common. The MA operators, $\theta_m(L)$, have their roots outside or on the unit circle and so components which are strictly non-invertible are permitted.

The classical approach enables formulae for the optimal estimators of the unobserved components to be constructed in terms of the observations. This leads to alternative algorithms for the computation of smoothed estimators. However, the main value of the classical formulae probably lies in the insight which they give into the nature of the smoothed estimators. The material presented here is simply intended to give the reader a flavour of the classical approach rather than going into any technical details. The subject is dealt with in some depth in Whittle (1983), Nerlove *et al.* (1979, ch. V) and Priestley (1981, ch. 10).

The most straightforward classical formulae relate to the estimation of an unobserved component in an infinite sample. From the practical point of view, these results are generally a reasonable approximation when the sample is moderately large and the point to be estimated is somewhere near the middle.

Suppose that the component to be extracted is the one corresponding to $m=1$, and let this component be denoted as μ_t. This implies no loss in generality, nor does it imply that the component is necessarily a trend. The MMSLE of μ_t based on an infinite sample is

$$m_{t|\infty} = \sum_{j=-\infty}^{\infty} w_j y_{t+j} \tag{4.7.2}$$

where the weights are given by the coefficients of the powers of L in the polynomial $w(\mathrm{L})$, determined from the expression

$$w(\mathrm{L}) = \frac{|\theta_1(\mathrm{L})|^2\sigma_1^2}{|\Delta_1(\mathrm{L})\varphi_1(\mathrm{L})|^2} \Bigg/ \sum_{m=0}^{M} \frac{|\theta_m(\mathrm{L})|^2\sigma_m^2}{|\Delta_m(\mathrm{L})\varphi_m(\mathrm{L})|^2} \tag{4.7.3}$$

where $|\theta_m(\mathrm{L})|^2 = \theta_m(\mathrm{L})\theta_m(\mathrm{L}^{-1})$ and similarly for $\phi_m(\mathrm{L})$ and $\Delta_m(\mathrm{L})$. This expression can be rewritten as

$$w(\mathrm{L}) = \frac{\left|\prod_{m\neq 1} \Delta_m(\mathrm{L})\right|^2 |\theta_1(\mathrm{L})|^2 |\varphi_1(\mathrm{L})|^{-2}\sigma_1^2}{g(\mathrm{L})} \tag{4.7.4}$$

where $g(\mathrm{L})$ is the autocovariance generating function of the stationary process

$$\left[\prod_{m=0}^{M} \Delta_m(\mathrm{L})\right] y_t$$

If desired, $g(\mathrm{L})$ can be expressed in terms of the coefficients of the reduced form ARMA model, that is

$$g(\mathrm{L}) = \sigma^2|\theta(\mathrm{L})|^2/|\varphi(\mathrm{L})|^2 \tag{4.7.5}$$

The coefficients of $w(\mathrm{L})$ can be computed from (4.7.4) by a suitable algorithm; see, for example, Box *et al.* (1978).

The MSEs of the smoothed estimators, together with the covariances between the estimation errors at different points in time, can be obtained from the covariance generating function of $m_{t|\infty} - \mu_t$. Bell (1984) shows that this is given by

$$v(\mathrm{L}) = [\sigma_1^2|\theta_1(\mathrm{L})|^2/|\varphi_1(\mathrm{L})|^2]\left[\sum_{m\neq 1} \sigma_m^2 \left|\prod_{j\neq 1,m} \Delta_j(\mathrm{L})\right|^2 |\theta_m(\mathrm{L})|^2/|\varphi_m(\mathrm{L})|^2\right] \Bigg/ g(\mathrm{L}) \tag{4.7.6}$$

The MSE of $m_{t|\infty}$ is given by the coefficient of L^0 in (4.7.6). An alternative way of evaluating the MSE is by integrating the spectral density of the estimation error. Thus

$$\mathrm{MSE}(m_{t|\infty}) = \frac{1}{2\pi}\int_{-\pi}^{\pi} v(e^{i\lambda})\,d\lambda \tag{4.7.7}$$

Example 4.7.1 Consider the following model, the significance of which will become apparent in sub-section 6.1.2:

$$y_t = \mu_t + \varepsilon_t^* \tag{4.7.8a}$$

$$\mu_t = \mu_{t-1} + \eta_t^* + \eta_{t-1}^* \tag{4.7.8b}$$

where ε_t^* and η_t^* are mutually uncorrelated white-noise disturbances with the same variance, σ_*^2. Thus

$$y_t = \left(\frac{1+\mathrm{L}}{1-\mathrm{L}}\right)\eta_t + \varepsilon_t \tag{4.7.9}$$

The reduced form of (4.7.8) is a random walk in which the variance of the disturbance term is four times that of the common variance of ε_t^* and η_t^*. The weights needed to extract the trend component, μ_t, from the observations can be obtained almost immediately from (4.7.4), which in this case is

$$w(\mathrm{L}) = \frac{|1+\mathrm{L}|^2}{4} = \frac{(1+\mathrm{L})(1+\mathrm{L}^{-1})}{4} = \tfrac{1}{2} + \tfrac{1}{4}\mathrm{L} + \tfrac{1}{4}\mathrm{L}^{-1} \tag{4.7.10}$$

yielding

$$m_{t|\infty} = \tfrac{1}{4}y_{t-1} + \tfrac{1}{2}y_t + \tfrac{1}{4}y_{t+1} \tag{4.7.11}$$

The same result can be obtained by solving the Riccati equation and substituting in the fixed-interval smoother; see Exercise 4.8. This is one of the few cases where an explicit expression like (4.7.11) can be obtained from a state space smoothing algorithm.

Evaluating the covariance generating function, $v(\mathrm{L})$, gives

$$\begin{aligned} v(\mathrm{L}) &= \sigma_*^2|1+\mathrm{L}|^2\sigma_*^2/(|1+\mathrm{L}|^2\sigma_*^2 + |1-\mathrm{L}|^2\sigma_*^2) \\ &= \sigma_*^2(\tfrac{1}{4}\mathrm{L}^{-1} + \tfrac{1}{2}\mathrm{L} + \tfrac{1}{4}\mathrm{L}^{-1}) \end{aligned}$$

Thus from the coefficient of L^0

$$\mathrm{MSE}\,(\tilde{\mu}_{t|\infty}) = \sigma_*^2/2 \tag{4.7.12}$$

Example 4.7.2 Consider

$$y_t = \mu_t + \varepsilon_t \tag{4.7.13a}$$

$$\mu_t = \varphi\mu_{t-1} + \eta_t \tag{4.7.13b}$$

with $\sigma_\eta^2 = q\sigma_\varepsilon^2$. The weights for extracting the trend, μ_t, can be obtained directly from (4.7.3) as

$$w(\mathrm{L}) = \frac{q/|1-\varphi\mathrm{L}|^2}{(q/|1-\varphi\mathrm{L}|^2)+1} = \frac{q}{q+|1-\varphi\mathrm{L}|^2}; \tag{4.7.14}$$

see Whittle (1983, pp. 34–5, 58–9). Setting $\varphi = 1$, which of course is the random

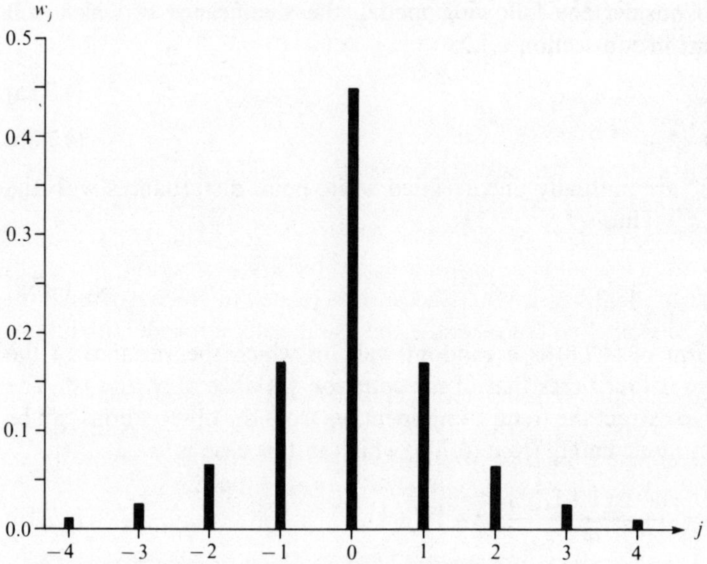

Fig. 4.7.1 Weights for signal extraction in a random walk plus noise model.

walk plus noise model yields

$$w(L)=\frac{(1-\lambda)q}{[1-(1-\lambda)L][1-(1-\lambda)L^{-1}]} \tag{4.7.15}$$

where λ is the smoothing constant defined in (4.1.24). The weights in $w(L)$ are

$$w_j=\frac{q(1-\lambda)^{|j|+1}}{\lambda(2-\lambda)}=[q/(4+q)]^{\frac{1}{2}}(1-\lambda)^{|j|}, \quad j=0, \pm 1, \pm 2, \ldots \tag{4.7.16}$$

When there is no measurement noise, that is $\sigma_\varepsilon^2=0$, it is easy to verify that $w_0=1$, while $w_j=0$ for $j\neq 0$. Conversely as q moves towards zero the weights become more evenly spread out. Figure 4.7.1 shows the weights when the measurement and signal noise are equal, i.e. $\sigma_\eta^2=\sigma_\varepsilon^2$. This corresponds to $\lambda=0.62$.

Finally it can be shown that

$$\text{MSE}(m_{t|\infty})=\frac{\sigma_\eta^2(1-\lambda)}{\lambda(2-\lambda)} \tag{4.7.17}$$

The above formulae for obtaining smoothed estimators and their MSEs can be generalised to cases where the sample is finite. As a special case the estimator of a component at time $t=T$ is the filtered estimator. The elegance of the approach is appealing and it is often very useful as a means of carrying out a theoretical analysis of certain aspects of time-invariant models. However, as noted in Whittle (1983, p. vi), the greater generality of the state space smoothing algorithms and the ease with which they can be applied makes them more attractive for computational purposes, except in certain special cases.

4.7.2 Conditions for unobserved components to be estimable

A fundamental question for any structural time series model is whether its components are estimable. In other words, for given values of the hyperparameters, can the components be estimated with finite MSE? If they cannot, the model specification is unable to produce a sensible decomposition. The issue is essentially one of identifiability, but because it relates to stochastic quantities which cannot be estimated consistently, the usual criteria for identifiability do not apply.

The classical solution is given in terms of the UCARIMA model of (4.7.1). The following result is given by Pierce (1979): *the estimation error of an unobserved component is stationary, and has finite MSE, if and only if the non-stationary operators, the $\Delta_m(L)$'s, have no common roots of unit modulus.*

The estimability of unobserved components can also be established via the state space form. The structural models considered in this chapter can all be expressed in state space form, with the unobserved components being given by a linear combination of the elements of the state vector. Hence, as noted in section 3.6, a sufficient condition for the unobserved components to be capable of being estimated with finite MSE is that the model be *observable*. It is important to note that this result applies to models containing deterministic as well as stochastic components. If all the components are deterministic then the observability condition reduces to the standard rank condition on the matrix of explanatory variables in regression. This is then a standard case of identifiability in the usual sense.

As an illustration of some of the above points, consider the dummy variable form of the BSM. The UCARIMA form is

$$y_t = \frac{(1+\theta L)}{\Delta^2}\xi_{1t} + \frac{\xi_{2t}}{S(L)} + \xi_{0t} \tag{4.7.18}$$

where $\xi_{2t} = \omega_t$, $\xi_{0t} = \varepsilon_t$ and $(1+\theta L)\xi_{1t} = \Delta\eta_t + \zeta_{t-1}$. Since Δ^2 and S(L) have no roots in common both the trend and seasonal components are estimable. Furthermore, as noted in section 4.1, the model is observable. The observability is not affected if, for example, σ_ω^2 is equal to zero. The second term on the right-hand side of (4.7.18) would, however, disappear in this case.

A minor amendment to the specification of the seasonal component in (4.7.18) is to let

$$\gamma_t = \gamma_{t-s} + \omega_t \tag{4.7.19}$$

where ω_t is a white-noise disturbance term. Rearranging (4.7.19) as

$$\gamma_t = \omega_t / \Delta_s \tag{4.7.20}$$

shows immediately that such a definition of a seasonal component is inadmissible because $\Delta_s = \Delta . S(L)$ and so Δ and Δ_s have a unit root in common. It is also straightforward to verify that the model is not observable. In the special case when the trend is deterministic and the variance of the disturbance in (4.7.19) is zero, the state space form is the same as for a standard regression model with s seasonal dummies, a constant and a time trend. A model of this kind is not identifiable and is a classic case of extreme multicollinearity induced by what is sometimes referred to as the 'dummy variable trap'.

A final point to note is that Pierce's result does not apply to the level and slope components of trend. As can be seen in the unobserved components form of (2.3.59) in (2.3.67), the slope is based on the operator Δ^2 which has a common factor of Δ with the level component of the trend. However, the slope is certainly observable.

EXERCISES

4.1 Consider the basic structural model. If $\text{Var}(\varepsilon_t)=0$, write the model in state space form as a minimal realisation. [*Hint*: Transform the observations to first differences.]

4.2 Put the cyclical trend model, (2.3.56a), (2.3.27b) and (2.3.64) in state space form and determine the conditions needed for the Kalman filter to converge to a steady-state solution exponentially fast.

4.3 How would you estimate the damped trend model, (2.3.66), in (i) the time domain, and (ii) the frequency domain?

4.4 Consider the following model:

$$y_t = \mu_{1t} + \mu_{2t} + \varepsilon_t$$

$$\mu_{i,t} = \mu_{i,t-1} + \eta_{i,t}, \quad i=1,2$$

where $\varepsilon_t \sim \text{NID}(0, \sigma_\varepsilon^2)$, $\eta_{i,t} \sim \text{NID}(0, \sigma_i^2)$, $i=1,2$, and ε_t, $\eta_{1,t}$ and $\eta_{2,t}$ are mutually independent.

(a) By calculating the correlogram of the stationary form show that the model is not identifiable.

(b) Is the model identifiable when it is known that $\sigma_1^2 = \sigma_2^2$?

(c) Is the model (i) controllable; (ii) stabilisable; (iii) observable; and (iv) detectable? Does knowing that $\sigma_1^2 = \sigma_2^2$ affect these properties?

(d) What are the implications of your answers to (c) for (i) a steady state solution to the Kalman filter; and (ii) the estimation of the unobserved components $\mu_{1,t}$ and $\mu_{2,t}$?

4.5 Use (4.7.17) to estimate the gain from smoothing, as compared with filtering, in the random walk plus noise model when μ_t is to be estimated and t is near the centre of a long sample.

4.6 Consider the BSM with seasonal dummies. It can be shown that the identifiability of the model is not affected if ω_t and η_t are allowed to be correlated. Find an expression for the s.g.f. of $\Delta\Delta_s y_t$ and hence show how the unknown parameters could be estimated by the method of scoring. Is the model still observable if η_t and ω_t are correlated? Can the seasonal component be estimated with finite MSE?

4.7 Determine whether the following seasonal model is identifiable

$$y_t = \gamma_t + \varepsilon_t \tag{a}$$

$$\Delta_s \gamma_t = \omega_t + \theta\omega_{t-s} \tag{b}$$

How does your answer relate to the general order condition for identifiability?

Given values of the parameters in the above model, is it possible to estimate the seasonal component, γ_t, with finite MSE? Is it possible to do this if a random walk component, μ_t, is added to the right-hand side of (a)?

4.8 Put model (4.7.8) in SSF and verify that it satisfies the necessary conditions to have a unique steady-state solution which it converges to exponentially fast. Show that the steady-state MSE matrix of $\mathbf{a}_t$ is

$$\bar{\mathbf{P}}^* = \begin{bmatrix} 0.75 & 0.25 \\ 0.25 & 0.75 \end{bmatrix}$$

Hence set up the Kalman filter and find an expression for the MMSLE of μ_T in terms of the current and past values of y_t.

Use the fixed-interval smoother to derive (4.7.11).

4.9 How would you handle the following model:

$$y_t = \mu_t + \mu_t^{\lambda}\gamma_t + \varepsilon_t$$

where μ_t, γ_t and ε_t are as in the BSM and $\lambda\,(\geqslant 0)$ is an unknown constant?

4.10 Show that the dummy variable seasonality version of the BSM is only controllable and stabilisable if σ_ω^2 and σ_ζ^2 are strictly positive.

4.11 Suppose that the observations are equal to a constant plus a dummy variable seasonal component, that is

$$y_t = \mu + \gamma_t$$

where $S(L)\gamma_t = \omega_t$.

(i) Derive expressions for efficient estimators of μ and σ_ω^2 based on moving averages of the observations.

(ii) Find an expression for making forecasts of future values of y_t. What can be said about the properties of the forecast function?

4.12 Find the MSE of the MMSE of y_{T+l} in a random walk plus drift model when the drift is estimated from T observations.

Chapter 5

Testing and model selection

This chapter describes the main statistical test procedures and the way in which they may be applied to structural time series models in both the time and frequency domains. Diagnostics and measures for assessing goodness of fit are described and the chapter finishes with a section on model selection methodology.

In setting up the various tests, it is assumed that all disturbances are normally distributed.

5.1 Principles of testing

5.1.1 *Classical test procedures*

Methods for testing hypotheses can be derived systematically using a maximum likelihood approach. The basic test procedure is the likelihood ratio test, but two other tests, the Wald test and the Lagrange multiplier test, have the same properties under a sequence of local alternatives. The tests are described briefly here. A fuller discussion can be found in a wide range of sources including Cox and Hinkley (1974), Harvey (1981a, ch. 5) and Silvey (1970).

The likelihood ratio (LR) test is primarily concerned with testing the validity of a set of restrictions on the $n \times 1$ parameter vector, $\boldsymbol{\psi}$. When these restrictions are linear, they may be expressed in the form

$$\mathbf{R}\boldsymbol{\psi} = \mathbf{r} \tag{5.1.1}$$

where $\mathbf{R}$ is an $m \times n$ matrix of fixed values, $\mathbf{r}$ is an $m \times 1$ vector of fixed values and m, the number of restrictions, is less than n.

Under the null hypothesis, H_0, $\boldsymbol{\psi}$ satisfies the restrictions in (5.1.1). When the restrictions are imposed, the ML estimator of $\boldsymbol{\psi}$ is denoted by $\tilde{\boldsymbol{\psi}}_0$ and this may be contrasted with the unrestricted estimator, $\tilde{\boldsymbol{\psi}}$. If the maximised likelihood function under H_0, $L(\tilde{\boldsymbol{\psi}}_0)$, is much smaller than the unrestricted maximised likelihood, $L(\tilde{\boldsymbol{\psi}})$, there is evidence against the null hypothesis. This result is formalised in the Neyman-Pearson lemma which shows that a test based on the likelihood ratio,

$$\lambda = L(\tilde{\psi}_0)/L(\tilde{\psi}) \qquad (5.1.2)$$

has certain desirable statistical properties.

It is sometimes possible to transform the likelihood ratio into a statistic, the exact distribution of which is known under H_0. When this cannot be done, a large sample test is carried out. This is based on the result that the statistic

$$LR = -2 \log \lambda \qquad (5.1.3)$$

is asymptotically distributed as χ^2_m under H_0. If the general model is time invariant

$$LR \simeq (T-d) \log(SSE_0/SSE) \qquad (5.1.4)$$

where SSE is the sum of squares of the one-step-ahead prediction errors obtained from any criterion function asymptotically equivalent to the likelihood, and SSE_0 is its value under H_0. Alternatively these sums of squares measures may be replaced by appropriate measures of the prediction error variance, σ^2, as defined in sub-section 5.5.1.

The disadvantage of the LR test is that the model must be estimated under both the null and alternative hypotheses. A different procedure, the *Wald test*, only requires an estimate of $\boldsymbol{\psi}$ from the unrestricted model. The usual form of the test statistic is

$$W = [\mathbf{R}\tilde{\boldsymbol{\psi}} - \mathbf{r}]'[\mathbf{R}\mathbf{I}^{-1}(\tilde{\boldsymbol{\psi}})\mathbf{R}']^{-1}[\mathbf{R}\tilde{\boldsymbol{\psi}} - \mathbf{r}] \qquad (5.1.5)$$

where $\mathbf{I}(\tilde{\boldsymbol{\psi}})$ is the information matrix evaluated at the unrestricted estimate $\tilde{\boldsymbol{\psi}}$. Under H_0, W, like LR, is asymptotically χ^2_m.

If the model is easier to estimate under the null hypothesis, a *Lagrange multiplier* (LM) test may be appropriate. The test statistic which again is asymptotically χ^2_m under H_0, takes the form

$$LM = \left[\frac{\partial \log L}{\partial \boldsymbol{\psi}}\right]' \mathbf{I}^{-1}(\tilde{\boldsymbol{\psi}}_0)\left[\frac{\partial \log L}{\partial \boldsymbol{\psi}}\right] \qquad (5.1.6)$$

where $\partial \log L/\partial \boldsymbol{\psi}$ is evaluated at the restricted estimate, $\tilde{\boldsymbol{\psi}}_0$. Estimation of the more general unrestricted model is therefore avoided.

The tests can also be applied in situations where the restrictions are non-linear. In this case (5.1.1) is written in the more general form

$$\mathbf{r}(\boldsymbol{\psi}) = 0 \qquad (5.1.7)$$

where $\mathbf{r}(\boldsymbol{\psi})$ is an $m \times 1$ vector of (possibly) non-linear functions of $\boldsymbol{\psi}$. The three tests are carried out as before; the $\mathbf{R}$ matrix in the Wald test is set equal to the $m \times n$ matrix of derivatives $\partial \mathbf{r}(\boldsymbol{\psi})/\partial \boldsymbol{\psi}'$.

The regularity conditions needed for the LR, LM and Wald tests to be valid are essentially the same as those required for the asymptotic distribution of the ML estimator of the parameter vector to be normal with a mean equal to the true parameter vector and a covariance matrix equal to the large sample information matrix. For structural time series models these conditions were set out in sub-section 4.5.1.

5.1.2 Classical tests when parameters lie on the boundary of the parameter space

Situations in which one or more of the parameters lie on the boundary of the parameter space are not uncommon in structural time series models. Whether or not the classical likelihood-based tests can be applied in these cases depends on whether the remaining regularity conditions are met. If they are, the LM test statistic has its usual asymptotic χ^2 distribution under H_0. The LR and Wald statistics do not have this distribution. Instead their asymptotic distribution under the null is a mixture of χ^2 distributions. Another statistic, known as the Kuhn-Tucker statistic, also has this asymptotic distribution. The main results are set out below. Further details can be found in Gourieroux *et al.* (1980, 1982), and Rogers (1986). Modifications to the LM test are discussed in sub-section 5.2.3.

When a single parameter is constrained to lie on the boundary of the parameter space under H_0, the LR statistic has the following asymptotic distribution under H_0:

$$\mathrm{LR} \sim \tfrac{1}{2}\chi_0^2 + \tfrac{1}{2}\chi_1^2; \tag{5.1.8}$$

see Chernoff (1954). The χ_0^2 distribution is a degenerate distribution with all its mass at the origin. Thus (5.1.8) means that in large samples LR has a 0.5 chance of taking a value of zero and a 0.5 chance of being drawn from a χ_1^2 distribution. The size of the LR test can therefore be set appropriately simply by using the 2α, rather than the α, significance point of a χ_1^2 distribution for a test of size α. The same modification is made to the Wald test.

When two parameters are constrained to lie on the boundary of the parameter space under H_0, the LR statistic has the following asymptotic distribution under H_0:

$$\mathrm{LR} \sim w\chi_0^2 + \tfrac{1}{2}\chi_1^2 + (\tfrac{1}{2} - w)\chi_2^2 \tag{5.1.9}$$

where w is the weight

$$w = (1/2\pi)\cos^{-1}\tilde{\rho} \tag{5.1.10}$$

The quantity $\tilde{\rho}$ is the correlation between $\mathbf{r}_1'\tilde{\boldsymbol{\psi}}$ and $\mathbf{r}_2'\tilde{\boldsymbol{\psi}}$ where $\mathbf{r}_1'$ and $\mathbf{r}_2'$ are the rows of the $2 \times n$ matrix $\mathbf{R}$ which defines the constraints in (5.1.1), that is $\mathbf{R}' = [\mathbf{r}_1 \quad \mathbf{r}_2]$. This quantity may be evaluated from the asymptotic covariance matrix. A table of critical values at the 5% and 10% level of significance can be found, for various values of $\tilde{\rho}$, in Gourieroux *et al.* (1982, p. 72). Standard theory, based on LR $\sim \chi_2^2$, would lead to the region of acceptance being too large. Thus at the 5% level of significance, standard theory leads to a critical value of 5.99 whereas for $\tilde{\rho}=0.5$ the appropriate critical value is 2.7.

Example 5.1.1 In the discussion of the asymptotic distribution of the random walk plus noise model in sub-section 4.5.2, it was observed that a value of σ_η^2 equal to zero violates regularity condition (iv). The unrestricted ML estimators of σ_η^2 and σ_ε^2 will not therefore have joint asymptotic normal distributions. As a result the classical likelihood tests cannot be applied to test whether σ_η^2 is zero, even if they are modified in the way suggested above. The situation is different when σ_η^2 is positive. In this case condition (iv) is satisfied even if σ_ε^2 is zero. Hence it is possible to carry out classical tests of $H_0\colon \sigma_\varepsilon^2=0$ against $H_1\colon \sigma_\varepsilon^2>0$. The LR and Wald statistics are taken to have the distribution of (5.1.8). Alternatively, the Wald test can simply be carried out by dividing the estimate of σ_ε^2 by its estimated standard error, and conducting a one-sided test based on the standard normal distribution.

The reduced form of the random walk plus noise model is the ARIMA(0, 1, 1) model, (4.5.4). A test that σ_η^2 is equal to zero corresponds to a test of $H_0\colon \theta=-1$ against $H_1\colon \theta>-1$. The model is therefore strictly non-invertible under the null and it follows from the results of Sargan and Bhargava (1983) that the classical procedures cannot be applied in this case; the Monte Carlo results reported in Plosser and Schwert (1977) show the effects of attempting to do so.

5.1.3 *Most-powerful-invariant tests*

Within the framework of linear regression models, most-powerful-invariant (MPI), or point-optimal, tests provide an alternative approach to certain testing problems. By a judicious formulation of the problem, it is possible to obtain a test procedure which is, in general, more powerful than the corresponding LM test. Furthermore, MPI tests can be applied in certain situations where the regularity conditions necessary for the likelihood tests to be applied break down. As was shown in Example 5.1.1, such situations are not uncommon in structural time series models.

A thorough review of the issues involved in constructing MPI tests may be found by consulting Berenblut and Webb (1973), Franzini and Harvey (1983), King (1985, 1986) and Lehmann (1959). Let a general linear regression model be written in matrix form as

$$\mathbf{y}=\mathbf{X}\boldsymbol{\alpha}+\mathbf{u} \tag{5.1.11}$$

where $\boldsymbol{\alpha}$ is a $k\times 1$ vector of unknown regression parameters and $\mathbf{u}$ is a $T\times 1$ vector of disturbances following a multivariate normal distribution with mean vector zero and covariance matrix

$$\mathrm{Var}(\mathbf{u})=\sigma_*^2\boldsymbol{\Omega}(\boldsymbol{\psi}_*) \tag{5.1.12}$$

The $T \times T$ matrix $\mathbf{\Omega}(\boldsymbol{\psi}_*)$ is assumed to depend on a set of parameters in $\boldsymbol{\psi}_*$ and σ_*^2 is a postive scalar. The aim is to construct a test which is invariant to transformations of the form $\mathbf{y}^* = \gamma_0 \mathbf{y} + \mathbf{X}\gamma$ where γ_0 is a positive scalar and γ is $k \times 1$, and which, for a given test size, maximises the probability of rejecting

$$\mathrm{H}_0: \boldsymbol{\psi}_* = \boldsymbol{\psi}_{*_0} \tag{5.1.13a}$$

against the alternative

$$\mathrm{H}_1: \boldsymbol{\psi}_* = \boldsymbol{\psi}_{*_1} \tag{5.1.13b}$$

Following Lehmann (1959), such a test is known as an MPI test.

It can be shown that the critical region of the MPI test is of the form

$$\frac{S(\boldsymbol{\psi}_{*_1})}{S(\boldsymbol{\psi}_{*_0})} < c \tag{5.1.14}$$

where

$$S(\boldsymbol{\psi}_{*_1}) = [\mathbf{y} - \mathbf{X}\tilde{\boldsymbol{\alpha}}]' \mathbf{\Omega}^{-1}(\boldsymbol{\psi}_{*_1})[\mathbf{y} - \mathbf{X}\tilde{\boldsymbol{\alpha}}] \tag{5.1.15}$$

$\tilde{\boldsymbol{\alpha}}$ being the GLS estimator of $\boldsymbol{\alpha}$. The quantity $S(\boldsymbol{\psi}_{*_0})$ is defined in an analogous fashion. All that remains is to compute the critical value, c, and this can be done using the method of Imhof (1961).

In many applications, the null hypothesis specifies that the disturbances are independently and identically distributed. In this case $\mathbf{\Omega}(\boldsymbol{\psi}_{*_0})$ becomes the identity matrix and $S(\boldsymbol{\psi}_{*_0})$ is simply the sum of squares of the OLS residuals, that is

$$S(\boldsymbol{\psi}_{*_0}) = [\mathbf{y} - \mathbf{X}\mathbf{a}]'[\mathbf{y} - \mathbf{X}\mathbf{a}] \tag{5.1.16}$$

where $\mathbf{a}$ is the OLS estimator of $\boldsymbol{\alpha}$. Since $\boldsymbol{\psi}_{*_1}$ is typically not specified exactly, the idea is to choose $\boldsymbol{\psi}_{*_1}$ so as to give the test high power for a wide range of values of $\boldsymbol{\psi}_{*_1}$ likely to occur in practice. Thus suppose that the disturbances are generated by an AR(1) process

$$u_t = \varphi u_{t-1} + \varepsilon_t \tag{5.1.17}$$

under the alternative. An MPI test can be constructed by setting φ equal to a pre-specified value. One possibility is to set φ equal to unity as in Berenblut and Webb (1973). This has good power characteristics for a wide range of high values of φ. At the other extreme it can be shown that as $\varphi \to 0$ under H_1, the limiting case of the MPI test is, apart from end corrections, the Durbin-Watson test. Thus the D-W test is approximately the *locally best invariant* (LBI) test for an AR(1) disturbance term; see King and Hillier (1985).

There are no set rules, in general, for determining how $\boldsymbol{\psi}_{*_1}$ should be set. If $\boldsymbol{\psi}_{*_1}$ contains only one parameter, Nyblom (1986) suggests a criterion based on Pitman efficiency, while King (1985) adopts a somewhat different approach. For several parameters a method given by Franzini and Harvey (1983) may be applied. The parameters in ψ_{*_1} are fixed in relative terms so that

$$\mathbf{\Omega}=\mathbf{I}+q\mathbf{\Omega}^* \tag{5.1.18}$$

where q is a variable scalar and $\mathbf{\Omega}^*$ is a $T \times T$ matrix defined implicitly by (5.1.18). The proportion of variance due to ψ_{*_1}, denoted by θ, is related to q by the expression

$$\theta=\frac{q\ \mathrm{tr}(\mathbf{M\Omega}^*)}{\mathrm{tr}(\mathbf{M})+q\ \mathrm{tr}(\mathbf{M\Omega}^*)} \tag{5.1.19}$$

where $\mathbf{M}=\mathbf{I}-\mathbf{X}(\mathbf{X}'\mathbf{X})^{-1}\mathbf{X}'$; see La Motte and McWhorter (1978). The evidence presented in Franzini and Harvey (1983) suggests that setting a value of q corresponding to θ equal one-half works quite well in practice. This evidence is reviewed in sub-section 5.3.5.

In the special case when $\theta=q=0$, the test statistic in (5.1.14) is inappropriate. However, the use of L'Hôpital's rule gives a test of the form

$$\frac{[\mathbf{y}-\mathbf{Xa}]'\mathbf{\Omega}^*[\mathbf{y}-\mathbf{Xa}]}{S(\psi_{*_0})}>c^* \tag{5.1.20}$$

This is, in fact, the LBI test.

Finally it should be stressed that $\mathbf{\Omega}(\psi_{*_0})$ is not always a scalar matrix. An example is the test proposed by King (1983) for testing AR(1) against MA(1) disturbances.

5.2 Lagrange multiplier tests

The LM test statistic takes the general form (5.1.6). For any state space model this statistic can, in principle, be computed in the time domain. The resulting test can be applied not only to linear models but also to non-linear conditionally Gaussian models of the form discussed in sub-section 3.7.1.

Evaluating the LM statistic in the time domain can be tedious when the model contains more than one disturbance term. This is true for most time-invariant structural models and in such cases the LM test is more easily carried out in the frequency domain.

5.2.1 LM test in the time domain

For a univariate model the likelihood function is usually written as in (3.4.9). In what follows, however, no distinction will be made between σ_*^2 and the other parameters. Indeed the derivations are valid irrespective of whether the likelihood function is set up as in (3.4.9) or (3.4.7). There is no advantage to working with (3.4.9) unless the information matrix is block diagonal with respect to σ_*^2 and the other parameters. If ψ denotes the complete set of parameters, the score vector is

$$\frac{\partial \log L}{\partial \boldsymbol{\psi}} = -\frac{1}{2}\sum_{t=1}^{T} \frac{\partial f_t}{\partial \boldsymbol{\psi}} \frac{1}{f_t}\left(1-\frac{v_t^2}{f_t}\right) - \sum_{t=1}^{T} \frac{\partial v_t}{\partial \boldsymbol{\psi}} \frac{v_t}{f_t} \tag{5.2.1}$$

The information matrix is obtained from (3.4.69). If the expectation in the second term is dropped, the following asymptotically equivalent information matrix is obtained:

$$\mathbf{I}^*(\psi) = \frac{1}{2}\sum_{t=1}^{T} \frac{1}{f_t^2} \frac{\partial f_t}{\partial \boldsymbol{\psi}} \frac{\partial f_t}{\partial \boldsymbol{\psi}'} + \sum_{t=1}^{T} \frac{1}{f_t} \frac{\partial v_t}{\partial \boldsymbol{\psi}} \frac{\partial v_t}{\partial \boldsymbol{\psi}'} \tag{5.2.2}$$

This expression, like the score vector, depends only on first derivatives. As was shown in sub-section 3.4.6, when the model is in state space form these derivatives may be evaluated either numerically or analytically.

Substituting for the score vector and the information matrix from (5.2.1) and (5.2.2) enables the LM statistic (5.1.6) to be written as

$$\mathrm{LM} = \left[\sum_{j=1}^{2T} v_j^* \mathbf{x}_j\right]' \left[\sum_{j=1}^{2T} \mathbf{x}_j \mathbf{x}_j'\right]^{-1} \left[\sum_{j=1}^{2T} v_j^* \mathbf{x}_j\right] \tag{5.2.3}$$

where v_j^* and the $n \times 1$ vector $\mathbf{x}_j$ are defined for $j=1,\ldots,2T$ by

$$v_t^* = 2^{-\frac{1}{2}}[1-(v_t^2/f_t)], \quad t=1,\ldots,T \tag{5.2.4a}$$

$$v_{T+t}^* = v_t/f_t^{\frac{1}{2}}, \quad t=1,\ldots,T \tag{5.2.4b}$$

and

$$\mathbf{x}_t = \frac{1}{\sqrt{2}} \frac{1}{f_t} \frac{\partial f_t}{\partial \boldsymbol{\psi}}, \quad t=1,\ldots,T \tag{5.2.5a}$$

$$\mathbf{x}_{T+t} = \frac{1}{f_t^{\frac{1}{2}}} \frac{\partial v_t}{\partial \boldsymbol{\psi}}, \quad t=1,\ldots,T \tag{5.2.5b}$$

Both sets of variables are evaluated under the null hypothesis.

An asymptotically equivalent test statistic can be constructed in terms of the coefficient of multiple correlation, R^2, from the regression of v_j^* on $\mathbf{x}_j$. The argument is as follows. Since the sum of the v_j's is approximately, and in some cases exactly, equal to zero, R^2 is approximately equal to the uncentred coefficient of multiple correlation

$$\frac{\left[\sum v_j^* \mathbf{x}_j\right]' \left[\sum \mathbf{x}_j \mathbf{x}_j'\right]^{-1} \left[\sum v_j^* \mathbf{x}_j\right]}{\sum v_j^{*2}}$$

where the summations are from $j=1,\ldots,2T$. The numerator in the above expression is the same as the numerator in (5.2.3). Furthermore

$$\operatorname{plim}\frac{\sum v_j^{*2}}{T}=\operatorname{plim}\frac{1}{2T}\sum_{t=1}^{T}[1-(v_t^2/f_t)]^2+\operatorname{plim}\frac{1}{T}\sum_{t=1}^{T}v_t^2/f_t$$
$$=2$$

since plim $\Sigma(v_t^4/Tf_t^2)=3$ under the normality assumption, and so the statistic

$$\text{LM}^*=2\text{TR}^2 \tag{5.2.6}$$

will have the same asymptotic distribution as (5.2.3). As in the cases noted by Koenker (1981), this statistic should be more robust to non-normality than (5.2.3).

Example 5.2.1 Consider the AR(1) model with ARCH disturbances:

$$y_t=\varphi y_{t-1}+\varepsilon_t,\quad \varepsilon_t|Y_{t-1}\sim N(0,\sigma_t^2) \tag{5.2.7a}$$

$$\sigma_t^2=\alpha_0+\alpha_1\varepsilon_{t-1}^2 \tag{5.2.7b}$$

with y_0 and ε_0 both fixed and equal to zero; see Example 3.7.2. Suppose that the null hypothesis is H_0: $\varphi=\alpha_1=0$. Although the model is non-linear, it is conditionally Gaussian and in terms of the general notation used above $v_t=y_t-\varphi y_{t-1}$ and $f_t=\sigma_t^2$. The variables in (5.2.4) are

$$v_t^*=2^{-\frac{1}{2}}[1-(y_t^2/\tilde{\alpha}_0)],\quad v_{T+t}^*=\tilde{\alpha}_0^{-\frac{1}{2}}y_t \tag{5.2.8a}$$

while the vectors in (5.2.5) consist of the elements

$$\left.\begin{aligned} x_t(\varphi)&=0, & x_{T+t}(\varphi)&=-\tilde{\alpha}_0^{-\frac{1}{2}}y_{t-1}\\ x_t(\alpha_0)&=2^{-\frac{1}{2}}\tilde{\alpha}_0^{-1}, & x_{T+t}(\alpha_0)&=0\\ x_t(\alpha_1)&=2^{-\frac{1}{2}}\tilde{\alpha}_0^{-1}y_{t-1}^2, & x_{T+t}(\alpha_1)&=0\end{aligned}\right\} \tag{5.2.8b}$$

for $t=2,\ldots,T$, where, for example, $x_t(\varphi)$ indicates the variable constructed by differentiation with respect to φ; that is

$$x_t(\varphi)=\frac{1}{\sqrt{2}}\frac{1}{f_t}\frac{\partial f_t}{\partial\varphi} \tag{5.2.8c}$$

These variables are evaluated under the null hypothesis and

$$\tilde{\alpha}_0=T^{-1}\sum_{t=1}^{T}y_t^2 \tag{5.2.9}$$

The test statistic, in the form LM or LM*, has a χ_2^2 distribution under the null hypothesis.

It is interesting to note that after some manipulation the LM statistic (5.2.3) can be expressed as

$$\mathrm{LM} = T.r^2(1) + T.\mathrm{rsq}^2(1) \tag{5.2.10}$$

where $\mathrm{rsq}^2(1)$ is the first-order autocorrelation between y_t^2 and y_{t-1}^2. Thus the first part of (5.2.10) is the standard LM test for an AR(1) disturbance term, while the second part is the LM test for an ARCH disturbance term.

In many models the parameters in $\boldsymbol{\psi}$ can be separated into two sets, $\boldsymbol{\psi}_1$ and $\boldsymbol{\psi}_2$, such that $\partial v_t/\partial\boldsymbol{\psi}_1 = \mathbf{0}$ and $\partial f_t/\partial\boldsymbol{\psi}_2 = \mathbf{0}$ for all t. The information matrix is then block diagonal. If the hypothesis to be tested involves only restrictions on $\boldsymbol{\psi}_1$, the LM statistic is

$$\mathrm{LM} = TR^2 \tag{5.2.11}$$

where R^2 is the coefficient of multiple correlation obtained from regressing v_t^* on $\mathbf{x}_t$ for $t = 1, \ldots, T$. If the null hypothesis involves only $\boldsymbol{\psi}_2$, the test statistic is again of the form of (5.2.11) but based on a regression of v_{T+t}^* on $\mathbf{x}_{T+t}$ for $t = 1, \ldots, T$. There are many examples of LM tests of this form in the literature.

5.2.2 LM test in the frequency domain

Consider a linear time-invariant model in which the frequency-domain likelihood function is of the form (4.3.1). Substituting in (5.1.6) from the expressions for the first derivatives, (4.3.26), and the information matrix, (4.3.29), gives

$$\mathrm{LM} = \frac{1}{2}\left[\sum_{j=0}^{T-1} \frac{1}{g_j^2}\frac{\partial g_j}{\partial\boldsymbol{\psi}} \upsilon_j\right]'\left[\sum_{j=0}^{T-1} \frac{1}{g_j^2}\frac{\partial g_j}{\partial\boldsymbol{\psi}}\frac{\partial g_j}{\partial\boldsymbol{\psi}'}\right]^{-1}\left[\sum_{j=0}^{T-1} \frac{1}{g_j^2}\frac{\partial g_j}{\partial\boldsymbol{\psi}} \upsilon_j\right] \tag{5.2.12}$$

where g_j and its derivatives are evaluated at $\boldsymbol{\psi} = \tilde{\boldsymbol{\psi}}_0$ and

$$\upsilon_j = 2\pi I(\lambda_j) - g_j, \quad j = 0, \ldots, T-1 \tag{5.2.13}$$

As in the time domain, LM is asymptotically χ_m^2 under the null hypothesis.

An alternative form of the test statistic is obtained by dividing (5.2.12) through by $T^{-1}\Sigma\upsilon_j^2/g_j^2$. Since, from (4.3.25), the variance of υ_j is g_j^2, it follows that

$$\operatorname{plim} T^{-1} \sum_{j=0}^{T-1} \upsilon_j^2/g_j^2 = 1 \tag{5.2.14}$$

and so the asymptotic distribution of the test statistic is unaltered. The amended test statistic may be written as

$$\mathrm{LM}^* = \frac{T}{2}\,\frac{\left[\sum_{j=0}^{T-1} g_j^{-2}\mathbf{z}_j\upsilon_j\right]'\left[\sum_{j=0}^{T-1} g_j^{-2}\mathbf{z}_j\mathbf{z}_j'\right]^{-1}\left[\sum_{j=0}^{T-1} g_j^{-2}\mathbf{z}_j\upsilon_j\right]}{\sum_{j=0}^{T-1}(\upsilon_j^2/g_j^2)} \tag{5.2.15}$$

where

$$\mathbf{z}_j = \left.\frac{\partial g_j}{\partial \boldsymbol{\psi}}\right|_{\psi=\tilde{\psi}_0} \tag{5.2.16}$$

Despite the definition of $\mathbf{z}_j$ in (5.2.16) it will, on occasion, be more convenient to define an element of $\mathbf{z}_j$ as being proportional to, rather than equal to, the corresponding first derivative. This is one of the reasons for the change in notation from (5.2.12). The other reason for the change in notation is that it makes it clearer that LM can be expressed as

$$\text{LM}^* = \tfrac{1}{2}TR^2 \tag{5.2.17}$$

where R^2 is the coefficient of determination in a weighted regression of υ_j on the elements $\mathbf{z}_j$. A constant term is not included unless it is already in $\mathbf{z}_j$. Note that it follows from (4.3.45) and (4.3.40) that the mean of the υ_j/g_j's is zero.

The appearance of the one-half in (5.2.17) may at first sight seem rather strange to those familiar with the TR^2 form of the LM statistic. The explanation lies in the fact that each observation is effectively counted twice when the summation in (5.2.15) is over T points. Redefining the summation as $j=0,\ldots,[\tfrac{1}{2}T]$ leaves the value of LM* unchanged but perhaps makes the appearance of $T/2$ rather than T more plausible.

Aside from its rather nice interpretation, (5.2.15) is a better statistic on which to base a test than is (5.2.12) because, like its time-domain counterpart (5.2.6), it is more robust to departures from the underlying normality assumption. Other variations are also possible. In particular the regression interpretation suggests carrying out an F-test based on

$$\text{LMF} = \frac{\tfrac{1}{2}T-n}{m}\,\frac{R^2}{1-R^2} \tag{5.2.18}$$

The critical region is based on an F-distribution with $(m, \tfrac{1}{2}T-n)$ degrees of freedom. In some circumstances a t-test may be appropriate. Such tests, which are known as *modified* LM tests, have been shown to have attractive properties in other areas of econometrics; see, for example, Harvey (1981a, pp. 174, 275–7) and Kiviet (1986).

The following examples provide some relatively straightforward applications of LM tests in the frequency domain and show how they can sometimes be interpreted in the time domain. Reference is frequently made to trigonometric identities; a summary of the main identities can be found in Harvey (1981b, ch. 3).

Example 5.2.2 Consider testing $\text{H}_0: \varphi=0$ against $\text{H}_1: \varphi\neq 0$ in the AR(1) model

$$y_t = \varphi y_{t-1} + \xi_t, \quad t=1,\ldots,T \tag{5.2.19}$$

with $\xi_t \sim \text{NID}(0, \sigma^2)$. Since

$$g_j = \sigma^2/(1+\varphi^2-2\varphi \cos \lambda_j) \tag{5.2.20}$$

we have

$$z_{1j} = \partial g_j/\partial\varphi = -2\sigma^2(\varphi - \cos \lambda_j)/(1+\varphi^2-2\varphi \cos \lambda_j)^2$$

which becomes

$$z_{1j} = 2\sigma^2 \cos \lambda_j, \quad j=0,\ldots,T-1$$

under the null hypothesis, and

$$z_{2j} = \partial g_j/\partial\sigma^2 = 1/(1+\varphi^2-2\varphi \cos \lambda_j), \quad j=0,\ldots,T-1$$

which is equal to unity for all j under H_0.

Under H_0 the information matrix is block diagonal because, with $g_j = \tilde{\sigma}^2$,

$$\sum_{j=0}^{T-1} g_j^{-2} z_{1j} z_{2j} = \tilde{\sigma}^{-4} \sum(-2\tilde{\sigma}^2 \cos \lambda_j) = 0$$

as $\Sigma \cos \lambda_j = 0$. Evaluating (5.2.12) gives

$$\text{LM} = \frac{1}{2}\left[\sum_{j=0}^{T-1} \frac{2\tilde{\sigma}^2(2\pi I(\lambda_j) - \tilde{\sigma}^2)\cos \lambda_j}{\tilde{\sigma}^4}\right]^2 \Bigg/ \sum_{j=0}^{T-1} \frac{4\tilde{\sigma}^4 \cos^2 \lambda_j}{\tilde{\sigma}^4}$$

Bearing in mind that $\Sigma \cos \lambda_j = 0$ and that $\Sigma \cos^2 \lambda_j = T/2$,

$$\text{LM} = T^{-1}\tilde{\sigma}^{-4}\left[\sum_{j=0}^{T-1} 2\pi I(\lambda_j) \cos \lambda_j\right]^2 \tag{5.2.21}$$

and under H_0, $\text{LM}^* \sim \chi_1^2$. As Example 5.2.1 showed, the LM statistic in the time domain is

$$\text{LM}^* = Tr^2(1) \tag{5.2.22}$$

where $r(1)$ is the first-order sample autocorrelation of the y_t's. However, since twice the term in square brackets in (5.2.21) is the inverse Fourier transform of the periodogram, the statistics in (5.2.21) and (5.2.22) are indeed identical.

Example 5.2.3 Consider the cyclical process, $y_t = \psi_t$, where ψ_t is as defined in (2.3.38). The s.g.f. is

$$g_{\psi j} = \frac{(1+\rho^2 - 2\rho \cos \lambda_c \cos \lambda_j)\sigma_\kappa^2}{1+\rho^4+4\rho^2\cos^2 \lambda_c - 4\rho(1+\rho^2)\cos \lambda_c \cos \lambda_j + 2\rho^2 \cos 2\lambda_j} \tag{5.2.23}$$

Suppose for the moment that λ_c is known, and that the objective is to test the null hypothesis that ρ is equal to zero. Differentiating (5.2.23) and setting ρ equal to zero gives

$$\frac{\partial g_{\psi j}}{\partial \rho} = (-2\cos\lambda_c\cos\lambda_j + 4\cos\lambda_c\cos\lambda_j)\sigma_\kappa^2$$
$$= 2\sigma_\kappa^2\cos\lambda_c\cos\lambda_j$$

$$\frac{\partial g_{\psi j}}{\partial \sigma_\kappa^2} = 1$$

and

$$g_{\psi j} = \sigma_\kappa^2, \quad j = 0, \ldots, T^* - 1$$

The LM* statistic is therefore obtained by regressing $\upsilon_j = 2\pi I(\lambda_j) - \tilde{\sigma}_\kappa^2$ on $2\tilde{\sigma}_\kappa^2\cos\lambda_c\cos\lambda_j$ and a constant, with $\tilde{\sigma}_\kappa^2$ being the estimated variance of y_t. However, a regression on $\cos\lambda_j$ gives exactly the same result. From the previous example we know that this yields the $Tr^2(1)$ test statistic, (5.2.22). This statistic does not depend on λ_c and so it is valid for all λ_c. The LM test of a cycle against white noise is therefore the same as the LM test of an AR(1) process. The test can be carried out by treating $T^{\frac{1}{2}}r(1)$ as having an N(0, 1) distribution under H_0. However, even though ρ is restricted to be non-negative, a one-sided test is not appropriate since the theoretical first-order autocorrelation, $\rho(1)$, may be positive or negative for the cyclical process. If, on the other hand, the sign of $\cos\lambda_c$ is known to be positive (negative), a one-sided test for positive (negative) serial correlation can be carried out using the von Neumann ratio or the d-statistic. King and Evans (1986) show that such a test is LBI.

Example 5.2.4 Consider an unobserved components model consisting of an AR(1) and a seasonal AR(1) process,

$$y_t = \frac{\varepsilon_t}{1 - \varphi L} + \frac{\omega_t}{1 - \Phi L^s} \tag{5.2.24}$$

Any test of the null hypothesis $\varphi = \Phi = 0$ immediately runs into difficulties because the model is not identifiable under H_0. The LM test can, however, be modified to cope with this situation. Specifically

$$g(e_j^{i\lambda}) = \frac{\sigma_\varepsilon^2}{1 + \varphi^2 - 2\varphi\cos\lambda_j} + \frac{\sigma_\omega^2}{1 + \Phi^2 - 2\Phi\cos\lambda_j s} \tag{5.2.25}$$

and taking derivatives with respect to $\boldsymbol{\psi} = (\sigma_\varepsilon^2, \sigma_\omega^2, \varphi, \Phi)'$, evaluating them under H_0, and substituting in the frequency-domain expression for the information matrix gives

$$\frac{1}{2}\sum_{j=0}^{T-1}\frac{1}{g_j^2}\frac{\partial g_j}{\partial \boldsymbol{\psi}}\frac{\partial g_j}{\partial \boldsymbol{\psi}'} = \frac{T}{2(\sigma_\varepsilon^2 + \sigma_\omega^2)^2}\begin{bmatrix} 1 & 1 & 0 & 0 \\ 1 & 1 & 0 & 0 \\ 0 & 0 & 2\sigma_\varepsilon^4 & 0 \\ 0 & 0 & 0 & 2\sigma_\omega^2 \end{bmatrix} \tag{5.2.26}$$

This matrix is singular and so an LM statistic cannot be constructed in the normal way. The solution is to introduce the constraint

$$\sigma_\varepsilon^2/(\sigma_\varepsilon^2+\sigma_\omega^2)=k, \quad 0\leqslant k\leqslant 1 \tag{5.2.27}$$

Following Aitchison and Silvey (1960), a factor of $(1-k)$ is added to the first diagonal element of (5.2.26) and a factor of k to the second. This gives a non-singular matrix. The value of k is not important because on evaluating the LM statistic, (5.2.15), the terms involving k drop out in view of Parseval's theorem. This leaves

$$\mathrm{LM}^* = \frac{1}{T\tilde{\sigma}^4}\left\{\left[\sum_{j=0}^{T-1} 2\pi I(\lambda_j)\cos\lambda_j\right]^2 + \left[\sum_{j=0}^{T-1} 2\pi I(\lambda_j)\cos\lambda_j s\right]^2\right\}$$

where $\tilde{\sigma}^2$ is the sample variance of y_t, and so

$$\mathrm{LM}^* = T[r^2(1)+r^2(s)] \tag{5.2.28}$$

Thus the test statistic has a time-domain interpretation in terms of the first-order and s-th order sample autocorrelations.

The LM statistic in (5.2.28) is also the LM statistic for testing $\varphi=\Phi=0$ in the autoregressive model with 'gaps'

$$(1-\varphi\mathrm{L}-\Phi\mathrm{L}^s)\,y_t=\xi_t \tag{5.2.29}$$

and the multiplicative model

$$(1-\varphi\mathrm{L})(1-\Phi\mathrm{L}^s)\,y_t=\xi_t \tag{5.2.30}$$

where, in both cases, $\xi_t \sim \mathrm{NID}(0,\sigma_\xi^2)$.

5.2.3 Parameters on the boundary of the parameter space

It was noted in sub-section 5.1.2 that when some of the parameters lie on the boundary of the parameter space under the null hypothesis, the distribution of the LR and Wald statistics does not have the usual asymptotic χ^2 distribution. The LM test statistic, however, does have this distribution. The objection to the use of a conventional LM test in these circumstances is that it takes no account of the one-sided nature of the alternative. Hence it can be expected to have low power compared to procedures such as the LR, Wald and Kuhn-Tucker, which use this information.

Fortunately, the LM test can be modified to take account of the one-sided nature of the alternative. This is relatively straightforward to do in cases where a single parameter is being tested. The more general situation is treated by Rogers (1986).

The LM* statistic in (5.2.17) is obtained by carrying out a frequency-domain weighted regression of υ_j, defined in (5.2.13), on the elements of $\mathbf{z}_j$. If the test to be carried out is that a single non-negative parameter in $\boldsymbol{\psi}$ is zero, the regression model in (4.3.36) implies the construction of an LM test based on the t-statistic of the appropriate element of $\mathbf{z}_j$ in the regression of v_j on $\mathbf{z}_j$. This t-statistic is the signed square root of the LMF statistic in (5.2.18) and should be treated in the same spirit. If T rather than $[T/2]$ data points are used in this regression, the t-statistic must be divided by $\sqrt{2}$. The alternative is to take the square root of LM* in (5.2.15) with the sign being that of the single non-zero element in the score vector, $\Sigma g_j^{-2}\mathbf{z}_j v_j$. Either way, the regression model in (4.3.36) makes it clear that the test is to be carried out with respect to the *positive* tail of the normal or t-distribution; compare the time-domain example given in Harvey (1981a, p. 174).

Example 5.2.5 Consider the AR(1) plus noise model

$$y_t = \frac{\eta_t}{1-\varphi \mathrm{L}} + \varepsilon_t, \quad |\varphi| < 1 \tag{5.2.31}$$

in which the null hypothesis is $\mathrm{H}_0: \sigma_\varepsilon^2 = 0$, and the alternative is $\mathrm{H}_1: \sigma_\varepsilon^2 > 0$. The s.g.f. is

$$g_j = \sigma_\eta^2/(1+\varphi^2 - 2\varphi \cos \lambda_j) + \sigma_\varepsilon^2 \tag{5.2.32}$$

but under the null hypothesis that the model is a pure AR(1) process, it is evaluated as

$$g_j = \tilde{\sigma}_\eta^2/(1+\tilde{\varphi}^2 - 2\tilde{\varphi} \cos \lambda)$$

The elements of $\mathbf{z}_j$ are as follows when evaluated under the null hypothesis:

$$z_{1j} = \frac{\partial g_j}{\partial \sigma_\eta^2} = \frac{1}{(1+\tilde{\varphi}^2 - 2\tilde{\varphi}\cos \lambda_j)} \tag{5.2.33a}$$

$$z_{1j} = \frac{\partial g_j}{\partial \sigma_\eta^2} = \frac{1}{(1+\tilde{\varphi}^2 - 2\tilde{\varphi}\cos \lambda_j)} \tag{5.2.33b}$$

$$z_{3j} = \frac{\partial g_j}{\partial \sigma_\varepsilon^2} = 1 \tag{5.2.33c}$$

The estimate of $\tilde{\sigma}_\eta^2$ is just a factor of proportionality and so can be omitted when the LM test is constructed via a weighted regression. The test is based on the t-statistic associated with the constant term z_{3j}, with the critical region taken to be the positive tail of a standard normal, or a t-distribution, according to preference.

The simulation results in Harvey and Hotta (1982) suggest that the power of the one-sided LM test is similar to that of the LR test based on the distribution in (5.1.8). As regards the Wald test, it appears that its size may often be considerably in excess of its nominal size.

Example 5.2.6 It was noted at the end of Example 5.2.3, that with λ_c known, a one-sided test of $H_0: \rho=0$ against $H_1: \rho>0$ is appropriate. This may be carried out within a regression framework by means of a t-test on the coefficient of $\partial g_{\psi j}/\partial \rho$.

5.3 Tests of specification for structural models

Tests of specification are tests of specific hypotheses. Tests of misspecification are tests which may be derived against a particular alternative, but which do not necessarily take that alternative seriously as a model which might be entertained as a possible final specification. Tests of misspecification are therefore diagnostics and are considered in the next section. Tests of specification are normally based on the LR, Wald or LM principles, although the last of these is also often used to derive tests of misspecification.

Specification testing in structural models raises a number of issues, primarily because of the breakdown of standard regularity conditions. At first sight this appears to make testing a much more complicated business that it is in ARIMA models. However, many of the same problems arise in ARIMA models, although they are not always explicitly recognised. An example would be testing for overdifferencing which is a situation in which the usual LR-based tests are invalid. A further point is that because the variance parameters in structural models have to be non-negative, taking account of this restriction leads to tests which, while being slightly more complicated than their reduced form equivalents, are actually more powerful.

5.3.1 Tests on the variances in the basic structural model

The basic structural model contains four parameters, $\sigma_\eta^2, \sigma_\zeta^2, \sigma_\omega^2$ and σ_ε^2, irrespective of whether it is in the dummy variable or trigonometric seasonal form. All four parameters are constrained to be non-negative since they are variances. Thus a value of zero is on the boundary of the parameter space. As noted in section 5.1, suitably modified LR-based tests can still be applied in this situation provided that the ML estimator of the parameter in question is asymptotically normally distributed when the restriction is not applied. As shown in section 4.5, the ML estimators of the parameters in a time-invariant structural model are asymptotically normal provided that the spectral density of the associated stationary process is nowhere zero in the range $[-\pi, \pi]$. This condition holds in the basic structural model provided that σ_ζ^2 and σ_ω^2 are both strictly positive.

Given that σ_ζ^2 and σ_ω^2 are both strictly positive, a test of the hypothesis that either σ_η^2 or σ_ε^2 is zero can be carried out using the LR, Wald or LM principles. For the LR or Wald tests, the statistics are computed in the usual way and their distributions taken to be a mixture of chi-square distributions, as in (5.1.8). A one-sided LM test can be carried out in the way suggested in sub-section 5.2.3.

Example 5.3.1 The results of estimating the basic structural model for the quarterly airline data were given in Table 2.7.1. Imposing the constraint $\sigma_\eta^2 = 0$, gave a prediction error variance of $\tilde{\sigma}^2 = 1.74$. Without this constraint $\tilde{\sigma}^2 = 1.40$. The LR statistic, (5.1.4), is therefore

$$LR = 43 \log(1.74/1.40) = 9.35 \tag{5.3.1}$$

The critical region for a test of $H_0: \sigma_\eta^2 = 0$ against $H_1: \sigma_\eta^2 > 0$ at the 5% level of significance is $LR > 2.71$, where 2.71 is the 10% significance point of a χ_1^2 variate. The null hypothesis is therefore rejected.

Obtaining the distribution of the LR, Wald and LM statistics for a joint test of $\sigma_\eta^2 = \sigma_\varepsilon^2 = 0$ is more complicated; see the discussion in sub-sections 5.1.2 and 5.2.3.

If σ_ζ^2 is known to be zero, it is no longer possible to test $\sigma_\eta^2 = 0$ using (modified) LR procedures. The hypothesis that $\sigma_\varepsilon^2 = 0$ can still be tested using such procedures, provided that both σ_η^2 and σ_ω^2 are strictly positive.

5.3.2 The discounted least squares trend restriction

The discounted least squares trend model imposes the restriction that $q_\zeta = (q_\eta/2)^2$; see the discussion at the end of sub-section 2.3.2. The restriction is a non-linear one. Nevertheless LR, Wald and LM tests can be carried out and since the parameters lie in the interior of the parameter space no modifications are needed. Thus, in the BSM, provided that σ_ζ^2 and σ_ω^2 are strictly positive, all three test statistics have a χ_1^2 distribution in large samples when the null hypothesis is true.

The LR and LM tests are relatively straightforward. The latter is carried out by regressing υ_j on $z_{\mu j}$, $z_{\beta j}$, $z_{\gamma j}$ and $z_{\varepsilon j}$ of (4.3.5) with g_j evaluated under the null hypothesis, and testing $\frac{1}{2}TR^2$. As regards the Wald test, we first write the restriction as

$$r(\psi) = \frac{\sigma_\zeta^2}{\sigma_\varepsilon^2} - \frac{1}{4}\left(\frac{\sigma_\eta^2}{\sigma_\varepsilon^2}\right)^2 = 0 \tag{5.3.2}$$

The vector of first derivatives, corresponding to the matrix $\mathbf{R}'$ in (5.1.5) is given by

$$\left.\begin{aligned}
\frac{\partial r(\psi)}{\partial \sigma_\eta^2} &= -\frac{1}{2}\frac{\sigma_\eta^2}{\sigma_\varepsilon^4} \\
\frac{\partial r(\psi)}{\partial \sigma_\zeta^2} &= \frac{1}{\sigma_\varepsilon^2} \\
\frac{\partial r(\psi)}{\partial \sigma_\omega^2} &= 0 \\
\frac{\partial r(\psi)}{\partial \sigma_\varepsilon^2} &= -\frac{\sigma_\zeta^2}{\sigma_\varepsilon^4} + \frac{1}{2}\frac{\sigma_\eta^4}{\sigma_\varepsilon^6}
\end{aligned}\right\} \tag{5.3.3}$$

Evaluating these derivatives and $\mathbf{r}(\psi)$ using estimates from the unrestricted model and substituting in (5.1.5) gives the required test statistic.

Example 5.3.2 In the quarterly airline model, the discounted least squares trend model had $\tilde{\sigma}^2 = 1.72$; see Table 2.7.1. The LR statistic is therefore

$$\text{LR} = 43 \log(1.72/1.40) = 8.85 \tag{5.3.4}$$

The 5% significance point for a χ_1^2 variate is 3.84 and so the null hypothesis is rejected.

5.3.3 Serial correlation in the disturbance terms

The additive nature of unobserved components models does introduce some pitfalls not normally found in ARIMA models. These pitfalls arise in formulating the alternative hypothesis when an LM test is to be carried out. The following example provides an illustration.

Example 5.3.3 Consider an LM test of the hypothesis that the disturbance term in a random walk plus noise model is an AR(1) process. The general model is:

$$y_t = \mu_t + \varepsilon_t \tag{5.3.5}$$

$$\mu_t = \mu_{t-1} + \eta_t \tag{5.3.6a}$$

$$\eta_t = \varphi \eta_{t-1} + \kappa_t, \quad |\varphi| < 1 \tag{5.3.6b}$$

where ε_t and κ_t are independent white-noise disturbances. The s.g.f. of Δy_t is

$$g_j = (1 + \varphi^2 - 2\varphi \cos \lambda_j)^{-1} \sigma_\kappa^2 + 2(1 - \cos \lambda_j)\sigma_\varepsilon^2 \tag{5.3.7}$$

Under the null hypothesis that $\varphi = 0$, the derivatives of g_j with respect to the unknown parameters are, respectively,

$$\frac{\partial g_j}{\partial \sigma_\kappa^2} = 1, \quad \frac{\partial g}{\partial \varphi} = 2\sigma_\kappa^2 \cos \lambda_j, \quad \frac{\partial g}{\partial \sigma_\varepsilon^2} = 2(1 - \cos \lambda_j) \tag{5.3.8}$$

Unfortunately the test cannot be implemented. In the terms of the regression used to construct the LM* statistic (5.2.15), the third regressor in (5.3.8) is a linear combination of the other two. This arises because the LM tests for AR(1) and MA(1) processes are the same. Under the null hypothesis Δy_t already contains an MA(1) term, and adding a second one to the model would leave it underidentified. The full model, on the other hand, is identifiable, and so both the LR and Wald tests can be implemented.

Suppose that the disturbance term in the level equation is modified so that the autoregressive lag is a second-order one,

$$\eta_t = \varphi \eta_{t-2} + \kappa_t, \quad |\varphi| < 1 \tag{5.3.9}$$

In this case

$$g_j = (1+\varphi^2 - 2\varphi \cos 2\lambda)^{-1}\sigma_\kappa^2 + 2(1 - \cos \lambda_j)\sigma_\varepsilon^2 \qquad (5.3.10)$$

and it is straightforward to check that the LM test of H_0: $\varphi = 0$ can be carried out.

The above example is an important pointer to the difficulties which can be encountered in formulating LM tests for structural models. Thus for the local linear trend model, it is not, in general, possible to set up an LM test against an AR(1) model for the disturbance term of either the level, μ_t, or the slope, β_t. In fact, for the slope, it is not even possible to test for a second-order process of the kind given in (5.3.9). However, as with (5.3.6) there is no problem in constructing an LM test for serial correlation in the measurement equation disturbance term, ε_t.

Curiously, the problems associated with testing for serial correlation in the level and slope disturbances of a stochastic trend disappear when a seasonal component is added as in the BSM. A set of diagnostic LM tests for the BSM is developed in sub-section 5.4.4.

5.3.4 *Cyclical components*

Testing for the presence of a cyclical component, or components, in a structural model raises a number of issues. The first is concerned with the identifiability problems which arise under the null hypothesis when a cycle is added to a white-noise disturbance term. In the simplest case

$$y_t = \psi_t + \varepsilon_t \qquad (5.3.11)$$

where ψ_t is the cyclical component (2.3.38). More generally (5.3.11) may include a stochastic trend component, μ_t, and a seasonal, γ_t, but the presence of such terms is irrelevant to the immediate issue at hand. A test for the presence of a cycle in (5.3.11) amounts to a test of H_0: $\rho = 0$ against H_1: $\rho > 0$. However an immediate problem arises because when $\rho = 0$, ψ_t reduces to white noise and so cannot be distinguished from ε_t. This lack of identifiability needs to be borne in mind if one is contemplating carrying out a Wald or an LM test. In the case of the LM test the solution is simply to drop ε_t from the unrestricted model; compare Example 5.2.4.

As was shown in Example 5.2.3, the fact that the frequency of the cycle, λ_c, may be unknown poses no problem for the LM test. However, for Wald and LR tests an unknown λ_c does present a problem since when ρ is zero, λ_c is not identifiable. This is true even if the irregular component, ε_t, is dropped from (5.3.11). The best strategy would seem to be to test for a cycle *before* estimating an unrestricted model. If the null hypothesis is true, such an approach avoids the computational problems, primarily non-convergence, associated with estimating a model which is not identifiable.

The implementation of an LM test in the trend plus cycle model, (4.1.11), is as follows. The unrestricted model is taken to be

$$y_t = \mu_t + \psi_t \qquad (5.3.12)$$

where μ_t is a stochastic trend and ψ_t is a cycle. The s.g.f. of $\Delta^2 y_t$ is

$$g_j = \sigma_\zeta^2 + 2(1 - \cos\lambda_j)\sigma_\eta^2 + 4(1 - \cos\lambda_j)^2 g_{\psi j} \tag{5.3.13}$$

where $g_{\psi j}$ is as defined in (5.2.23). The LM test of H_0: $\rho = 0$ is then constructed by a weighted regression of v_j, as defined in (5.2.13), on a constant term, $2(1 - \cos\lambda_j)$, $4(1 - \cos\lambda_j)^2$ and $(1 - \cos\lambda_j)^2 \cos\lambda_j$. The weights, g_j, are given by (5.3.13) with $g_{\psi j}$ equal to the estimator of σ_κ^2 under the null. (This is the same as the estimator of σ_ε^2 in the local linear trend model.) The resulting test statistic, LM*, has a χ_1^2 distribution under H_0.

The construction of the LM statistic for the trend plus cycle model suggests that for the cyclical trend, the appropriate unrestricted model is obtained by dropping η_t from the level equation. The LM statistic would then be formed by the same regression as was used for the trend plus cycle but with the final regressor $(1 - \cos\lambda_j)^2 \cos\lambda_j$ replaced by $(1 - \cos\lambda_j)\cos\lambda_j$. However, this procedure does not work because of multicollinearity among the regressors. The explanation lies in Examples 5.2.2 and 5.3.3. The first of these showed that testing for a cycle is equivalent to testing for an AR(1) component, while the second pointed to the difficulty which arises because the LM test treats AR(1) and MA(1) processes in the same way. If ε_t is dropped from the model, the problem disappears. An example of an LM test for a cyclical trend component is given in sub-section 5.7.3.

Once a seasonal component is brought into the model, the above problems associated with testing for a cycle in the level equation disappear. The precise nature of the LM tests for cycles in the BSM is discussed in section 5.4.

5.3.5 Deterministic trend and seasonal components

As was observed in sub-section 5.3.1, the standard regularity conditions for carrying out likelihood-based tests break down when certain variances are zero under the null hypothesis. This corresponds to a situation in which the model contains *deterministic* components. A partial solution to the problem is to set up a test prior to estimating the model. The parameter values under both the null and the alternative are pre-specified and an MPI test is constructed. The discussion of MPI tests in sub-section 5.1.3 was in terms of a linear regression model. The first step in applying MPI tests to structural models is therefore to put them in a regression framework. In sub-section 4.2.2 it was shown how the general model, (4.1.3), could be written in regression form by conditioning on the non-stationary part of the state vector at $t = 0$. Thus

$$\mathbf{y} = \mathbf{X}_0 \boldsymbol{\alpha}_0^\dagger + \mathbf{u}, \quad \text{Var}(\mathbf{u}) = \sigma_*^2 \boldsymbol{\Omega}_0(\boldsymbol{\psi}_*) \tag{5.3.14}$$

where $\boldsymbol{\Omega}_0$ is given by (4.2.7) and $\boldsymbol{\psi}_*$ denotes the hyperparameters relative to σ_*^2. Within this framework a test of H_0: $\boldsymbol{\psi}_* = \boldsymbol{\psi}_{*_0}$ against H_1: $\boldsymbol{\psi}_* = \boldsymbol{\psi}_{*_1}$ may be constructed by setting up a test based on the ratio $S(\boldsymbol{\psi}_{*_1})/S(\boldsymbol{\psi}_{*_0})$ as indicated in

(5.1.14). Fortunately, conditioning on $\boldsymbol{\alpha}_0^\dagger$ is not crucial to such a test. The generalised sum-of-squares function, $S(\psi_*)$, is the same irrespective of the point in time at which the conditioning takes place. This includes conditioning at some point in the remote past, which is effectively the same as starting off with a diffuse prior. Indeed the equivalence between $S(\psi_*)$ calculated from (4.2.11b) and $S(\psi_*)$ calculated from the Kalman filter initiated with a diffuse prior was explicitly noted in sub-section 4.2.2. In what follows it will be assumed that the MPI tests are being applied to a model initiated with a diffuse prior and that $S(\psi_*)$ is being calculated from (4.2.4b).

Deterministic trend Consider a test of the hypothesis $\sigma_\eta^2=0$ in the local level model with drift,

$$y_t=\frac{\eta_t}{\Delta}+\beta t+\varepsilon_t \tag{5.3.15}$$

The null is just the deterministic linear trend model (2.3.3). As observed at the end of sub-section 5.3.1, a likelihood-based test cannot be constructed. However, an MPI test can. Writing $\sigma_\eta^2=q\sigma_\varepsilon^2$, the construction of the test hinges on the choice of q. Nyblom (1986), using the criterion of Pitman efficiency, suggests setting

$$q=375.1/(T-2)^2 \tag{5.3.16}$$

so that q moves towards zero as T goes to infinity. This choice tends to give a slightly higher power than setting q according to expression (5.1.18) with θ equal to one-half. It gives a much higher power than the test proposed by La Motte and McWhorter (1978).

The numerator and denominator of the MPI test statistic can be computed by running the Kalman filter for the local linear trend model and recording the sum of squares of the standardised innovations. To obtain $S(\psi_{*_1})$ set $\sigma_\eta^2/\sigma_\varepsilon^2$ equal to the value of q given by (5.3.16) and σ_ζ^2 equal to zero. To obtain $S(\psi_{*_0})$ set $\sigma_\eta^2=\sigma_\zeta^2=0$. Alternatively $S(\psi_{*_0})$ is given simply as the sum of squares of the OLS residuals from regressing y_t on a constant and a time trend. The null hypothesis that σ_η^2 is zero is rejected at the α level if the statistic $(T-2)[1-S(\psi_{*_1})/S(\psi_{*_0})]/375.1$ is less than the appropriate critical value given in Table 5.3.1. Nyblom chose to tabulate this statistic because it has a non-degenerate limiting distribution.

Tests of the null hypothesis of a deterministic trend could also be constructed by allowing the slope, as well as the level, to be stochastic under the alternative. This would involve specifying both $\sigma_\eta^2/\sigma_\varepsilon^2$ and $\sigma_\zeta^2/\sigma_\varepsilon^2$. However, the evidence presented in Franzini and Harvey (1983) suggests that the MPI test based on a fixed slope will still have relatively high power when the data really are generated by a local linear trend model in which the slope is stochastic.

An LBI test of the hypothesis that σ_η^2 is zero can also be constructed. The test

Table 5.3.1 *Critical values of* $(T-2)[1-S(\Psi_{*1})/S(\Psi_{*0})]/375.1$

	α			
$T-2$	0.10	0.05	0.025	0.01
10	0.0199	0.0206	0.0212	0.0218
20	0.0263	0.0280	0.0295	0.0313
30	0.0285	0.0308	0.0328	0.0353
40	0.0294	0.0320	0.0344	0.0374
50	0.0299	0.0327	0.0354	0.0386
60	0.0302	0.0332	0.0360	0.0394
80	0.0306	0.0337	0.0367	0.0404
100	0.0307	0.0340	0.0371	0.0410
∞	0.0312	0.0350	0.0385	0.0431

This test is the most efficient in the Pitman sense when the limiting power is 0.80 at the significance level $\alpha = 0.05$. The transformed statistic tabulated here has significant large values.

statistic, obtained by dividing (5.1.20) by T, is

$$\frac{1}{T}\frac{\mathbf{e}'\mathbf{\Omega}^*\mathbf{e}}{\mathbf{e}'\mathbf{e}} \tag{5.3.17}$$

where $\mathbf{e}$ denotes the $T \times 1$ vector of OLS residuals from regressing the observations on a constant and a time trend and the element (s, t) of $\mathbf{\Omega}^*$ is just $\min(s, t)$. The main attraction of this approach is that the test statistic has a known asymptotic distribution. In fact the asymptotic distribution is valid even in cases where the disturbances are not normally distributed, as assumed in the derivation of the test. For (5.3.15) the 5% critical value, assuming that μ_0 is fixed but unknown, is 0.148. If the slope term is not included in the trend, so that the general model is just a random walk and the elements of the vector $\mathbf{e}$ are deviations from the mean, the limiting distribution of the test statistic is the same as that of the Cramer-von Mises statistic and the 5% critical value is 0.461. Further details may be found in Nabeya and Tanaka (1988).

Deterministic trend and seasonal If σ_η^2, σ_ζ^2 and σ_ω^2 in the BSM are all zero, the model collapses to the deterministic trend and seasonal model of (2.3.1). For quarterly data, Franzini and Harvey set up a test of the null hypothesis that this model is true against the more general alternative of a BSM by letting $\sigma_\eta^2 = q\sigma_\varepsilon^2$, $\sigma_\zeta^2 = 0$ and $\sigma_\omega^2 = q\sigma_\varepsilon^2$. The value of q is determined from (5.1.19) by setting θ equal to one-half; see Table 5.3.2. The resulting test statistic is termed the *b-statistic.* It can be computed by running the Kalman filter for the BSM, and the null hypothesis of a deterministic trend and seasonal is rejected if b is less than the appropriate critical value given in Table 5.3.2. Note that this table assumes the seasonal dummy variable formulation of the BSM.

Table 5.3.2 *Critical values for b at 5% level of significance, $\theta=0.5$*

T	q	Critical value	T	q	Critical value	T	q	Critical value
12	0.384	0.437	44	0.136	0.570	76	0.082	0.651
16	0.314	0.447	48	0.126	0.583	80	0.078	0.659
20	0.265	0.465	52	0.117	0.595	88	0.072	0.672
24	0.229	0.485	56	0.109	0.606	96	0.066	0.684
28	0.201	0.504	60	0.102	0.616	104	0.061	0.695
32	0.180	0.523	64	0.096	0.626	112	0.057	0.705
36	0.162	0.540	68	0.091	0.635	120	0.053	0.714
40	0.148	0.555	72	0.087	0.643			

Table 5.3.3 *Critical values for b* at 5% level of significance, $\theta=0.5$*

T	q	Critical value	T	q	Critical value	T	q	Critical value
12	0.156	0.421	44	0.051	0.611	76	0.030	0.692
16	0.125	0.453	48	0.047	0.624	80	0.029	0.699
20	0.103	0.486	52	0.044	0.637	88	0.026	0.712
24	0.088	0.514	56	0.041	0.648	96	0.024	0.724
28	0.077	0.538	60	0.038	0.658	104	0.022	0.734
32	0.068	0.560	64	0.036	0.668	112	0.021	0.743
36	0.061	0.579	68	0.034	0.677	120	0.020	0.752
40	0.056	0.595	72	0.032	0.685			

The number of differenced observations is $T-1$.

Partially deterministic trend and seasonal In the partially deterministic model, the trend is taken to be a random walk plus drift while the seasonals are fixed. In order to complete the specification under the null hypothesis the value of σ_ε^2 is set to zero. Thus σ_*^2 is now taken to be σ_η^2 while the remaining parameters, σ_ζ^2, σ_ω^2 and σ_ε^2 are all zero. The alternative hypothesis has $\sigma_\zeta^2=q\sigma_\eta^2$ and $\sigma_\omega^2=q\sigma_\eta^2$. Suitable values of q are given in Table 5.3.3, together with critical values for the test statistic, b^*. The numerator of b^* can be obtained by applying the Kalman filter to a BSM in the state space form (4.1.3) with $h=0$ and $\mathbf{Q}=\text{diag}(1,q,q)$. The denominator is given by setting $q=0$. The denominator can also be calculated as the residual sum of squares obtained by subtracting seasonal means from the first differenced series; see equation (5.5.16) below.

The partially deterministic model is more likely to arise in practice than a model with a completely deterministic trend. Indeed it is for this reason that the partially deterministic model is suggested as a baseline for the goodness-of-fit statistic, R_s^2, in sub-section 5.5.5. Note that if the model contains no seasonal, the first test (deterministic trend) described in this sub-section can be adopted to test the null hypothesis of a random walk plus drift against the alternative that the drift is stochastic. The random walk plus drift forms the baseline for the R_D^2 goodness-of-fit statistic.

Airline passengers For the quarterly airline data, introduced in sub-section 2.7.5, the test statistic for a deterministic model, b, is 0.353. This gives a clear rejection since the critical value from Table 5.3.2 is 0.583. A clear rejection is also obtained with the Durbin-Watson test, the d-statistic taking a value of 0.57.

The partially deterministic model gives a much better fit to the model, as witnessed by the second row in Table 2.7.1. Furthermore it survives the Durbin-Watson test quite easily since $d = 1.87$ and the 5% critical value is 1.47. However, it is rejected by the b^* test: the critical value is 0.624 while b^* is 0.458.

5.4 Diagnostics

In a well-specified model, the residuals should be approximately random. This can be checked by graphical procedures and various statistical tests. The statistical tests may be derived using the LM principle so as to be powerful against certain alternatives. On the other hand, they may be statistics whose distributions are known when the model is correctly specified and whose forms are such that they can be expected to have high power against plausible, but perhaps rather vaguely defined, alternatives.

This section presents various graphical procedures and tests appropriate for structural models. An indication is given for each as to the type of misspecifications which they are likely to be able to detect.

5.4.1 *Residuals and graphical procedures*

The main time-domain diagnostics are based on the innovations obtained by running the Kalman filter initialised with a diffuse prior. If the n hyperparameters are partitioned as $\psi = [\psi_*' \quad \sigma_*^2]'$, the filter does not depend on the scalar variance parameter σ_*^2. For a given value of ψ_*, the *residuals* are then defined as the standardised innovations

$$\tilde{v}_t = v_t / f_t^{\frac{1}{2}}, \quad t = d+1, \ldots, T \tag{5.4.1}$$

When the model is correctly specified, and the parameters in ψ_* are known, the residuals have the property:

$$\tilde{v}_t \sim \text{NID}(0, \sigma_*^2) \tag{5.4.2}$$

In the more usual case when some of the parameters in ψ_* have been estimated, (5.4.2) holds approximately. However some care must be exercised in constructing 'naive' tests in which the estimated parameters in ψ_* are treated as though they were known.

The basic way of examining the behaviour of the residuals is by plotting them directly against time. A *standardised plot* is based on the residuals divided by the estimate of the standard deviation given by (4.2.5), that is $\tilde{\sigma}_*^{-1}\tilde{v}_t$, $t=1,\ldots, T$. These quantities can be treated as being approximately NID(0, 1). Note that although the second moment of the $\tilde{\sigma}_*^{-1}\tilde{v}_t$'s is unity, the variance is not necessarily equal to unity as the mean need not be equal to zero. An alternative standardised plot can be based on $(\tilde{v}_t-\bar{\tilde{v}})/\hat{\sigma}_*$, where $\hat{\sigma}_*$ is defined in (5.4.3b) below.

Plots of the cumulative sum (CUSUM) and the cumulative sum of squares are also useful, and a good deal of information can be obtained simply by inspecting them; see Brown *et al.* (1975) and Harvey (1981a, pp. 151–4). Then CUSUM is defined as

$$\text{CUSUM}(t)=\hat{\sigma}_*^{-1}\sum_{j=d+1}^{t}\tilde{v}_j,\quad t=d+1,\ldots, T \tag{5.4.3a}$$

where

$$\hat{\sigma}_*^2=(T-d-1)^{-1}\sum_{t=d+1}^{T}(\tilde{v}_t-\bar{\tilde{v}})^2 \tag{5.4.3b}$$

with $\bar{\tilde{v}}$ being the mean of the residuals. In large samples $\hat{\sigma}_*^2$ may be replaced by the usual estimator $\tilde{\sigma}_*^2$. A formal assessment of the CUSUM plot is obtained by determining whether it crosses either of two predefined significance lines drawn above and below the horizontal axis, CUSUM$(t)=0$. The equation of these lines is given by

$$\text{CUSUM}=\pm[a\sqrt{T-d}+2a(t-d)/\sqrt{T-d}]$$

where $a=0.948$ for a significance level of 5% and 0.850 for 10%. The CUSUM procedure is particularly valuable for detecting structural change and an example of its use in this context is given later in sub-section 7.5.2.

The CUSUM of squares is based on a plot of the quantities

$$\text{CUSUMSQ}(t)=\sum_{j=d+1}^{t}\tilde{v}_j^2\Big/\sum_{t=d+1}^{T}\tilde{v}_t^2 \tag{5.4.4}$$

and the way in which a formal test can be constructed may be found in the references cited above. The CUSUM of squares can also be used to detect structural change. Its other role is as a test for heteroscedasticity in the residuals.

If, instead of initialising the Kalman filter with a diffuse prior, the elements of the initial state vector are treated as fixed, a different set of innovations, v_t, $t=1,\ldots, T$, are obtained; compare (3.4.27). When σ_*^2 is the only unknown hyperparameter, these innovations are normally distributed with mean zero. Unlike the residuals of (5.4.1) they are not mutually independent in small samples. However, when divided by $f_t^{\frac{1}{2}}$, they are approximately NID$(0,\sigma_*^2)$, and this remains true when parameters other than σ_*^2 have to be estimated. Hence they can be used as diagnostics. On the whole, though, the residuals based on a diffuse prior seem to be preferable, and there seems to be little point in computing the alternative set unless the model is being estimated with fixed initial conditions.

A set of statistics which do offer the possibility of providing useful additional information are the estimates of the irregular disturbance term. For a general model of form (4.1.1), these quantities are defined by

$$e_{t|T} = y_t - \mathbf{z}_t'\mathbf{a}_{t|T}, \quad t = 1, \ldots, T \tag{5.4.5}$$

Given the properties of $\mathbf{a}_{t|T}$; the smoothed estimate of $\boldsymbol{\alpha}_t$, it can be shown that if the hyperparameter vector is partitioned as $[\boldsymbol{\psi}_*' \quad \sigma_*^2]$ and $\boldsymbol{\psi}_*$ is known, the $e_{t|T}$'s are normally distributed with mean zero and variance $\sigma_*^2(h_t - \mathbf{z}_t'\mathbf{P}_{t|T}\mathbf{z}_t)$. However, they are not, in general, serially independent; see Kohn and Ansley (1989). Plots or standardised plots of the $e_{t|T}$'s may nevertheless provide useful information. It is perhaps misleading to refer to the $e_{t|T}$'s as residuals, since they primarily reflect the unexplained part of the model associated with the irregular component. Thus, unlike the residuals of (5.4.1), they cannot be used as the basis for a general assessment of misspecification. However, it is for this very reason that they may provide additional insight.

Example 5.4.1 The deterministic linear trend model

$$y_t = \alpha + \beta t + \varepsilon_t, \quad \varepsilon_t \sim \text{NID}(0, \sigma_*^2), \quad t = 1, \ldots, T$$

is a special case of a classical linear regression model and the $T-2$ residuals of (5.4.1) are the recursive residuals. The $e_{t|T}$'s of (5.4.5) are the OLS residuals. Since there is only a single disturbance term in a regression model, the recursive and OLS residuals contain the same information but presented in different ways. The recursive residuals are exactly $\text{NID}(0, \sigma_*^2)$ since there are is no $\boldsymbol{\psi}_*$ vector containing unknown parameters to be estimated. As is well known, the OLS residuals in a regression model are, in general, neither independent nor homoscedastic in small samples.

In a regression model the innovations, v_t, obtained using a Kalman filter with fixed initial conditions also correspond to the OLS residuals.

5.4.2 Tests of misspecification based on residuals

A number of tests of misspecification can be based directly on the residuals defined in (5.4.1).

Serial correlation The residual sample autocorrelations are defined by

$$r_v(\tau) = \frac{\sum_{t=d+1+\tau}^{T} (\tilde{v}_t - \bar{\tilde{v}})(\tilde{v}_{t-\tau} - \bar{\tilde{v}})}{\sum_{t=d+1}^{T} (\tilde{v}_t - \bar{\tilde{v}})^2}, \quad \tau = 1, 2, \ldots \tag{5.4.6}$$

and the resulting correlogram gives an indication of any serial correlation. Approximate standard errors for the sample autocorrelations may be obtained by the method of McLeod (1978), with the appropriate number of degrees of freedom equal to $n^* = n-1$, the number of fitted hyperparameters excluding σ_*^2.

A joint test of significance of the first P residual autocorrelations is given by a portmanteau statistic based on the sums of squares of these autocorrelations. The Box-Ljung form of the test statistic is

$$Q^* = T^*(T^*+2) \sum_{\tau=1}^{P} (T^*-\tau)^{-1} r_v^2(\tau) \tag{5.4.7}$$

where $T^* = T-d$. This test statistic is a modified version of the Box-Pierce statistic; Ljung and Box (1978) argue that it has better small sample properties. When an ARIMA(p, d, q) has been fitted, Q^* is asymptotically $\chi^2_{P-(p+q)}$. This asymptotic result requires that P increases with T, so that, for example, P may be determined as $P = \sqrt{T}$ or $\log T$. In a structural model it may be conjectured that Q^* is also asymptotically χ^2 but with degrees of freedom given by $P - n^*$.

Other tests for serial correlation can be constructed by means of the LM principle in the frequency domain. These tests are described in sub-section 5.4.4.

Non-linearity It may be useful to compute the sample autocorrelations for functions of the residuals. In particular, the sample autocorrelations of the squared residuals, denoted by $\text{rsq}_v(\tau)$, can provide an indication of certain types of non-linear effects which may be present; see Example 5.2.1 and section 6.5. These sample autocorrelations,

$$\text{rsq}_v(\tau) = \frac{\sum(\tilde{v}_t^2 - \tilde{\sigma}_*^2)(\tilde{v}_{t-\tau}^2 - \tilde{\sigma}_*^2)}{\sum(\tilde{v}_t^2 - \tilde{\sigma}_*^2)^2}, \quad \tau = 1, 2, \ldots \tag{5.4.8}$$

can be used to construct a Box-Ljung type test for non-linearity by replacing $r_v(\tau)$ by $\text{rsq}_v(\tau)$ in (5.4.7). As shown in McLeod and Li (1983), the asymptotic distribution of this statistic is χ^2_P.

Heteroscedasticity A simple diagnostic test for heteroscedasticity can be constructed from the residuals. Suppose that h is the nearest integer to $T^*/3$. The test statistic is

$$H(h) = \sum_{t=T-h+1}^{T} \tilde{v}_t^2 \Big/ \sum_{t=d+1}^{d+1+h} \tilde{v}_t^2 \tag{5.4.9}$$

If the only unknown parameter in the model were σ_*^2, this statistic would have an $F(h, h)$ distributed under the null hypothesis. It is therefore suggested that the $H(h)$ statistic be tested against an $F(h, h)$ distribution in more general situations. The alternative is to base the test on the asymptotic distribution of $hH(h)$, which is χ^2_h under the null hypothesis. If it is thought that the variances may be bigger (smaller) towards the end of the sample, then the upper (lower) tail of the

F-distribution should be used as the critical region in a one-sided test. A two-sided test allows for both possibilities but at the expense of a loss in power.

A heteroscedasticity test can also be based on the CUSUM of squares, as was noted below (5.4.4).

A more specific test, against the ARCH form of heteroscedasticity was described in Example 5.2.1. The form of the resulting test statistic as given in (5.2.10) suggests, as a more general test for ARCH, the analogue of the Box-Ljung test in which the residual autocorrelations in (5.4.7) are replaced by the autocorrelations of the squared residuals, (5.4.8).

Normality The standardised third and fourth moments of the residuals about the mean are

$$\sqrt{b_1} = \hat{\sigma}_*^{-3} \sum(\tilde{v}_t - \bar{\tilde{v}})^3/T^* \tag{5.4.10}$$

and

$$b_2 = \hat{\sigma}_*^{-4} \sum(\tilde{v}_t - \bar{\tilde{v}})^4/T^* \tag{5.4.11}$$

where $\hat{\sigma}_*^2$ is as defined in (5.4.3b). These statistics are the basic measures of skewness and kurtosis, and for a normal distribution they should be centred around zero and three respectively. They are asymptotically normal, with

$$\sqrt{b_1} \sim \text{AN}(0, 6/T^*)$$

and $b_2 \sim \text{AN}(3, 24/T^*)$

when the model is correctly specified; see Bowman and Shenton (1975). A test for non-normality may therefore be based on the statistic

$$N = (T^*/6)b_1 + (T^*/24)(b_2 - 3)^2 \tag{5.4.12}$$

Under the null hypothesis, this statistic has a χ_2^2 distribution in large samples. As pointed out in Jarque and Bera (1980), the test can be obtained by using the LM principle.

It is sometimes desirable to test skewness and kurtosis individually. A test on the latter is particularly useful since if it is significant it may be an indication of the presence of outliers; see sub-section 6.4.2.

The drawback of basing tests on the measures of skewness and kurtosis is that their behaviour may be rather erratic in small samples. Other tests of non-normality, such as the Shapiro-Wilk test, may therefore be considered.

5.4.3 Cumulative periodogram

If a model is estimated in the frequency domain, the cumulative residual periodogram becomes an attractive diagnostic checking procedure. The residual periodogram ordinates are defined by

$$p_j = 2\pi I(\lambda_j)/\tilde{g}_j, \quad j = 0, \dots, [T^*/2] \tag{5.4.13}$$

where $I(\lambda_j)$ is the periodogram of the (differenced) observations, $\Delta(L)y_t$, and g_j is the spectral generating function evaluated at the estimated parameter values. The residual periodogram ordinates are used to construct a series of statistics,

$$s_i = \sum_{j=1}^{i} \tilde{p}_j^2 \Big/ \sum_{j=1}^{[T^*/2]} \tilde{p}_j^2, \quad i = 1, \dots, [T^*/2] \tag{5.4.14}$$

The test procedure is based on a plot of s_i against i, which is known as the cumulative periodogram. This differs from the periodogram itself, in that the highly unstable behaviour of the $\tilde{p}_j$'s is, to a large extent, ironed out by the process of accumulation. Thus, although a visual inspection of the periodogram is of limited value, the cumulative periodogram is a useful diagnostic tool.

For a white-noise series, the s_i's will lie close to the 45° line on the graph of s_i against i. On the other hand, the cumulative periodogram for a process with an excess of low-frequency will tend to lie above the 45° line. By way of contrast, a process with an excess of high-frequency components will tend to have a cumulative periodogram which lies below the 45° line. A formal test for departures from randomness is obtained by constructing two lines parallel to the 45° line, $s = i/[T^*/2]$. These are defined by

$$s = \pm c_0 + i/[T^*/2] \tag{5.4.15}$$

where c_0 is a significance value which depends on $[T^*/2]$ and may be read off directly from a table given in Durbin (1969). This table is reproduced in Harvey (1981a). The appropriate significance value is obtained by entering the table at $[T^*/2]-1$. For a two-sided test of size α, c_0 is read from the column headed '$\alpha/2$'. The null hypothesis is rejected at the α level of significance if the sample path, $s_1, \dots, s_{[T^*/2]}$, crosses either of the lines in (5.4.15). For a one-sided test the significance value is found in exactly the same way except that the column headed 'α' is now the one to be consulted.

The test can be carried out without actually graphing the s_i's. The rule for a two-sided procedure is to reject H_0 if

$$\max_i |s_i - i/[T^*/2]| > c_0$$

The cumulative periodogram is similar to the CUSUM of squares test. It can be regarded as a test for heteroscedasticity in the frequency domain, and therefore it is a test for serial correlation in the time domain. The drawback with the procedure is that the test described above is not strictly valid, even in large samples, if hyperparameters, other than σ_*^2, are estimated. As pointed out in Durbin (1975), the test is 'naive'. Nevertheless, it may still provide useful information and the cumulative periodogram plot itself is certainly a valuable tool for visual diagnostic checking.

5.4.4 Lagrange multiplier diagnostics for the basic structural model

While the Box-Ljung test based on (5.4.7) is easy to carry out, it may not always be very powerful. This is because P must be reasonably large for the asymptotic theory upon which the test is based to be valid and with a large value of P the effect of a misspecification may become diluted. An LM test, on the other hand, can be based on any number of degrees of freedom. In ARIMA modelling there is evidence to suggest that suitably constructed LM tests can yield more powerful diagnostic checking procedures than the Box-Ljung test; see Poskitt and Tremayne (1981). The same is likely to be true for structural models.

Consider a basic structural model in which both σ_ζ^2 and σ_ω^2 are strictly positive. LM tests can be constructed by a weighted frequency-domain regression of v_j on the four basic regressors $z_{\mu j}$, $z_{\beta j}$, $z_{\gamma j}$ and $z_{\varepsilon j}$, defined in (4.3.5), together with additional regressors selected from Table 5.4.1. The resulting LM* statistic, (5.2.17), is then tested against a χ^2 distribution with degrees of freedom equal to the total number of additional regressors included. Tests I to IV can be carried out jointly or separately. Modified versions of the tests can be based on (5.2.18).

Test I is formally a test against an AR(P) or MA(P) process in the irregular component. However if $P=1$ it is also, as Example 5.2.3 showed, the LM test against a cycle. Similarly test II with $P=1$ is the LM test against a cyclical trend as well as the test against η_t following an AR(1) or MA(1) process. Thus both tests are designed to be powerful against a number of different alternatives and so should be reasonably effective as tests of misspecification.

One way of rationalising the higher-order trend test is by letting the disturbance term in the growth equation follow an AR(1) process. Thus (4.1.6b) becomes

$$\beta_t = \beta_{t-1} + \zeta_t$$

where

$$\zeta_t = \varphi\zeta_{t-1} + \zeta_t^*, \quad \zeta_t^* \sim \text{NID}(0, \sigma_{\zeta^*}^2)$$

Provided that $|\varphi| < 1$, the stationary form of the model is

$$\Delta\Delta_s y_t = \Delta_s y_t + \frac{\text{S(L)}\zeta_{t-2}^*}{1-\varphi \text{L}} + \Delta\Delta_s \varepsilon_t$$

and test IV then emerges as the LM test against $\varphi \neq 0$. Since $\varphi = 1$ yields a higher-order trend, namely a local approximation to a quadratic, the test can be expected to have some power against such an alternative.

The rationale for the first seasonal misspecification test lies in the modification of the (dummy variable) seasonal component to either

Table 5.4.1 *Construction of LM tests for the BSM in the frequency domain*

	Test	Additional regressors		d.f.
I	Serial correlation in measurement equation	$z_{\varepsilon j} \cos k\lambda_j$,	$k=1, 2, \ldots, P$	P
II	Serial correlation in level equation	$z_{\mu j} \cos k\lambda_j$,	$k=1, 2, \ldots, P$	P
III	Higher-order trend	$z_{\beta j} \cos \lambda_j$		1
IV	Seasonal misspecification	$z_{\gamma j} \cos ks\lambda_j$, and $z_{\gamma j} \cos l\lambda_j$,	$k=0, 1, \ldots, Q$ $l=0, 1, \ldots, P$	$P+Q$

$$S(L)\gamma_t = (1+\theta_s L^s)\omega_t \quad \text{or} \quad S(L)\gamma_t = (1-\varphi_s L^s)^{-1}\omega_t \tag{5.4.16}$$

The technical details may be deduced from Example 5.2.3. Specifications similar to those in (5.4.16) are favoured by some statisticians and in fact the unobserved components model which approximately underlies the X-11 seasonal adjustment procedure contains seasonal moving average terms; see (6.2.4) and (6.2.15). Test IV may also be used with trigonometric seasonality with $z_{\gamma j}$ suitably redefined. In this case Q should be set equal to zero.

The above principles may be used to construct frequency-domain LM tests of misspecification in other structural models. However, two points should be noted. Firstly, the definitions of regressors, such as $z_{\mu j}$, depend on the transformation needed to make the model as a whole stationary. Secondly, not all the LM tests can be carried out because of identifiability problems under the null. Some examples were given in sub-sections 5.3.3 and 5.4.4. It is particularly important to stress that test III cannot be carried out when there is no seasonal component present, and that test II cannot employ an additional regressor with $k=1$.

5.5 Goodness of fit

The prediction error variance (p.e.v.) is the basic measure of goodness of fit in a time series model. The first sub-section below shows how the prediction error variance of a fitted model can be estimated in either the time or the frequency domain. Sub-section 5.5.3 provides a method of estimating the p.e.v. of a series before a model is fitted. The use of the mean deviation as a measure of goodness of fit is discussed in sub-section 5.5.2.

Relative measures of goodness of fit are discussed in sub-sections 5.5.4 and 5.5.5. The second of these sub-sections introduces coefficients of determination, R_D^2 and R_S^2, which are more useful than the conventional R^2 when trend and seasonality are present.

5.5.1 Prediction error variance

The prediction error variance of a time-invariant model is the variance of the one-step-ahead prediction errors in the steady state. Thus if the variances in the model are expressed relative to σ_*^2, the prediction error variance is defined by

$$\sigma^2 = \sigma_*^2 \bar{f} \tag{5.5.1a}$$

where $\bar{f}$ is the steady-state value of f_t, namely

$$\bar{f} = \lim_{t \to \infty} f_t \tag{5.5.1b}$$

The prediction error variance is the same as the variance of the disturbance term in the reduced form and is a natural measure of goodness of fit. When σ_*^2 is estimated by (4.2.5), the corresponding estimator of σ^2 will be written as

$$\tilde{\sigma}^2 = s^2 = \tilde{\sigma}_*^2 \bar{f} \tag{5.5.1c}$$

As we shall see in chapter 7, the addition of explanatory variables to the model leads to a slight difference in definition between $\tilde{\sigma}$ and s.

On some occasions it will be useful to quote the *finite* prediction error variance

$$\sigma_f^2 = \sigma_*^2 f_T \tag{5.5.2}$$

With σ_*^2 estimated by (4.2.5), the estimator σ_f^2 is written as $\tilde{\sigma}_f^2$. The difference between $\tilde{\sigma}^2$ and $\tilde{\sigma}_f^2$ becomes small as the sample size becomes large. A large sample size also allows both estimators to be expressed directly in terms of one-step-ahead prediction errors:

$$\tilde{\sigma}_f^2 \simeq \tilde{\sigma}^2 = \frac{\bar{f}}{T^*} \sum_t \tilde{v}_t^2 = \frac{1}{T^*} \sum_t \frac{v_t^2}{f_t} \bar{f} \simeq \frac{1}{T^*} \sum_t v_t^2 \tag{5.5.3}$$

where $T^* = T - d$.

An alternative way of estimating σ^2 is in the frequency domain. For any stationary indeterministic process with strictly positive spectral density everywhere in the range $[-\pi, \pi]$, the prediction error variance is given by the classical formula of Kolmogorov:

$$\hat{\sigma}^2 = \exp\left[\frac{1}{2\pi} \int_{-\pi}^{\pi} \log 2\pi f(\lambda) d\lambda\right] \tag{5.5.4}$$

If a model has been fitted, (5.5.4) may be estimated in finite samples by

$$\hat{\sigma}^2 = \exp\left[\frac{1}{T^*} \sum_{j=0}^{T^*-1} \log \tilde{g}_j\right] \tag{5.5.5a}$$

$$= \left[\prod_{j=0}^{T^*-1} \tilde{g}_j\right]^{\frac{1}{T^*}} \tag{5.5.5b}$$

where $\tilde{g}_j$ denotes the s.g.f. evaluated at the ML estimator $\tilde{\psi}$.

Table 5.5.1 *Estimates of the prediction error variance for Chicago purse-snatching data*

	FD	FD*	TD(finite)	TD	Initial
Local linear trend	45.20	42.60	42.70	42.61	45.51
Local level	38.94	38.93	38.94	38.93	33.61

Estimating the prediction error variance via (5.5.5) is particularly convenient if ML estimation is carried out in the frequency domain. If a parameter, σ_*^2, has been concentrated out of the likelihood function, then by substituting (4.3.43) into (5.5.5) it can be seen that

$$\hat{\sigma}^2 = (2\pi + 1)^{-1}(L_c)^{-2/T^*} \tag{5.5.6}$$

where L_c is the concentrated likelihood function defined in (4.3.46).

The asymptotic distribution of the estimator of the prediction error variance can be obtained by noting that in the ARMA reduced form model, the ML estimator of σ^2 is asymptotically independent of the ML estimators of the AR and MA parameters, even though the latter are subject to restrictions. Taking expectations of $\partial^2 \log L/\partial\sigma^4$ in (4.3.20) leads to

$$\tilde{\sigma}^2 \sim \text{AN}(\sigma^2, 2\sigma^4/T) \tag{5.5.7}$$

In the reduced form of a structural model, the AR and MA parameters will normally be subject to restrictions. However, as can be seen from (5.5.7) the distribution of $\tilde{\sigma}^2$ is not affected by these restrictions.

Purse snatching in Chicago Estimation results for the Chicago purse-snatching data were presented in sub-section 4.5.4. Table 5.5.1 shows various estimates of the p.e.v. for the two models fitted. The two frequency-domain figures were calculated from (5.5.5); as in Table 4.5.1, FD* denotes the estimates before the 'fine tuning' of concentrating σ_ε^2 out of the likelihood function in the time domain. The initial estimates were calculated by a method to be discussed in sub-section 5.5.3.

Much greater discrepancies can be found between the various measures in seasonal models, particularly if σ_ω^2 is close to zero.

5.5.2 Prediction error mean deviation

The direct estimator of the mean deviation of the one-step-ahead prediction errors is, by analogy with (5.5.3),

$$\widehat{\text{m.d.}} = \frac{\bar{f}}{T^*} \sum_t |\tilde{v}_t| \simeq \frac{1}{T^*} \sum_t |v_t| \tag{5.5.8}$$

If the sample size is large and the specification of the model, including the normality assumption is correct, then

$$\text{plim}(\widehat{\text{m.d.}}) \simeq (2/\pi)^{\frac{1}{2}} \sigma = 0.80\sigma \tag{5.5.9}$$

Thus in a correctly specified model $(2/\pi)\tilde{\sigma}^2/(\widehat{\text{m.d.}})^2$ should be approximately equal to unity. A high value could be an indication of higher kurtosis than is consistent with normality.

The mean deviation is perhaps of limited value in the sample period. Comparing it with $\tilde{\sigma}$ may give an indication of non-normality, perhaps due to outliers, but a proper test is best conducted via (5.4.12). In section 5.6, it is suggested that the mean deviation may play a useful role in a post-sample-period evaluation of the model.

Despite the limited value of the direct estimator of the mean deviation (5.5.7), the idea of the average (absolute) prediction error is one which is more easily understood by non-statisticians. It is therefore often useful to present an estimate of the mean deviation. However, if the diagnostics, including the normality test, indicate that the model is acceptable, it is quite legitimate to estimate the mean deviation indirectly via (5.5.9), i.e.

$$\widehat{\text{m.d.}} = (2/\pi)^{\frac{1}{2}} \tilde{\sigma} \tag{5.5.10}$$

In fact this estimator is more efficient, asymptotically, than (5.5.8). It has an asymptotic variance of $(1/\pi)\sigma^2/T^*$ whereas the asymptotic variance of m.d. is $[(\pi-2)/\pi]\sigma^2/T^*$. Hence the efficiency of $\widehat{\text{m.d.}}$ is 0.876; see Cramér (1946, p.485).

5.5.3 Initial non-parametric estimator of the prediction error variance

The prediction error variance can be estimated prior to any model fitting by replacing the spectral density in (5.5.4) by the periodogram. Thus

$$\hat{\sigma}_0^2 = \exp\left\{\frac{1}{T^*} \sum_{j=0}^{T^*-1} \log\left[2\pi\, I(\lambda_j)\right] + \gamma\right\} \tag{5.5.11}$$

where $I(\lambda_j)$ is the periodogram of the stationary series and γ is Euler's constant, which is 0.57721. The need for the factor $\exp(\gamma)$ arises from the fact that log $[2\pi I(\lambda_j)]$ has expectation $-\gamma$ when the observations are NID(0, 1).

If estimation of a model is being carried out in the frequency domain, it is easy to compute (5.5.11). The condition under which it is sensible to use this estimator is that the spectral density, $f(\lambda)$, should be strictly positive everywhere in the range $[-\pi, \pi]$. It will be recalled from sub-section 4.5.1 that this same condition is also required for the ML estimators of the model parameters to possess the usual asymptotic distribution. Thus, for example, if the parameter σ_ζ^2 in a basic structural model is zero, the prediction error variance of the series should be estimated from the sample spectral density of $\Delta_s y_t$ rather than $\Delta\Delta_s y_t$.

In moderately large samples, log $\hat{\sigma}_0^2$ may be treated as normal with mean log σ^2 and variance $2\pi^2\sigma^4/6T^*$. The two distributions are equivalent asymptotically, but it is likely that the first suggestion, which amounts to $\hat{\sigma}_0^2$ being treated as log-normally distributed, is preferable; see Hannan and Nicholls (1977, p.836). When σ^2 is estimated from a correctly specified model, its estimator is asymptotically normally distributed with mean σ^2 and variance $2\sigma^4/T^*$; see (5.5.7). Since $2\pi^2/6 = 3.290$, the efficiency of the non-parametric estimator, $\hat{\sigma}_0^2$, is 61%, irrespective of the form of the process.

A non-parametric estimator of the p.e.v. may be constructed in the time domain by fitting a long autoregression to the differenced series. Alternatively a long autoregression may be fitted to the levels of the observations. If the series is non-stationary, this levels autoregression will normally contain one or two unit roots. This issue is discussed further in sub-section 6.1.4.

Provided the sample size is reasonably large, the non-parametric estimator can give a useful indication of the prediction error variance which a parametric model can be expected to attain. However, in small samples, experience suggests that $\hat{\sigma}_0^2$ is too erratic to serve as a reliable guide. This is particularly so when seasonality is present, and in such circumstances it may be better to treat the seasonal effects as fixed. In the time domain this means including a set of seasonal dummies in the long autoregression. In the frequency domain the methods of sub-section 4.3.6 are appropriate.

5.5.4 Relative measures of error

If the observations have been transformed to natural logarithms prior to estimation of the model, σ and m.d., or rather their respective estimators, may be regarded as relative measures of error. Thus $100 \times$ m.d. is, approximately, the average absolute prediction error expressed as a percentage of the (unlogged) level of the process. An analogous interpretation is possible for σ.

The reason for the above interpretation is as follows. Let $\hat{y}$ denote an estimator of the logarithm of the observation and let $\hat{e}$ denote a measure of the error. Then a measure of the error in estimating the level of the observation is:

$$\exp(\hat{y}+\hat{e})-\exp(\hat{y})$$

Combining this with the error in estimating the observations when $\hat{e}$ has the same absolute value but the opposite sign, gives an average error of

$$\frac{\exp(\hat{y}+\hat{e})-\exp(y)+\exp(\hat{y})-\exp(\hat{y}-\hat{e})}{2\exp(\hat{y})}=\hat{e}+\frac{\hat{e}^3}{3!}+\frac{\hat{e}^5}{5!}+\cdots \simeq \hat{e} \tag{5.5.12}$$

A value of $\hat{e} = 0.2500$ gives 0.2526 when the average error is evaluated exactly. Hence the approximation in (5.5.12) is likely to be satisfactory for most practical purposes.

Airline passengers For the quarterly airline data, estimation of the basic structural model yields $\tilde{\sigma}^2 = 1.40 \times 10^{-3}$. Hence $\tilde{\sigma} = 0.037$ and m.d. $= 0.030$. Thus, on average, forecast errors are about 3% of the forecasts.

5.5.5 Coefficient of determination

In regression analysis the coefficient of determination, R^2, is almost always presented as a measure of goodness of fit. This measure is not usually given for time series models, primarily because fitting a mean to the data does not provide a useful yardstick for assessing goodness of fit. Time series observations normally show strong upward or downward movements and any model which is able to pick up a trend reasonably well will have an R^2 close to unity. The statistic is therefore of little value, except when the series is stationary or close to being stationary. Indeed, the situation is very similar when a regression is carried out on time series data, but the use of R^2 is so well entrenched that it is not only invariably quoted but is quite often used as evidence that the model is a good one.

The measures presented below are an attempt to provide goodness-of-fit criteria which are useful for non-stationary time series data. As will be shown in section 7.4, they are applicable to regression models as well as to univariate time series models.

The residual sum of squares for a univariate time series model may be defined as

$$\mathrm{SSE} = \bar{f} \sum_t \tilde{v}_t^2 = \bar{f}\, S(\psi_*) = (T-d)\tilde{\sigma}^2 \tag{5.5.13}$$

where $\tilde{\sigma}^2$ is the time-domain estimator of the prediction error variance based on (5.5.1) and (4.2.5). The conventional measure of goodness of fit, R^2, is obtained by dividing SSE by the sum of squares of the observations about the mean and subtracting from unity. A better measure for time series data, R_D^2, is obtained by replacing the observations by their first differences, that is

$$R_D^2 = 1 - \mathrm{SSE} \Big/ \sum_{t=2}^{T} (\Delta y_t - \overline{\Delta y})^2 \tag{5.5.14}$$

where $\overline{\Delta y}$ is the mean of the first differences. The yardstick being adopted in (5.5.14) is the random walk plus drift,

$$y_t = y_{t-1} + \beta + \eta_t, \quad t = 2, \ldots T \tag{5.5.15}$$

This is a very simple model in which next period's forecast is taken to be the current observation plus the average increase over the sample period. Despite its simplicity the model can yield quite good forecasts.

Setting β equal to zero in (5.5.15) yields a pure random walk and the simple forecasting procedure which this leads to is often used as a naive model in studies of forecasting performance (see, for example, Makridakis *et al.*, 1982). More formally it provides the basis for the U-statistic proposed by Theil (1966). If R_D^2 is redefined with $\overline{\Delta y}$ set equal to zero it is straightforward to show that it is equal to $1-U^2$. The rationale for retaining $\overline{\Delta y}$ in the definition of R_D^2 is that it is more in line with the definition of R^2 and it provides a slightly more stringent criterion. The random walk with drift is still a very simple model and any model which gives a worse fit, i.e. has $R_D^2<0$, should not be seriously entertained.

When the observations are monthly or quarterly, seasonal effects are likely to be present in unadjusted data, and even a naive forecaster will want to take them into account. If there are s seasons, the simplest extension to (5.5.15) is to add $s-1$ seasonal dummies to the right-hand side. Alternatively β can be dropped, thereby allowing the model to contain s dummies,

$$\Delta y_t = \sum_{j=1}^{s} \gamma_j^* z_{tj} + \eta_t, \quad t=2, \ldots, T \tag{5.5.16}$$

where the z_{tj}'s are dummy variables taking the value in one season j and zero otherwise, and the γ_j^*'s are the unknown parameters. This formulation is rather more convenient because the OLS estimators of $\gamma_1^*, \ldots, \gamma_s^*$ are simply the means of the differenced observations in each of the seasons; compare (4.3.61). A forecasting procedure based on (5.5.16) is, therefore, still very simple. At the same time Pierce (1978) has noted that the model gives quite a good fit to many economic time series, a view which is backed up by the evidence presented in Table 2.7.1; see the discussion in the next sub-section. This suggests the use of the goodness-of-fit criterion

$$R_s^2 = 1 - \text{SSE/SSDSM} \tag{5.5.17}$$

where SSDSM is the sum of squares of first differences around the seasonal means. Any model which has R_s^2 negative can be rejected, whereas if R_s^2 is positive but close to zero, the gains from what is presumably a more complex procedure are marginal.

5.5.6 *Comparison between different models*

Two different models may be compared on the basis of their respective p.e.v.'s. As shown in (5.5.3), this is essentially the same as comparing the sums of squares of their one-step-ahead prediction errors.

The maximised likelihood functions may also be used as a basis for comparison. However, this is the same as comparing the p.e.v.'s if the sample is large. Indeed it may be identical to comparing the p.e.v.'s, depending on the precise definition of the likelihood function and the p.e.v.; see, for example, (5.5.6). If the rival models contain different numbers of parameters, comparison may be made on the basis of the Akaike information criterion (AIC) or the Bayes information criterion (BIC); see (2.6.11) and (2.6.12). Expressing the AIC in terms of the p.e.v. gives the criterion

$$\mathrm{AIC}^{\dagger} = \tilde{\sigma}^2 \exp[2(n+d)/T] \tag{5.5.18}$$

where d is the number of non-stationary elements in the state vector and n is the number of hyperparameters. The criterion $\mathrm{BIC}^{\dagger}$ is defined in a similar way, with the '2' replaced by 'log T'. The reason for including the number of non-stationary elements in the state vector in the criterion function is to allow comparisons involving models with deterministic components.

Airline passengers Table 2.7.1 showed the results of fitting various models to the quarterly airline passenger data. All the models contain trend and seasonal components and so $d=5$. This includes the ARIMA model since the order of the $\Delta\Delta_s$ polynomial is five. The difference between, say, the BSM and the deterministic trend and seasonal model, (2.3.1), is that the former contains three extra hyperparameters, σ_η^2, σ_ζ^2 and σ_ω^2, which allow the trend and seasonal components to change over time. (Both models contain the irregular component variance hyperparameter.) The BSM is clearly better in terms of both $\mathrm{AIC}^{\dagger}$ and $\mathrm{BIC}^{\dagger}$. In fact the deterministic model would never have been seriously entertained since it fails the diagnostic checks with an unacceptably high value for the Q-statistic.

The second model detailed in Table 2.7.1 is (5.5.16) which is the one which provides the basis for the goodness-of-fit measure R_s^2. As can be seen, R_s^2 is equal to $1-(3.02/2.05) = -0.47$ for the deterministic model. On the other hand, the BSM has an R_s^2 of 0.32 indicating a 32% reduction in variance as compared with (5.5.16).

The various goodness-of-fit criteria can also be used to compare models in levels and logarithms. To do this it is necessary to make an amendment to the estimator of the p.e.v. in the logarithmic model by multiplying it by a factor of $\exp[2/T)\Sigma \log y_t]$; see Harvey (1981a, p.177). Thus the AIC expression in (5.5.18) has $(n+d)$ replaced by $(n+d+\Sigma \log y_t)$.

5.6 Post-sample predictive testing and model evaluation

The aim of the test procedures described in the preceding sections is to select an appropriate model from the data. Once a suitable model has been specified, its parameters are estimated from the same set of data. Since several specifications may be tried, it is important to guard against 'data-mining'. Data-mining may be defined as the application of model selection procedures to a wide range of models, leading to the uncritical acceptance of a particular specification on the basis of its goodness of fit. The way in which the class of structural models is set up on the basis of *a priori* considerations should make data-mining less of a problem than, say, with ARIMA models where the class of models is much wider. Nevertheless, the only way in which the adequacy of a model may be truly assessed is by its performance outside the sample period. In what follows it will be assumed that the post-sample period consists of the observations $y_{T+1}, \ldots, y_{T+l}$. These post-sample observations are used as a yardstick by which to judge the forecasting accuracy of models selected and estimated on the basis of the sample observations, $y_1, \ldots, y_T$.

5.6.1 Post-sample predictive testing

Suppose that a model is correctly specified and that all the hyperparameters, apart from σ_*^2, are known. The one-step-ahead prediction errors in the post-sample period, $v_{T+j}, j=1, \ldots, l$ will then be normally distributed with mean zero and variance $\sigma_*^2 f_{T+j}$. The *standardised prediction errors* are then defined in exactly the same way as the residuals in (5.4.1), namely

$$\tilde{v}_{T+j} = v_{T+j}/f_{T+j}^{\frac{1}{2}}, \quad j=1, \ldots, l \tag{5.6.1}$$

and so

$$\tilde{v}_t \sim \text{NID}(0, \sigma_*^2), \quad t=d+1, \ldots, T+l \tag{5.6.2}$$

It therefore follows that, under these assumptions, the distribution of the *post-sample predictive test statistic,*

$$\xi(l) = \left[\sum_{j=1}^{l} \tilde{v}_{T+j}^2/l\right] \Bigg/ \left[\sum_{t=d+1}^{T} \tilde{v}_t^2/(T-d)\right] = \sum_{j=1}^{l} \tilde{v}_{T+j}^2/(l\,\tilde{\sigma}_*^2) \tag{5.6.3}$$

is $F(l, T-d)$. In the more usual case when parameters other than σ_*^2 are estimated it can be shown that $l\xi(l)$ is asymptotically χ_l^2. Nevertheless it is suggested that the F-distribution will provide a better approximation to the small-sample distribution of $\xi(l)$.

When the model is misspecified, and a spuriously good fit has been obtained in the sample period, the value of $\xi(l)$ will be inflated. The test will therefore lead to a rejection of the model. However, an insignificant value of $\xi(l)$ should not necessarily be taken as proof that the model is a good one; it may simply mean that the fits in the sample and post-sample periods are equally poor.

Airline passengers Fitting the BSM to the quarterly airline passenger series for the first forty observations and using the remaining eight observations as the basis for a post-sample test gave a value of $\xi(8)$ equal to 0.295. Thus the fit in the post-sample period is better than in the sample period, indicating that this classic testbed series is a rather easy one to forecast!

UK macroeconomic time series Prothero and Wallis (1976) fitted ARIMA models to a set of quarterly UK macroeconomic time series using what was, at the time, generally accepted to be the Box-Jenkins methodology. In Harvey and Todd (1983), these ARIMA models were compared with the BSM, this being chosen on the grounds that for a relatively short economic time series the main features are a trend and seasonality. Estimation was over the period 1957Q3 to 1966Q3 with the next eight observations being used for post-sample predictive testing. For most of the series the results for the ARIMA and BSM models were similar, but a dramatic difference arose in the series on imports. The model preferred by Prothero and Wallis was a seasonal ARIMA of order $(0,0,0)\times(4,1,0)$ plus constant. This specification was chosen 'on account of its small residual variance and small value of the Q-statistic'. It had a p.e.v. of 1,259, smaller than the p.e.v. of the BSM, which was 1,532. However, the post-sample performance of the ARIMA model was disastrous, with $\xi(8)$ taking a value of 59.98 against a 5% critical value of 2.25 for an $F_{2,32}$ distribution. The BSM also failed the post-sample predictive test with $\xi(8)$ equal to 4.75, but at least the forecasts bore some relation to the actual values. In fact any univariate model would have had problems in forecasting over this particular post-sample period because of the devaluation of the pound in 1967, but the spectacular failure of the ARIMA model is indicative of the dangers inherent in a methodology which is open to data mining.

The post-sample predictive test may be supplemented by a plot of the standardised prediction errors and a plot of the CUSUM. The CUSUM is particularly useful when the model is systematically under- or overpredicting in the post-sample period. It is defined as

$$\text{CUSUM}(T,h)=\tilde{\sigma}_*^{-1}\sum_{j=1}^{h}\tilde{v}_{T+j},\quad h=1,\ldots,l \tag{5.6.4}$$

where the estimator of σ_* is computed from the sample residuals in the usual way. The use of $\hat{\sigma}_*$, as defined in (5.4.3b), is still legitimate, but the case for it is less compelling here than it is when the CUSUM is being computed for the sample residuals. In fact if the model has been found to give a good fit within the sample period, the mean of the residuals should be close to zero, and it will not make much difference which estimator of σ_* is used. Predetermined significance lines can be drawn on the CUSUM plot as indicated below (5.4.3) and a formal test may be carried out if desired. A test may also be based on the statistic

$$\psi(T,l)=\sum_{j=1}^{l}\tilde{v}_{T+j}/\tilde{\sigma}_*\sqrt{l}=\text{CUSUM}(T,l)/\sqrt{l} \tag{5.6.5}$$

If all the parameters apart from σ_*^2 are known, $\psi(T,l)$ has a t-distribution with $T-d$ degrees of freedom when the model is correctly specified. If σ_*^2 is estimated from (5.4.3b), the degrees of freedom are $T-d-1$.

5.6.2 *Multi-step predictions*

The predictions used to assess the performance of the model so far have been one-step-ahead predictions. However, it is also possible to extrapolate at time

T by making a series of multi-step predictions, namely $\tilde{y}_{T+j|T}, j=1,\ldots,l$. A plot of these predictions gives the forecast function and such a plot can be extremely informative in exposing the shortcomings of a model.

The multi-step predictions give rise to a set of j-step-ahead prediction errors

$$v_{T+j|T} = y_{T+j} - \tilde{y}_{T+j|T}, \quad j=1,\ldots,l \tag{5.6.6}$$

Although the $v_{T+j|T}$'s can be standardised, they are not independent of each other and the construction of a valid post-sample predictive test would have to take account of this dependence. However, it turns out that proceeding in this way is ultimately pointless since, as Box and Tiao (1976) have shown, all the relevant information is effectively contained in the one-step-ahead prediction errors. One is therefore led back to the test based on $\xi(l)$ of (5.6.3).

Prediction errors of more than one step ahead, therefore, provide no additional information for assessing the internal validity of a model. However, they are useful in providing a measure of predictive performance which can be used as a basis for comparison with rival models. The obvious statistic to consider is what we might call the *extrapolative sum of squares*

$$\text{ESS}(T,l) = \sum_{j=1}^{l} v_{T+j|T}^2 \tag{5.6.7}$$

An alternative would be the sum of the absolute values of the prediction errors

$$\text{ESAV}(T,l) = \sum_{j=1}^{l} |v_{T+l|T}| \tag{5.6.8}$$

UK macroeconomic time series In the study by Prothero and Wallis (1976) referred to earlier, a seasonal ARIMA model of order $(0,1,0)\times(4,0,0)$ was fitted to the series on investment. The p.e.v. in the BSM was found by Harvey and Todd (1983) to be only slightly bigger at 1,823 as opposed to 1,745. The models gave similar one-step-ahead predictions in the post-sample period, and both passed the predictive test with $\xi(8)$ equal to 0.86 for the ARIMA model and 0.95 for the BSM. However the multi-step predictions for the BSM were more accurate. The ESS was 7,551 while for the ARIMA model it was almost double at 15,942. The eventual forecast function for the ARIMA model is a horizontal line but this seems inappropriate for a series which shows a clear upward movement over time. The forecast function for the BSM tracks the series quite well.

5.7 Strategy for model selection

The first sub-section below sets out an overall strategy for the selection of a univariate structural time series model, keeping in mind the basic specification criteria which were laid down in section 1.5. Certain aspects of this strategy are illustrated in the applications presented in the sub-sections which follow. Some of these applications were first introduced in section 2.7.

5.7.1 Model selection

The initial stage in model selection is a preliminary analysis of the data and the formulation of a possible model or models to be estimated. Once a model has been estimated, it is subject to tests of misspecification, that is diagnostic checking, and tests of specification. A model which satisfies these checking and testing procedures may then be validated internally, by post-sample predictive testing, or externally by comparing its fit with that of a rival specification.

Preliminary analysis and model specification The essential step in preliminary analysis is the graphing of the series. It is this, combined with prior knowledge of the nature of the series, which provides the basis for model specification. It may also be useful to graph the series after differencing transformations, including subtracting seasonal means from first differences. Plots may also be carried out after the observations have been subject to certain instantaneous transformations, such as the taking of logarithms or square roots. These graphs should give an indication as to whether a time-invariant model is, in fact, appropriate or whether the series is subject to structural changes, either throughout the series or at particular points in time.

If a time-invariant model is appropriate it will generally be possible to reduce the series to stationarity by appropriate differencing. The measures of skewness and kurtosis, $\sqrt{b_1}$ and b_2, may then be computed and used to give an indication of non-normality. Lomnicki (1961) shows that these statistics will have the asymptotic distribution indicated in sub-section 5.4.2 but with the modification that their variances are inflated when serial correlation is present. Specifically

$$\text{Avar}(\sqrt{b_1}) = (6/T^*) \sum_{-\infty}^{\infty} \rho(\tau)^3 \quad \text{and} \quad \text{Avar}(b_2) = (24/T^*) \sum_{-\infty}^{\infty} \rho(\tau)^4$$

The correction terms may be estimated by taking finite sums of powers of sample autocorrelations. Granger and Newbold (1977, p. 315) cite evidence which suggests that the resulting test statistics will be reasonably well behaved in moderate-sized samples, but may be less satisfactory when the sample is small. Nevertheless, they can give a useful indication as to whether taking logarithms is appropriate or whether there are outliers in the series. It may be possible to detect the latter by visual inspection.

If it is felt that the series can be reduced to stationarity by differencing transformations, the correlogram and related plots, such as the sample partial autocorrelation function and inverse autocorrelation, may provide useful supplementary information. Thus, one would not normally want to select a structural model in which the theoretical autocorrelation function was inconsistent with the correlogram. For example, it would be inappropriate to attempt to fit a random walk plus noise model if the first-order sample autocorrelation of the first-differenced observations was found to be strongly positive. In the frequency domain, the estimated power spectrum provides complementary information to that in the correlogram and this may be particularly useful when pseudo-cyclical behaviour is suspected. Calculating the sample spectrum for the raw data yields the pseudo-spectrum and this has the attraction that, since the series is not differenced, the information may be presented in a manner which is easier to interpret. Note that it is generally inadvisable to carry out detrending prior to analysis as it can lead to misleading inferences being drawn about the properties of the series; this matter is discussed further in sub-section 6.1.3.

It is important to stress that the correlogram does not play the same prominent role as in ARIMA modelling. Because it rests on the assumption of stationarity, it may be distorted in a variety of ways, and this could lead to an inappropriate model being chosen. The presence of outliers provides a good example of the way in which distortions can arise. More fundamentally, the series may be subject to structural changes. This suggests that important information may be gained by dividing the series into two parts and comparing the two correlograms.

As a rule, a reasonably general model should be chosen at the outset. This may subsequently be reduced to a more parsimonious form. The only exception to formulating a general model is when such a formulation might lead to identifiability problems. Thus a cyclical component should only be included in a model if there are reasonably strong grounds for believing one to be present. This matter was discussed in sub-section 5.3.4, where it was suggested that some preliminary testing might be appropriate.

Tests and diagnostics Tests of specification are primarily carried out to see if the model can be simplified. For example, it may be possible to set a variance hyperparameter equal to zero. Tests of this kind are generally of the Wald form, although LR tests may be appropriate in some cases. On occasions, a test of specification will be against a more general model than the one fitted. An LM test for a second stochastic cycle in a model is one such case. In addition to formal statistical tests certain parameter values may be examined to see if they are consistent with known properties of the series. This applies, for example, to the cyclical component where preliminary analysis or prior knowledge may have given some indication as to the period.

The diagnostics described in section 5.4 are computed to determine whether the residuals are serially uncorrelated and normally distributed with zero mean and constant variance. Failure to satisfy the diagnostics may indicate a variety of misspecifications. This includes the possibility that a time-invariant univariate model cannot be constructed.

Once a model has been found to satisfy the diagnostic checks within the sample, a post-sample predictive testing is carried out to determine whether it performs equally well outside the sample. The formal tests are based on one-step-ahead prediction errors. However the multi-step forecast function in the post-sample period can be just as informative if not more so. Multi-step predictions which are close to the actual values give a more convincing demonstration of the effectiveness of a forecasting model, and in the event of post-sample predictive failure they may give a clearer indication as to what has gone wrong.

Rival specifications The goodness-of-fit statistics R_D^2 and R_s^2 compare the fitted model with very simple baseline specifications. If they are less than zero, one may as well revert to the simpler model. The initial non-parametric estimator of the p.e.v., described in sub-section 5.5.3, gives an indication of the goodness of fit that could, in principle, be obtained by fitting a time-invariant model. The estimated $\tilde{\sigma}^2$ should not compare unfavourably with the initial non-parametric estimate, though it should be borne in mind that the latter can be highly variable in small samples.

It may happen that two or more models satisfying the various internal specification criteria have been fitted to a series. Discrimination between rival models may be made on a goodness-of-fit criterion. Account may also be taken of performance in a post-sample period, especially with regard to multi-step predictions. Finally a preferred model should be encompassing, in that it can explain the results given by its rivals.

5.7.2. Trends and cycles in US Real GNP

Estimates were presented for a cyclical trend model fitted to US Real GNP 1909–47 in sub-section 2.7.4. The model passes the diagnostics and $R_D^2=0.20$. Thus there is a 20% improvement in goodness of fit over a random walk plus drift. In the case of the trend plus cycle model, R_D^2 is only 0.05.

It was noted earlier in sub-section 5.3.4, that it is inadvisable to fit a cycle model unless there is some evidence that such a model is appropriate. The correlogram in Figure 2.7.8(a) clearly indicates the possibility of some sort of cyclical movement in the data. In fact, it is straightforward to carry out an LM test for a cyclical trend model against a random walk plus drift if σ_ζ^2 in the cyclical trend is assumed to be zero and σ_ε^2 is also assumed to be zero. The general model is then

$$\Delta y_t = \psi_t + \eta_t \qquad (5.7.1)$$

which is the same form as (5.3.11). The LM test takes $Tr^2(1)$ to be χ_1^2 under the null hypothesis that a cyclical component is not present. For the 1909–47 period $Tr^2(1)=5.34$ and so the null hypothesis is easily rejected at the 5% level of significance. In order to justify a one-sided test, an *a priori* assumption of a period less than four years would have been necessary. Note also that if the decision as to whether to include a cyclical component had been on the basis of the portmanteau test statistic, it would not have been so clear-cut: $Q(5)$ is 10.73 and the 5% critical value of a χ_5^2 distribution is 11.07.

In the case of the 1948–70 period, the correlogram in Figure 2.7.8(b) shows little evidence of cyclical behaviour. The negative value of $r(1)$ indicates that if a cyclical trend model was appropriate, the period of the cycle would have to be less than four years. This is not implausible, but, on the other hand, $Tr^2(1)$ is only 0.28, while $Q(5)$ is a mere 0.43. It may be that a cycle would show up with quarterly data. Nevertheless, with annual data, the preliminary analysis suggests nothing more ambitious than a local linear trend model which when estimated gives

$$\underset{(4.28\times 10^{-4})}{\tilde{\sigma}_\eta^2 = 7.52\times 10^{-4}}, \quad \tilde{\sigma}_\zeta^2 = 0, \quad \underset{(1.92\times 10^{-4})}{\tilde{\sigma}_\varepsilon^2 = 0.65\times 10^{-4}}$$

$$s = 0.030, \quad R_D^2 = 0.01, \quad Q(8) = 9.26, \quad H(7) = 0.58, \quad N = 0.27$$

The slope term is constant as $\tilde{\sigma}_\zeta^2 = 0$. Furthermore, $\tilde{\sigma}_\varepsilon^2$ is statistically insignificant; recall from section 5.3.1, that the critical value for a test of $\sigma_\varepsilon^2 > 0$ at the 5% level is the 10% significance value of a χ_1^2 variate, which is 2.71. In fact, as R_D^2 shows, the gain from including ε_t in the model is only 1%. It would therefore appear that US Real GNP over the period 1948 to 1970 can be quite adequately characterised by a random walk plus drift.

Although the preliminary analysis suggests that attempting to fit a cyclical trend model is inadvisable, it is interesting to see what happened when this was done. The optimisation procedure converged giving the following results:

$$\tilde{\sigma}_\eta^2 = 6.89\times 10^{-4}, \quad \tilde{\sigma}_\zeta^2 = 0.0, \quad \tilde{\sigma}_\varepsilon^2 = 0.0$$

$$\tilde{\sigma}_\kappa^2 = 1.68\times 10^{-4}, \quad \tilde{\rho} = 0.37, \quad \tilde{\lambda}_c = 3.14$$

$$s = 0.030, \quad R_D^2 = 0.01, \quad Q(8) = 9.00, \quad H(7) = 0.58$$

The diagnostics are almost identical to those noted for the previous model, and the goodness of fit is the same. What has happened is that because $\tilde{\lambda}_c$ is equal to π, the cyclical component has reduced to the AR(1) process

$$\psi_t = -0.37\,\psi_{t-1} + \kappa_t \tag{5.7.2}$$

Since $\tilde{\sigma}_\varepsilon^2$ is zero, it is this process which is picking up the mild negative first-order autocorrelation in Δy_t.

5.7.3 *Rainfall in north-east Brazil*

The correlogram of the observations on annual rainfall in Fortaleza, Brazil was shown in Figure 2.7.5. The LM test statistic for the presence of a cyclical component in model (2.7.4), takes the value of $Tr^2(1) = 7.55$ which is clearly statistically significant on a χ_1^2 distribution. Coupled with the prior notion that cyclical behaviour might be present in these data, it seems reasonable to start off by fitting model (2.7.4). The results are as given in sub-section 2.7.2 with the following diagnostic and goodness-of-fit statistics:

$$s=46.3, \quad R^2=0.078, \quad Q(10)=5.27, \quad H(43)=1.09, \quad N=2.86$$

If the model is correctly specified, the large sample distribution of $Q(10)$ is χ^2_7. The value of 5.27 gives no indication of model inadequacy, and nor does the heteroscedasticity statistic. Since the series is presumed to be stationary, R^2, rather than R^2_D, is the appropriate measure of goodness of fit.

The decision not to take logarithms is justified by the normality test statistic, $N=2.86$. Under the null hypothesis, N should have a χ^2_2 distribution for which the 5% critical value is 3.94. The N-statistics obtained for the data before fitting a model were 3.00 and 7.58 for unlogged and logged data respectively. As noted in sub-section 5.7.1, these tests can still be used to give an indication of non-normality in the presence of serial correlation. The N-statistic for logged data is relatively high. Further examination shows this is due to high negative skewness, with $\sqrt{b_1}=-0.56$, and this is a clear indication that the logarithmic transformation is inappropriate. The non-normality continued to show up in the residuals when an attempt was made to fit the model in logarithms.

The case for adding a second cyclical component to the model is not a strong one. As noted in sub-section 2.7.4, the spectrum implied by the fitted model is very similar to the estimated spectrum. Furthermore the value of the LM test statistic was very small. The only other possibility one might consider for extending the model is the replacement of μ by a stochastic component, μ_t, following a random walk. This would allow for movements in the underlying level of rainfall which might conceivably be taking place due to changes in environmental factors. However, when this extended model was estimated in the time domain, it collapsed to the original one since the estimate of σ^2_η was zero.

The low value of R^2 suggests that the cyclical component is dominated by the irregular component. This is clear from Figure 5.7.1 where the estimated cycle, originally shown in Figure 2.7.6, has been superimposed on the original series. The practical implications for forecasting are also clear from Figure 5.7.1. The extrapolation of the cyclical component beyond the end of the sample in 1979 represents the best forecasts of rainfall which can be made from model (2.7.4). The forecasts, together with their estimated root mean square errors (RMSE), are shown in Table 5.7.1. As can be seen, fitting the cycle leads to a 4.5% saving on RMSE for the one-year-ahead forecast. This saving rapidly tends to zero as the forecast horizon increases, and the forecasts tend towards the mean value of the series, 142.

Table 5.7.1 also shows the actual figures for rainfall in the early 1980s. These figures, which were obtained after the model had been estimated, are shown in Figure 5.7.1 by a dotted line. The forecasts for 1980–83 are below the average for the series, and they show that the model was predicting the trough of a rainfall cycle. The forecast values would not, in themselves, have indicated a drought, but

Table 5.7.1 *Forecasts from the model using data up to and including 1979*

Year	1980	1981	1982	1983	1984	1985	1986	1987	...	2000
Forecast	127.5	126.4	128.2	131.7	136.0	140.1	143.3	145.5	...	142.0
RMSE	46.4	47.5	48.0	48.2	48.2	48.3	48.3	48.4	...	48.6
Actual	109.5	110.0	104.0	88.4	198.0	—	—	—	...	—

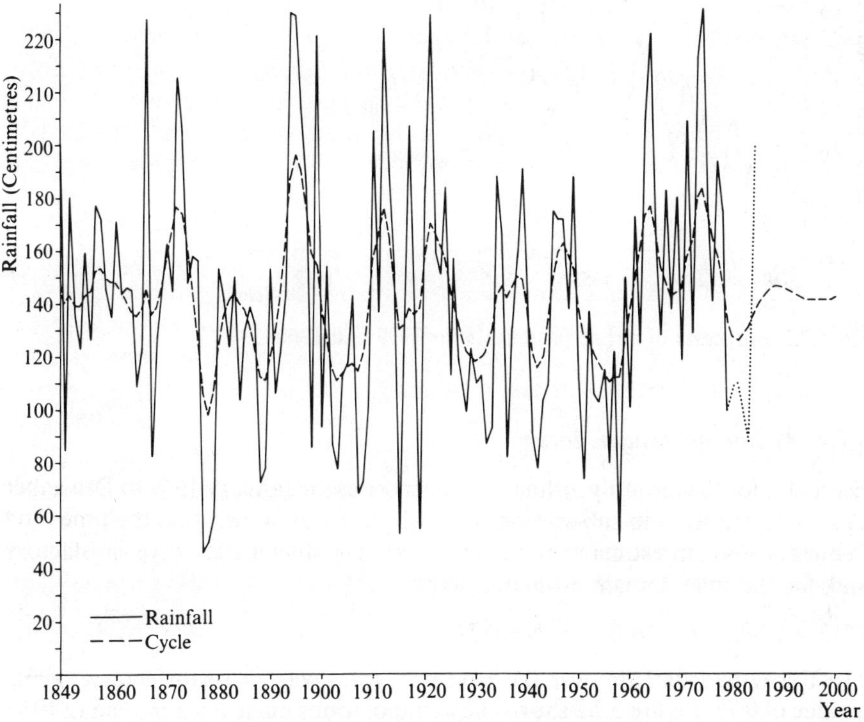

Fig. 5.7.1 Estimated stochastic cycle and forecasts for rainfall in Fortaleza using data up to 1979.

they do show that the area was vulnerable at this time. As it turned out, the rainfall during these years was lower than predicted for 1980–83 and was exceptionally low in 1983, when a severe drought did, in fact, ensue. Our analysis of the data suggests that a value as anomalous as the one in 1983 arises mainly due to chance and would have been very difficult to predict back in 1979. Even if data up to 1982 had been used to predict 1983, the forecast would have been 123.6. This forecast is well below average because the stochastic nature of the cycle allows it to adapt to the sequence of low values in the years immediately below. Nevertheless it is still well above the realised value of 88.4.

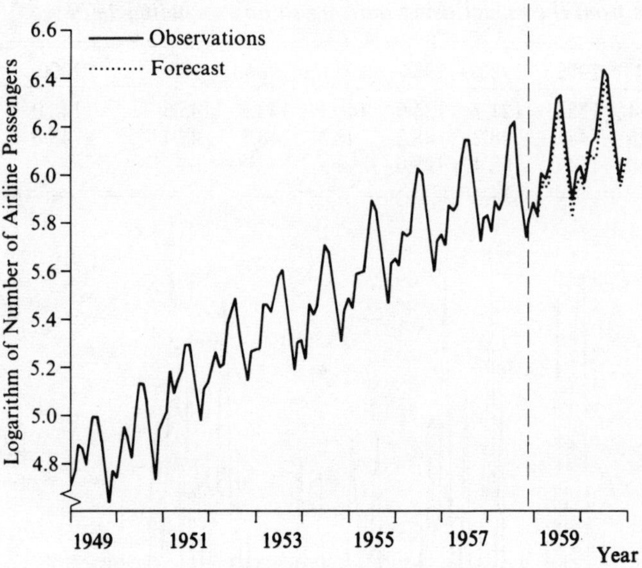

Fig. 5.7.2 Forecasts of airline passengers for 1959 and 1960.

5.7.4 *Airline passenger data*

Estimates for the monthly airline passenger series for January 1949 to December 1958 were reported in sub-section 4.5.4, where it was shown that the time- and frequency-domain estimates were very close. The diagnostics were satisfactory and, for the time-domain estimates, were:

$Q(12)=7.30, \quad H(35)=0.47, \quad N=0.74$

The Chow test statistic over the next two years was also satisfactory, taking a value of 0.75. Figure 5.7.2 shows the extrapolations made from the end of 1957, compared with the actual values.

If estimated without taking logarithms, the diagnostics were:

$Q(12)=58.37, \quad H(35)=3.22, \quad N=1.64$

Curiously enough, the deficiencies of the model do not show up in the normality test statistic. However, the heteroscedasticity statistic indicates a tendency for the residual variance to increase over time. This is exactly what one would expect if it is appropriate to take logarithms. Perhaps more surprising is the strong evidence of serial correlation in the residuals. Attempting to remove this serial correlation by fitting a more elaborate time series model would clearly be misguided, since the correct solution is simply to fit the BSM in logarithms. The Chow statistic is 2.01. This is less than the 5% critical value on an $F_{24,107}$ distribution. The fit is

Table 5.7.2 *Multi-step predictions for the airline passengers series: January 1959 to December 1960*

Month	Actual	Level model	Log model (TD)	Log model (FD)
1959				
Jan	360	353.9	354.2	354.2
Feb	342	336.1	339.1	338.1
Mar	406	381.5	393.0	391.1
Apr	396	369.4	382.1	380.2
May	420	383.0	392.2	392.4
Jun	472	454.0	464.0	466.7
Jul	548	508.4	517.0	521.4
Aug	559	522.5	525.6	532.4
Sep	463	425.2	439.0	439.9
Oct	407	382.0	389.7	390.9
Nov	362	335.3	342.3	342.3
Dec	405	363.8	380.0	378.0
1960				
Jan	417	380.7	396.8	395.2
Feb	391	362.8	379.9	377.3
Mar	419	408.3	440.2	436.4
Apr	461	396.2	428.1	424.2
May	472	409.8	439.4	437.8
Jun	535	480.8	519.8	520.7
Jul	622	535.1	579.2	581.8
Aug	606	549.3	588.7	594.0
Sep	508	452.0	491.7	490.8
Oct	461	408.8	436.6	436.2
Nov	390	362.1	383.4	381.9
Dec	432	392.5	425.7	421.7
Sum of squares of prediction errors		42636.4	11638.4	11171.3
Sum of absolute values of prediction errors		900.5	468.7	463.1

therefore not significantly worse in the post-sample period, which is perhaps not surprising as there has been no attempt at data-mining. The shortcomings of the model show up more clearly in the extrapolations, which underpredict the actual values. Table 5.7.2 compares these predictions with those obtained by the logarithmic model.

EXERCISES

5.1 Consider the model

$$y_t = \psi_{1t} + \psi_{2t}$$

where ψ_{1t} and ψ_{2t} are stochastic cyclical processes as in (2.3.38), with frequencies λ_1 and λ_2 respectively and damping factors ρ_1 and ρ_2.

(a) Explain why it is not possible to carry out a two degrees of freedom LM test of the hypothesis that $\rho_1 = \rho_2 = 0$.

(b) Suppose that $y_t = \psi_{1t}$ has been fitted. How would you set up a test for the presence of a second cycle?

5.2 Suppose that the ARCH model of (5.2.7) is fitted with $\varphi = 0$. Formulate an LM test of the hypothesis $H_0: \varphi = 0$ against $H_1: \varphi \neq 0$.

5.3 A portmanteau test statistic for serial correlation in the variance of a time series is

$$\text{QSQ}(P) = T \sum_{\tau=1}^{P} \text{rsq}^2(\tau)$$

where $\text{rsq}(\tau)$ is the autocorrelation between y_t^2 and $y_{t-\tau}^2$. Formulate a model against which a test based on QSQ(P) is the LM test. What is the distribution of QSQ(P) under the null hypothesis?

5.4 When would you amend the test in Example 5.2.2 if you knew, *a priori*, that λ_c was equal to $2\pi/7$?

5.5 It is often argued that when a series is time-invariant, the degree of differencing needed to induce stationarity is the one which minimises the variance of the transformed series. Discuss whether or not this argument is correct by reference to the damped trend model (2.3.66).

5.6 Construct a frequency-domain LM test of the hypothesis that, in the BSM, ω_t and η_t are correlated.

5.7 Fit a pure AR model to the data on rainfall in Fortaleza. Comment on the result.

5.8 Construct a frequency-domain LM test of the hypothesis that $\sigma_\varepsilon^2 = 0$ in the random walk plus noise model. Show that this test can be converted to an equivalent test in the time domain.

Chapter 6

Extensions of the univariate model

This chapter examines a number of different topics relating to structural time series models. The first two sections deal with certain fundamental questions concerning trend and seasonality, and provide a justification of the statistical models adopted and the reasons for the shortcomings of certain other approaches. Various extensions of the trend and seasonal components of structural models are also considered.

Section 6.3 looks at the consequences of different observation and model timing intervals and shows that the principal structural models are relatively robust to changes in the observation timing interval. Data irregularities are examined in section 6.4. The Kalman filter is an invaluable tool for handling such problems as missing observations, outliers and data revisions, and the structural approach appears to be the natural way to tackle model formulation.

The potential of state space methods for handling various types of non-linearity and structural change is explored in section 6.5, while the last section sets up models appropriate for dealing with count data and qualitative observations. Again it is argued that the structural approach is the natural way to proceed.

6.1 Trends, detrending and unit roots

This section discusses various aspects of trends. The first two sub-sections focus on the fundamental definition of a trend and the way in which a series may be decomposed into a trend and other components. It is assumed that the series in question do not contain components, such as seasonal and daily effects, which tend to repeat their pattern within a given time period. The extension of the various concepts to take account of such factors is made in section 6.2.

The pitfalls inherent in prior detrending are discussed in sub-section 6.1.3, while 6.1.4 explores the links between structural models with stochastic trends and autoregressive models with unit roots. These issues are both of considerable importance in applied work.

The last two sub-sections are concerned with introducing non-linear trends into structural models. Sub-section 6.1.5 sets out the generalisation of the local linear trend model to higher-order polynomials. From the technical point of view this is a straightforward extension of what has gone before. The non-linear trends considered in sub-section 6.1.6 are more interesting and perhaps more useful. However, there is no obvious solution to the way in which they should be handled and a number of possible approaches are discussed.

6.1.1 What is a trend?

The question of defining a trend is one which has exercised the minds of economists and statisticians for many years. Most people would claim to be able to recognise a trend when they saw one, but few would be able to go beyond the rather vague definition in the *Concise Oxford Dictionary* which is that a trend is 'a general direction and tendency'. Indeed there is a strong temptation to echo the sentiments expressed by Cairncross (1971, p. 139): 'A trend is a trend is a trend . . .'.

Actually, the *Concise Oxford Dictionary*'s definition is not a bad one, in that it defines the trend in terms of prediction. This is the view taken here. In much of the statistical literature, however, a trend is conceived of as that part of a series which changes relatively slowly over time. In other words, smoothness properties play a key role in the definition. There is no fundamental reason, though, why a trend should be smooth, except that it is somewhat easier on the eye. Suppose, for example, that a series, such as a stock-market price, follows a random walk. The general direction of such a series at the current point in time is a horizontal line passing through the last observation. The last observation therefore *is* the trend. There is no difference between the trend and the observations and so the trend, like the series itself, is not smooth.

What then is a trend? Viewed in terms of prediction, *the estimated trend is that part of the series which when extrapolated gives the clearest indication of the future long-term movements in the series.* Note that a trend does not necessarily have to show an upward or downward movement and in fact a series will always contain a trend unless the long-run forecasts are equal to zero. The definition makes no mention of smoothness and it is consistent with the idea of indicating a 'general direction'.

Having defined the trend in terms of its properties when extrapolated, we need a mechanism for making this extrapolation, just as we need a mechanism for making predictions of future values of the series itself. A mechanism for making predictions of the series is provided by a statistical model and such a model is fitted in the hope that it will provide the best possible predictions. A statistical model for the trend component can also be set up as part of the overall model for y_t. This sub-model should be such that the optimal estimator of the trend at the end of the series gives rise to a forecast function, satisfying the criterion of the previous paragraph. The optimal estimator of the trend component within the series is then defined automatically. The properties of the estimated trend within the series therefore emerge as a consequence of the required properties of the trend forecast function and the characteristics of the data.

The trend components in structural time series models are always set up in such a way that their forecast functions indicate the long-term movements in the series. Indeed, as section 2.3 showed, this was the main consideration motivating their formulation in the first place. Thus, in the absence of seasonal and daily effects, the forecast function for the trend component tends towards the forecast function for the series as a whole, that is

$$\lim_{l \to \infty} (\tilde{y}_{T+l|T} - m_{T+l|T}) = 0 \tag{6.1.1a}$$

where $m_{T+l|T}$ is the MMSLE of the trend made at time T. For a model with disturbances which are independent, rather than merely being uncorrelated, the MMSE, $\tilde{\mu}_{T+l|T}$, displays exactly the same characteristics and, indeed, the discussion in this sub-section could just have easily been framed in terms of MMSEs. In any case the distinction disappears in a Gaussian model.

Since the trend component in a structural model can usually be thought of as providing a local approximation to a continuous function of time, its forecast function can also be regarded as a continuous function of time and written as $m(T+l|T)$ for $l \geqslant 0$. This continuous forecast function is *anchored* at the estimated trend at the end of the series, that is

$$m(T+l|T) = m_T \quad \text{at} \quad l = 0 \tag{6.1.1b}$$

Example 6.1.1 Consider the model

$$y_t = \mu_t + \upsilon_t + \varepsilon_t \tag{6.1.2a}$$

$$\mu_t = \mu_{t-1} + \eta_t \tag{6.1.2b}$$

$$\upsilon_t = \rho \upsilon_{t-1} + \kappa_t \quad |\rho| < 1 \tag{6.1.2c}$$

where η_t, κ_t and ε_t are mutually uncorrelated white-noise disturbances. The forecast function for future values of the series is

$$\tilde{y}_{T+l|T} = m_T + \rho^l \tilde{\upsilon}_T, \quad l = 0, 1, 2, \ldots \tag{6.1.3a}$$

where $\tilde{\upsilon}_T$ is the MMSLE of υ_T at the time T. The forecast function for the trend is

$$m_{T+l|T} = m_T, \quad l = 1, 2, \ldots \tag{6.1.3b}$$

and since $|\rho| < 1$ it is easily seen that it converges to the forecast function for the series as a whole as the lead time increases. However, because it is simpler than (6.1.3a), it gives a clearer indication of the long-run direction of the series. Indeed the continuous trend forecast function, $m(T+l|T)$, is simply a horizontal line at a height of m_T.

Example 6.1.2 In the local linear trend model the continuous trend forecast function is a straight line starting off from m_T and having a slope of b_T; compare (2.3.30).

Example 6.1.3 In the damped trend model, (2.3.66), the trend forecast function was derived in Example 3.5.2 and is

$$m_{T+l|T}=m_T+[(1-\rho^l)/(1-\rho)]b_T, \quad l=0,1,2,\ldots \tag{6.1.4}$$

The right-hand side of (6.1.4) can also be regarded as a continuous forecast function, $m(T+l|T)$ for $l\geqslant 0$.

The structural time series models formulated in continuous time in chapter 9 yield estimated trends with similar properties to those set up in discrete time models. The same is true of structural models, which although discrete, are set up for a timing interval which is less than the observation timing interval; see section 6.3. It is also the case that the trends that emerge from the common factor multivariate models of sections 8.5, 8.8 and 9.4 satisfy our general definition of a trend and the long-run forecast and continuity properties which it implies.

Finally, let us return to the question of smoothness. Other things being equal, it is desirable to have a smooth trend if only because it is more appealing to policy makers. However, the view which has been put forward here is that once a suitable structural model has been selected and estimated, the properties of the estimated trend are fixed. Unless the variable is a flow and the model is formulated in continuous time or at a finer timing interval than the observation timing interval, a matter taken up in sub-section 6.3.4, there are no degrees of freedom left with which to impose smoothness. Smoothness can only be imposed on the trend by bringing in some restrictions. In the local linear trend model, the smoothness of the trend depends on the relative parameters q_η and q_ζ, but if q_η is constrained to be zero, as in Kitagawa (1981), Gersch and Kitagawa (1983) and Theil and Wage (1964), the trend component becomes

$$\Delta^2\mu_t=\zeta_{t-1} \tag{6.1.5}$$

and the resulting estimated trend within the series is relatively smooth. The argument is given by Akaike (1980) in terms of *smoothness priors*. Since the model is still a structural one, the properties required of a trend, namely (6.1.1a) and (6.1.1b), remain satisfied. The argument against setting σ_η^2 equal to zero is that such a model may give relatively poor predictions compared to a model where σ_η^2 is allowed to be positive. An obvious example would be if the data were generated by a random walk. It is interesting to note that the rationale for the smoothness induced by (6.1.5) was originally given by Whittaker (1923). However, he was working with actuarial life tables where the case for imposing smoothness is much stronger than any conditions pertaining to predictions outside the range of the sample. The same is true when the corresponding continuous time version of the local linear trend model is used for fitting a spline function to cross-sectional data, as in Wecker and Ansley (1983).

6.1.2 Decompositions based on ARIMA models

The approach to trend estimation favoured by some statisticians is to first fit an unrestricted reduced form ARIMA model to the data and then to decompose this model into components. If the decomposition is to be into a trend and an irregular, one criterion which has been adopted is to maximise the variance of the irregular component, thereby making the trend as smooth as possible. Tiao and Hillmer (1978) call this the *canonical decomposition* while Pierce (1979) refers to it as the 'principle of minimum extraction'. Although Box *et al.* (1987) show that the trend emerging from the canonical decomposition can be regarded as being defined in terms of prediction, its forecast function is not anchored at the trend estimate at the end of the series.

The way in which the canonical decomposition works can be illustrated by an ARIMA(0, 1, 1) process,

$$\Delta y_t = \xi_t + \theta \xi_{t-1}$$

Such a process can be decomposed as follows:

$$y_t = \mu_t^* + \varepsilon_t^* \tag{6.1.6a}$$

$$\mu_t^* = \mu_{t-1}^* + \eta_t^* + \theta^* \eta_{t-1}^* \tag{6.1.6b}$$

where $|\theta^*| \leqslant 1$, and ε_t^* and η_t^* are mutually uncorrelated, zero mean, white-noise disturbances, with variances σ_ε^2 and σ_η^2 respectively.

The model can be reduced to stationarity by taking first differences, that is

$$\Delta y_t = \eta_t^* + \theta^* \eta_{t-1}^* + \varepsilon_t^* - \varepsilon_{t-1}^*$$

The right-hand side of this expression is equivalent to an MA(1) process since the autocorrelations are zero beyond lag one. The first-order autocorrelation is

$$\rho(1) = \frac{\theta^* q - 1}{(1 + \theta^{*2})q + 2} \tag{6.1.7}$$

where $q = \sigma_\eta^2 / \sigma_\varepsilon^2$. An immediate problem now arises with (6.1.6) since it contains three parameters, σ_η^2, σ_ε^2 and θ^*, rather than the two parameters associated with an MA(1) process. This is reflected in the two parameters, θ^* and q, in the expression for $\rho(1)$. There is an infinite number of combinations of values of θ^* and q giving the same value of $\rho(1)$. Hence, as it stands, the model is not identifiable for normally distributed observations; see section 4.4. Restrictions must therefore be placed on it. The standard structural model has θ^* equal to zero, which reduces (6.1.6) to a random walk plus noise. In the canonical decomposition, the idea is to minimise q for a given value of $\rho(1)$ in (6.1.7), thereby determining the value of θ^*. It is not difficult to see that in the special case when the reduced form is a random walk, so that $\rho(1) = 0$, the canonical decomposition has $\theta^*=1$ and $q=1$. In fact it can be shown that the canonical decomposition has $\theta^*=1$ for any value of $\rho(1)$; see Box *et al.* (1978).

If n_T^* denotes the MMSLE of η_T^*, the forecast function for the trend, which in this case is just the level of the process, is

$$m_{T+l|T}^* = m_T^* + n_T^*, \quad l=1, 2, \ldots \tag{6.1.8}$$

This is also the forecast function for the observations. The trend forecast function can be regarded as a continuous horizontal line for $l \geqslant 1$. However, this line cannot be extended back to pass through the estimator of the current level, μ_T^*, unless η_T^* happens to be identically equal to zero. This compares with the structural model in Example 6.1.1, which reduces to the random walk plus noise when ρ is zero and has as its continuous trend forecast function a horizontal straight line starting at $l=0$. The implications of this failure to yield a continuous forecast function anchored at the estimated trend at the end of the series are brought home most clearly in the special case where the reduced form is a random walk. It was shown in Example 4.7.1 that the MMSLE of the trend is the weighted average given in (4.7.11). It can also be shown that at the end of the series

$$m_T^* = \tfrac{3}{4} y_T + \tfrac{1}{4} y_{T-1}; \tag{6.1.9}$$

see Exercise 4.7 and Box *et al.* (1978, p. 319). Of course the final forecast function is just

$$\tilde{y}_{T+l|T} = m_{T+l|T}^* = y_T, \quad l=1, 2, \ldots \tag{6.1.10}$$

denoting the fact that the optimal forecast of future values of a random walk is the current value. It is difficult to see what m_T^* represents since it cannot be regarded as an estimator of the current level of the process. Similarly the estimates of the trend within the sample, given by (4.7.11), reflect an attempt to smooth a process which is inherently unsmoothable.

The paper by Beveridge and Nelson (1981) proposes a definition of trend which is based primarily on prediction. The underlying philosophy is therefore very close to that expounded in the previous sub-section. As with the structural approach, the Beveridge-Nelson methodology indicates that the trend in a random walk process coincides with the observations themselves. Indeed they cite this as a check on the reasonableness of their results.

Beveridge and Nelson focus attention on fitted ARIMA(p, 1, q) models which contain a constant term. For such models the final forecast function is linear, and the Beveridge-Nelson definition of the trend at the end of the series is the value obtained when the final forecast function is extrapolated back to the end of the series. The decomposition of the series is then expressed in terms of the ARIMA disturbance term. In the ARIMA(0, 1, 1) case the decomposition is:

$$y_t = \mu_t^\dagger + \varepsilon_t^\dagger \tag{6.1.11}$$

where

$\mu_t^\dagger=(1+\theta)\xi_t/\Delta$ and $\varepsilon_t^\dagger=-\theta\xi_t$

The model is therefore of the form of a random walk plus noise in which the components are correlated and we may write

$$y_t=\frac{\eta_t^\dagger}{\Delta}+\varepsilon_t^\dagger \tag{6.1.12}$$

where $\text{Var}(\eta_t^\dagger)=(1+\theta)^2\sigma^2$ and $\text{Var}(\varepsilon_t^\dagger)=\theta^2\sigma^2$, with σ^2 being the variance of ξ_t. As can be seen, $\mu_t^\dagger$ does indeed become equal to y_t when θ is equal to zero.

In the corresponding structural random walk plus noise model, the filtered estimate of the trend component is equal to the long-run prediction of the observations made at that point in time. This is equal, by definition, to the trend component in the Beveridge-Nelson decomposition. Thus, in terms of (6.1.11), $\mu_t^\dagger$ is estimated with zero MSE and there is no need to even contemplate smoothing. However, in the structural model, a better estimator of the underlying trend, μ_t, can be obtained by smoothing and, except when θ is equal to zero or minus one, it will generally be different to the filtered estimator. Hence it will also be different to the trend, $\mu_t^\dagger$, given by the Beveridge-Nelson decomposition. The fact that observations beyond time t are ignored in constructing the Beveridge-Nelson trend within the series must surely lessen its appeal.

The Beveridge-Nelson definition of trend will not always correspond to the filtered estimate of trend in an analogous structural model. Thus in the damped trend model, the trend forecast function, (6.1.4), only goes towards its final form, which is a horizontal straight line, as l goes to infinity. Hence

$$\mu_t^\dagger=m_t+b_t/(1-\rho)$$

In the special case when $\sigma_\varepsilon^2=\sigma_\eta^2=0$ in the damped trend model, the trend is given by the observations themselves. The Beveridge-Nelson decomposition, on the other hand, yields the trend

$$\mu_t^\dagger=y_t+\rho\Delta y_t/(1-\rho)=\zeta_{t-1}/[(1-\rho)\Delta]$$

This trend is a random walk in which the variance of the disturbance term is $\sigma_\xi^2/(1-\rho)^2$. This suggests that, for $\rho>0$, it will be more erratic than the actual observations which are driven by a disturbance term with variance σ_ξ^2.

6.1.3 *Detrending*

It is common practice, particularly in economics, to detrend a series before subjecting it to analysis. The best advice to anyone contemplating such a course of action is not to do it.

Detrending is usually carried out by regressing the observations on time. The detrended series consists of the residuals, and these are analysed and a model fitted to them. Forecasts are then made by adding the forecasts of the detrended series to the fitted deterministic trend.

A deterministic linear trend is a special case of the local linear trend used in structural time series models. It corresponds to a situation in which the two variance parameters, σ_η^2 and σ_ζ^2, are both zero. As is evident from the applications reported in section 2.7, a deterministic trend is the exception rather than the rule for economic time series and there is no justification for attempting to impose it at the outset. The forecasts made on the basis of an inappropriate deterministic trend may be very misleading. Furthermore the distorting effect on the residuals may be such that spurious inferences are drawn about the nature of the underlying process. The nature of these distortions is illustrated in the paper by Nelson and Kang (1981). They analyse the properties of the residuals from a regression on time when the true process is a random walk, and conclude that inappropriate detrending 'will tend to produce apparent periodicity which is not in any meaningful sense a property of the underlying system'. They also suggest that the dynamics of econometric models estimated from detrended data 'may be wholly, or in part, an artifact of the trend removal procedure'.

Further evidence on the effect of fitting a deterministic time trend to a random walk is provided in a later paper by Nelson and Kang (1984). They report a Monte Carlo experiment for 100 observations from a random walk in which the average R^2 from a regression on time was 0.44. The estimated intercept and slope terms were statistically significant at the nominal 5% level with frequencies of 80% and 87% respectively. The standard regression statistics therefore exaggerate the extent to which the movement of the data is actually accounted for by time. When the underlying process is a random walk plus drift these spurious effects become even more pronounced with R^2 being driven close to unity. A recent paper by Phillips (1986) provides the distributional theory underlying these results.

US GNP The data on US Real GNP in the period 1948 to 1970 can be used to illustrate the above findings. The analysis in sub-sections 2.7.4 and 5.7.2 showed the logarithm of this series to be very close to a random walk plus drift. Regressing it on time yields:

$$\hat{y}_t = \underset{(0.015)}{5.755} + \underset{(0.0011)}{0.0366}\, t$$

with

$$R^2 = 0.981, \quad s = 0.035$$

and the first three residual autocorrelations taking the values

$$r(1) = 0.63, \quad r(2) = 0.36, \quad r(3) = 0.12$$

This might be taken to suggest that a deterministic trend model with a stationary AR(1) disturbance term is appropriate.

Rather than simply regressing on time, some people prefer to regress on a higher-order polynomial. For example in Nerlove *et al.* (1979), all series are detrended by regressing on t and t^2. While this may be slightly more flexible it is still the case that attempting to force a deterministic pattern on a series which is inherently stochastic is likely to cause serious distortions.

In view of the above discussion it may be tempting to detrend by fitting a local linear trend model to the data. However, such a procedure is not appropriate. What will tend to happen is that the estimates of σ_η^2 and σ_ζ^2 will take values which enable the trend to respond to movements in the series which are more suitably modelled by other components. The only case where the trend could be removed is when the model consists of a deterministic trend plus a stationary process. This, of course, is the one case where regressing on time is legitimate; see, for example, Anderson (1971, ch. 2).

Detrending is sometimes carried out by smoothing the series by a moving average filter as in (2.2.26). As was shown in section 4.7, a particular specification for a structural model implies that a certain filter is optimal. The best that can be said for a moving average filter is that it may not cause too much damage if it corresponds roughly to the optimal filter. If it does not, it may cause considerable distortion and if several filters are applied spurious cycles may be induced in the series by the Yule-Slutsky effect; see Harvey (1981b, pp. 81-3).

To summarise, therefore, the trend should not be treated as a separate entity which can be estimated in isolation from the rest of the series. In any case, given the benefits of working with a full structural model, there seems to be little point in subjecting a series to detrending in the first place.

6.1.4 Stochastic trends and autoregressions with unit roots

There has been considerable interest in the use of autoregressive processes for modelling non-stationary time series. Fuller (1985) provides a review. The non-stationarity leads to the presence of unit roots in the autoregressive polynomial and the problem of testing for these units has been studied at some length; see, for example, Dickey and Fuller (1979), Fuller (1976, section 8.5) and Phillips (1987).

The purpose of the present sub-section is to provide an interpretation of non-stationary autoregressions within the framework of structural time series models. We first consider a model in which the trend, μ_t, is a random walk plus drift and the remaining component, v_t, is stationary and invertible, that is

$$y_t = \mu_t + v_t \tag{6.1.13a}$$

$$\mu_t = \mu_{t-1} + \beta + \eta_t \tag{6.1.13b}$$

The stationary form of the model is

$$\Delta y_t = \eta_t + \beta + \Delta v_t \tag{6.1.14}$$

and the reduced form is such that Δy_t is equal to a constant plus an ARMA process. The autoregressive approximation to the reduced form is obtained by approximating the ARMA process by an AR process of order p. Thus

$$\Delta y_t = \beta + \xi_t/\varphi(L)$$

where $\varphi(L)$ is a polynomial in the lag operator of order p and ξ_t is the reduced form disturbance term. Now consider an autoregression of the form

$$\varphi^*(L)y_t = \beta^* + \xi_t \tag{6.1.15}$$

If this is derived from the previous equation then $\varphi^*(L) = \varphi(L)(1-L)$ and $\beta^* = \beta\varphi(1)$. However, a straightforward regression of y_t on $p+1$ lagged values of itself provides estimators of the coefficients of $\varphi^*(L)$ without imposing the unit root restriction.

If, in a model of the form (6.1.15), $\varphi^*(L)$ is stationary, that is, all its roots are outside the unit circle, the interpretation of β^* changes to a quantity which is proportional to the mean of the process. A trend component can be brought into the model by introducing a time trend. Thus

$$\varphi^*(L)y_t = \beta^* + \gamma^* t + \xi_t \tag{6.1.16}$$

and this is equivalent to a deterministic trend plus a stationary autoregressive disturbance term. However, if $\varphi^*(L)$ contains a unit root, a non-zero value for γ^* implies a quadratic forecast function.

By the classic result of Frisch and Waugh (1933), including a time trend in a regression is equivalent to first detrending the variables by regressing them individually on time. The danger with formulating model (6.1.16) should therefore be clear from the discussion on detrending in the previous sub-section. If the true model contains a stochastic trend, implying a unit root in $\varphi^*(L)$, the time trend in (6.1.16) will tend to be statistically significant and the estimated autoregressive coefficients will tend to be stable (stationary) rather than explosive. Dropping the time trend and working with an unrestricted version of (6.1.15) may also be unsatisfactory. Suppose that the trend in (6.1.13) is close to being deterministic. This means that the value of σ_η^2 will be relatively small and so, as can be seen from (6.1.14), the reduced form ARMA process for Δy_t will lie close to the invertibility boundary. As a result a long autoregressive process will be needed to provide a reasonable approximation. In the extreme case when the trend is deterministic, the AR approximation will fail.

The distributional theory for the estimators of the AR parameters in (6.1.15) and (6.1.16) is discussed in Fuller (1985) and Phillips (1986). Valid tests are most conveniently carried out by taking the first difference to be the left-hand-side variable. Thus, for $p \geqslant 1$, (6.1.16) is expressed as

$$\Delta y_t = (\varphi - 1)y_{t-1} + \sum_{j=1}^{p} \varphi_j^\dagger \Delta y_{t-j} + \beta^* + \gamma^* t + \xi_t \tag{6.1.16$'$}$$

where

$$\varphi_j^{\dagger} = -\sum_{k=j+1}^{p+1} \varphi_k^*, \quad j=1,2,\ldots,p$$

and

$$\varphi = \sum_{k=1}^{p+1} \varphi_k^*$$

Carrying out a regression on this model is equivalent to a regression of y_t on y_{t-1} to y_{t-p-1}; it does not impose the unit root restriction which regressing Δy_t on Δy_{t-1} to Δy_{t-p} would do. An additional attraction of working with (6.1.16)′ is that it is more numerically stable than the corresponding regression in levels. As regards inference, a unit root in the autoregressive polynomial corresponds to a coefficient of zero for y_{t-1} since $\varphi=1-\varphi^*(1)$ and $\varphi^*(1)=0$. However when a unit root is present the distribution of the estimator of this coefficient is shifted over to the left. The distribution of the 't-statistic' associated with y_{t-1} is tabulated in Fuller (1976, Table 8.5.2) and these tables, which are known as the Dickey–Fuller tables, need to be consulted if a valid test of the unit root hypothesis is to be carried out. On the other hand, Fuller (1985) shows that the t-statistics associated with the differenced right-hand-side variables in (6.1.16)′ are asymptotically standard normal.

US GNP Carrying out a regression of the form (6.1.16)′ using the data on US Real GNP referred to in the previous sub-section gives

$$\widehat{\Delta y_t} = \underset{(0.837)}{1.654} + \underset{(0.0072)}{0.0134t} - \underset{(0.196)}{0.374y_{t-1}} + \underset{(0.243)}{0.052\Delta y_{t-1}}$$

where the observations on Δy_t run from 1950 to 1971. The t-statistic for y_{t-1} is -1.91. A one-sided test of the null hypothesis of a unit root against the alternative of a stationary autoregressive process would lead to a rejection of the unit root at the 5% level if the t-statistic was treated as being asymptotically normal and -1.64 were taken to be the critical value. Table 8.5.2 in Fuller (1976), on the other hand, gives a 5% critical value of -3.60 for $T=25$. Inference on the coefficient of Δy_{t-1} can be carried out in the usual way, and it is clear that it is not statistically significant. Dropping this variable from the regression gives

$$\widehat{\Delta y_t} = \underset{(0.705)}{1.574} + \underset{(0.0062)}{0.0127t} - \underset{(0.165)}{0.355y_{t-1}}$$

where the observations on Δy_t now start at 1949. The t-statistic for y_{t-1} is -2.15, but, as before, the null hypothesis of a unit root cannot be rejected at any reasonable level of significance when the Dickey-Fuller tables are used. Note that if the above equation is rearranged so that y_t is the dependent variable, the coefficient of y_{t-1} is 0.645, a value which the uninitiated might well feel was comfortably within the stationarity region; indeed, when this series was examined in the previous sub-section, it was observed that similar conclusions might easily be drawn from the correlogram of the detrended data. Note also that the 't-statistic' of the time trend is 2.07, a value which would normally be thought of as significant.

Testing for a unit root is related to the problem of testing for a deterministic trend. As was pointed out in chapter 5, the standard regularity conditions do not hold when testing for a deterministic trend and this is also the case when testing for a unit root. However, although the source of the statistical difficulties is essentially the same, the formulation of the testing problem is somewhat different in the two cases. In a structural model, such as (6.1.13), the test is of σ_η^2 equal to zero against the alternative that it is positive. Thus the null hypothesis is that the trend is deterministic. Testing that the slope, β, is zero is a subsidiary, and optional, hypothesis. In the context of an unrestricted autoregression of the form (6.1.15), the null hypothesis implies that the model contains a stochastic trend. Under the alternative the process is stationary. If the model is formulated with a time trend as in (6.1.16), a model with a deterministic trend emerges under the alternative, while the null implies a stochastic trend with fixed linear and quadratic terms.

The attraction of autoregressions is that they are easy to specify and estimate. They can be expected to yield good short-term forecasts in many situations. However, although they can be regarded as approximations to the reduced forms of structural models, the information which they provide about the dynamic characteristics of a series may be somewhat muddled. Indeed the small sample properties of the (unrestricted) estimators in (6.1.15) and (6.1.16) are such that they may be quite misleading.

6.1.5 Higher-order polynomial trends

So far attention has been focussed on the notion of a linear trend. This sub-section generalises the idea of a local linear trend to higher order polynomials. While such trends are non-linear in the sense that they lead to, say, quadratic or cubic forecast functions, they can still be formulated as linear time series models. This is not true of the models presented in the next sub-section.

A deterministic h-th order polynomial trend model may be written as

$$y_t = \alpha_0 + \alpha_1 t + \alpha_2 \frac{t^2}{2} + \cdots + \alpha_h \frac{t^h}{h!} + \varepsilon_t, \quad t = 1, \ldots, T \qquad (6.1.17)$$

The corresponding local trend model is obtained by setting up a transition equation in which the $(h+1) \times (h+1)$ transition matrix, $\mathbf{T}$, is an upper triangular matrix with elements $t_{ij} = 1/(i-j)!$ for $i \leqslant j$. The first element in the state vector is the current level of the trend and so $\mathbf{z}_t' = [1 \quad \mathbf{0}_h']$. The remaining elements are the first to the h-th derivatives of the trend at time t. As in the local linear trend model the disturbances in the transition equation are taken to be uncorrelated with each other.

The local polynomial trend model can be reduced to stationarity by differencing $h+1$ times. The controllability condition is that the variance of the disturbance corresponding to the last element of the state vector should be strictly positive. When this condition is fulfilled, estimation can be carried out in the frequency domain in the manner described in chapter 4, and the regularity conditions of section 4.5 are satisfied.

As a specific example, consider the local quadratic trend model. The state space form is

$$y_t = [1 \quad 0 \quad 0]\boldsymbol{\alpha}_t + \varepsilon_t, \quad t=1,\ldots,T \tag{6.1.18a}$$

$$\boldsymbol{\alpha}_t = \begin{bmatrix} \mu_t \\ \beta_t \\ \gamma_t \end{bmatrix} = \begin{bmatrix} 1 & 1 & \frac{1}{2} \\ 0 & 1 & 1 \\ 0 & 0 & 1 \end{bmatrix} \begin{bmatrix} \mu_{t-1} \\ \beta_{t-1} \\ \gamma_{t-1} \end{bmatrix} + \begin{bmatrix} \eta_t \\ \zeta_t \\ \kappa_t \end{bmatrix} \tag{6.1.18b}$$

where β_t and γ_t are, respectively, the local slope and the local 'acceleration'. The unobserved components form of the model is

$$y_t = \frac{\eta_t}{\Delta} + \frac{\zeta_{t-1} + 0.5\kappa_{t-1}}{\Delta^2} + \frac{\kappa_{t-2}}{\Delta^3} + \varepsilon_t \tag{6.1.19}$$

and if σ_κ^2 is strictly positive it is necessary to difference three times to achieve stationarity. The reduced form is an ARIMA(0, 3, 3) process. A local quadratic trend model may be plausible for the logarithm of the price level; see, for example, the discussion in Jacobs and Jones (1980). Since the first difference of the logarithm of the price level is the rate of inflation, the acceleration term corresponds to a growth term in the rate of inflation. Of course, if σ_ζ^2 is zero, the model effectively reduces to a local linear trend model for the rate of inflation.

6.1.6 Growth curves

Certain non-linear trend functions, like the logistic and Gompertz functions, may be attractive in situations where there is thought to be a saturation level to the series. Such situations arise where a new product is entering a market. Typically penetration into the market is slow at first, there then follows a period of acceleration, and finally the growth rate slows again as the sales of the product reach a saturation level. The trend used to model such a process is known as a *growth curve*. Growth curves may equally well apply to the stock of a good, such as the total number of telephones in a country, or to the related concept of the proportion of households owning that good.

The traditional formulation of a growth curve model is:

$$y_t = \mu_t + \varepsilon_t, \quad t=1,\ldots,T \tag{6.1.20}$$

where μ_t is a deterministic function of time. In the logistic case

$$\mu_t = \alpha/(1+\beta e^{\gamma t}) \tag{6.1.21}$$

where α, β and γ are parameters such that $\alpha, \beta > 0$ and $\gamma > 0$. Even though μ_t is deterministic, the model is intrinsically non-linear and ML estimation has to be carried out by non-linear least squares. Generalising these models so that they can handle local, as well as global, trends is therefore not easy. On the other hand, the desirability of introducing some discounting into past observations was recognised specifically in the pioneering work on trend curve fitting by Gregg *et al.* (1964, pp. 15–16).

Before proceeding to suggest ways in which growth curves may be incorporated in time series models, we examine some of the functional forms for growth curves which have been proposed in the literature. These curves are best regarded as continuous functions of time and, as such, will be denoted by $\mu(t)$.

The logistic curve is given by the right-hand side of (6.1.21). As $t \to \infty$, $\mu(t)$ tends asymptotically to its saturation level of α, while as $t \to -\infty$ it goes towards zero. The slope at any point is given by

$$d\mu(t)/dt = \mu(t)^2 \exp(\delta + \gamma t) \tag{6.1.22}$$

where $\delta = -\beta\gamma/\alpha$, or

$$d\mu(t)/dt = (-\gamma/\alpha)\, \mu(t)\, [\alpha - \mu(t)] \tag{6.1.23}$$

The second of these expressions enables one to interpret the rate of change of $\mu(t)$ with respect to t as being proportional to the current level of $\mu(t)$ multiplied by the distance below the saturation level. The first derivative is positive for all values of t. Evaluating the second derivative and setting it equal to zero shows that there is a point of inflexion at $t = (-1/\gamma) \log \beta$ with $\mu(t) = \alpha/2$.

The general modified exponential function takes the form

$$\mu(t) = \alpha(1+\beta e^{\gamma t})^{\kappa} \tag{6.1.24}$$

When κ is equal to minus one, this becomes the logistic, while setting κ equal to one gives the simple modified exponential. The logarithm of a Gompertz curve, a function which has been used quite widely in demography, is also obtained by setting κ equal to one. The slope of (6.1.24) is given by

$$d\mu(t)/dt = \mu(t)^{\rho} \exp(\delta + \gamma t) \tag{6.1.25}$$

where δ is defined as for (6.1.22).

There is no clear-cut solution regarding the best way to incorporate growth curves into the class of structural time series models. Indeed the solution will partly depend on the nature of the problem. A distinction needs to be drawn between the three cases alluded to in the opening paragraph, where it was pointed out that the series to be modelled may be a stock, a flow or a proportion.

Levels There are a number of ways in which non-linear global trends may be modified so as to become local trends. One possibility is simply to allow the parameters to follow random walks. However, this does not, in general, work since it fails to preserve a degree of continuity. As was observed in the treatment of polynomial trends in the previous sub-section, it is necessary to re-parameterise so that the model is set up in terms of the current level. This is difficult for curves which are intrinsically non-linear.

In the case of the logistic curve, the most satisfactory solution proceeds from the observation that the growth rate, obtained by dividing (6.1.23) by $\mu(t)$, is a linear function of $\mu(t)$, that is

$$\frac{d\log\mu(t)}{dt}=\frac{1}{\mu(t)}\frac{d\mu(t)}{dt}=-\gamma+\gamma^{\dagger}\mu(t) \tag{6.1.26}$$

where $\gamma^{\dagger}=\gamma/\alpha$. If the irregular component combines multiplicatively with the trend, (6.1.26) suggests the following model:

$$\log y_t=\mu_t^{\dagger}+\varepsilon_t \tag{6.1.27a}$$

$$\mu_t^{\dagger}=\mu_{t-1}^{\dagger}-\gamma_{t-1}+\gamma^{\dagger}\exp(\mu_{t-1}^{\dagger})+\eta_t \tag{6.1.27b}$$

$$\gamma_t=\gamma_{t-1}+\zeta_t \tag{6.1.27c}$$

where $\mu_t^{\dagger}=\log\mu_t$ and ε_t, η_t and ζ_t are mutually independent normally distributed white-noise disturbances. When there is no saturation level, and α is equal to infinity, $\gamma^{\dagger}$ is zero and the term involving $\exp(\mu_{t-1}^{\dagger})$ in (6.1.27b) disappears. The model then collapses to the local linear trend model with minus γ_t in (6.1.27) being equal to the growth rate, β_t. A further extension to the model would let $\gamma^{\dagger}$ follow a random walk but this may be adding too much flexibility into the model to make it a practical proposition.

Model (6.1.27) can be handled by the extended Kalman filter. All that happens is that $\mu_{t-1}^{\dagger}$ in (6.1.27b) is replaced by its estimator $\hat{\mu}_{t-1}^{\dagger}$, computed at time $t-1$. If $\mu_t^{\dagger}$ were used instead of μ_{t-1} in (6.1.27b), the estimator would be $\mu_{t|t-1}^{\dagger}$. Note that even if $\gamma^{\dagger}$ is kept constant, it can still be included in the state vector if it is convenient to do so.

The growth rate expression, (6.1.26), is used in Levenbach and Reuter (1976) as the basis for the model

$$\Delta\log y_t=-\gamma+\gamma^{\dagger}y_t+\eta_t \tag{6.1.28}$$

This formulation is a special case of that in (6.1.27) and is appropriate if γ is fixed and the trend is observed directly with no measurement error or irregular term obscuring it.

Levenbach and Reuter also suggest a generalisation of (6.1.28), which includes the reciprocal of y_t as an additional term. This model is written as

$$\Delta\log y_t=-\gamma+\gamma^{\dagger}y_t+\gamma^{*}y_t^{-1}+\eta_t \tag{6.1.29}$$

and the resulting path of y_t is known as a *Riccati growth curve*. This extension could also be made to (6.1.27) by including the term $\gamma^* \exp(1/\mu_{t-1}^\dagger)$ in (6.1.27b).

The way in which the trend component is handled in (6.1.27) poses no problem if additional components are to be brought into the model. Thus a seasonal or cycle may be added to (6.1.27a) and treated in the usual way.

A final possibility for handling situations where there is a saturation level is to abandon the idea of using one of the standard growth curves and instead to fit the damped trend model (2.3.66). This option may be a viable one at certain points in time although it is not able to capture some of the important features inherent in the growth curve formulations.

Differences Let Y_t, $t=1,\ldots,T$ denote the stock of a variable and suppose that this stock is subject to an unknown saturation level. The corresponding flow, or net increase, in the stock will be denoted by $y_t=\Delta Y_t$, $t=2,\ldots,T$. Here, attention is focussed on the way in which y_t may be modelled and forecasts constructed for it. Forecasts for the stock, Y_t, then emerge as a by-product. The methods presented can only be applied if y_t is always strictly positive, i.e. $y_t>0$, $t=2,\ldots,T$.

Taking logarithms in the expression (6.1.25) for the slope of $\mu(t)$ in a general modified exponential function and assuming an additive disturbance term suggests the model

$$\log y_t=\rho \log \mu_{t-1}+\delta+\gamma t+\varepsilon_t \tag{6.1.30}$$

The inclusion of μ_{t-1} means that the long-term movements in y_t are affected by the build-up in the total stock.

Since μ_{t-1} is unobservable, it may be replaced by Y_{t-1} to yield

$$\log y_t=\rho \log Y_{t-1}+\delta+\gamma t+\varepsilon_t \tag{6.1.31}$$

This model may then be estimated by OLS. If ρ is given, then $\log(y_t/Y_{t-1}^{\rho})$ is simply regressed on t. The l-step-ahead forecasts, $\tilde{y}_{T+l|T}$ and $\tilde{Y}_{T+l|T}$ can be computed from the recursions

$$\tilde{y}_{T+l|T}=\tilde{Y}_{T+l-1|T}^{\rho} \exp[\delta+\gamma(T+l)] \tag{6.1.32a}$$

$$\tilde{Y}_{T+l|T}=Y_{T+l-1|T}+\tilde{y}_{T+l|T}, \quad l=1,2,\ldots \tag{6.1.32b}$$

where $\tilde{Y}_{T|T}=Y_T$. The forecast function for the stock takes the form of a general modified exponential and gradually approaches the saturation level, α. Although model (6.1.31) contains a deterministic linear trend component, it yields a local trend predictor for the growth curve for the stock variable, Y_t.

Tractors in Spain The official figures on tractor ownership in Spain over the period 1951–76 were used in a study of the logistic curve by Mar-Molinero (1980). Estimating (6.1.31) by OLS gave

$$\widehat{\log y_t}=\underset{(0.421)}{1.799} \log Y_{t-1}-\underset{(0.143)}{1.509}-\underset{(0.0623)}{0.1612}t, \quad t=2,\ldots T \tag{6.1.33}$$

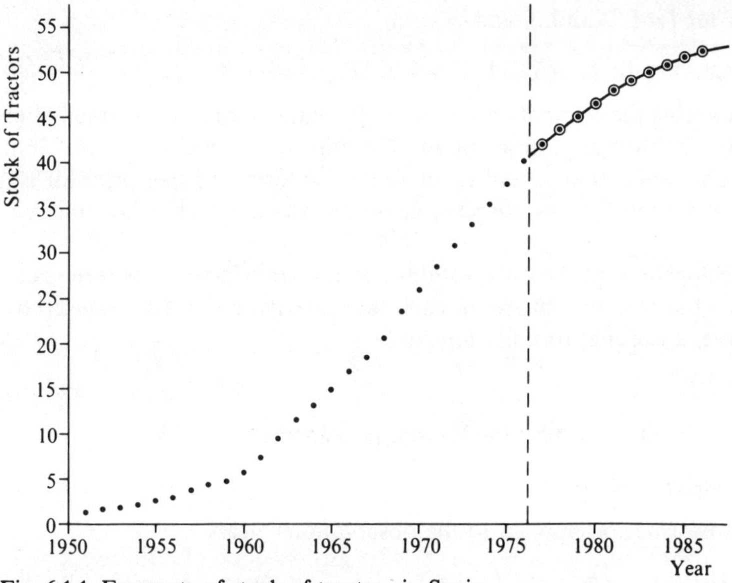

Fig. 6.1.1 Forecasts of stock of tractors in Spain.

with $\tilde{\sigma}=0.284$. The estimate of ρ is not significantly different from two, which suggests that a model corresponding to the logistic curve is appropriate. Re-estimating the parameters α^* and γ by regressing $\log(y_t/Y_{t-1}^2)$ on time gave

$$\widehat{\log y_t}=2\log Y_{t-1}-\underset{(0.130)}{1.535}-\underset{(0.0083)}{0.1907}t, \quad t=2,\ldots,T \tag{6.1.34}$$

with $\tilde{\sigma}=0.285$. The residuals in (6.1.34) are reasonably well behaved, although there is some indication of serial correlation with a Durbin-Watson d-statistic of 1.33. This is just significant at the 5% level according to the tables in King (1981).

The predictions for the stock of tractors, Y_t, are shown in Figure 6.1.1. A comparison of these predictions with predictions based on a global logistic model, (6.1.20), can be found in Harvey (1984).

The model in (6.1.31) could be modified and extended in a number of ways. For example, rather than using Y_{t-1} as an estimator of μ_{t-1}, an alternative estimator could be built up recursively. A modification of this kind becomes rather more important if the model is extended so as to include seasonal components. A more fundamental extension is to let the deterministic linear component in (6.1.31) be stochastic. This gives

$$\log y_t=\rho\log Y_{t-1}+\mu_t^*+\varepsilon_t, \quad t=2,\ldots,T \tag{6.1.35}$$

where μ_t^* is specified as in (4.1.6). Further modification would replace Y_{t-1} by a more appropriate estimator of μ_{t-1}, so that

$$\log y_t=\rho\log\hat{\mu}_{t-1}+\mu_t^*+\varepsilon_t, \quad t=2,\ldots,T \tag{6.1.36a}$$

where $\hat{\mu}_t = Y_t$ for $t=1$, 2 and 3, and

$$\hat{\mu}_t = \hat{\mu}_{t-1} + \exp(\rho \log \hat{\mu}_{t-1} + m^*_{t|t-1}), \quad t=4, \ldots T \tag{6.1.36b}$$

with $m^*_{t|t-1}$ denoting the optimal estimator of μ^*_t obtained from the Kalman filter by treating $\hat{\mu}_{t-1}$ as though it were known. The reason the recursion in (6.1.36b) can only start at $t=4$ is that y_2 and y_3 are needed to form a proper prior for μ^*_t. Clearly a number of variations are possible on the way in which μ_t is estimated.

Proportions Suppose that the observations are constrained to lie between zero and unity, as is the case with proportions. If the underlying trend is modelled by a logistic curve, α is equal to unity and so

$$\mu(t) = 1/(1+\beta e^{\gamma t}) \tag{6.1.37}$$

The curve may be linearised by the logistic transformation

$$\log \{\mu(t)/[1-\mu(t)]\} = \log \beta + \gamma t \tag{6.1.38}$$

The same transformation applied to the observations yields

$$y^*_t = \log [y_t/(1-y_t)], \quad t=1, \ldots, T \tag{6.1.39}$$

where the transformed observations lie in the range $-\infty$ to ∞ if the original are in the range 0 to 1. This suggests the model

$$y^*_t = \log \beta + \gamma t + \varepsilon_t, \quad t=1, \ldots, T \tag{6.1.40}$$

As it stands, (6.1.40) has a global trend, but since it is linear, it can be converted into a local model in the usual way. In fact, having made the transformation (6.1.39), any linear structural model may be formulated. The main issue is whether combining the components additively after the logistic transformation corresponds to an appropriate way of combining them in the untransformed series.

The question of making predictions for the original observations is considered by Wallis (1987); he extends the results on instantaneous data transformations noted in sub-section 4.6.1.

6.2 Seasonality and seasonal adjustment

The first sub-section below considers the way in which a seasonal component is defined for a univariate time series. The question of seasonal adjustment is then considered. A model-based seasonal adjustment procedure is described in sub-section 6.2.2 and this is contrasted with the X-11 procedure in 6.2.3. As in sub-sections 6.1.1 and 6.1.2, the discussion is framed in terms of optimal linear estimators.

Although the treatment is formally for seasons, normally months or quarters, which repeat themselves every year, most of the material applies equally well to days repeating themselves every week.

6.2.1 Seasonality

As with a trend, a seasonal component is defined in terms of the predictions it yields. *The estimated seasonal is that part of the series which, when extrapolated, repeats itself over any one-year time period and averages out to zero over such a time period.* In a structural model, the seasonal forecast function satisfies the condition:

$$c_{T+l|T} = -\sum_{j=1}^{s-1} c_{T+l-j|T}, \quad l=1,2,\ldots \tag{6.2.1}$$

Hence the forecast function depends solely on the current estimates of the seasonal effects over the last $s-1$ periods, that is $c_{T-j|T}$ for $j=0, 1, \ldots, (s-2)$. This is somewhat akin to the continuity property defined for a trend in (6.1.1b).

The seasonal forecast function contains no information on the general direction of the series, either in the long run or the short run. It is therefore often sensible to focus attention on the seasonally adjusted forecast function for the series which is

$$y^a_{T+l|T} = \tilde{y}_{T+l|T} - c_{T+l|T}, \quad l=1, 2, \ldots \tag{6.2.2}$$

Replacing $\tilde{y}_{T+l|T}$ by $y^a_{T+l|T}$ in (6.1.1) allows the desired properties of a trend to be extended to a seasonal series.

Both the dummy variable seasonal model and the trigonometric model satisfy (6.2.1). This is immediately apparent in the dummy variable case as was observed when the MMSE of the seasonal component was written down in (2.3.44). In the case of trigonometric seasonality it follows from (4.6.2) that

$$c_{T+l|T} = \sum_{j=1}^{[s/2]} (c_{jT} \cos \lambda_j l + c^*_{jT} \sin \lambda_j l), \quad l=0, 1, 2, \ldots \tag{6.2.3}$$

and from standard trigonometric identities (6.2.1) holds for the forecast function $c_{T+l|T}$. More generally, if $S(L)\gamma_t \sim MA(s-2)$, the forecast function satisfies (6.2.1). The seasonal component in the canonical decomposition of Hillmer and Tiao (1982) is such that $S(L)\gamma_t \sim MA(s-1)$ and in this case the seasonal forecast function only satisfies the property displayed by (6.2.1) for $l=2$ onwards. Similarly the seasonal components

$$S(L)\gamma_t = (1+\theta_s L^s)\omega_t \tag{6.2.4}$$

and

$$S(L)\gamma_t = (1+\theta_s L^s + \theta_{2s} L^{2s})\omega_t \tag{6.2.5}$$

where ω_t is white noise, satisfy (6.2.1) from $l=3$ onwards and $l=s+3$ onwards respectively. The rationale behind (6.2.4) and (6.2.5) is discussed in Cleveland and Tiao (1976) and Burridge and Wallis (1984).

The model

$$\gamma_t = \gamma_{t-s} + \omega_t \tag{6.2.6}$$

where ω_t is white noise is sometimes used for modelling seasonality. It is not suitable for this purpose. The forecast function repeats itself every year, but the sum of the terms over a year will not, in general, be zero. Thus the predictions of the seasonal component are confounded with the predictions of the trend. For similar reasons, it is not possible to separate out the trend and seasonal components in the sample, a matter which was discussed when the model was introduced in (4.7.19).

Introducing a parameter φ into (6.2.6) yields the stationary model

$$\gamma_t = \varphi\gamma_{t-s} + \omega_t, \quad |\varphi| < 1 \tag{6.2.7}$$

This model has a forecast function which damps down to zero as $l \to \infty$. There may be occasions where a component of this kind is useful for picking up certain seasonal effects, but these effects are transient and do not constitute a seasonal component as such. As Bell and Hillmer (1984, p. 304) argue, it would be inappropriate to attempt to remove them as part of a process of seasonal adjustment.

We now consider briefly how the notion of seasonality may be generalised. The crucial feature of a seasonal component is that it should be based on the seasonal summation operator, S(L). Thus the notion of a seasonal component might be generalised by defining it such that $S^2(L)\gamma_t$ follows an MA process. In the dummy variable seasonal model, the seasonal effects could be allowed to increase over time by adding a slope term to (2.3.43). If this slope term is denoted by $\beta_t^{(s)}$, the model becomes

$$\sum_{j=0}^{s-1} \gamma_{t-j} = \beta_{t-1}^{(s)} + \omega_t \tag{6.2.7a}$$

$$\sum_{j=0}^{s-1} \beta_{t-j}^{(s)} = \zeta_t^{(s)} \tag{6.2.7b}$$

where $\zeta_t^{(s)}$ is a white-noise disturbance term. Using the seasonal summation operator the model can be rewritten as

$$S^2(L)\gamma_t = \zeta_{t-1}^{(s)} + S(L)\omega_t \tag{6.2.8}$$

which shows that $S^2(L)\gamma_t \sim MA(s-1)$. Trigonometric seasonality can also be extended by the introduction of an additional component in a 2×1 vector, $\boldsymbol{\beta}_{jt}^{(s)}$, at each seasonal frequency. Thus if (2.3.50) is written as

$$\boldsymbol{\gamma}_{jt} = \mathbf{T}_j \boldsymbol{\gamma}_{j,t-1} + \boldsymbol{\omega}_{jt}, \quad j = 1, \ldots, [s/2] \tag{6.2.9}$$

it becomes

$$\boldsymbol{\gamma}_{jt} = \mathbf{T}_j \boldsymbol{\gamma}_{j,t-1} + \boldsymbol{\beta}_{jt}^{(s)} + \boldsymbol{\omega}_{jt} \tag{6.2.10a}$$

$$\boldsymbol{\beta}_{jt}^{(s)} = \mathbf{T}_j \boldsymbol{\beta}_{j,t-1}^{(s)} + \boldsymbol{\zeta}_{jt}^{(s)} \tag{6.2.10b}$$

where $\boldsymbol{\zeta}_{jt}^{(s)}$ contains two mutually uncorrelated white-noise disturbances with common variance. Whether models of this kind are a useful extension of the notion of seasonality remains to be seen.

There is an example of the use of a seasonal component of the form (6.2.7) in Kitagawa and Gersch (1984, p. 386). In fact, they impose the constraint that σ_ω^2 is zero, so that (6.2.8) simply has a white-noise disturbance term on the right-hand side.

6.2.2 *Model-based seasonal adjustment*

Seasonal adjustment entails the removal of the seasonal component from a series. In a structural model, the various components are defined explicitly. Given a linear model, the mechanics of seasonal adjustment are straightforward. Once the parameters have been estimated, the optimal estimator of the seasonal component can be obtained by a smoothing algorithm and subtracted from the original series to yield the seasonally adjusted series

$$y_t^a = y_t - c_{t|T}, \quad t = 1, \ldots, T \tag{6.2.11}$$

The estimated RMSE of $c_{t|T}$, and hence y_t^a, is also given by the smoother. As Hausman and Watson (1985) note, the President's Committee to Appraise Employment and Unemployment Statistics in the US recommended, as early as 1962, 'that estimates of the standard errors of seasonally adjusted data be prepared and published as soon as the technical problems have been solved'.

The seasonally adjusted figures at the end of the series will be subject to revisions as new observations become available. The nature and extent of these revisions may be investigated by setting up a fixed-point smoother. It should be noted that such revisions are inevitable if the information in the later observations is to be used to obtain optimal estimators of the seasonal effects. The question of revisions arising from the fact that the latest observations are often preliminary is a separate one, which is dealt with in sub-section 6.4.4. Suffice it to say that such revisions can be handled by a suitable extension of the model.

Seasonal adjustment can be carried out for any structural model containing a seasonal component. The usual choice will be the BSM, but the model may possibly contain a cycle or, as in Hausman and Watson (1985), an irregular component which reflects the sampling scheme. Because y_t^a is constructed by fitting a model to the series, the procedure is known as *model-based seasonal adjustment.*

The notion of model-based seasonal adjustment could be extended further by introducing explanatory variables into the model. The model for the seasonal component then becomes

$$\gamma_t^{\dagger} = \gamma_t + \gamma^* x_t \tag{6.2.12}$$

where γ_t is the standard dummy variable or trigonometric seasonality model, x_t is an observable explanatory variable and γ^* is an unknown coefficient. The most likely candidates for x_t are weather variables such as temperature or rainfall. If the x_t's are measured in terms of deviations from the average for each particular season, the estimators of the $\gamma_t^{\dagger}$'s will still satisfy the condition in (6.2.1) as the values of x_t entering into the forecast function will all be zero. Calendar effects can also be handled by means of explanatory variables as discussed in section 6.4.3.

A final aspect of model-based seasonal adjustment is that the state space form enables data irregularities, such as missing observations, to be handled. It also provides a framework for dealing with outliers.

Energy consumption The data on energy consumption by 'Other final users' was discussed in sub-section 2.7.6. There the BSM was used. A minor refinement may be introduced by supplementing the BSM by a variable, x_t, as in (6.2.12), recording the discrepancy between the temperature in each particular quarter and the average temperature for that quarter. For the data on coal consumption the coefficient on this variable was estimated as -0.0678, the minus sign being what one would expect. The estimates of the hyperparameters are not too different from those reported in sub-section 2.7.6. The seasonally adjusted series is shown in Figure 6.2.1. It is more variable than the trend shown in Figure 1.4.1 since it contains the irregular component.

For the electricity consumption series, there is an outlying observation in 1974Q1 created by the miners' strike. This suggests the model

$$y_t = \mu_t + \gamma_t + \gamma^* x_t + \delta z_t + \varepsilon_t$$

where z_t is unity in 1974Q1 and zero otherwise, and y_t is in logarithms. The results of estimating this model by the method of scoring using the data up to 1983Q4 are as follows:

$$\tilde{\sigma}_\eta^2 = \underset{(12.5\times 10^{-5})}{23.0\times 10^{-5}}, \quad \tilde{\sigma}_\zeta^2 = \underset{(0.17\times 10^{-5})}{0.16\times 10^{-5}}, \quad \tilde{\sigma}_\omega^2 = \underset{(5.0\times 10^{-5})}{15.5\times 10^{-5}}, \quad \tilde{\sigma}_\varepsilon^2 = \underset{(28.1\times 10^{-5})}{25.0\times 10^{-5}}$$

$$\text{Temperature} = \underset{(0.005)}{-0.016}, \quad \text{Miners' strike 74Q1} = \underset{(0.038)}{-0.217}$$

Again a seasonally adjusted series can be constructed by removing the stochastic seasonal component and the temperature effect.

Model-based seasonal adjustment can also be carried out by fitting a seasonal ARIMA model to the series and then decomposing it into trend, seasonal and irregular components. This is the approach adopted by Burman (1980) and

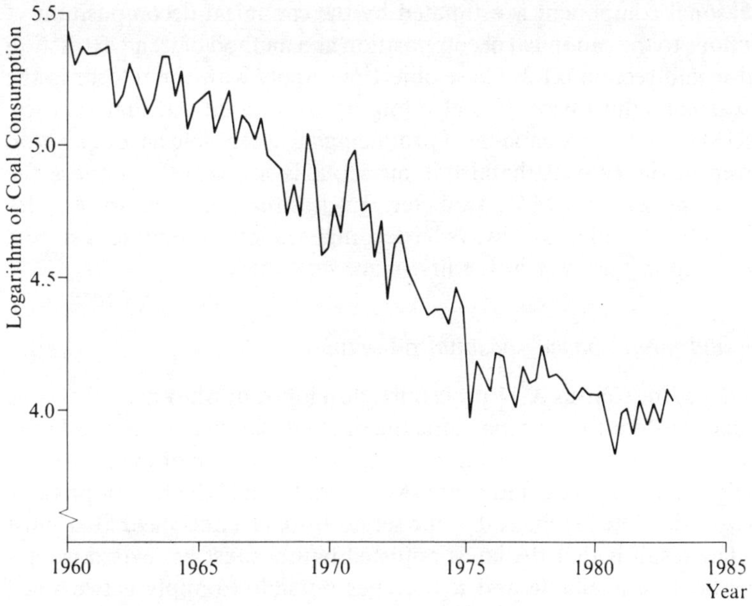

Fig. 6.2.1 Seasonally adjusted UK coal consumption.

Hillmer and Tiao (1982). Hillmer and Tiao (1982) examine three models which give rise to what they call 'an acceptable decomposition'. The most important of these is the airline model, (2.5.16), where the decomposition is such that

$$\begin{aligned} \Delta^2 \mu_t &\sim \mathrm{MA}(2) \\ S(L)\gamma_t &\sim \mathrm{MA}(s-1) \end{aligned} \tag{6.2.13}$$

while the irregular component is white noise. Without further restrictions the components would not be identifiable. This problem is solved by means of the canonical decomposition whereby the variance of the irregular component is maximised. The mechanics of the canonical decomposition were described for a simple case in sub-section 6.1.2; for a seasonal model the technical details are considerably more complex.

The decomposition obtained from the airline model is very similar to the UCARIMA form of the BSM. The difference is that, in the BSM, the orders of the MA components for $\Delta^2 \mu_t$ and $S(L)\gamma_t$ are one less than in (6.2.13), that is they are one and $s-1$ repectively. It was shown in sub-section 2.5.5 that the BSM and airline models can be applied to much the same kind of series. If both models are fitted to such a series it follows from the discussion in sub-section 6.1.2 that the trend extracted by the canonical decomposition will be smoother than the trend estimated for the BSM. The same is true for the seasonal component. A corollary to this is that the seasonally adjusted series will be correspondingly less smooth when the seasonal component is estimated by the canonical decomposition.

The objections to the canonical decomposition as a method of trend extraction were set out in sub-section 6.1.2. These objections apply with equal force in the context of seasonal adjustment. It is also important to point out that very few seasonal ARIMA models are capable of producing an acceptable decomposition and that, even in the case of the airline model, it is necessary to impose the restriction that the seasonal MA parameter Θ is less than or equal to zero. By contrast, a structural model can always be decomposed into components since it is explicitly set up in that way in the first place.

6.2.3 X-11 and model-based seasonal adjustment

The US Bureau of the Census X-11 procedure, developed by Shiskin *et al.* (1967), has been widely used for the seasonal adjustment of official time series. It is based on a series of filters and is a somewhat more elaborate version of the procedure described below (2.2.26). These filters are two-sided, but it is clearly not possible to apply a two-sided filter at the end of the series. Instead a one-sided filter must be applied. The result is that the latest adjusted figures must be revised as new observations become available and it becomes possible to apply a two-sided filter. Dagum (1975) suggested that a more satisfactory approach would be to fit an ARIMA model to the series, forecast future values of the series and then seasonally adjust the whole series, actual and predicted, by X-11. In this way the latest observations are actually adjusted by a two-sided filter. Revisions are still necessary as observations come in to replace the predicted values, but they should be smaller than before. This modified version of X-11 is known as X-11-ARIMA.

The basic drawback of X-11 is its inflexibility. Although there is some scope for adjustment, the same procedure is essentially applied irrespective of the properties of the series. This can lead to the adjusted series having very undesirable properties, something which has now been well documented; see Pierce (1978) and Hausman and Watson (1985).

A model-based seasonal adjustment procedure is tailor-made to a particular series. As noted in the previous section, the model specification may not be the same for all series. Furthermore, for a particular specification, such as the BSM, there is the additional flexibility deriving from the estimation of the model hyperparameters. Once these parameters have been estimated, the Kalman filter and smoother produce the optimal estimates of the trend and seasonal components. There is no need to consider some modification based on forecasting future observations as in X-11-ARIMA. Revisions will still be needed as new observations become available, but, as pointed out in the previous sub-section, such revisions are inevitable if full use is to be made of the information in the new observations.

The theoretical argument in favour of model-based seasonal adjustment is very strong. However, since X-11 has been found to perform reasonably well for many

Table 6.2.1 *Autocorrelation function of* BSM *and autocorrelation function implied by X-11*

τ	X-11	BSM
1	−0.061	−0.065
2	0.266	0.260
3	0.226	0.225
4	0.201	0.200
5	0.175	0.175
6	0.150	0.150
7	0.125	0.125
8	0.100	0.100
9	0.075	0.075
10	0.046	0.050
11	0.178	0.175
12	−0.326	−0.320
13	0.153	0.150
14	−0.004	0

series, it is important to determine whether the BSM is applicable to such series. This question is addressed in Maravall (1985). If y_t denotes a monthly series for which X-11 is appropriate, Cleveland (1972) has shown that the a.c.f. of $\Delta\Delta_{12}\, y_t$ is as shown in the X-11 column of Table 6.2.1. It can be seen that all the constraints in (2.4.35), the a.c.f. of the dummy variable BSM, are satisfied. In particular, setting

$$q_\eta = 0.133, \quad q_\zeta = 0.167 \quad \text{and} \quad q_\omega = 0.067 \tag{6.2.14}$$

gives the a.c.f. in the last column of Table 6.2.1. The two a.c.f.'s are practically identical. Thus the BSM can certainly be fitted to series for which X-11 is appropriate. On the other hand, an examination of the estimated parameters in the BSM fitted to, say, the car drivers KSI series in sub-section 2.7.1, shows them to be some way removed from the values in (6.2.14). For real series, σ_ζ^2 is usually dominated by σ_η^2 while σ_η^2 is often of a similar size, or larger, than σ_ε^2. The seasonal variance, σ_ω^2, is often close to zero; see Pierce (1978). The trend and seasonal components extracted from a BSM with hyperparameters set as in (6.2.14) will therefore typically be smoother than if the parameters had been estimated.

A second issue considered by Maravall (1985) is the nature of the X-11 and BSM decompositions for series in which X-11 is appropriate. Cleveland (1972) has shown that the following unobserved components model yields a decomposition corresponding to the one given by X-11:

$$y_t = \frac{1+0.26L+0.30L^2-0.32L^3}{\Delta^2}\xi_{1t} + \frac{1+0.26L^{12}}{S(L)}\xi_{2t} + \xi_{0t} \tag{6.2.15}$$

where ξ_{1t}, ξ_{2t} and ξ_{0t} are independent white-noise disturbances with

$$\mathrm{Var}(\xi_{1t})/\mathrm{Var}(\xi_{0t})=0.099 \quad \text{and} \quad \mathrm{Var}(\xi_{2t})/\mathrm{Var}(\xi_{0t})=0.030 \tag{6.2.16}$$

It follows that $\mathrm{Var}(\Delta\Delta_{12}y_t)=6.067\ \mathrm{Var}(\xi_{0t})$. In the case of the BSM with relative hyperparameters given by (6.2.14), $\mathrm{Var}(\Delta\Delta_{12}y_t)=6.667\ \sigma_\varepsilon^2$. The net result is that the variance of the X-11 irregular component is approximately 10% greater than that of the BSM. The implicit model underlying X-11 is therefore quite similar to the UCARIMA form of the BSM. The only difference is the additional MA terms in (6.2.15) which result in some additional smoothing for the trend and seasonal components and a corresponding increase in the variance of the irregular component.

For most series, therefore, X-11 will tend to produce a smoother trend component than the BSM. This arises both because of the implied parameter values in the underlying reduced form and because of the decomposition given by X-11 for such a reduced form. Nevertheless, there are occasions when the BSM will give a smoother trend and it follows from the discussion at the end of sub-section 6.1.1, that one such case is when σ_η^2 is found to be small relative to σ_ζ^2.

6.2.4 *Why seasonally adjust anyway?*

Although the pattern of seasonal effects may change slowly over time, seasonality is basically a repetitive feature of a time series. This emerges explicitly in the seasonal forecast function and there is an obvious rationale for looking at a forecast function for the series with the seasonal effects removed, as in (6.2.2). By a similar token, it could be argued that it is useful to look at a series in order to gain some idea of its history and that, if this is to be done, it is helpful to abstract from its seasonal movements; hence the need for seasonal adjustment.

Why would one want to look at a seasonally adjusted series apart from historical interest? One reason is the desire to extrapolate. However, if a series has been seasonally adjusted by fitting a model to it, this becomes pointless since optimal predictions can be made directly from the model. Indeed, in a structural model all the information needed to make predictions is explicitly available in the final estimated state vector. Thus the ability to carry out model-based seasonal adjustment effectively removes one of the main reasons for wishing to seasonally adjust in the first place!

There is perhaps some case to be made for working with a seasonally adjusted series at the model formulation stage. The use of a relatively robust procedure, such as X-11, may be helpful in enabling one to identify non-seasonal movements. For example, the seasonally adjusted series may give a clearer indication as to whether a trend is subject to a saturation level, in which case a damped trend might be fitted in preference to the usual local linear trend. It may sometimes be of assistance in detecting breaks and structural changes, though there is also the possibility that it could obscure such irregularities.

The production of seasonally adjusted series is standard practice for government agencies. While adjusted series may be marginally easier for the casual user to interpret, it has to be recognised that the original series has been distorted in what is often a rather arbitrary way. There are usually better and more direct ways of providing the information which the user actually requires. Certainly the idea that a seasonally adjusted series should be published *instead of* the original series is open to very serious criticism.

6.3 Different timing intervals for the model and observations

Time series models are usually formulated for a timing interval which corresponds to the time between observations. Such an approach is not always satisfactory since there may be good reasons for setting up the model in terms of a finer timing interval. For example, suppose a series is generated by a random walk process at a timing interval of one month. If observations are made quarterly on the sum of the monthly variables over the quarter, then it can be shown that the first-order autocorrelation for the first differences of the quarterly observations is 0.21 rather than zero. Thus a rejection of the random walk hypothesis at the quarterly level does not imply rejection of the same hypothesis at the monthly level. This point was originally made by Working (1960).

This section examines the statistical implications of formulating models at a timing interval which is shorter than the observation interval. The statistical problems considered are:
(a) time-domain estimation of the model parameters by maximum likelihood;
(b) estimation of the unobserved components at the observation points and at intermediate points;
(c) estimation of what the observations themselves would have been at intermediate points;
(d) prediction of future observations.

Estimation at points between observations will be termed *interpolation* for a stock variable and *distribution* for a flow. This distinction between stocks and flows is important. Stocks are variables such as interest rates or temperature which can be measured at a particular point in time, while flows are variables such as income which are defined with respect to an interval of time. The issues raised by flow variables tend to be more complex.

Results are derived for a fairly general linear time series model. This model includes ARIMA processes, as well as structural models, as special cases. However, ARIMA model specification is rather difficult in the absence of any available observations at the model timing interval. This problem is less severe with structural models because their form is more dependent on prior considerations. Furthermore, for stock variables, the forms of the principal structural components turn out to be invariant to the observation interval. This is not, in general, true for ARIMA models, as shown, for example, in Brewer (1973),

Nijman (1985) and Stram and Wei (1986). This invariance of specification with respect to the frequency with which the variable is measured is an attractive property of the structural class.

A continuous time model can be regarded as a limiting case of the set-up proposed in this section. A full discussion of continuous time models can be found in chapter 9.

6.3.1 General form of the model

The model considered is a general linear time-invariant specification of the kind adopted in (4.1.3), that is

$$y_t^{\dagger} = \mathbf{z}'\boldsymbol{\alpha}_t + \varepsilon_t, \quad \mathrm{Var}(\varepsilon_t) = \sigma_\varepsilon^2 \tag{6.3.1a}$$

$$\boldsymbol{\alpha}_t = \mathbf{T}\boldsymbol{\alpha}_{t-1} + \mathbf{R}\boldsymbol{\eta}_t, \quad \mathrm{Var}(\boldsymbol{\eta}_t) = \mathbf{Q} \tag{6.3.1b}$$

A 'dagger' has been added to y_t in order to make the point that the series is not necessarily observed at all the points in time $t = 1, 2, 3, \ldots$. Instead, observations denoted as $y_\tau, \tau = 1, \ldots, T$, are available every δ time periods, where δ is a positive integer. For a stock variable this means that

$$y_\tau = y_{\delta\tau}^{\dagger}, \quad \tau = 1, \ldots, T \tag{6.3.2}$$

while for values of $t \neq \delta\tau$, $y_t^{\dagger}$ is unobservable. For a flow variable the observations consist of the temporal aggregates

$$y_\tau = \sum_{r=0}^{\delta-1} y_{\delta\tau-r}^{\dagger}, \quad \tau = 1, \ldots, T \tag{6.3.3}$$

Sometimes for a stock variable the average over the period is recorded. An example would be a monthly price index which is averaged over the year when the annual figure is given. In such cases

$$y_\tau = (1/\delta) \sum_{r=0}^{\delta-1} y_{\delta\tau-r}^{\dagger}, \quad \tau = 1, \ldots, T \tag{6.3.4}$$

A variable measured in this way is known as a *time-averaged stock*. From the statistical point of view it is handled as though it were a flow.

In order to handle situations where the observation timing interval is greater than the model timing interval, a suitable state space form must be constructed. If the state space form is set up for the unit time interval, i.e. indexed $t = 1, \ldots, \delta T$, it will be referred to as SSF(t, 1). If, on the other hand, it is set up for the observation timing interval and indexed $\tau = 1, \ldots, T$ it will be denoted by SSF(τ, δ). Both forms can be used to estimate the hyperparameters. However, for interpolation and distribution, it is SSF(t, 1) which is appropriate. On some occasions it may be required to interpolate on some other interval, Δ, which is also an integer and is such that δ/Δ is also an integer. The index in this case will be $i = 1, \ldots, (\delta/\Delta)T$ and the state space form will be written as SSF(i, Δ).

The transition equations for both SSF(τ, δ) and SSF(i, Δ) are obtained by substituting repeatedly for lagged values of the state vector in (6.3.1b). In the case of SSF(τ, δ) this yields

$$\boldsymbol{\alpha}_{\delta\tau} = \mathbf{T}^{\delta}\boldsymbol{\alpha}_{\delta(\tau-1)} + \sum_{s=1}^{\delta} \mathbf{T}^{\delta-s}\mathbf{R}\boldsymbol{\eta}_{\delta(\tau-1)+s}, \quad t = \delta\tau, \quad \tau = 1, \ldots, T \tag{6.3.5}$$

Redefining the index on the state vector by dividing by δ gives a transition equation at a timing of δ namely

$$\boldsymbol{\alpha}_{\tau} = \mathbf{T}^{\delta}\boldsymbol{\alpha}_{\tau-1} + \bar{\boldsymbol{\eta}}_{\tau} \tag{6.3.6}$$

with

$$\text{Var}(\bar{\boldsymbol{\eta}}_{\tau}) = \sum_{s=1}^{\delta} \mathbf{T}^{\delta-s}\mathbf{RQR}'(\mathbf{T}')^{\delta-s} \tag{6.3.7}$$

6.3.2 Stock variables

If the series, $y_t^{\dagger}$, generated by (6.3.1) is a stock variable observed every δ time periods as in (6.3.2), SSF(t, 1) consists of (6.3.1b) together with a measurement equation which takes the form of (6.3.1a), but which is only regarded as being defined at $t = \delta\tau$, $\tau = 1, \ldots, T$. The Kalman filter for such a state space model can be run straightforwardly, simply by skipping the updating equations at the intermediate times. The only point to note is that if some of the components in the model relate to a time period shorter than δ, they may effectively become redundant due to aliasing. The model as a whole does not then satisfy the observability condition, (3.3.5), although it can always be made to do so by dropping the redundant components. This question is examined further during the discussion on seasonal models which follows later in this section.

As regards SSF(τ, δ), the transition equation is as given in (6.3.6). The corresponding measurement equation is

$$y_{\tau} = \mathbf{z}'\boldsymbol{\alpha}_{\tau} + \varepsilon_{\tau}, \quad \tau = 1, \ldots, T \tag{6.3.8}$$

where $\text{Var}(\varepsilon_{\tau}) = \sigma_{\varepsilon}^2$, since ε_{τ} is equal to the original measurement equation disturbance, $\varepsilon_{\delta\tau}$, $\tau = 1, \ldots, T$ appearing in (6.3.1). The likelihood function for the observations $y_1, \ldots, y_T$ can be constructed by running the Kalman filter for SSF(t, 1) or SSF(τ, δ). If the state vector contains d_{τ} observable non-stationary components and these are regarded as having an initial diffuse prior, the likelihood function is formed from the prediction errors at time $\tau = d_{\tau} + 1, \ldots, T$, for SSF($\tau, \delta$) or equivalently from those at $t = \delta(d_{\tau} + 1), \ldots, \delta T$ for SSF(t, 1).

Interpolation is straightforward using a fixed-interval smoother applied to SSF(t, 1). The estimators of the intermediate observations are given by

$$\tilde{y}_{t|\delta T}^{\dagger} = \mathbf{z}'\mathbf{a}_{t|\delta T}, \quad t \neq \delta\tau, \quad \tau = 1, \ldots, T \tag{6.3.9}$$

where $\mathbf{a}_{t|\delta T}$ denotes the smoothed estimator of the state vector based on the information at time $t=\delta T$. Since $\mathbf{a}_{t|\delta T}$ is independent of ε_t when the corresponding $y_t^\dagger$ is not observed,

$$\text{MSE}(\tilde{y}_{t|\delta T}^\dagger)=\text{MSE}(\mathbf{z}'\mathbf{a}_{t|\delta t})+\sigma_\varepsilon^2 \tag{6.3.10}$$

Interpolation on another interval, Δ, is trivial for a stock variable. The required estimates can simply be obtained from the smoother applied to SSF$(t, 1)$. Alternatively SSF(i, Δ) can be constructed as in (6.3.5) with δ and τ replaced by Δ and i respectively, and the measurement equation defined only at $i=(\delta/\Delta)\tau$, $\tau=1,\ldots, T$.

What are the implications of the above discussion for structural models? Since a structural model is usually separable into independent components as in (4.1.4), the form of SSF(τ, δ) – and hence the form of the model at the observation timing interval – can be built up component by component.

Trend For the trend component, (4.1.6), repeated substitution, as in (6.3.5), gives:

$$\begin{bmatrix}\mu_{\delta\tau}\\ \beta_{\delta\tau}\end{bmatrix}=\begin{bmatrix}1 & \delta\\ 0 & 1\end{bmatrix}\begin{bmatrix}\mu_{\delta(\tau-1)}\\ \beta_{\delta(\tau-1)}\end{bmatrix}+\sum_{s=1}^{\delta}\begin{bmatrix}1 & \delta-s\\ 0 & 1\end{bmatrix}\begin{bmatrix}\eta_{\delta(\tau-1)+s}\\ \zeta_{\delta(\tau-1)+s}\end{bmatrix} \tag{6.3.11}$$

Converting this equation to a timing interval of δ then yields

$$\begin{bmatrix}\mu_\tau\\ \beta_\tau\end{bmatrix}=\begin{bmatrix}1 & \delta\\ 0 & 1\end{bmatrix}\begin{bmatrix}\mu_{\tau-1}\\ \beta_{\tau-1}\end{bmatrix}+\begin{bmatrix}\bar{\eta}_\tau\\ \bar{\zeta}_\tau\end{bmatrix}, \quad \tau=1, 2,\ldots \tag{6.3.12a}$$

where

$$\text{Var}\begin{bmatrix}\bar{\eta}_\tau\\ \bar{\zeta}_\tau\end{bmatrix}=\sum_{j=0}^{\delta-1}\begin{bmatrix}1 & j\\ 0 & 1\end{bmatrix}\begin{bmatrix}\sigma_\eta^2 & 0\\ 0 & \sigma_\zeta^2\end{bmatrix}\begin{bmatrix}1 & 0\\ j & 1\end{bmatrix}$$

$$=\delta\begin{bmatrix}\sigma_\eta^2+\frac{1}{6}(\delta-1)(2\delta-1)\sigma_\zeta^2 & \frac{1}{2}(\delta-1)\sigma_\zeta^2\\ \frac{1}{2}(\delta-1)\sigma_\zeta^2 & \sigma_\zeta^2\end{bmatrix} \tag{6.3.12b}$$

Although the covariance matrix in (6.3.12b) is not diagonal, this has no important implications for the dynamic properties of the model. Hence the trend model is essentially invariant to a change in the timing interval.

Cycle Converting the cycle, (2.3.38), to a timing interval of δ yields a model of exactly the same form provided that κ_t and κ_t^* are uncorrelated with each other and have a common variance, σ_κ^2. In terms of the original parameters, the new damping factor and frequency are equal to ρ^δ and $\lambda_c\delta$ respectively. The covariance matrix of the disturbances is equal to $\sigma_\kappa^2[1+\rho^2+\cdots+\rho^{2(\delta-1)}]I_2$. All this assumes that $\delta\lambda_c\leqslant\pi$ so that the cycle is observable.

Seasonal Since each of the $[s/2]$ trigonometric seasonal components is just a cycle with ρ equal to unity, the frequencies become $\delta\lambda_j$ while $\text{Var}(\bar{\omega}_{j\tau})=\delta\sigma_j^2$. If the seasonal component is formulated at the unit interval with a full complement of trigonometric components, those components at a frequency of $\delta\lambda_j > \pi$ will not be observable when the observations are at an interval of δ. They are therefore redundant and their effects are incorporated either within the level term, μ_τ, or the trigonometric components which remain. This can be illustrated by considering a monthly model which is observed at quarterly intervals. The frequencies in the monthly model are $\lambda_j = 2\pi j/12$, $j=1,\ldots,6$, but when observed every quarter these become $\lambda_j^* = 3\lambda_j = 6\pi j/12$, $j=1,\ldots,6$. Only the first two of these frequencies are observable. As regards the others, consider first $j=3$, corresponding to the frequency $\lambda_3^* = 3\pi/2 = \lambda_1^* + \pi$. Since $\cos(\lambda_1^* + \pi) = \cos\lambda_1^*$ and $\sin(\lambda_1^* + \pi) = -\sin\lambda_1^*$, all that happens is that the cyclical component at λ_3^* is included in the component at λ_1^*; the disturbance terms associated with λ_3^* are simply added to those associated with λ_1^* and the variance of the latter is correspondingly increased. Taking λ_4^* next, we have $\cos 2\pi = 1$ and $\sin 2\pi = 0$. Hence the variance of the disturbances is added on to the level component in the trend since the trigonometric component at λ_4^* has become

$$\gamma_{4,\tau}^* = \gamma_{4,\tau-1}^* + \bar{\omega}_{4,\tau}, \quad \text{Var}(\bar{\omega}_{4,\tau}) = \delta\sigma_4^2$$

The components corresponding to frequencies at $j=5$ and 6 become part of the components at λ_1^* and λ_2^* respectively. As this example illustrates, if the variances in the trigonometric seasonal components are all the same at one timing interval, they are not necessarily the same at a coarser timing interval.

Taking all the above results together it follows that the form of an additive structural model remains unchanged when observations are made at a multiple of the original model timing interval. This property is an important one. The relationship between the parameters does, however, change. For example in the simplest case of a random walk plus noise, $\text{Var}(\eta_\tau) = \delta\sigma_\eta^2$ while $\text{Var}(\varepsilon_\tau) = \sigma_\varepsilon^2$ and so the signal–noise ratio in the model at a timing interval of τ is δ times what it is in the original model.

6.3.3 *Flow variables*

State space models for handling a flow variable subject to temporal aggregation can be constructed by defining the cumulator variable

$$y_{\delta(\tau-1)+r}^f = \sum_{s=1}^{r} y_{\delta(\tau-1)+s}^\dagger, \quad \tau=1,\ldots,T, \quad r=1,\ldots,\delta \tag{6.3.13}$$

Substituting from model (6.3.1) then gives

$$\begin{aligned} y_t^f &= \psi_t y_{t-1}^f + \mathbf{z}'\boldsymbol{\alpha}_t + \varepsilon_t \\ &= \psi_t y_{t-1}^f + \mathbf{z}'\mathbf{T}\boldsymbol{\alpha}_{t-1} + \mathbf{z}'\mathbf{R}\boldsymbol{\eta}_t + \varepsilon_t \end{aligned} \tag{6.3.14}$$

with the indicator variable, ψ_t, defined as

$$\psi_t = \begin{cases} 0, & t=\delta(\tau-1)+1, \quad \tau=1,\ldots,T \\ 1, & \text{otherwise} \end{cases} \tag{6.3.15}$$

The cumulator variable, y_t^f, is used to augment the state vector to give the transition equation for SSF$(t, 1)$ as

$$\begin{bmatrix} \boldsymbol{\alpha}_t \\ y_t^f \end{bmatrix} = \begin{bmatrix} \mathbf{T} & \mathbf{0} \\ \mathbf{z}'\mathbf{T} & \psi_t \end{bmatrix} \begin{bmatrix} \boldsymbol{\alpha}_{t-1} \\ y_{t-1}^f \end{bmatrix} + \begin{bmatrix} \mathbf{R} & \mathbf{0} \\ \mathbf{z}'\mathbf{R} & 1 \end{bmatrix} \begin{bmatrix} \boldsymbol{\eta}_t \\ \varepsilon_t \end{bmatrix} \tag{6.3.16a}$$

while the measurement equation is

$$y_\tau = [\mathbf{0}' \quad 1] \begin{bmatrix} \boldsymbol{\alpha}_t \\ y_t^f \end{bmatrix}, \quad t=\delta\tau, \quad \tau=1,\ldots,T \tag{6.3.16b}$$

No starting-value problems are posed by the introduction of y_t^f into the state vector since

$$y_0^f \equiv 0$$

In order to construct SSF(τ, δ), repeated substitution is carried out in the state vector so that it can be written as

$$\boldsymbol{\alpha}_{\delta(\tau-1)+r} = \mathbf{T}^r \boldsymbol{\alpha}_{\delta(\tau-1)} + \sum_{s=1}^{r} \mathbf{T}^{r-s} \mathbf{R} \boldsymbol{\eta}_{\delta(\tau-1)+s}, \quad \tau=1,\ldots,T, \quad r=1,\ldots,\delta \tag{6.3.17}$$

The cumulator variable is therefore

$$\begin{aligned} y_{\delta\tau}^f &= \sum_{r=1}^{\delta} \mathbf{z}'\boldsymbol{\alpha}_{\delta(\tau-1)+r} + \sum_{r=1}^{\delta} \varepsilon_{\delta(\tau-1)+r} \\ &= \mathbf{z}'\left[\sum_{r=1}^{\delta} \mathbf{T}^r\right] \boldsymbol{\alpha}_{\delta(\tau-1)} + \mathbf{z}' \sum_{r=1}^{\delta} \sum_{s=1}^{r} \mathbf{T}^{r-s} \mathbf{R} \boldsymbol{\eta}_{\delta(\tau-1)+s} + \sum_{r=1}^{\delta} \varepsilon_{\delta(\tau-1)+r} \\ &= \mathbf{z}'(\mathbf{W}_\delta - \mathbf{I}) \boldsymbol{\alpha}_{\delta(\tau-1)} + \mathbf{z}' \sum_{r=1}^{\delta} \mathbf{W}_{\delta-r} \mathbf{R} \boldsymbol{\eta}_{\delta(\tau-1)+r} + \sum_{r=1}^{\delta} \varepsilon_{\delta(\tau-1)+r}, \\ &\qquad \tau=1,\ldots,T, \end{aligned} \tag{6.3.18}$$

where

$$\mathbf{W}_r = \sum_{s=0}^{r} \mathbf{T}^s, \quad r=0, 1, 2, \ldots; \tag{6.3.19}$$

see (4.6.18). Redefining the index on the state vector and the cumulator variable and noting that the latter gives the observations, the augmented state space form, SSF(τ, δ), is

$$\begin{bmatrix} \boldsymbol{\alpha}_\tau \\ y_\tau \end{bmatrix} = \begin{bmatrix} \mathbf{T}^\delta & \mathbf{0} \\ \mathbf{z}'(\mathbf{W}_\delta - \mathbf{I}) & 0 \end{bmatrix} \begin{bmatrix} \boldsymbol{\alpha}_{\tau-1} \\ y_{\tau-1} \end{bmatrix} + \begin{bmatrix} \mathbf{I} & \mathbf{0} \\ \mathbf{0}' & \mathbf{z}' \end{bmatrix} \begin{bmatrix} \bar{\boldsymbol{\eta}}_\tau \\ \bar{\boldsymbol{\eta}}_\tau^f \end{bmatrix} + \begin{bmatrix} 0 \\ \varepsilon_\tau^f \end{bmatrix} \tag{6.3.20a}$$

and

$$y_\tau = [\mathbf{0}' \quad 1]\begin{bmatrix} \boldsymbol{\alpha}_\tau \\ y_\tau \end{bmatrix}, \quad \tau = 1, \ldots, T \tag{6.3.20b}$$

where

$$\varepsilon_\tau^f = \sum_{r=1}^{\delta} \varepsilon_{\delta(\tau-1)+r} \tag{6.3.20c}$$

has variance $\delta\sigma_\varepsilon^2$, and

$$\operatorname{Var}\begin{bmatrix} \bar{\boldsymbol{\eta}}_\tau \\ \bar{\eta}_\tau^f \end{bmatrix} = \sum_{s=0}^{\delta-1} \begin{bmatrix} \mathbf{T}^s\mathbf{R}\mathbf{Q}\mathbf{R}'\mathbf{T}^{s\prime} & \mathbf{T}^s\mathbf{R}\mathbf{Q}\mathbf{R}'\mathbf{W}_s' \\ \mathbf{W}_s\mathbf{R}\mathbf{Q}\mathbf{R}'\mathbf{T}^{s\prime} & \mathbf{W}_s\mathbf{R}\mathbf{Q}\mathbf{R}'\mathbf{W}_s' \end{bmatrix} \tag{6.3.20d}$$

Although ε_τ^f could be put in the measurement equation rather than the transition equation, it is necessary to place it in the transition equation when more complex situations are to be handled.

It is worth remarking that while the SSF for a stock variable observed every δ periods is of the same dimension as the SSF of the underlying data generation process, (6.3.1), the dimension of the state vector required to handle a temporally aggregated series is increased by one. There is a parallel here with known results for an ARMA model; see Brewer (1973). If a stock variable ARMA($p, p-1$) process is observed every $\delta > 1$ periods it remains an ARMA($p, p-1$) process. If, however, it is a flow, it becomes ARMA(p, p) and the dimension of the state vector in a state space representation would need to be increased by one.

Maximum likelihood estimation of the hyperparameters proceeds almost exactly as in the stock case using either SSF(t, 1) or SSF(τ, δ). Similarly, smoothed estimators of the elements of $\boldsymbol{\alpha}_t$ can be computed using SSF(t, 1). However, two points need to be noted. First, if σ_ε^2 is equal to zero, the covariance matrix of the estimator of the complete state vector, $[\boldsymbol{\alpha}_t' \quad y_t^f]'$, at times $t = \delta(\tau-1)+1$, $\tau = 1, \ldots, T$, made in the previous time period will be singular. Some modification therefore needs to be made to the fixed-interval smoother. Two (equivalent) possibilities are open: either y_t^f can be removed from the state vector at times $t = \delta(\tau-1)+1$, $\tau = 1, \ldots, T$ or a generalised inverse can be used to handle the singular covariance matrix as in Kohn and Ansley (1983). The second point to be noted is that although estimators of $y_t^\dagger$ can be obtained from the estimators of y_t^f, i.e.

$$\tilde{y}_{t|\delta T}^\dagger = \begin{cases} \tilde{y}_{t|\delta T}^f - \tilde{y}_{t-1|\delta T}^f, & t \neq \delta(\tau-1)+1, \quad \tau = 1, \ldots, T \\ \tilde{y}_{t|\delta T}^f, & t = \delta(\tau-1)+1, \quad \tau = 1, \ldots, T \end{cases} \tag{6.3.21}$$

their MSEs are not immediately available. Computation of these MSEs requires the addition of $y_t^\dagger$ itself to the state vector and the augmentation of the transition equation by

$$y_t^\dagger = \mathbf{z}'\mathbf{T}\boldsymbol{\alpha}_{t-1} + \mathbf{z}'\mathbf{R}\boldsymbol{\eta}_t + \varepsilon_t, \quad t=1,\ldots,\delta T \tag{6.3.22}$$

Note that the estimators of the $y_t^\dagger$'s will satisfy the constraint implied by (6.3.3), that is

$$y_\tau = \sum_{r=0}^{\delta-1} \tilde{y}^\dagger_{(\delta\tau-r)|\delta T}, \quad \tau=1,\ldots,T \tag{6.3.23}$$

This property is not shared by the quantities $\mathbf{z}'\mathbf{a}_{t|\delta T}$, $t=1,\ldots,T$, except when σ_ε^2 is zero. This is why $\tilde{y}^\dagger_{t|\delta T}$ cannot, in general, be computed from an expression of the form (6.3.9) as in the stock case.

Suppose that estimators of m^* linear combinations of the state vector are required at the intermediate points Δ time periods apart. Let $\mathbf{Z}$ be an $m^* \times m$ matrix which forms these combinations from $\boldsymbol{\alpha}_t$. Then what is required is

$$\boldsymbol{\alpha}^f_{\Delta i} = \sum_{s=1}^{\delta} \mathbf{Z}\boldsymbol{\alpha}_\Delta(i-1)+s, \quad i=1,2,\ldots,(\delta/\Delta)T \tag{6.3.24}$$

Estimators of these quantities can clearly be formed from the smoothed estimates obtained from SSF$(t,1)$. However, if MSEs are needed, $\boldsymbol{\alpha}_t^f$ must be added explicitly to the state vector. This leads to a modified form of SSF$(t,1)$ with a transition eq::ation given by

$$\begin{bmatrix}\boldsymbol{\alpha}_t\\ y_t^f\\ \boldsymbol{\alpha}_t^f\end{bmatrix} = \begin{bmatrix}\mathbf{T} & \mathbf{0} & \mathbf{0}\\ \mathbf{z}'\mathbf{T} & \psi_t & \mathbf{0}\\ \mathbf{ZT} & \mathbf{0} & \psi_t^*\mathbf{I}\end{bmatrix}\begin{bmatrix}\boldsymbol{\alpha}_{t-1}\\ y_{t-1}^f\\ \boldsymbol{\alpha}_{t-1}^f\end{bmatrix} + \begin{bmatrix}\mathbf{R} & \mathbf{0}\\ \mathbf{z}'\mathbf{R} & 1\\ \mathbf{ZR} & \mathbf{0}\end{bmatrix}\begin{bmatrix}\boldsymbol{\eta}_t\\ \varepsilon_t\end{bmatrix}, \quad t=1,\ldots,\delta T \tag{6.3.25}$$

where ψ_t is as defined in (6.3.15) while

$$\psi_t^* = \begin{Bmatrix}0, & t=\Delta(i-1)+1, \quad i=1,\ldots,(\delta/\Delta)T\\ 1, & \text{otherwise}\end{Bmatrix} \tag{6.3.26}$$

The calculations can also be based on SSF(i,Δ). The construction of SSF(i,Δ) is relatively straightforward given the techniques already developed for forming SSF(τ,δ). The form of SSF(i,Δ) is, in fact, directly analogous to the SSF(i,Δ) derived from the continuous time flow model in section 9.3.

Finally, optimal predictions of future observations and of future elements of the state vector can be computed in the usual way by applying the Kalman filter prediction equations without the updating equations. Either SSF$(t,1)$ or SSF(τ,δ) can be used. In the former case the indicator variable, ψ_t of (6.3.15), must be set equal to zero at $t=T+\delta(l-1)+1$ for $l=1,2,3,\ldots$.

Example 6.3.1 The random walk plus noise model

$$y_t^\dagger = \mu_t + \varepsilon_t, \quad \text{Var}(\varepsilon_t) = \sigma_\varepsilon^2 \tag{6.3.27a}$$

$$\mu_t = \mu_{t-1} + \eta_t, \quad \text{Var}(\eta_t) = \sigma_\eta^2 \tag{6.3.27b}$$

can be used to illustrate some of the points made in this sub-section. Thus SSF(τ, δ) is

$$y_\tau = [0 \quad 1] \begin{bmatrix} \mu_\tau \\ y_\tau \end{bmatrix} \tag{6.3.28a}$$

$$\begin{bmatrix} \mu_\tau \\ y_\tau \end{bmatrix} = \begin{bmatrix} 1 & 0 \\ \delta & 0 \end{bmatrix} \begin{bmatrix} \mu_{\tau-1} \\ y_{\tau-1} \end{bmatrix} + \begin{bmatrix} \bar{\eta}_\tau \\ \bar{\eta}_\tau^f \end{bmatrix} + \begin{bmatrix} 0 \\ \varepsilon_\tau^f \end{bmatrix} \tag{6.3.28b}$$

with $\text{Var}(\varepsilon_\tau^f) = \delta\sigma_\varepsilon^2$ and

$$\text{Var}\begin{bmatrix} \bar{\eta}_\tau \\ \bar{\eta}_\tau^f \end{bmatrix} = \sigma_\eta^2 \delta \begin{bmatrix} 1 & \frac{1}{2}(\delta+1) \\ \frac{1}{2}(\delta+1) & \frac{1}{6}(\delta+1)(2\delta+1) \end{bmatrix} \tag{6.3.28c}$$

The disturbance term ε_τ^f can alternatively be put in the measurement equation rather than the transition equation.

Estimators of μ_t and $y_t^\dagger$ can be computed from SSF(t, 1). If the MSE of the estimators of $y_t^\dagger$ is needed, SSF(t, 1) must be further augmented to give

$$\begin{bmatrix} \mu_t \\ y_t^f \\ y_t^\dagger \end{bmatrix} = \begin{bmatrix} 1 & 0 & 0 \\ 1 & \psi_t & 0 \\ 1 & 0 & 0 \end{bmatrix} \begin{bmatrix} \mu_{t-1} \\ y_{t-1}^f \\ y_{t-1}^\dagger \end{bmatrix} + \begin{bmatrix} 1 & 0 \\ 1 & 1 \\ 1 & 1 \end{bmatrix} \begin{bmatrix} \eta_t \\ \varepsilon_t \end{bmatrix} \tag{6.3.29a}$$

and

$$y_\tau = [0 \quad 1 \quad 0] \begin{bmatrix} \mu_t \\ y_t^f \\ y_t^\dagger \end{bmatrix}, \quad t = \delta\tau, \quad \tau = 1, \ldots, T \tag{6.3.29b}$$

Table 6.3.1 shows the smoothed estimates of the trend, μ_t, and the observations, $y_t^\dagger$, for $\delta = 4$ and $T = 5$, under the assumption that $\sigma_\eta^2 = \sigma_\varepsilon^2 = 1$. The observations y_τ, $\tau = 1, \ldots, 5$, were chosen, arbitrarily, as 4, 8, 0, 8 and 10. The estimated MSEs for the estimates of the trend vary over time but are about 0.80 on average. Note that the estimates of the $y_t^\dagger$'s satisfy the distribution constraint, (6.3.23). Because the estimates of the μ_t's do not have to satisfy this constraint their pattern is somewhat smoother.

Table 6.3.1 *Optimal estimates of the trend and observations in a random walk plus noise model assuming* $\sigma_\eta^2 = \sigma_\varepsilon^2 = 1$

t	Trend	Observations	
1	0.89	0.84	
2	0.95	0.89	4
3	1.00	0.97	
4	1.44	1.29	
5	1.85	2.12	
6	1.95	2.23	8
7	1.77	2.05	
8	1.31	1.60	
9	0.57	0.22	
10	0.19	−0.17	0
11	0.17	−0.19	
12	0.50	0.14	
13	1.19	1.35	
14	1.73	1.89	8
15	2.11	2.27	
16	2.34	2.50	
17	2.42	2.55	
18	2.47	2.52	10
19	2.51	2.49	
20	2.53	2.44	

6.3.4 Temporal aggregation in structural models

It was observed in sub-section 6.3.2 that the form of the principal structural time series models is unaltered when they are observed at a multiple of the original model timing interval. On the other hand, the treatment of flows in the previous sub-section required an additional element in the state vector to accommodate the temporal aggregation. The question is what effect this has on the structure of the model.

In order to get a feel of the effects of temporal aggregation, consider Working's result on the temporal aggregation of a random walk alluded to at the beginning of this section. The underlying model is:

$$y_t^\dagger = \eta_t / \Delta \tag{6.3.30}$$

but what is observed is y_τ, $\tau = 1, \ldots, T$ as defined in (6.3.3). Using the summation operator, (2.1.10), this may be written as

$$y_\tau = \mathrm{S}_\delta(\mathrm{L})\, y_{\delta\tau}^\dagger, \quad \tau = \delta, 2\delta, \ldots \tag{6.3.31}$$

First-differencing y_τ is equivalent to differencing at an interval of δ on the original time scale and so the stationary series corresponding to the observations is:

$$\Delta_\delta y_\tau = \Delta_\delta S_\delta(L)\, y^{\dagger}_{\delta\tau} = S^2_\delta(L)\eta_{\delta\tau}, \quad \tau=\delta, 2\delta, \ldots \tag{6.3.32}$$

or

$$\Delta_\delta y_\tau = \sum_{j=1}^{\delta} j\, \eta_{t-j+1} + \sum_{j=1}^{\delta} (\delta-j)\, \eta_{t-\delta-j+1} \tag{6.3.33}$$

Thus $\Delta_\delta y_\tau$ is made up not only of the disturbances in the previous δ time periods but also of disturbances before that. Evaluating the autocovariance function for $\Delta_\delta y_\tau$ yields

$$\left.\begin{aligned} \gamma(0) &= \sigma^2_\eta\, \delta(2\delta^2+1)/3 \\ \gamma(1) &= \sigma^2_\eta\, \delta(\delta^2-1)/6 \\ \gamma(\tau) &= 0, \qquad \tau \geqslant 2 \end{aligned}\right\} \tag{6.3.34}$$

and so

$$\rho(1) = \frac{\delta^2-1}{2(2\delta^2+1)} \tag{6.3.35}$$

For $\delta=3$, that is a monthly model observed in aggregated form every quarter, $\rho(1)$ is 0.21. The limit of $\rho(1)$ as $\delta \to \infty$ is 0.25.

The above result can be generalised to the random walk plus noise model, (6.3.27), to show that the temporally aggregated model now allows the first-order autocorrelation coefficient to lie in the range $[-0.5, 0.25]$ rather than $[-0.5, 0]$. Similarly, the range of the MA parameter in the reduced form ARIMA(0, 1, 1) model is expanded to $[-1, 0.268]$; see also Tiao (1972).

Returning to the question of whether temporal aggregation fundamentally changes the form of a structural model, consider SSF(τ, δ) in (6.3.20). Rather than augmenting the state vector, the second equation in (6.3.20a),

$$y_\tau = \mathbf{z}'(\mathbf{W}_\delta - \mathbf{I})\boldsymbol{\alpha}_{\tau-1} + \mathbf{z}'\boldsymbol{\eta}^f_\tau + \varepsilon^f_\tau, \quad \tau=1, \ldots, T \tag{6.3.36}$$

can be treated as a measurement equation. Defining

$$\boldsymbol{\alpha}^*_\tau = \boldsymbol{\alpha}_{\tau-1}$$

enables (6.3.36) to be written as

$$y_\tau = \mathbf{z}'_\tau \boldsymbol{\alpha}^*_\tau + \varepsilon_\tau, \quad \tau=1, \ldots, T \tag{6.3.37a}$$

where $\mathbf{z}_\tau = \mathbf{z}'(\mathbf{W}_\delta - \mathbf{I})$ and $\varepsilon_\tau = \mathbf{z}'\boldsymbol{\eta}^f_\tau + \varepsilon^f_\tau$. The corresponding transition equation is

$$\boldsymbol{\alpha}^*_{\tau+1} = \mathbf{T}^\delta \boldsymbol{\alpha}^*_\tau + \bar{\boldsymbol{\eta}}_\tau, \quad \tau=1, \ldots, T \tag{6.3.37b}$$

Taken together, the system in (6.3.37) is of the form (3.1.1a) and (3.1.4) with the measurement disturbance, ε_τ, and the transition equation disturbance, $\bar{\boldsymbol{\eta}}_\tau$, correlated. If $\mathbf{Q}^\dagger_\delta$ denotes the covariance matrix in (6.3.20d), the covariance matrix

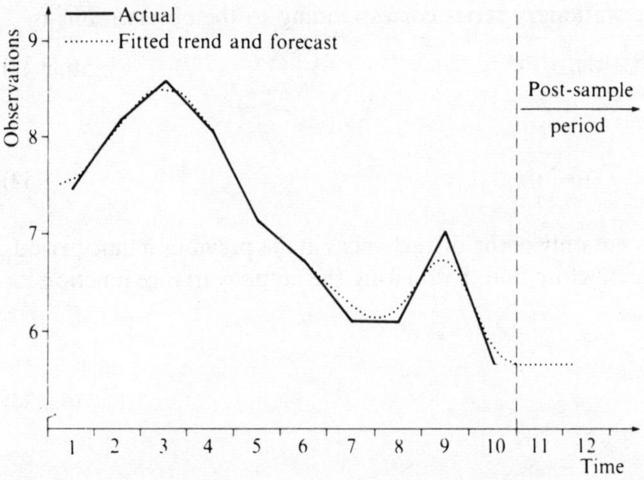

Fig. 6.3.1 Trend from a series following a random walk after temporal aggregation.

of $[\bar{\boldsymbol{\eta}}_\tau' \quad \varepsilon_\tau]'$ is given by

$$\mathrm{Var}\begin{bmatrix}\boldsymbol{\eta}_\tau \\ \varepsilon_\tau\end{bmatrix}=\begin{bmatrix}\mathbf{Q}_\delta & \mathbf{g}_\delta \\ \mathbf{g}_\delta' & \mathbf{H}_\delta\end{bmatrix}=\begin{bmatrix}\mathbf{I} & \mathbf{0} \\ \mathbf{0}' & \mathbf{z}'\end{bmatrix}\mathbf{Q}_\delta^\dagger\begin{bmatrix}\mathbf{I} & \mathbf{0}' \\ \mathbf{0} & \mathbf{z}\end{bmatrix}+\begin{bmatrix}\mathbf{0} & \mathbf{0} \\ \mathbf{0} & \delta\sigma_\varepsilon^2\end{bmatrix} \tag{6.3.38}$$

The Kalman filter may be applied to (6.3.37) in the modified form noted in (3.2.21) and (3.2.22). However, the important point to note is that the state space form of the aggregated system is basically as in the stock case, the main difference being the correlation between the measurement and transition equation disturbances. Thus the principal structural time series models do not really change in any fundamental way when they are subject to temporal aggregation.

So far nothing has been said about the choice of δ; it has been assumed given, Attempts to estimate δ as a free parameter would almost certainly run into difficulties as it is not identifiable. However, there is another issue, that of smoothness. Other things being equal, a higher value of δ corresponds to a smoother trend component. This can again be illustrated using the random walk plus noise model, (6.3.27). The first-order autocorrelation for Δy_τ in (6.3.28) is $\rho(1)=\{\frac{1}{6}q(\delta^2-1)-1\}/\{\frac{1}{3}q(2\delta^2+1)+2\}$ while $\rho(\tau)=0$ for $\tau\geqslant 2$. Thus aggregating a series with $q=0.4$ over four time periods, that is $\delta=4$, yields a random walk. Thus although it was argued in section 6.1.1 that the trend in a random walk is just the series itself, it turns out that if the model is formulated at a finer timing interval some of the noise can be removed to give a slightly smoother series. Figure 6.3.1 shows the results of extracting a trend from ten points generated by a random walk.

6.3.5 *Estimation in the frequency domain*

Suppose that $y_t^\dagger$ is generated by a stationary stochastic process. For a stock variable observed every δ time periods, as in (6.3.2), the s.g.f. of y_τ, $g(e^{i\lambda})$, is related to the s.g.f. of $y_t^\dagger$, $g^\dagger(e^{i\omega_h})$, by the 'folding formula'

$$g(e^{i\lambda}) = \delta^{-1} \sum_{h=0}^{\delta-1} g^\dagger(e^{i\omega_h}) \tag{6.3.39a}$$

where

$$\omega_h = (\lambda + 2\pi h)/\delta, \quad h = 0, \ldots, \delta - 1; \tag{6.3.39b}$$

see, for example, Robinson (1980). This expression for the s.g.f. can be inserted in the frequency-domain likelihood function, (4.4.1). Maximisation of this function yields the ML estimators of the parameters in the process generating $y_t^\dagger$.

For a flow variable, y_τ is related to $y_t^\dagger$ by (6.3.3) and the s.g.f. of y_τ is obtained as follows. Suppose the right-hand side of (6.3.3) were observed for $t = 1, \ldots, \delta T$. In this case the s.g.f. of the resulting moving average would be

$$|S_\delta(e^{i\omega})|^2 g^\dagger(e^{i\omega}) \tag{6.3.40}$$

where

$$S_\delta(e^{i\omega}) = 1 + e^{i\omega} + e^{i2\omega} + \cdots + e^{i(\delta-1)\omega} = \sum_{h=0}^{\delta-1} e^{ih\omega} \tag{6.3.41}$$

The derivation of (6.3.41) follows straightforwardly by noting that a moving average of length δ may be written as

$$\sum_{r=0}^{\delta-1} y_{t-r}^\dagger = S_\delta(L) y_t^\dagger \tag{6.3.42}$$

The second step is simply to replace $g^\dagger(.)$ in (6.3.39) by (6.3.40) giving

$$g(e^{i\lambda}) = \delta^{-1} \sum_{h=0}^{\delta-1} |S(e^{i\omega_h})|^2 g^\dagger(e^{i\omega_h}) \tag{6.3.43}$$

This follows because the moving average is only observed every δ time periods. As with a stock, substitution of (6.3.43) in (4.4.1) yields the required likelihood function.

The above results may be extended to non-stationary models. What is needed is to find the s.g.f. of the observation series after it has been converted to stationarity by appropriate differencing operations. Suppose that the underlying process, $y_t^\dagger$, is stationary in first differences and that the s.g.f. of $\Delta y_t^\dagger$ is $g^\dagger(.)$. Let $y_t^\dagger$ be observed every δ periods as a stock, as in (6.3.2). First-differencing the observations, $y_\tau, \tau = 1, \ldots, T$, is equivalent to taking δ-th differences of the

$y_t^\dagger$ process, because

$$y_\tau - y_{\tau-1} = y_{\delta\tau}^\dagger - y_{\delta\tau-\delta}^\dagger = \Delta_\delta y_{\delta\tau}, \quad \tau = 1, \ldots, T \tag{6.3.44}$$

Since $\Delta_\delta = \Delta . S_\delta(L)$ the s.g.f. of $\Delta_\delta y_t^\dagger$ is the same as the s.g.f. of $S_\delta(L)\Delta y_t$, that is

$$|S_\delta(e^{i\omega})|^2 g^\dagger(e^{i\omega}) \tag{6.3.45}$$

However, when $\Delta_\delta y_t^\dagger$ is only observed every δ time periods its spectrum, and hence the spectrum of $y_\tau - y_{\tau-1}$, is given by

$$g(e^{i\lambda}) = \delta^{-1} \sum_{h=0}^{\delta-1} |S_\delta(e^{i\omega_h})|^2 g^\dagger(e^{i\omega_h}) \tag{6.3.46}$$

where ω_h is as defined in (6.3.39b). This formula is exactly the same as the formula obtained for a temporally aggregated stationary process in (6.3.43).

When $y_t^\dagger$ is a flow variable, so that y_τ is defined by (6.3.3), it follows from what has been done previously that the s.g.f. of $y_\tau - y_{\tau-1}$ is

$$g(e^{i\lambda}) = \delta^{-1} \sum_{h=0}^{\delta-1} |S_\delta(e^{i\omega_h})|^4 g^\dagger(e^{i\omega_h}) \tag{6.3.47}$$

Now suppose that $y_t^\dagger$ is stationary in d-th differences. Observing d-th differences of y_τ is equivalent to observing the process $\Delta_\delta^d y_t$ every δ time periods. Since $\Delta_\delta^d = S_\delta^d(L)\Delta^d$ the s.g.f. of d-th differences of y_τ is:

$$g(e^{i\lambda}) = \delta^{-1} \sum_{h=0}^{\delta-1} |S_\delta(e^{i\omega_h})|^{2d} g^\dagger(e^{i\omega_h}) \tag{6.3.48}$$

where $g^\dagger(.)$ is the s.g.f. of $\Delta^d y_t^\dagger$. Similarly if $y_t^\dagger$ is a flow, the s.g.f. of the second differences of y_τ is

$$g(e^{i\lambda}) = \delta^{-1} \sum_{h=0}^{\delta-1} |S_\delta(e^{i\omega_h})|^{2(d+1)} g^\dagger(e^{i\omega_h}) \tag{6.3.49}$$

On a computational point, it follows from (2.1.12) and standard trigonometric identities that

$$\begin{aligned} |S[e^{i(\lambda+2\pi h)/d}]|^2 &= \{1 - \cos\lambda\}/\{1 - \cos[(\lambda+2\pi h)/h]\} \\ &= \frac{\sin^2(\lambda/2)}{\sin^2 \frac{1}{2}\left(\frac{\lambda+2\pi h}{\delta}\right)}, \quad h = 0, \ldots, \delta-1 \end{aligned} \tag{6.3.50}$$

The above results can be used to construct the likelihood functions of the main structural time series models. Thus, for the random walk plus noise, observed as a stock, substituting the appropriate expression for $g^\dagger\{\exp(i\omega_h)\}$, namely (4.4.30), into (6.3.43) yields:

$$g(e^{i\lambda})=\delta^{-1}\sum_{h=0}^{\delta-1}|S_\delta(e^{i\omega_h})|^2[\sigma_\eta^2+2(1-\cos\omega_h)\sigma_\varepsilon^2]$$

$$=\frac{\sigma_\eta^2}{\delta}\sum_{h=0}^{\delta-1}|S_\delta(e^{i\omega_h})|^2+\delta^{-1}\sum_{h=0}^{\delta-1}\frac{(1-\cos\lambda)}{(1-\cos\omega_h)}2(1-\cos\omega_h)\sigma_\varepsilon^2$$

$$=\frac{\sigma_\eta^2}{\delta}\sum_{h=0}^{\delta-1}|S_\delta(e^{i\omega_h})|^2+2(1-\cos\lambda)\sigma_\varepsilon^2$$

$$=\delta\sigma_\eta^2+2(1-\cos\lambda)\sigma_\varepsilon^2 \tag{6.3.51}$$

The last step follows from the identity

$$\sum_{h=0}^{\delta-1}|S_\delta(e^{i\omega_h})|^2=\delta^2 \tag{6.3.52}$$

Expression (6.3.51) is consistent with the spectrum obtained by noting that the δ-th differences of the process can be written as:

$$y_{\delta\tau}^{\dagger}-y_{\delta\tau-\delta}^{\dagger}=\sum_{j=0}^{\delta-1}\eta_{\delta\tau-j}+\varepsilon_{\delta\tau}-\varepsilon_{\delta(\tau-1)} \tag{6.3.53}$$

For more complex models, attempting a more direct approach to the evaluation of $g(e^{i\lambda})$ by working out an expression analogous to (6.3.53) can be difficult. The appropriate route is by working through a derivation similar to the one above (6.3.51).

6.3.6 *Gains from more frequent observations*

There are two sources of improvement when observations are made at more frequent intervals. The first is that the elements of the state vector can be estimated more accurately. This translates into more accurate estimates of the unobserved components of the model within the sample, and into more accurate predictions of the components and the observations outside the sample. The second source of improvement is the greater accuracy of the estimators of the parameters, $\boldsymbol{\psi}$. As has already been shown, the principal structural time series models have the property that they depend on the same set of parameters when the observations are at different timing intervals.

In order to formalise matters, suppose that the finer timing interval is the unit interval, and that this corresponds to the model timing interval. We wish to evaluate the gain from having observations at the unit interval, rather than every δ time periods. The problem could have been posed in other ways, for example, by formulating a model at the unit interval and then considering the gains from having observations at intervals of $1/\delta$. The attraction of the chosen approach is that it ties in somewhat more easily with the material of the previous sub-sections. Finally, in order to simplify matters, it will be assumed that no elements of the state vector are lost, owing to aliasing, in moving from a unit timing interval to a timing interval of δ.

It is self-evident that sampling at a finer timing interval will give more accurate estimators of unobserved stochastic components at points which are not observed when sampling is less frequent. Even at the points where observations are made, there will tend to be a gain from using the smoothed estimators from the finer timing interval scheme. The more interesting questions concern the gains which arise when predictions are made. In order to analyse this problem it will be assumed that $\boldsymbol{\psi}$ is known. There are additional gains from the increased precision with which $\boldsymbol{\psi}$ can be estimated; see the discussion at the end of section 3.5.

Observations at the finer interval are made at times $t=1,\ldots,\delta T$. When observations are made every δ periods, they are at times $t=\delta, 2\delta,\ldots,\delta T$. The analysis of the coarser sampling situation will always be in terms of SSF(t, 1). The comparison to be made is between the predictions at times $t=\delta T+\delta l$, $l=1,2,3,\ldots$ since predictions from the model observed at intervals of δ will normally be made at the same interval. As will be seen below, the reduction in prediction MSE from sampling more frequently comes solely from the reduction in the MSE of the estimator of the state vector at time $T\delta$.

For a stock variable, the optimal predictor of $y_{\delta T+\delta l}$ is given by

$$\tilde{y}_{\delta T+\delta l|\delta T}=\mathbf{z}'\mathbf{T}^{\delta l}\mathbf{a}_{\delta T}, \quad l=1,2,\ldots \tag{6.3.54}$$

The predictions obtained from using more frequent observations will tend to be more accurate because $\mathbf{a}_{\delta T}$ is estimated with a smaller MSE. However, the error from estimating $\boldsymbol{\alpha}_{\delta T}$ is only a part of the forecasting error and the remainder is common to forecasts made from any observation timing interval. The full prediction MSE is given by expression (4.6.3) with l replaced by δl.

In the case of the random walk plus noise, it follows from (3.5.8b) that

$$\text{MSE}(\tilde{y}_{\delta T+\delta l|\delta T})=(p_T+l\delta q+1)\sigma_\varepsilon^2 \tag{6.3.55}$$

If T is large and $q>0$, then from (4.1.22), observations at the unit interval have

$$p_T=\bar{p}-q=(-q+\sqrt{q^2+4q})/2$$

while at the δ interval, p_T is given by the same expression but with q replaced by δq. If Eff(δ, l) denotes the ratio of the MSE of the forecasts made from the δ interval to the forecasts made at the unit interval, then

$$\text{Eff}(\delta,l)=\frac{-\delta q+\sqrt{\delta^2q^2+4\delta q}+2l\delta q+2}{-q+\sqrt{q^2+4q}+2l\delta q+2} \tag{6.3.56}$$

Since p_T is of $O(1)$, it is dominated by the term involving l in (6.3.56) as l increases. As $l \to \infty$, $\text{Eff}(\delta, l) \to 1$.

6.3.7 *Mixed observation timing intervals*

A series may sometimes consist of observations at two different timing intervals. For example, observations may, at first, only be available on an annual basis, whereas later on they are collected every quarter. A model could, of course, be constructed for the quarterly observations, and the annual observations ignored. This would, however, be wasting information about movements in the trend and the loss of information could be quite severe if most of the available observations were annual ones.

Let the finer observation timing interval, the quarterly one in the preceding paragraph, be the unit interval and let this also be the model timing interval. When observations are available less frequently, they are recorded every δ time periods. This corresponds to the situation considered in the previous sub-sections. Thus if the model is (6.3.1) and the less frequent observations come first, these observations are defined by (6.3.2), or (6.3.3), for $\tau = 1, \ldots, T_1$. The remaining $T - T_1$ observations are the values of $y_t^\dagger$ from $t = T_1\delta + 1, \ldots, T$. All we need to do is to combine the information in the two parts of the sample.

An approximation to the log-likelihood function could be constructed, in the time domain or the frequency domain, by treating the two parts of the sample separately and summing their respective log-likelihoods. The loss of information is asymptotically negligible, but it can be avoided altogether in the time domain by formulating a state space model which is able to cope with both parts of the sample. The resulting Kalman filter can then be used as the basis for forecasting future observations and estimating missing observations.

Consider the specific case of mixed annual and quarterly observations and suppose that the underlying quarterly model is the BSM. Treating the two parts of the sample separately would mean a lack of continuity and the loss of two observations. This is remedied as follows. For the annual observations the Kalman filter is applied to SSF(t, 1) or SSF(τ, δ) with the first two observations providing starting values. The seasonal component is obviously unobservable for annual data and so the elements associated with it do not appear in the state vector at this stage. Once the quarterly observations are reached, the state vector is expanded to include the three seasonal elements. These elements are initialised with a diffuse prior. A quarterly model would normally require five observations as starting values but in the present situation estimators of the level and slope are provided by the annual observations. Only the first three quarterly observations are needed to give starting values for the remainder of the sample. The exact likelihood function is constructed via the prediction error decomposition using the prediction errors at times $t = \delta\tau, \tau = 3, \ldots, T_1$ and $t = T_1 + 4, \ldots, T$.

Applying the Kalman filter in the way described above yields the optimal estimator of the state vector at the end of the sample together with its MSE matrix. The forecast function is constructed from these values in the usual way. Estimates of quarterly observations during the annual period can be made by smoothing, assuming that the Kalman filter has been applied to SSF(t, 1) in the annual period.

As regards model selection, if there are enough observations at the unit timing interval, standard techniques can be used on this part of the sample alone. However, likelihood-based tests, including diagnostics based on the LM principle, can be constructed using all the sample; see the discussion of missing observation diagnostics in the next section.

6.4 Data irregularities

It is not uncommon for observations to be missing at various points in a series. This poses the questions of how to estimate a model for such data and how to estimate the missing observations if these values are of interest in themselves. Another problem is that a sample may sometimes contain outlying observations, that is, observations which appear to be inconsistent with the rest of the sample. Outliers may occur as a result of measurement error or there may be some special reason for their existence. Thus, they may arise from some identifiable event, such as a strike. A failure to deal with outliers in an appropriate way may have serious consequences when a model is constructed and used for forecasting.

The question of measurement error is raised quite explicitly when an initial observation is regarded as being preliminary and is subject to revision at a later stage. Such revisions are quite common in the statistics produced by government agencies and it is clear that some account must be taken of the additional uncertainty in preliminary observations in making forecasts.

A final source of data irregularities is calendar effects and trading day variations. Both lead to irregular movements in a series which would otherwise be perfectly behaved.

Solutions to all the above problems are described in the sub-sections below. It is assumed that in the absence of data irregularities, the model is a time-invariant one of the form (4.1.3). Handling the various kinds of data irregularity normally requires some modification of the measurement equation and may also involve augmentation of the transition equation.

Data irregularities can sometimes cause considerable distortion in analytical tools such as the correlogram. This may pose particular difficulties for the application of ARIMA model selection methodology. The model selection strategy outlined in section 5.7, with its emphasis on the *a priori* specification of components, is less vulnerable in this respect.

6.4.1 Missing observations and temporal aggregation

A framework for handling missing observations was set out in sub-section 3.4.7. The underlying model generates a series of values $y_t^\dagger$, $t = 1, \ldots, T^\dagger$ and the ones which are actually observed are denoted by y_τ, $\tau=1,\ldots,T$ where

$$y_\tau = y^\dagger_{t_\tau}, \quad \tau=1,\ldots,T \tag{6.4.1}$$

and the t_τ's are integers, denoting the values of t at which observations are available. This equation corresponds to (3.4.77), the matrix $\mathbf{W}_\tau$ being superfluous in the context of a univariate series.

The underlying time-invariant structural model, (4.1.3), can be expressed as in (6.3.1). The measurement equation in the state space form is obtained by combining (6.3.1a) and (6.4.1). If the transition equation remains formulated for a unit time interval, as in (6.3.1b), the measurement equation is not defined for $t \neq t_\tau$, and at these points the Kalman filter updating equations are omitted. Following the terminology of the previous section, a set-up of this kind will be referred to as SSF(t, 1). The alternative is to redefine the transition equation as in (6.3.6). The measurement equation is then (6.3.8). If we let

$$\delta_\tau = t_\tau - t_{\tau-1}, \quad \tau=2,\ldots,T \tag{6.4.2}$$

this system may be denoted by SSF(τ, δ_τ). The skipping of updating equations is avoided in SSF(τ, δ_τ), but the transition equation is normally time-varying. The likelihood function may be obtained from either SSF(t, 1) or SSF(τ, δ_τ). If d consecutive values of $y^\dagger_t$ are available at the beginning of the sample, i.e. $y_\tau = y^\dagger_t$, $t=\tau=1,\ldots,d$, a proper prior can be formed and the likelihood function constructed via the prediction error decomposition as in (4.2.3). When d initial consecutive observations are not available, difficulties may arise since the first d observations may not necessarily yield a proper prior for all the elements of the state vector. Thus, with monthly data, an additional observation in March is of no help in estimating the seasonal effect in June. One solution to this problem is to reverse the order of the observation. This effectively means that a likelihood function is constructed for $y_{T-d-\tau}$, $\tau=1,\ldots,T-d$; as observed in Harvey and Pierse (1984) this is quite a legitimate device. Of course this approach fails if some of the observations are missing at the end of the series. A more general solution is to adopt the algorithms of de Jong (1989) or Ansley and Kohn (1985); see section 3.4.

Irrespective of the way in which ML estimation is carried out, it is SSF(t, 1) which is used when the missing observations are estimated by a smoothing algorithm. In the previous section, the use of the fixed-interval smoother was advocated for interpolation. Clearly this smoother can also be used to estimate missing observations, but if the number of missing observations is relatively small, a fixed-point smoother may be computationally more attractive; see sub-section 3.6.1. Dummy variables may also be used to handle missing observations. Rather than adopting the framework implied by (6.4.1), we set $y^\dagger_t = 0$ when it is not observed and pretend that the sample is of size $T+M$, where M is the number of missing observations. The model is then written as

$$y_t = z_t'\alpha_t + \sum_{j=1}^{M} \lambda_j w_{jt} + \varepsilon_t, \quad t=1,\ldots,T+M \tag{6.4.3}$$

where w_{jt} is a dummy variable which takes the value of unity at the point at which the j-th missing observation occurs and is zero otherwise. This model can be estimated by any of the ML procedures described in section 7.3, with the w_{jt}'s treated as exogenous variables and the λ_j's concentrated out of the likelihood function. The procedure is effectively the same as that suggested by Sargan and Drettakis (1974) except that they treat the observations themselves as unknown parameters rather than introducing additional variables into the model. Thus the parameter representing the j-th missing observation is equal to *minus* λ_j. However, the point of the Sargan and Drettakis article is to show that a correction needs to be made to the determinantal term in the likelihood function if it is to be correct; see also Harvey and McKenzie (1984) and Exercise 6.9. If the number of missing observations is relatively small, failure to make this correction is unlikely to make a great deal of difference in practice. If it is felt that the correction should be made, the dummy variable method loses any attraction it might otherwise have over modifying the Kalman filter to take account of the missing observations.

When the value of a flow variable is missing, it may be included in the figure for the next observation which is actually recorded. This is *temporal aggregation*, and it means that (6.4.1) is replaced by

$$y_\tau = \sum_{s=1}^{\delta_\tau} y_{t_{\tau-1}+s}, \quad \tau = 1, \ldots, T \tag{6.4.4}$$

Such a situation may be handled by including a cumulator variable in the state vector. Following on from (6.3.13), this variable is defined as

$$y^f_{t_{\tau-1}+r} = \sum_{s=1}^{r} y_{t_{\tau-1}+s}, \quad r = 1, \ldots, \delta_\tau, \quad \tau = 1, \ldots, T \tag{6.4.5}$$

The estimation of parameters and the subsequent distribution of the temporal aggregates may be carried out along the lines of sub-section 6.3.3. The only difficulty arises in handling temporal aggregation when a transformation has been applied to the data. Suppose, to take the most common example, that the $y_t^\dagger$ variables are the logarithms of some original variable. The problem is that it will usually be the sum of the original variables which is observed rather than the sum of the logarithms, and these two quantities are not equal. An approximate solution to this problem based on the extended Kalman filter was suggested for ARIMA models in Harvey and Pierse (1984), but how well such techniques would perform in the present context has yet to be investigated.

Model selection is made more difficult by missing observations. This is particularly so when the initial specification is dependent on tools such as the correlogram. In a stationary series, a single missing observation effectively means that two points are lost in the numerator term of $r(\tau)$, at least for low values of τ. The alternative is to give the missing observation a value of zero, but this could lead to distortion. When differencing has to be carried out to make a series stationary, the situation is even more serious. A single missing observation leads to two observations missing in the first-differenced series, and four observations missing in a doubly-differenced series.

As regards diagnostics, it is still possible to define a set of residuals which are NID $(0, \sigma^2)$ when the model is correctly specified and the hyperparameters are known; compare (5.4.1). For many tests, such as those for normality and heteroscedasticity, the spacing between the observations is irrelevant and these tests may be constructed in the same way as before using the residuals which are actually available. A Box-Ljung test may also be constructed on this basis but the unequal spacing of the observations may have an adverse effect on power. A better approach may be to formulate a test based on estimates of the autocorrelations which make an explicit allowance for the missing observations. Let $\tilde{v}_t^\dagger$ denote the residual defined by (5.4.1) when $y_t^\dagger$ is observed and let it be set at zero for all other values of t for $t=d+1,\ldots,T^\dagger$. A suitable estimator of the residual autocorrelation at lag k is

$$r(k)=\left[\sum_{t=d+1}^{T^\dagger} \tilde{v}_t^\dagger \tilde{v}_{t-k}^\dagger / T(k)\right] \Bigg/ \left[\sum_{t=d+1}^{T^\dagger} \tilde{v}_t^{\dagger 2}/(T-d)\right]$$

where $T(k)$ is the number of non-zero cross-products of residuals in the numerator of the statistic. The residuals may be expressed in deviation-from-the-mean form if desired. Provided $T(k)>0$ for $k=1,\ldots,P$, the following variant of the Box-Pierce statistic may be constructed:

$$Q_m=\sum_{k=1}^{P} T(k) r^2(k)$$

When the residuals are from a static regression model, Robinson (1985) has shown that Q_m is the LM test against an AR(P) disturbance term and that it has a chi-square distribution with P degrees of freedom when the disturbances are white noise. Against an AR(p) alternative, it can be shown to have a higher asymptotic power than the corresponding test which ignores the irregular spacing of the observations provided that $P \geqslant p$. In the present context, when unknown hyperparameters are estimated, the distribution of Q_m is not known, but if it is to be tested against a chi-square distribution, it at least seems appropriate to amend the degrees of freedom in the same way as for the Box-Ljung test of sub-section 5.4.2.

More generally the most efficient way to proceed is to construct diagnostics via the LM principle. The LM test is a likelihood-based test and the derivatives needed to compute it can be computed recursively within a state space framework using the recursions described in sub-section 3.4.6. Note that, as shown in sub-section 3.4.5, the information matrix depends only on first derivatives. The information matrix can also be used to construct Wald tests.

Rather than simply being a nuisance, missing observations may sometimes be of interest in themselves and estimates of them may be made of smoothing.

However, it may be possible to obtain more accurate estimates of missing observations, and variables subject to temporal aggregation, by bringing in additional information from related series. This matter is pursued in sub-section 8.7.1.

6.4.2 Outliers

An *outlier* is an observation which is inconsistent with a model which is thought to be appropriate for the overwhelming majority of the observations. As a result the parameters in the model will be sensitive to its inclusion, as will the resulting forecasts.

Within the time series literature, a distinction is often made between *innovation outliers* and *additive outliers.* In an innovation outlier ARMA model, the disturbance term is assumed to have a long-tailed distribution, such as Cauchy, a t-distribution or a double exponential; see, for example, Martin and Yohai (1985). In such a model, the influence of a large disturbance will be felt on subsequent observations. In a structural model, letting any disturbance term appearing in the transition equation take extreme values will similarly have an effect on future observations. If the corresponding component is a non-stationary one, such as a trend or seasonal, the effect will be permanent. This issue is taken up further in sub-section 6.5.2 under the heading of 'Breaks in components'. It is the concept of an additive outlier therefore, which accords with the definition given in the opening paragraph. Additive outliers affect observations in isolation and are viewed as error terms added to the underlying model. Thus the actual observation is

$$y_t = y_t^\dagger + \varepsilon_t^*, \quad t=1,\ldots,T \tag{6.4.6}$$

where $y_t^\dagger$ is the value of the underlying process at time t and ε_t^* is an error term which is zero for non-outlying observations.

The additive outlier formulation fits naturally into the framework of structural time series models. The measurement equation, (4.1.3a), becomes

$$y_t = \mathbf{z}_t'\boldsymbol{\alpha}_t + \varepsilon_t + \varepsilon_t^*, \quad t=1,\ldots,T \tag{6.4.7}$$

If one were to assume that $\varepsilon_t^* \sim \text{NID}(0, k_t^2\sigma_\varepsilon^2)$ with k_t fixed and known for all t, the model could be handled within the conventional state space framework by treating $(\varepsilon_t + \varepsilon_t^*)$ as a composite disturbance term with variance $h_t\sigma_\varepsilon^2$ where $h_t = 1 + k_t^2$. In practice the difficulty lies in identifying outliers and assigning a suitable positive value to k_t. Probably the only case where the solution is clear cut is when an observation is known to be *incorrectly recorded.* Since such an observation is felt to be completely unreliable, the most appropriate course of action is to discard it completely and treat it as though it were missing. This is effectively the same as setting k_t equal to infinity.

It may sometimes be possible to associate outliers with *identifiable events.* In this case it is appropriate to treat ε_τ^* as a fixed effect, by introducing into the model an intervention variable which takes the value unity for an outlying observation and is zero elsewhere; see equation (6.4.3) and the general discussion in section 7.6. An example of treating an outlier in this way was given in modelling electricity consumption in sub-section 6.2.2 where a dummy variable was used to allow for the effect of the miners' strike. As was noted in the discussion below (6.4.3), the use of a dummy variable has almost exactly the same effect as treating the relevant observation as missing. However, there is an important conceptual difference. For an identifiable event the observation is a correct one, and by retaining it in the sample an estimate is made of the effect of the event.

Outliers which come about as a result of incorrect observation or an identifiable event have a clear-cut solution. However, unless the presence and location of such outliers is known at the start of the analysis, they must be detected during the analysis. The first question to ask, therefore, is what effect do outliers have on the model if they are not specifically allowed for? We need to determine the effect on (a) the estimators of the hyperparameters and (b) the estimates of the state. The asymptotic results in sub-section 4.5.5 indicate that if the disturbances can be regarded as having finite fourth moments, the ML estimators of the hyperparameters computed under the normality assumption will at least be consistent. This is reassuring, but it doesn't necessarily tell us a great deal about the likely effects of outliers in small samples, and it seems difficult to draw any systematic conclusions about these effects. As regards the influence of outliers on the state, some insight is possible for given values of the (relative) hyperparameters. Consider the random walk plus noise with q known. In the steady state, the optimal estimator of μ_T is an exponentially weighted average of past observations, (2.2.3). If at time τ, $y_\tau = y_\tau^\dagger + \varepsilon_\tau^*$, whereas elsewhere $y_t = y_t^\dagger$, then

$$\hat{\mu}_T = \lambda \sum_{j=0}^{T-1} (1-\lambda)^j y_{T-j} = \lambda \sum_{j=0}^{T-1} (1-\lambda)^j y_{T-j}^\dagger + \lambda(1-\lambda)^{T-\tau}\varepsilon_\tau^* \tag{6.4.8}$$

where λ, the smoothing constant, is a function of q as given in (4.1.24). The point to note about (6.4.8) is that when λ is close to one, the effect of the outlier on the current level, μ_T, diminishes rapidly. For a random walk, it is only the current estimate of the state which is affected. At the other extreme as $\lambda \to 0$, $q \to 0$ and the model becomes deterministic. The estimator of the state is then the sample mean and, because past observations are not discounted, a single outlier can lead to serious distortions. Overall the general conclusion is that components which are subject to a high degree of discounting will not be seriously affected by outliers. The degree of discounting which applies to different components in a model will, of course, depend on the estimates of relative hyperparameters such as q_η, q_ζ, q_ω.

Hopefully outliers will show up in the residuals of an estimated model, with their presence being indicated by a high kurtosis coefficient. However, there is no guarantee that this will happen and it is also quite possible that observations which are not outliers will be identified as such. Furthermore, it is not unusual to find that when an outlier is removed, other observations, which were previously well-behaved, now become outliers. An alternative way of trying to determine the position of outliers is by examining the $e_{t|T}$'s, the smoothed estimates of the irregular component defined in (5.4.5). Experience suggests that this approach works well if the irregular term is relatively important. If it is not, the smoothed trend should also be examined for evidence of outliers.

A different approach, which may be more robust, is to remove trend and seasonal effects by using *moving medians* to smooth a series, rather than moving averages as in (2.2.26); see Cleveland *et al.* (1978). The seasonal effects are then estimated by medians and outliers are identified by examining the irregular series. Another possibility is to apply the $\Delta(L)$ operator in order to yield what would, in the absence of outliers, be a stationary series. A robust measure of scale may then be calculated, and relatively large values of $\Delta(L)y_t$ noted. Unfortunately this can create serious distortions; for example the $\Delta\Delta_S$ operator produces four outlying transformed observations for just one in the original series.

The methods outlined above may not always be successful in detecting outliers. An alternative approach is to adopt a procedure which yields estimates of the state vector which are *robust* to outlying observations. A number of possibilities are open but only two will be discussed here. In the first robust estimation procedure, the model is specified in the usual way, that is without the outlier error term, ε_t^*, of (6.4.6), but the assumption of normality on the measurement equation disturbance term, ε_t, is relaxed. Instead ε_t is assumed to have a heavy-tailed distribution, such as a double exponential or a t-distribution. (The normality assumption on the disturbances in the transition equation *is* retained.) The attraction of the double exponential distributional assumption is that, when the state vector is deterministic, we have a regression model being estimated by the method of minimum absolute deviations (MAD). In the general case an exact filter may be computed using the techniques described in sub-section 3.7.3; see Kitagawa (1987). The drawback to this approach is that it requires a great deal of computing time. The second procedure is based on what are called *approximate maximum-likelihood type estimates* (*AM-estimates*). This approach has been advocated by Martin *et al.* (1983); a review can be found in Martin and Yohai (1985, section 6). The method is applied to ARIMA models by these authors. However, it uses a robust modification of the Kalman filter and could easily be adapted to structural models.

Once a model has been estimated by a robust procedure, it may be possible to detect additive outliers of the kind implied by (6.4.6) by examining smoothed estimates of the irregular component. If these outliers can be shown to be the result of incorrect observation or identifiable events, the model may be re-estimated under the normality assumption with the appropriate allowance made for the outliers. However, it may not be possible to classify all the outliers in this way. Indeed, there may not be the time or resources available to do so. In such cases, no explicit judgement is made as to what is, and what is not, an outlier, and it is the robust model itself which is used for forecasting.

The above robust procedures do have their limitations. They are being operated within a framework in which it is assumed that a linear, time-invariant, univariate model is capable of representing the data generation process. However, an outlying observation may be symptomatic of something other than an excessively large disturbance in the measurement equation. It is, for example, possible to construct non-linear models which give rise to what might be regarded as outliers in a linear framework. More fundamentally, the presence of outliers may indicate that a univariate model is inappropriate. Hence the solution may be to extend the model so as to include explanatory variables.

6.4.3 Calendar effects

It is not unusual for the level of a monthly time series to be influenced by calendar effects. Such effects arise because of changes in the level of activity resulting from variations in the composition of the calendar between years. The two main sources of calendar effects are trading day variation and moving festivals. They may both be introduced into a time series model and estimated along with the other components in the model. Thus, for example, the BSM is extended so as to become

$$y_t = \mu_t + \gamma_t + \tau_t + \varphi_t + \varepsilon_t \tag{6.4.9}$$

where τ_t is the trading day variation component and φ_t is the moving festival component.

Calendar effects should be modelled so as not to affect the level of the trend. Thus when the forecast function is constructed, they should cancel out under temporal aggregation in the same way as the seasonal component. Furthermore, because they represent what are basically artificial movements in the series, there is a clear case for removing them as part of the process of seasonal adjustment; see the discussion surrounding (6.2.12).

Trading day variation Trading day variation occurs when the activity of an industry or business varies with the day of the week. Thus for a flow variable, or a time-averaged stock, the observation recorded for a particular month will depend on which days of the week occur five times. Accounting and reporting practices can also create trading day effects in a time series. For example, businesses that perform their bookkeeping on Fridays tend to report higher sales in months with five Fridays than in months with four. Time series other than economic time series may also exhibit analogous effects to trading day variation. For example, road accidents tend to be higher on Fridays and Saturdays.

The standard way of allowing for trading day variation is to set up the model

$$\tau_t = \sum_{j=1}^{6} \theta_j (n_{jt} - n_{7t}) \tag{6.4.10}$$

The variable $n_{jt}, j=1, \ldots, 7$ is the number of times day j occurs in month t and θ_j is an unknown parameter associated with it. The effect associated with the seventh day is

$$\theta_7 = -\sum_{j=1}^{6} \theta_{jt} \tag{6.4.11}$$

The formulation in (6.4.10) is adopted by Kitagawa and Gersch (1984) and by Bell and Hillmer (1983), although in the second of these references the remaining part of the model is of the ARIMA form, rather than being a structural model as in (6.4.9). Bell and Hillmer (1983) also include in the model the variable

$$n_t = \sum_{j=1}^{7} n_{jt} \tag{6.4.12}$$

This variable, which is the total number of days in month t, is able to account for effects due to leap year Februaries. However, if there are no leap year effects, or if the February figure is adjusted prior to any model building, n_t becomes superfluous. In what follows n_t will not be included in the model.

Summing the trading day effect for each month over a period equal to a whole number of weeks yields zero, as

$$\sum_t \tau_t = \sum_t \sum_j \theta_j (n_{jt} - n_{7t}) = \sum_j \theta_j \left(\sum_t n_{jt} - \sum_t n_{7t} \right) = 0$$

The effect of including a trading day component in the manner suggested by (6.4.10) is therefore to allow for variations in the series due to differing day-of-the-week compositions without removing part of the trend. Over a year the sum of trading day effects will be almost, but not exactly, equal to zero, as 52 weeks is equal to 364 rather than 365 or 366 days.

The trading day model in (6.4.10) may be derived from the daily effects component defined in sub-section 2.3.5. We will simplify this model somewhat by suppressing the disturbance terms, χ_{jt}, so that the effects remain constant over time. However, the notion that different days may give rise to the same effect will be retained thereby allowing more parsimonious models than (6.4.10). Summing the daily effects defined in sub-section 2.3.5 over one month, and noting the constraint on θ_w in (2.3.55) yields:

$$\tau_t = \sum_{j=1}^{w} \theta_j n_{jt} = \left(\sum_{j=1}^{w-1} \theta_j n_{jt} \right) + n_{wt} \left(\frac{-1}{k_w} \sum_{j=1}^{w-1} k_j \theta_j \right) = \sum_{j=1}^{w-1} \theta_{jt} \left(n_{jt} - \frac{k_j n_{wt}}{k_w} \right) \tag{6.4.13}$$

Thus, for example, if all weekdays are the same, and Saturdays and Sundays are the same, τ_t contains a single variable, that is

$$\tau_t = \theta_1 n^*_{1t} \tag{6.4.14}$$

where $n^*_{1t} = n_{1t} - n_{2t}(5/2)$, n_1 being the number of weekdays in the month and n_2 being the number of Saturdays and Sundays in the month. When all days are different, (6.4.13) and (6.4.10) are identical.

The statistical treatment of the trading day model in (6.4.13) follows by regarding the variables, $n_{jt} - (k_j/k_w)n_{wt}, j = 1, \ldots, w-1$, as explanatory variables. Methods for handling explanatory variables are described in chapter 7. One approach, which is the one used by Kitagawa and Gersch (1984), is to extend the state space model by putting the θ_j's in the state vector even though they are time-invariant. Although Kitagawa and Gersch do not suggest it, this formulation leads itself naturally to an extension to a model in which the trading day effects are allowed to change over time. A formal derivation of such a model from the daily effects model would follow from the methods described in sub-section 6.3.4. An implementation of a stochastic trading day effects model can be found in Dagum and Quenneville (1988).

The examples in Hillmer (1982), Bell and Hillmer (1983) and Kitagawa and Gersch (1984) suggest that the additive formulation adopted in (6.4.10), and generalised in (6.4.13), performs reasonably well in practice. However, it is not satisfactory in all respects. For example, suppose that a particular activity is only carried out on weekdays but not at weekends. This would suggest amending the data before any model-fitting by dividing the monthly total by the number of working days. (It may also be multiplied by the average number of working days per month, although this is not important in the present context.) The result will not be the same as using the trading day models given above. Suppose that we amend (6.4.14) somewhat, so that it becomes

$$\tau_t = \theta n_{1t} \tag{6.4.15}$$

If the structural model is in levels, there is no way that defining τ_t as in (6.4.15) can be equivalent to dividing y_t by n_1. This is the case even if y_t is in logarithms, because there is no value of θ which makes $\exp(\theta n_{1t})$ equal to unity for all n_{1t}.

Another problem is the effect of public holidays on modelling trading day variation. A public holiday could be treated as an eighth day of the week and given its own effect, or it could be treated as a Sunday. There may, however, be other effects arising from public holidays. For example, if a holiday falls on a Friday, the usual Friday effect may be transferred to a Thursday.

Moving festivals The month in which certain holidays and religious festivals fall can vary from year to year. A prime example is Easter, which can fall anywhere from 22 March to 25 April. Many series are affected by Easter, including, for obvious reasons, industrial production, retail sales and air traffic.

In connection with retail sales, Bell and Hillmer (1983) suggest modelling

Easter as

$$\varphi_t = \alpha h_t \qquad (6.4.16)$$

where h_t is the proportion of the time period H days before Easter that falls in month t. This model can be defined for any positive H and if $H \leqslant 22$ the only months for which h_t will ever be non-zero are March and April. A similar model could be used for road and air traffic except that in this case the time period up to and including Easter Monday might be the relevant one. The value of H would probably be four or five.

As it stands, (6.4.16) does not have the property that the φ_t's sum to zero over a year. Fortunately this is easily remedied. In addition, the form of the moving festival component may be generalised. Suppose that φ_t is modelling any moving festival effect, not necessarily Easter, and that h_t is now a weight given to month t. Let the sum of the h_t's over any one year be unity. The pattern of the h_t's depends on the location of the moving festival in question and its postulated effect on the surrounding days. Thus, for example, the weight pattern for a series on road accidents might be derived by assigning initial weights of $\frac{1}{3}$, $\frac{1}{6}$, $\frac{1}{6}$ and $\frac{1}{3}$ to the days from Good Friday to Easter Monday. If Easter Monday were 1 April in a particular year, this would imply that h_t for March would be $\frac{2}{3}$, while for April it would be $\frac{1}{3}$. A moving festival may now be formulated as

$$\varphi_t = \alpha h_t^* \qquad (6.4.17a)$$

where

$$h_t^* = h_t - 1/s \qquad (6.4.17b)$$

where s is twelve unless the timing interval is lunar months, in which case it is thirteen.

Further generalisation is possible. The parameter α may be allowed to change over time by modelling it as a random walk. The weight function, h_t, then appears in the corresponding position in the z_t vector in the measurement equation.

A final issue, which is relevant to both trading day variation and moving festivals, concerns model selection. If there is reason to suspect calendar effects are present, they should be included in the model at the outset. If a model is fitted without calendar effects, then significant Box-Ljung or other serial correlation statistics may be an indication that seasonal effects are present. More specific methods of detecting calendar effects from fitted models are discussed in Cleveland and Devlin (1980, 1982). As in the case with outliers, calendar effects can distort the correlogram of the series. An example is given in Liu (1980) where the series is affected by the varying placement of the Chinese New Year. The distortion in the correlogram of a series because of trading day variation is illustrated in Hillmer (1982, p. 388). The series examined by Hillmer was the monthly outward station movements (disconnections) of the Wisconsin telephone company from January

1951 to October 1966. An earlier analysis of this series, using standard ARIMA methodology, had been carried out by Thompson and Tiao (1971). They had obtained the model

$$(1-0.49L^3)(1-1.005L^{12})y_t=(1-0.23L^9-0.33L^{12}-0.17L^{13})\xi_t \qquad (6.4.18)$$

After allowing for trading day variation, Hillmer selected the airline model.

6.4.4 *Data revisions*

The economic time series produced by government agencies are often subjected to revisions. The first figure is almost invariably regarded as being preliminary and it is revised, perhaps several times, as more information becomes available. This distinction between preliminary and final observations is usually ignored when forecasts are made from econometric and time series models, but the size of the revisions is often of such an order that the forecasts are seriously affected. Indeed in an interview reported in *The Times* (9 December 1980), Professor Lawrence Klein pinpointed 'big data revisions' as one of the major technical reasons for the poor performance of econometric forecasts.

The Kalman filter offers a means of handling the information in preliminary observations within a properly defined statistical framework. A similar framework may be used to incorporate the information from *benchmarks* into prediction of future observations. The use of benchmarks is discussed in Cholette (1982). An example might be a scenario put forward by a group of experts for the level of unemployment at the end of the year. The problem is to combine this piece of information with the predictions made by a statistical model and to produce predictions consistent with the benchmark for all the months of the coming year, not just the last one.

The treatment below concentrates on a situation where there is a single revision to a preliminary observation; see Howrey (1978, 1984) and Conrad and Corrado (1979). Methods for handling situations where there are several revisions to the same observation are described in Harvey *et al.* (1983).

Let $y_t^\dagger$ denote the true value of a variable at time t and let $y_t^{(0)}$ denote a preliminary observation which is available M time periods prior to the actual value of $y_t^\dagger$. A model relating $y_t^{(0)}$ to $y_t^\dagger$ may be constructed on the basis of past values of both variables. Following Howrey (1978), let $y_t^{(0)}$ be linearly related to $y_t^\dagger$ with an AR(1) disturbance term. Thus

$$y_t^{(0)}=\gamma+\delta y_t^\dagger+u_t^{(0)} \qquad (6.4.19a)$$

$$u_t^{(0)}=\psi u_{t-1}^{(0)}+\varepsilon_t^{(0)}, \quad |\psi|<1 \qquad (6.4.19b)$$

where $\varepsilon_t^{(0)}$ is a white-noise disturbance term, with variance σ_0^2, which is assumed to be uncorrelated with the true observations. If $\gamma=0$ and $\delta=1$, there are no *systematic* biases in the preliminary observations. In general, one would not expect such biases since, if they began to appear, the statistical agency would presumably make the appropriate adjustments. However, it must be remembered that statistical agencies are trying to gather information rather than produce optimal estimates and so the model in (6.4.19) seems a reasonable starting point. Some autoregressive behaviour in the preliminary estimation error is quite plausible and if the autoregressive process were not stationary, the preliminary and actual observations might soon bear very little resemblance to each other. An interesting discussion of the type of behaviour which could be expected from statistical agencies if they were 'rational' can be found in de Jong (1987).

The full model, (4.1.3), together with (6.4.19) can be put in state space form by expanding the state vector to allow for lagged values of the series up to $y^\dagger_{t-M}$. The serial correlation in $u_t^{(0)}$ is handled by putting this variable in the state vector as well. The transition equation is

$$\boldsymbol{\alpha}_t^\dagger = \begin{bmatrix} \boldsymbol{\alpha}_{t+1} \\ y_t^\dagger \\ \mathbf{y}_{t-1}^\dagger \\ u_t^{(0)} \end{bmatrix} = \begin{bmatrix} \mathbf{T} & \vdots & \mathbf{0} & \vdots & \mathbf{0} & \vdots & \mathbf{0} \\ \mathbf{z}' & \vdots & 0 & \vdots & \mathbf{0}' & \vdots & 0 \\ \mathbf{0} & \vdots & \mathbf{I}_M & & \mathbf{0} & \vdots & \mathbf{0} \\ \mathbf{0}' & \vdots & 0 & \vdots & \mathbf{0}' & \vdots & \psi \end{bmatrix} \begin{bmatrix} \boldsymbol{\alpha}_t \\ y_{t-1}^\dagger \\ \mathbf{y}_{t-2}^\dagger \\ u_{t-1}^{(0)} \end{bmatrix} + \begin{bmatrix} \mathbf{R}\boldsymbol{\eta}_{t+1} \\ \varepsilon_t \\ \mathbf{0} \\ \varepsilon_t^{(0)} \end{bmatrix} \tag{6.4.20a}$$

where $\mathbf{y}_{t-1}^\dagger$ is the $M \times 1$ vector $[y_{t-1}^\dagger \cdots y_{t-M}^\dagger]'$. The measurement equation is

$$\mathbf{y}_t = \begin{bmatrix} y_t^{(0)} \\ y_{t-M}^\dagger \end{bmatrix} = \begin{bmatrix} \mathbf{0}' & \delta & \mathbf{0}' & 1 \\ \mathbf{0}' & 0 & \mathbf{0}' \; 1 & 0 \end{bmatrix} \boldsymbol{\alpha}_t^\dagger + \begin{bmatrix} \gamma \\ 0 \end{bmatrix} \tag{6.4.20b}$$

The first row in the measurement equation corresponds to (6.4.19a); the second row simply records the information that $y_{t-M}^\dagger$ is observed exactly at time t for the first time. There is no disturbance term in (6.4.20b), although if φ is zero, so that the serial correlation disappears, $u_t^{(0)}$ does not need to appear in the augmented state vector and $\varepsilon_t^{(0)}$ then plays the role of a measurement equation disturbance term.

If $y_t^\dagger$ is modelled as a pure AR process, with or without differencing, the SSF can be set up so that $\boldsymbol{\alpha}_t$ contains lagged values of $y_t^\dagger$; see (3.1.9b). In this case it is unnecessary to augment the state vector by any values of $y_t^\dagger$, which already appear in $\boldsymbol{\alpha}_t$.

At time $t = T$, true values of $y_t^\dagger$ are available up to and including time $t = T - M$. The hyperparameters in the time series model, (4.1.3), may therefore be estimated from these observations using one of the standard ML procedures described in chapter 4. The preliminary observation model, (6.4.19), may be estimated using the same data-set for the true observations, together with the corresponding preliminary observations. Once this has been done, the SSF of (6.4.20) may be set up. All that is required now is to construct the appropriate starting values for the augmented state vector, $\boldsymbol{\alpha}_t^\dagger$. The augmented model may then be used to make optimal predictions of $y_t^\dagger$ for the period $t = T - M + 1$ to $t = T$ and for $t > T$. It may also be updated, and the process of making predictions repeated, as new observations become available.

Given estimates of the hyperparameters, applying the Kalman filter to the SSF (4.1.3) yields the optimal estimator of $\boldsymbol{\alpha}_{T-M+1}$ based on the observations up to $y^{\dagger}_{T-M}$. This may be written as $\mathbf{a}_{T-M+1|T-M}$, while its MSE matrix is $\mathbf{P}_{T-M+1|T-M}$. The optimal estimator of $\boldsymbol{\alpha}^{\dagger}_{T-M}$ based on the same data-set is, together with its MSE matrix,

$$\mathbf{a}^{\dagger}_{T-M}=\begin{bmatrix}\mathbf{a}_{T-M+1|T-M}\\ y^{\dagger}_{T-M}\\ \mathbf{y}^{\dagger}_{T-M-1}\\ u^{(0)}_{T-M}\end{bmatrix},\quad \mathbf{P}^{\dagger}_{T-M}=\begin{bmatrix}\mathbf{P}_{T-M+1|T-M} & \mathbf{0} & \mathbf{0} & \mathbf{0}\\ \mathbf{0}' & 0 & \mathbf{0}' & 0\\ \mathbf{0} & \mathbf{0} & \mathbf{0} & \mathbf{0}\\ \mathbf{0}' & 0 & \mathbf{0}' & 0\end{bmatrix} \tag{6.4.21}$$

The preliminary measurement error,

$$u^{(0)}_{T-M}=y^{(0)}_{T-M}-\gamma-\delta y^{\dagger}_{T-M} \tag{6.4.22}$$

is treated as though it were known exactly although this will not be the case if γ and δ are estimated. In many instances γ and δ will be set at 0 and 1 respectively and so the problem does not arise.

Starting from (6.4.21), the Kalman filter can be used to update the augmented state vector by bringing in the preliminary observations, $y^{(0)}_{T-M+1},\ldots,y^{(0)}_{T}$ one at a time. Since the true values $y^{\dagger}_{t-M}$, $t=T-M+1,\ldots,T$ have already been used in constructing (6.4.21), they are not new observations and so only the first row of (6.4.20b) need be employed as the measurement equation. However, since the elements $y^{\dagger}_{t-M}$, $t=T-M+1,\ldots,T$ are included in the estimated state vector with a zero MSE, working with the full measurement equation (6.4.20b) will give exactly the same result as only working with its first row. At time T, the estimated state vector, $\mathbf{a}^{\dagger}_{T}$, contains the optimal estimates of $y^{\dagger}_{T-M+1},\ldots,y^{\dagger}_{T}$ based on the actual values of $y^{\dagger}_{t}$ up to $t=T-M$ and the preliminary observations up to $t=T$. This is the full information set available at time T. The diagonal elements of $\mathbf{P}^{\dagger}_{T}$ contain the MSEs of the estimated values of $y^{\dagger}_{t}$ and the components of the state vector conditional on the estimated hyperparameters in the model.

As new observations become available, the Kalman filter may be applied to (6.4.20) and the optimal estimates of the last M values of $y^{\dagger}_{t}$ are automatically given in the estimated augmented state vector. Future values of $y^{\dagger}_{t}$ may be forecast optimally from the multi-step prediction equations.

Example 6.4.1 Suppose that $y^{\dagger}_{t}$ is modelled as a random walk plus noise. Suppose also that $M=1$ so that a preliminary observation is followed by the final observation one period later. The augmented SSF is:

$$\mathbf{y}_t=\begin{bmatrix}y^{(0)}_t\\ y^{\dagger}_{t-1}\end{bmatrix}=\begin{bmatrix}0 & 1 & 0\\ 0 & 0 & 1\end{bmatrix}\boldsymbol{\alpha}^{\dagger}_t+\begin{bmatrix}\varepsilon^{(0)}_t\\ 0\end{bmatrix} \tag{6.4.23a}$$

$$\boldsymbol{\alpha}_t^\dagger = \begin{bmatrix} \mu_{t+1} \\ y_t^\dagger \\ y_{t-1}^\dagger \end{bmatrix} = \begin{bmatrix} 1 & 0 & 0 \\ 1 & 0 & 0 \\ 0 & 1 & 0 \end{bmatrix} \begin{bmatrix} \mu_t \\ y_{t-1}^\dagger \\ y_{t-2}^\dagger \end{bmatrix} + \begin{bmatrix} \eta_t \\ \varepsilon_t \\ 0 \end{bmatrix} \tag{6.4.23b}$$

The model for $y_t^\dagger$ is estimated by ML using $y_t^\dagger, t=1,\ldots,T-1$ while

$$\tilde{\sigma}_0^2 = (T-1)^{-1} \sum_{t=1}^{T-1} (y_t^\dagger - y_t^{(0)}) \tag{6.4.24}$$

The initial conditions, (6.4.21), are

$$\mathbf{a}_{T-1}^\dagger = \begin{bmatrix} m_{T|T-1} \\ y_{T-1}^\dagger \\ y_{T-2}^\dagger \end{bmatrix}, \quad \mathbf{P}_{T-1}^\dagger = \begin{bmatrix} p_{T|T-1} & 0 & 0 \\ 0 & 0 & 0 \\ 0 & 0 & 0 \end{bmatrix} \tag{6.4.25}$$

where $m_{T|T-1}$ is the optimal predictor of μ_T, given Y_{T-1}, in the random walk plus noise model and $p_{T|T-1} = \sigma_\varepsilon^{-2}\text{MSE}(m_{T|T-1})$. Applying the Kalman filter prediction equations for the augmented SSF, (6.4.23), to the starting values in (6.4.25) gives:

$$\mathbf{a}_{T|T-1}^\dagger = \begin{bmatrix} m_{T|T-1} \\ m_{T|T-1} \\ y_{T-1}^\dagger \end{bmatrix}, \quad \mathbf{P}_{T|T-1}^\dagger = \begin{bmatrix} p_{T|T-1}+q & p_{T|T-1} & 0 \\ p_{T|T-1} & p_{T|T-1}+1 & 0 \\ 0 & 0 & 0 \end{bmatrix} \tag{6.4.26}$$

The updating equation gives

$$\mathbf{a}_T^\dagger = [\tilde{\mu}_{T+1|T} \quad \tilde{y}_T^\dagger \quad y_{T-1}^\dagger]' \tag{6.4.27}$$

where $\tilde{\mu}_{T+1|T}$ and $\tilde{y}_T^\dagger$ are the optimal estimators of μ_{T+1} and $y_T^\dagger$ respectively based on the information at time T. The expressions are as follows:

$$\tilde{\mu}_{T+1|T} = m_{T|T-1} + \frac{p_{T|T-1}}{p_{T|T-1}+1+\bar{\sigma}_0^2}(y_T^{(0)} - m_{T|T-1}) \tag{6.4.28}$$

and

$$\tilde{y}_T^\dagger = m_{T|T-1} + \frac{p_{T|T-1}+1}{p_{T|T-1}+1+\bar{\sigma}_0^2}(y_T^{(0)} - m_{T|T-1}) \tag{6.4.29}$$

where $\bar{\sigma}_0^2 = \sigma_0^2/\sigma_\varepsilon^2$. When σ_0^2 is zero, (6.4.28) collapses to the standard expression (4.1.22) while (6.4.29) simply states that $\tilde{y}_T^\dagger$ is equal to $y_T^{(0)}$. The effect of including a positive value of σ_0^2 in (6.4.28) is to give less influence to the preliminary observations in making predictions of future observations and in estimating the current value of $y_t^\dagger$.

If an optimal estimator of μ_T is required it can be obtained by smoothing.

The above framework may be used to handle benchmarks, simply by regarding time T as a point in the future at which a benchmark or scenario has been proposed. There is no difficulty in bringing several such preliminary observations into the measurement equation. The only problem likely to arise is the practical one of whether there is enough past information to assess the variances and the covariances of their estimation errors.

6.5 Time-varying and non-linear models

This section examines the main types of time-varying structures which are likely to arise in modelling economic and social time series. All the models can be set up within a state space framework. The classifications made are, to some extent, arbitrary, since the different problems can interlink in rather complex ways. This is partly a reflection of the fact that the notion of time-variation is bound up with non-linearity and non-normality. The introductory paragraphs below attempt to clarify the relationship between these concepts.

Structural time series models typically include components, such as trends and seasonals, which are allowed to evolve stochastically over time. However, the rate at which these components change depends on parameters which are assumed to be constant over time. As a result the model can be reduced to stationarity by an appropriate operator, $\Delta(L)$. The ability of a time series model to be reduced to stationarity is a useful property but it is not an essential one. Indeed it may be considered unduly restrictive. Once the need for a stationary form is abandoned, time variation may be introduced into the variance parameters, and into other parameters such as the damping factor in the stochastic cycle model. This introduces a wealth of possibilities. However, outside an engineering environment, detailed information on how parameters might change in each time period is rarely available. It is therefore necessary to set up models which can capture the sort of structural changes which appear to be plausible in a given situation. These models need to be formulated using a limited number of parameters and incorporating as much prior information as possible.

Within the state space framework, the shift from time-invariant to time-varying structures means working with (4.1.1) rather than (4.1.3). The system in (4.1.1) has a *linear state space form* in that the system matrices are *non-stochastic* and the disturbances follow white-noise processes. The additional assumption that the disturbances and the initial state vector are normally distributed ensures that the model is linear. A *linear model* is defined as one in which the observations can be represented as a linear combination of current and past values of a series of independent random variables; see Priestley (1981, p. 816). This definition must be understood to apply to models in which the weights attached to the current and past independent random variables can change over time in a deterministic fashion.

As regards prediction, the linearity of a model guarantees that the MMSEs of future observations are linear combinations of past and present observations.

However, unless the observations are normal, it may be difficult to determine the full distribution of these predictions. On the other hand, a Gaussian linear model has the characteristic that, conditional on the current information, the distribution of future observations is known exactly; each one is normally distributed with its mean and variance given by the Kalman filter.

The class of time-varying models can be widened further by allowing the system matrices to depend on past observations. The general class of such models was defined in (3.7.1). The changes in the system matrices over time are *endogenous* and, as a result, the models are *non-linear*. The statistical handling of such models is facilitated by their being conditionally Gaussian. The exact likelihood function can be constructed in the time domain, and the derivatives and information matrix computed in the same way as for a linear model. This in turn means that the various likelihood-based test statistics can be formulated; an illustration was given in Example 5.2.1. Further possibilities for time-varying structures arise once the requirement that the model be conditionally Gaussian is dropped. The drawback is that approximations, such as the extended Kalman filter, need to be employed and an exact likelihood can no longer be computed.

Although conditionally Gaussian models are non-linear, the MMSEs of future observations may or may not be linear. Examples where they are not linear are easily constructed; see Exercise 6.10. A linear example was provided by the ARCH process in sub-section 3.7.1. Indeed in this case the MSEs of forecasts could also be computed, but as expression (3.7.8) makes clear the distribution of forecasts more than one step ahead is not easy to determine.

Although a time-varying linear model does not have a stationary form, non-linear models can sometimes be reduced to stationarity. When this is the case, it is no longer sufficient to restrict attention to second-order properties, as characterised by the autocorrelation function. For example, important information may be contained in the a.c.f. of the *squares* of the observations from their mean. This contrasts with the situation for a stationary linear model where it can be shown that all the dynamic properties are captured by the a.c.f. For example, the a.c.f. of the squared observations is simply equal to the square of the conventional a.c.f.; see Maravall (1983).

Example 6.5.1 Suppose that the observations are generated by a simple ARCH process in which, conditional on Y_{t-1}, y_t is normal with mean zero and variance

$$\sigma_t^2 = \alpha_0 + \alpha_1 y_{t-1}^2$$

Repeated use of the conditional expectation operator shows that the unconditional mean and variance of y_t are zero and $\alpha_0/(1-\alpha_1)$ respectively and that the observations are uncorrelated. However, the unconditional distribution is not normal. It is shown in Engle (1982a, p. 992) that the kurtosis is $3(1-\alpha_1^2)/(1-3\alpha_1^2)$. This exceeds three for any positive value of α_1, giving an impression of a heavier-tailed distribution than the normal.

The ARCH model is therefore white noise, but it is not a linear process because successive observations are not independent. (Some authors use the term *strict* white noise for observations which are serially independent.) The serial dependence in the observations shows up, not in the correlogram of y_t, but in the correlogram of the square of y_t. Assuming finite kurtosis, which requires $3\alpha_1^2 < 1$, the theoretical a.c.f. of y_t^2 is such that the τ-th autocorrelation is α_1^τ. Thus it has the same form as the a.c.f. of an AR(1) process and this is why the LM test for ARCH is based on the first-order autocorrelation of y_t^2; see Example 5.2.1.

The above results generalise to higher-order ARCH models. An ARCH(p) model for y_t has

$$\sigma_t^2 = \alpha_0 + \alpha_1 y_{t-1}^2 + \cdots + \alpha_p y_{t-p}^2$$

The LM test in this case is the generalisation of the portmanteau test based on the first p autocorrelations of the squared observations. This test was given at the end of sub-section 5.4.2, where it was noted that it is often regarded as a general test for non-linearity.

If an ARIMA model has disturbances which are independent, rather than merely being uncorrelated, it is a linear model and, for given initial conditions, the linear predictions computed by the method outlined in sub-section 2.6.1 are MMSEs. Normality of the disturbances is not required. On the other hand, when a model with a linear state space form has more than one disturbance term, the assumption of independence is not, in general, sufficient for the Kalman filter to yield MMSE predictions. In other words independence of the disturbances in the state space model does not, in the absence of normality, imply independence of the disturbances in the reduced form. Nevertheless, as long as the disturbances are uncorrelated, there is the compensation that the Kalman filter at least gives the optimal *linear* predictor. If MMSEs are required, the more general filter described in sub-section 3.7.3 must be applied.

The fact that normality is not a requirement for the MMSEs of future observations in ARIMA models to be linear and easily computable should not be regarded as a powerful argument in favour of this class of models. As was noted earlier in sub-section 6.4.2, allowing the disturbances in ARIMA models to be non-normal is not, in general, a particularly useful way of handling outliers. Nor do ARIMA models with non-normal disturbances provide a viable basis for modelling count data and qualitative observations. The next section develops models for dealing with this kind of data. These models are essentially structural but are not based on the traditional state space form.

Once one starts to modify a univariate model in order to allow for time-variation, the simplicity of the univariate approach begins to disappear. Indeed it could be argued that, in some cases, the apparent time-variation may be an indication of the desirability of setting up a behavioural model. At the most basic level this means bringing in explanatory variables. It may sometimes be the case that a stable structure can be achieved by conditioning on such variables.

Chapter 7 is devoted to the issues surrounding the treatment of explanatory variables in structural models.

6.5.1 *Heteroscedasticity*

When a model contains a single disturbance term, heteroscedasticity exists where the variance of this disturbance term is not constant over time. In a structural time series model, there is typically more than one disturbance term. Each of these disturbances may have a variance which changes over time and which may be modelled in a particular way. This allows enormous flexibility, but the full potential of such models has yet to be explored. For present purposes, attention will be focussed on a restricted form of heteroscedasticity which affects all the disturbances in the same way. Thus we will consider heteroscedastic structural models of the form (4.1.3), but with

$$\text{Var}(\varepsilon_t)=g(.)h \tag{6.5.1a}$$

$$\text{Var}(\boldsymbol{\eta}_t)=g(.)\mathbf{Q} \tag{6.5.1b}$$

where $g(.)$ is a scalar function of time and observable variables.The relative importance of the various disturbances is unaffected by this specification. If $g(.)$ is equal to unity throughout the sample period, the model is homoscedastic and reduces to the time-invariant form of (4.1.1).

The viability of (6.5.1) depends on being able to find a suitable form for $g(.)$. If the model is to be a linear one, $g(.)$ must be deterministic. The simplest option is to let it be a function of time. Possible formulations might include $g(t) = 1 + \gamma t$ or $g(t) = \exp(\gamma t)$, where γ is a parameter to be estimated. A more general formulation would have $g(.)$ a function of a set of observable variables, $\mathbf{x}_t$, so that we could write $g(.)=g(t, x_t)$. The additional parameter, or parameters, in $g(.)$ will normally need to be estimated along with the hyperparameters as part of the numerical optimisation.

The reduced form of a linear heteroscedastic structural time series model will have the same specification as the reduced form of the time-invariant model obtained by setting $g(.)$ equal to unity. However, once $g(.)$ is allowed to change over time, the AR and MA parameters in the reduced form are no longer time-invariant. In other words the effect on the reduced form is not simply to multiply the variance of the disturbance by $g(.)$. This can be seen quite easily in the random walk plus noise model, where taking first differences gives

$$\Delta y_t=\eta_t+\varepsilon_t-\varepsilon_{t-1} \tag{6.5.2}$$

When $g(.)$ is unity, (6.5.2) is an MA(1) process. But if $g(.)$ changes, so that $\text{Var}(\varepsilon_t)\neq\text{Var}(\varepsilon_{t-1})$, the MA(1) parameter in the reduced form must also change.

Heteroscedasticity can be made endogenous to the system by introducing past observations of y_t into the function determining the changing variances in (6.5.1).

Thus g(.) becomes $g(t, Y_{t-1})$, where Y_{t-1} denotes all past observations up to, and including, time $t-1$. Such models are non-linear but, because $g(t, Y_{t-1})$ is determined at time $t-1$, a conditionally Gaussian model can be set up. In the formulation

$$g_t(t, Y_{t-1}) = 1 + \gamma v_{t-1}^2 \tag{6.5.3}$$

the variance is assumed to depend on the innovation in the previous time period. (There is a minor technical problem here, since even in a time-invariant model, the use of a diffuse prior means that $\text{Var}(v_t)$ is not constant until the Kalman filter reaches a steady state; see sub-section 3.3.4. It is difficult to correct for this, but failure to do so is unlikely to be important in practice.) Further lags of the squared innovations can be added to (6.5.3). Another extension is to let $g(.)$ depend on its own lagged values. The simplest example of such a model is

$$g_t(t, Y_{t-1}) = 1 + \gamma^{\dagger} g_{t-1}(t-1, Y_{t-2}) + \gamma v_{t-1}^2 \tag{6.5.4}$$

where $\gamma^{\dagger}$ and γ are unknown parameters. Again this model may be generalized to include higher-order terms, and observable variables may be included as suggested earlier for linear heteroscedastic models. Provided the observations are conditionally Gaussian, obtaining the exact likelihood function is straightforward.

When the model contains only a single disturbance term, the mechanism in (6.5.3) is the standard first-order ARCH model; see Examples 3.7.2, 5.2.1 and 6.5.1. The disturbance term and the innovation, v_t, are then the same. Such models have a good deal of intuitive appeal and have found application in a number of areas including the models of inflation and the foreign exchange rate; see Engle (1982a), Domowitz and Hakkio (1985) and Pagan and Ullah (1986). The extension to include lagged values of $g(.)$, as in (6.5.4), was suggested by Bollerslev (1986) and is known as generalised ARCH, or GARCH. One is tempted to refer to the modifications suggested in the previous paragraph for structural models as 'STARCH' models.

Autoregressive conditional heteroscedasticity can also feed back into the mean of the process. Such a mechanism has been put forward by Engle *et al.* (1987) for modelling the relative excess holding yield on a long bond and it has been christened an ARCH-*M* model. Again such a model can be applied within a stuctural framework with equation (4.1.3a) being modified to

$$y_t = \mathbf{z}_t' \boldsymbol{\alpha}_t + \delta g_t + \varepsilon_t \tag{6.5.5}$$

where g_t is a mechanism like (6.5.4) and δ is an unknown parameter. As before g_t can include higher-order lags and observable variables. Further generalisation within a structural framework can, in principle, be made by allowing various components to depend on g_t.

6.5.2 Breaks in components

The essence of a structural time series model is that it allows the various components in the model to change slowly over time. On occasion these components may be subject to sudden shifts. This kind of situation is parallel to the problem of outliers, as discussed in sub-section 6.4.2. The difference is that its root cause lies in the transition equation rather than the measurement equation. Outliers are a temporary phenomenon which we do not want to affect the basic model; breaks in components are a permanent effect which we would like the model to adjust to as quickly as possible. The consequences of ignoring such shifts are as follows. For given values of the hyperparameters, the model will usually adjust to allow for breaks in components, but this may take some time. When the hyperparameters need to be estimated, they will be subject to some distortion. Thus in a random walk plus noise model, a sudden change in the level at some point will result in the estimator of the variance of the level disturbance term, σ_η^2, being larger than it might otherwise have been.

As is the case with outliers, the treatment of breaks in components is clear cut when they are seen to be the result of *identifiable events*. They can then be handled explicitly by the introduction of dummy variables into the model. This is known as intervention analysis and the technical details are set out in section 7.6. Any component which appears in the state vector can be treated in this way. An example of a shift in level which is due to an identifiable event is the drop in the series of car drivers killed and seriously injured, shown in Figure 1.2.2. This can be attributed to the seat belt law of 1983 and it is modelled as such in section 7.6. Unfortunately not all shifts in components have such straightforward solutions. For example, consider the fall in UK manufacturing output which can be seen in Figure 1.2.1(b). This took place at the start of Mrs Thatcher's period as Prime Minister of the United Kingdom and it can be attributed to a number of causes such as a high exchange rate. The question of whether this warrants a 'Thatcher effect' dummy variable is not an easy one to answer, particularly as the fall took place over several observations.

If the components in a model are subject to breaks at unknown points in time, the problem becomes even more difficult. Detection of breaks in components is as difficult, if not more difficult, than detecting outliers. A somewhat different approach is to set up a model in which the disturbances in the transition equation have long-tailed distributions. The more general filter described in sub-section 3.7.3 may then be applied. Kitagawa (1987) gives some examples of how such an approach may work in practice.

6.5.3 Breaks in structure and switching regimes

As was shown in sub-section 2.7.4, an analysis of the series on US Real GNP indicates that its structure changes after 1947. There is a change in regime in that the values taken by the relative hyperparameters in the two periods are quite different. This change is attributable to the success of stabilisation policies in the post-war period brought about, in large part, by the Keynesian revolution in macroeconomics.

Changes in regime at known points in time require appropriate modification to the state space model at these points. The construction of a likelihood function still proceeds via the prediction error decomposition, the only difference being that there are now more parameters to estimate. If all the parameters change when there is a change in regime, as in the US GNP example, it may be easier, from the practical point of view simply to estimate separate models for each regime. This at least means that one parameter can be concentrated out of the likelihood function for each regime. If all the regimes are handled together, there is a saving on observations needed to construct starting values for non-stationary components, but only one parameter can be concentrated out of the likelihood function for the whole series. Of course, if the components are also subject to a break when there is a change in regime, estimating each regime separately becomes the appropriate procedure.

Example 6.5.2 Consider the random walk plus noise model with two regimes $\psi_1=[\sigma^2_{1\varepsilon} \quad \sigma^2_{1\eta}]'$ for $t=1,\ldots,T_1$ and $\psi_2=[\sigma^2_{2\varepsilon} \quad \sigma^2_{2\eta}]'$ for $t=T_1+1,\ldots,T$. If the two regimes are handled together, one of the variances, say $\sigma^2_{1\varepsilon}$, can be concentrated out of the likelihood function. The others are expressed relative to it. A likelihood function is then formed for $y_2,\ldots,y_T$, with y_1 being used to obtain a starting value for μ_t. If the two regimes are estimated separately, then a parameter can be concentrated out of each likelihood function. However, the observation at time T_1+1 is then needed to construct a starting value for μ_t in the second regime.

The point at which a regime changes may be endogenous to the model. Thus it is possible to have a finite number of regimes each with a different set of hyperparameters. If the signal as to which regime holds depends on past values of the observations, the model is conditionally Gaussian. Two possible models spring to mind. The first is a two-regime model in which the regime is determined by the sign of Δy_{t-1}. The second is a threshold model, in which the regime depends on whether or not y_t has crossed a certain threshold value in the previous period. Thus for two thresholds, c_1 and c_2, with $c_1>c_2$ the signals may be:

$$\left.\begin{array}{ll}\text{Regime 1:} & y_{t-1}>c_1\\ \text{Regime 2:} & y_{t-1}<c_2\\ \text{Regime 3:} & c_2\leqslant y_{t-1}\leqslant c_1\end{array}\right\}\tag{6.5.6}$$

Some applications of threshold models can be found in Tong and Lim (1980) and Pemberton and Tong (1983).

More generally, the switch may depend on the estimate of the state based in information at time $t-1$. Such a model is still conditionally Gaussian and allows a fair degree of flexibility in model formulation.

Example 6.5.3. In work on the business cycle, it has often been observed that the downward movement into a recession proceeds at a more rapid rate than the subsequent recovery. This suggests some modification to the cyclical components in structural models formulated for macroeconomic time series. A switch from one frequency to another can be made endogenous to the system by letting

$$\lambda_c = \begin{cases} \lambda_1 & \text{if } \tilde{\psi}_{t|t-1} - \tilde{\psi}_{t-1} > 0 \\ \lambda_2 & \text{if } \tilde{\psi}_{t|t-1} - \tilde{\psi}_{t-1} \leqslant 0 \end{cases}$$

where $\tilde{\psi}_{t|t-1}$ and $\tilde{\psi}_{t-1}$ are the MMSEs of the cyclical component based on the information at time $t-1$. A positive value of $\tilde{\psi}_{t|t-1} - \tilde{\psi}_{t-1}$ indicates that the cycle is in an upswing and hence λ_1 will be set to a smaller value than λ_2. In other words the period in the upswing is larger.

The multi-regime model of Harrison and Stevens (1976) also allows for the regime to switch endogenously. However, in this case it is assumed that the parameters in the different regimes are known and that there are known transition probabilities from one regime to the next.

A final way of allowing for changes in the structure of the model is to let the hyperparameters change over time according to some stochastic process. Thus, for example, in the random walk plus noise model, the signal–noise ratio, q, may be modelled as a random walk or may perhaps be allowed to change slowly over time in some other way. However, allowing q to change over time may be asking too much of the data. The method proposed by Trigg and Leach (1967) allows the smoothing 'constant', λ, in the EWMA to change over time and this approach, known as 'adaptive filtering', is essentially the same as letting q change over time. The difficulty in applying Trigg and Leach in practice concerns the trade-off between speed of adjustment and stability. In a more recent paper, Ekern (1981) argues that keeping λ constant generally yields a much better forecasting performance than Trigg and Leach.

6.6 Non-normality, count data and qualitative observations

The normality test, the N test of (5.4.12), is one of the standard diagnostic tests. However, the detection of non-normality in the residuals should not necessarily be taken as an indication that the appropriate way to proceed is to formulate a model with non-normal disturbances. Non-normality in the residuals may arise for a number of reasons. For example, there may be an outlier, which, if it can be associated with an identifiable event, is best modelled by a dummy variable. Alternatively a non-linear model, such as ARCH, may be appropriate. Finally the non-normality may be a symptom of a failure to make an appropriate transformation, such as taking logarithms.

The initial reaction to non-normality is therefore to attempt to reformulate the model in such a way that normality of the disturbances can be assumed. If this cannot be done, then non-normality is intrinsic to the problem. The fundamental way in which intrinsic non-normality arises stems from the nature of the data. This being the case it should be recognised at the outset. Thus the observations may record the number of events which occur in each time period. This is known as *count data.* An example is provided by the Chicago purse-snatching data introduced in sub-section 2.7.3. In that case a Gaussian model was used but if the number of events in each period is relatively small, a normal approximation is unreasonable. In order to be data-admissible the model should explicitly take account of the fact that the observations must be non-negative integers. A more extreme example is when the data are dichotomous and can take one of only two values, zero and one. The structural approach to time series model-building attempts to take such data characteristics into account.

Count data models are usually based on distributions such as the Poisson or negative binomial. If the means of these distributions are constant, or can be modelled in terms of observable variables, then estimation is relatively easy; see, for example, the book on GLIM models by McCullagh and Nelder (1983). The essence of time series models, however, is that the mean of a series cannot be modelled in terms of observable variables but depend on some stochastic mechanism. The nature of count data makes ARIMA models inappropriate unless the values of the observations are large enough to justify the assumption of normally distributed disturbances as a reasonable approximation. The structural approach is more appealing in that it explicitly takes into account the notion that there may be two sources of randomness, one affecting the underlying level and the other affecting the distribution of the observations around that level. Thus one can consider setting up a model in which the distribution of an observation, y_t, conditional on the mean, μ_t, is Poisson or negative binomial, while the mean itself follows a stochastic process such that it is always positive. The same ideas can be used to handle *qualitative* variables. The simplest such case is that of binary data, where the two possible outcomes are dependent on a binomial distribution. The set-up may be generalized to several outcomes, dependent on a multinomial distribution.

The essence of the problem is to formulate a model which allows the distribution of y_t, given past observations, to be obtained. If this can be done, the likelihood function can be formed and used as the basis for estimating unknown parameters in the model. Predictions of future observations may then be made. The solution to the problem rests on the use of natural-conjugate distributions of the type used in Bayesian statistics. However, the approach taken here is still essentially a classical one and an attempt is made to develop a model-fitting procedure based on the kind of methodology used for Gaussian models.

We focus our attention on formulating models for count and qualitative data which are analogous to the random walk plus noise model

$$y_t = \mu_t + \varepsilon_t, \quad t = 1, \ldots, T \tag{6.6.1a}$$

$$\mu_t = \mu_{t-1} + \eta_t \tag{6.6.1b}$$

in that they allow the underlying level of the process to change over time. By introducing a hyperparameter, ω, into these local level models, past observations are discounted in making forecasts of future observations. Indeed it transpires that in all cases the predictions can be constructed by an *exponentially weighted moving average* (EWMA). This is exactly what happens in the random walk plus noise model under the normality assumption.

Explanatory variables can be introduced into our local level models via the kind of link functions which appear in GLIM models; see section 7.9. Time trends and seasonal effects can be included as special cases. The framework does not extend to allowing these effects to be stochastic, as is typically the case in linear structural models. This may not be a serious restriction. Even with data on continuous variables, it is not unusual to find that the slope and seasonal effects are close to being deterministic; see, for example, the fitted seat belt model in sub-section 2.7.1. With count and qualitative data it seems even less likely that the observations will provide enough information to pick up changes in the slope and seasonal effects over time.

The use of natural conjugate distributions to formulate local level models for count and qualitative observations was suggested by J. Q. Smith (1979, 1981). He observed that such procedures gave rise to EWMA predictions. His models were set up within a Bayesian framework, however, and he did not advocate the estimation of the hyperparameter, ω, by maximum likelihood. The same is true of West *et al.* (1985) and West and Harrison (1986) where various approximations are used in order to tackle a more general problem in which components other than the level are allowed to change over time. The approach adopted in this paper is more along the lines of that employed by R. L. Smith and Miller (1986) in their study on predicting records in athletics. However, their paper is not concerned with count or qualitative observations but rather with observations which, when transformed, are exponentially distributed.

The opening sub-section sets out the basic approach and applies it to modelling Poisson observations. Sub-section 6.6.2 extends these ideas to data from binomial and multinomial distributions. The negative binomial is examined in sub-section 6.6.3. Some applications, taken from Harvey and Fernandes (1989), are presented in sub-sections 6.6.4 and 6.6.5. The final sub-section looks at models for exponential and extreme value distributions.

6.6.1 Poisson observations

Suppose that the observations at time t are drawn from a Poisson distribution,

$$p(y_t | \mu_t) = \mu_t^{y_t} e^{-\mu_t} / y_t! \tag{6.6.2}$$

This corresponds to the measurement equation of (6.6.1a).

The conjugate prior for a Poisson distribution is the gamma distribution. Let $p(\mu_{t-1}|Y_{t-1})$ denote the p.d.f. of μ_{t-1} conditional on the information at time $t-1$. Suppose that this distribution is gamma, that is it is given by

$$p(\mu; a, b) = \frac{e^{-b\mu}\mu^{a-1}}{\Gamma(a)b^{-a}}, \quad a, b > 0 \tag{6.6.3}$$

with $\mu = \mu_{t-1}$, $a = a_{t-1}$ and $b = b_{t-1}$ where a_{t-1} and b_{t-1} are computed from the first $t-1$ observations, Y_{t-1}. In model (6.6.1) with normally distributed observations, $\mu_{t-1} \sim N(m_{t-1}, p_{t-1})$ at time $t-1$ implies that $\mu_t \sim N(m_{t-1}, p_{t-1} + \sigma_\eta^2)$ at time $t-1$. In other words the mean of $\mu_t|Y_{t-1}$ is the same as that of $\mu_{t-1}|Y_{t-1}$ but the variance increases. The same effect can be induced in the gamma distribution by multiplying a and b by a factor less than one. We therefore suppose that $p(\mu_t|Y_{t-1})$ follows a gamma distribution with parameters $a_{t|t-1}$ and $b_{t|t-1}$ such that

$$a_{t|t-1} = \omega a_{t-1} \tag{6.6.4a}$$

$$b_{t|t-1} = \omega b_{t-1} \tag{6.6.4b}$$

and $0 < \omega \leqslant 1$. Then

$$\mathrm{E}(\mu_t|Y_{t-1}) = a_{t|t-1}/b_{t|t-1} = a_{t-1}/b_{t-1} = \mathrm{E}(\mu_{t-1}|Y_{t-1})$$

while

$$\mathrm{Var}(\mu_t|Y_{t-1}) = a_{t|t-1}/b_{t|t-1}^2 = \omega^{-1}\mathrm{Var}(\mu_{t-1}|Y_{t-1})$$

The stochastic mechanism governing the transition of μ_{t-1} to μ_t is therefore defined implicitly rather than explicitly. However, it is possible to show that it is formally equivalent to a multiplicative transition equation of the form

$$\mu_t = \omega^{-1}\mu_{t-1}\eta_t \tag{6.6.5}$$

where η_t has a beta distribution, of the form (6.6.19), with parameters ωa_{t-1} and $(1-\omega)a_{t-1}$; see the discussion in Smith and Miller (1986).

Once the observation y_t becomes available, the posterior distribution, $p(\mu_t|Y_t)$, is obtained by evaluating an expression similar to (3.7.24). This yields a gamma distribution with parameters

$$a_t = a_{t|t-1} + y_t \tag{6.6.6a}$$

$$b_t = b_{t|t-1} + 1 \tag{6.6.6b}$$

The initial prior gamma distribution, that is the distribution of μ_t at time $t=0$, tends to become diffuse, or non-informative, as $a, b \to 0$, although it is actually degenerate at $a = b = 0$ with $\Pr(\mu = 0) = 1$. However, none of this prevents the recursions (6.6.4) and (6.6.6) being initialised at $t=0$ with $a_0 = b_0 = 0$. A proper distribution for μ_t is then obtained at time $t = \tau$ where τ is the index of the first non-zero observation. It follows that, conditional on Y_τ, the joint density of the observations $y_{\tau+1},\ldots,y_T$ is

$$p(y_{\tau+1},\ldots,y_T;\omega)=\prod_{t=\tau+1}^{T} p(y_t|Y_{t-1}) \tag{6.6.7}$$

The predictive p.d.f.'s are given by

$$p(y_t|Y_{t-1})=\int_0^\infty p(y_t|\mu_t)p(\mu_t|Y_{t-1})d\mu_t \tag{6.6.8}$$

and for Poisson observations and a gamma prior, this operation yields a negative binomial distribution

$$p(y_t|Y_{t-1})=\binom{a+y_t-1}{y_t}b^a(1+b)^{-(a+y_t)} \tag{6.6.9}$$

where $a=a_{t|t-1}$ and $b=b_{t|t-1}$ and

$$\binom{a+y_t-1}{y_t}=\frac{\Gamma(a+y)}{\Gamma(y+1)\Gamma(a)}$$

although since y is an integer, $\Gamma(y+1)=y!$ Hence the log-likelihood function for the unknown hyperparameter ω is

$$\log L(\omega)=\sum_{t=\tau+1}^{T}\{\log\Gamma(a_{t|t-1}+y_t)-\log y_t!-\log\Gamma(a_{t|t-1})$$
$$+a_{t|t-1}\log b_{t|t-1}-(a_{t|t-1}+y_t)\log(1+b_{t|t-1})\} \tag{6.6.10}$$

It follows from the properties of the negative binomial that the mean and variance of the predictive distribution of y_{T+1} given Y_T are respectively

$$\tilde{y}_{T+1|T}=\mathrm{E}(y_{T+1}|Y_T)=a_{T+1|T}/b_{T+1|T}=a_T/b_T \tag{6.6.11a}$$

and

$$\mathrm{Var}(y_{T+1}|Y_T)=a_{T+1|T}(1+b_{T+1|T})/b^2_{T+1|T}$$
$$=\omega^{-1}\mathrm{Var}(\mu_T|Y_T)+E(\mu_T|Y_T) \tag{6.6.11b}$$

Repeated substitution from (6.6.4) and (6.6.6) shows that the forecast function is

$$\tilde{y}_{T+1|T}=a_T/b_T=\sum_{j=0}^{T-1}\omega^j y_{T-j}\Big/\sum_{j=0}^{T-1}\omega^j \tag{6.6.12}$$

This is a weighted mean in which the weights decline exponentially. It has exactly the same form as (2.2.14), the discounted least squares estimate of a mean. In large samples the denominator of (6.6.12) is approximately equal to $1/(1-\omega)$ when $\omega<1$ and the forecasts can be obtained recursively by the EWMA scheme

$$\tilde{y}_{t+1|t}=(1-\lambda)\tilde{y}_{t|t-1}+\lambda y_t,\quad t=1,\ldots,T \tag{6.6.13}$$

where $y_{1|0}=0$ and $\lambda=1-\omega$ is the smoothing constant. When $\omega=1$, the right-hand side of (6.6.12), is equal to the sample mean. Regarding this as an estimate of μ, the choice of zeros as initial values for a and b in the filter is seen to be justified insofar as it yields the classical solution. It is also worth noting that, unlike the Gaussian case, no approximations are involved in the use of a diffuse prior in this model.

Now consider multi-step prediction. The l-step-ahead predictive distribution at time T is given by

$$p(y_{T+l}|Y_T)=\int_0^\infty p(y_{T+l}|\mu_{T+l})p(\mu_{T+l}|Y_T)\,d\mu_{T+l} \tag{6.6.14}$$

It could be argued that the assumption embodied in (6.6.4) suggests that $p(\mu_{T+l}|Y_T)$ has a gamma distribution with parameters

$$a_{T+l|T}=\omega^l a_T \tag{6.6.15a}$$

$$b_{T+l|T}=\omega^l b_T \tag{6.6.15b}$$

This would mean the predictive distribution for y_{T+l} was negative binomial, (6.6.9), with a and b given by $a_{T+l|T}$ and $b_{T+l|T}$ in (6.6.15). Unfortunately the evolution which this implies for μ_t is not consistent with that which would occur if observations were made at times $T+1, T+2, \ldots, T+l-1$. In the latter case, the distribution of y_{T+l} at time T is

$$p(y_{T+l}|Y_T)=\sum_{y_{T+l-1}}\cdots\sum_{y_{T+1}}\prod_{j=1}^{l}p(y_{T+j}|Y_{T+j-1}) \tag{6.6.16}$$

This is the analogue of (3.7.8) for discrete observations. It is difficult to derive a closed form expression for $p(y_{T+l|T})$ from (6.6.16) for $l>1$ but it can, in principle, be evaluated numerically.

Although finding a closed form expression for $p(y_{T+l}|Y_T)$ is difficult, it is possible to show that

$$\mathrm{E}(y_{T+l}|Y_T)=a_T/b_T \tag{6.6.17}$$

for all lead times. To see this result, first note that taking the conditional expectation of y_{T+l} at time $T+l-1$ gives, from (6.6.11a),

$$\underset{T+l-1}{\mathrm{E}}(y_{T+l})=a_{T+l-1}/b_{T+l-1}$$

Using (6.6.4) and (6.6.6), and taking conditional expectations at time $T+l-2$ gives

$$\underset{T+l-2}{\mathrm{E}}\ \underset{T+l-1}{\mathrm{E}}(y_{T+l})=\underset{T+l-2}{\mathrm{E}}\left[\frac{\omega a_{T+l-2}+y_{T+l-1}}{\omega b_{T+l-2}+1}\right]$$

$$=\frac{a_{T+l-2}}{b_{T+l-2}},\quad l\geqslant 2$$

Repeating this procedure by taking conditional expectations at time $T+l-3$ and so on gives (6.6.17).

6.6.2 Binomial and multinomial observations

If the observations at time t are generated from a binomial distribution then

$$p(y_t|\pi_t)=\binom{n_t}{y_t}\pi_t^{y_t}(1-\pi_t)^{n_t-y_t}, \quad y_t=0,\ldots,n_t \tag{6.6.18}$$

where π is the probability that y_t is unity when n_t is one. The value of n_t is assumed to be fixed and known. Thus observations from the binomial can be regarded as a special case of count data where there is a fixed number of opportunities for the event in question to occur. When n_t is one, the data are *binary* or *dichotomous.*

The conjugate prior for the binomial distribution is the beta distribution

$$p(\pi; a, b)=[B(a, b)]^{-1}\pi^{a-1}(1-\pi)^{b-1} \tag{6.6.19}$$

where the beta function is

$$B(a, b)=\Gamma(a)\Gamma(b)/\Gamma(a+b)$$

Let $p(\pi_{t-1}|Y_{t-1})$ have a beta distribution with parameters a_{t-1} and b_{t-1}. Assume that $p(\pi_t|Y_{t-1})$ is also beta with parameters given by (6.6.4). This again ensures that the mean of $\pi_t|Y_{t-1}$ is the same as that of $\pi_{t-1}|Y_{t-1}$ but again the variance increases. Specifically

$$\mathrm{E}(\pi_t|Y_{t-1})=a_{t|t-1}/(a_{t|t-1}+b_{t|t-1})=a_{t-1}/(a_{t-1}+b_{t-1})$$

and

$$\begin{aligned}\mathrm{Var}(\pi_t|Y_{t-1})&=\frac{a_{t|t-1}b_{t|t-1}}{(a_{t|t-1}+b_{t|t-1})^2(a_{t|t-1}+b_{t|t-1}+1)}\\&=\frac{a_{t-1}b_{t-1}}{(a_{t-1}+b_{t-1})^2(\omega a_{t-1}+\omega b_{t-1}+1)}\end{aligned}$$

Once the t-th observation becomes available, the distribution of $\pi_t|Y_t$ is beta with parameters

$$a_t=a_{t|t-1}+y_t \tag{6.6.20a}$$

$$b_t=b_{t|t-1}+n_t-y_t \tag{6.6.20b}$$

The predictive distribution, $p(y_t|Y_{t-1})$ is beta-binomial

$$p(y_t|Y_{t-1})=\frac{1}{n_t+1}\,\frac{B(a+y_t, b+n_t-y_t)}{B(y_t+1, n_t-y_t+1)\,B(a, b)} \tag{6.6.21}$$

where $a=a_{t|t-1}$ and $b=b_{t|t-1}$. The likelihood function is again (6.6.7) with

τ defined as the first time period for which

$$0<\sum_{t=1}^{\tau} y_t<\sum_{t=1}^{\tau} n_t$$

This condition ensures that a_τ and b_τ are strictly positive, although again there is nothing to prevent us starting the recursions (6.6.4) and (6.6.20) at $t=1$ with $a_0=b_0=0$; see the comments in Lehmann (1983, p. 243). (This does not correspond to the use of a uniform prior. Since the range of a beta distribution is between zero and one, a uniform prior is a proper prior and the summation in the likelihood runs from $t=1$ to T. A uniform distribution is obtained by setting the beta parameters, a and b, equal to unity; alternatively Jeffreys (1961) has argued that it is more appropriate to have $a=b=\frac{1}{2}$, corresponding to arc sin $(\pi^{\frac{1}{2}})$ having a uniform distribution.)

From the properties of the beta-binomial distribution, the mean and variance of y_{T+1} conditional on the information at time T are

$$\tilde{y}_{T+1|T}=\mathrm{E}(y_{T+1}|Y_T)=n_{T+1}a_T/(a_T+b_T) \tag{6.6.22a}$$

$$\mathrm{Var}\,(y_{t+1}|Y_t)=\frac{n_{T+1}a_Tb_T(a_T+b_T+\omega^{-1}n_{T+1})}{(a_t+b_T)^2(a_T+b_T+\omega^{-1})} \tag{6.6.22b}$$

By substituting repeatedly from the recursive equations (6.6.20) it can be seen that, for n_t constant, $\tilde{y}_{T+1|T}$ is effectively an EWMA.

For binary data, $n_t=1$, the beta-binomial distribution in (6.6.21) reduces to a binomial distribution with

$$\Pr(y_t=1|Y_{t-1})=a_{t|t-1}/(a_{t|t-1}+b_{t|t-1}) \tag{6.6.23}$$

The log-likelihood function can be written very simply. As regards forecasts, it can be shown, by evaluating (6.6.16), that the distribution of $y_{T+l}|Y_T$ is binomial with expected value $a_T/(a_T+b_T)$ for all $l=1, 2, 3, \ldots$. Hence its variance does not increase with the lead time.

The model for binary data can easily be extended to handle Markov chains in which there are two parameters evolving over time but the one which pertains at time t depends on the observation at $t-1$. Thus if

$y_{t-1}=1$ then $\Pr(y_t=1)=\pi_{t|t-1}$

while if

$y_{t-1}=0$ then $\Pr(y_t=1)=\pi^*_{t|t-1}$

When $y_{t-1}=1$, the parameters $a_{t|t-1}$ and $b_{t|t-1}$ associated with $\pi_{t|t-1}$ are used to form the predictive distribution for y_t and are updated via (6.6.20) when y_t becomes available. From the point of view of π^*_t, y_t is treated as though it were missing. When $y_{t-1}=0$, the situation is reversed.

When there are more than two categories, the observations are said to be *polytomous* and the multinomial distribution is appropriate. Let there be $m+1$ possible categories and suppose that the probability that, at time t, an object belongs to the i-th category is π_{it}. If there are n_t trials and the number of objects in the i-th category is y_{it}, then

$$p(y_{0t}, \ldots, y_{mt}) = \binom{n_t}{y_{1t}, \ldots, y_{mt}} \prod_{i=0}^{m} \pi_{it}^{y_{it}} \tag{6.6.24}$$

with

$$\sum_{i=0}^{m} y_{it} = n_t \quad \text{and} \quad \sum_{i=0}^{m} \pi_{it} = 1$$

The conjugate prior for the multinomial distribution is the multivariate beta or *Dirichlet* distribution

$$p(\pi_0, \ldots, \pi_m; a_0, \ldots, a_m) = \frac{\Gamma(\Sigma a_i)}{\Pi \Gamma(a_i)} \prod_{i=0}^{m} \pi_i^{a_i - 1} \tag{6.6.25}$$

where the summations are from $i=0$ to m. (When $m=1$ this collapses to the beta distribution with $a_0 = a$ and $a_1 = b$.) Proceeding as in the previous section, it is not difficult to show that the recursive equations corresponding to (6.6.4) and (6.6.20) become

$$a_{i,t|t-1} = \omega a_{i,t-1} \tag{6.6.26a}$$

$$a_{it} = a_{i,t|t-1} + y_{it}, \quad i = 0, \ldots, m \tag{6.6.26b}$$

The likelihood for ω is as in (6.6.7) with τ the first value of t which yields $a_{it} > 0$ for all $i = 0, \ldots, m$. The predictive distribution in this case is known as the Dirichlet-multinomial. The forecasts can again be expressed in terms of EWMAs.

6.6.3 *Negative binomial observations*

The negative binomial distribution is

$$p(y_t | \pi_t) = \binom{\upsilon + y_t - 1}{y_t} \pi_t^{\upsilon} (1 - \pi_t)^{y_t} \quad y_t = 0, 1, 2, \ldots \tag{6.6.27}$$

where $0 < \pi_t < 1$ and $\upsilon > 0$. This is known as the Pascal distribution if υ is an integer and if $\upsilon = 1$ it corresponds to the geometric distribution. The mean and variance are

$$\mathrm{E}(y_t | \pi_t) = \upsilon(1 - \pi)/\pi \tag{6.6.28a}$$

$$\mathrm{Var}(y_t | \pi_t) = \mathrm{E}(y_t | \pi_t)[1 + \upsilon^{-1} \mathrm{E}(y_t | \pi_t)] \tag{6.6.28b}$$

The distribution therefore exhibits overdispersion compared with the Poisson distribution, that is the variance exceeds the mean. However, if the mean is kept constant, the negative binomial tends towards the Poisson distribution as $\upsilon \rightarrow \infty$. The conjugate prior distribution for the negative binomial is the beta distribution. At first sight it might appear that the recursions in (6.6.4) are again appropriate. However, in view of (6.6.28a), it is the expected value of $(1-\pi)/\pi$, rather than π, which needs to be kept constant while the variance increases. For a beta distribution, (6.6.19),

$$E[(1-\pi)/\pi]=\int_0^1 \pi^{a-2}(1-\pi)^b\,d\pi$$

$$=\frac{B(a-1,b+1)}{B(a,b)}=\frac{b}{a-1} \tag{6.6.29}$$

provided that $a>1$. Hence we require that

$$\frac{b_{t|t-1}}{a_{t|t-1}-1}=\frac{b_{t-1}}{a_{t-1}-1} \tag{6.6.30}$$

This can be achieved by multiplying the numerator and denominator in the expression on the right-hand side of (6.6.30) by ω. The prediction equation, (6.6.4a), is therefore modified to

$$a_{t|t-1}=\omega a_{t-1}+(1-\omega), \quad 0<\omega\leqslant 1 \tag{6.6.31}$$

while (6.6.4b) remains unchanged. The updating equations have the more standard form

$$a_t=a_{t|t-1}+\upsilon \tag{6.6.32a}$$

$$b_t=b_{t|t-1}+y_t \tag{6.6.32b}$$

The predictive distribution is the beta-Pascal

$$p(y_t|Y_{t-1})=\frac{1}{\upsilon+y_t}\frac{B(\upsilon+a_{t|t-1},y_t+b_{t|t-1})}{B(\upsilon,y_t+1)\,B(a_{t|t-1},b_{t|t-1})} \tag{6.6.33}$$

and the likelihood function is as in (6.6.7) with τ the first value of t for which y_t is non-zero.

The expected value of the one-step-ahead predictive distribution at time T is

$$\tilde{y}_{T+1|T}=\mathrm{E}(y_{T+1}|Y_T)$$

$$=\int_0^1 \mathrm{E}(y_{T+1}|\pi_{T+1})p(\pi_{T+1}|Y_T)d\pi_{T+1}$$

$$=\upsilon\frac{b_{T+1|T}}{a_{T+1|T}-1}=\frac{\upsilon b_T}{a_T-1} \tag{6.6.34}$$

in view of (6.6.29) and the way in which prediction operates via (6.6.30). As in the previous models b_T can be written as an exponentially weighted average of past weights, while repeatedly substituting from (6.6.31) and (6.6.32a) gives

$$a_T = \upsilon \sum_{j=0}^{T-1} \omega^j + (1-\omega) \sum_{j=0}^{T-1} \omega^j \tag{6.6.35}$$

As $T \to \infty$, $(a_T - 1) \to \upsilon/(1-\omega)$ and so $\tilde{y}_{T+1|T}$ again has the EWMA form of (6.6.10). Furthermore, a similar argument to that used to show (6.6.17) can be employed to demonstrate that the optimal l-step-ahead forecasts remain at the level in (6.6.34).

The parameter υ can be estimated by ML along with ω. Alternatively it may be pre-set; see the discussion in Cameron and Trivedi (1986).

6.6.4 Model selection and applications

Models for count data are usually based on the Poisson or negative binomial distributions. If there are a fixed number of trials the binomial distribution is appropriate. It is also possible to conceive of situations where there are counts on the number of objects in several different categories. Multivariate set-ups of this kind will not be considered here. Suffice to say that the multinomial distribution is appropriate when there are a fixed number of trials; when this is not the case the negative multinomial becomes relevant.

Many of the issues which arise in the selection of GLIM models are also relevant here. However there is the additional problem of testing for serial correlation. The standardised (Pearson) residuals are defined by

$$v_t = \frac{y_t - E(y_t|Y_{t-1})}{\mathrm{SD}(y_t|Y_{t-1})} \tag{6.6.36}$$

If the parameters in the model are known, it follows from the decomposition of the likelihood in (6.6.7) that these residuals are independently distributed with mean zero and unit variance. However, they are not, in general, identically distributed. Thus some care needs to be exercised in constructing suitable diagnostic test statistics.

The following diagnostic checks may be carried out:

(a) Examine the plot of the residuals against time and against an estimate of the level;

(b) Check whether the sample variance of the Pearson residuals is close to one. A value greater than one indicates overdispersion relative to the model which is being fitted.

Goals scored by England against Scotland Figure 1.1.3 showed the number of goals scored by England in international football matches played against Scotland at Hampden Park in Glasgow. Apart from the war years these matches

Table 6.6.1 *Predictive probability distribution of goals in next match*

Number of goals					
0	1	2	3	4	>4
0.471	0.326	0.138	0.046	0.013	0.005

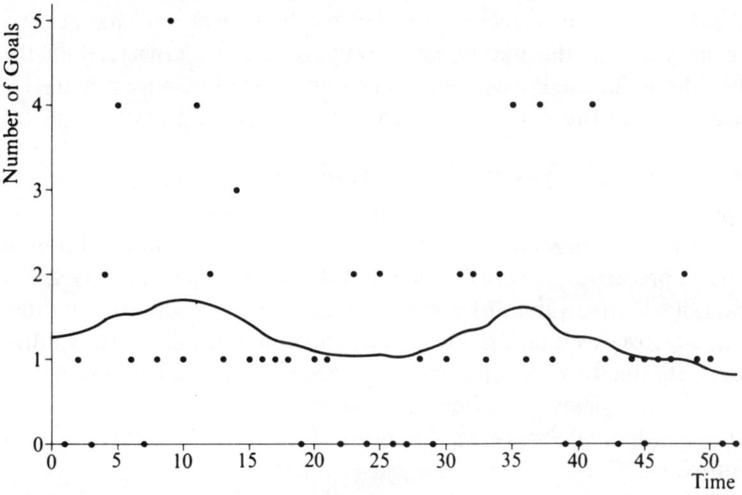

Fig. 6.6.1 Goals scored by England against Scotland at Hampden Park and underlying trend.

were played in Glasgow every other year. (The year 1985 was also an exception; the match should have been played at Wembley but Mrs Thatcher decreed that it be played in Scotland to save Londoners from the ravages of marauding Scottish football supporters.) Treating the observations as though they were evenly spaced, estimation of the Poisson-gamma model gives

$$\tilde{\omega}=0.844$$

The variance of the standardised residuals is 1.269 and a plot of them shows no indication of misspecification.

The forecast is 0.82. This corresponds to the forecasts that would have been obtained from the Gaussian random walk plus noise model (6.6.1) by setting $q=0.029$. The general formula is

$$q=(1+\omega^2-2\omega)/\omega; \tag{6.6.37}$$

see Exercise 6.12. The full one-step-ahead predictive distribution is shown in Table 6.6.1. The smooth line in Figure 6.6.1 shows the estimate of the level of the process obtained by applying the fixed-interval smoothing algorithm to a random walk plus noise model with $q=0.029$; see (3.6.17). Since there is no firm theoretical foundation for constructing a smoother in this way we will refer to it as the *quasi-smoother*.

Fitting the negative binomial-beta model using a crude grid search for υ yields an estimate of $\upsilon=5$, with the corresponding estimate of ω being 0.916. Thus the introduction of an adjustable scale parameter has resulted in less movement in the level. The variance of the standardised residuals is 1.077 and the prediction is 1.187. The likelihood function is relatively insensitive with respect to changes in υ. Furthermore its value at the maximum is only marginally greater than the maximised likelihood for the Poisson-gamma model. If an allowance is made for the extra parameter via the AIC, the Poisson-gamma model gives a better fit.

Purse snatching in Chicago The Gaussian random walk plus noise model was fitted to the purse-snatching data in sub-section 2.7.3. However the model is not, strictly speaking, data-admissible. The forecast function is horizontal and cannot be negative but a prediction interval of one RMSE on either side rapidly strays into the region of negative values of y. A logarithmic formulation, on the other hand, is not satisfactory as it fails the Bowman-Shenton normality test. A much better model is obtained by carrying out a square root transformation before fitting the model. This yields an estimated signal–noise ratio of $q=0.132$, while squaring the forecasted values gives predictions of 7.432 and a much narrower prediction interval.

Of course, the purse snatchings are an example of count data, but since the numbers are not too small, fitting various Gaussian models is a useful preliminary exercise. For example extending the model to include a stochastic slope indicates that such a component is unnecessary. It should be noted that the square root transformation is the variance-stabilising transformation for a Poisson distribution; see McCullagh and Nelder (1983, pp. 129–30).

When the data are treated explicitly as count data, a negative binomial-beta model with $\upsilon=20$ seems to give the best fit. The estimate of ω is

$$\tilde{\omega}=0.697$$

The predictions are 7.573, corresponding to predictions from the Gaussian model with $q=0.131$. A plot of the residuals shows no evidence of heteroscedasticity, while the sample variance of the standardised residuals is 1.008.

6.6.5 *Observations with exponential and related distributions*

Suppose that the observations follow an exponential distribution

$$p(y_t|\theta_t)=\theta_t \exp(-\theta_t y_t), \quad y_t>0 \tag{6.6.38}$$

This has a mean of $1/\theta_t$. If $\theta_{t-1} \sim \Gamma(a_{t-1}, b_{t-1})$, then the recursive equations are

$$a_t = \omega a_{t-1} + 1 \tag{6.6.39a}$$

$$b_t = \omega b_{t-1} + y_t \tag{6.6.39b}$$

The mean of the posterior distribution of θ_T is

$$\mathrm{E}(\theta_T | Y_T) = \frac{a_T}{b_T} = \frac{1}{\mathrm{EWMA}(y)}$$

where EWMA(y) denotes the exponentially weighted average given in (6.6.12).

The predictive distribution is

$$p(y_t | Y_{t-1}) = a_{t|t-1} b_{t|t-1}^{a_{t|t-1}} / (b_{t/t-1} + y_t)^{a_{t|t-1}+1}, \quad y_t > 0 \tag{6.6.40}$$

This is a Pareto distribution. The properties of the Pareto distribution are such that the predictive distribution for y_{T+1}, given Y_T, has mean

$$\underset{T}{\mathrm{E}}(y_{T+1}) = \frac{b_{T+1|T}}{a_{T+1|T} - 1} = \frac{\omega b_T}{\omega a_T - 1} \tag{6.6.41}$$

for $a_{T+1} > 1$. However, it may be preferable to define the prediction equation for $a_{t|t-1}$ in the same way as for the negative binomial, (6.6.31). Thus (6.6.39a) becomes

$$a_t = \omega a_{t-1} + (1 - \omega) + 1 \tag{6.6.42}$$

As a result, from (6.6.30),

$$\underset{T}{\mathrm{E}}(y_{T+1}) = b_T/(a_T - 1) = \mathrm{EWMA}(y) \tag{6.6.43}$$

As regards the variance

$$\mathrm{Var}(y_{T+1} | Y_T) = a_{T+1|T} b_{T+1|T}^2 (a_{T+1|T} - 1)^{-2} (a_{T+1|T} - 2)^{-1}$$

provided that $a_{T+1|T} > 2$. From (6.6.30) and (6.6.43)

$$\mathrm{Var}(y_{T+1} | Y_T) = \frac{a_{T+1|T}}{a_{T+1|T} - 2} \left[\underset{T}{E}(y_{T+1}) \right]^2 \tag{6.6.44}$$

Censored observations are easily handled within the framework of an exponential distribution. Such observations arise when the only information recorded is that $y \geqslant y_{\max}$. With exponentially distributed observations, the probability of such an occurence is

$$\int_{y_{\max}}^{\infty} \frac{1}{\theta} e^{-\theta y} dy = \exp(y_{\max}) \tag{6.6.45}$$

The application of Bayes theorem for a censored observation leads to no change in the updating equations for b_t. However, a_t is affected. Since, from (6.6.45) above, $p(y_t|\theta_t)$ is just equal to $\exp(y_t)$ for a censored observation, the recursive equation in (6.6.42) becomes

$$a_t = \omega a_{t-1} + (1-\omega) + \delta_t \tag{6.6.46}$$

where

$$\delta_t = \begin{cases} 0, & \text{censored observation} \\ 1, & \text{otherwise} \end{cases}$$

The likelihood function can be written down in terms of one-step-ahead predictive distributions as in (6.6.7). When there is no censoring, the predictive distribution is as in (6.6.40). For a censored value, (6.6.44) must be integrated from $y_{\max}$ to ∞ to yield

$$p(y_t|Y_{t-1}) = [b_{t|t-1}/(b_{t|t-1} + y_t)]^{a_{t|t-1}} \tag{6.6.47}$$

A further attraction of the exponential-gamma set-up is that it can be extended to handle observations which are generated by certain distributions which are related to the exponential. Two examples of distributions of a variable, x, and the relationship of this variable to the exponential, y, via the one-to-one transformation $y = g(x)$ are as follows:

(i) Weibull: $y = x^{\varphi}$
(ii) Gumbel: $y = \exp(\pm x/\varphi)$

Both distributions are for x positive. The scale parameter, φ, must either be fixed on prior grounds or estimated along with the other parameters in the model. The log-likelihood function of x is equal to the corresponding log-likelihood function of y plus the Jacobian term, that is

$$\log L(x) = \log L(y) + \sum_t \partial g(x_t)/\partial x_t \tag{6.6.48}$$

In their study of the prediction of records, Smith and Miller (1986) use the Gumbel, or extreme value, distribution. They also make an allowance for censoring. This arises in their application because, for any year in which the record is not broken, the best performance in that year is a censored value; all that is known is that it is bigger (or smaller) than the current record.

EXERCISES

6.1 Show that including a time trend in a regression is equivalent to first detrending all the variables by regressing on time.

6.2 Fitting an autoregression of the form (6.1.16)′ to the purse-snatching data of sub-section 2.7.3 gives

$$\widehat{\Delta y_t} = 3.916 - \underset{(0.122)}{0.286 y_{t-1}} - \underset{(0.146)}{0.412 \Delta y_{t-1}} - \underset{(0.126)}{0.022 \Delta y_{t-2}}$$

Interpret these results.

6.3 It is not unusual to estimate the current growth rate of a series by calculating the relative increase over the same period one year ago. Thus if y_t denotes the logarithm of the series in question, the estimator of the growth rate is

$$g_T = (y_T - y_{T-s})/s$$

Suppose the series can be represented by a BSM. If g_T is regarded as an estimator of β_{T-1}, show that its estimation error has zero expectation and that

$$\text{MSE}(g_T) = \text{Var}(g_T - \beta_{T-1})$$
$$= \frac{(s-1)(2s-1)}{6s}\sigma_\zeta^2 + \frac{\sigma_\eta^2}{s} + \frac{2\sigma_\omega^2}{s^2} + \frac{2\sigma_\varepsilon^2}{s^2}$$

Derive an analogous expression for when g_T is regarded as an estimator of β_T. Comment on these results.

6.4 Find an expression for the forecast function for the local quadratic trend model, (6.1.18).

6.5 Verify the identity (6.3.52).

6.6 Consider the data revisions problem of Example 6.4.1

(a) Confirm that expressions (6.4.28) and (6.4.29) are indeed obtained from the starting values given in (6.4.25) and find the corresponding MSE matrix, $\mathbf{P}_T^\dagger$.

(b) Carry out the Kalman filter recursions when $y_{T+1}^{(0)}$ and $y_{T-M+1}^\dagger$ become available. Compare the results with (6.4.28) and (6.4.29).

(c) Consider a naive estimation procedure in which μ_{T-1} is estimated from final observations as in (6.4.25), but the preliminary observation, $y_T^{(0)}$, is treated as though it were a final observation. Derive an expression for the forecasts of future observations, $y_{T+l}^\dagger$, $l = 1, 2, \ldots$, obtained in this way and find the MSE of these forecasts. Comment on the result.

(d) Explain how you would estimate the trend, μ_T, using two different smoothing procedures. Which do you prefer?

6.7 Derive the SSF, (6.3.37), for a BSM with time-varying trading day effects starting from a BSM formulated at the daily level with daily effects.

6.8 Consider a stationary AR(p) model in which some of the observations are subject to temporal aggregation. If the time between the observations, δ_τ, is never greater that p, explain how the AR parameters may be estimated, and the temporal aggregates distributed, without augmenting the state vector by the cumulator variable, (6.4.4).

6.9 Show that in Example 3.4.2, treating the missing observation, $y_t^{\dagger *}$, a parameter to be estimated, leads to the estimator obtained in (3.6.18) for a given value of φ. Write down the joint density function for the full set of variables, $y_1^{\dagger}, \ldots, y_{T+1}^{\dagger}$ (including the missing observation), and show that replacing $y_t^{\dagger *}$ by the estimator in (3.6.18) leads to a likelihood function which is the same as (3.4.83) apart from the determinantal and constant terms. Show that setting the missing observation equal to zero and introducing a dummy variable into the model, as in (6.4.3), leads to the same result.

6.10 Consider the process

$$y_t = \varepsilon_t + \beta \varepsilon_{t-1} \varepsilon_{t-2}, \quad t = 1, \ldots, T$$

where ε_t is a sequence of independent, identically distributed random variables with mean zero and constant variance and $\varepsilon_0 = \varepsilon_{-1} = 0$. Show that y_t is white noise. What is the MMSE of y_{T+1}? Compare this with the MMSLE.

Is the model conditionally Gaussian?

6.11 Find an expression for the MMSE of y_{T+1} in the model

$$y_t = \varphi_t y_{t-1} + \varepsilon_t, \quad t = 1, \ldots, T$$

where $\varphi_t = 0.8$ for t even and 0.5 for t odd, and ε_t is a sequence of independent random variables. Is the process stationary?

6.12 By equating the first-order autocorrelation for the stationary form of a random walk plus noise with that of an ARIMA(0, 1, 1), find an expression for the signal–noise ratio, q, in terms of θ. Hence, given that $\omega = -\theta$, verify expression (6.6.37)

Chapter 7

Explanatory variables

A structural time series model with explanatory variables collapses to a standard regression model when the stochastic components other than the irregular term are dropped. Thus many of the concepts and modelling procedures associated with regression are relevant to the models considered in this chapter. Some of these ideas, particularly those developed in econometrics, are reviewed in section 7.1 and an indication is given as to how they fit in with the structural approach to time series modelling.

Estimation of structural models with explanatory variables is covered in section 7.3. The preceding section lays some of the groundwork by reviewing the methods by which classical regression models may be estimated in the frequency domain. The tests set out in section 7.4 are essentially generalisations of the tests given in chapter 5 and modifications of tests used in regression. A model selection strategy is developed in section 7.5. The applications illustrate how some of the key ideas concerning model selection used in econometrics can be taken on board in the structural approach. This methodology is extended to modelling the effects of interventions in section 7.6 and a number of new diagnostics specifically designed for interventions are introduced.

The last three sections deal with areas which are, as yet, relatively undeveloped. The first is concerned with models in which the parameters of the explanatory variables are allowed to be time-varying. The technical treatment of such models is fairly straightforward, but there is, as yet, little practical experience of the way in which these models may be formulated and applied. The same is true of the models for count data described in the last section. However, the results for the two applications to count data presented are very encouraging and seem to indicate that the approach taken is a viable one. The penultimate section deals with the application of instrumental variables.

7.1 Introduction

So far the variable y_t has been modelled in terms of past values of itself and its position with respect to time. In the basic structural model its movements are explained in terms of a stochastic time trend and a stochastic seasonal component. Suppose now that the information set is expanded to include

k observable variables, and that these variables are able to explain some of the movements in y_t. If the additional variables are (weakly) exogenous and the relationship between them and y_t is linear, the model may be written as

$$y_t = \mu_t + \gamma_t + \mathbf{x}_t'\boldsymbol{\delta} + \varepsilon_t, \quad t = 1, \ldots, T \tag{7.1.1}$$

The $k \times 1$ vector $\mathbf{x}_t$ contains the explanatory variables while the $k \times 1$ vector $\boldsymbol{\delta}$ contains the unknown parameters associated with them. Thus the linear combination $\mathbf{x}_t'\boldsymbol{\delta}$ has been added to the basic structural model. More generally, other components such as cycles or daily effects may be employed as well as, or instead of, the trend and seasonal components.

The rationale for a model of the form (7.1.1) was discussed briefly in the introductory chapter. The explanatory variables are only partially successful in explaining the level of y_t. If they were completely successful, the trend would reduce to a constant term. Similarly, the seasonal component would be unnecessary if the seasonal movements in y_t could be fully explained by corresponding movements in $\mathbf{x}_t$.

The condition that the variables in $\mathbf{x}_t$ are weakly exogenous is a crucial one. Weak exogeneity as defined by Engle *et al.* (1983) means that we can condition on $\mathbf{x}_t$ without losing any information relevant to the estimation of the unknown parameters in the model. Hence it is not necessary to construct a model for $\mathbf{x}_t$. A more formal definition is given in sub-section 7.1.4. The penultimate section in the chapter gives an instrumental variable estimator which at least has desirable properties when some of the explanatory variables are not weakly exogenous.

Forecasts of y_t are made conditional on values of the explanatory variables. In general these values will be unknown as they are future values. Hence the forecasts are conditional on predictions of the explanatory variables themselves or on some future *scenario*. Either way, if efficient forecasts are to be based on a single equation, the explanatory variables must satisfy the more stringent requirement of strong exogeneity, as opposed to weak exogeneity. Again this concept is defined formally in sub-section 7.1.4.

If lagged values of an exogenous variable enter into equation (7.1.1), the variable is said to be a *leading indicator*. In this case some of the lagged values of the exogenous variables will be known for a limited number of future time periods. The gains from leading indicators are discussed in Box and Jenkins (1976).

7.1.1 State space form

The basic structural model was put into state space form in sub-section 4.1.1. Model (7.1.1) can be similarly expressed by retaining the same transition equation but having the measurement equation as

$$y_t = \mathbf{z}_t'\boldsymbol{\alpha}_t + \mathbf{x}_t'\boldsymbol{\delta} + \varepsilon_t, \quad t = 1, \ldots, T \tag{7.1.2}$$

In terms of (3.1.2), the general definition of a measurement equation for a univariate time series, d_t, here is equal to $\mathbf{x}_t'\boldsymbol{\delta}$. The equation in (7.1.2) can be taken to represent a much wider class of models than (7.1.1) simply by defining $\mathbf{z}_t$ and $\boldsymbol{\alpha}_t$ as appropriate for the required unobserved components.

If $\boldsymbol{\delta}$ were known, the addition of $\mathbf{x}_t'\boldsymbol{\delta}$ to the measurement equation would make no real difference to the operation of the Kalman filter. However, in most cases of interest, $\boldsymbol{\delta}$ is unknown. It is often useful to incorporate it into the state vector. This gives an augmented state vector $\boldsymbol{\alpha}_t^\dagger = [\boldsymbol{\alpha}_t' \quad \boldsymbol{\delta}_t']'$ which satisfies the state space model

$$y_t = [\mathbf{z}_t' \quad \mathbf{x}_t']\boldsymbol{\alpha}_t^\dagger + \varepsilon_t, \quad t=1,\ldots,T \tag{7.1.3a}$$

and

$$\boldsymbol{\alpha}_t^\dagger = \begin{bmatrix} \boldsymbol{\alpha}_t \\ \boldsymbol{\delta}_t \end{bmatrix} = \begin{bmatrix} \mathbf{T} & \mathbf{0} \\ \mathbf{0} & \mathbf{I} \end{bmatrix} \begin{bmatrix} \boldsymbol{\alpha}_{t-1} \\ \boldsymbol{\delta}_{t-1} \end{bmatrix} + \begin{bmatrix} \boldsymbol{\eta}_t \\ \mathbf{0} \end{bmatrix} \tag{7.1.3b}$$

The lower part of the transition equation simply reflects the fact that $\boldsymbol{\delta} = \boldsymbol{\delta}_t$ is time-invariant. Including it in the state vector allows it to be estimated simultaneously with $\boldsymbol{\alpha}_t$. In addition it opens up the generalisation to a time-varying parameter model in which

$$\boldsymbol{\delta}_t = \boldsymbol{\delta}_{t-1} + \boldsymbol{\upsilon}_t, \tag{7.1.4}$$

where $\boldsymbol{\upsilon}_t$ is a $k \times 1$ vector of white-noise disturbances with a p.s.d. covariance matrix. The time-varying parameter regression model has been studied at some length. Recent reviews of the literature can be found in Chow (1984) and Nicholls and Pagan (1985).

The augmented SSF in (7.1.3) is convenient for forecasting since it allows the estimator of $\boldsymbol{\delta}$ to be updated as each new observation becomes available. If multi-step forecasts are to be made, the MSE of $\tilde{y}_{T+l|T}$ obtained from (7.1.3) will reflect the estimation error in the estimator of $\boldsymbol{\delta}$ as well as the uncertainty associated with the state variables in $\boldsymbol{\alpha}_t$. If forecasts of y_t are made without including $\boldsymbol{\delta}_t$ in the state vector, the resulting MSE is conditional on $\boldsymbol{\delta}$ as well as on the relative hyperparameters, $\boldsymbol{\psi}_*$.

Lagged values of the dependent variable may occur in structural models. Thus

$$y_t = \varphi_1 y_{t-1} + \cdots + \varphi_r y_{t-r} + \mathbf{z}_t'\boldsymbol{\alpha}_t + \mathbf{x}_t'\boldsymbol{\delta} + \varepsilon_t, \quad t=r+1,\ldots,T \tag{7.1.5}$$

The dynamic properties of such models are described in the next sub-section and an application is given in sub-section 7.5.2. If the exogenous variables are removed from (7.1.5), the model reduces to a univariate model of the kind first introduced in (2.3.75).

There are two ways in which (7.1.5) may be handled. The first is to treat the lagged dependent variables in the same way as exogenous variables. Estimation can then be carried out using the time- or frequency-domain procedures described in section 7.3. However, when forecasts are made more than one step ahead, it is necessary to replace the lagged values of the dependent variable by predicted values. Thus the l-step-ahead forecast is

$$\tilde{y}_{T+l|T} = \sum_{i=1}^{r} \varphi_i \tilde{y}_{T+l-i|T} + \mathbf{z}_t' \mathbf{a}_{T+l|T} + \mathbf{x}_{T+l}' \mathbf{d}_T \tag{7.1.6}$$

where $\tilde{y}_{T+j|T} = y_{T+j}$ if $j \leqslant 0$, and the predicted values are built up recursively.

The problem with treating lagged dependent variables in the same way as exogenous variables is that no account is taken of the contribution to the prediction MSE arising from the use of predicted values. One solution is to employ a state space representation in which y_t and its lagged values are included in the state vector. The SSF is

$$y_t = [\mathbf{0}_m' \quad 1 \quad \mathbf{0}_{r-1}']\boldsymbol{\alpha}_t^* \tag{7.1.7a}$$

$$\boldsymbol{\alpha}_t^* = \begin{bmatrix} \boldsymbol{\alpha}_t \\ \mathbf{y}_t \\ \boldsymbol{\delta}_t \end{bmatrix} = \begin{bmatrix} \mathbf{T} & \mathbf{0} & \mathbf{0} \\ \mathbf{z}'\mathbf{T} & \boldsymbol{\varphi}' & \mathbf{0}' \\ \mathbf{0} \quad & \mathbf{I}_{r-1} \quad \mathbf{0} & \mathbf{0} \\ \mathbf{0} & \mathbf{0} & \mathbf{I} \end{bmatrix} \begin{bmatrix} \boldsymbol{\alpha}_{t-1} \\ \mathbf{y}_{t-1} \\ \boldsymbol{\delta}_{t-1} \end{bmatrix} + \begin{bmatrix} \mathbf{R}\boldsymbol{\eta}_t \\ \mathbf{z}_t'\mathbf{R}\boldsymbol{\eta}_t + \varepsilon_t \\ \mathbf{0} \\ \mathbf{0} \end{bmatrix} \tag{7.1.7b}$$

where $\mathbf{y}_t = [y_t, \ldots, y_{t-r+1}]'$ and $\boldsymbol{\varphi} = [\varphi_1, \ldots, \varphi_r]'$. (The Kalman filter can be started off at $t=0$ with a diffuse prior for the full state vector, or at $t=r$ with a diffuse prior for $\boldsymbol{\alpha}_t$, $\mathbf{y}_t$ and $\boldsymbol{\delta}_t$, and the lagged values $y_1, \ldots, y_r$ set equal to their observed values.) By including lagged values of y_t in the state vector, the computation of the predicted values of (7.1.6) is automatically accomplished. This augmented state space model in (7.1.6) is different to the one which would have been obtained if the lagged y_t's had been treated in the same way as exogenous variables and the $\boldsymbol{\varphi}$ vector had been included in the state vector in the manner of (7.1.3). The SSF in (7.1.7) cannot be used to estimate $\boldsymbol{\varphi}$ simultaneously with $\boldsymbol{\alpha}_t$, and hence the MSE of $\tilde{y}_{T+l|T}$ obtained from the prediction equations is conditional on $\boldsymbol{\varphi}$ as well as on the relative hyperparameters in the model.

Example 7.1.1 An AR(1) model, (2.3.6), is a special case of (7.1.5). If y_{t-1} is treated in the same way as an exogenous variable, MSE($\tilde{y}_{T+l|T}$) will be computed as σ^2 rather than $\sigma^2(1-\varphi^{2l})/(1-\varphi^2)$.

Another attraction of the SSF in (7.1.7) is that it can be used to handle missing observations. Attempting to deal with missing observations by means of dummy variables, as in (6.4.3), becomes very messy in the presence of lagged dependent variables.

7.1.2 Distributed lags

The explanatory variables can be made to exhibit dynamic effects in a number of ways, all of which are well documented in the econometric, engineering and time series literature. The methods used in econometrics are normally presented in the context of a regression model, but employing them in the somewhat more general context of (7.1.1) is equally valid.

Unconstrained distributed lags The simplest way of introducing dynamic effects into an explanatory variable is to include lagged values in the model. Thus

$$y_t = \mathbf{z}_t'\boldsymbol{\alpha}_t + \sum_{\tau=0}^{h} \mathbf{x}_{t-\tau}'\boldsymbol{\delta}_\tau + \varepsilon_t, \quad t=1,\ldots,T \tag{7.1.8}$$

The assumption that all the variables are subject to the same lag length, h, is made for notational convenience. There is no difficulty, in principle, in estimating the parameters in (7.1.8). However, if the object of the exercise is to obtain a reasonably precise estimate of the lag structure, a formulation of this kind may not always be satisfactory. The reason is that economic time series are typically slowly changing and so the various lagged values of each explanatory variable will tend to be highly correlated with each other. There are various ways of tackling this multicollinearity problem. However, they all have the same objective, which is to impose some constraints on the lag structure, thereby reducing the number of parameters to be estimated.

Polynomial distributed lags Almon (1965) suggested approximating the distributed lag structure by a polynomial. Thus suppose, for simplicity, that (7.1.8) contains only a single explanatory variable so that it is written as

$$y_t = \mathbf{z}_t'\boldsymbol{\alpha}_t + \sum_{\tau=0}^{h} \delta_\tau x_{t-\tau} + \varepsilon_t \tag{7.1.9}$$

Rather than attempting to estimate all $h+1$ coefficients, it is assumed that they lie on a polynomial of degree $g<h$. This means that the lag structure is modelled in terms of only $g+1$ parameters.

Let $P(\tau)$ be a polynomial of degree g which is a continuous function of τ. This depends on $g+1$ coefficients $\delta_0^*, \ldots, \delta_g^*$ and is expressed as

$$P(\tau) = \sum_{l=0}^{g} \delta_l^* \tau^l \tag{7.1.10}$$

Under the polynomial lag hypothesis, the lag coefficients in (7.1.9) are defined by

$$\delta_\tau = P(\tau)$$

for the integers $\tau = 0, 1, \ldots, h$. Note that $\delta_0 = P(0) = \delta_0^*$. As a simple illustration suppose that h is five, but that $P(\tau)$ is a second degree polynomial

$$P(\tau) = 2 + 5\tau - \tau^2$$

Because the coefficients all lie on a quadratic curve, the lag structure depends on only three parameters, $\delta_0^* = 2$, $\delta_1^* = 5$ and $\delta_2^* = -1$.

Estimation of a polynomial distributed lag can be carried out by noting that if δ_τ is set equal to $P(\tau)$ as in (7.1.11) the lag component in (7.1.9) can be written as

$$\sum_{\tau=0}^{h} \delta_\tau x_{t-\tau} = \sum_{l=0}^{g} \delta_l^* w_{lt} \tag{7.1.11a}$$

where

$$w_{lt} = \sum_{\tau=0}^{h} \tau^l x_{t-\tau} \tag{7.1.11b}$$

Hence the w_t's are treated as the explanatory variables and estimates of the δ_l^*'s are computed by one of the methods set out in section 7.3. The original lag coefficients are then obtained from (7.1.10) as

$$\tilde{\delta}_\tau = \sum_{l=0}^{g} \tilde{\delta}_l^* \tau^l \tag{7.1.12}$$

The covariance matrix of $\tilde{\boldsymbol{\delta}}_\tau = [\delta_0 \quad \ldots \quad \delta_h]'$ is given by

$$\text{Var}(\tilde{\boldsymbol{\delta}}) = \mathbf{S}\,\text{Var}(\tilde{\boldsymbol{\delta}}^*)\mathbf{S}'$$

where $\mathbf{S}$ is the $(h+1)\times(g+1)$ matrix, defined by $\mathbf{S} = [\mathbf{s}_0 \quad \ldots \quad \mathbf{s}_g]'$ where $\mathbf{s}_0 = [1 \quad 0 \ldots 0]'$ and $\mathbf{s}_\tau = [1 \quad \tau \quad \tau^2 \quad \ldots \quad \tau^g]'$, $\tau = 1, \ldots, g$.

Apart from ease of estimation, an important attraction of the polynomial distributed lag structure is that it enables testing and model selection to be carried out in a systematic way; see Sargan (1980).

Rational distributed lags A lag structure may be represented by the ratio of two polynomials in the lag operator. This technique was suggested in econometrics by Jorgenson (1966) who called it a *rational distributed lag*, and it provides the basis for a good deal of lag modelling in engineering and time series analysis. A structural model with a rational distributed lag is written as

$$y_t = \mathbf{z}_t' \boldsymbol{\alpha}_t + \sum_{i=1}^{k} \frac{\omega_i(\mathrm{L})}{\lambda_i(\mathrm{L})} x_{it} + \varepsilon_t \tag{7.1.13}$$

where $\omega_i(\mathrm{L})$ and $\lambda_i(\mathrm{L})$ are finite-order polynomials in the lag operator for $i = 1, \ldots, k$. The reduced form is

$$y_t = \sum_{i=1}^{k} \frac{\omega_i(\mathrm{L})}{\lambda_i(\mathrm{L})} x_{it} + u_t \tag{7.1.14}$$

where, following the discussion of sub-section 2.5.3, u_t is an ARIMA process. A model of this kind with u_t modelled as an unrestricted ARIMA process is known as a *transfer function* model. It is widely used, particularly in engineering, and was advocated by Box and Jenkins (1976). The idea of having the lag structure represented by the ratio of two polynomials in the lag operator parallels the representation of an ARIMA model in (2.4.19).

When the transfer function model contains more than one explanatory variable, handling it in the time domain becomes messy. Furthermore, its formulation is not particularly amenable to a systematic approach to model selection; see the discussion in Harvey (1981a, pp. 245 and 262). For these reasons, the transfer function distributed lag model is not recommended.

Lagged dependent variable A structural time series model with a lagged dependent variable is defined as

$$y_t = \varphi_1 y_{t-1} + \cdots + \varphi_r y_{t-r} + \mathbf{z}_t' \boldsymbol{\alpha}_t + \sum_{i=1}^{k} \omega_i(\mathrm{L}) x_{it} + \varepsilon_t \tag{7.1.15}$$

where the $\omega_i(\mathrm{L})$'s are a set of polynomials in the lag operator and the parameters $\varphi_1, \ldots, \varphi_r$ are the coefficients in a polynomial $\varphi(\mathrm{L})$. The model can be rewritten as

$$y_t = \frac{\mathbf{z}_t' \boldsymbol{\alpha}_t}{\varphi(\mathrm{L})} + \sum_{i=1}^{k} \frac{\omega_i(\mathrm{L})}{\varphi(\mathrm{L})} x_{it} + \frac{\varepsilon_t}{\varphi(\mathrm{L})} \tag{7.1.16}$$

showing that the lag structure has many of the features of the transfer function model (7.1.13). The difference is that each component on the right-hand side of (7.1.16) contains the common factor divisor $\varphi(\mathrm{L})$ and this has important implications for the properties of the model as a whole. Removing the stochastic components in $\mathbf{z}_t' \boldsymbol{\alpha}_t$ leads to the *autoregressive distributed lag* model which is widely used in econometrics.

Reparameterisation of unconstrained lags If constraints are not to be introduced into the lag structure, it may be desirable to reparameterise the lag structure. The model in (7.1.8) may be rewritten as

$$y_t = \mathbf{z}_t' \boldsymbol{\alpha}_t + \mathbf{x}_t' \boldsymbol{\delta} + \sum_{\tau=0}^{h-1} \Delta \mathbf{x}_{t-\tau}' \boldsymbol{\delta}_\tau^\dagger + \varepsilon_t \tag{7.1.17}$$

where

$$\boldsymbol{\delta}_\tau^\dagger = -\sum_{j=\tau+1}^{h} \boldsymbol{\delta}_j, \quad \tau = 0, 1, \ldots, h-1 \tag{7.1.18}$$

and

$$\boldsymbol{\delta} = \sum_{j=0}^{h} \boldsymbol{\delta}_j \tag{7.1.19}$$

Thus $\boldsymbol{\delta}$ is the *total multiplier*. This formulation is more stable numerically because the multicollinearity between the transformed variables $\mathbf{x}_t, \Delta\mathbf{x}_t, \ldots, \Delta\mathbf{x}_{t-h+1}$ will typically be considerably less than the multicollinearity between the original variables. The fact that $\mathbf{x}_t$ will not usually be strongly correlated with its first differences makes it clear why its coefficient, $\boldsymbol{\delta}$, may be estimated reasonably accurately even though the shape of the lag distribution may be difficult to determine precisely; see, for example, Hatanaka and Wallace (1980).

As with the unconstrained distributed lag, the structure of (7.1.15) may be rearranged for convenience and numerical stability; see also sub-section 6.1.4. Thus

$$y_t = \varphi y_{t-1} + \sum_{j=1}^{r-1} \varphi_j^\dagger \Delta y_{t-j} + \mathbf{z}_t'\boldsymbol{\alpha}_t + \mathbf{x}_t'\boldsymbol{\omega} + \sum_{i=0}^{s-1} \Delta\mathbf{x}_{t-i}'\boldsymbol{\omega}_i^\dagger + \varepsilon_t \tag{7.1.20}$$

where $\boldsymbol{\omega}, \boldsymbol{\omega}_0^\dagger, \ldots, \boldsymbol{\omega}_{s-1}^\dagger$ are defined analogously to $\boldsymbol{\delta}, \boldsymbol{\delta}_0^\dagger, \ldots, \boldsymbol{\delta}_{s-1}^\dagger$ in (7.1.18) and

$$\varphi_j^\dagger = -\sum_{k=j+1}^{r} \varphi_k, \quad j=1,2,\ldots,r-1 \tag{7.1.21}$$

$$\varphi = \sum_{k=1}^{r} \varphi_k \tag{7.1.22}$$

The vector of total multipliers is given by

$$\boldsymbol{\delta} = (1-\varphi)^{-1}\boldsymbol{\omega} \tag{7.1.23}$$

If the dependent variable is taken as Δy_t, the coefficient of y_{t-1} is equal to $\varphi - 1$ and the total multiplier is equal to ω divided by minus this coefficient.

Suppose that there is a single exogenous variable. It may often be more appropriate to have x_{t-1}, rather than x_t, appearing as the levels explanatory variable in the model. The lag on this variable then corresponds to the lag on the level of the dependent variable, and the model may be written as

$$\Delta y_t = (\varphi-1)y_{t-1} + \sum_{j=1}^{r-1} \varphi_j^\dagger \Delta y_{t-j} + \mathbf{z}_t'\boldsymbol{\alpha}_t + \omega_0 \Delta x_t + \omega x_{t-1} + \sum_{i=1}^{s-1} \omega_i^\dagger \Delta x_{t-i} + \varepsilon_t \tag{7.1.24}$$

The contributions from two levels explanatory variables may be written together as

$$(\varphi-1)y_{t-1} + \omega x_{t-1} = (\varphi-1)[y_{t-1} - \delta x_{t-1}]$$

The model is then expressed in the form

$$\Delta y_t = \sum_{j=1}^{r} \varphi_j^\dagger \Delta y_{t-j} + \mathbf{z}_t'\boldsymbol{\alpha}_t + \omega_0 \Delta x_t + \sum_{i=1}^{s-1} \omega_i^\dagger \Delta x_{t-i} + (\varphi-1)[y_{t-1} - \delta x_{t-1}] + \varepsilon_t \tag{7.1.25}$$

If $\mathbf{z}_t'\boldsymbol{\alpha}_t$ were absent, (7.1.25) would be an *error correction model* with the long-run relationship, or target relation, being

$$\bar{y}_t = \delta \bar{x}_t \tag{7.1.26}$$

As a rule the variables in (7.1.25) are in logarithms, in which case δ is the long-run elasticity of y with respect to x. If δ is known to take some particular value, then the term in square brackets is actually an explanatory variable. For example, in modelling the relationship between income and consumption, Davidson *et al.* (1978) argued that δ should be unity and so $(y_{t-1}-x_{t-1})$ is included as an explanatory variable in an equation which would otherwise be entirely in differences.

Returning to (7.1.25), with $\mathbf{z}_t'\boldsymbol{\alpha}_t$ equal to a stochastic trend, μ_t, the equation can be rearranged as

$$\Delta y_t = \sum_{j=1}^{r} \varphi_j^\dagger \Delta y_{t-j} + \omega_0 \Delta x_t + \sum_{i=1}^{s-1} \omega_i^\dagger \Delta x_{t-i} + (\varphi - 1)(y_{t-1} - \mu_t^\dagger - \delta x_{t-1}) + \varepsilon_t \quad (7.1.27)$$

where $\mu_t^\dagger = \mu_t/(1-\varphi)$. The term in square brackets can still be regarded as an error correction mechanism even though it contains a non-stationary stochastic component. The long-run relationship is

$$\bar{y}_t = \mu_{t+1}^\dagger + \delta \bar{x}_t \quad (7.1.28)$$

7.1.3 *Detrending and differencing*

We now consider the key issues of detrending and differencing. The discussion will be in terms of the model

$$y_t = \mu_t + \mathbf{x}_t'\boldsymbol{\delta} + \varepsilon_t, \quad t = 1, \ldots, T \quad (7.1.29)$$

where μ_t is the local linear trend component, (2.3.27). The implications for models containing other unobserved components will be readily apparent. The vector of explanatory variables in (7.1.29) may include lagged values. Furthermore, the results noted below remain true if the elements of $\boldsymbol{\delta}$ are subject to constraints, as in the polynomial distributed lag, or if $\mathbf{x}_t$ is redefined to include the possibility of lagged values of the dependent variable.

As set up in (7.1.29) the model includes a stochastic trend. However, if $\sigma_\eta^2 = \sigma_\zeta^2 = 0$, the stochastic trend collapses to a deterministic trend and the model may be written as

$$y_t = \alpha + \beta t + \mathbf{x}_t'\boldsymbol{\delta} + \varepsilon_t, \quad t = 1, \ldots, T \quad (7.1.30)$$

Now suppose that prior detrending of the dependent and explanatory variables in (7.1.29) is carried out by regressing each of them individually on time and a constant term. If the detrended dependent variable is now regressed on the detrended explanatory variables, the resulting estimator of $\boldsymbol{\delta}$ can be shown to be identical to the estimator of $\boldsymbol{\delta}$ obtained by applying OLS to the original model (7.1.30). This is a special case of a classic result in regression which was first pointed out by Frisch and Waugh (1933). However, if the trend in (7.1.29) is not a deterministic one, prior detrending is invalid. As shown in Nelson and Kang

(1984) it can lead to poor forecasts and misleading inferences about $\boldsymbol{\delta}$. In particular, if μ_t in (7.1.29) is a random walk, there is a relatively high probability that if the regression in (7.1.30) is run, the estimator of β will appear to be statistically significant.

Taking second differences in (7.1.29) leads to a regression model with a stationary disturbance term:

$$\Delta^2 y_t = (\Delta^2 \mathbf{x}_t)'\boldsymbol{\delta} + w_t, \quad t = 3, \ldots, T \tag{7.1.31a}$$

where

$$w_t = \Delta\eta_t + \zeta_{t-1} + \Delta^2\varepsilon_t \tag{7.1.31b}$$

As was shown in sub-section 2.4.3, (7.1.31) corresponds to the stationary form of the local linear trend model and its reduced form is an MA(2) process. In the important special case when σ_ζ^2 is zero, it is only necessary to difference once in order to obtain a stationary disturbance term. Thus

$$\Delta y_t = \beta + (\Delta \mathbf{x}_t)'\boldsymbol{\delta} + w_t, \quad t = 2, \ldots, T \tag{7.1.32a}$$

where

$$w_t = \eta_t + \Delta\varepsilon_t \tag{7.1.32b}$$

corresponds to an MA(1) process. If σ_ε^2 is equal to zero, the model is

$$\Delta y_t = \beta + (\Delta \mathbf{x}_t)'\boldsymbol{\delta} + \eta_t, \quad t = 2, \ldots, T \tag{7.1.33}$$

and a simple OLS regression of Δy_t on $\Delta \mathbf{x}_t$ and a constant term gives efficient estimators of β and $\boldsymbol{\delta}$.

To summarise, therefore, the levels model with a time trend, (7.1.30), and the first-difference model, (7.1.33), emerge from (7.1.29) as special cases. Only in the first of these cases will prior detrending be a valid procedure. As a final point, note that if the first-difference model is formulated in levels with an unconstrained lag structure on the dependent and explanatory variables, the lag polynomials will all contain a unit root. The application in section 7.5.2 provides an illustration.

7.1.4 Exogeneity

The ability to treat a model like (7.1.2) within a single equation framework depends crucially on the exogeneity of the explanatory variables, $\mathbf{x}_t$. Efficient estimation of the parameters requires that no information on these parameters is lost by conditioning on the explanatory variables. In other words, the explanatory variables may be treated as though they are fixed in repeated samples, even though they may be generated by a stochastic mechanism in the same way as y_t. If this condition is satisfied, the explanatory variables are said to be weakly exogenous. For purposes of prediction, stronger conditions must be placed on the explanatory variables. Specifically, there must be no feedback between them and the dependent variable. If this condition holds, the explanatory variables are said to be strongly exogenous. Strong exogeneity implies weak exogeneity, but not vice versa.

A formal definition of weak exogeneity requires that we are able to conceive of a joint probability density function for $\mathbf{y}=[y_1,\ldots,y_T]'$ and $\mathbf{X}=[\mathbf{x}_1,\ldots,\mathbf{x}_T]'$. Following (3.4.2), this may be written as

$$L(\mathbf{y},\mathbf{X};\boldsymbol{\lambda})=\prod_{t=1}^{T} p(y_t,\mathbf{x}_t|\mathbf{Y}_{t-1},\mathbf{X}_{t-1};\boldsymbol{\lambda}) \tag{7.1.34}$$

where $\boldsymbol{\lambda}$ denotes the full set of parameters upon which the joint p.d.f. of $\mathbf{y}$ and $\mathbf{X}$ depends. Suppose that the model may be re-parameterised in terms of a new set of parameters, $\boldsymbol{\theta}^\dagger$, which may be partitioned as $\boldsymbol{\theta}^\dagger=[\boldsymbol{\theta}' \quad \boldsymbol{\theta}_x']'$ where $\boldsymbol{\theta}$ and $\boldsymbol{\theta}_x$ are *variation-free* in the sense that for any specific admissible value of $\boldsymbol{\theta}_x$, $\boldsymbol{\theta}$ can take any value in its parameter space and vice versa. Suppose also that the *parameters of interest* are a function only of $\boldsymbol{\theta}$. The explanatory variables, $\mathbf{x}_t$, are *weakly exogenous* for $\boldsymbol{\theta}$ over the sample period, if the joint p.d.f. in (7.1.34) can be factored as

$$L(\mathbf{y},\mathbf{X};\boldsymbol{\theta}^\dagger)=\left[\prod_{t=1}^{T} p(y_t|\mathbf{Y}_{t-1},\mathbf{X}_t;\boldsymbol{\theta})\right]\left[\prod_{t=1}^{T} p(\mathbf{x}_t|\mathbf{X}_{t-1},\mathbf{Y}_{t-1};\boldsymbol{\theta}_x)\right] \tag{7.1.35}$$

This being the case, the marginal distribution of $\mathbf{x}_t$, the second term on the right-hand side of (7.1.35), can be ignored as it contains no information on the parameters of interest. Inference on $\boldsymbol{\theta}$ can be based on the conditional distribution of y_t, which is the first term on the right-hand side of (7.1.35), that is

$$L(\mathbf{y}|\mathbf{X};\boldsymbol{\theta})=\prod_{t=1}^{T} p(y_t|\mathbf{Y}_{t-1},\mathbf{X}_t;\boldsymbol{\theta}) \tag{7.1.36}$$

Constructing the likelihood function from (7.1.36) is equivalent to regarding the explanatory variables as being fixed in repeated samples.

In order to be able to concentrate exclusively on (7.1.2) for prediction purposes, the distribution of $\mathbf{x}_t$ must be independent of past values of y_t. Thus

$$p(\mathbf{x}_t|\mathbf{Y}_{t-1},\mathbf{X}_{t-1};\boldsymbol{\theta}_x)=p(\mathbf{x}_t|\mathbf{X}_{t-1};\boldsymbol{\theta}_x), \quad t=1,\ldots,T \tag{7.1.37}$$

If this is the case, then $\mathbf{Y}_{t-1}$ does not *Granger-cause* $\mathbf{x}_t$. When (7.1.37) holds, $\mathbf{x}_t$ is *strongly exogenous* with respect to θ.

Example 7.1.2 Consider the following bivariate model for y_t and a single explanatory variable, x_t:

$$y_t=\varphi_{11}y_{t-1}+\varphi_{12}x_{t-1}+\varepsilon_{1t} \tag{7.1.38a}$$

$$x_t=\varphi_{22}x_{t-1}+\varepsilon_{2t} \tag{7.1.38b}$$

where, conditional on $\mathbf{Y}_{t-1}$ and $\mathbf{X}_{t-1}$, the disturbance vector $[\varepsilon_{1t} \quad \varepsilon_{2t}]'$ has a multivariate normal distribution with mean zero and p.d. covariance matrix

$$\Sigma=\begin{bmatrix}\sigma_{11} & \sigma_{12}\\ \sigma_{12} & \sigma_{22}\end{bmatrix}$$

A single equation for y_t can be formulated by conditioning on current as well as past values of the explanatory variable. Making use of the results on the properties of the multivariate normal distribution noted in the appendix to chapter 3 (and interchanging the roles of y and x) enables us to assert that, by conditioning on current values of x_t, y_t is normally distributed with mean

$$\begin{aligned}E(y_t|\mathbf{Y}_{t-1},\mathbf{X}_t;\boldsymbol{\theta})&=\varphi_{11}y_{t-1}+\varphi_{12}x_{t-1}+(\sigma_{12}/\sigma_{22})(x_t-\varphi_{22}x_{t-1})\\ &=\varphi_{11}y_{t-1}+(\sigma_{12}/\sigma_{22})x_t+[\varphi_{12}-(\varphi_{22}\sigma_{12}/\sigma_{22})]x_{t-1}\end{aligned} \tag{7.1.39a}$$

and variance

$$\mathrm{Var}(y_t|\mathbf{Y}_{t-1},\mathbf{X}_t;\boldsymbol{\theta})=\sigma_{11}-\sigma_{12}^2/\sigma_{22} \tag{7.1.39b}$$

This leads to the autoregressive distributed lag model

$$y_t=\varphi y_{t-1}+\delta_0 x_t+\delta_1 x_{t-1}+\varepsilon_t \tag{7.1.40}$$

where the parameters φ, δ_0, δ_1 and σ^2 are related to the original parameters via equations (7.1.39a) and (7.1.39b). The two sets of parameters, $\boldsymbol{\theta}=[\varphi\quad\delta_0\quad\delta_1\quad\sigma^2]'$ and $\boldsymbol{\theta}_x=[\varphi_{22}\quad\sigma_2^2]'$ are variation-free. The equation for x_t remains as specified in (7.1.38b), and from the properties of the multivariate normal distribution ε_{2t} and ε_t are distributed independently of each other; hence the factorisation in (7.1.35) is possible.

As can be seen from equation (7.1.38b), the distribution of x_t does not depend on past values of y_t and so (7.1.37) is satisfied. Hence x_t is strongly exogenous with respect to the parameters of interest in $\boldsymbol{\theta}$.

It is difficult to test directly whether the explanatory variables are weakly exogenous without specifying the general multivariate model. This is unfortunate since one of the main reasons for working with a single equation is to avoid the need to specify a general model. Exogeneity can, however, be tested indirectly since if it does not hold, the model is unlikely to be stable and this is likely to show up when it is subjected to diagnostic checking. Further details on exogeneity and testing for exogeneity can be found in Engle *et al.* (1983) and Engle (1984).

7.2 Estimation in the frequency domain

In order to develop the frequency-domain estimator, consider a model with a $k\times 1$ vector of exogenous variables, $\mathbf{x}_t$, and a disturbance term, u_t, which is generated by a stationary stochastic process with zero mean and a continuous power spectrum, $f(\lambda)$, which is everywhere positive in the interval $[0,\pi]$. Such a model may be written

$$y_t=\mathbf{x}_t'\boldsymbol{\delta}+u_t,\quad t=1,\ldots,T \tag{7.2.1}$$

where $\boldsymbol{\delta}$ is a $k \times 1$ vector of unknown parameters. In the context of structural time series modelling, the observations will usually need to be differenced in some way before the disturbance term is stationary; these matters are dealt with explicitly in sub-section 7.3.3.

When $f(\lambda)$ is known, the estimation of $\boldsymbol{\delta}$ in (7.2.1) is a problem in generalised least squares (GLS) and it is shown below how the GLS estimator can be computed in the frequency domain. When $f(\lambda)$ depends on a set of unknown parameters, $\boldsymbol{\psi}$, an ML estimation procedure is appropriate. Repeated computation of the GLS estimator of $\boldsymbol{\delta}$ is an integral part of this procedure.

As noted in section 4.3 frequency-domain methods are exact when applied to circular processes and are asymptotically valid even when this assumption does not hold. In the context of (7.2.1) it is important to stress that it is the circularity of the disturbance term, u_t, which is relevant. The question of whether the elements of $\mathbf{x}_t$ are circular does not enter into the discussion at all except in the special methods described for distributed lags in sub-section 7.2.3. More importantly there is no reason, in general, for $\mathbf{x}_t$ to be stationary. It is the stationarity of u_t which is crucial. Conditions on $\mathbf{x}_t$ are needed in order to derive asymptotic properties of the estimators, but, as Hannan (1963) makes clear, these conditions can be much weaker than a requirement of stationarity.

7.2.1 *Generalised least squares*

Model (7.2.1) may be written in matrix terms as

$$\mathbf{y} = \mathbf{X}\boldsymbol{\delta} + \mathbf{u} \tag{7.2.2}$$

where $\mathbf{y}$ is a $T \times 1$ vector, $\mathbf{X}$ is a $T \times k$ matrix, and $\mathbf{u}$ is a $T \times 1$ vector with covariance matrix $\mathrm{E}(\mathbf{uu}') = \mathbf{V}$. The GLS estimator of $\boldsymbol{\delta}$ is obtained by minimising

$$S(\boldsymbol{\delta}) = (\mathbf{y} - \mathbf{X}\boldsymbol{\delta})'\mathbf{V}^{-1}(\mathbf{y} - \mathbf{X}\boldsymbol{\delta}) \tag{7.2.3}$$

On comparing the last terms in (4.3.6) and (4.3.14) it can be seen that when u_t is a circular process, $S(\boldsymbol{\delta})$ can be written in the frequency domain as

$$S(\boldsymbol{\delta}) = \sum_{j=0}^{T-1} \frac{I(\lambda_j)}{f(\lambda_j)} \tag{7.2.4}$$

where $I(\lambda_j)$ is the sample spectrum of $(y_t - \mathbf{x}_t'\boldsymbol{\delta})$, that is

$$I(\lambda_j) = \frac{1}{2\pi T}\left| \sum_{t=1}^{T} y_t e^{-i\lambda_j t} - \boldsymbol{\delta}' \sum_{t=1}^{T} \mathbf{x}_t e^{-i\lambda_j t} \right|^2 \tag{7.2.5}$$

Suppose initially that there is only a single exogenous variable. Let $I_y(\lambda_j)$, $I_x(\lambda_j)$ and $I_{xy}(\lambda_j)$ denote the sample spectra of y_t and x_t, and the cross-spectrum of x_t and y_t respectively. The cross-spectrum is a complex quantity given by

$$I_{xy}(\lambda_j) = \frac{1}{2\pi T}\left(\sum_{t=1}^{T} x_t e^{-i\lambda_j t} \right)\left(\sum_{t=1}^{T} y_t e^{i\lambda_j t} \right) \tag{7.2.6}$$

Using these definitions (7.2.5) can be expanded to give

$$\begin{aligned} I(\lambda_j) &= I_y(\lambda_j) - \delta I_{yx}(\lambda_j) - \delta I_{xy}(\lambda_j) + \delta^2 I_x(\lambda_j) \\ &= I_y(\lambda_j) - 2\delta I^*_{xy}(\lambda_j) + \delta^2 I_x(\lambda_j) \end{aligned} \tag{7.2.7}$$

where $I^*_{xy}(\lambda_j)$ denotes the real part of the cross-spectrum between x_t and y_t. This is the same as the real part of the cross-spectrum between y_t and x_t. The complex parts in (7.2.7) cancel. Note that

$$I^*_{xy}(\lambda_j) = (2\pi T)^{-1}[(\Sigma x_t \cos \lambda_j t)(\Sigma y_t \cos \lambda_j t) + (\Sigma x_t \sin \lambda_j t)(\Sigma y_t \sin \lambda_j t)] \tag{7.2.8}$$

with all summations running from $t = 1$ to T.

In the general case when the model contains k exogenous variables, (7.2.7) becomes

$$I(\lambda_j) = I_y(\lambda_j) - 2\boldsymbol{\delta}'\mathbf{I}^*_{xy}(\lambda_j) + \boldsymbol{\delta}'\mathbf{I}^*_{xx}(\lambda_j)\boldsymbol{\delta} \tag{7.2.9}$$

where $\mathbf{I}_{xy}(\lambda_j)$ is a $k \times 1$ vector of the sample cross-spectra between y_t and the elements of $\mathbf{x}_t$, and $\mathbf{I}_{xx}(\lambda_j)$ is a $k \times k$ matrix containing the sample spectra of the exogenous variables on the main diagonal and the sample cross-spectra in the off-diagonal positions. This matrix is Hermitian, i.e. equal to its complex conjugate transpose, and hence the complex parts cancel in the quadratic form $\boldsymbol{\delta}'\mathbf{I}_{xx}(\lambda_j)\boldsymbol{\delta}$.

Substituting (7.2.9) into (7.2.4) and minimising with respect to $\boldsymbol{\delta}$ yields the frequency-domain GLS estimator

$$\tilde{\boldsymbol{\delta}} = \left[\sum_{j=0}^{T-1} \frac{1}{f(\lambda_j)} \mathbf{I}^*_{xx}(\lambda_j) \right]^{-1} \sum_{j=0}^{T-1} \frac{1}{f(\lambda_j)} \mathbf{I}^*_{xy}(\lambda_j) \tag{7.2.10}$$

This estimator has a mean of $\boldsymbol{\delta}$ and a covariance matrix

$$\mathrm{Var}(\tilde{\boldsymbol{\delta}}) = \left[\sum_{j=0}^{T-1} \frac{1}{f(\lambda_j)} \mathbf{I}^*_{xx}(\lambda_j) \right]^{-1} \tag{7.2.11}$$

When u_t is normally distributed, $\tilde{\boldsymbol{\delta}}$ has a multivariate normal distribution. If the circularity assumption for u_t does not hold, (7.2.10) must be regarded as an approximation to the GLS estimator, but it has the same asymptotic distribution.

The GLS estimator can also be derived by transforming the observations in (7.2.2) by pre-multiplying by the Fourier matrix, $\mathbf{W}$, defined in (4.3.7). This gives

$$\mathbf{Wy} = \mathbf{WX}\boldsymbol{\delta} + \mathbf{Wu} \tag{7.2.12}$$

The transformed disturbances are heteroscedastic with covariance matrix $\mathbf{F}$; see (4.3.8). The GLS estimator formed by applying weighted least squares to (7.2.12) is exactly as given by (7.2.10). It is interesting to note that when $\mathbf{V} = \sigma^2\mathbf{I}$, OLS applied to the transformed model, (7.2.12), is identical to OLS applied to the original model, (7.2.2).

The above discussion has assumed that the spectrum of the disturbance term, $f(\lambda)$, is known. When it is unknown, a non-parametric estimator of $\boldsymbol{\delta}$ can be obtained by replacing $f(\lambda_j)$ in (7.2.10) by a consistent estimator, computed using one of the standard procedures – for example, a Blackman–Tukey or Parzen window; see Harvey (1981b, ch. 3, section 6 and ch. 7, section 4). The resulting estimator of $\boldsymbol{\delta}$ has the same asymptotic distribution as the GLS estimator. Estimation of $\boldsymbol{\delta}$ when a parametric model is specified for the process generating the disturbance term is considered in the next sub-section.

7.2.2 *Maximum likelihood*

Now consider the estimation of (7.2.1) when u_t depends on a set of unknown parameters, $\boldsymbol{\psi}$, and is assumed to be normally distributed. The log-likelihood function is of the form given in (4.3.1), that is

$$\log L(\boldsymbol{\delta}, \boldsymbol{\psi}) = -\tfrac{1}{2}T \log 2\pi - \frac{1}{2}\sum_{j=0}^{T-1} \log g_j - \pi \sum_{j=0}^{T-1} \frac{I(\lambda_j)}{g_j} \tag{7.2.13}$$

where $I(\lambda_j)$ is as defined in (7.2.5).

For a given value of $\boldsymbol{\psi}$, the ML estimator of $\boldsymbol{\delta}$ is the GLS estimator (7.2.10). However, since the likelihood function in (7.2.13) is expressed in terms of g_j rather than $f(\lambda_j)$, it is more convenient to write the GLS estimator in terms of g_j also. Thus

$$\tilde{\boldsymbol{\delta}}(\boldsymbol{\psi}) = \left[\sum_{j=0}^{T-1} \frac{1}{g_j} \mathbf{I}^*_{xx}(\lambda_j)\right]^{-1} \sum_{j=0}^{T-1} \frac{1}{g_j} \mathbf{I}^*_{xy}(\lambda_j) \tag{7.2.14}$$

Maximisation of the likelihood function can be carried out by concentrating $\boldsymbol{\delta}$ out of the likelihood function. Thus $\tilde{\boldsymbol{\delta}}(\boldsymbol{\psi})$ is substituted for $\boldsymbol{\delta}$ in (7.2.9) and the resulting concentrated likelihood function is maximised with respect to $\boldsymbol{\psi}$ by a numerical optimisation procedure.

An alternative way of computing ML estimates is by the method of scoring. The information matrix is block diagonal with respect to $\boldsymbol{\delta}$ and $\boldsymbol{\psi}$ in large samples – see (7.3.4) – and so the scoring algorithm consists of two parts, one for $\boldsymbol{\psi}$ and one for $\boldsymbol{\delta}$. The part for $\boldsymbol{\delta}$ consists simply of the repeated computation of the GLS estimator, (7.2.14), while the part for $\boldsymbol{\psi}$ is as it would be for a model without exogenous variables.

7.2.3 *Distributed lags*

Suppose that the model consists of an unconstrained distributed lag in a single explanatory variable, that is

$$y_t = \sum_{\tau=0}^{h} \delta_\tau x_{t-\tau} + u_t, \qquad t=1,\ldots,T \tag{7.2.15}$$

where u_t is a stationary disturbance term. The model is therefore a special case of (7.2.1) with the $\mathbf{x}_t$ vector consisting of the $(h+1)\times 1$ vector of current and lagged variables, $[x_t \quad x_{t-1} \quad \ldots \quad x_{t-h}]'$. Although the estimator of $\boldsymbol{\delta}$ in (7.2.10) is perfectly valid, its computation, as Fishman (1969, p. 154) notes, can be simplified by observing that the periodogram in (7.2.5) can be expressed as

$$I(\lambda_j) \simeq \frac{1}{2\pi T}\left| \sum_{t=1}^{T} y_t e^{-i\lambda_j t} - (\delta_0 + \delta_1 e^{-i\lambda_j} + \cdots + \delta_h e^{-i\lambda_j h}) \sum_{t=1}^{T} x_t e^{-i\lambda_j t} \right|^2 \tag{7.2.16}$$

In order to see how this approximation arises, consider the case of a single lag, $h=1$. The term involving x_t and its lagged value in the expression for $I(\lambda_j)$ is

$$\delta_0 \sum_{t=1}^{T} x_t e^{-i\lambda_j t} + \delta_1 \sum_{t=1}^{T} x_{t-1} e^{-i\lambda_j t}$$

and this may be re-written as

$$\delta_0 \sum_{t=1}^{T} x_t e^{-i\lambda_j t} + \delta_1 e^{-i\lambda_j} \sum_{t=1}^{T} x_t e^{-i\lambda_j t} + \delta_1 e^{-i\lambda_j}(x_0 - x_T e^{-i\lambda_j T})$$

$$= (\delta_0 + \delta_1 e^{-i\lambda_j}) \sum_{t=1}^{T} x_t e^{-i\lambda_j t} + \delta_1 e^{-i\lambda_j}(x_0 - x_T)$$

The simplification in the last term arises because $\exp(-i\lambda_j T) = 1$. Since the other terms involve summations over T terms, the last term will normally be negligible in large samples. In fact, if $x_0 = x_T$, it disappears completely irrespective of the sample size. Thus a direct calculation of the periodogram quantities involving the lagged explanatory variable is avoided.

The above argument extends to the more general model, (7.2.15) and so any distortion induced by the approximation in (7.2.16) will be relatively minor if the sample is large and/or the differences between the last m observations and the initial observations, $x_{-h+1}, \ldots, x_0$, are small. The use of this approximation may therefore not be advisable in a small sample when x_t has a strong trend. On the other hand, when x_t is a circulant, the approximation in (7.2.16) becomes an equality.

Let $\mathbf{e}_j$ denote an $(h+1) \times 1$ vector with $\exp(-i\lambda_j p)$ in the $(t+1)$-th position for $p = 0, \ldots, h$. Expanding (7.2.16) then gives

$$I(\lambda_j) = I_y(\lambda_j) - 2\boldsymbol{\delta}' \mathrm{Re}[\mathbf{e}_j I_{xy}(\lambda_j)] + \boldsymbol{\delta}' \mathbf{e}_j \bar{\mathbf{e}}_j' \boldsymbol{\delta} I_x(\lambda_j) \tag{7.2.17}$$

Substituting for $I(\lambda_j)$ in the criterion function (7.2.4), differentiating with respect to $\boldsymbol{\delta}$ and then setting to a vector of zeros gives the spectral distributed lag estimator

$$\tilde{\boldsymbol{\delta}} = \left[\sum_{j=0}^{T-1} \mathbf{e}_j \bar{\mathbf{e}}_j' \frac{I_x(\lambda_j)}{f(\lambda_j)} \right]^{-1} \sum_{j=0}^{T-1} \frac{1}{f(\lambda_j)} \mathrm{Re}[\mathbf{e}_j I_{xy}(\lambda_j)] \tag{7.2.18}$$

A similar device can be used in the treatment of polynomial distributed lags in order to compute the parameter vector $\boldsymbol{\delta}^*$. The same device provides the key to computing estimators of the parameters in a rational distributed lag.

7.3 Estimation of models with explanatory variables and structural time series components

This section considers various aspects of estimating structural time series models with explanatory variables. Time-domain estimation follows from the general procedures described in section 3.4, while the frequency-domain procedures are obtained by combining the material presented in the previous section and section 4.3.

7.3.1 OLS and semi-parametric estimation

The parameter vector, $\boldsymbol{\delta}$, attached to the explanatory variables in a model of the form (7.1.2) can be estimated without estimating the hyperparameters, $\boldsymbol{\psi}$. The first step is to transform to a regression model with a stationary disturbance term as in (7.1.16). Thus, in general,

$$\Delta(\mathrm{L})\, y_t = \Delta(\mathrm{L})\mathbf{x}_t'\boldsymbol{\delta} + w_t, \quad t = d+1, \ldots, T \tag{7.3.1}$$

where w_t is the stationary form of the structural components in the model and $\Delta(\mathrm{L})$ is the non-stationary operator defined in (2.4.28). In the case of (7.1.1), $\Delta(\mathrm{L})$ is $\Delta\Delta_s$.

Applying OLS to the transformed observations gives an estimator of $\boldsymbol{\delta}$, $\mathbf{d}$, which is consistent but not efficient. More precisely the OLS estimator is asymptotically normal with a mean of $\boldsymbol{\delta}$ and a covariance matrix

$$\mathrm{Var}(\mathbf{d}) = \left[\sum_j \mathbf{I}_{xx}^*(\lambda_j)\right]^{-1} \sum_j f(\lambda_j)\mathbf{I}_{xx}^*(\lambda_j) \left[\sum_j \mathbf{I}_{xx}^*(\lambda_j)\right]^{-1} \tag{7.3.2}$$

where in the case of (7.3.1), $\mathbf{I}_{xx}(\lambda_j)$ now refers to $\Delta(\mathrm{L})\mathbf{x}_t$ rather than $\mathbf{x}_t$, $f(\lambda)$ is the power spectrum of w_t and the summations run from $j=0$ to $T-d-1$.

The evaluation of (7.3.2) requires that the spectral density ordinates, $f(\lambda_j)$, be estimated. This may be done using the residuals from the OLS regression, which may be run either in the time domain or in the frequency domain. Note that the spectrum does not have to be estimated consistently, using a window, for the estimator of Var($\mathbf{d}$) to be consistent. The raw periodogram ordinates will suffice. Compare a similar result in White (1980).

A semi-parametric estimator of $\boldsymbol{\delta}$ which is asymptotically efficient may be constructed by estimating $f(\lambda_j)$ consistently and substituting in a feasible GLS estimator of the form given in (7.3.10). Unlike the OLS estimator, this estimator requires that $f(\lambda)$ should be everywhere positive over the range $[-\pi, \pi]$; compare condition (iv) in sub-section 4.5.1.

7.3.2 ML estimation in the time domain

Maximum likelihood estimators of the parameters in (7.1.2) can be constructed in the time domain via the prediction error decomposition. Following the discussion in sub-section 4.2.2, the non-stationary elements of $\boldsymbol{\alpha}_t$ are taken to have a diffuse prior. This leaves two possible ML estimators, depending on the way in which $\boldsymbol{\delta}$ is treated. If $\boldsymbol{\delta}$ is added to the state vector, as in (7.1.3), the summation in the prediction error decomposition is from $t=d+k+1$ to T. On the other hand, the GLS transformation method of sub-section 3.4.2 may be used to transform y_t and $\mathbf{x}_t$ by the Kalman filter appropriate to the stochastic part of the model, $y_t-\mathbf{x}_t'\boldsymbol{\delta}$. The likelihood function is then

$$\log L=-\frac{(T-d)}{2}\log 2\pi-\frac{(T-d)}{2}\log\sigma_*^2-\frac{1}{2}\sum_{t=d+1}^{T}\log f_t$$

$$-\frac{1}{2\sigma_*^2}\sum_{t=d+1}^{T}\frac{v_t^2}{f_t} \tag{7.3.3a}$$

where

$$v_t=y_t^*-\mathbf{x}_t^{*\prime}\boldsymbol{\delta},\quad t=d+1,\ldots,T \tag{7.3.3b}$$

the y_t^* and $\mathbf{x}_t^*$ variables being the 'innovations' obtained by applying the Kalman filter appropriate to the stochastic part of the model. The ML estimator of $\boldsymbol{\delta}$, conditional on $\boldsymbol{\psi}_*$, is obtained by a WLS regression of y_t^* on $\mathbf{x}_t^*$, that is

$$\tilde{\boldsymbol{\delta}}=\left[\sum_{t=d+1}^{T}f_t^{-1}\,\mathbf{x}_t^*\mathbf{x}_t^{*\prime}\right]^{-1}\sum_{t=d+1}^{T}f_t^{-1}\,\mathbf{x}_t^*\,y_t^* \tag{7.3.4}$$

If σ_*^2 is concentrated out of the likelihood function, the criterion function can be taken to be the minimand

$$S^\dagger(\boldsymbol{\delta},\boldsymbol{\psi}_*)=S(\boldsymbol{\delta},\boldsymbol{\psi}_*)\left[\prod_{t=d+1}^{T}f_t\right]^{\frac{1}{T-d}} \tag{7.3.5a}$$

where

$$S(\boldsymbol{\delta},\boldsymbol{\psi}_*)=\sum_{t=d+1}^{T}v_t^2/f_t \tag{7.3.5b}$$

For a steady-state filter, the minimand is simply

$$\bar{S}(\boldsymbol{\delta},\boldsymbol{\psi}_*)=\sum_{t=d+1}^{T}v_t^2 \tag{7.3.6}$$

If $\boldsymbol{\delta}$ is concentrated out of the likelihood function, the criterion function in (7.3.5) becomes

$$S^\dagger(\boldsymbol{\psi}_*)=S(\boldsymbol{\psi}_*)\left[\prod_{t=d+1}^{T}f_t\right]^{\frac{1}{T-d}} \tag{7.3.7a}$$

where

$$S(\boldsymbol{\psi}_*)=\sum_{t=d+1}^{T}\tilde{v}_t^2/f_t \tag{7.3.7b}$$

and

$$v_t = y_t^* - \mathbf{x}_t^{*\prime}\tilde{\boldsymbol{\delta}}, \quad t = d+1, \ldots, T \tag{7.3.7c}$$

Kohn and Ansley (1985) observe that, for a given value of $\boldsymbol{\psi}_*$, $\tilde{\boldsymbol{\delta}}$ can be efficiently and accurately computed using the QR algorithm and that (7.3.7a) can be efficiently minimised with respect to $\boldsymbol{\psi}_*$ by viewing it as a sum of squares function.

Example 7.3.1 In the model

$$y_t = \mu_t + \mathbf{x}_t'\boldsymbol{\delta} + \varepsilon_t \tag{7.3.8a}$$

$$\mu_t = \mu_{t-1} + \eta_t \tag{7.3.8b}$$

the Kalman filter for $y_t - \mathbf{x}_t'\boldsymbol{\delta}$ depends on the signal–noise ratio, q. From (4.2.15)

$$y_{t+1}^* = \Delta y_{t+1} + y_t^*/f_t \tag{7.3.9a}$$

$$\mathbf{x}_{t+1}^* = \Delta \mathbf{x}_{t+1} + f_t^{-1}\mathbf{x}_t^*, \quad t = 2, \ldots, T-1 \tag{7.3.9b}$$

where f_t depends on q and is given by (4.2.15b). For a given value of q, $\tilde{\boldsymbol{\delta}}(q)$ may be computed by (7.3.4), and, if desired, concentrated out of the likelihood function.

The first ML procedure, based on the augmented state vector, is theoretically the correct one to use if $\boldsymbol{\delta}$ is viewed as a random variable. As noted earlier it has the attraction of leading on to the case when the regression parameters are time-varying. The second method is correct when $\boldsymbol{\delta}$ is regarded as being fixed in repeated samples. In practice, the difference between the estimators obtained from the two procedures is likely to be small. As shown in sub-section 3.4.2, the only difference in the two likelihood functions is in the determinantal term, and asymptotically they are the same.

A final point concerns the estimation of σ_*^2. For a given value of the vector of relative hyperparameters, $\boldsymbol{\psi}_*$, the residual sum of squares, $S(\boldsymbol{\psi}_*)$, obtained from including $\boldsymbol{\delta}$ in the state vector is the same as the residual sum of squares obtained from the GLS transformation. The ML estimators are different, however, as the first has a divisor of $T-d-k$ while the second has a divisor of $T-k$; see (7.4.1) and (7.4.2) respectively. Given $\boldsymbol{\psi}_*$, dividing by $T-d-k$ gives an unbiased estimator of σ_*^2.

7.3.3 *ML estimation in the frequency domain*

Once the model has been written as (7.3.1), the frequency domain likelihood function is seen to be as in (7.2.13) with T replaced by $T-d$, the summations running from $j=0$ to $T-d-1$, and $I(\lambda_j)$ defined in terms of $\Delta(\mathrm{L})y_t$ and $\Delta(\mathrm{L})\mathbf{x}_t$ in expressions (7.2.5) and (7.2.9). Because of the block diagonality of the information matrix with respect to $\boldsymbol{\psi}$ and $\boldsymbol{\delta}$, the scoring algorithm operates by alternately computing expressions of the form (4.3.33) and (7.2.14). The first step in the algorithm is the estimation of $\boldsymbol{\delta}$ by OLS as described in sub-section 7.3.1.

Table 7.3.1 *Estimation of model (7.3.3) for car drivers KSI, January 1969 to December 1981*

(a) Estimates of hyperparameters (multiplied by 10^6)

Iteration	σ_η^2	σ_ζ^2	σ_ω^2	σ_ε^2
1 (OLS)	−865[a]	20.0	10.2	3654
2 (two-step)	987	−13.7[a]	11.6	2941
3	537	0.261	11.5	3171
4	406	0.416	11.3	3317
⋮	⋮	⋮	⋮	⋮
10	274	0.430	11.6	3531
⋮	⋮	⋮	⋮	⋮
21	259	0.433	11.6	3557
Final	242	0.405	10.8	3322
Exact ML	308	0	0	4198

[a] Reset to a positive value.

(b) Estimates of coefficients of explanatory variables

	δ_1	δ_2
Scoring (21 iterations)	0.03	−0.35
Final	0.08	−0.32
Exact ML	0.08	−0.31
Standard errors	0.14	−0.11

Some feel for the operation of the scoring algorithm may be obtained by considering a specific application. The series on car drivers killed and seriously injured was introduced in sub-section 2.7.1 where it was handled by the BSM. Two possible explanatory variables for this series are the car mileage index, x_{1t} and the real price of petrol, x_{2t}. The reason for considering these variables is discussed later in sub-section 7.5.1. The model is therefore of the form (7.1.1), namely

$$y_t = \mu_t + \gamma_t + \delta_1 x_{1t} + \delta_2 x_{2t} + \varepsilon_t \tag{7.3.10}$$

with the sample running from January 1969 to December 1981. The progress of the scoring algorithm is shown in Table 7.3.1. The estimates of the hyperparameters at the first iteration are given by applying (4.3.37) to the periodogram ordinates obtained from the OLS residuals. The estimates at the second iteration are asymptotically efficient. The algorithm converged in 21 iterations. The final estimates were then obtained in the time domain by running through the Kalman filter with σ_η^2, σ_ω^2 and σ_ζ^2 expressed relative to σ_ε^2. The last row of Table 7.3.1(a) shows the estimates obtained by exact ML, while Table 7.3.1(b) gives the estimates of the coefficients of the explanatory variables.

The estimates of σ_ζ^2 and σ_ω^2 are both close to zero in the frequency domain and so are consistent with the zero estimates given by exact ML; recall the discussion of sub-section 4.5.3. Although the frequency domain estimates of the other two variance parameters are slightly smaller than the corresponding time-domain estimates, their ratios are very close. As can be seen from Table 7.3.1(b), the small differences in the scoring and exact ML estimates of the hyperparameters have little effect on the estimates of the coefficients of the explanatory variables. Finally, note that the two-step estimates are not very close to the final estimates but that the estimates obtained after two more iterations are quite reasonable.

7.3.4 Lagged dependent variables

Maximum likelihood estimators of the parameters in a lagged dependent variable model, (7.1.15), can be obtained by treating the lagged values of the dependent variable as though they were exogenous variables. However, there are some additional complications. An initial estimator of the vector $[\boldsymbol{\varphi}' \quad \boldsymbol{\delta}']'$ obtained by regressing $\Delta(\mathrm{L})y_t$ on $\Delta(\mathrm{L})y_{t-1}, \ldots, \Delta(\mathrm{L})y_{t-r}$, and $\Delta(\mathrm{L})\mathbf{x}_t$ will not be consistent because of the correlation between the lagged values of the dependent variable and the disturbance term. Furthermore once ML estimators have been obtained, estimators of asymptotic standard errors will be incorrect if calculated analytically in the usual way. This is because the asymptotic information matrix is not block diagonal with respect to $\boldsymbol{\psi}$ and $[\boldsymbol{\phi}' \quad \boldsymbol{\delta}']'$.

An initial consistent estimator of $[\boldsymbol{\varphi}' \quad \boldsymbol{\delta}']'$ can be obtained by using an instrumental variable estimator. Lagged values of the $\mathbf{x}_t$'s would provide valid instruments for lagged values of the y_t's. An asymptotically efficient two-step estimator could, however, only be constructed by taking account of the structure of the information matrix. A similar situation arises when a lagged dependent variable is coupled with an autoregressive disturbance term; see Hatanaka (1974).

The information matrix is most easily derived in the frequency domain. It has the following structure

$$\mathbf{I}\begin{bmatrix}\boldsymbol{\psi}\\ \boldsymbol{\delta}\\ \boldsymbol{\varphi}\end{bmatrix}=\left[\begin{array}{cc:c}\mathbf{I}_{\psi\psi} & \mathbf{0} & \mathbf{I}_{\psi\varphi}\\ \mathbf{0} & \mathbf{I}_{\delta\delta} & \mathbf{I}_{\delta\varphi}\\ \hdashline \mathbf{I}_{\varphi\psi} & \mathbf{I}_{\varphi\delta} & \mathbf{I}_{\varphi\varphi}\end{array}\right] \tag{7.3.11}$$

Without the lagged dependent variables, the information matrix would be block diagonal.

7.4 Tests and measures of goodness of fit

This section discusses how the various testing procedures of chapter 5 may be extended to a model with explanatory variables. When the stochastic components of $\mathbf{z}_t'\boldsymbol{\alpha}_t$ are not present, (7.1.2) collapses to a linear regression model and many of the tests reduce to tests which are familiar in the context of such a model; see Harvey (1981a, chapter 5).

7.4.1 Residuals

Two sets of time-domain residuals may be calculated for the model in (7.1.2). Both are obtained by standardising the innovations from the Kalman filter. The difference stems from whether or not $\boldsymbol{\delta}$ is included in the state vector; see the discussion in sub-section 7.3.2. If the explanatory variables are absent, both sets of residuals reduce to the univariate model residuals, $\tilde{v}_t$, of section 5.4.

A third set of residuals could be obtained by regarding the initial non-stationary elements in $\boldsymbol{\alpha}_0$ as being fixed but these residuals will not be used in this book.

Generalised recursive residuals If $\boldsymbol{\delta}$ is included in the state vector, a set of $T-d-k$ one-step-ahead prediction errors is produced. When these are standardised by dividing by $f_t^{\dagger}$, the result is the generalised recursive residuals, $\tilde{v}_t^{\dagger}, t=d+k+1, \ldots, T$. If the stochastic components, $\mathbf{z}_t'\boldsymbol{\alpha}_t$, are not included in the model, the Kalman filter would be equivalent to the OLS recursions and the generalised recursive residuals would reduce to the recursive residuals; see Harvey (1981a, 1981b). The known behaviour of the recursive residuals under various kinds of misspecification of regression models is helpful in determining the type of testing and diagnostic procedures which it is useful to carry out with generalised recursive residuals. When σ_*^2 is concentrated out of the likelihood function and $\boldsymbol{\psi}_*$ is known, $\tilde{v}_t^{\dagger} \sim \text{NID}(0, \sigma_*^2)$.

Generalised least squares residuals Given the GLS estimator of $\boldsymbol{\delta}$, a set of $T-d$ innovations, the v_t's of (7.3.7c), are produced when the Kalman filter is applied to the 'observations' $y_t - \mathbf{x}_t'\tilde{\boldsymbol{\delta}}, t=d+1, \ldots, T$. When divided by $f_t^{\dagger}$ these are known as the generalised least squares (GLS) residuals, and are denoted by $\tilde{v}_t$, $t=d+1, \ldots, T$. If the model does not contain the stochastic components in $\mathbf{z}_t'\boldsymbol{\alpha}_t$, these residuals reduce to the OLS residuals. Unlike the recursive residuals, the OLS residuals are not independently distributed with constant variance in small samples.

When $\boldsymbol{\delta}$ is regarded as being random, the ML estimator of σ_*^2 emerges as a function of the generalised recursive residuals, that is

$$s_*^2 = (T-d-k)^{-1} \sum_{t=d+k+1}^{T} \tilde{v}_t^{\dagger 2} \tag{7.4.1}$$

On the other hand, when $\boldsymbol{\delta}$ is assumed to be fixed, the ML estimator of σ_*^2 is a function of the GLS residuals:

$$\tilde{\sigma}_*^2 = (T-d)^{-1} \sum_{t=d+1}^{T} \tilde{v}_t^2 \tag{7.4.2}$$

However, as was noted in sub-section 7.3.2, the sums of squares in (7.4.1) and (7.4.2) are identical; the only difference lies in the respective divisors.

For testing for normality, heteroscedasticity and serial correlation, using the Box-Ljung test, the GLS residuals are appropriate. The main use of the generalised recursive residuals is in procedures to detect structural change. This includes structural change in the post-sample period or in a period immediately after an intervention; see sub-sections 7.4.4 and 7.6.3 respectively. The CUSUM procedure, described in sub-section 5.4.1, is particularly useful for detecting structural change. The variance, σ_*^2, is estimated by a formula analogous to (5.4.3b), namely

$$\hat{s}_*^2 = (T-d-k-1)^{-1} \sum_{t=d+k+1}^{T} (\tilde{v}_t^\dagger - \bar{\tilde{v}}^\dagger)^2; \tag{7.4.3}$$

compare the more usual estimator given in (7.4.1). Another test based on generalised recursive residuals is the *recursive t-test*. The test statistic is given by

$$\begin{aligned}\psi &= \sum_{d+k+1}^{T} \tilde{v}_t/\hat{s}_*\sqrt{T-d-k} \\ &= \text{CUSUM}\ (T)/\sqrt{T-d-k}\end{aligned} \tag{7.4.4}$$

If ψ_* is known, and there are no lagged dependent variables, the test statistic has a t-distribution with $T-d-k-1$ degrees of freedom. Applications of the recursive t-test include testing for functional misspecification as well as testing for structural change; see Harvey and Collier (1977).

Frequency-domain residuals Tests based on the residual periodogram were described in sub-section 5.4.3. In a model with explanatory variables the residual periodogram ordinates are defined by

$$\tilde{p}_j = 2\pi\ I(\lambda_j)/\tilde{g}_j, \quad j=0, \ldots, [(T-d)/2] \tag{7.4.5}$$

where $I(\lambda_j)$ is the periodogram of the series $\Delta(\mathrm{L})y_t - \Delta(\mathrm{L})\mathbf{x}_t'\tilde{\boldsymbol{\delta}}$, $t=d+1, \ldots, T$. If estimation has been carried out in the frequency domain, $I(\lambda_j)$ is immediately available. Thus it follows from (7.2.9) that for a model with k exogenous variables

$$I(\lambda_j) = I_y(\lambda_j) - 2\tilde{\boldsymbol{\delta}}'\mathbf{I}_{xy}^*(\lambda_j) + \tilde{\boldsymbol{\delta}}'\mathbf{I}_{xx}^*(\lambda_j)\tilde{\boldsymbol{\delta}} \tag{7.4.6}$$

where it is understood that y_t and $\mathbf{x}_t$ have both been transformed by the $\Delta(\mathrm{L})$ operator.

The main use of the residual periodogram ordinates is in the construction of the cumulative periodogram described earlier in sub-section 5.4.3.

7.4.2 *Lagrange-multiplier and most-powerful-invariant tests*

The Lagrange-multiplier (LM) tests described in sections 5.2 and 5.3 carry over to models of the form (7.1.2). The only difference is that $I(\lambda)$ in (5.2.13) is defined as the periodogram of $\Delta(L)y_t - \Delta(L)\mathbf{x}_t'\boldsymbol{\delta}$ as at the end of the previous sub-section.

The reason the form of the LM tests is unchanged for (7.1.2) is that the information matrix is block diagonal with respect to $\boldsymbol{\delta}$ and $\boldsymbol{\psi}$. When the model contains a lagged dependent variable this is no longer the case and LM tests are affected. A similar situation arises in a lagged dependent variable model when testing for serial correlation. In that case the Durbin h-test, rather than the Durbin-Watson test, is appropriate; see Harvey (1981a, ch. 8). LM tests can be set up for a model with a lagged dependent variable by working with the full information matrix, which takes the form (7.3.11).

Most-powerful-invariant (MPI) tests as described in sub-section 5.3.5 can be carried out in a model with explanatory variables. Model (5.3.14) now becomes

$$\mathbf{y} = \mathbf{X}_0\boldsymbol{\alpha}_0^\dagger + \mathbf{X}\boldsymbol{\delta} + \mathbf{u} = [\mathbf{X}_0 \quad \mathbf{X}]\begin{bmatrix}\boldsymbol{\alpha}_0^\dagger \\ \boldsymbol{\delta}\end{bmatrix} + \mathbf{u}, \quad \mathrm{Var}(\mathbf{u}) = \sigma_*^2\boldsymbol{\Omega}_0(\boldsymbol{\psi}_*) \tag{7.4.7}$$

where $\mathbf{X}$ is the $T \times k$ matrix of observations on the explanatory variables. Test statistics can be calculated by using the Kalman filter to evaluate $S(\boldsymbol{\psi}_{*1})$ and $S(\boldsymbol{\psi}_{*0})$. However, the distribution of each test statistic will depend on the actual values of the explanatory variables. Thus a critical value needs to be computed each time a test is carried out on a new model. This could be avoided by constructing a bounds test, along the lines of the Durbin-Watson test. An alternative approach would be to formulate large sample tests using LBI statistics like (5.3.17), since the asymptotic distribution of such statistics is invariant to $\mathbf{X}$.

7.4.3 *Goodness of fit*

The prediction error variance can be estimated as

$$s^2 = s_*^2\bar{f} \tag{7.4.8}$$

or

$$\tilde{\sigma}^2 = \tilde{\sigma}_*^2\bar{f} \tag{7.4.9}$$

where s_*^2 and $\tilde{\sigma}_*^2$ are as defined in (7.4.1) and (7.4.2) respectively. In both cases $\bar{f}$ is the steady-state value of f_t in the Kalman filter applied to the SSF in which the fixed elements, $\boldsymbol{\delta}$, do not appear in the state vector.

An appropriate estimator of the prediction error variance can be obtained by using the unstandardised GLS innovations, v_t, in expression (5.5.3). The frequency-domain estimator of the prediction error variance is given directly by (5.5.5).

As regards the coefficient of determination, the residual sum of squares is defined as

$$\mathrm{SSE} = (T-d)\tilde{\sigma}^2 = (T-d-k)s^2 \tag{7.4.10}$$

and this may be used in R_D^2, (5.5.14), and R_s^2, (5.5.17). By making an adjustment for degrees of freedom, measures analogous to the $\bar{R}^2$ of classical regression may be defined. These are

$$\bar{R}_D^2 = 1 - \frac{s^2}{\sum_{t=2}^{T} (\Delta y_t - \bar{\Delta y})^2/(T-2)} \tag{7.4.11}$$

and

$$\bar{R}_s^2 = 1 - \frac{s^2}{\mathrm{SSDSM}/(T-s-1)} \tag{7.4.12}$$

where SSDSM is as defined in (5.5.17). The rationale for these measures is as follows. Conditional on ψ_*, s^2 is an unbiased estimator of σ^2. Similarly the divisors $T-2$ and $T-s-1$ make the denominators in (7.4.11) and (7.4.12) unbiased estimators of σ^2 in models (5.5.15) and (5.5.16) respectively.

In a model with a moderately high number of explanatory variables, the modified coefficient may be noticeably smaller. In a univariate model, the coefficient of determination and its modified 'bar' form are usually, but not necessarily, the same. For example, in the BSM, $d = s+1$ and so $R_s^2 = \bar{R}_s^2$.

7.4.4 *Post-sample predictive testing*

The standardised one-step-ahead prediction errors in the post-sample period are defined in a similar way to the generalized recursive residuals, that is

$$\tilde{v}_{T+j}^{\dagger} = v_{T+j}^{\dagger}/(f_{T+j}^{\dagger})^{\frac{1}{2}}, \quad j = 1, \ldots, l \tag{7.4.13}$$

The post-sample predictive test statistic, which was defined for a univariate model in (5.6.3), is therefore

$$\xi(l) = \sum_{j=1}^{l} v_{T+j}^{\dagger 2}/ls_*^2 \tag{7.4.14}$$

If ψ_* is known and no lagged dependent variables are present, the standardised prediction errors are normally and independently distributed with mean zero and variance σ_*^2. Therefore $\xi(l)$ is distributed as $F(l, T-n-k)$ when the model is correctly specified. When the stochastic components of $\mathbf{z}_t'\boldsymbol{\alpha}_t$ are not present, so that (7.1.2) collapses to a classical linear regression model, the test based on $\xi(l)$ is known as the *Chow test*.

The standardised prediction errors can also be used in CUSUM and ψ-tests. The relevant test statistics are as defined in (5.6.4) and (5.6.5) respectively, with $\hat{\sigma}_*^2$ replaced by $\hat{s}_*^2$ as defined in (7.4.3). The ψ-test is carried out with respect to a t-distribution with $T-n-k-1$ degrees of freedom.

Finally, multi-step predictions may be used to assess the model in the way suggested in sub-section 5.6.2. The j-steps-ahead prediction errors are defined by

$$v_{T+j|T} = y_{t+j} - \tilde{y}_{T+j|T}, \quad j = 1,\ldots,l \tag{7.4.15}$$

7.5 Model selection strategy and applications

Before starting to build a model with explanatory variables, it is advisable to fit a univariate time series model to the dependent variable. This serves a number of purposes. In particular, it provides a description of the salient features of the series, the 'stylised facts' as they were called in section 2.7. This in turn indicates whether there is a case for including components such as seasonals and cycles in an initial specification of the model since the explanatory variables may, or may not, be able to account for all of these effects. If a trend is present in the dependent variable, it will normally be desirable to include a trend component in the dynamic regression. The only exception would be if it is known *a priori* that there is a levels relationship between the dependent and explanatory variables. If there is some doubt it is better to include the trend and then to drop it at a later stage if it becomes clear that it is unnecessary.

An initial analysis of the potential explanatory variables may also prove helpful. In fact simply comparing a graph of an explanatory variable with the dependent variable may indicate which of the movements in the dependent variable are capable of being explained. If a model has been fitted to an explanatory variable, it will serve as an indication as to what properties the variable has in common with the dependent variable. In particular the order of integration of the variables will be known. It is not difficult to see that, if the model is correctly specified, the order of integration of the dependent variable cannot be less than the order of integration of any of the explanatory variables. This implies that certain explanatory variables may need to be differenced prior to their inclusion in a model. A further point is that if the order of integration of the dependent variable is greater than that of each of the explanatory variables, a stochastic trend component must be present.

It may be possible to gain some idea of the functional form and lag structures of potential explanatory variables by carrying out a regression after an appropriate non-stationary operator has been applied. The model is then in the form (7.3.1). The effectiveness of such an approach depends on the properties of the unobserved components and their relation to the $\Delta(L)$ operator. If there is only a single explanatory variable, it may be useful to examine the cross-correlogram as in Box and Jenkins (1976, ch. 11). However, this requires that the explanatory variable be 'pre-whitened' and that the same transformation be applied to the dependent variable; a critical discussion can be found in Harvey (1981a, p. 245). An additional problem is that the method requires that the order of integration of the two variables be the same. A regression based on (7.3.1) is therefore by far the most appealing procedure, particularly as it can be applied with more than one explanatory variable.

Once any initial investigations have been carried out, a tentative model may be estimated by maximum likelihood. Other things being equal, a fairly general model is to be preferred; this may be tested down so as to achieve a more parsimonious specification. As in univariate modelling, diagnostic checking is applied at all stages. In addition, the estimated coefficients of the explanatory variables should satisfy any prior knowledge concerning their sign and magnitude.

To be acceptable a model should satisfy all the internal checks, including the post-sample predictive test. It should also provide a fit at least as good as any rival specification, including the preferred univariate model. Furthermore it should be encompassing in that it should be able to explain the results obtained by its competitors.

7.5.1 Road accidents in Great Britain

The series on car drivers KSI was modelled by fitting the BSM in sub-section 2.7.1. The question of including explanatory variables was first discussed in section 1.2. Two possible explanatory variables are:

(i) the car traffic index, which measures the number of kilometres travelled by cars in a month, and

(ii) the real price of petrol, i.e. the price of petrol per litre at the pump divided by the retail price index.

The use of the car traffic index as an explanatory variable calls for no explanation, but perhaps a little should be said about the inclusion of the real price of petrol. During the period under review there were substantial changes in this variable and one effect of petrol price increases was probably to induce some drivers to drive more slowly and with less braking and acceleration. This could be expected to reduce accident rates. The variable can also be regarded as a proxy for such factors as petrol rationing and the introduction of lower speed limits during the oil crisis period of 1973–74. Lagged values of the petrol price index were originally included but their coefficients were found to be small and statistically insignificant.

The model with current traffic index and petrol price is as in (7.3.10). Estimating this model for the period January 1969 to December 1981 by exact ML gave the results shown in the last rows of Tables 7.3.1, (a) and (b). The goodness-of-fit statistics and diagnostics are

$$s=0.074, \qquad R^2=0.78, \qquad R_s^2=0.31$$
$$H(47)=1.43, \qquad Q(15)=17.35, \qquad \text{Normality}=1.19$$

Because the variables are in logarithms the coefficients of the car traffic index and the petrol price may be interpreted as elasticities. Thus a 1% rise in the traffic index gives a 0.08% rise in casualties, while a 1% rise in the price of petrol gives a 0.31% fall in casualties. The coefficient of the traffic index is statistically insignificant, and refitting the model without it gives virtually the same results; see Durbin and Harvey (1985, p. A7). The diagnostics were satisfactory and the post-sample predictive test statistic is $\xi(12)=0.562$ indicating that the model gives good predictions for 1982.

The report by Durbin and Harvey (1985) examines a number of series on road accidents in Great Britain. The models fitted are of a similar form to the one reported for car drivers KSI. The series on pedestrian fatalities provides an illustration of the use of the CUSUM technique to detect and assess model breakdown.

The model fitted to the series on the logarithm of pedestrians killed included a single explanatory variable, the motor traffic index. Using data from January 1969 to December 1982 gave the following results:

$$\tilde{\sigma}_\eta^2=0.152\times 10^{-3},\quad \tilde{\sigma}_\zeta^2=0,\quad \tilde{\sigma}_\omega^2=0.948\times 10^{-5},\quad \tilde{\sigma}_\varepsilon^2=7.665\times 10^{-3}$$

Estimated coefficient of total motor traffic index $=0.93$
(0.20)

$$s=0.108,\qquad R^2=0.85,\qquad R_s^2=0.53$$
$$H(51)=1.187,\qquad Q(15)=27.23,\qquad \text{Normality}=2.66$$

As can be seen the Q-statistic is rather high; it is statistically significant at the 5% level and is almost significant at the 1% level. Although the other diagnostics are acceptable, the model cannot be regarded as being satisfactory. One possible explanation is that after allowing for the increase in road traffic, the model indicates an average annual fall in pedestrian fatalities of 6.9%. This figure remains constant throughout the series since σ_ζ^2 is estimated to be zero However, the series shows some tendency to level off in 1982. This shows up in the CUSUM of the generalised recursive residuals, which is plotted in Figure 7.5.1 from January 1981 onwards. The steady rise in the CUSUM from the beginning of 1982 is indicative of a systematic tendency to underpredict. The fact that the 10% significance lines are not crossed is not critical since the CUSUM is best regarded as a diagnostic rather than a formal test procedure. Overall, the general impression is of a model which is starting to break down in 1982.

The risk compensation hypothesis, discussed in Adams (1985), suggests that the introduction of compulsory seat belt wearing for car drivers will have an adverse effect on pedestrian casualties. Hence the series on pedestrian fatalities is of some importance in assessing the overall effect of seat belt legislation on road accidents. This matter is discussed further in the next section. The point to note here is that the model breakdown in 1982 indicated by Figure 7.5.1 would make one reluctant to use the model reported above as the basis for assessing the effect of the 1983 seat belt law on pedestrians.

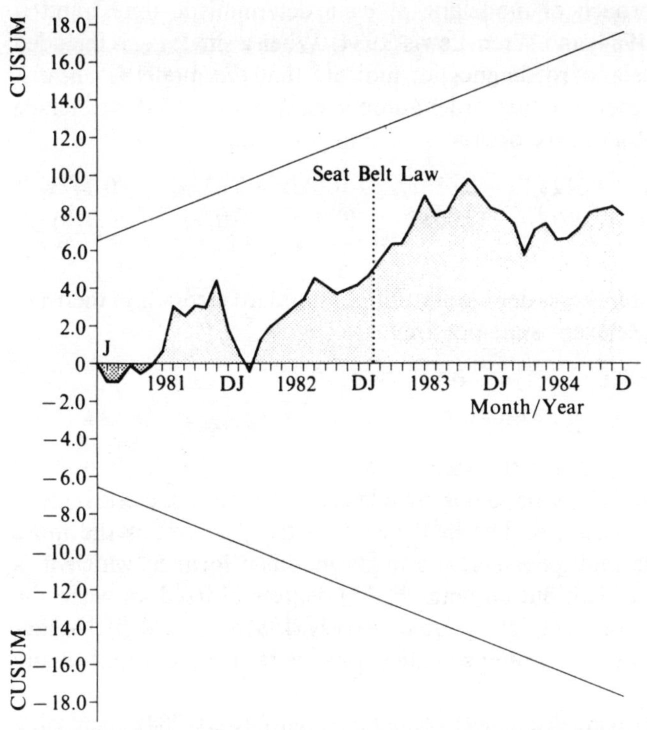

Fig. 7.5.1 CUSUM of generalised recursive residuals for pedestrians killed (with 10% significance lines).

7.5.2 Employment–output equation

The economic theory underlying the employment–output equation was reviewed in section 1.2. This leads to an equation of the general form (1.2.1), and it was suggested in section 1.2 that the productivity effect should be stochastic. Hence there is an *a priori* case for the inclusion of a stochastic trend component in the model. The economic theory also suggests a single lagged dependent variable as well as an unspecified set of lags on output. If a logarithmic formulation is adopted, therefore, an initial *a priori* specification of the model is

$$y_t = \mu_t + \varphi y_{t-1} + \sum_{\tau=0}^{h} \delta_\tau x_{t-\tau} + \varepsilon_t \qquad (7.5.1)$$

where μ_t is a stochastic trend component and y_t and x_t are, respectively, the logarithms of UK manufacturing employment and output, these variables being defined as in section 1.2.

Before estimating (7.5.1), it is enlightening to examine what happens when the more traditional approach of modelling μ_t by a deterministic time trend is adopted; see Nickell (1984) and Wren-Lewis (1984). When a single lag is included on employment, the standard diagnostics indicate that the model is unsatisfactory, with strong evidence of first-order autocorrelation. If, instead, we include two lags on y_t and let $h=2$, we obtain

$$\underset{}{\hat{y}_t=} \underset{(0.117)}{0.288} - \underset{(0.00010)}{0.00024t} + \underset{(0.069)}{1.612y_{t-1}} - \underset{(0.061)}{0.653y_{t-2}} + \underset{(0.015)}{0.103x_t} - \underset{(0.022)}{0.029x_{t-1}} - \underset{(0.018)}{0.047x_{t-2}} \tag{7.5.2}$$

where the figures in parentheses denote asymptotic standard errors, and there are $T=81$ observations. Relevant statistics are

$$s=2.77\times 10^{-3},\quad R_D^2=0.89,\quad r(1)=-0.13$$
$$Q(5)=3.56,\quad Q(8)=5.46,\quad Q^{\dagger}(4,70)=0.80$$

The Box-Ljung statistic is not the ideal means of testing for residual serial correlation in a model of this kind, but is included since the same statistic is given for the stochastic trend model. The final test statistic, $Q(P, T^*)$, is the more appropriate Lagrange multiplier statistic in its modified form in which it is treated as having an F-distribution with (P, T^*) degrees of freedom when the model is correctly specified; see, for example, Harvey (1981a, pp. 273–9). Neither this statistic nor the two Box-Ljung statistics indicate serial correlation to any significant degree.

Equations of this form are discussed in detail in Wren-Lewis (1984). Increasing returns to scale are observed with an output elasticity in the long run of 0.66. The time trend is conventionally thought of as picking up underlying productivity growth, which in this case is 2.36% per annum, i.e. if output were constant, employment would, on average fall by this amount each year. However, despite the superficial plausibility of (7.5.2), the coefficient of t appears *not* to be estimating the growth rate of productivity. Exactly why this is so will become clear shortly. For the moment consider re-estimating the model without the trend term:

$$\hat{y}_t = \underset{(0.041)}{-0.029} + \underset{(0.056)}{1.710y_{t-1}} - \underset{(0.058)}{0.709y_{t-2}} + \underset{(0.015)}{0.109x_t} - \underset{(0.021)}{0.040x_{t-1}} - \underset{(0.016)}{0.066x_{t-2}} \tag{7.5.3}$$

with

$$s=2.84\times 10^{-3},\quad R_D^2=0.88,\quad r(1)=-0.18$$
$$Q(5)=4.76,\quad Q(8)=5.26,\quad Q^{\dagger}(4,71)=1.15$$

The estimated coefficients in (7.5.2) and (7.5.3) are similar, despite the exclusion of the trend term from (7.5.3). Furthermore the diagnostics in (7.5.3) are satisfactory, although the mild negative first-order serial correlation has become slightly stronger. At first sight it is rather surprising, considering Figure 1.2.1, that dropping the measure of technical progress should make so little difference to the estimated employment–output relationship. This is one indication that the trend in (7.5.2) is not in fact measuring this underlying trend at all.

Now consider the stochastic trend model, (7.5.1). Although the theory specifies only one lag on employment, an equation was initially estimated with two lags and h correspondingly set equal to two. The coefficients on both y_{t-2} and x_{t-2} were small and statistically insignificant and so were dropped. Estimating the model by exact ML gave

$$\left.\begin{aligned} &y_t = m_{t|T} + \underset{(0.041)}{0.755}y_{t-1} + \underset{(0.014)}{0.112}x_t + \underset{(0.016)}{0.058}x_{t-1} + e_{t|T} \\ &\tilde{\sigma}_\varepsilon^2 = \underset{(0.955\times10^{-6})}{1.505\times10^{-6}}, \quad \tilde{\sigma}_\eta^2 = \underset{(1.695\times10^{-6})}{4.831\times10^{-6}}, \quad \tilde{\sigma}_\zeta^2 = 0.000\times10^{-6} \end{aligned}\right\} \tag{7.5.4}$$

where $m_{t|T}$ and $e_{t|T}$ denote the smoothed estimates of the trend and irregular components respectively. The standard errors in parentheses are asymptotic standard errors computed in the frequency domain. Since the model did not involve second-order lags, (7.5.4) was estimated using $T=82$ observations. The goodness-of-fit and diagnostic statistics are:

$$s = 2.76\times10^{-3}, \quad R_D^2 = 0.89, \quad r(1) = -0.02$$

$$Q(5) = 2.91, \quad Q(8) = 4.39$$

Re-arranging the fitted equation in (7.5.4) in line with (7.1.25) and (7.1.27) gives

$$\Delta y_t = 0.112\Delta x_t - 0.245(y_{t-1} - m_{t|T}^{\dagger} - 0.682x_{t-1}) + e_{t|T} \tag{7.5.5}$$

Thus the long-run output elasticity is 0.682.

Equation (7.5.4) seems preferable to (7.5.2) on both economic and statistical grounds. It contains only the single lagged dependent variable suggested by the basic theoretical model, while some auxiliary hypothesis is required to justify the term in y_{t-2} in (7.5.2). The negative lagged terms on output in (7.5.2) are also difficult to rationalise, but they disappear in (7.5.4). The diagnostics in both models are satisfactory, though it is worth noting that first-order serial correlation is virtually absent from (7.5.4). Although the goodness-of-fit statistics are not strictly comparable, because (7.5.4) was estimated using one extra observation, they indicate a similar fit for each model. In fact, if we do not count σ_ζ^2 as a parameter, since it is zero, (7.5.4) contains one less parameter than (7.5.2).

In addition to satisfying the economic and statistical criteria, the stochastic trend model is encompassing. Bearing in mind that $\tilde{\sigma}_\zeta^2 = 0$, equation (7.5.4) implies a first difference model of the form (7.1.32), estimated as

$$\Delta y_t = -0.00159 + 0.755\Delta y_{t-1} + 0.112\Delta x_t + 0.058\Delta x_{t-1} + \hat{w}_t \tag{7.5.6}$$

where the constant term is the estimate of β_T, and $\hat{w}_t$ is the fitted MA(1) process. Strictly speaking, regressing Δy_t on Δy_{t-1}, Δx_t and Δx_{t-1} without taking account of the serial correlation in the disturbance term should lead to inconsistent estimators. However, since η_t dominates ε_t, with the result that the implied first-order autocorrelation in the disturbance term, w_t, is only -0.14, it is perhaps not surprising that a simple regression in differences gives coefficients fairly close to those in (7.5.3).

Expanding the first-difference operator in (7.5.6) and rearranging gives

$$y_t = -0.00159 + 1.755y_{t-1} - 0.755y_{t-2} + 0.112x_t - 0.054x_{t-1} - 0.058x_{t-2} + \hat{w}_t \tag{7.5.7}$$

A comparison of this equation with (7.5.3) clearly shows why (7.5.4) encompasses (7.5.3). In fact, with hindsight it is now possible to see something very close to a common factor of unity in both (7.5.3) and (7.5.2). Furthermore, it is apparent that it is the constant term in (7.5.2) which should be most closely identified with the slope of the stochastic trend. The role of the time trend in (7.5.2) is unclear; the fact that it is 'significant' is almost certainly a reflection of the spurious regression phenomenon which arises when time is erroneously included as an explanatory variable in a model containing a unit root; see sub-section 6.1.4. It should also be noted in this regard that the sum of coefficients on y_{t-1} and y_{t-2} is smaller in (7.5.2) than in (7.5.3). This reflects the underestimation of the unit root that tends to occur when time is used as an explanatory variable.

As a final point note that the -0.18 value of $r(1)$ for (7.5.3) is not far from the theoretical first-order autocorrelation of -0.14 suggested by (7.5.7).

One additional reason for preferring (7.5.4) over (7.5.2) is that it allows for stochastic movements in the underlying trend in productivity. A fixed-interval smoothing algorithm was used to compute optimal estimates of the trend component, $m_{t|T}$, for the time period covered by the sample. Figure 7.5.2 shows a graph of $m_{t|T}$ against time.

The smoothing algorithm allows root mean square errors (RMSEs) to be calculated for the estimators of the trend and slope components. These RMSEs are conditional on the estimates of σ_η^2 and σ_ζ^2. The full set of RMSEs for the trend component is not given here, but in the case of $m_{T|T}(=m_T)$ the estimate was 1.33 with a RMSE of 0.29. Since the variance of the disturbance in the slope equation, σ_ζ^2, was estimated to be zero, the slope is constant. Its value, b_T, is -0.00159 with a RMSE, or standard error, of 0.00032. Thus the underlying annual growth rate in the employment equation (before allowing for the influence of the lagged dependent variable) is $-0.000159 \times 4 \times 100$, which is -0.64%. Its standard error is 0.13%. It follows that, on the average, if output were constant, employment would fall, and productivity increase, by 2.6% p.a.

Although the equation estimates the rate of growth to be constant, it is clear from Figure 7.5.2 that important shifts in underlying productivity did take place between 1974 and 1978. This finding is consistent with *a priori* ideas about a reduced rate of technical progress following the 1974/5 recession. It is interesting that the equation interprets these movements as shifts in the level of

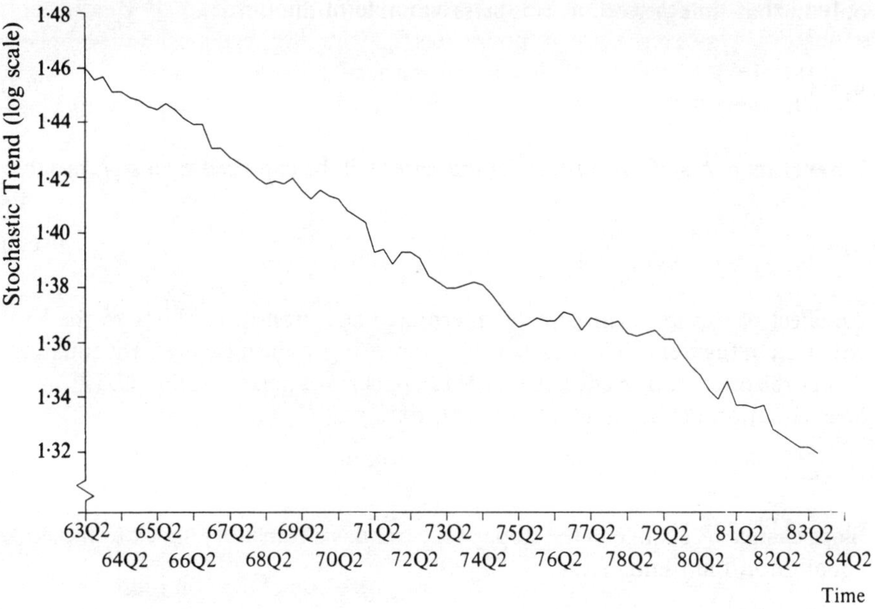

Fig. 7.5.2 Smoothed estimates of the stochastic trend component in the employment–output equation.

underlying productivity rather than changes in its rate of growth, that is as changes in μ_t rather than β_t. It is also worth noting the absence of any major favourable changes in underlying productivity growth during the 1980s.

7.6 Intervention analysis

Intervention analysis is concerned with making inferences about the effects of known events. These effects are measured by including intervention, or dummy, variables in a dynamic regression model. In pure intervention analysis no other explanatory variables are present.

Model (7.1.2) may be generalised to yield the intervention model

$$y_t = \mathbf{z}_t'\boldsymbol{\alpha}_t + \mathbf{x}_t'\boldsymbol{\delta} + \lambda w_t + \varepsilon_t \tag{7.6.1}$$

where w_t is the intervention variable and λ is its coefficient. The definition of w_t depends on the form which the intervention effect is assumed to take. If the model contains stochastic trend and seasonal components, four main cases may be distinguished.

Transitory effects If the intervention takes place at time $t = \tau$ and has an effect only in that time period, w_t is a *pulse* variable of the form

$$w_t = \begin{cases} 0, & t \neq \tau \\ 1, & t = \tau \end{cases} \tag{7.6.2}$$

Level change A shift in the level of the series will be captured by a *step* variable

$$w_t = \begin{cases} 0, & t < \tau \\ 1, & t \geqslant \tau \end{cases} \tag{7.6.3}$$

An effect of this kind can also be interpreted as a transitory shock to the level equation in the trend. Thus, rather than appearing in the measurement equation, (7.6.1), the intervention effect can instead appear as a pulse variable, (7.6.2), in the level equation of the trend component, that is

$$\mu_t = \mu_{t-1} + \beta_{t-1} + \lambda w_t + \eta_t \tag{7.6.4}$$

Slope change A change in the slope of the trend is a transitory shock to the slope equation in the trend. Thus

$$\beta_t = \beta_{t-1} + \lambda w_t + \zeta_t \tag{7.6.5}$$

where w_t is a pulse variable. Such an effect can be captured in (7.6.1) by defining the variable

$$w_t = \begin{cases} 0, & t < \tau \\ t - \tau, & t \geqslant \tau \end{cases} \tag{7.6.6}$$

Change in seasonal pattern It may sometimes happen that the seasonal pattern changes as the result of an intervention. An example would be the change in the system of registering cars in the UK a few years ago. The single letter on a UK number-plate indicates the year in which the car was registered, and when the first month in the 'year' was changed from January to August there was a marked effect on the seasonal pattern of new car sales. Modelling an effect of this kind requires the introduction of a set of $s-1$ dummy variables from time τ onwards, the effects of which are constrained to be zero over s consecutive time periods; compare (2.3.2). This is equivalent to introducing $s-1$ pulse variables into the seasonal transition equation.

It is quite possible for an intervention to give rise to several of the effects listed above. Thus, for example, both the level and the slope of the trend may be affected in which case the two intervention variables, (7.6.3) and (7.6.6), must be introduced into the model. There is also the possibility of a dynamic response to the intervention. Thus if a transitory effect dies away gradually it might be appropriate to model it by the intervention variable.

$$w_t = \begin{cases} 0, & t < \tau \\ \varphi^{t-\tau}, & t \geqslant \tau \end{cases} \tag{7.6.7}$$

with φ between zero and one. An interesting property of this specification is that w_t becomes a pure pulse variable when φ is zero and a pure step variable when φ is one.

7.6.1 Estimation

Estimation of a model of the form (7.6.1) can be carried out in both the time- and frequency-domains by treating the intervention variable just like any other explanatory variable. The only points to note arise when λ is put in an augmented state vector. Irrespective of the way in which ML estimation is carried out, running the Kalman filter with $\boldsymbol{\delta}$ and λ in the state vector is useful because of the value of the generalised recursive residuals in diagnostic checking.

In the absence of an intervention variable, the use of a diffuse prior for both $\boldsymbol{\delta}$ and $\boldsymbol{\alpha}_0$ leads to a proper prior being formed from the initial $d+k$ observations. Generalised recursive residuals are defined for $t=d+k+1$ onwards. Now suppose a step or pulse intervention variable is included in the state vector. The state space model is then

$$y_t = \mathbf{z}_t^{*\prime}\boldsymbol{\alpha}_t^* + \varepsilon_t \tag{7.6.8a}$$

$$\boldsymbol{\alpha}_t^* = \begin{bmatrix} \mathbf{T}_t & \mathbf{0} \\ \mathbf{0}' & 1 \end{bmatrix} \boldsymbol{\alpha}_{t-1}^* + \begin{bmatrix} \mathbf{R}_t\boldsymbol{\eta}_t \\ 0 \end{bmatrix} \tag{7.6.8b}$$

where in terms of the notation of (7.1.3),

$\boldsymbol{\alpha}_t^* = [\boldsymbol{\alpha}_t^{\dagger\prime} \quad \lambda]'$ and $\mathbf{z}_t^* = [\mathbf{z}_t^{\dagger\prime} \quad w_t]'$

If $\tau \leqslant d+k+1$, a proper prior for λ is formed along with the proper prior for $\boldsymbol{\alpha}_t$ and $\boldsymbol{\delta}$ once $d+k+1$ observations have been processed. If, however, τ is greater than $d+k+1$, the fact that w_t is zero until $t=\tau$ means that a proper estimator of λ can only be constructed once the τ-th observation has been processed. Nevertheless a proper prior for the state vector and $\boldsymbol{\delta}$ is given by the initial $d+k$ observations and it is not difficult to show that the MSE matrix of the estimator of the augmented state vector at $t=d+k$ is

$$\mathbf{P}_{d+k}^* = \begin{bmatrix} \mathbf{P}_{d+k}^\dagger & \mathbf{0} \\ \mathbf{0}' & \kappa \end{bmatrix} \tag{7.6.9}$$

where $\mathbf{P}_{d+k}^\dagger$ is the MSE matrix of the estimator of $[\boldsymbol{\alpha}_{d+k}' \quad \boldsymbol{\delta}']$ which would have been obtained if λ had not been added to the state vector. Since, in the measurement equation, $\mathbf{z}_t^* = [\mathbf{z}_t' \quad \mathbf{x}_t' \quad w_t]'$, the fact that w_t is zero for $t=1,\ldots,\tau-1$, effectively isolates the estimator of λ and its associated 'large κ' MSE from the rest of the Kalman filter. At time $t=\tau$, an estimator of λ with a finite MSE is obtained and $v_\tau^\dagger$ is identically equal to zero. If the likelihood function is being constructed in this way then $f_\tau^\dagger$ should not appear in the determinantal term. In other words, the summation in the likelihood function is over $t=d+k+1$ to $\tau-1$ and $t=\tau+1$ to T.

An alternative way of proceeding is not to include λ in the state vector at $t=0$. The filter proceeds to give an estimator, $\mathbf{a}_{\tau-1}^\dagger$, of $\boldsymbol{\alpha}_{\tau-1}^\dagger=[\boldsymbol{\alpha}_{\tau-1}' \quad \boldsymbol{\delta}_{\tau-1}']'$ at time $\tau-1$, together with a covariance matrix proportional to $\mathbf{P}_{\tau-1}^\dagger$. The estimator of the augmented state vector $\boldsymbol{\alpha}_\tau^*=[\boldsymbol{\alpha}_\tau' \quad \boldsymbol{\delta}' \quad \lambda]'$ at time τ is given by:

$$\mathbf{a}_\tau^*=\begin{bmatrix}\mathbf{a}_{\tau|\tau-1}^\dagger \\ y_\tau-\mathbf{z}_\tau^{\dagger\prime}\mathbf{a}_{\tau|\tau-1}\end{bmatrix} \tag{7.6.10a}$$

with

$$\mathbf{P}_\tau^*=\begin{bmatrix}\mathbf{P}_{\tau|\tau-1}^\dagger & \mathbf{P}_{\tau|\tau-1}\mathbf{z}_\tau^* \\ \mathbf{z}_\tau^{*\prime}\mathbf{P}_{\tau|\tau-1} & f_\tau^\dagger\end{bmatrix} \tag{7.6.10b}$$

After that the Kalman filter proceeds to operate on the state space model (7.6.8). A similar device was used by Brown *et al.* (1975) in the context of computing recursive residuals for a regression model.

If the intervention variable is a slope change, the modifications described above take place at time $\tau+1$ rather than time τ. Thus the generalised recursive residual is zero at time $\tau+1$. A seasonal change leads to $s-1$ zero generalised recursive residuals at times τ to $\tau+s-2$.

7.6.2 Assessing the impact of an intervention

Suppose that a step intervention occurs at time τ. The question arises, how accurately can the effect be measured and how does this accuracy improve as more observations become available? In order to answer this question we analyse the simple model

$$\begin{aligned} y_t&=\mu_t+\lambda w_t+\varepsilon_t, \quad \mathrm{Var}(\varepsilon_t)=\sigma_\varepsilon^2 \\ \mu_t&=\mu_{t-1}+\eta_t, \quad \mathrm{Var}(\eta_t)=\sigma_\varepsilon^2 q \end{aligned} \tag{7.6.11}$$

where w_t is as defined in (7.6.3). The signal–noise ratio will be assumed to be known and τ will be taken to be large.

The GLS method for estimating λ in (7.6.11) is to apply the Kalman filter appropriate for the random walk plus noise model to both y_t and w_t, and then to do a WLS regression of the innovations from y_t on the innovations from w_t. The variance of the resulting estimator of λ can then be obtained directly as

$$\mathrm{Var}(\tilde{\lambda})=\sigma_\varepsilon^2\left[\sum_{t=2}^{T} w_t^{*2}/f_t\right]^{-1} \tag{7.6.12}$$

where w_t^*, $t=2,\ldots,T$ are the innovations from applying the Kalman filter appropriate to the random walk plus noise model to w_t. The innovations in a random walk plus noise model can be obtained directly from the recursion given in (4.2.14). In the steady state, when $f_t=\bar{f}$, applying this recursion to w_t gives

$$w_t^*=\begin{cases}0, & t<\tau\\ (1/\bar{f})^{t-\tau}, & t\geqslant\tau\end{cases}\tag{7.6.13}$$

and so, on substituting in (7.6.12),

$$\operatorname{Var}(\tilde{\lambda})=\sigma_\varepsilon^2\left[\sum_{t=\tau}^{T}(1/\bar{f})^{2(t-\tau)}/\bar{f}\right]^{-1}=\sigma^2\Big/\sum_{t=\tau}^{T}(1/\bar{f})^{2(t-\tau)}\tag{7.6.14}$$

as $\sigma^2=\sigma_*^2\bar{f}$. Thus if $T=\tau$, $\operatorname{Var}(\tilde{\lambda})$ is equal to σ^2 which is the variance of the one-step-ahead prediction error. If q is strictly positive, $\bar{f}$ is greater than one, and the terms in square brackets in (7.6.14) can be summed as a geometric series yielding

$$\operatorname{Var}(\tilde{\lambda})=\sigma^2\frac{[1-(1/\bar{f})^2]}{1-(1/\bar{f})^{2(T-\tau+1)}}\tag{7.6.15}$$

This expression may be evaluated for any signal–noise ratio, q, since from (3.3.16),

$$\bar{f}=\bar{p}+1=[2+q+\sqrt{q^2+4q}]/2\tag{7.6.16}$$

As $T-\tau\rightarrow\infty$,

$$\operatorname{Var}(\tilde{\lambda}_\infty)=\sigma^2(\bar{f}^2-1)/\bar{f}^2\tag{7.6.17}$$

Thus λ cannot be estimated consistently when q is strictly positive. If there are $j=T-\tau$ observations after the intervention, the relative variance of $\tilde{\lambda}$ is given by the ratio of (7.6.17) to (7.6.15), that is

$$\begin{aligned}\operatorname{Var}(\tilde{\lambda}_\infty)/\operatorname{Var}(\tilde{\lambda})&=1-(1/\bar{f})^{2(j+1)}\\&=1-[2/(2+q+\sqrt{q^2+4q})]^{2(j+1)}\end{aligned}\tag{7.6.18}$$

This formula holds for all positive q, including q equal to infinity, when the ratio is unity for all $T\geqslant\tau$. Evaluation of (7.6.15) and (7.6.17) is not possible in this case, but it is straightforward to show directly that $\operatorname{Var}(\tilde{\lambda})=\sigma_\eta^2$ for all $T\geqslant\tau$. The value of (7.6.18) for different values of j and q is shown in Table 7.6.1. The main point to note is the rapidity with which $\tilde{\lambda}$ reaches its minimum variance. Thus all the relevant information on the effect of an intervention tends to be in the observations immediately afterwards.

The only case when λ can be estimated consistently is when q is zero. In this case the level is constant rather than stochastic, and it follows from (7.6.16) that

Table 7.6.1 *Relative variance of GLS estimator of λ after j time periods*

	Time periods, *j*, after intervention								
q	0	1	2	3	4	5	6	...	10
0.01	0.18	0.33	0.45	0.55	0.63	0.70	0.75	...	0.91
0.05	0.36	0.59	0.74	0.83	0.89	0.93	0.96	...	0.99
0.1	0.47	0.72	0.85	0.92	0.96	0.98	0.99	...	1.00
1	0.85	0.98	1.00						
10	0.99	1.00							
∞	1.00								

$\bar{f}=1$ and so (7.6.14) becomes

$$\mathrm{Var}\,(\tilde{\lambda})=\sigma^2/(T-\tau+1) \tag{7.6.19}$$

7.6.3 Testing the specification of an intervention variable

The dynamics following an intervention are rarely known, although *a priori* knowledge sometimes gives an indication. When *a priori* knowledge is available it usually, but not always, suggests that the effect of the intervention is immediate, i.e. there are effectively no dynamics. Another, even more fundamental, question concerns whether the intervention is a pulse, a step or a slope change. This is absolutely crucial to any evaluation of the effects of the intervention. A pulse means that there are no permanent effects, whereas a step or slope change does. When the dynamics of the intervention are unknown as well, determining whether it is a pulse, a step or a slope change can become extremely difficult.

A large part of the specification problem in intervention analysis arises from the fact that because a time series model typically involves discounting, the period during which an intervention makes itself felt on the series is limited; see the discussion in sub-section 7.4.2. Hence elaborate nested models incorporating all types of change and dynamics are rarely a viable proposition. Even a very simple model, such as (7.6.7), may be very difficult to estimate with any degree of accuracy. The only reasonable strategy may therefore be to use as much *a priori* knowledge as possible to construct an intervention model and then to submit it to diagnostic checking. The usual diagnostics, such as the Box-Ljung test, are of limited value in this respect since any distortion in the residuals immediately after the intervention will be diluted in the full set of residuals. Intervention misspecification diagnostics should therefore concentrate on the period immediately after the intervention.

Suppose, first of all, that an intervention occurs at time τ, and that the hyperparameters are estimated from the first $\tau-1$ observations. Thus the estimators of the hyperparameters will be unaffected by any misspecification in the intervention. For the purposes of argument, it will be assumed that $\boldsymbol{\psi}_*$ can be treated as known. Any statements regarding exact distributions must be regarded as conditional on this assumption. Now suppose that the pattern of the dynamics is known but that the overall effect is not. Thus for example in terms of (7.6.7), φ is given but λ is not. This assumption essentially reduces the problem to one which is equivalent to a simple intervention with no dynamics. The suggested *post-intervention* test statistic is

$$\xi_\tau(l)=\left[\sum_{t=\tau+1}^{\tau+l} \tilde{v}_t^{\dagger 2}/l\right]\Bigg/\left[\sum_{t=d+k+1}^{\tau-1} \tilde{v}_t^{\dagger 2}/(\tau-1-d-k)\right] \tag{7.6.20}$$

where $v_t^\dagger$ is the generalised recursive residual at time t, the denominator in $\xi_\tau(l)$ is the unbiased estimator of σ_*^2 based on the first $\tau-1$ observations, and $t=\tau+l$ is the point beyond which the effect of the intervention is felt to be negligible. The choice of l will depend partly on the structure of the series and partly on the assumed dynamics of the intervention. If the preferred value of $\tau+l$ is much smaller than T it may be more advantageous to use the modified statistic given in (7.6.21) below.

The rationale behind (7.6.20) is similar to the rationale behind the Chow statistic, (7.4.14), for post-sample predictive testing. The alternative hypothesis is that the response structure is different to the assumed one and that it is unrestricted. There are $l+1$ coefficients in this response structure but since the null hypothesis specifies one unknown parameter, λ, the degrees of freedom in the numerator of $\xi_\tau(l)$ are l not $l+1$. Indeed this is apparent from the summation in the numerator which goes from $\tau+1$ to $\tau+l$, because $\tilde{v}_\tau^\dagger$ is identically zero. When the model is correctly specified, $\tilde{v}_t^\dagger \sim \text{NID}(0, \sigma_*^2)$ for $t=d+k+1,\ldots,\tau-1$, $\tau+1,\ldots,\tau+l$ and so $\xi_\tau(l)$ has an F-distribution with $(l, \tau-1-d-k)$ degrees of freedom. If the assumption that the elements of $\boldsymbol{\psi}_*$ are known is relaxed, the exact distribution of $\xi_\tau(l)$ is unknown. In large samples $l\xi_\tau(l) \sim \chi_m^2$, but for practical purposes it may be better to use the F-distribution when the sample is small.

If the intervention occurs relatively early on in the series, a more powerful test may be obtained by using the residuals formed after the effect of the intervention has worn off to get a better estimator of σ_*^2. The test statistic is

$$\xi_\tau^*(l)=\left[\sum_{t=\tau+1}^{\tau+l} \tilde{v}_t^{\dagger 2}/l\right]\Bigg/\left\{\left[\sum_{d+k+1}^{\tau-1} \tilde{v}_t^{\dagger 2}+\sum_{\tau+l^*+1}^{T} \tilde{v}_t^{\dagger 2}\right]\Bigg/(T-l^*-d-k)\right\} \tag{7.6.21}$$

where $l^* \geqslant l$. Setting $l^*>l$ means that some residuals are not included in the test statistic since it is unclear whether or not they are influenced by the dynamics of the intervention. Under the null hypothesis $\xi_\tau(l)^*$ has an F-distribution with $(l, T-l^*-d-k)$ degrees of freedom when $\boldsymbol{\psi}_*$ is known.

Other tests can be carried out to detect misspecification of the intervention variable. One possibility is to plot the CUSUM of the post-intervention residuals $\tilde{v}_{\tau+1}^\dagger,\ldots,\tilde{v}_{\tau+M}^\dagger$. This is defined as

$$\text{CUSUM}_\tau(h)=\sum_{\tau+1}^{\tau+h} \tilde{v}_t^\dagger/s_*(\tau-1) \qquad h=1,\ldots,l \tag{7.6.22}$$

where $s_*^2(\tau-1)$ is as defined in (7.4.1) but with the summation to $\tau-1$ rather than T, that is, it is the same as the denominator of (7.6.20). A recursive t-test may also be constructed. This is based on the statistic

$$\psi_\tau(l)=\sum_{t=\tau+1}^{\tau+l}\tilde{v}_t^\dagger/l^{\frac{1}{2}}s_*(\tau-1)=\text{CUSUM}_\tau(l)/\sqrt{l} \tag{7.6.23}$$

Under the null hypothesis, (7.6.23) has a t-distribution with $\tau-1-d-k$ degrees of freedom. If there is a high proportion of observations after the intervention, the numerator of this statistic may be amended in the same way as (7.6.20) was amended to give (7.6.21).

The discussion so far has assumed that the intervention effect involves the estimation of only one unknown parameter. If there are several parameters, there is a corresponding reduction in the number of residuals which can be used in the numerators of post-intervention test statistics described above. As a result it becomes relatively more difficult to detect misspecification.

7.6.4 Model selection and application to the UK seat belt law

If the intervention occurs near the end of the series a suitable model may be constructed on the basis of the observations prior to the intervention. The intervention variable is then added, and its specification is tested using the techniques developed in the previous section. However, if the intervention does not take place near the end of the series the specification of the model and the intervention must be carried out jointly.

In the case of the UK seat belt law study, the intervention took place near the end of the sample period. As a result models could be specified on the basis of observations prior to the change in the law. For car drivers KSI, details of the preferred model, (7.3.10), and the specification process by which it was arrived at, were given in sub-sections 7.3.3 and 7.5.1. We now consider modelling the effect of the seat belt law on this series, and on some related series.

The effect of the seat belt law on car drivers The most straightforward hypothesis to adopt is that the introduction of the seat belt law on 31 January 1983, induced a once and for all downward shift in the level of the series on car drivers KSI. This implies a step intervention variable, (7.6.3). However, since the seat belt wearing rate rose from 40% in December 1982 to 50% in January 1983 in anticipation of the introduction of the law, (7.6.3) was modified slightly by setting $w_t=0.18$ in January 1983. The relative variances estimated using data up to the end of 1982 were used when the intervention parameter, λ, was estimated using the data up to and including December 1984. The resulting estimate of λ was

$$\tilde{\lambda}=\underset{(0.053)}{-0.262}$$

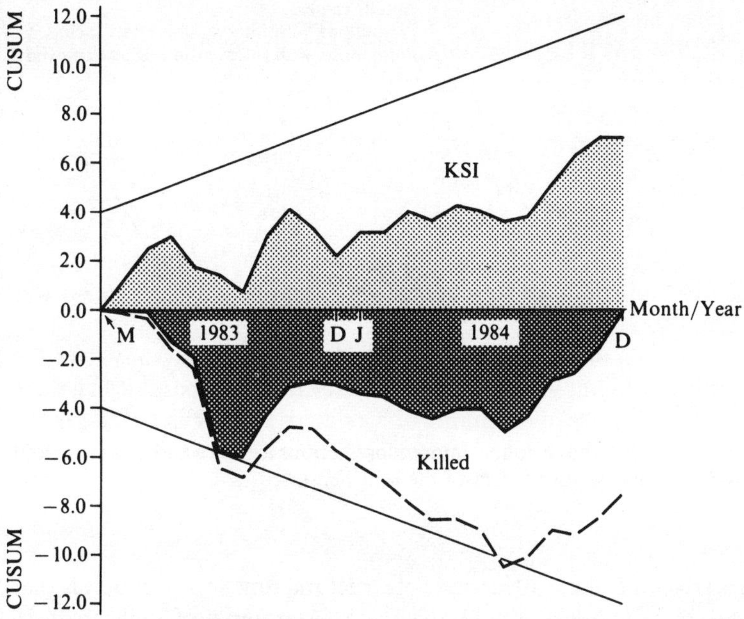

Fig. 7.6.1 CUSUM of generalised recursive residuals for car drivers killed and seriously injured and car drivers killed (with 10% significance lines). Lower broken line shows CUSUM for drivers killed under the risk homeostasis hypothesis.

Since $\exp(-0.262)=0.770$, the estimated reduction in drivers KSI was 23.0%. The 50% confidence interval for this reduction is 20.2% to 25.8% while the 95% confidence interval is 14.7% to 30.6%. The relationship between the normal and log-normal distributions suggests the use of $\exp[\tilde{\lambda}+\frac{1}{2}\operatorname{var}(\tilde{\lambda})]$ instead of $\exp(\tilde{\lambda})$. However the value of this gives an estimated reduction of 22.9% so the difference is negligible.

The diagnostics are based on the residuals from February 1983 onwards, that is τ is January 1983. The post-intervention predictive test statistics for $l=3$, 6 and 23 are as follows:

$$\xi_\tau(3)=1.28,\quad \xi_\tau(6)=0.93,\quad \xi_\tau(23)=0.67$$

None of these indicates a statistically significant increase in the variance of the residuals following the intervention. Similarly the CUSUM up to December 1984, which can be found plotted in Figure 7.6.1, does not cross the 10% boundary lines. Finally, Figure 7.6.2 shows the predictions for 1983 and 1984. These are obtained using observations of the explanatory variables for 1983 and 1984 but not using observations of the car drivers KSI series itself for 1983 and 1984. Including the intervention variable, which was subsequently estimated from the 1983 and 1984 data, gives very accurate results.

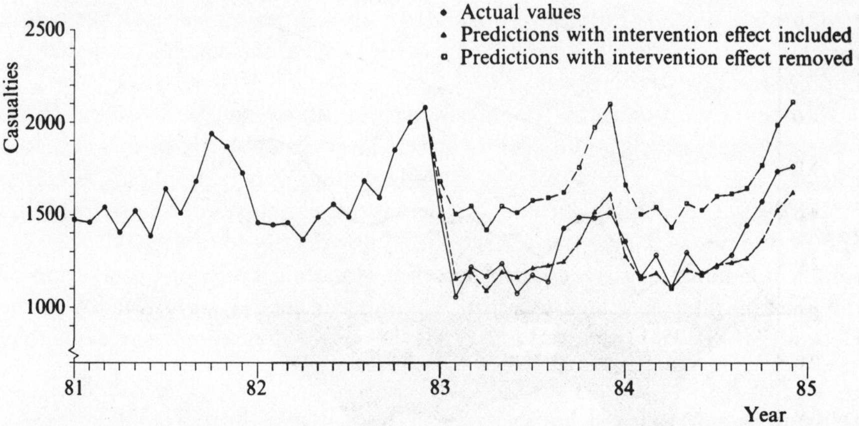

Fig. 7.6.2 Car drivers killed and seriously injured: predictions for 1983 and 1984 with and without the estimated intervention effect of the seat belt law.

Sensitivity analysis One of the attractions of structural time series models is that they lend themselves to sensitivity analysis. As an example of such analysis, consider the series for the logarithm of pedestrians killed by cars, using the logarithm of pedestrians KSI by heavy goods vehicles (HGVs) and public service vehicles (PSVs) as an explanatory variable. (The reason for the choice of this variable as a control variable is discussed in more detail in Durbin and Harvey (1985) together with the reasons for wishing to study the effect of the law on a group not directly affected by it; the details are not important in the present context.) The result of fitting this model to data up to December 1982 was to produce deterministic trend and seasonal components, i.e. $\sigma_\eta^2 = \sigma_\zeta^2 = \sigma_\omega^2 = 0$. The diagnostics were acceptable and $s = 0.149$ while $R_s^2 = 0.44$ and $R^2 = 0.76$.

It has been argued throughout this book that a deterministic trend is unusual and needs to be handled with some care. Thus some caution is needed in assessing the estimate of the intervention effect of the seat belt law which is

$$\tilde{\lambda} = \underset{(0.066)}{0.133}$$

and is statistically significant at the 5% level in a two-sided test. It was therefore decided to examine the sensitivity of this estimate to changes in the variance parameters. The key parameter in this respect is σ_η^2, since in most of the models fitted this tended to be significantly different from zero. Setting $\sigma_\eta^2/\sigma_\varepsilon^2 = 0.1$ yields

$$\tilde{\lambda} = \underset{(0.098)}{0.095}$$

Making this modification therefore yields an estimate smaller than the original estimate and this new estimate is not statistically significant. Nevertheless it does indicate a non-negligible increase in this series and so the conclusion is that the original result is fairly robust.

Another aspect of sensitivity analysis concerns the treatment of outliers. In the present context observations with relatively large residuals are often associated with extreme weather conditions, as in the exceptionally cold month of December 1981. One way of dealing with the problem is to estimate models both including and excluding such outlying observations in order to determine whether the results are unduly sensitive to their presence. Handling a missing observation by the Kalman filter is straightforward. A number of models were fitted with the December 1981 value included and excluded but the differences were negligible.

Dynamic response and risk homeostasis In the context of the seat belt law, the risk homeostasis hypothesis advocated by Wilde (1982) states that car drivers will eventually readjust their driving behaviour so as to keep the probability of their being killed constant. Stated in this general form the risk homeostasis hypothesis is virtually impossible to prove or disprove for a time series with a stochastic trend component. The reason for this is the discounting of observations as one moves further away from the time at which the intervention occurred; see sub-section 7.4.2. However, if a specific hypothesis on the form of the dynamic response is put forward it can be tested using the methods outlined in the previous sub-section. Thus suppose the effect of the seat belt law declines linearly until it is eliminated after two years. This means that the intervention variable w_t is defined as

$$w_t = \begin{cases} 0, & t < \text{January 1983} \\ 0.18, & t = \text{January 1983} \\ 1-(t-\text{February 1983})/24, & t = \text{February 1983}, \ldots, (\text{February 1983}+24) \end{cases}$$

Fitting (7.3.10) with an intervention variable w_t, defined as above, to the series on car drivers killed gave

$$\tilde{\lambda} = \underset{(0.075)}{-0.206}$$

with the post-intervention test statistic $\zeta_\tau(23)$, taking the value 1.240. This is not statistically significant at any conventional level of significance, and it is not much higher than the value of 1.207 obtained when the original intervention variable was fitted. Thus although one would prefer the original model on grounds of goodness of fit in the post-intervention period, the fit is not dramatically better than that of the postulated risk homeostasis model and the forecast errors from the latter model are comparable to the forecast errors obtained before the intervention. However, where this particular version of the dynamic risk homeostasis model does break down is in the CUSUM. Figure 7.6.1 shows the CUSUM as a broken line. As can be seen it clearly crosses the lower 10% significance line. Again a one-sided test is appropriate as one would expect the dynamic risk homeostasis model to overpredict if the seat belt law had led to a once and for all downward shift in the level of fatalities.

7.7 Time-varying parameters

At the beginning of this chapter it was suggested that the coefficients of the explanatory variables could be made time-varying by allowing them to be random walks. The first sub-section below addresses a number of issues raised by such models. Sub-section 7.7.2 considers a slightly different class of models in which the time-varying parameters follow stationary processes.

7.7.1 *Random walk models*

If the parameters associated with the explanatory variables in (7.1.2) are allowed to follow a multivariate random walk process as in (7.1.4), the SSF is

$$y_t = \mathbf{z}_t'\boldsymbol{\alpha}_t + \mathbf{x}_t'\boldsymbol{\delta}_t + \varepsilon_t \tag{7.7.1a}$$

$$\boldsymbol{\alpha}_t = \begin{bmatrix} \boldsymbol{\alpha}_t \\ \boldsymbol{\delta}_t \end{bmatrix} = \begin{bmatrix} \mathbf{T} & \mathbf{0} \\ \mathbf{0} & \mathbf{I} \end{bmatrix} \begin{bmatrix} \boldsymbol{\alpha}_{t-1} \\ \boldsymbol{\delta}_{t-1} \end{bmatrix} + \begin{bmatrix} \boldsymbol{\eta}_t \\ \boldsymbol{\upsilon}_t \end{bmatrix} \tag{7.7.1b}$$

Assuming a diffuse prior, estimation is carried out via the prediction error decomposition using the innovations for $t = d+k+1, \ldots, T$.

If the model contains a lagged dependent variable, this may also have a time-varying parameter. Thus

$$y_t = \varphi_t y_{t-1} + \mathbf{z}_t'\boldsymbol{\alpha}_t + \mathbf{x}_t'\boldsymbol{\delta}_t + \varepsilon_t \tag{7.7.2}$$

where φ_t follows a random walk. This model may also be handled in the time domain by adding φ_t to the state vector. The only difference is that the model is conditionally Gaussian rather than linear. Of course, there is a conceptual problem in allowing the coefficient of the lagged dependent variable to be time-varying if it is felt that it ought always to lie within the stability region, $|\varphi_t| < 1$.

A distributed lag structure on the exogenous variables in the model raises somewhat different issues. Consider (7.1.8) with a single exogenous variable. Simply letting the parameters, δ_τ, change according to independent random walks is not very attractive. One possibility is to let the total multiplier evolve over time in a different way to the shape of the lag distribution. There are a number of ways in which this may be done. One could make use of the formulation in (7.1.17), in which the lagged variables are rearranged into a single level variable and first differences. The coefficient of the level variable is then the total multiplier and its movements can be modelled separately from those of other coefficients. A different way of setting up the problem is to let

$$\delta_\tau = \delta/(h+1) + \delta_\tau^{\#}, \quad \tau = 0, \ldots, h \tag{7.7.3}$$

where δ is the total multiplier. The definition of the total multiplier in (7.1.19) implies that

$$\sum_{\tau=0}^{h} \delta_\tau^{\#} = 0 \tag{7.7.4}$$

Substituting (7.7.3) in (7.1.8) gives:

$$y_t = \mathbf{z}_t'\boldsymbol{\alpha}_t + \delta\left[\sum_{\tau=0}^{h} x_{t-\tau}/(h+1)\right] + \sum_{\tau=0}^{h} \delta_\tau^{\#} x_{t-\tau} + \varepsilon_t \tag{7.7.5}$$

The total multiplier is the long-run effect. The remaining coefficients give the shape of the lag distribution. These coefficients could be allowed to evolve independently of the total multiplier by a mechanism which ensures that they sum to zero as required by (7.7.4); a possible mechanism is the daily effects model of sub-section 2.3.5. Alternatively, one of the $\delta_\tau^{\#}$'s can be removed from (7.7.5) by means of (7.7.4). This yields

$$y_t = \mathbf{z}_t'\boldsymbol{\alpha}_t + \delta\left[\sum_{\tau=0}^{h} x_{t-\tau}/(h+1)\right] + \sum_{\tau=1}^{h} \delta_\tau^{\#}(x_{t-\tau} - x_t) + \varepsilon_t \tag{7.7.6}$$

The $\delta_\tau^{\#}$ coefficients can now be allowed to evolve as independent random walks with a common variance.

Time-variation can be introduced into an Almon lag. The transformation in (7.1.11) means that the variable associated with the first polynomial coefficient, δ_0^*, is the moving sum of the observations. A comparison with (7.7.5) shows that multiplying δ_0^* by $h+1$ gives the total multiplier. The other polynomial coefficients, δ_1^* to δ_g^*, capture various aspects of the shape of the lag distribution.

A univariate time series model is a special case of a time-varying parameter regression model in which the explanatory variables are functions of time. However, a key feature of a univariate time series model is that it is set up to preserve some degree of continuity when the parameters change. This needs to be borne in mind when a more general time-varying parameter model is formulated. Consider the model

$$y_t = \alpha + \delta x_t + \varepsilon_t \tag{7.7.7}$$

Rather than simply letting α and δ follow random walks, it may be better to feed changes emanating from the explanatory variable into the level, particularly when the explanatory variable is non-stationary. Thus

$$y_t = \mu_t + \varepsilon_t \tag{7.7.8a}$$

$$\mu_t = \mu_{t-1} + \delta_{t-1}\Delta x_t + \eta_t \tag{7.7.8b}$$

$$\delta_t = \qquad \delta_{t-1} \qquad + \zeta_t \tag{7.7.8c}$$

When $x_t = t$, (7.7.8) reduces to the standard local linear trend model. Very little attention has been paid in the literature to the way in which time-variation should be introduced into the coefficients of explanatory variables and the issue may be a crucial one in practice.

Testing for time-variation in the coefficients of the explanatory variables in (7.7.1) is subject to the problems already encountered in carrying out tests on certain of the variance hyperparameters in structural time series models. The difficulties stem from the random walk nature of the time-varying parameters and the fact that $\boldsymbol{\delta}_t$ is not stabilisable under the null hypothesis that $\text{Var}(\boldsymbol{\upsilon}_t) = \mathbf{0}$. An LM test statistic can be constructed but, as noted in Tanaka (1983), its distribution is difficult to determine since the usual likelihood regularity conditions break down. A possible solution is to employ an MPI test. Tests of this kind were advocated for testing for deterministic trend and seasonal components in sub-sections 5.3.5 and 7.4.2.

7.7.2 Random coefficients and the return to normality model

If the variation in the parameters of the explanatory variables is modelled by a stationary process, there is no longer the discounting of past observations which is a feature of the random walk formulation. Nevertheless there may be *a priori* reasons for wishing to regard the parameter variation as being stationary. The simplest model is

$$\boldsymbol{\delta}_t - \bar{\boldsymbol{\delta}} = \boldsymbol{\Phi}(\boldsymbol{\delta}_{t-1} - \bar{\boldsymbol{\delta}}) + \boldsymbol{\upsilon}_t \tag{7.7.9}$$

where $\boldsymbol{\upsilon}_t$ is a $k \times 1$ vector with a p.s.d. covariance matrix. If $\boldsymbol{\Phi} = \mathbf{I}$, the model becomes (7.1.4). However, if the roots of $\boldsymbol{\Phi}$ lie inside the unit circle the model is stationary. This type of parameter variation is sometimes referred to as *return to normality*, because the parameters move around a constant mean, $\bar{\boldsymbol{\delta}}$. Applications can be found in Rosenberg (1973) and Schaefer *et al.* (1975); the second of these papers is concerned with modelling a share's market risk.

In principle $\boldsymbol{\delta}_t$ may be modelled by any multivariate ARMA process. The problem is that specifying an appropriate model from such a wide class is virtually impossible. Furthermore, a large number of parameters need to be estimated. Even the model in (7.7.9) may really only be a viable proposition if $\boldsymbol{\Phi}$ and $\text{Var}(\boldsymbol{\upsilon}_t)$ are constrained to be diagonal. Some Monte Carlo evidence on the small sample properties of the ML estimator for (7.7.9) may be found in Harvey and Phillips (1982).

If $\boldsymbol{\delta}_t$ in (7.7.9) is substituted into (7.7.1), the result is

$$y_t = \mathbf{z}_t'\boldsymbol{\alpha}_t + \mathbf{x}_t'\boldsymbol{\delta}_t^* + \mathbf{x}_t'\bar{\boldsymbol{\delta}} + \varepsilon_t \tag{7.7.10}$$

where $\boldsymbol{\delta}_t^* = \boldsymbol{\delta}_t - \bar{\boldsymbol{\delta}}$. The model is therefore in SSF. Since $\boldsymbol{\delta}_t^*$ is stationary, its initial conditions in the Kalman filter are a mean of zero and a covariance matrix obtained by solving (3.3.18). In the special case when $\text{Var}(\boldsymbol{\upsilon}_t)$ and $\boldsymbol{\Phi}$ are diagonal, the i-th diagonal element of this covariance matrix is given immediately as $\text{Var}(\upsilon_{it})/(1-\varphi_i^2)$, $i=1,\ldots,k$. When $\mathbf{z}_t'\boldsymbol{\alpha}_t$ is deterministic, there is also the possibility of constructing a two-step estimator; see Harvey (1981b, p. 203) or Nicholls and Pagan (1985). As regards $\boldsymbol{\delta}$, this may be estimated like any fixed parameter, either by augmenting the state vector or by applying the Rosenberg or GLS algorithms.

When $\boldsymbol{\Phi} = \mathbf{0}$, (7.7.9) and (7.7.10) collapse to the *random coefficient* model. This may be written in the form

$$y_t = \mathbf{z}_t'\boldsymbol{\alpha}_t + \mathbf{x}_t'\bar{\boldsymbol{\delta}} + u_t \tag{7.7.11a}$$

where

$$u_t = \mathbf{x}_t'\boldsymbol{\delta}_t^* + \varepsilon_t \tag{7.7.11b}$$

Clearly u_t is a random disturbance term with mean zero and variance $\mathbf{x}_t'\text{Var}(\boldsymbol{\upsilon}_t)\mathbf{x}_t + \sigma_\varepsilon^2$, $t=1,\ldots,T$. There is no serial correlation in u_t, only heteroscedasticity. Hence the model is very easy to handle. However, the absence of a dynamic structure in the time path of the coefficients makes its appeal limited.

The problems which arise in testing for parameter variation in (7.7.9) are somewhat different to those which arise when the alternative hypothesis is that the parameters follow random walks. The model is stabilisable, but there is the additional problem that when $\boldsymbol{\Phi} = \mathbf{0}$, the parameters in $\text{Var}(\boldsymbol{\upsilon}_t)$ cease to be identifiable. Again an MPI test represents a possible solution. In the random coefficient model, a standard LM test for heteroscedasticity may be used, and Nicholls and Pagan (1985, p. 429) suggest that this test may have high power against the more general return to normality model.

7.8 Instrumental variables

The methods proposed in this chapter have, up to now, been based on the assumption that the explanatory variables in the models are *exogenous.* In many applications involving economic data, however, an equation may be part of a larger system of simultaneous equations. Some, or all, of the explanatory variables in the equation of interest may be *endogenous* to this system. If the current values of these endogenous variables enter into the equation of interest, estimation procedures based on a likelihood function obtained by conditioning on these variables are inappropriate. In fact, because these variables will, in general, be correlated with the disturbances in the stochastic part of the model, such ML procedures are likely to yield inconsistent estimators of the parameters in the model. Lagged values of endogenous variables do not give rise to such difficulties and are classed, together with exogenous variables, as *predetermined.*

If the complete system of equations can be specified, a full information maximum likelihood (FIML) procedure may be employed. If only a sub-system is specified, but all the predetermined variables are named, a limited information maximum likelihood (LIML) procedure is appropriate. The way in which FIML and LIML might be applied is outlined in section 8.9. When the rest of the system has not been specified at all, ML methods cannot be applied, but a valid instrumental variable (IV) estimator can be obtained. The IV procedure is fairly general and is often appropriate outside the context of simultaneous equation systems.

7.8.1 The principle of instrumental variable estimation

In order to develop the method of instrumental variables, consider the equation of interest written in matrix notation as

$$\mathbf{y} = \mathbf{Z}\boldsymbol{\delta} + \mathbf{u} \tag{7.8.1}$$

where $\mathbf{Z}$ is a $T \times k$ matrix of observations on explanatory variables and $\mathbf{u}$ is a $T \times 1$ vector of disturbances with mean zero and covariance matrix, $\sigma_*^2 \mathbf{V}$. The explanatory variables may include variables which are not exogenous. A set of K instrumental variables is available. These are contained in a $T \times K$ matrix, $\mathbf{X}$. In order to be valid, or admissible, instruments, these variables should be uncorrelated with the disturbances in large samples. In order to be effective, they should be highly correlated with the explanatory variables in (7.8.1). If $\mathbf{Z}$ contains some weakly exogenous variables, these will also be contained within $\mathbf{X}$, and will act as their own instruments.

Suppose initially that $\mathbf{V} = \mathbf{I}$. All that needs to be done is to reduce the $K \geqslant k$ instruments to a set of k optimal instruments. These are formed by carrying out a multivariate regression of $\mathbf{Z}$ on $\mathbf{X}$. Thus the $T \times k$ matrix of optimal instruments is

$$\mathbf{W} = \mathbf{X}(\mathbf{X}'\mathbf{X})^{-1}\mathbf{X}'\mathbf{Z} \tag{7.8.2}$$

and so the IV estimator is:

$$\tilde{\boldsymbol{\delta}} = (\mathbf{W}'\mathbf{Z})^{-1}\mathbf{W}'\mathbf{y} \tag{7.8.3a}$$

$$= (\mathbf{Z}'\mathbf{P}\mathbf{Z})^{-1}\mathbf{Z}'\mathbf{P}\mathbf{y} \tag{7.8.3b}$$

where $\mathbf{P}$ is the projection matrix

$$\mathbf{P} = \mathbf{X}(\mathbf{X}'\mathbf{X})^{-1}\mathbf{X}' \tag{7.8.4}$$

In a system of simultaneous equations, where $\mathbf{X}$ is the full set of exogenous variables, (7.8.3) is the two-stage least squares (2SLS) estimator.

In the more general case when $\mathbf{V}$ is any p.d. matrix, a number of options are open. Two will be described here. Both are based on first transforming (7.8.1) by multiplying through by a $T \times T$ matrix $\mathbf{L}$ with the property that $\mathbf{L}'\mathbf{L} = \mathbf{V}^{-1}$. This yields

$$\mathbf{Ly} = \mathbf{LZ}\boldsymbol{\delta} + \mathbf{Lu} \tag{7.8.5}$$

The disturbance term in this equation has a scalar covariance matrix, that is, $\text{Var}(\mathbf{Lu}) = \sigma_*^2\mathbf{I}$. Given (7.8.5), the main issue is whether to apply the same transformation to the instruments, $\mathbf{X}$.

If the transformation is applied to $\mathbf{X}$, the matrix of optimal instruments, $\mathbf{W}$, is formed by replacing $\mathbf{X}$ and $\mathbf{Z}$ in (7.8.2) by $\mathbf{LX}$ and $\mathbf{LZ}$ respectively. The resulting IV estimator is then

$$\mathbf{d}^{\dagger} = [\mathbf{Z}'\mathbf{V}^{-1}\mathbf{X}(\mathbf{X}'\mathbf{V}^{-1}\mathbf{X})^{-1}\mathbf{X}'\mathbf{V}^{-1}\mathbf{Z}]^{-1}\mathbf{Z}'\mathbf{V}^{-1}\mathbf{X}(\mathbf{X}'\mathbf{V}^{-1}\mathbf{X})^{-1}\mathbf{X}'\mathbf{V}^{-1}\mathbf{y} \tag{7.8.6}$$

This can be rewritten as

$$\mathbf{d}^{\dagger} = (\mathbf{Z}'\mathbf{L}'\mathbf{P}_v\mathbf{LZ})^{-1}\mathbf{Z}'\mathbf{L}'\mathbf{P}_v\mathbf{Ly} \tag{7.8.7}$$

where $\mathbf{P}_v$ is the idempotent projection matrix

$$\mathbf{P}_v = \mathbf{LX}(\mathbf{X}'\mathbf{V}^{-1}\mathbf{X})^{-1}\mathbf{X}'\mathbf{L}'$$

Bowden and Turkington (1984, pp. 70–1) refer to $\mathbf{d}^{\dagger}$ as the *GLS analogue* since if $\mathbf{X} = \mathbf{Z}$ it is equivalent to the usual GLS estimator. In the context of a simultaneous equation system, where it was first used by Theil (1961), it is known as *generalised two-stage least squares* (G2SLS).

Following Bowden and Turkington (1984, p. 26), if it is assumed that
(i) plim $T^{-1}\mathbf{X}'\mathbf{V}^{-1}\mathbf{u} = \mathbf{0}$;
(ii) plim $T^{-1}\mathbf{X}'\mathbf{V}^{-1}\mathbf{X}$ exists and is p.d.;
(iii) plim $T^{-1}\mathbf{X}'\mathbf{V}^{-1}\mathbf{Z}$ exists and has full column rank,
it is easy to show that $\mathbf{d}^{\dagger}$ is consistent, that is plim $\mathbf{d}^{\dagger} = \mathbf{d}$. If furthermore it is assumed that
(iv) $T^{-\frac{1}{2}}\mathbf{X}'\mathbf{V}^{-1}\mathbf{u}$ has a limiting normal distribution with mean zero and covariance matrix plim $T^{-1}\mathbf{X}'\mathbf{V}^{-1}\mathbf{X}$
then $T^{\frac{1}{2}}\mathbf{d}^{\dagger}$ has a limiting normal distribution, and we can say that $\mathbf{d}^{\dagger}$ is asymptotically normally distributed with mean $\boldsymbol{\delta}$ and covariance matrix,

$$\text{Avar}(\mathbf{d}^{\dagger}) = \sigma_*^2(\mathbf{Z}'\mathbf{L}'\mathbf{P}_v\mathbf{LZ})^{-1} \tag{7.8.8}$$

These conditions could be weakened by using the equivalent of Grenander's conditions. Furthermore, if $\mathbf{V}$ is unknown, but depends on a finite number of parameters which can be estimated consistently, the asymptotic distribution is unaffected; see Wickens (1969).

The alternative approach is not to transform the instruments. The matrix of optimal instruments, $\mathbf{W}$, is then formed by regressing $\mathbf{LZ}$ on $\mathbf{X}$, and the IV estimator is

$$\tilde{\mathbf{d}}^* = (\mathbf{Z}'\mathbf{L}'\mathbf{PLZ})^{-1}\mathbf{Z}'\mathbf{L}'\mathbf{PLy} \tag{7.8.9}$$

where **P** is the projection matrix defined in (7.8.4). Again, subject to appropriate regularity conditions, $\tilde{\mathbf{d}}^*$ may be shown to be asymptotically normal with mean δ and covariance matrix

$$\text{Avar}(\tilde{\mathbf{d}}^*) = \sigma_*^2(\mathbf{Z}'\mathbf{L}'\mathbf{PLZ})^{-1} \tag{7.8.10}$$

It is not possible to make general statements about the relative efficiency of the above estimators. However, Wickens (1969) shows that in a simultaneous equation system, the G2SLS estimator, $\tilde{\mathbf{d}}^\dagger$, is at least as efficient as 2SLS or the $\tilde{\mathbf{d}}^*$ estimator (7.8.9) provided that the system contains no lagged endogenous variables and the set of instruments, **X**, corresponds to the exogenous variables in the system. Further insight can only be obtained by looking at the system in more detail, and this is done in section 8.9.

7.8.2 Instrumental variable estimation for models with structural time series components

We now consider the estimation of models which contain structural time series components as well as explanatory variables. Attention will be focussed on the situation when only a stochastic trend is present. The model is then

$$y_t = \mu_t + \mathbf{z}_t'\boldsymbol{\delta} + \varepsilon_t, \quad t = 1, \ldots, T \tag{7.8.11}$$

This model can be written in matrix form as in (7.8.1), with $\sigma_*^2\mathbf{V}$ being the covariance matrix of $\mu_t + \varepsilon_t$. From the development of the GLS estimator in section 7.3.2, it follows that the transformation **Ly** and **LZ** may be carried out by applying the Kalman filter based on the stochastic part of the model. If the GLS analogue estimator is to be computed, the same Kalman filter is applied to the instrumental variables in **X**.

The fact that the **L** transformation converts a non-stationary process to a stationary one seems to point even more forcefully to the idea that the GLS analogue is the appropriate estimator to employ. Even though the elements of **Z** and **X** may be highly correlated, applying the **L** transformation only to **Z** could result in the correlation becoming much smaller.

In general, the hyperparameters in (7.8.11) are unknown. If the model is cast in the form of (7.3.1),

$$\Delta(\mathrm{L})y_t = \Delta(\mathrm{L})\mathbf{z}_t'\boldsymbol{\delta} + w_t, \quad t = d+1, \ldots, T, \tag{7.8.12}$$

an estimator of $\boldsymbol{\delta}$ may be obtained using the IV estimator, $\tilde{\mathbf{d}}$, as in (7.8.3). This estimator will be consistent, providing that $\mathbf{z}_t$ does not contain lagged values of the dependent variable. Consistent estimators of the hyperparameters may then be obtained by applying any of the methods of chapter 4 to the residuals, $y_t - \mathbf{z}_t'\tilde{\mathbf{d}}$,

$t=1,\ldots,T$. These estimators may then be used to construct a feasible GLS analogue estimator which has the asymptotic distribution set out for $\tilde{\mathbf{d}}^{\dagger}$ in the previous sub-section.

When the hyperparameters are known, the criterion function for the GLS analogue estimator is

$$S(\boldsymbol{\delta})=(\mathbf{y}-\mathbf{Z}\boldsymbol{\delta})'\mathbf{L}'\mathbf{P}_v\mathbf{L}(\mathbf{y}-\mathbf{Z}\boldsymbol{\delta}) \tag{7.8.13}$$

This needs some modification when the hyperparameters, $\boldsymbol{\psi}_*$, are unknown. Let $\bar{\mathbf{L}}$ be defined as a lower triangular matrix with ones on the diagonal such that

$$\bar{\mathbf{L}}'\mathbf{F}^{-1}\bar{\mathbf{L}}=\mathbf{V}^{-1} \tag{7.8.14}$$

where $\mathbf{F}=\text{diag}\,[f_{d+1},\ldots,f_T]$. The transformation

$$\mathbf{v}=\bar{\mathbf{L}}(\mathbf{y}-\mathbf{Z}\boldsymbol{\delta}) \tag{7.8.15}$$

then gives a $(T-d)\times 1$ vector of elements analogous to those defined by (7.3.3b). The IV criterion function is analogous to the criterion function in (7.3.5) being

$$S^{\dagger}_{\text{IV}}(\boldsymbol{\delta},\boldsymbol{\psi}_*)=S_{\text{IV}}(\boldsymbol{\delta},\boldsymbol{\psi}_*)\left[\prod_{t=d+1}^{T} f_t\right]^{\frac{1}{T-d}} \tag{7.8.16}$$

where $S_{\text{IV}}(\boldsymbol{\delta},\boldsymbol{\psi}_*)$ is the right-hand side of (7.8.13) regarded as a function of $\boldsymbol{\delta}$ and $\boldsymbol{\psi}_*$. In order to make the link with (7.3.5) clearer, we can write

$$S_{\text{IV}}(\boldsymbol{\delta},\boldsymbol{\psi}_*)=\mathbf{v}'\mathbf{F}^{-\frac{1}{2}}\mathbf{P}_v\mathbf{F}^{-\frac{1}{2}}\mathbf{v} \tag{7.8.17}$$

For a steady-state filter, the criterion function is

$$\bar{S}_{\text{IV}}(\boldsymbol{\delta},\boldsymbol{\psi}_*)=\mathbf{v}'\mathbf{P}_v\mathbf{v} \tag{7.8.18}$$

If the instrumental variables are not transformed, the criterion function is as in (7.8.16), but with $S_{\text{IV}}(\boldsymbol{\delta},\boldsymbol{\psi}_*)$ redefined as

$$S^{*}_{\text{IV}}(\boldsymbol{\delta},\boldsymbol{\psi}_*)=\mathbf{v}'\mathbf{F}^{-\frac{1}{2}}\mathbf{P}\mathbf{F}^{-\frac{1}{2}}\mathbf{v} \tag{7.8.19}$$

The only difference is the replacement of $\mathbf{P}_v$ by $\mathbf{P}$. Campos (1986) uses a criterion function of this form in the estimation of an equation with ARMA disturbances.

Estimation proceeds by concentrating $\boldsymbol{\delta}$ out of the criterion function. In the case of (7.8.16), this leaves $S^{\dagger}_{\text{IV}}(\boldsymbol{\psi}_*)$ to be minimised with respect to $\boldsymbol{\psi}_*$ since $S_{\text{IV}}(\boldsymbol{\delta},\boldsymbol{\psi}_*)$ is replaced by

$$S_{\text{IV}}(\boldsymbol{\psi}_*)=\mathbf{v}'\mathbf{F}^{-\frac{1}{2}}\mathbf{P}_v\mathbf{F}^{-\frac{1}{2}}\mathbf{v} \tag{7.8.20a}$$

where

$$\mathbf{v}=\bar{\mathbf{L}}(\mathbf{y}-\mathbf{Z}\tilde{\mathbf{d}}^{\dagger}) \tag{7.8.20b}$$

Once IV estimators of $\boldsymbol{\delta}$ and $\boldsymbol{\psi}_*$ have been computed, σ^2_* may be estimated as

$$\hat{\sigma}^2_*=(T-d)^{-1}\mathbf{v}'\mathbf{F}^{-1}\mathbf{v}=(T-d)^{-1}\sum v_t^2/f_t \tag{7.8.21}$$

One might be tempted to consider a criterion function in which $S_{IV}(\psi_*)$ is replaced by

$$S(\psi_*) = \mathbf{v}'\mathbf{F}^{-1}\mathbf{v} \tag{7.8.22}$$

This corresponds exactly to the criterion function, (7.3.7), obtained from the likelihood function for the case of exogenous explanatory variables, except that $\boldsymbol{\delta}$ is concentrated out of the likelihood function by an IV procedure. If $\mathbf{X}=\mathbf{Z}$ the two criterion functions are, of course, identical. Setting $\mathbf{X}=\mathbf{Z}$, on the other hand, causes the IV criterion functions (7.8.16) and (7.8.19) to become identically equal to zero, irrespective of the value of ψ_*. The same is true if the equation is exactly identified rather than being overidentified.

7.8.3 Instrumental variable estimation in the frequency domain

Just as ML estimation of a model of the form (7.1.2) can be conveniently carried out in the frequency domain, so too can IV estimation. Consider first the construction of IV estimators for (7.8.1). The frequency-domain expression for the GLS analogue estimator, (7.8.6), is obtained by substituting for $\mathbf{V}^{-1}$ from (4.3.11) and then noting that the use of expressions similar to (4.3.13) yields:

$$\tilde{\boldsymbol{\delta}}^{\dagger} = \left\{\left[\sum_{j=0}^{T-1}\frac{1}{f_j}\mathbf{I}_{zx}(\lambda_j)\right]\left[\sum_{j=0}^{T-1}\frac{1}{f_j}\mathbf{I}_{xx}(\lambda_j)\right]^{-1}\left[\sum_{j=0}^{T-1}\frac{1}{f_j}\mathbf{I}_{xz}(\lambda_j)\right]\right\}^{-1}$$

$$\times\left[\sum_{j=0}^{T-1}\frac{1}{f_j}\mathbf{I}_{zx}(\lambda_j)\right]\left[\sum_{j=0}^{T-1}\frac{1}{f_j}\mathbf{I}_{xx}(\lambda_j)\right]^{-1}\sum_{j=0}^{T-1}\frac{1}{f_j}\mathbf{I}_{xy}(\lambda_j) \tag{7.8.23}$$

where $f_j = f(\lambda_j)$ and $\mathbf{I}_{zx}(\lambda_j)$ is the $k \times K$ cross-periodogram matrix between $\mathbf{z}_t'$ and $\mathbf{x}_t$ at frequency λ_j. The asymptotic covariance matrix of $\tilde{\boldsymbol{\delta}}^{\dagger}$ is given by the inverse of the matrix in curly brackets in (7.8.23).

The alternative estimator, $\tilde{\boldsymbol{\delta}}^*$ of (7.8.9), is obtained by noting that transforming (7.8.1) to the frequency domain as in (7.2.12) gives

$$\mathbf{Wy} = \mathbf{WZ}\boldsymbol{\delta} + \mathbf{Wu} \tag{7.8.24}$$

where

$$\text{Var}(\mathbf{Wu}) = \mathbf{WVW}^{\dagger} = \mathbf{F}$$

with the diagonal matrix $\mathbf{F}$ containing the spectral ordinates, $f(\lambda_{j-1})$, in the j-th position for $j=1,\ldots,T$. In terms of the notation of sub-section 7.8.1, $\mathbf{L}=\mathbf{F}^{-\frac{1}{2}}\mathbf{W}$ and $\mathbf{L}'=\mathbf{W}^{\dagger}\mathbf{F}^{-\frac{1}{2}}$. Substituting for $\mathbf{L}$ in (7.8.9) therefore gives

$$\tilde{\boldsymbol{\delta}}^* = (\mathbf{Z}'\mathbf{W}^{\dagger}\mathbf{F}^{-\frac{1}{2}}\mathbf{P}\mathbf{F}^{-\frac{1}{2}}\mathbf{WZ})^{-1}\mathbf{Z}'\mathbf{W}^{\dagger}\mathbf{F}^{-\frac{1}{2}}\mathbf{PWy} \tag{7.8.25}$$

with

$$\mathbf{P} = \mathbf{WX}(\mathbf{X}'\mathbf{W}^{\dagger}\mathbf{WX})^{-1}\mathbf{W}^{\dagger}\mathbf{X}'$$

Hence

$$\tilde{\boldsymbol{\delta}}^* = \left\{ \left[\sum \frac{1}{f_j^{\frac{1}{2}}} \mathbf{I}_{zx}(\lambda_j) \right] \left[\sum \mathbf{I}_{xx}(\lambda_j) \right]^{-1} \left[\sum \frac{1}{f_j^{\frac{1}{2}}} \mathbf{I}_{xz}(\lambda_j) \right] \right\}^{-1}$$

$$\times \sum \frac{1}{f_j^{\frac{1}{2}}} \mathbf{I}_{zx}(\lambda_j) \left[\sum \mathbf{I}_{xx}(\lambda_j) \right]^{-1} \sum \frac{1}{f_j^{\frac{1}{2}}} \mathbf{I}_{zy}(\lambda_j) \tag{7.8.26}$$

(Note that from (4.3.9), $\mathbf{I}_{xx}(\lambda_j) = \mathbf{X}'\mathbf{W}'\mathbf{W}\mathbf{X} = (1/2\pi)\mathbf{X}'\mathbf{X}$ and so it is not actually necessary to compute the cross-periodogram matrix of $\mathbf{X}$ explicitly.)

The estimation of a structural model is carried out by first putting it in the form (7.8.12) and recalling that $f_j = g_j/2\pi$ and that g_j, the s.g.f., depends on the hyperparameters, $\boldsymbol{\psi}$. For the GLS analogue estimator, the criterion function can be expressed as the minimand

$$L_{\mathrm{IV}}^{\dagger}(\boldsymbol{\delta}, \boldsymbol{\psi}) = \sum_j \log f_j + \left[\sum_j \frac{1}{f_j} \mathbf{I}_{wx}(\lambda_j) \right] \left[\sum_j \frac{1}{f_j} \mathbf{I}_{xx}(\lambda_j) \right]^{-1} \left[\sum_j \frac{1}{f_j} \mathbf{I}_{xw}(\lambda_j) \right] \tag{7.8.27}$$

where $\mathbf{I}_{wx}(\lambda_j)$ is the cross-periodogram matrix at frequency λ_j between the disturbance term w_t in (7.8.12) and $\Delta(\mathrm{L})\mathbf{x}_t$. Since

$$\mathbf{I}_{wx}(\lambda_j) = \mathbf{I}_{yx}(\lambda_j) - \boldsymbol{\delta}'\mathbf{I}_{zx}(\lambda_j)$$

it can be seen that minimising (7.8.26) with respect to $\boldsymbol{\delta}$ yields (7.8.22).

The alternative estimator uses the minimand

$$L_{\mathrm{IV}}^{*}(\boldsymbol{\delta}, \boldsymbol{\psi}) = \sum_j \log f_j + \left[\sum_j f_j^{-\frac{1}{2}} \mathbf{I}_{wx}(\lambda_j) \right] \left[\sum_j \mathbf{I}_{xx}(\lambda_j) \right]^{-1} \left[\sum_j f_j^{-\frac{1}{2}} \mathbf{I}_{xw}(\lambda_j) \right] \tag{7.8.28}$$

Since the reduced form of the disturbance term in (7.8.12) is an ARMA process, the asymptotic properties of the estimators obtained by minimising (7.8.28) are given by expressions similar to those derived by Campos (1986).

If g_j is expressed as $\sigma_*^2 g_j^*$, where g_j^* depends on ψ_*, in (4.3.43), the criterion functions are analogous to those given for the time-domain IV estimator. Thus for the GLS analogue

$$S_{\mathrm{IV}}^{\dagger}(\boldsymbol{\delta}, \boldsymbol{\psi}_*) = S_{\mathrm{IV}}(\boldsymbol{\delta}, \boldsymbol{\psi}_*)[\Pi g_j^*]^{\frac{1}{T-d}}$$

where

$$S_{\mathrm{IV}}(\boldsymbol{\delta}, \boldsymbol{\psi}_*) = \left[\sum_j \frac{1}{g_j^*} \mathbf{I}_{wx}(\lambda_j) \right] \left[\sum_j \frac{1}{g_j^*} \mathbf{I}_{xx}(\lambda_j) \right]^{-1} \left[\sum_j \frac{1}{g_j^*} \mathbf{I}_{xw}(\lambda_j) \right] \tag{7.8.29}$$

Once $\boldsymbol{\psi}_*$ and $\boldsymbol{\delta}$ have been estimated, σ_*^2 may be estimated from the periodogram of the residuals using an expression analogous to (4.3.45).

7.9 Count data

In a model with Poisson, binomial or negative binomial observations, but no dynamic structure, explanatory variables are introduced via a *link* function; see the discussion of the GLIM framework in McCullagh and Nelder (1983). For a Poisson model, the exponential link function

$$\mu_t = \exp(\mathbf{x}_t'\boldsymbol{\delta}) \tag{7.9.1}$$

ensures that μ_t remains positive. For a binomial model, the logit link function

$$\pi_t = \exp(\mathbf{x}_t'\boldsymbol{\delta})/[1+\exp(\mathbf{x}_t'\boldsymbol{\delta})] \tag{7.9.2}$$

ensures that π_t remains between zero and one. Recent applications of GLIM models to count data include Hausman *et al.* (1984) who studied the number of patents applied for by firms and Cameron and Trivedi (1986) who studied the number of consultations with a doctor. Note that it does not make sense to include a lagged dependent variable as an explanatory variable when the observations are small and discrete.

Explanatory variables can be introduced into the dynamic structural models of section 6.6, at least for count data. Consider the Poisson model introduced for observations in sub-section 6.6.1. As in (7.9.1), the level, μ_t, may be thought of as a component which has a separate effect from that of the explanatory variables in $\mathbf{x}_t$, none of which is a constant. Suppose that $\mu_{t-1} \sim \Gamma(a_{t-1}, b_{t-1})$ and that, conditional on Y_{t-1}, $\mu_t \sim \Gamma(\omega a_{t-1}, \omega b_{t-1})$. This level component may be combined multiplicatively with an exponential link function for the explanatory variables so that the distribution of y_t conditional on μ_t is Poisson with mean

$$\mu_t^\dagger = \mu_t \exp(\mathbf{x}_t'\boldsymbol{\delta}) \tag{7.9.3}$$

It follows from the properties of the gamma distribution, that, conditional on Y_{t-1}, $\mu_t^\dagger \sim \Gamma(a_{t|t-1}^\dagger, b_{t|t-1}^\dagger)$ where

$$a_{t|t-1}^\dagger = \omega a_{t-1} \quad \text{and} \quad b_{t|t-1}^\dagger = \omega b_{t-1}\exp(-\mathbf{x}_t'\boldsymbol{\delta}) \tag{7.9.4}$$

respectively. The log-likelihood of the observations is therefore as in (6.6.10) with $a_{t|t-1}$ and $b_{t|t-1}$ replaced by $a_{t|t-1}^\dagger$ and $b_{t|t-1}^\dagger$. This must be maximised with respect to ω and $\boldsymbol{\delta}$.

As regards updating, $\mu_t^\dagger \sim \Gamma(a_t^\dagger, b_t^\dagger)$ where $a_t^\dagger$ and $b_t^\dagger$ are obtained from $a_{t|t-1}^\dagger$ and $b_{t|t-1}^\dagger$ via updating equations of the form (6.6.6). Therefore the posterior distribution of μ_t is $\Gamma(a_t, b_t)$, where a_t is equal to $a_t^\dagger$ and b_t is equal to $b_t^\dagger$ multiplied by $\exp(\mathbf{x}_t'\boldsymbol{\delta})$. Hence

$$a_t = \omega a_{t-1} + y_t \tag{7.9.5a}$$

and

$$b_t = \omega b_{t-1} + \exp(\mathbf{x}_t'\boldsymbol{\delta}), \quad t = \tau+1, \ldots, T \tag{7.9.5b}$$

Thus the only amendment as compared with the recursions in sub-section 6.6.1 is the replacement of unity by $\exp(\mathbf{x}_t'\boldsymbol{\delta})$ in the equation for b_t.

For a given value of $\boldsymbol{\delta}$, we can proceed as in (6.6.17) to show that the mean of the predictive distribution of y_{T+l} is

$$\begin{aligned}\underset{T}{\mathrm{E}}(y_{T+l}) &= \exp(\mathbf{x}_{T+l}'\boldsymbol{\delta})\,\Sigma\,\omega^j y_{T-j}/\Sigma\,\omega^j \exp(\mathbf{x}_{T-j}'\boldsymbol{\delta}) \\ &= \exp(\mathbf{x}_{T+l}'\boldsymbol{\delta})\ \mathrm{EWMA}(y)/\mathrm{EWMA}[\exp(\mathbf{x}'\boldsymbol{\delta})]\end{aligned} \tag{7.9.6}$$

where EWMA(y) denotes the exponentially weighted average of the observations given by (6.6.12) and EWMA[$\exp(\mathbf{x}'\boldsymbol{\delta})$] is defined similarly.

It is interesting to compare (7.9.6) with the result obtained from the Gaussian model

$$\log y_t = \mu_t + \mathbf{x}_t'\boldsymbol{\delta} + \varepsilon_t \tag{7.9.7a}$$

$$\mu_t = \mu_{t-1} + \eta_t \tag{7.9.7b}$$

for the same discount factor, ω. Since the level and explanatory variables are combined multiplicatively in (7.9.3), it seems sensible to make the comparison with a Gaussian model in which logarithms have been taken. The optimal estimator of μ_t is obtained by applying the EWMA operation to $\log y_t - \mathbf{x}_t'\boldsymbol{\delta}$, and so the optimal estimator of $\log y_{T+l}$ can be expressed as

$$\underset{T}{\mathrm{E}}(\log y_{T+l}) = \mathbf{x}_{T+l}'\boldsymbol{\delta} + \mathrm{EWMA}(\log y) - \mathrm{EWMA}(\mathbf{x}'\boldsymbol{\delta}) \tag{7.9.8}$$

The other point of comparison with the Gaussian model is in the maximisation of the respective likelihood functions. In the Gaussian case, the computational burden is eased considerably by the fact that $\boldsymbol{\delta}$ may be concentrated out of the likelihood function as discussed in sub-section 7.2.3. This suggests the possibility of using estimates from the Gaussian model, (7.9.7), as starting values. However, this is only likely to be useful if the observations are not too small; apart from anything else, there is the problem of how to handle zero observations when logarithms are being taken.

Explanatory variables can also be introduced into a Gaussian model via the level. Thus (7.9.7) can be reformulated as

$$\log y_t = \mu_t^* + \varepsilon_t \tag{7.9.9a}$$

$$\mu_t^* = \mu_{t-1}^* + (\Delta\mathbf{x}_t)'\boldsymbol{\delta} + \eta_t \tag{7.9.9b}$$

The only difference is that μ_t^* includes the effect of the exogenous variables while μ_t did not; in fact $\mu_t^* = \mu_t + \mathbf{x}_t'\boldsymbol{\delta}$. Following Smith and Miller (1986), explanatory variables can be brought into a Poisson model in an analogous way. If $\mu_{t-1}^* \sim \Gamma(a_{t-1}^*, b_{t-1}^*)$, then, conditional on Y_{t-1}, μ_t^* is gamma with

$$a_{t|t-1}^* = \omega a_{t-1}^*, \quad b_{t|t-1}^* = \omega b_{t-1}^* \exp(-\Delta\mathbf{x}_t'\boldsymbol{\delta}) \tag{7.9.10}$$

The posterior distribution of μ_t^* is then $\Gamma(a_t^*, b_t^*)$, where a_t^* and b_t^* are obtained from $a^*_{t|t-1}$ and $b^*_{t|t-1}$ via equations of the form (6.6.6). Repeated substitution shows that

$$b^*_T = 1 + \sum_{j=1}^{T-1} \omega^j \exp(-\Delta_j \mathbf{x}'_T \boldsymbol{\delta})$$

where $\Delta_j = 1 - \mathrm{L}^j$, and further rearrangement yields a forecast function which is exactly the same as (7.9.6).

The appropriate way of proceeding with negative binomial observations is to introduce the explanatory variables directly into the distribution of $y_t|\pi_t$ via an exponential link function. This may be done by replacing υ by $\upsilon_t = \upsilon \exp(\mathbf{x}'_t \boldsymbol{\delta})$. Such a negative binomial distribution has, for a constant π, a constant variance–mean ratio; see the discussion in Cameron and Trivedi (1986, p. 33). Proceeding in this way leads to the updating equation (6.6.32a) being modified to

$$a_t = a_{t|t-1} + \upsilon \exp(\mathbf{x}'_t \boldsymbol{\delta}) \tag{7.9.11}$$

while (6.6.32b) remains unchanged. Combining the prediction and updating equations for a_t gives

$$a_t = \omega a_{t-1} + (1-\omega) + \upsilon \exp(\mathbf{x}'_t \boldsymbol{\delta})$$

The mean of the predictive distribution is

$$\mathop{\mathrm{E}}_T(y_{T+l}) = \upsilon_{T+l} b_{T+l|T}/(a_{T+l|T} - 1) = \upsilon \exp(\mathbf{x}'_{T+l} \boldsymbol{\delta})\, b_T/(a_T - 1)$$

and it is not difficult to deduce that it can be expressed in terms of an equation identical to (7.9.6).

Goals scored by England against Scotland One of the examples given in sub-section 6.6.4 concerned the number of goals scored by England against Scotland in international football matches at Hampden Park. A Poisson-gamma model was found to fit the data quite well. We now consider the complete series by including observations on the number of goals scored by England in matches played at Wembley. Playing at home tends to confer an advantage, and so we extend the model by introducing a dummy explanatory variable which takes a value of unity when England are at home and zero when they are away. The ML estimates of the parameters are:

$$\tilde{\omega} = 0.903, \quad \tilde{\delta} = 0.498$$

As expected, the estimate of δ is positive. The likelihood ratio test statistic, (5.1.3), is 10.57: this statistic is asymptotically χ^2_1 under the null hypothesis that δ is zero, and so is clearly highly significant. Since exp(0.498) is equal to 1.64, the results can be interpreted as saying that the expected number of goals scored by England rises by 64% when they are playing at home.

It was noted in section 6.6 that bringing stochastic slope and seasonal components into count data models is not easy. They can, however, enter in a deterministic fashion and this is done by treating them as explanatory variables. A slope is introduced by setting one of the elements of $\mathbf{x}_t$ equal to time, t. The seasonals are modelled by $s-1$ explanatory variables constructed as in (2.3.2) so that the seasonal effects sum to zero over a period of one year. The form of (7.9.3) means that the trend and seasonals combine multiplicatively, just as in a logarithmic Gaussian model. As in such a model, the coefficient of the slope is to be interpreted as a growth rate, while the seasonal coefficients are multiplicative seasonal factors.

The extension of count data models to include explanatory variables opens up the possibility of carrying out *intervention analysis*. As in section 7.6, the explanatory variables $\mathbf{x}_t$ are replaced or augmented by a variable w_t which is designed to pick up the effect of some event or policy change. The variable may be a pulse, as in (7.6.2), a step, as in (7.6.3), or it may model a slope change as in (7.6.6).

Effect of the seat belt law on van drivers in Great Britain The effect of the seat belt law of January 1983 on various categories of road users in Great Britain was examined in Harvey and Durbin (1986); the analysis for the series on car drivers killed and seriously injured was described in sub-section 7.6.4. For certain categories the numbers involved are relatively small with the result that a Gaussian model cannot be regarded as a reasonable approximation. One such series is the monthly totals of drivers of light goods vehicles (LGV) killed. Here the numbers, from January 1969 to December 1984, range from two to seventeen.

Since the series contains no zero observations, a Gaussian model can be fitted to the logarithms of the observations. This gives preliminary estimates for the seasonal and intervention effects which can be used as starting values in the iterative procedure used to calculate the ML estimators in a count data model. However, it is clear from doing this that a Gaussian model is not at all satisfactory in these circumstances and the results are very different for different specifications. In particular, fitting a model with fixed seasonals and no slope gives an estimate of the intervention effect which implies a 45% fall in fatalities as a result of the seat belt law. This is quite out of line with estimates obtained for other series, and indeed with the results obtained when a slope is included.

For the Poisson model, it is reassuring to note that the conclusions regarding the effect of the seat belt law are affected very little by the inclusion or otherwise of a slope term. In fact, the preferred specification does not have a slope. The explanatory variables are therefore an intervention and seasonals, and fitting the model gives the following estimates of ω and the intervention effect:

$$\tilde{\omega}=0.934, \quad \tilde{\lambda}=-0.276$$

The estimate of λ implies a 24.1% reduction in fatalities which is quite close to the figures reported earlier for car drivers in sub-section 7.6.4. The likelihood ratio test statistic for the inclusion of the intervention variable is 25.96 and this is

Table 7.9.1. *Estimated seasonal factors for LGV drivers killed*

J	F	M	A	M	J	J	A	S	O	N	D
1.16	0.79	0.94	0.89	0.91	1.06	0.97	0.92	0.92	1.16	1.19	1.19

clearly significant when set against a χ_1^2 distribution. Finally the estimated seasonal factors (Table 7.9.1), given by exponentiating the estimated seasonal coefficients, are very reasonable and not dissimilar to the seasonal factors reported in sub-section 2.7.1 for car drivers killed and seriously injured.

EXERCISES

7.1 In the model

$$y_t = \mu_t + \delta x_{t-2} + \varepsilon_t^*, \quad \mathrm{Var}(\varepsilon_t^*) = 1$$

$$\mu_t = \mu_{t-1} + \eta_t^*, \qquad \mathrm{Var}(\eta_t^*) = 0.5$$

the explanatory variable, x_t, follows a local linear trend model with $\sigma_\varepsilon^2 = 2$, $\sigma_\eta^2 = 1$ and $\sigma_\zeta^2 = 0.2$.

(a) What kind of univariate process does y_t follow? What are the values of its parameters?

(b) What gains, if any, does the use of x_t offer in forecasting future values of y_t? State any assumptions you make.

7.2 Suppose that a preliminary estimator of δ in (7.3.1) is computed by pre-setting the vector of relative hyperparameters, $\boldsymbol{\psi}_*$, to some arbitrary, but admissible, value. Write down an expression for the covariance matrix of this estimator similar in form to (7.3.2). Might an estimator of this kind be more attractive than OLS?

Chapter 8

Multivariate models

In discussing univariate models, it was argued that the nature of the problem allows fairly strong restrictions to be imposed. These restrictions are not normally enforced within the traditional ARIMA framework. In a multivariate set-up, the number of parameters to be estimated increases rapidly as more series are included and in a vector ARMA model the issues concerned with identifiability become quite complicated; see Hannan (1969). Hence it is even more important to formulate models which take account of the nature of the problem. Apart from saving on the number of parameters to be estimated, such models are also likely to provide more useful information on the dynamic properties of the series.

In section 1.3 a distinction was drawn between multivariate models for cross-sections of time series and multivariate models for interactive systems. This distinction is important in considering the kind of multivariate structural time series models to be entertained. For cross-sections of time series, the class of univariate structural time series models generalises in a rather natural way, as discussed in sections 8.2 to 8.4. However, the fact that several series are now being modelled together suggests the possibility of common factors. Models of this kind are introduced in section 8.5. Section 8.6 examines the way in which control groups can be handled within the statistical framework of multivariate structural time series models, while section 8.7 looks at the handling of various data irregularities. Dynamic interactions between variables are considered in section 8.8, and a class of vector autoregressive models with trend components, possibly in common, is proposed. The final section looks briefly at some of the issues raised by simultaneous equation systems when stochastic trend components are present. Before embarking on these topics, some of the basic concepts of multivariate time series are reviewed.

8.1 Stochastic properties of multivariate models

The first sub-section below generalises autoregressive and ARMA processes to a multivariate setting. The next two sub-sections examine the properties of multivariate stationary processes in the time and frequency domains. This is essentially a matter of generalising the concepts of section 2.4. The final sub-section, on the other hand, introduces a concept which is only relevant in a multivariate system, namely co-integration.

8.1.1 Multivariate stochastic processes

The first-order vector autoregressive process, originally introduced in (2.3.16), plays a fundamental role in state space models irrespective of whether the observations are a univariate or a multivariate process. As such, a good deal has already been said about its properties. An important special case is the multivariate random walk,

$$\mathbf{y}_t = \mathbf{y}_{t-1} + \boldsymbol{\xi}_t \tag{8.1.1}$$

where $\boldsymbol{\xi}_t$ is multivariate white noise with mean zero and covariance matrix $\boldsymbol{\Sigma}$. Just as the univariate random walk plays a key role in setting up univariate models, so (8.1.1) plays a similar key role in multivariate modelling.

The first-order process may be generalised to

$$\mathbf{y}_t = \boldsymbol{\Phi}_1 \mathbf{y}_{t-1} + \cdots + \boldsymbol{\Phi}_p \mathbf{y}_{t-p} + \boldsymbol{\xi}_t \tag{8.1.2}$$

where $\boldsymbol{\Phi}_i$, $i=1,\ldots,p$ are $N \times N$ matrices of parameters. This is a first-order vector autoregressive process, indicated by writing $\mathbf{y}_t \sim \text{VAR}(p)$. By defining a matrix polynomial in the lag operator,

$$\boldsymbol{\Phi}(\text{L}) = \mathbf{I} - \boldsymbol{\Phi}_1 \text{L} - \cdots - \boldsymbol{\Phi}_p \text{L}^p \tag{8.1.3}$$

it may be written more concisely as

$$\boldsymbol{\Phi}(\text{L})\mathbf{y}_t = \boldsymbol{\xi}_t \tag{8.1.4}$$

The multivariate random walk is non-stationary because its individual elements are non-stationary. However, it does not follow from this statement that stationarity of all the individual components in a multivariate process is a sufficient condition for the process as a whole to be (covariance) stationary. In addition to the conditions required of the individual elements, namely (2.4.1), (2.4.2) and (2.4.3), the cross-covariances between different elements must be independent of their position in time for all lags. If y_{it} and y_{jt} denote the i-th and j-th elements in the vector $\mathbf{y}_t$, the cross-covariance between y_{it} and $y_{j,t-\tau}$ is

$$\gamma_{ij}(\tau) = \text{E}[(y_{it} - \mu_i)(y_{j,t-\tau} - \mu_j)], \quad \tau = 0, \pm 1, \pm 2, \ldots \tag{8.1.5}$$

for $i, j = 1, \ldots, N$.

The condition for a VAR(1) process to be stationary is that the roots of the matrix polynomial, (8.1.3), should all lie outside the unit circle; see Harvey (1981b, section 2.7). The multivariate random walk, (8.1.1), has all its roots on the unit circle.

Any linear stationary multivariate process satisfies the Wold decomposition and hence can be written as an infinite multivariate MA process:

$$\mathbf{y}_t = \sum_{j=0}^{\infty} \mathbf{\Psi}_j \boldsymbol{\xi}_{t-j} = \mathbf{\Psi}(\mathrm{L})\boldsymbol{\xi}_t \qquad (8.1.6)$$

where the $\mathbf{\Psi}_j$'s are $N \times N$ matrices of parameters, $\mathbf{\Psi}_0$ is the identity matrix and the matrix polynomial, $\mathbf{\Psi}(\mathrm{L})$, is absolutely summable; compare (2.5.1). As a generalisation of what happens in the univariate case, a process of the form (8.1.6) can be approximated, to any level of accuracy, by a model within the vector ARMA class

$$\mathbf{y}_t = \mathbf{\Phi}_1 \mathbf{y}_{t-1} + \cdots + \mathbf{\Phi}_p \mathbf{y}_{t-p} + \boldsymbol{\xi}_t + \mathbf{\Theta}_1 \boldsymbol{\xi}_{t-1} + \cdots + \mathbf{\Theta}_q \boldsymbol{\xi}_{t-q} \qquad (8.1.7)$$

The stationarity conditions for (8.1.7) are as for a VAR(p) model. Invertibility requires that the roots of the MA matrix polynomial

$$\mathbf{\Theta}(\mathrm{L}) = \mathbf{I} + \mathbf{\Theta}_1 \mathrm{L} + \cdots + \mathbf{\Theta}_q \mathrm{L}^q \qquad (8.1.8)$$

lie outside the unit circle.

A vector ARMA process implies a particular specification of its individual elements in terms of univariate ARMA processes. First write (8.1.7) as

$$y_t = \mathbf{\Phi}^{-1}(\mathrm{L})\mathbf{\Theta}(\mathrm{L})\boldsymbol{\xi}_t \qquad (8.1.9)$$

The power series expansion of $\mathbf{\Phi}^{-1}(\mathrm{L})$ is

$$\mathbf{\Phi}^{-1}(\mathrm{L}) = \mathbf{\Phi}^{\dagger}(\mathrm{L})/|\mathbf{\Phi}(\mathrm{L})| \qquad (8.1.10)$$

where $\mathbf{\Phi}^{\dagger}(\mathrm{L})$ is the adjoint matrix of $\mathbf{\Phi}(\mathrm{L})$. Substituting into (8.1.9) and rearranging gives the autoregressive final form,

$$|\mathbf{\Phi}(\mathrm{L})|\mathbf{y}_t = \mathbf{\Phi}^{\dagger}(\mathrm{L})\mathbf{\Theta}(\mathrm{L})\boldsymbol{\xi}_t \qquad (8.1.11)$$

The right-hand side of each of the N equations in (8.1.11) consists of a linear combination of MA processes each of order $p+q$. However, each of these linear combinations can be expressed as an MA process of order $p+q$. Thus the equations in (8.1.11) can be written as

$$\varphi_i^*(\mathrm{L})y_{it} = \theta_i^*(\mathrm{L})\xi_{it}^*, \; i = 1, \ldots N, \qquad (8.1.12)$$

where ξ_{it}^* is white noise, $\theta_i^*(\mathrm{L})$ is an MA polynomial in the lag operator of order $p+q$ and $\varphi_i^*(\mathrm{L}) = |\mathbf{\Phi}(\mathrm{L})|$ is an AR polynomial of order Np. The implication of this result is that each variable in $\mathbf{y}_t$ can be modelled as a univariate ARMA process. However, if the variables are considered together, (8.1.12) also implies that the disturbances in the different ARMA models will be correlated and the autoregressive components will be identical. In practice though, common AR components may not be observed because of common factors in $\varphi_i^*(\mathrm{L})$ and $\theta_i^*(\mathrm{L})$ in some equations.

8.1.2 Time-domain properties of stationary processes

If the expected value of the stationary multivariate process $\mathbf{y}_t$ is $\boldsymbol{\mu}$, the autocovariance matrix at lag τ is given by

$$\boldsymbol{\Gamma}(\tau)=\mathrm{E}[(\mathbf{y}_t-\boldsymbol{\mu})(\mathbf{y}_{t-\tau}-\boldsymbol{\mu})'], \quad \tau=0,\pm 1,\pm 2,\ldots \tag{8.1.13}$$

The covariance matrix of $\mathbf{y}_t$ is obtained when $\tau=0$. This matrix is symmetric, but at non-zero lags, $\boldsymbol{\Gamma}(\tau)$ is not, in general, symmetric. However, it follows from (8.1.5) that it is always the case that

$$\boldsymbol{\Gamma}(\tau)=\boldsymbol{\Gamma}'(-\tau), \quad \tau=0, 1, 2,\ldots \tag{8.1.14}$$

for any stationary process.

Example 8.1.1 The vector MA(1) process

$$\mathbf{y}_t=\boldsymbol{\xi}_t+\boldsymbol{\Theta}\boldsymbol{\xi}_{t-1} \tag{8.1.15}$$

is stationary, irrespective of the values of the parameters in $\boldsymbol{\Theta}$. Since $\mathrm{E}(\mathbf{y}_t)=\mathbf{0}$, the covariance matrix of $\mathbf{y}_t$ is

$$\boldsymbol{\Gamma}(0)=\mathrm{E}(\mathbf{y}_t\mathbf{y}_t')=\boldsymbol{\Sigma}+\boldsymbol{\Theta}\boldsymbol{\Sigma}\boldsymbol{\Theta}' \tag{8.1.16}$$

while the autocovariance matrices are given by

$$\boldsymbol{\Gamma}(\tau)=\mathrm{E}(\mathbf{y}_t\mathbf{y}_{t-\tau}')=\left\{\begin{array}{ll}\boldsymbol{\Theta}\boldsymbol{\Sigma}, & \tau=1\\ \boldsymbol{\Sigma}\boldsymbol{\Theta}', & \tau=-1\\ \mathbf{0}, & |\tau|\geqslant 2\end{array}\right\} \tag{8.1.17}$$

Note that $\boldsymbol{\Gamma}'(-1)=\boldsymbol{\Gamma}(1)$, but that there is an abrupt cut-off for $|\tau|\geqslant 2$. This behaviour exactly parallels that in the univariate MA(1) process.

Example 8.1.2 The first-order vector autoregressive process 2..16) is stationary if the roots of $\boldsymbol{\Phi}$ have modulus less than one. Given that this condition is satisfied, the autocovariance matrices may be derived by post-multiplying $\mathbf{y}_t$ by $\mathbf{y}_{t-\tau}$ and taking expectations. Thus

$$\mathrm{E}(\mathbf{y}_t\mathbf{y}_{t-\tau}')=\boldsymbol{\Phi}\mathrm{E}(\mathbf{y}_{t-1}\mathbf{y}_{t-\tau}')+\mathrm{E}(\boldsymbol{\xi}_t\mathbf{y}_{t-\tau}')$$

For $\tau\geqslant 1$, the last term is a matrix of zeros, and so

$$\boldsymbol{\Gamma}(\tau)=\boldsymbol{\Phi}\boldsymbol{\Gamma}(\tau-1), \quad \tau\geqslant 1 \tag{8.1.18}$$

This is a vector difference equation with solution

$$\boldsymbol{\Gamma}(\tau)=\boldsymbol{\Phi}^{\tau}\boldsymbol{\Gamma}(0), \quad \tau\geqslant 0; \tag{8.1.19}$$

compare (2.4.96).

When $\tau=0$,

$$\mathrm{E}(\boldsymbol{\xi}_t\mathbf{y}_t)=\mathrm{E}[\boldsymbol{\xi}_t(\boldsymbol{\Phi}\mathbf{y}_{t-1}+\boldsymbol{\xi}_t)']=\mathrm{E}(\boldsymbol{\xi}_t\boldsymbol{\xi}_t')=\boldsymbol{\Sigma}$$

Furthermore, in view of (8.1.14) and (8.1.19),

$$E(\mathbf{y}_{t-1}\mathbf{y}_t') = \mathbf{\Phi\Gamma}(-1) = \mathbf{\Phi\Gamma}'(1) = \mathbf{\Phi\Gamma}(0)\mathbf{\Phi}'$$

and so

$$\mathbf{\Gamma}(0) = \mathbf{\Phi\Gamma}(0)\mathbf{\Phi}' + \mathbf{\Sigma} \tag{8.1.20}$$

A method of solving these equations for $\mathbf{\Gamma}(0)$ was given in (3.3.21).

An autocovariance matrix may be standardised to yield the corresponding *autocorrelation matrix*. The *ij*-th element in $\mathbf{\Gamma}(\tau)$ is simply divided by the square roots of the variances of y_i and y_j to give the corresponding autocorrelation or cross-correlation. In matrix terms the autocorrelation matrix at lag τ, $\mathbf{P}(\tau)$, is defined by

$$\mathbf{P}(\tau) = \mathbf{D}_0^{-1}\mathbf{\Gamma}(\tau)\mathbf{D}_0^{-1}, \quad \tau = 0, \pm 1, \pm 2, \ldots \tag{8.1.21}$$

where $\mathbf{D}_0^2 = \text{diag}[\gamma_{11}(0), \ldots, \gamma_{NN}(0)]$. The *ij*-th element of $\mathbf{P}(\tau)$ gives the cross-correlation between y_i and y_j at lag τ, i.e.

$$\rho_{ij}(\tau) = \gamma_{ij}(\tau)/\sqrt{\gamma_{ii}(0)\gamma_{jj}(0)} \tag{8.1.22}$$

The cross-correlation function between y_i and y_j is therefore

$$\rho_{ij}(\tau), \quad \tau = 0, \pm 1, \pm 2, \ldots$$

An alternative definition of the autocorrelation matrix has been suggested by Chitturi (1974). This is

$$\mathbf{P}^{\dagger}(\tau) = \mathbf{\Gamma}(\tau)\mathbf{\Gamma}^{-1}(0), \quad \tau = 0, \pm 1, \pm 2, \ldots \tag{8.1.23}$$

The a.c.g.f. of a multivariate process is defined as

$$\mathbf{G}(\mathrm{L}) = \sum_{\tau=-\infty}^{\infty} \mathbf{\Gamma}(\tau)\mathrm{L}^{\tau} \tag{8.1.24}$$

For the multivariate ARMA model of (8.1.7), the a.c.g.f. is

$$\mathbf{G}(\mathrm{L}) = \mathbf{\Phi}^{-1}(\mathrm{L})\mathbf{\Theta}(\mathrm{L})\mathbf{\Sigma\Theta}'(\mathrm{L}^{-1})\mathbf{\Phi}^{-1\prime}(\mathrm{L}^{-1}) \tag{8.1.25}$$

If a process is constructed by adding together a set of mutually uncorrelated stationary processes, its a.c.g.f. is the sum of the individual a.c.g.f.'s. Then (2.4.52) generalises to

$$\mathbf{G}(\mathrm{L}) = \sum_{j=0}^{n} \mathbf{G}_j(\mathrm{L}) \tag{8.1.26}$$

Finally, $\mathbf{\Gamma}(\tau)$ can be estimated in an obvious fashion by

$$\hat{\mathbf{\Gamma}}(\tau) = \mathbf{C}(\tau) = T^{-1}\sum_{t=\tau+1}^{T} (\mathbf{y}_t - \bar{\mathbf{y}})(\mathbf{y}_{t-\tau} - \bar{\mathbf{y}})' \tag{8.1.27}$$

The corresponding estimates of $\mathbf{P}(\tau)$ and $\mathbf{P}^{\dagger}(\tau)$ will be denoted by $\mathbf{R}(\tau)$ and $\mathbf{R}^{\dagger}(\tau)$ respectively.

8.1.3 Frequency-domain properties

The multivariate spectrum of a stationary process is

$$\mathbf{F}(\lambda)=(2\pi)^{-1}\sum_{\tau=-\infty}^{\infty}\mathbf{\Gamma}(\tau)e^{-i\lambda\tau},\quad -\pi\leqslant\lambda\leqslant\pi \tag{8.1.28}$$

Using the definition of the a.c.g.f. in (8.1.24), it may be written as

$$\mathbf{F}(\lambda)=(2\pi)^{-1}\mathbf{G}(e^{-i\lambda}) \tag{8.1.29}$$

The diagonal elements of $\mathbf{F}(\lambda)$ are the power spectra of the individual processes. The ij-th element is the cross-spectrum between the i-th and the j-th variable for $j>i$. It is the cross-spectrum which contains all the information concerning the relationship between the two series in the frequency domain. The cross-spectrum is, in general, a complex quantity and $f_{ji}(\lambda)$ is the complex conjugate of $f_{ij}(\lambda)$. Hence $\mathbf{F}(\lambda)$ is Hermitian, i.e. $\mathbf{F}(\lambda)=\bar{\mathbf{F}}(\lambda)'$. When $\mathbf{\Gamma}(\tau)$ is symmetric, $\mathbf{F}(\tau)$ is real and (8.1.28) can be written as

$$\mathbf{F}(\lambda)=\frac{1}{2\pi}\left[\mathbf{\Gamma}(0)+2\sum_{\tau=1}^{\infty}\mathbf{\Gamma}(\tau)\cos\lambda\tau\right] \tag{8.1.30}$$

The multivariate spectrum can be estimated as

$$\mathbf{I}^{\#}(\lambda_j)=\frac{1}{2\pi}\sum_{\tau=-(T-1)}^{T-1}\mathbf{C}(\tau)e^{-i\lambda_j\tau} \tag{8.1.31}$$

where $\mathbf{C}(\tau)$ is as defined in (8.1.27). This expression may be rearranged in a similar way to the univariate sample spectrum, (2.4.47), to give

$$\mathbf{I}^{\#}(\lambda_j)=\frac{1}{2\pi T}\left[\sum_{t=1}^{T}(\mathbf{y}_t-\bar{\mathbf{y}})e^{-i\lambda_j t}\right]\left[\sum_{t=1}^{T}(\mathbf{y}_t-\bar{\mathbf{y}})'e^{i\lambda_j t}\right] \tag{8.1.32}$$

The off-diagonals of this matrix, the sample cross-spectra, were defined earlier in (7.2.7).

8.1.4 Co-integration

The elements in the multivariate random walk of (8.1.1) are non-stationary and so do not move around a constant level. Furthermore, as long as $\mathbf{\Sigma}_\eta$ is p.d., there is no long-run relationship between the series. This may be shortcoming for a time series model, particularly in economics where notions of equilibrium suggest that series cannot go on haphazardly drifting further and further apart. The idea that non-stationary series may satisfy long-run relationships is captured by the concept of co-integration; see Engle and Granger (1987).

A preliminary definition is that of an integrated series. If a series with no deterministic component has a stationary, invertible ARMA representation after differencing d times, it is said to be *integrated of order d*; see sub-section 2.5.2. This may be expressed concisely by writing $y_t \sim I(d)$. Thus if a series is $I(0)$, it is stationary, while if it is $I(1)$ it is stationary in first differences. Clearly a local linear trend model is $I(2)$, provided, of course, that the variance of the slope disturbance term, σ_ζ^2, is positive.

If two series, y_{1t} and y_{2t}, are both $I(d)$, it will normally be the case that any linear combination is also $I(d)$. However, it is possible that there is a linear combination of the two series for which the order of integration is smaller than d. In this case the series are said to be co-integrated. More generally we have the following definition. The components of the vector y_t are said to be *co-integrated of order d, b* if (i) all components of $\mathbf{y}_t$ are $I(d)$; and (ii) there exists a non-null vector, $\boldsymbol{\alpha}$, such that $\boldsymbol{\alpha}'\mathbf{y}_t$ is $I(d-b)$ with $b>0$. This may be expressed as $\mathbf{y}_t \sim \mathrm{CI}(d, b)$. The vector $\boldsymbol{\alpha}$ is called the *co-integrating vector*.

The presence of co-integration implies the need to impose certain constraints on a multivariate time series model. Such restrictions are not easy to impose on a multivariate ARIMA model, that is a multivariate ARMA model of the form (8.1.7) applied to d-th differences; see Engle and Granger (1987, pp. 255–9). In the structural time series framework, co-integrating restrictions are imposed explicitly by setting up common factor models.

8.2 Seemingly unrelated time series equations

Suppose that the $N \times 1$ vector $\mathbf{y}_t$ denotes a set of observations on a cross-section of, say, firms, countries or individuals. The data, $\mathbf{y}_t, t=1, \ldots, T$, therefore consists of a cross-section of time series. It is assumed that the different series are not subject to any cause-and-effect relationships between them. However, they are subject to the same overall environment, such as the prevailing business climate, and so a multivariate model will seek to link them together. With a structural framework this is done by allowing the various components to be contemporaneously correlated. Such a model is a time series analogue of the seemingly unrelated regression equation (SURE) model introduced into econometrics by Zellner (1963). It is therefore appropriate to refer to it as a system of *seemingly unrelated time series equations* – a SUTSE model.

The simplest SUTSE model is the multivariate random walk plus noise process:

$$\mathbf{y}_t = \boldsymbol{\mu}_t + \boldsymbol{\varepsilon}_t, \quad t=1, \ldots, T \tag{8.2.1a}$$

$$\boldsymbol{\mu}_t = \boldsymbol{\mu}_{t-1} + \boldsymbol{\eta}_t \tag{8.2.1b}$$

where $\boldsymbol{\mu}_t$ is an $N \times 1$ vector of local level components and $\boldsymbol{\varepsilon}_t$ and $\boldsymbol{\eta}_t$ are $N \times 1$ vectors of multivariate white noise with mean zero and covariance matrices $\boldsymbol{\Sigma}_\varepsilon$ and $\boldsymbol{\Sigma}_\eta$ respectively. As in the univariate model, $\boldsymbol{\varepsilon}_t$ and $\boldsymbol{\eta}_t$ are assumed to be uncorrelated with each other in all time periods. The N series are linked via the off-diagonal elements in $\boldsymbol{\Sigma}_\eta$ and $\boldsymbol{\Sigma}_\varepsilon$. Each of these matrices contains $N(N+1)/2$ parameters.

The other principal univariate structural time series models may be converted to SUTSE systems in a similar way. Thus in terms of the single equation representation of (2.4.26), the SUTSE model is

$$\mathbf{y}_t = \sum_{k=0}^{g} \frac{\theta_k(L)}{\varphi_k(L)\Delta_k(L)} \boldsymbol{\varepsilon}_{kt} \tag{8.2.2a}$$

where the $\boldsymbol{\varepsilon}_{kt}$'s are $N \times 1$ vectors of white-noise disturbances such that

$$\left.\begin{array}{l} E(\boldsymbol{\varepsilon}_{kt})=0, \quad k=0,\ldots,g, \quad t=1,\ldots,T \\ \text{and} \\ E(\boldsymbol{\varepsilon}_{kt}\boldsymbol{\varepsilon}'_{js})=\begin{cases}\boldsymbol{\Sigma}_k, & k=j, \quad t=s \\ \mathbf{0}, & \text{otherwise}\end{cases} \end{array}\right\} \tag{8.2.2b}$$

where the $\boldsymbol{\Sigma}_k$'s are p.s.d. The ratio of polynomials, $[\theta_k(L)/\varphi_k(L)\Delta_k(L)]$, is a scalar quantity which is identical for all N time series. If a cyclical component is included, therefore, it has the same frequency, λ_c, and the same damping factor, ρ, for all N series.

An important property of the SUTSE system is that its form remains unaltered when it is subject to contemporaneous aggregation. Suppose that an $N^\dagger \times 1$ vector of variables, $\mathbf{y}_t^\dagger$, is generated by a model of the form (8.2.2), but that $N \leqslant N^\dagger$ linear combinations are observed as an $N \times 1$ vector $\mathbf{y}_t$. Thus

$$\mathbf{y}_t = \mathbf{W}\mathbf{y}_t^\dagger, \quad t=1,\ldots,T \tag{8.2.3}$$

where $\mathbf{W}$ is an $N \times N^\dagger$ matrix of rank N. On pre-multiplying the model for $\mathbf{y}_t^\dagger$ through by $\mathbf{W}$ it follows that the model for $\mathbf{y}_t$ is of exactly the same form, (8.2.2), with

$$\operatorname{Var}(\boldsymbol{\varepsilon}_{kt}) = \boldsymbol{\Sigma}_k = \mathbf{W}\boldsymbol{\Sigma}_k^\dagger\mathbf{W}', \quad k=0,\ldots,g \tag{8.2.4}$$

where $\boldsymbol{\Sigma}_k^\dagger$ is the covariance matrix of $\boldsymbol{\varepsilon}_k^\dagger$, the disturbance vector in the model for $\mathbf{y}_t^\dagger$.

The definition of contemporaneous aggregation in (8.2.3) is a very general one, allowing for various weighted averages of the disaggregated series to be observed. The important special case when the sum of the individual series are observed is obtained by setting $\mathbf{W}=\mathbf{i}'$, where $\mathbf{i}$ is an $N \times 1$ vector of ones. It is also worth noting that the aggregated series can overlap. Thus with N equal to three, having

$$\mathbf{W} = \begin{bmatrix} 1 & 1 & 1 \\ 0 & 0 & 1 \end{bmatrix}$$

would mean observing the sum of the first three series and the third series.

The treatment of SUTSE models presented here will be limited to linear time-invariant systems. Generalisations to cover various types of non-linearities and time variations are, however, possible.

8.2.1 *Stochastic properties and the reduced form*

For the multivariate random walk plus noise model, (8.2.1),

$$\Delta \mathbf{y}_t = \boldsymbol{\eta}_t + \boldsymbol{\varepsilon}_t - \boldsymbol{\varepsilon}_{t-1} \tag{8.2.5}$$

is a stationary process. The autocovariance matrices are:

$$\left.\begin{aligned} \boldsymbol{\Gamma}(0) &= \boldsymbol{\Sigma}_\eta + 2\boldsymbol{\Sigma}_\varepsilon \\ \boldsymbol{\Gamma}(1) &= -\boldsymbol{\Sigma}_\varepsilon \\ \boldsymbol{\Gamma}(\tau) &= \mathbf{0}, \quad \tau \geqslant 2 \\ \boldsymbol{\Gamma}(-\tau) &= \boldsymbol{\Gamma}(\tau) \end{aligned}\right\} \tag{8.2.6}$$

The symmetry of the autocovariance function, that is

$$\boldsymbol{\Gamma}(\tau) = \boldsymbol{\Gamma}'(\tau) = \boldsymbol{\Gamma}(-\tau)$$

arises because $\boldsymbol{\Sigma}_\varepsilon$ is symmetric. As was noted above (8.1.14), the autocovariance function is not, in general, symmetric, but it is a characteristic of all SUTSE models that their autocovariance functions do, in fact, possess this property. Furthermore, just as the form of the autocovariance function in (8.2.6) mirrors that of the corresponding univariate autocovariance function in (2.4.32), so the form of any multivariate autocovariance function for a SUTSE model mirrors the corresponding univariate model. All that is required is to replace variances such as σ_η^2 and σ_ζ^2 by the corresponding covariance matrices, $\boldsymbol{\Sigma}_\eta$ and $\boldsymbol{\Sigma}_\zeta$.

The stationary series obtained from the general SUTSE model defined in (8.2.2) is $\Delta(\mathrm{L})\mathbf{y}_t$ where $\Delta(\mathrm{L})$ is as defined in (2.4.28). Thus as a generalisation of (2.4.29), the a.c.g.f. is

$$\mathbf{G}(\mathrm{L}) = \sum_{k=0}^{g} z_k(\mathrm{L})\boldsymbol{\Sigma}_k \tag{8.2.7}$$

where $z_k(\mathrm{L})$ is the scalar polynomial

$$z_k(\mathrm{L}) = \Delta_k^{\ddagger}(\mathrm{L})\Delta_k^{\ddagger}(\mathrm{L}^{-1})\theta_k(\mathrm{L})\theta_k(\mathrm{L}^{-1})/\varphi_k(\mathrm{L})\varphi_k(\mathrm{L}^{-1})$$

This expression immediately shows why the autocovariance function of a SUTSE model has the same form as the corresponding univariate model and why it is symmetric.

As regards frequency-domain properties, the symmetry of the autocovariance function means that the spectral matrix is real and is symmetric around $\lambda = 0$.

Setting L equal to $\exp(i\lambda)$ in (8.2.7) gives:

$$\mathbf{G}(\lambda)=\sum_{k=0}^{g} z_k(e^{i\lambda})\boldsymbol{\Sigma}_k \tag{8.2.8}$$

Thus for the multivariate random walk plus noise model, (8.2.1),

$$\mathbf{G}(\lambda)=\boldsymbol{\Sigma}_\eta+2(1-\cos\lambda)\boldsymbol{\Sigma}_\varepsilon \tag{8.2.9}$$

It follows from what has already been said that the reduced form of a SUTSE model is a multivariate ARIMA(p, d, q) model with p, d and q taking the same values as in the corresponding univariate case. For (8.2.1) the reduced form is the multivariate ARIMA(0, 1, 1) model

$$\Delta\mathbf{y}_t=\boldsymbol{\xi}_t+\boldsymbol{\Theta}\boldsymbol{\xi}_{t-1} \tag{8.2.10}$$

In the univariate case, the structural form implies that θ must lie between zero and minus one in the reduced form ARIMA(0, 1, 1) model; see (2.5.11). Hence only half the parameter space is admissible. In the multivariate model, the structural form in (8.2.1) not only implies restrictions on the parameter space in the reduced form, (8.2.10), but also reduces its dimension. The total number of parameters in the structural form is $N(N+1)$ while in the unrestricted reduced form, the covariance matrix of $\boldsymbol{\xi}_t$, $\boldsymbol{\Sigma}$, consists of $N(N+1)/2$ different elements while the MA parameter matrix contains N^2. Thus if N is five, the structural form contains thirty parameters while the unrestricted reduced form has forty. The restrictions are even tighter when the structural model contains several components.

The reduced form of a SUTSE model is always invertible although it may not always be strictly invertible. In other words some of the roots of the MA polynomial for the reduced form may lie on, rather than outside, the unit circle. In the case of the multivariate random walk plus noise, the condition for strict invertibility of the stationary form is that $\boldsymbol{\Sigma}_\eta$ should be p.d. If a model is not strictly invertible, then the spectral matrix, $\mathbf{G}(\lambda)$, is not p.d. at every point in the range $-\pi\leqslant\lambda\leqslant\pi$. These results generalise to other SUTSE models in an obvious way as suggested by the discussion in sub-section 4.5.2. Thus, for example, the multivariate BSM has a strictly invertible reduced form if $\boldsymbol{\Sigma}_\zeta$ and $\boldsymbol{\Sigma}_\omega$ are both p.d. An important practical point to remember is that if a model is strictly non-invertible it cannot be represented by a vector autoregression.

8.2.2 Estimation in the time domain

A linear time-invariant univariate structural model can be written in the state space form (4.1.3). If N such processes form a SUTSE system, the model may be written

$$\mathbf{y}_t=(\mathbf{z}'\otimes\mathbf{I}_N)\boldsymbol{\alpha}_t+\boldsymbol{\varepsilon}_t \tag{8.2.11a}$$

$$\boldsymbol{\alpha}_t=(\mathbf{T}\otimes\mathbf{I}_N)\boldsymbol{\alpha}_{t-1}+(\mathbf{R}\otimes\mathbf{I}_N)\boldsymbol{\eta}_t \tag{8.2.11b}$$

with $\text{Var}(\boldsymbol{\varepsilon}_t)=\boldsymbol{\Sigma}_\varepsilon$ and $\text{Var}(\boldsymbol{\eta}_t)$ a block diagonal matrix with the blocks being $\boldsymbol{\Sigma}_k$, $k=1,\ldots,g$. Thus for the seasonal dummy form of the multivariate BSM, $\boldsymbol{\eta}_t=[\eta_{1t}\ \ldots\ \eta_{Nt}, \zeta_{1t}\ \ldots\ \zeta_{Nt}, \omega_{1t}\ \ldots\ \omega_{Nt}]'$ and

$$\text{Var}(\boldsymbol{\eta}_t)=\begin{bmatrix} \boldsymbol{\Sigma}_\eta & 0 & 0 \\ 0 & \boldsymbol{\Sigma}_\zeta & 0 \\ 0 & 0 & \boldsymbol{\Sigma}_\omega \end{bmatrix}$$

In fact a more general formulation of the SUTSE model would not constrain $\text{Var}(\boldsymbol{\eta}_t)$ in (4.1.3) to be diagonal and hence $\text{Var}(\boldsymbol{\eta}_t)$ in (8.2.11b) need not be block diagonal. Indeed the SUTSE formulation can be generalised further to allow quantities such as $\mathbf{z}$, $\boldsymbol{\Sigma}_\varepsilon$, $\mathbf{T}$, $\mathbf{R}$ and $\text{Var}(\boldsymbol{\eta}_t)$ to change deterministically over time. As shown in Harvey (1986), the time-domain treament still goes through.

The Kalman filter may be applied to (8.2.11), the number of sets of observations needed to form an estimator of $\boldsymbol{\alpha}_t$ with finite MSE matrix being the same as in the univariate case. The conditions for the filter to converge to a steady state are an obvious generalisation of the conditions in the univariate case. Thus for the multivariate BSM the Kalman filter converges exponentially fast to a steady state if $\boldsymbol{\Sigma}_\zeta$ and $\boldsymbol{\Sigma}_\omega$ are p.d. For model (8.2.1) the steady-state recursions are the multivariate generalisation of the EWMA; see Jones (1966).

Given normality of the disturbances, the log-likelihood function is of the prediction error decomposition form (3.4.5). The summations run over $t=d+1,\ldots,T$, where d is the number of non-stationary elements in each of the univariate models.

It is not, in general, possible to concentrate any of the covariance matrices, $\Sigma_0,\ldots,\Sigma_g$, out of the likelihood function. The best that can be done is to concentrate out a single diagonal element from one of them. Let this element be denoted by σ_*^2 and define the covariance matrices relative to σ_*^2 according to $\boldsymbol{\Sigma}_k=\sigma_*^2\boldsymbol{\Sigma}_k^*$, $k=0,\ldots,g$. The likelihood function is then

$$\log L=-\frac{(T-d)N}{2}\log\sigma_*^2-\frac{1}{2}\sum_{t=d+1}^{T}\log|\mathbf{F}_t|-\frac{1}{2\sigma_*^2}\sum_{t=d+1}^{T}\mathbf{v}_t'\mathbf{F}_t^{-1}\mathbf{v}_t \tag{8.2.12}$$

where $\mathbf{v}_t$ and $\mathbf{F}_t$ are now independent of σ_*^2. Conditional on the remaining (relative) parameters, $\boldsymbol{\psi}_*$, in the model the ML estimator of σ_*^2 is

$$\tilde{\sigma}_*^2=\frac{1}{(T-d)N}\sum_{t=d+1}^{T}\mathbf{v}_t'\mathbf{F}_t^{-1}\mathbf{v}_t=\frac{S(\boldsymbol{\psi}_*)}{(T-d)N} \tag{8.2.13}$$

Maximising the concentrated likelihood function is therefore equivalent to minimising

$$S^\dagger(\boldsymbol{\psi}_*)=S(\boldsymbol{\psi}_*)\left(\prod_{t=d+1}^{T}|\mathbf{F}_t|\right)^{\frac{1}{(T-d)N}} \tag{8.2.14}$$

with respect to $\boldsymbol{\psi}_*$.

Rather than obtain exact ML estimators, approximate ML estimators may be obtained by assuming a steady state. In this case the criterion function to be minimised is

$$\bar{S}(\boldsymbol{\psi}) = \left| \sum_{t=d+1}^{T} \mathbf{v}_t \mathbf{v}_t' \right|; \tag{8.2.15}$$

compare (3.4.13) and (4.2.12).

The preferred criterion function must be maximised or minimised with respect to the elements of the covariance matrices, $\boldsymbol{\Sigma}_k, k=0,\ldots,g$ and any other hyperparameters such as ρ and λ_c in a cyclical component. The condition that the covariance matrices be p.s.d. is easily enforced by carrying out numerical optimisation with respect to the elements of the corresponding square root matrix, that is the lower triangular matrix $\mathbf{L}_k$ such that $\mathbf{L}_k'\mathbf{L}_k = \boldsymbol{\Sigma}_k$. This is much easier than attempting to constrain the MA parameters in a multivariate ARMA model to be invertible.

8.2.3 *Estimation in the frequency domain*

By generalising the derivation in sub-section 4.3.1, it can be shown that the log-likelihood function for a circular stationary multivariate process is

$$\log L = -\frac{NT}{2}\log 2\pi - \frac{1}{2}\sum_{j=0}^{T-1}\log|\mathbf{G}_j| - \pi \operatorname{tr}\sum_{j=0}^{T-1}\mathbf{G}_j^{-1}\mathbf{I}(\lambda_j) \tag{8.2.16}$$

where $\mathbf{G}_j$ is the spectral generating function, $\mathbf{G}(e^{-i\lambda_j})$, and $\mathbf{I}(\lambda_j)$ is the multivariate sample spectrum (8.1.31); see, for example, Nicholls (1976). In a SUTSE model the spectral generating function is given by the expression in (8.2.8) with the terms $z_k[\exp(i\lambda)]$ evaluated as in section 4.3. Since $\mathbf{G}_j$ is real, only the real part of $\mathbf{I}(\lambda_j)$ need be computed.

A scoring algorithm can be developed by differentiating the likelihood function with respect to the elements of the covariance matrices, $\boldsymbol{\Sigma}_k, k=0,\ldots,g$ or their square roots. The information matrix may also be evaluated in this way. The details may be found in Fernández (1986). Dunsmuir (1979) provides the general asymptotic theory.

Deterministic components may be handled by generalising the results given for univariate models in sub-sections 4.3.6 and 4.5.4. Thus if a drift term is added to the right-hand side of (8.2.1b), it may be estimated as

$$\tilde{\boldsymbol{\beta}} = (T-1)^{-1}(\mathbf{y}_T - \mathbf{y}_1) \tag{8.2.17}$$

while

$$\operatorname{Var}(\tilde{\boldsymbol{\beta}}) = (T-1)^{-1}\mathbf{G}_0 \tag{8.2.18}$$

where $\mathbf{G}_0$ is the s.g.f. of $\Delta\mathbf{y}_t$ at $\lambda = 0$.

8.2.4 *Explanatory variables*

Explanatory variables can be included in a SUTSE model, just as explanatory variables were included in univariate models in chapter 7. The measurement equation of the general SUTSE system, (8.2.11), is extended to become

$$\mathbf{y}_t = (\mathbf{z}' \otimes \mathbf{I}_N)\boldsymbol{\alpha}_t + \mathbf{X}_t\boldsymbol{\delta} + \boldsymbol{\varepsilon}_t \tag{8.2.19}$$

where $\mathbf{X}_t$ is an $N \times K$ matrix of explanatory variables and $\boldsymbol{\delta}$ is a $K \times l$ vector of parameters. The typical form of the $\mathbf{X}_t$ matrix will be

$$\mathbf{X}_t = \begin{bmatrix} \mathbf{x}'_{1t} & 0 & \cdots & 0 \\ 0 & \mathbf{x}'_{2t} & \cdots & 0 \\ \vdots & \vdots & \ddots & \\ 0 & 0 & & \mathbf{x}'_{Nt} \end{bmatrix} \tag{8.2.20}$$

corresponding to individual equations of the form

$$y_{it} = \mathbf{z}'\boldsymbol{\alpha}_{it} + \mathbf{x}'_{it}\boldsymbol{\delta}_i + \varepsilon_{it}, \quad i = 1, \ldots, N \tag{8.2.21}$$

where $\mathbf{x}_{it}$ and $\boldsymbol{\delta}_i$ are $k_i \times 1$ vectors and $\boldsymbol{\delta} = [\boldsymbol{\delta}'_1 \ \ \ldots \ \ \boldsymbol{\delta}'_N]'$. One attraction of this formulation is that it can easily handle situations where there are constraints on the parameters in $\boldsymbol{\delta}$ across equations; see Harvey (1981a, p. 71). The special case in which the same variables appear in each equation is of some interest, particularly for the homogeneous systems described in the next section. In this case, $\mathbf{X}_t = (\mathbf{I} \otimes \mathbf{x}'_t)$, where $\mathbf{x}_t$ is the $k \times 1$ vector of common explanatory variables.

Equation (8.2.19) is a measurement equation of the form (3.4.33). Hence the multivariate GLS algorithm, described in sub-section 3.4.2, can be used to estimate the model. Alternatively a frequency-domain approach can be employed, as described in Fernández (1986).

8.3 Homogeneous systems

A vector process, $\mathbf{y}_t$, is said to be *homogeneous* if all linear combinations of its N elements have the same stochastic properties. In other words, if $\mathbf{w}$ is any $N \times 1$ vector of fixed weights, the power spectrum and autocorrelation function of the stationary univariate process, $\Delta(\mathrm{L})\mathbf{w}'\mathbf{y}_t$, are independent of $\mathbf{w}$.

The multivariate random walk plus noise model, (8.2.1), is a homogeneous system if and only if

$$\boldsymbol{\Sigma}_\eta = q\boldsymbol{\Sigma}_\varepsilon \tag{8.3.1}$$

where q is a non-negative scalar. Thus the two covariance matrices in the model must be proportional to each other. The fact that (8.3.1) implies homogeneity is easily shown since the linear combination, $\mathbf{w}'\mathbf{y}_t$, forms the univariate model

$$\mathbf{w}'\mathbf{y}_t = \mathbf{w}'\boldsymbol{\mu}_t + \mathbf{w}'\boldsymbol{\varepsilon}_t \tag{8.3.2a}$$

$$\mathbf{w}'\boldsymbol{\mu}_t = \mathbf{w}'\boldsymbol{\mu}_{t-1} + \mathbf{w}'\boldsymbol{\eta}_t \tag{8.3.2b}$$

and

$$\frac{\mathrm{Var}\,(\mathbf{w}'\boldsymbol{\eta}_t)}{\mathrm{Var}\,((\mathbf{w}'\boldsymbol{\varepsilon}_t)} = q\frac{\mathbf{w}'\boldsymbol{\Sigma}_\varepsilon\mathbf{w}}{\mathbf{w}'\boldsymbol{\Sigma}_\varepsilon\mathbf{w}} = q \tag{8.3.3}$$

Hence the univariate model in (8.3.2) has a signal–noise ratio of q and the autocorrelation function and the power spectrum of the stationary form depend only on this ratio. Now consider the converse proposition, namely that homogeneity of the series implies (8.3.1). If each series has the same stochastic properties, then

$$\mathrm{Var}(\eta_{it})/\mathrm{Var}(\varepsilon_{it}) = q, \quad i = 1, \dots, N \tag{8.3.4}$$

Considering a linear combination of any two series

$$\mathrm{Var}(\mathbf{w}'\boldsymbol{\varepsilon}_t) = w_i^2\,\mathrm{Var}(\varepsilon_{it}) + w_j^2\,\mathrm{Var}(\varepsilon_{jt}) + 2w_iw_j\mathrm{Cov}(\varepsilon_{it}\varepsilon_{jt})$$

while

$$\mathrm{Var}(\mathbf{w}'\boldsymbol{\eta}_t) = w_i^2\,\mathrm{Var}(\eta_{it}) + w_j^2\,\mathrm{Var}(\eta_{jt}) + 2w_iw_j\mathrm{Cov}(\eta_{it}\eta_{jt}), \quad i, j = 1, \dots, N$$

where w_i and w_j are the i-th and j-th elements respectively of $\mathbf{w}$. Now since (8.3.4) holds, it follows that $\mathrm{Cov}(\eta_{it}\eta_{jt}) = q\,\mathrm{Cov}(\varepsilon_{it}\varepsilon_{jt})$ since if it did not, (8.3.3) would not hold. Hence it follows that all elements of $\boldsymbol{\Sigma}_\varepsilon$ and $\boldsymbol{\Sigma}_\eta$ are proportional, that is (8.3.1) holds.

By following a similar line of argument, it can be shown that a general SUTSE model of the form (8.2.2) is homogeneous if and only if

$$\boldsymbol{\Sigma}_k = q_k\boldsymbol{\Sigma}_*, \quad k = 1, \dots, g$$

and

$$\boldsymbol{\Sigma}_0 = \boldsymbol{\Sigma}_\varepsilon = h\boldsymbol{\Sigma}_* \tag{8.3.5}$$

where $q_k, k = 1, \dots, g$ and h are non-negative scalars and $\boldsymbol{\Sigma}_*$ is an $N \times N$ p.d. matrix. As the notation indicates, an important practical implication of the homogeneity restriction is that it allows $\boldsymbol{\Sigma}_*$ to be concentrated out of the likelihood function. Numerical optimisation is then carried out with respect to the parameters $q_1, \dots, q_g$ and h; one of these is normally set at a fixed value, usually unity. The fact that (8.3.1) allows $\boldsymbol{\Sigma}_\varepsilon$ to be concentrated out of the likelihood function in the case of model (8.2.1) was exploited by Enns *et al.* (1982). However, they gave no rationale for this condition in terms of homogeneity. Nor did they utilise the fact that the Kalman filter becomes decoupled, in the sense that the model can be handled by applying a univariate filter to each series in turn; see sub-section 8.3.2.

Viewed as homogeneity restrictions, (8.3.1) and (8.3.5) are not unreasonable constraints, since in many situations there may be *a priori* reasons for feeling that the series follow similar processes. In small samples the case for imposing homogeneity is even stronger; see the argument in Sims (1985). Consider, for example, a situation in which N series may be aggregated. In a homogeneous system, seasonal adjustment based on a linear SUTSE model will be such that the sum of the individually adjusted series is equal to the adjusted aggregate.

When a multivariate model contains explanatory variables, as in (8.2.19), and the same variables appear in each equation, homogeneity again means that each equation can be handled separately. This is a generalisation of a well-known result for SURE models: when the same variables appear in each equation, the SURE estimator can be obtained by applying OLS to each equation in turn.

8.3.1 Stochastic properties and the reduced form

When a SUTSE system is homogeneous, its a.c.g.f., (8.2.7), can be written as

$$\mathbf{G}(\mathrm{L}) = \mathrm{g}_*(\mathrm{L})\mathbf{\Sigma}_* \tag{8.3.6a}$$

where

$$\mathrm{g}_*(\mathrm{L}) = \mathrm{z}_0(\mathrm{L})h + \sum_{k=1}^{g} \mathrm{z}_k(\mathrm{L})q_k \tag{8.3.6b}$$

The scalar polynomial $\mathrm{g}_*(\mathrm{L})$ is the same as the a.c.g.f. of the stationary form of a univariate process (2.4.29) in which $\sigma_0^2 = h$ and $\sigma_k^2 = q_k$ for $k = 1, \ldots, g$. If the autocovariance at lag τ for such a model is denoted by $\gamma_*(\tau)$, it follows that the autocovariance matrices of the stationary process $\Delta(\mathrm{L})\mathbf{y}_t$ are given by

$$\mathbf{\Gamma}(\tau) = \gamma_*(\tau)\mathbf{\Sigma}_*, \quad \tau = 0, \pm 1, \pm 2, \ldots \tag{8.3.7}$$

If the autocorrelation matrices are defined as in (8.1.23), then they are scalar since

$$\mathbf{P}^{\dagger}(\tau) = \mathbf{\Gamma}(\tau)\mathbf{\Gamma}^{-1}(0) = \gamma_*(\tau)\mathbf{\Sigma}_*[\gamma_*(0)\mathbf{\Sigma}_*]^{-1} = \rho(\tau)\mathbf{I}_N, \quad \tau = 0, \pm 1, \pm 2, \ldots \tag{8.3.8}$$

where $\rho(\tau)$ is the autocorrelation at lag τ for the univariate process. The knowledge that the autocorrelation matrices have this simple structure is a useful aid to recognition of a homogeneous system.

The structure of the autocovariance matrix function in (8.3.7) implies that the reduced form ARMA model for $\Delta(\mathrm{L})\mathbf{y}_t$ has scalar matrix polynomials:

$$\mathbf{\Phi}(\mathrm{L}) = \varphi(\mathrm{L})\mathbf{I}_N \text{ and } \mathbf{\Theta}(\mathrm{L}) = \theta(\mathrm{L})\mathbf{I}_N \tag{8.3.9}$$

where $\phi(\mathrm{L})$ and $\theta(\mathrm{L})$ are the polynomials associated with the reduced form in the univariate model. This can be seen by substituting (8.3.9) in the a.c.g.f. of a vector ARMA process, (8.1.25), to give

$$\mathbf{G}(\mathrm{L}) = [|\theta(\mathrm{L})|^2/|\varphi(\mathrm{L})|^2]\mathbf{\Sigma} \tag{8.3.10}$$

The parameters in θ(L) and φ(L) are such that a univariate ARMA model with this specification has the autocorrelation function, $\rho(\tau)$, given in (8.3.8).

The AR and MA parameter matrices in a SUTSE system are not, in general, diagonal. Thus the reduced form does not correspond to what Nelson (1976) calls a system of 'seemingly unrelated ARMA processes'. (Nelson's motive in studying this latter class stemmed from (8.1.12).) In the case of a homogeneous system the AR and MA matrices are not only diagonal but are subject to the further restriction that all the diagonal elements in any one parameter matrix are the same.

The autoregressive representation of a homogeneous model is

$$\mathbf{\Pi}(L)\Delta(L)\mathbf{y}_t = \boldsymbol{\xi}_t$$

where

$$\mathbf{\Pi}(L) = \pi(L)\mathbf{I}_N$$

with π(L) being an infinite-order scalar polynomial in the lag operator. Since **Π**(L) is diagonal, we have a *Granger non-causal system*; in the terminology of sub-section 7.1.4, none of the series Granger-causes any of the others. Causality tests could be used to provide indirect evidence on homogeneity. However, if homogeneity is to be tested, a better approach is to use a test specifically designed for the purpose. Such a test is described in sub-section 8.4.4.

8.3.2 Estimation in the time domain

When a system is homogeneous, the Kalman filter becomes decoupled. All the information needed for estimation, prediction and smoothing can be obtained by applying the same univariate filter to each series in turn. The decoupling of the Kalman filter is related to the result which arises in a SURE system where OLS applied to each equation in turn is fully efficient if each equation contains the same regressors.

Consider the multivariate random walk plus noise model (8.2.1) with the homogeneity restriction, (8.3.1). The Kalman filter for this model is

$$\mathbf{m}_{t+1|t} = \mathbf{m}_{t|t-1} + \mathbf{K}_t(\mathbf{y}_t - \mathbf{m}_{t|t-1}), \quad t = 2, \dots, T \tag{8.3.11a}$$

and

$$\mathbf{P}_{t+1|t} = \mathbf{P}_{t|t-1} - \mathbf{P}_{t|t-1}\mathbf{F}_t^{-1}\mathbf{P}_{t|t-1} + q\mathbf{\Sigma}_\varepsilon \tag{8.3.11b}$$

where

$$\mathbf{K}_t = \mathbf{P}_{t|t-1}\mathbf{F}_t^{-1} \tag{8.3.11c}$$

and

$$\mathbf{F}_t = \mathbf{P}_{t|t-1} + \mathbf{\Sigma}_\varepsilon \tag{8.3.11d}$$

Let w_t denote a positive scalar for $t=2,\ldots,T$ and suppose that $\mathbf{P}_{t|t-1}$, the MSE matrix of the $N \times 1$ vector $\mathbf{m}_{t|t-1}$, is proportional to $\mathbf{\Sigma}_\varepsilon$, i.e. $\mathbf{P}_{t|t-1}=w_t\mathbf{\Sigma}_\varepsilon$. It then follows from (8.3.11b) that $\mathbf{P}_{t+1|t}$ is of the same form, that is, $\mathbf{P}_{t+1|t}=w_{t+1}\mathbf{\Sigma}_\varepsilon$ with $w_{t+1}=(w_t+w_tq+q)/(w_t+1)$. Furthermore if $\mathbf{P}_{t|t-1}=w_t\mathbf{\Sigma}_\varepsilon$ it follows from (8.3.11c) that the gain matrix in (8.3.11a) is diagonal, that is

$$\mathbf{K}_t=w_t\mathbf{\Sigma}_\varepsilon(w_t\mathbf{\Sigma}_\varepsilon+\mathbf{\Sigma}_\varepsilon)^{-1}=[w_t/(w_{t+1})]\mathbf{I}_N \tag{8.3.12}$$

Suppose that the above Kalman filter is started off in such a way that $\mathbf{P}_{2|1}$ is proportional to $\mathbf{\Sigma}_\varepsilon$; that is $\mathbf{P}_{2|1}=p_{2|1}\mathbf{\Sigma}_\varepsilon$, where $p_{2|1}$ is a scalar. Since $\mathbf{P}_{t|t-1}$ must continue to be proportional to $\mathbf{\Sigma}_\varepsilon$, it follows from (8.3.12) that the elements of $\mathbf{m}_{t+1|t}$ can be computed from univariate recursions of the form (3.2.8). It also follows that w_t must be equal to $p_{t|t-1}$ for all $t=2,\ldots,T$.

The starting values $\mathbf{m}_{2|1}=\mathbf{y}_1$ and $\mathbf{P}_{2|1}=\mathbf{\Sigma}_\eta+\mathbf{\Sigma}_\varepsilon=(1+q)\mathbf{\Sigma}_\varepsilon$ correspond to the use of a diffuse prior, and the use of these starting values leads to the exact likelihood function for $\mathbf{y}_2,\ldots,\mathbf{y}_T$ in the prediction error decomposition form

$$\log L=-\frac{(T-1)N}{2}\log 2\pi-\frac{1}{2}\sum_{t=2}^{T}\log|\mathbf{F}_t|-\frac{1}{2}\sum_{t=2}^{T}\mathbf{v}_t'\mathbf{F}_t^{-1}\mathbf{v}_t \tag{8.3.13}$$

However, the decoupling of the Kalman filter allows the elements of $\mathbf{v}_t$ to be computed from the univariate recursions. Furthermore

$$\mathbf{P}_{t|t-1}=p_{t|t-1}\mathbf{\Sigma}_\varepsilon,$$

and so

$$\mathbf{F}_t=\mathbf{P}_{t|t-1}+\mathbf{\Sigma}_\varepsilon=f_t\mathbf{\Sigma}_\varepsilon,\quad t=3,\ldots,T \tag{8.3.14}$$

where $f_t=(p_{t|t-1}+1)$. Substituting from (8.3.14) into (8.3.13) gives

$$\log L=-\frac{(T-1)N}{2}\log 2\pi+\frac{(T-1)}{2}\log|\mathbf{\Sigma}_\varepsilon^{-1}|-\frac{N}{2}\sum_{t=2}^{T}\log f_t-\frac{1}{2}\sum_{t=2}^{T}\frac{1}{f_t}\mathbf{v}_t'\mathbf{\Sigma}_\varepsilon^{-1}\mathbf{v}_t \tag{8.3.15}$$

Differentiating (8.3.15) with respect to the distinct elements of $\mathbf{\Sigma}_\varepsilon^{-1}$ leads to the ML estimator of $\mathbf{\Sigma}_\varepsilon$ being

$$\tilde{\mathbf{\Sigma}}_\varepsilon=(T-1)^{-1}\sum_{t=2}^{T}f_t^{-1}\mathbf{v}_t\mathbf{v}_t' \tag{8.3.16}$$

for any given value of q. The ML estimators of q and $\mathbf{\Sigma}_\varepsilon$ can therefore be obtained by maximising the concentrated likelihood function

$$\log L_c=-\frac{(T-1)N}{2}\log 2\pi-\frac{(T-1)}{2}\log|\tilde{\mathbf{\Sigma}}_\varepsilon|-\frac{N}{2}\sum_{t=2}^{T}\log f_t \tag{8.3.17}$$

with respect to q. Carrying out numerical optimisation with respect to a single parameter is obviously much easier than when there are $N(N+1)$ parameters as in the non-homogeneous version of the model.

Once the parameters have been estimated, prediction and smoothing can be carried out. The predictions of future observations are obtained from the univariate recursions, while

$$\text{MSE}(\tilde{\mathbf{y}}_{T+l|T}) = f_{T+l|T}\boldsymbol{\Sigma}_\varepsilon, \quad l = 1, 2, \ldots \tag{8.3.18}$$

where

$$f_{T+l|T} = p_{T+l|T} + 1$$

The decoupling of the Kalman filter can be shown in a similar way for any SUTSE model, (8.2.2), with the homogeneity restriction (8.3.5). Indeed one can go further and generalise (8.2.11) so that the system changes deterministically over time. Thus

$$\mathbf{y}_t = (\mathbf{z}_t' \otimes \mathbf{I}_N)\boldsymbol{\alpha}_t + \boldsymbol{\varepsilon}_t, \quad \text{Var}(\boldsymbol{\varepsilon}_t) = h_t\boldsymbol{\Sigma}_* \tag{8.3.19a}$$

$$\boldsymbol{\alpha}_t = (\mathbf{T}_t \otimes \mathbf{I}_N)\boldsymbol{\alpha}_{t-1} + (\mathbf{R}_t \otimes \mathbf{I}_N)\boldsymbol{\eta}_t, \quad \text{Var}(\boldsymbol{\eta}_t) = \mathbf{Q}_t \otimes \boldsymbol{\Sigma}_* \tag{8.3.19b}$$

In the case of model (8.2.2), $\mathbf{Q}_t = \text{diag}(q_1, \ldots, q_k)$. The more general formulation does not constrain $\mathbf{Q}_t$ to be diagonal, although, as in the univariate model, restrictions are needed on $\mathbf{Q}_t$ for the model to be identifiable. The fact that the Kalman filter for (8.3.19) can be shown to be decoupled suggests a more general definition of a homogeneous SUTSE system. All the results on estimation and prediction carry through, with $\mathbf{P}_{t+1|t} = \mathbf{P}^*_{t+1|t} \otimes \boldsymbol{\Sigma}_*$, where $\mathbf{P}^*_{t+1|t}$ is the MSE matrix for the univariate model; see Harvey (1986).

8.3.3 *Exponential smoothing*

Provided q is positive, the Kalman filter for the random walk plus noise model converges to a steady-state recursion which is the same as the EWMA; see sub-section 4.1.2. Starting the Kalman filter off at $t = 1$ with $p_{2|1} = \bar{p}$ and $m_{2|1} = y_1$, where $\bar{p}$ is given by (4.1.22), yields the steady state, and hence the EWMA, at the outset. Similarly if the Kalman filter given in (8.3.11) is started off with $m_{2|1} = y_1$ and $\mathbf{P}_{2|1} = \bar{p}\boldsymbol{\Sigma}_\varepsilon$, the univariate recursions are of the EWMA form with a common smoothing constant, λ, given by (4.1.24). If $\mathbf{v}_t$ now denotes the vector of EWMA residuals, $\mathbf{y}_t - \hat{\mathbf{y}}_{t|t-1}$, $t = 2, \ldots, T$, the smoothing constant λ may be found by minimising

$$S(\lambda) = \left| \sum_{t=2}^{T} \mathbf{v}_t \mathbf{v}_t' \right| \tag{8.3.20}$$

As was noted in the discussion surrounding (8.2.15), minimising a criterion function of the form (8.3.20) can be justified as an approximate ML procedure.

A similar line of reasoning justifies the use of Holt's local linear trend recursions applied to each series in turn, with the smoothing constants being obtained by minimising a criterion function of a form similar to (8.3.20).

Predictions of future observations are obtained from the univariate recursions in the usual way. The MSE matrix for the one-step-ahead prediction is given by

$$\text{MSE}\,(\tilde{\mathbf{y}}_{T+1|T})=(T-d)^{-1}\sum_{t=d+1}^{T}\mathbf{v}_t\mathbf{v}_t' \tag{8.3.21}$$

8.3.4 Estimation in the frequency domain and properties of the estimators

For a homogeneous model, it follows from (8.3.6) that the spectral generating function is

$$\mathbf{G}(e^{i\lambda})=\mathrm{g}_*(e^{i\lambda})\mathbf{\Sigma}_* \tag{8.3.22}$$

where the terms $\mathrm{z}_k(e^{i\lambda})$ in $\mathrm{g}_*(e^{i\lambda})$ can be evaluated as in section 4.3. Substituting (8.3.22) in the frequency-domain likelihood function, (8.2.16), gives

$$\log L=-\frac{N(T-d)}{2}\log 2\pi-\frac{N}{2}\sum_{j=0}^{T-d-1}\log \mathrm{g}_{*j}-\frac{(T-d)}{2}\log|\mathbf{\Sigma}_*|$$
$$-\pi\,\text{tr}\sum_{j=0}^{T-d-1}\mathrm{g}_{*j}^{-1}\mathbf{\Sigma}_*^{-1}\mathbf{I}(\lambda_j) \tag{8.3.23}$$

where $\mathrm{g}_{*j}=\mathrm{g}_*[\exp(i\lambda_j)]$. Only the real part of the multivariate sample spectrum need be computed. For given values of $q_1,\ldots,q_g$ and h, the ML estimator of $\mathbf{\Sigma}_*$ is

$$\tilde{\mathbf{\Sigma}}_*=\frac{2\pi}{T-d}\sum_{j=0}^{T-d-1}\mathrm{g}_{*j}^{-1}\mathbf{I}(\lambda_j) \tag{8.3.24}$$

The concentrated likelihood function is therefore

$$\log L_c=-\tfrac{1}{2}N(T-d)(1+\log 2\pi)-\tfrac{1}{2}(T-d)\log|\tilde{\mathbf{\Sigma}}_*|-\frac{N}{2}\sum_{j=0}^{T-d-1}\log \mathrm{g}_{*j} \tag{8.3.25}$$

The asymptotic properties of a homogeneous model are most easily derived in the frequency domain. In the case of the multivariate random walk plus noise model, the ML estimators of q and $\mathbf{\Sigma}_\varepsilon$ are consistent and have a limiting multivariate normal distribution provided that $q>0$ and $\mathbf{\Sigma}_\varepsilon$ is p.d. As shown in Fernández (1986, pp. 121–5 and 164–8), the finite sample asymptotic covariance matrix is

$$\text{Avar}(\tilde{q})=2\Bigg/\left\{N\left[\sum_{j=0}^{T-2}\frac{1}{g_{\varepsilon j}^2}-\frac{1}{T-1}\left(\sum_{j=0}^{T-2}\frac{1}{g_{\varepsilon j}}\right)^2\right]\right\} \tag{8.3.26}$$

where

$$g_{\varepsilon j}=\mathrm{g}_{*j}=q+2(1-\cos\lambda_j) \tag{8.3.27}$$

The main point to note about (8.3.26) is that it does not depend on $\boldsymbol{\Sigma}_\varepsilon$ and so the degree of correlation between the series has no effect, asymptotically, on the estimator of q. (The requirement that $\boldsymbol{\Sigma}_\varepsilon$ be strictly p.d. rules out perfect correlation.) Furthermore the appearance of the factor N in (8.3.26) means that the estimator of q obtained by pooling the N series is N times more efficient than the estimator obtained from a single series of length T; compare expression (4.5.3). This result generalises to other homogeneous models.

In summary, therefore, if the hyperparameters in a homogeneous model are known, it is unnecessary to use a multivariate Kalman filter to obtain optimal predictions of future observations and smoothed estimates of the components. However, if the hyperparameters are unknown they can be estimated more efficiently by pooling the information in the N series.

8.4 Testing and model selection

This section generalises the tests and goodness-of-fit statistics of chapter 5 to multivariate SUTSE models. The penultimate sub-section introduces a test specifically designed for multivariate models, namely a test for homogeneity. The final sub-section illustrates the multivariate model selection strategy with an application.

As in univariate modelling an important role is played by the residuals. In a model estimated under the homogeneity assumption, the $N \times 1$ vector of residuals is obtained by dividing the vector of innovations by the scalar $f_t^{\frac{1}{2}}$. Thus

$$\tilde{\mathbf{v}}_t = f_t^{-\frac{1}{2}} \mathbf{v}_t, \quad t = d+1, \ldots, T \tag{8.4.1}$$

and it follows from (8.3.14) that, conditional on the $n^* = n - 1$ parameters in $\boldsymbol{\psi}_*$,

$$\tilde{\mathbf{v}}_t \sim \text{NID}(\mathbf{0}, \boldsymbol{\Sigma}_*) \tag{8.4.2}$$

The ML estimator of $\boldsymbol{\Sigma}_*$ is

$$\tilde{\boldsymbol{\Sigma}}_* = (T-d)^{-1} \sum_{t=d+1}^{T} \tilde{\mathbf{v}}_t \tilde{\mathbf{v}}_t'; \tag{8.4.3}$$

compare expression (8.3.16).

When homogeneity is not assumed, it is appropriate to define an $N \times 1$ vector of *standardised residuals*

$$\tilde{\tilde{\mathbf{v}}}_t = \mathbf{F}_t^{-\frac{1}{2}} \mathbf{v}_t, \quad t = d+1, \ldots, T \tag{8.4.4}$$

If all the parameters, $\boldsymbol{\psi}$, were known, $\tilde{\tilde{\mathbf{v}}}_t$ would have a multivariate standardised normal distribution, that is

$$\tilde{\tilde{\mathbf{v}}}_t \sim \text{NID}(\mathbf{0}, \mathbf{I}_N) \tag{8.4.5}$$

8.4.1 *Testing for serial correlation*

The vector of residuals may be used to construct a multivariate portmanteau test statistic. The form of the test statistic proposed by Hosking (1980) is

$$Q(P)=T^*\sum_{\tau=1}^{P}[\text{vec}\,\mathbf{C}_v(\tau)]'\,\mathbf{C}_v^{-1}(0)\otimes\mathbf{C}_v^{-1}(0)[\text{vec}\,\mathbf{C}_v(\tau)] \tag{8.4.6}$$

where $\mathbf{C}_v(\tau)$ is the autocovariance matrix at lag τ of the residuals. Using a standard result on the vec operator, the $Q(P)$ statistic may be expressed in the alternative form

$$Q(P)=T^*\sum_{\tau=1}^{P}\text{tr}[\mathbf{C}_v'(\tau)\mathbf{C}_v^{-1}(0)\mathbf{C}_v(\tau)\mathbf{C}_v^{-1}(0)]=T^*\sum_{\tau=1}^{P}\text{tr}[\mathbf{R}_v^{\dagger}(-\tau)\mathbf{R}_v^{\dagger}(\tau)] \tag{8.4.7}$$

where $\mathbf{R}_v^{\dagger}(\tau)$ is the residual autocorrelation matrix defined analogously to (8.1.23). Hosking (1980) shows that for residuals from an unrestricted VARMA(p, q) process, the multivariate Q-statistic is asymptotically distributed as χ^2 with $N^2(P-p-q)$ degrees of freedom when the model is correctly specified. The asymptotic distribution of the modified test statistic recommended by Li and McLeod (1981, p. 237),

$$Q^*=Q+N^2P(P+1)/2T^* \tag{8.4.8}$$

is the same.

For a model estimated under the homogeneity assumption, the Q or Q^* statistic can be computed from the residuals defined in (8.4.1). The loss of degrees of freedom is n^*, and so the statistic has a χ^2 distribution with N^2P-n^* degrees of freedom under the null hypothesis. For a non-homogeneous model, the Q-statistic can be computed from the standardised residuals, (8.4.4). However, it is not clear in this case what allowance should be made for the loss of degrees of freedom. Note that, in the homogeneous case, $\mathbf{R}_v(0)=\tilde{\mathbf{\Sigma}}_*$ as defined in (8.4.3), while for the standardised residuals of (8.4.4), $\mathbf{R}_v(0)=\mathbf{I}$.

A more restricted, but potentially more powerful, version of the Q-test may be constructed. This takes the form

$$Q^{\dagger}(P)=T^*\sum_{\tau=1}^{P}\{\text{tr}[\mathbf{R}_v^{\dagger}(\tau)]\}^2/N \tag{8.4.9}$$

In a homogeneous model, the distribution of $\mathbf{Q}^{\dagger}$ under the null hypothesis is χ^2 with $P-n^*$ degrees of freedom. Thus the test is based on considerably fewer degrees of freedom than the test based on Q or Q^*. The rationale underlying this test is as follows. Consider the multivariate AR(P) model, (8.1.2). A test of the null hypothesis $H_0\colon \mathbf{\Phi}_1=\mathbf{\Phi}_2=\cdots=\mathbf{\Phi}_P=\mathbf{0}$, can be constructed via the LM principle. This leads to the portmanteau statistic in (8.4.4) with the residuals being the same as the observations $\mathbf{y}_t$. A more restricted alternative hypothesis is obtained by making the autoregressive matrices in (8.1.2) scalar, that is $\mathbf{\Phi}_i=\varphi_i\mathbf{I}_N$, $i=1,\ldots,P$

where the φ_i's are scalars. Setting up an LM test of $H_0: \varphi_1 = \varphi_2 = \cdots = \varphi_P = 0$ leads to the statistic in (8.4.9) being tested as χ^2 with P degrees of freedom. If this restricted alternative provides a reasonable proxy to the type of departures from the null hypothesis which might arise in practice, then a test based on P, rather than N^2P, degrees of freedom can be expected to be more powerful. Rationalising the Q test as an LM test is difficult to do for a SUTSE model. However, in the homogeneous case, the scalar nature of the AR and MA parameter coefficients, (8.3.9), in the reduced form, lends some support to a test based on (8.4.9). More generally a test based on (8.4.9) can be justified on the grounds that, in a SUTSE system, an inadequate specification will be reflected in each of the equations in a similar way.

The strengths and weaknesses of a test based on (8.4.9) can be seen clearly by considering the special case when $C_v(0)$ is diagonal. In this case (8.4.9) becomes

$$Q^{\dagger}(P) = T^* \sum_{\tau=1}^{P} \left[\sum_{j=1}^{N} r_j(\tau) \right]^2 \Big/ N \tag{8.4.10}$$

where $r_j(\tau)$ is the τ-th order autocorrelation of the residuals in the j-th equation. Suppose, for the sake of argument, that for each lag, the $r_j(\tau)$'s are the same across the N equations. The test statistic in (8.4.10) is then N times as large as each of the $Q(P)$ statistics computed from the individual equations. However, it is based on the same number of degrees of freedom as the $Q(P)$ test carried out on the residuals from a single equation estimated in isolation. Hence the test should be relatively powerful when the residuals in the N series follow similar patterns in a misspecified model. If, on the other hand, the patterns of residuals are very different for different series, cancellation may occur in which case the value of $Q^{\dagger}$ will be relatively small.

In a homogeneous system the $\mathbf{P}^{\dagger}(\tau)$ matrices are scalar; see (8.3.8). Suppose that a model is estimated under the homogeneity assumption but is dynamically misspecified. To the extent that the $\mathbf{R}_v(\tau)$ matrices are scalar, the $Q^{\dagger}$-statistic will be N times the size of each of the Q-statistics calculated for a single equation, and will be the same size as the multivariate portmanteau test statistic of (8.4.7). This would suggest that a test based on $Q^{\dagger}$ could potentially be far more effective than Q-tests based on individually estimated equations, and more powerful than a test based on (8.4.7). However, it should be borne in mind that since the $\mathbf{R}_v(\tau)$'s are likely to be dominated by sampling error, they may be far from scalar even if the underlying system is homogeneous.

A test for serial correlation can also be constructed by generalising the LM frequency-domain procedures of sub-sections 5.3.3 and 5.4.4. Thus suppose we wish to test for serial correlation in the irregular component, this corresponds to Test I given for a univariate model in sub-section 5.4.4. Under the alternative hypothesis the irregular component is taken to be AR(P) or MA(P), but in a multivariate model such an alternative would lead to a test based on N^2P degrees of freedom. For the reasons given in the discussion following (8.4.9), it is sensible in the present context to reduce the degrees of freedom by letting the AR or MA matrices be scalar under the alternative. Thus a one degree of freedom test is based on a model in which the irregular component is formulated as

$$\mathbf{u}_t = \mathbf{\Phi u}_{t-1} + \boldsymbol{\varepsilon}_t, \quad \text{with } \mathbf{\Phi} = \varphi \mathbf{I}_N \tag{8.4.11a}$$

or

$$\mathbf{u}_t = \boldsymbol{\varepsilon}_t + \mathbf{\Theta} \boldsymbol{\varepsilon}_{t-1}, \quad \text{with } \mathbf{\Theta} = \theta \mathbf{I}_N \tag{8.4.11b}$$

where φ and θ are scalars. The null hypothesis is $\mathrm{H}_0 : \varphi = 0$ or $\mathrm{H}_0 : \theta = 0$.

8.4.2 *Goodness of fit*

The *prediction error covariance matrix* is defined as

$$\mathbf{\Sigma} = \bar{\mathbf{F}} = \lim_{t \to \infty} \mathbf{F}_t \tag{8.4.12}$$

If a scalar parameter, σ_*^2, is concentrated out of the likelihood function as in (8.2.13), $\mathbf{\Sigma}$ is estimated by

$$\tilde{\mathbf{\Sigma}} = \tilde{\sigma}_*^2 \bar{\mathbf{F}} \tag{8.4.13}$$

where $\bar{\mathbf{F}}$ depends on the n^* parameters $\boldsymbol{\psi}_*$.

A single measure of goodness of fit, known as the *generalised prediction error variance*, is given by the determinant of $\tilde{\mathbf{\Sigma}}$. Thus

$$|\tilde{\mathbf{\Sigma}}| = \tilde{\sigma}_*^{2N} |\bar{\mathbf{F}}| \tag{8.4.14}$$

In a homogeneous model it follows from (8.3.14) that

$$|\tilde{\mathbf{\Sigma}}| = \bar{f}^N |\tilde{\mathbf{\Sigma}}_*| \tag{8.4.15}$$

The generalised p.e.v. can also be computed in the frequency domain, as suggested by Jones (1976). The multivariate analogue of (5.5.5a) is

$$|\hat{\mathbf{\Sigma}}| = \exp\left[\frac{1}{T^*} \sum_{j=0}^{T^*-1} \log \mathbf{G}_j\right] \tag{8.4.16}$$

As in a univariate model, there is a good case to be made for concentrating out a parameter, σ_*^2, before the p.e.v. is computed in the frequency domain; see the discussion in sub-section 5.5.1.

8.4.3 *Post-sample predictive testing*

As in a univariate model the *standardised prediction errors* are defined in a similar fashion to the standardised residuals, namely

$$\tilde{\mathbf{v}}_{T+j} = \mathbf{F}_{T+j}^{-\frac{1}{2}} \mathbf{v}_{T+j}, \quad j = 1, \ldots, l \tag{8.4.17}$$

If all the parameters, $\boldsymbol{\psi}$, were known, the quadratic form $\mathbf{v}_t'\mathbf{F}_t^{-1}\mathbf{v}_t = \tilde{\tilde{\mathbf{v}}}_t'\tilde{\tilde{\mathbf{v}}}_t$ would be χ^2_N. In this case the distribution of the *post-sample predictive test statistic*

$$\xi(l) = \left[\frac{1}{Nl}\sum_{t=T+1}^{T+l}\tilde{\tilde{\mathbf{v}}}_t'\tilde{\tilde{\mathbf{v}}}_t\right]\Bigg/\left[\frac{1}{NT^*}\sum_{t=d+1}^{T}\tilde{\tilde{\mathbf{v}}}_t'\tilde{\tilde{\mathbf{v}}}_t\right] \qquad (8.4.18)$$

would be an F-distribution with (Nl, NT^*) degrees of freedom. This would also be the distribution if the model contained a single unknown parameter σ^2_* which was estimated via (8.2.13). The denominator in (8.4.18) would then be $\tilde{\sigma}^2_*$, while $\tilde{\tilde{\mathbf{v}}}_{T+j}$ in the numerator would effectively be inflated by $\tilde{\sigma}_*$ because of the different definition of $\mathbf{F}_t$ in (8.4.17). A statistic of this kind is a direct generalisation of the univariate test statistic (5.6.3).

Since there will typically be more unknown parameters than σ^2_*, the distribution of $\xi(l)$ will not, in general, be an F-distribution. However, $Nl\xi(l)$ will be χ^2_{Nl} in large samples. Because of the large number of parameters in a multivariate model, the argument for using the F-distribution as a small sample approximation is perhaps less compelling than it is in the univariate case.

Finally note that in a homogeneous model, the prediction errors can be defined analogously to the residuals in (8.4.1) namely

$$\tilde{\mathbf{v}}_{T+j} = f_{T+j}^{-\frac{1}{2}}\mathbf{v}_{T+j}, \quad j = 1, \ldots, l \qquad (8.4.19)$$

Using this definition the post-sample predictive test statistic can be written as

$$\xi(l) = \left[\frac{1}{Nl}\sum_{t=T+1}^{T+l}\tilde{\mathbf{v}}_t'\tilde{\boldsymbol{\Sigma}}_*^{-1}\tilde{\mathbf{v}}_t\right]\Bigg/\frac{1}{NT^*}\sum_{t=d+1}^{T}\tilde{\mathbf{v}}_t'\tilde{\boldsymbol{\Sigma}}_*^{-1}\tilde{\mathbf{v}}_t \qquad (8.4.20)$$

8.4.4 Testing for homogeneity

A multivariate structural model is relatively easy to estimate when the homogeneity constraint is imposed. The obvious way to test for homogeneity, therefore, is to employ the Lagrange-multiplier procedure. The test is most easily formulated in the frequency domain.

Consider the local level model, (8.2.1). The frequency-domain likelihood function is (8.2.16), and the LM statistic, (5.1.6), is evaluated using the score vector and information matrix evaluated under the null hypothesis $\text{H}_0\!: \boldsymbol{\Sigma}_\eta = q\boldsymbol{\Sigma}_\varepsilon$. The estimates of q and $\boldsymbol{\Sigma}_\varepsilon$ can be computed either in the time domain or the frequency domain, as described in section 8.3. Following Fernández (1986), differentiating (8.2.16) with respect to the full set of parameters in $\boldsymbol{\Sigma}_\eta$ and $\boldsymbol{\Sigma}_\varepsilon$ yields

$$\partial \log L/\partial\boldsymbol{\psi} = \frac{1}{2}\sum_{j=0}^{T^*-1}\mathbf{X}_j\mathbf{M}_j\mathbf{m}_j \qquad (8.4.21a)$$

while the information matrix is:

$$\mathbf{I}(\boldsymbol{\psi}) = \frac{1}{2}\sum_{j=0}^{T^*-1}\mathbf{X}_j\mathbf{M}_j\mathbf{X}_j' \qquad (8.4.21b)$$

where

$$\mathbf{X}_j'=\left[\begin{bmatrix}\mathbf{z}_j\\1\end{bmatrix}\otimes\mathbf{I}_{\frac{1}{2}N(N+1)}\right]\mathbf{D}' \tag{8.4.22a}$$

$$\mathbf{M}_j=(\tilde{q}+z_j)^{-2}(\tilde{\mathbf{\Sigma}}_\varepsilon^{-1}\otimes\tilde{\mathbf{\Sigma}}_\varepsilon^{-1}) \tag{8.4.22b}$$

$$\mathbf{m}_j=\text{vec}[2\pi\mathbf{I}(\lambda_j)-(\tilde{q}+z_j)\tilde{\mathbf{\Sigma}}_\varepsilon] \tag{8.4.22c}$$

with $z_j=2(1-\cos\lambda_j)$ and $\mathbf{D}$ the $N^2\times\frac{1}{2}N(N+1)$ duplication matrix; see Magnus and Neudecker (1980).

The unrestricted model has $N(N+1)$ parameters while the homogeneous model has only $1+\frac{1}{2}N(N+1)$. Therefore under the usual regularity conditions the LM statistic is asymptotically distributed as χ^2 with $\frac{1}{2}N(N+1)-1$ degrees of freedom. The test may be generalised to more elaborate structural models in a straightforward way.

Automobile data The data used by Enns *et al.* (1982) consisted of 109 seasonally adjusted monthly unit sales of a large US automobile manufacturer. Fernández (1986) analysed these data, taking the first 96 observations as the sample, and leaving the remaining observations for post-sample predictive testing.

Enns *et al.* estimated a multivariate local level model under the homogeneity restriction. However, for the differenced observations, the sample autocorrelation matrix at lag one, corresponding to (8.1.23), is

$$\mathbf{R}^\dagger(1)=\begin{bmatrix}-.49 & .82 & .17\\ -.01 & -.18 & -.01\\ .07 & -.61 & -.07\end{bmatrix}$$

Under homogeneity, the theoretical matrix, $\mathbf{P}^\dagger(1)$, should be scalar, as indicated by (8.3.8), but $\mathbf{R}^\dagger(1)$ appears to be some way from being scalar. More formally, the LM statistic for testing for homogeneity is 17.71. This leads to a rejection of the null hypothesis of homogeneity at the 5% level of significance since the 5% critical value for a χ_5^2 distribution is 11.07.

8.4.5 Telephone calls from Australia

Figure 1.3.1 showed three series, representing the number of paid minutes of telephone calls from Australia to three countries. Figure 8.4.1 shows the same series in logarithms, and it is immediately clear that it is the logarithmic formulation which is most appropriate. The three series exhibit similar characteristics, namely a pronounced trend and seasonality, and so a multivariate BSM would seem to be appropriate. Certainly fitting a BSM to each of the individual series in turn gives no grounds for doubting such a judgement.

Given the decision to fit a multivariate model, the initial step is to estimate such a model under the homogeneity assumption. Estimation was carried out in the

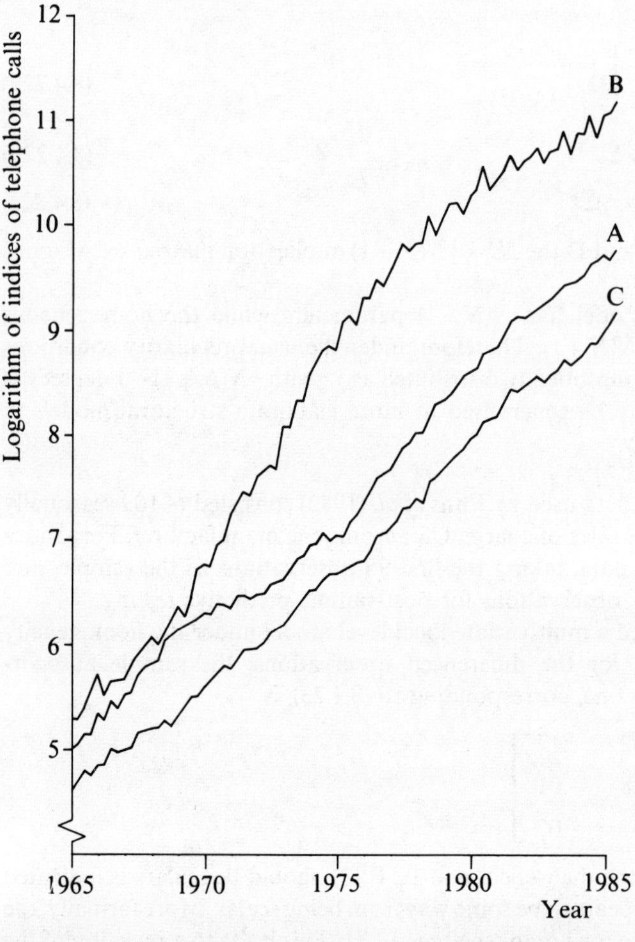

Fig. 8.4.1 Paid minutes of telephone calls from Australia to three other countries (logarithmic scale).

frequency domain by the method of scoring using the observations from 1965Q2 to 1984Q4. The final estimates were obtained by re-estimating Σ_ε in the time domain using (8.4.3); it will be recalled that this kind of fine tuning of frequency-domain estimates was also recommended for univariate models. The results were as follows:

$$\tilde{q}_\eta = \underset{(0.81)}{1.33} \qquad \tilde{q}_\zeta = \underset{(0.0281)}{0.0567} \qquad \tilde{q}_\omega = \underset{(0.075)}{0.137}$$

$$\tilde{\Sigma}_\varepsilon = \begin{bmatrix} 5.95 & & \\ 2.14 & 18.54 & \\ 2.16 & 1.73 & 3.96 \end{bmatrix} \times 10^{-4}$$

The estimated prediction error covariance matrix is

$$\tilde{\Sigma}=\begin{bmatrix}3.09 & & \\ 1.11 & 9.63 & \\ 1.12 & 0.90 & 2.06\end{bmatrix}\times 10^{-3}$$

and

$$\log|\tilde{\Sigma}|=-16.85$$

The estimates of the ratios q_η, q_ζ and q_ω are not too different from the estimates obtained by estimating each series in turn. This is borne out by the value of the homogeneity test statistic which is 12.38. Under the null hypothesis this test statistic has a χ^2_{15} distribution, the 5% critical value of which is 25.00.

As regards the diagnostics,

$$Q(6)=54.05 \quad \text{and} \quad Q^{\dagger}(6)=3.49$$

If the model is correctly specified, these statistics are asymptotically χ^2 with 51 and 3 degrees of freedom respectively. Neither is significant at any reasonable level of significance.

The four observations in 1985 were reserved for post-sample predictive testing. The test statistic is

$$\xi(4)=0.67$$

indicating that the model gives a good fit in the post-sample period.

When the seasonal component was dropped from the model the serial correlation diagnostics were

$$Q(6)=83.36 \quad \text{and} \quad Q^{\dagger}(6)=26.99$$

Both statistics clearly indicate misspecification, since the 5% critical values for χ^2 distributions with 52 and 4 degrees of freedom are 69.83 and 9.49 respectively. However the rejection with the $Q^{\dagger}$ statistic appears to be more decisive. The less dramatic misspecification of treating the slope components as fixed illustrates the potentially higher power of the $Q^{\dagger}$ test even more clearly. The statistics in this case are

$$Q(6)=57.84 \quad \text{and} \quad Q^{\dagger}(6)=11.86$$

The degrees of freedom for the relevant χ^2 distribution are again 52 and 4 respectively, and so the $Q^{\dagger}$ test rejects at the 5% level of significance while the Q test does not.

8.5 Dynamic factor analysis

In classical factor analysis, a model is set up in which it is assumed that each of N variables is a linear combination of $K<N$ common factors plus a random

disturbance term. The technique is usually applied to cross-sectional data, although there are one or two examples of its use in time series. Thus Ahamad (1967) used factor analysis, or more precisely, the closely related technique of principal components, in a study of annual data on various types of crimes in the UK. Recent theoretical work on factor analysis for time series can be found in Brillinger (1975, ch. 9), Geweke (1977), Geweke and Singleton (1981), Sims (1981), Box and Tiao (1977) and Velu *et al.* (1986). The approach adopted in most of these papers is based on the assumption that the vector of observations, $\mathbf{y}_t$, follows a stationary process.

The essence of a structural time series model is that it is formulated in terms of components which have distinctive dynamic properties. A natural generalisation of the SUTSE class of models is therefore to allow them to have certain of their components in common. Just as prior considerations may help in formulating a model in terms of components, so they may help in deciding which components are candidates for common factors. The fact that some of these components may be non-stationary does not pose any difficulties; rather it is an asset. The more different are the properties of components, the more easy they are to distinguish.

The discussion in this section is limited to dynamic factor analysis within a framework obtained from SUTSE models. Further generalisation to models where there may be dynamic interaction between the series within various components is made in sub-section 8.2.

8.5.1 Common trends

Consider the random walk plus noise SUTSE model, (8.2.1), with a slope term, $\boldsymbol{\beta}$, included. A common factor model for the trend components would lead to (8.2.1) becoming

$$\mathbf{y}_t = \boldsymbol{\Theta}\boldsymbol{\mu}_t + \boldsymbol{\mu}_0 + \boldsymbol{\varepsilon}_t, \quad \mathrm{Var}(\boldsymbol{\varepsilon}_t) = \boldsymbol{\Sigma}_\varepsilon \tag{8.5.1a}$$

$$\boldsymbol{\mu}_t = \boldsymbol{\mu}_{t-1} + \boldsymbol{\beta} + \boldsymbol{\eta}_t, \quad \mathrm{Var}(\boldsymbol{\eta}_t) = \boldsymbol{\Sigma}_\eta \tag{8.5.1b}$$

where $\boldsymbol{\mu}_t$ is a $K \times 1$ vector of *common trends*, $\boldsymbol{\Theta}$ is an $N \times K$ matrix of factor loadings and $0 \leqslant K \leqslant N$. The covariance matrices $\boldsymbol{\Sigma}_\varepsilon$ and $\boldsymbol{\Sigma}_\eta$ are $N \times N$ and $K \times K$ respectively and are p.d., while $\boldsymbol{\mu}_0$ is an $N \times 1$ vector which has zeros for its first K elements while its last N–K elements consist of an unconstrained vector $\bar{\boldsymbol{\mu}}$.

As it stands, (8.5.1) is not identifiable. For any non-singular $K \times K$ matrix $\mathbf{H}$, the matrix of factor loadings and the trend component could be redefined as $\boldsymbol{\Theta}^\dagger = \boldsymbol{\Theta}\mathbf{H}^{-1}$ and $\boldsymbol{\mu}_t^\dagger = \mathbf{H}\boldsymbol{\mu}_t$ respectively, and so

$$\mathbf{y}_t = \boldsymbol{\Theta}^\dagger\boldsymbol{\mu}_t^\dagger + \boldsymbol{\mu}_0 + \boldsymbol{\varepsilon}_t \tag{8.5.2a}$$

$$\boldsymbol{\mu}_t^\dagger = \boldsymbol{\mu}_{t-1}^\dagger + \boldsymbol{\beta}^\dagger + \boldsymbol{\eta}_t^\dagger \tag{8.5.2b}$$

where $\boldsymbol{\eta}_t^\dagger = \mathbf{H}\boldsymbol{\eta}_t$, $\boldsymbol{\beta}^\dagger = \mathbf{H}\boldsymbol{\beta}$ and $\mathrm{Var}(\boldsymbol{\eta}_t^\dagger) = \mathbf{H}\boldsymbol{\Sigma}_\eta\mathbf{H}'$. This model is indistinguishable from (8.5.1). There are an infinite number of parameter sets which give the same joint density function for the observations; see the discussion on identifiability in section 4.4.

In order for the model to be identifiable, restrictions must be placed on Σ_η and $\boldsymbol{\Theta}$. In classical factor analysis, the covariance matrix of the common factors is taken to be an identity matrix. However, this is not sufficient to make the model identifiable since if $\mathbf{H}$ is an orthogonal matrix, (8.5.2) still satisfies all the restrictions of the original model because $\text{Var}(\boldsymbol{\eta}_t^\dagger) = \mathbf{HH}' = \mathbf{I}$. Some restrictions are needed on $\boldsymbol{\Theta}$, and one way of imposing them is to require that the ij-th element of $\boldsymbol{\Theta}$, Θ_{ij}, be zero for $j > i$, $i = 1, \ldots, K-1$. Alternatively, Σ_η can be set equal to a diagonal matrix while $\Theta_{ij} = 0$ for $j > i$ and $\Theta_{ii} = 1$ for $i = 1, \ldots, K$. Note that when $K = N$, the model reverts to (8.2.1) since $\boldsymbol{\Theta\mu}_t$ in (8.5.1) may be redefined as $\boldsymbol{\mu}_t$ and the variance of the corresponding $\boldsymbol{\eta}_t$ is then the p.s.d. matrix $\boldsymbol{\Theta}\Sigma_\eta\boldsymbol{\Theta}'$.

The identifiability restrictions mean that the common trends are uncorrelated with each other. This is quite an attractive property. The restrictions on the $\boldsymbol{\Theta}$ matrix are less appealing, since they imply that y_{1t} depends only on the first common trend and not the others. Similarly y_{2t} depends only on the first two common trends, and so on until we reach y_{Kt}. This depends on all the common trends, as do $y_{K+1,t}, \ldots, y_{N,t}$. Clearly this is arbitrary, and defining the common trends in this way may not lead to a particularly useful interpretation. However, once the model has been estimated, an orthogonal $\mathbf{H}$ matrix can be used to give a *factor rotation*. The new common trends are then the elements of $\boldsymbol{\mu}_t^\dagger$ in (8.5.2).

A number of methods for carrying out factor rotation have been developed in the classical factor analysis literature. There is no reason why these should not be employed in the present context. Often one of the aims in factor rotation is to give a factor positive loadings for some variables while the other variables get a loading near zero. Thus the movements in a variable may be identified with only a subset of the factors. This may enable the factors to have a useful interpretation. If certain subsets of the variables can be associated with certain subsets of the factors it may be possible to put the variables into *clusters*. Thus if there are, say, three clusters, the loading matrix takes the form

$$\boldsymbol{\Theta} = \begin{bmatrix} \boldsymbol{\Theta}_1 & \mathbf{0} & \mathbf{0} \\ \mathbf{0} & \boldsymbol{\Theta}_2 & \mathbf{0} \\ \mathbf{0} & \mathbf{0} & \boldsymbol{\Theta}_3 \end{bmatrix} \tag{8.5.3}$$

The common trends model has the important property that $N-K$ linear combinations are stationary, even though all the elements of $\mathbf{y}_t$ are only stationary in first differences. In the terminology introduced in sub-section 8.1.4, the model is said to be co-integrated of order (1, 1). The co-integrating vectors are the $N-K$ rows of an $(N-K) \times N$ matrix $\mathbf{A}$ which has the property that $\mathbf{A\Theta} = \mathbf{0}$. Hence

$$\mathbf{Ay}_t = \mathbf{A}\boldsymbol{\mu}_0 + \mathbf{A}\boldsymbol{\varepsilon}_t \tag{8.5.4}$$

and $\mathbf{Ay}_t$ is an $(N-K)\times 1$ stationary process. In fact in this case it is simply multivariate while noise with mean $\mathbf{A}\boldsymbol{\mu}_0$ and covariance matrix $\mathbf{A}\boldsymbol{\Sigma}_\varepsilon\mathbf{A}'$.

Example 8.5.1 Suppose that $N=2$ and $K=1$. The model may be written as

$$\begin{bmatrix} y_{1t} \\ y_{2t} \end{bmatrix} = \begin{bmatrix} 1 \\ \theta \end{bmatrix} \mu_t + \begin{bmatrix} 0 \\ \bar{\mu} \end{bmatrix} + \begin{bmatrix} \varepsilon_{1t} \\ \varepsilon_{2t} \end{bmatrix} \tag{8.5.5a}$$

$$\mu_t = \mu_{t-1} + \beta + \eta_t \tag{8.5.5b}$$

with $\text{Var}(\eta_t) = \sigma_\eta^2$. The co-integrating vector may be normalised as $\mathbf{A} = [1 \quad \alpha]$. It must be such that

$$1 + \alpha\theta = 0$$

and so

$$\alpha = -1/\theta$$

Multiplying (8.5.5a) through by $\mathbf{A}$ gives

$$y_{1t} = (1/\theta)y_{2t} + (-1/\theta)\bar{\mu} + \varepsilon_t \tag{8.5.6}$$

where $\varepsilon_t = \varepsilon_{1t} - \varepsilon_{2t}/\theta$. Thus there is a levels relationship between y_{1t} and y_{2t}.

The attractions of a common trend model are threefold. Firstly, it is more parsimonious than a model without common trends. Secondly, it preserves certain levels relationships between the variables when forecasts are made. Thirdly, the common trends themselves may have an interesting interpretation, usually after an appropriate rotation has been made. The next sub-section explains how the common trends model may be estimated. It also addresses the key question of how K, the number of common trends, is determined.

The specifications of the common trends can be extended so as to include stochastic slopes. Thus

$$\boldsymbol{\mu}_t = \boldsymbol{\mu}_{t-1} + \boldsymbol{\Theta}_\beta \boldsymbol{\beta}_{t-1} + \boldsymbol{\beta}_0 + \boldsymbol{\eta}_t \tag{8.5.7a}$$

$$\boldsymbol{\beta}_t = \qquad \boldsymbol{\beta}_{t-1} + \qquad \boldsymbol{\zeta}_t \tag{8.5.7b}$$

where $\boldsymbol{\beta}_t$ is $K_\beta \times 1, 0 \leqslant K_\beta \leqslant K$, $\text{Var}(\boldsymbol{\zeta}_t) = \mathbf{I}$, $\boldsymbol{\Theta}_\beta$ is a $K \times K_\beta$ matrix with $\Theta_{\beta,ij} = 0$ for $j > i$. The disturbance vectors $\boldsymbol{\eta}_t$ and $\boldsymbol{\zeta}_t$ are mutually uncorrelated. Finally the $K \times 1$ vector $\boldsymbol{\beta}_0$ has its first K_β elements zero, so that $\boldsymbol{\beta}_0 = [\mathbf{0}' \quad \boldsymbol{\beta}']'$.

When $K_\beta = 0$, (8.5.7) collapses to the original fixed-slope model of (8.5.1) with $\boldsymbol{\beta} = \boldsymbol{\beta}_0$. When $K_\beta = K$, the model is equivalent to a SUTSE model with local linear trend components for all the variables. This system is easily seen to be co-integrated of order (2, 2). Indeed for any positive value of K_β the system will be co-integrated of order (2, 2) provided that $\boldsymbol{\Theta}$ and $\boldsymbol{\Theta}_\beta$ contain null rows. Whether or not allowing for different trend components to contain common slopes is a useful extension of the model in practice remains to be seen.

8.5.2 Estimation and testing

The model in (8.5.1) can be put in SSF almost immediately. The only issue is how to handle the unknown vectors, $\boldsymbol{\mu}_0$ and $\boldsymbol{\beta}$. Conceptually, $\boldsymbol{\mu}_0$ is most easily handled by including its non-zero part, $\bar{\boldsymbol{\mu}}$, in an augmented state vector, $\boldsymbol{\mu}_t^\dagger = [\boldsymbol{\mu}_t' \quad \bar{\boldsymbol{\mu}}']'$. The model is then

$$\mathbf{y}_t = \begin{bmatrix} \boldsymbol{\Theta} & \begin{matrix} \mathbf{0} \\ \mathbf{I} \end{matrix} \end{bmatrix} \begin{bmatrix} \boldsymbol{\mu}_t \\ \bar{\boldsymbol{\mu}}_t \end{bmatrix} + \boldsymbol{\varepsilon}_t \tag{8.5.8a}$$

$$\boldsymbol{\mu}_t^\dagger = \begin{bmatrix} \boldsymbol{\mu}_t \\ \bar{\boldsymbol{\mu}}_t \end{bmatrix} = \begin{bmatrix} \mathbf{I} & \mathbf{0} \\ \mathbf{0} & \mathbf{I} \end{bmatrix} \begin{bmatrix} \boldsymbol{\mu}_{t-1} \\ \bar{\boldsymbol{\mu}}_{t-1} \end{bmatrix} + \begin{bmatrix} \boldsymbol{\beta} \\ \mathbf{0} \end{bmatrix} + \begin{bmatrix} \mathbf{I} \\ \mathbf{0} \end{bmatrix} \boldsymbol{\eta}_t \tag{8.5.8b}$$

Assume, for the moment, that $\boldsymbol{\beta}$ is known. If a diffuse prior is used to start off the Kalman filter, a proper prior is obtained for $\boldsymbol{\mu}_1^\dagger$ from $\mathbf{y}_1$. The likelihood function is then written down in the prediction error decomposition form with the summations running from $t=2$ to T. This approach requires very little amendment to the algorithm which one would use for the model without trends in common. An alternative approach is to keep only $\boldsymbol{\mu}_t$ in the state vector, and to treat $\bar{\boldsymbol{\mu}}$ as a vector of unknown parameters by writing the model in the form (3.4.32) and applying the GLS algorithm. Since only K elements of $\mathbf{y}_1$ are needed to construct starting values for the state vector, the remaining elements contribute directly to the likelihood function. This is accomplished automatically if the general algorithm of de Jong (1989) is adopted.

As regards $\boldsymbol{\beta}$, there are three possibilities. Firstly it can be added to the state vector. This is the best way to proceed if one wishes to leave open the possibility of generalising the model to allow for a stochastic slope as in (8.5.7). The second approach is to estimate $\boldsymbol{\beta}$ by the GLS algorithm. Finally, for a given value of $\boldsymbol{\Theta}$ it is shown below that the estimator

$$\bar{\boldsymbol{\beta}}(\boldsymbol{\Theta}) = (\boldsymbol{\Theta}'\boldsymbol{\Theta})^{-1}\boldsymbol{\Theta}'\overline{\Delta\mathbf{y}} \tag{8.5.9}$$

where $\overline{\Delta\mathbf{y}} = (\mathbf{y}_T - \mathbf{y}_1)/(T-1)$ is asymptotically efficient. Thus if $\boldsymbol{\beta}$ is to be concentrated out of the likelihood function, (8.5.9) would seem to be the easiest way of doing it. Note that (8.5.9) collapses to (8.2.17) when there are no common trends.

As regards estimation in the frequency domain, the likelihood function for (8.5.1) when there are no common trends is (8.2.16) with

$$\mathbf{G}_j = \boldsymbol{\Sigma}_\eta + 2(1-\cos\lambda_j)\boldsymbol{\Sigma}_\varepsilon, \quad j=0,\ldots,T-1 \tag{8.5.10}$$

In the common trends model, $\boldsymbol{\Sigma}_\eta$ in (8.5.10) is replaced by $\boldsymbol{\Theta}\boldsymbol{\Sigma}_\eta\boldsymbol{\Theta}'$. This creates a difficulty at $j=0$, since $\mathbf{G}_0 = \boldsymbol{\Theta}\boldsymbol{\Sigma}_\eta\boldsymbol{\Theta}'$ and this is of rank $N<K$. However, as shown in Fernández (1986), the term involving $\mathbf{G}_0$ in (8.2.16), that is

$$-\tfrac{1}{2}\log|\mathbf{G}_0| - \pi\,\mathrm{tr}\,[\mathbf{G}_0^{-1}\,\mathbf{I}(\lambda_0)]$$

may be replaced by

$$-\tfrac{1}{2}\log|\boldsymbol{\Sigma}_\eta| - \mathrm{tr}[\boldsymbol{\Sigma}_\eta^{-1}\boldsymbol{\Theta}^*\mathbf{I}(\lambda_0)\boldsymbol{\Theta}^{*\prime}] \tag{8.5.11}$$

where

$$\boldsymbol{\Theta}^* = (\boldsymbol{\Theta}'\boldsymbol{\Theta})^{-1}\boldsymbol{\Theta}' \tag{8.5.12}$$

The likelihood function formed in this way is for the observations $\Delta\mathbf{y}_t - \boldsymbol{\Theta\beta}$, $t=2,\ldots,T$. However, $\boldsymbol{\beta}$ drops out of all the sample spectral matrices, $\mathbf{I}(\lambda_j)$, except the one at $\lambda_j=0$. When it is concentrated out of the likelihood function, the estimator (8.5.9) is obtained.

The only problem which remains is determining the number of common trends. A series of tests may be carried out based on the results derived by Stock and Watson (1988). Consider first the case of testing the null hypothesis that the model is not a common trend model against the alternative that it has one common trend. In terms of (8.5.1), this is a test of $\mathrm{H}_0: K=N$ against $\mathrm{H}_1: K=N-1$. The test statistic is based on the $N\times N$ matrix

$$\hat{\boldsymbol{\Phi}}_c = \left[T^{-2}\sum_{t=2}^{T}(\mathbf{y}_t-\bar{\mathbf{y}})(\mathbf{y}_{t-1}-\bar{\mathbf{y}})' - T^{-1}\hat{\mathbf{M}}\right] \times \left[T^{-2}\sum_{t=2}^{T}(\mathbf{y}_{t-1}-\bar{\mathbf{y}})(\mathbf{y}_{t-1}-\bar{\mathbf{y}})'\right]^{-1} \tag{8.5.13}$$

where, in general, $\hat{\mathbf{M}}$ is a consistent estimator of

$$\mathbf{M} = \sum_{j=1}^{\infty}\mathrm{Cov}(\Delta\mathbf{y}_t\Delta\mathbf{y}'_{t-j}) \tag{8.5.14}$$

In the case of (8.5.1), $\mathrm{Cov}(\Delta\mathbf{y}_t\Delta\mathbf{y}'_{t-j}) = \mathbf{0}$ for $j>1$ and so a possible estimator is

$$\hat{\mathbf{M}} = T^{-1}\sum_{t=3}^{T}[(\mathbf{y}_t-\bar{\mathbf{y}}) - \hat{\boldsymbol{\Phi}}(\mathbf{y}_{t-1}-\bar{\mathbf{y}})][(\mathbf{y}_{t-1}-\bar{\mathbf{y}}) - \hat{\boldsymbol{\Phi}}(\mathbf{y}_{t-2}-\bar{\mathbf{y}})]' \tag{8.5.15}$$

where ψ is given by (8.5.13) but without the term $\mathrm{T}^{-1}\hat{\mathbf{M}}$. The test statistic is

$$q_c = T(|\hat{\lambda}_{(K)}|-1) \tag{8.5.16}$$

where $\hat{\lambda}_{(K)}$ is the smallest eigenvalue of $\hat{\boldsymbol{\Phi}}_c$. The limiting distribution of this statistic is given by Stock and Watson (1988).

Carrying out further tests, for example $\mathrm{H}_0: K=N-1$ against $\mathrm{H}_1: K=N-2$ is more complicated and reference should be made to Stock and Watson for details.

8.5.3 Applications and extensions

Common cycles may play a role in dynamic factor models. A set of K_ψ cyclical components, each of the form (2.3.38), may be introduced into a multivariate model by defining an $N \times K_\psi$ loading matrix $\boldsymbol{\Theta}_\psi$ with the property that $\Theta_{\psi,ij}=0$ for $j>i$, and letting the disturbance terms in each stochastic cycle, κ_{jt} and κ_{jt}^*, $j=1,\ldots,K_\psi$ be mutually uncorrelated with unit variance. The example of rainfall in north-east Brazil, described in sub-section 2.7.2, suggests an application of a model with a common cycle. Suppose observations are available at other weather stations in the neighbourhood of Forteleza. It might be reasonable to suppose that the underlying cyclical movements are the same throughout the area, but that there are local differences which are reflected in the irregular term and in the overall level of each series. A possible model for the $N \times 1$ vector of observations is, therefore,

$$\mathbf{y}_t = \boldsymbol{\mu} + \boldsymbol{\Theta}_\psi \psi_t + \boldsymbol{\varepsilon}_t \tag{8.5.17}$$

with K_ψ equal to unity and $\boldsymbol{\mu}$ an $N \times 1$ vector of constants. The model collapses to (2.3.60) when N is one. The covariance matrix of $\boldsymbol{\varepsilon}_t$ could reflect the type of structure known as spatial autocorrelation.

Common seasonal components may also be introduced into a model. The techniques are much the same as for common trends. Common seasonality also leads to the idea of extending the definition of co-integration to include seasonal effects. With trigonometric seasonal components it is possible to set up models which are co-integrated at only some of the seasonal frequencies.

Finally exogenous variables may be added to a common factor model. An application may be found in Engle and Watson (1981). They set up a model in which the wage rates in five industries in Los Angeles are related to the wage rates in the same industries in the whole of the US and to an unobserved component which reflects the overall wage rate in metropolitan Los Angeles. Thus the model is

$$y_{it} = \theta_i \mu_t + \beta_i x_{it} + \mu_{oi} + \varepsilon_{it}, \quad i=1,\ldots,5, \quad t=1,\ldots,T \tag{8.5.18}$$

where y_{it} and x_{it} are the logarithms of the Los Angeles and national wage rates in industry i and year t, μ_t is the unobserved component representing the Los Angeles wage effect, and ε_{it} is an AR(1) disturbance term for the i-th industry. The unobserved component is assumed to be stationary with a mean of zero and hence an unknown constant μ_{oi} is included for each industry. The other unknown constants are $\beta_i, i=1,\ldots,5$ and the loadings $\theta_i, i=2,\ldots,5$; θ_1 is set equal to unity to ensure identifiability.

As it stands, the model in (8.5.18) appears to have little relation to the factor models discussed so far. However, Engle and Watson specify μ_t to be an AR(2) process and when estimated this becomes

$$\mu_t = 1.61\,\mu_{t-1} - 0.62\,\mu_{t-2} + \eta_t \tag{8.5.19}$$

On examination it can be seen that the process is effectively non-stationary since $1-1.61\,L+0.62\,L^2 \simeq (1-L)(1-0.62L)$. This point is also noted by Engle and Watson. The non-stationarity is confirmed by the smoothed estimates which show a steady upward movement over time reflecting the relatively faster growth of wages in the Los Angeles area. Although μ_t in (8.5.19) is virtually the same as a damped trend model, it would be interesting to see the effect of fitting a local linear trend model.

8.6 Intervention analysis with control groups

Intervention analysis is concerned with assessing the impact of an event, such as a policy change, on a time series. The technique was described in section 7.6, with the series of interest modelled in terms of time series components with explanatory variables, and the effect of the intervention being assessed by the introduction of a dummy variable. The aim of this section is to set up a framework within which a control group, or groups, can be used to obtain a more accurate estimate of the effect of the intervention. Control groups are normally a key feature of scientific experiments and it would seem important to try to utilise such groups, if they can be located, in analysing non-experimental data. A general discussion of the methodological aspects of control groups in time series can be found in Glass *et al.* (1975).

To qualify as a control group, a time series should not be influenced by the intervention which is supposed to affect the series of interest. In other respects it should be subject to much the same influences as operate on the series of interest. It is therefore appropriate to handle control groups within a SUTSE framework. In the absence of exogenous variables, the SUTSE model is of the general form (8.2.11). Without loss of generality, the first equation can be regarded as the one subject to the intervention, while the remaining $N-1$ variables are the control groups. The measurement equation in (8.2.11a) therefore becomes

$$\mathbf{y}_t = (\mathbf{z}' \otimes \mathbf{I}_N)\boldsymbol{\alpha}_t + \lambda \mathbf{w}_t + \boldsymbol{\varepsilon}_t, \quad t = 1, \ldots, T \tag{8.6.1}$$

where $\mathbf{w}_t$ is an $N \times 1$ vector, the first element of which is an intervention variable, w_t, defined as in section 7.6, while the remaining elements are zeros. The ML estimator of the scalar parameter λ is the appropriate estimator of the effect of the intervention when the information in the control groups is taken into account.

In order to investigate the effect of including control groups in intervention analysis, consider the multivariate random walk plus noise model. Including an intervention variable in the measurement equation means that (8.2.1a) is modified to

$$\mathbf{y}_t = \boldsymbol{\mu}_t + \lambda \mathbf{w}_t + \boldsymbol{\varepsilon}_t, \quad t = 1, \ldots, T \tag{8.6.2}$$

As in sub-section 7.6.2, we require an expression for the variance of the ML estimator of λ, conditional on the hyperparameters in the model. Subtracting the left- and right-hand sides of the Kalman filter state recursion, (8.3.11a), from $\mathbf{y}_{t+1}$ yields

$$\mathbf{y}_{t+1} - \mathbf{m}_{t+1|t} = \mathbf{y}_{t+1} - \mathbf{m}_{t|t-1} - \mathbf{P}_{t|t-1}\mathbf{F}_t^{-1}(\mathbf{y}_t - \mathbf{m}_{t|t-1}) \tag{8.6.3}$$

The left-hand side of this equation is the vector of innovations, $\mathbf{v}_t$, and so

$$\begin{aligned}\mathbf{v}_{t+1} &= \Delta\mathbf{y}_{t+1} + (\mathbf{I} - \mathbf{P}_{t|t-1}\mathbf{F}_t^{-1})\mathbf{v}_t \\ &= \Delta\mathbf{y}_{t+1} + (\mathbf{F}_t - \mathbf{P}_{t|t-1})\mathbf{F}_t^{-1}\mathbf{v}_t \\ &= \Delta\mathbf{y}_{t+1} + \mathbf{\Sigma}_\varepsilon\mathbf{F}_t^{-1}\mathbf{v}_t, \quad t=2,\ldots,T-1 \end{aligned} \tag{8.6.4}$$

the last line following from the definition of $\mathbf{F}_t$ in (8.3.11d). Expression (8.6.4) is the multivariate generalisation of the innovation recursion derived in (4.2.15a). Proceeding as in sub-section 7.6.2 gives

$$\mathrm{Var}(\tilde{\lambda}_{N,T}) = \left\{[1 \quad \mathbf{0}'_{N-1}]\left[\sum_{t=\tau}^{T}(\mathbf{\Sigma}^{-1}\mathbf{\Sigma}_\varepsilon)^{T-\tau}\mathbf{\Sigma}^{-1}(\mathbf{\Sigma}_\varepsilon\mathbf{\Sigma}^{-1})^{T-\tau}\right]\begin{bmatrix}1 \\ \mathbf{0}_{N-1}\end{bmatrix}\right\}^{-1} \tag{8.6.5}$$

where $\tilde{\lambda}_{N,T}$ denotes the ML estimator of λ based on N series, each with T observations. In a homogeneous system, it follows from (8.3.14) that $\mathbf{\Sigma}_\varepsilon\mathbf{F}_t^{-1} = (1/f_t)\mathbf{I}_N$ and so in the steady state $\mathbf{\Sigma}_\varepsilon\mathbf{\Sigma}^{-1} = (1/\bar{f})\mathbf{I}_N$. This being the case, expression (8.6.5) simplifies dramatically and may be written as

$$\mathrm{Var}(\tilde{\lambda}_{N,T}) = \mathrm{Var}(\tilde{\lambda}_T).(1-\rho^2) \tag{8.6.6}$$

where ρ^2 is the coefficient of multiple correlation between the innovations in the first series and the innovations in the $N-1$ control groups and $\mathrm{Var}(\tilde{\lambda}_T)$ is the GLS estimator of λ based on the first series alone. As (8.6.6) clearly shows, the gain in efficiency from using the control groups depends on the extent to which they are correlated with the series subjected to the intervention. However, if $q>0$, a consistent estimator of λ can still not be obtained unless $\rho^2=1$.

8.6.1 Single equation estimation

Rather than estimating a multivariate time series model, an alternative approach might be to estimate a single equation of the form (7.6.1), in which the exogenous variables, $\mathbf{x}_t$, are replaced by the control groups $y_{2t}, \ldots, y_{Nt}$. As a special case y_{1t} might simply be regressed on w_t and $y_{2t}, \ldots, y_{Nt}$. Given that the observations are generated by a multivariate model of the form (8.2.11), it is important to determine whether such a procedure is valid. The problem will be analysed within the framework of the multivariate random walk plus noise model, (8.2.1). Once this has been done, the extension to more general SUTSE models is relatively straightforward. The general conclusions are presented at the end of the sub-section.

Suppose that there are only two series and that $\mathbf{\Sigma}_\eta = \mathbf{0}$. This being the case, $[y_{1t} y_{2t}]'$ has a multivariate normal distribution with mean $[\mu_1 \quad \mu_2]'$ and covariance matrix $\mathbf{\Sigma}_\varepsilon$. When the first series is subject to an intervention, it follows from the properties of the multivariate normal that

$$y_{1t} = \mu + \beta y_{2t} + \lambda w_t + \varepsilon_t \tag{8.6.7}$$

where $\beta = \text{Cov}(\varepsilon_{1t}\varepsilon_{2t})/\text{Var}(\varepsilon_{2t})$, $\mu = \mu_1 - \beta\mu_2$ and $\varepsilon_t = \varepsilon_{1t} - \beta\varepsilon_{2t}$; see the appendix to chapter 3. By construction ε_t and y_{2t} are independent of each other. In the terminology of sub-section 7.1.4, y_{2t} is weakly exogenous in (8.6.7) and OLS applied to this equation yields an efficient estimator of λ. The OLS estimator clearly satisfies (8.6.6) since

$$\text{Var}(\varepsilon_t) = \text{Var}(\varepsilon_{1t}) - [\text{Cov}(\varepsilon_{1t}\varepsilon_{2t})]^2/\text{Var}(\varepsilon_{2t}) = \text{Var}(\varepsilon_{1t}).(1-\rho)^2$$

Now consider the general case with both Σ_η and Σ_ε specified to be p.d. If the system is homogeneous then

$$\beta = \frac{\text{Cov}(\varepsilon_{1t}\varepsilon_{2t})}{\text{Var}(\varepsilon_{2t})} = \frac{\text{Cov}(\eta_{1t}\eta_{2t})}{\text{Var}(\eta_{2t})} \tag{8.6.8}$$

Thus the multivariate model may be rewritten as

$$y_{1t} = \beta y_{2t} + \lambda w_t + \frac{\eta_t}{\Delta} + \varepsilon_t \tag{8.6.9a}$$

$$y_{2t} = \frac{\eta_{2t}}{\Delta} + \varepsilon_{2t} \tag{8.6.9b}$$

where $\eta_t = \eta_{1t} - \beta\eta_{2t}$. By construction $\text{E}(\eta_t\eta_{2t}) = 0$ and $\text{E}(\varepsilon_t\varepsilon_{2t}) = 0$. If q is known, the likelihood function for (y_{1t}, y_{2t}) may be factored into two parts, one involving the unknown parameters in (8.6.9a), i.e. β, λ and $\text{Var}(\varepsilon_{2t})$. Thus y_{2t} is weakly exogenous in (8.6.9a) and, in particular, it is weakly exogenous for the parameter of interest, λ. As a result, all the sample information concerning λ is in the partial likelihood function associated with equation (8.6.9a) and λ can be estimated efficiently from (8.6.9a) by applying the methods used to estimate equation (7.6.1). Note that the signal–noise ratio is still q just as it is in the two individual series. This is a direct consequence of homogeneity.

If q is unknown, y_{2t} is no longer weakly exogenous in equation (8.6.9a). This is because factorising the likelihood function as before leaves q in both parts. However, estimating q from equation (8.6.9a) alone still yields a consistent estimator, $\tilde{q}_1$, with the property that $\sqrt{T}(\tilde{q}_1 - q)$ has a limiting normal distribution. Thus in large samples $\tilde{\lambda}(\tilde{q}_1)$, the ML estimator of λ from (8.6.9a) will have approximately the same distribution as the GLS estimator, $\tilde{\lambda}(q)$, computed using the true value of q. More formally we can say that $\sqrt{T}[\tilde{\lambda}(\tilde{q}_1) - \tilde{\lambda}(q)]$ is bounded in probability or that the difference between the two converges in probability at rate $(1/\sqrt{T})$, i.e. $\tilde{\lambda}(\tilde{q}_1) - \tilde{\lambda}(q) = O_p(1/\sqrt{T})$.[1] A similar statement can be made about $\lambda(\tilde{q})$, the ML estimator of λ computed from the full likelihood function, even though the estimator of q in this case is asymptotically efficient. Thus in large samples it can be argued that inference about λ may just as well be based on the single equation likelihood. However, in small samples, using the

1. On the other hand if $\hat{\lambda}(q)$ is the OLS estimator of λ then $\hat{\lambda}(q) - \tilde{\lambda}(q) = O_p(1)$ for $q > 0$.

information in y_{2t} to obtain a better estimator of q may well lead to an improved estimator of λ.

When the system is not homogeneous it is not possible, in general, to choose a value of β in (8.6.9a) which results in $E(\eta_t \eta_{2t})$ and $E(\varepsilon_t \varepsilon_{2t})$ being zero simultaneously. The correlation between y_{2t} and the disturbance terms makes a single equation estimator inappropriate since it will be biased for any value of the signal–noise ratio. (It is not helpful to say that the estimator is inconsistent since λ cannot be estimated consistently in this model.)

If the assumption that Σ_η and Σ_ε are p.d. is relaxed so that they only need be p.s.d., single equation methods are valid in two special cases where the homogeneity property does not hold. These are: (i) $\text{Var}(\varepsilon_{2t})=0$; and (ii) $\text{Var}(\eta_{2t}) = 0$. In fact, single equation estimators in these two cases are fully efficient. When in case (i), η_{1t} and η_{2t} are perfectly correlated, the variable y_{2t} effectively replaces the stochastic trend in the equation for y_{1t} and OLS is the appropriate estimation technique.

The results for the random walk plus noise model all carry over to the more general SUTSE model, (8.2.11). Under the homogeneity assumption, (8.3.5), the following results hold.

(i) When the hyperparameters $q_1, \ldots, q_g$ and h are given, the single equation GLS estimator of λ, $\tilde{\lambda}(q_1, \ldots, q_g, h)$, is fully efficient.

(ii) When $q_1, \ldots, q_g$ and h are unknown they can only be estimated efficiently from the full multivariate model.

(iii) Notwithstanding result (ii) the difference between the single equation estimator of λ and the GLS estimator, $\tilde{\lambda}(q_1, \ldots, q_g, h)$, converges to zero in probability at the same rate, $(1/\sqrt{T})$, as does the difference between the multivariate estimator of λ and the GLS estimator.

8.6.2 Explanatory variables

If explanatory variables are included in the multivariate model, the set of equations in (8.6.1) is extended so as to become

$$\mathbf{y}_t = (\mathbf{z}' \otimes \mathbf{I}_N)\boldsymbol{\alpha}_t + \lambda \mathbf{w}_t + \mathbf{D}\mathbf{x}_t + \boldsymbol{\varepsilon}_t \qquad (8.6.10)$$

where $\mathbf{D}$ is an $N \times K$ matrix of parameters and $\mathbf{x}_t$ is a $K \times 1$ vector of explanatory variables; compare the somewhat different formulations in (8.2.19). Estimating this complete model will give an asymptotically efficient estimator of λ. The only questions concern the efficiency of single equation procedures. Again the analysis will be based on the random walk plus noise model with $N=2$, in which case (8.6.10) specialises to

$$y_{1t} = \mu_{1t} + \mathbf{x}'_{1t}\boldsymbol{\delta}_1 + \varepsilon_{1t} \qquad (8.6.11a)$$

$$y_{2t} = \mu_{2t} + \mathbf{x}'_{2t}\boldsymbol{\delta}_2 + \varepsilon_{2t}, \quad t=1, \ldots, T \qquad (8.6.11b)$$

The single equations do not necessarily contain all the explanatory variables in $\mathbf{x}_t$.

It is clear from the analysis of the previous sub-section that a necessary condition for a single equation procedure to be valid is that the system be homogeneous. Given that this is the case, (8.6.10) can be decomposed in the same way as in (8.6.9) to give

$$y_{1t} = \beta y_{2t} + \lambda w_t + \mathbf{x}_t'\boldsymbol{\delta} + \frac{\eta_t}{\Delta} + \varepsilon_t \tag{8.6.12a}$$

$$y_{2t} = \mathbf{x}_{2t}'\boldsymbol{\delta}_2 + \frac{\eta_{2t}}{\Delta} + \varepsilon_{2t} \tag{8.6.12b}$$

where $\boldsymbol{\delta}$ is such that

$$\mathbf{x}_t'\boldsymbol{\delta} = \mathbf{x}_{1t}'\boldsymbol{\delta}_1 - \mathbf{x}_{2t}'\boldsymbol{\delta}_2\beta \tag{8.6.13}$$

Suppose that q is known. The intervention parameter, λ, could be estimated by applying the single equation methods of section 7.6 to (8.6.12a). All the explanatory variables in the system are included. However, the estimator of the parameter of interest, λ, will only be efficient if the likelihood function for y_{1t} and y_{2t} can be decomposed into two parts as can be done for (8.6.9). This requires that the parameters in (8.6.12a) and (8.6.12b) should be variation-free. Given that it has already been established that the variances of the disturbances in the two equations are variation-free, the issue is whether β, λ and $\boldsymbol{\delta}$ are variation-free with respect to $\boldsymbol{\delta}_2$. This is the case if, and only if, $\mathbf{x}_{1t} = \mathbf{x}_t$; in other words, $\mathbf{x}_{1t}$ must contain all the explanatory variables in the system. This being the case, $\mathbf{x}_t$ and $\boldsymbol{\delta}_1$ can be partitioned conformably as:

$$\mathbf{x}_t = \begin{bmatrix} \bar{\mathbf{x}}_{2t} \\ \mathbf{x}_{2t} \end{bmatrix}, \quad \boldsymbol{\delta}_1 = \begin{bmatrix} \bar{\boldsymbol{\delta}}_{1,2} \\ \boldsymbol{\delta}_{1,2} \end{bmatrix}$$

Then

$$\mathbf{x}_t'\boldsymbol{\delta} = \bar{\mathbf{x}}_{2t}'\bar{\boldsymbol{\delta}}_{1,2} + \mathbf{x}_{2t}'(\boldsymbol{\delta}_{1,2} - \beta\boldsymbol{\delta}_2) \tag{8.6.14}$$

and so $\boldsymbol{\delta}$ can take any set of values in the parameter space, irrespective of the value assigned to $\boldsymbol{\delta}_2$. Thus y_{2t}, $\mathbf{x}_t$ and w_t are weakly exogenous for the parameter of interest, λ.

If $\mathbf{x}_{1t}$ does not include all the elements of $\mathbf{x}_{2t}$, the estimator of λ given by applying single equation methods to (8.6.10a) will be unbiased, but it could be very inefficient. Single equation estimation can only be recommended if $\mathbf{x}_{1t} = \mathbf{x}_t$. When q is unknown, the same considerations apply as in the previous sub-section. Finally note that when $\boldsymbol{\Sigma}_\eta = \mathbf{0}$, (8.6.10) is a SURE system and λ can be estimated efficiently simply by regressing y_{1t} on y_{2t}, w_t and $\mathbf{x}_t$.

8.6.3 *Application to the UK seat belt law*

The use of intervention analysis to assess the effects of the UK seat belt law on car drivers killed and seriously injured (KSI) was described in sub-section 7.6.4. Drivers of heavy goods vehicles (HGVs) are not subject to the seat belt law and this suggests that the series on HGV drivers KSI might be used as a control group for car drivers KSI.

In order to model the series on HGV drivers, it was found that the square root transformation, $y=2(\sqrt{\text{HGV drivers KSI}}-1)$ was necessary in order to give a model with stable variance throughout the series. Such a transformation arises because of the relatively small number of casualties each month and the fact that the square root transformation is the variance-stabilising transformation for a Poisson distribution; see the discussion on count data in the context of the Chicago purse snatchers in sub-section 6.6.4.

Two exogenous explanatory variables were tried in the model: the HGV mileage index and the real price of petrol (gasoline). The former was found to be significant while the latter was not. This is perhaps not surprising since the petrol price variable was introduced for cars in order to reflect the reduction in speed associated with a sharp rise in the price of petrol. The estimated model for HGVs using data up to and including December 1982 was:

$$\tilde{\sigma}_\varepsilon^2=1.296, \quad \tilde{\sigma}_\eta^2=0.0672, \quad \tilde{\sigma}_\zeta^2=0.00033, \quad \tilde{\sigma}_\omega^2=0.00516$$

$$\text{HGV mileage index}=\underset{(0.0013)}{0.0033}$$

There is a case for using a control variable without explanatory variables being included, on the grounds that the inclusion of explanatory variables is not always firmly grounded in any theory. The pure time series bivariate model, (8.6.1), was therefore estimated first, using the data from 1969 to 1982 and imposing the homogeneity constraint. However, the LM statistic for testing homogeneity, described in sub-section 8.4.4 gave a value of 18.48. Since the 5% significance value for the χ_6^2 distribution is 12.6 the null hypothesis of homogeneity is clearly rejected.[1] If HGV casualties are to be used as a control group in a model without explanatory variables, therefore, it would be advisable to carry out intervention analysis based on the unrestricted bivariate model.

Estimating the homogeneous bivariate model with explanatory variables[2]

1. The fact that estimating the car drivers' equation in isolation gave $\tilde{\sigma}_\zeta^2$ and $\tilde{\sigma}_\omega^2$ equal to zero casts doubt on the validity of the asymptotic distribution of the test statistic in this case. In addition the normality assumption for the measurement equation disturbance in the HGV model is clearly an approximation, though it does not seem to be an unreasonable one.

2. Estimation was carried out using the program for a pure time series model, but first subtracting the effect of the explanatory variables from the casualty figures. Although this does not exploit the full potential of the model in providing efficient estimators of the coefficients of the explanatory variables, it does not affect the asymptotic efficiency of the estimators of the elements of the covariance matrices $\Sigma_\varepsilon, \Sigma_\eta, \Sigma_\zeta$ and Σ_ω. The large-sample properties of the LM test are also unaffected.

included gave the following estimates for car drivers:

$$\tilde{\sigma}_\varepsilon^2 = 3.464 \times 10^{-3}, \quad \tilde{\sigma}_\eta^2 = 0.320 \times 10^{-3}, \quad \tilde{\sigma}_\zeta^2 = 5.64 \times 10^{-7}, \quad \tilde{\sigma}_\omega^2 = 4.47 \times 10^{-4}$$

while for HGV drivers

$$\tilde{\sigma}_\varepsilon^2 = 1.693, \quad \tilde{\sigma}_\eta^2 = 0.156, \quad \tilde{\sigma}_\zeta^2 = 2.76 \times 10^{-4}, \quad \tilde{\sigma}_\omega^2 = 0.219$$

These values are not too far from the values estimated by taking each equation in isolation. The correlation between each pair of disturbances was estimated as $\rho = 0.273$. The value of the LM statistic for homogeneity was 13.95. Although this is still significant at the 5% level, it is only marginally so, and hence an assumption of homogeneity may not be too unreasonable. In these circumstances formula (8.6.6) suggests a reduction of 7.5% in the variance of the estimator of the intervention effect, γ.

Estimating a univariate structural model for car drivers KSI with the control variable taken to be

$$y_{2t}^* = 2(\sqrt{\text{HGV drivers KSI}} - 1) - 0.0033 \text{ (HGV mileage index)}$$

gave, for 1969 to 1982,

$$\tilde{\sigma}_\varepsilon^2 = 3.804 \times 10^{-3}, \quad \tilde{\sigma}_\eta^2 = 3.178 \times 10^{-4}, \tilde{\sigma}_\zeta^2 = 0, \quad \tilde{\sigma}_\omega^2 = 0$$

$$\text{HGV control} = \underset{(0.0038)}{0.0102}, \quad \text{petrol price} = \underset{(0.103)}{-0.303}$$

with

$$s = 0.716, \quad R^2 = 0.79, \quad R_s^2 = 0.34$$

$$H(51) = 1.005, \quad Q(15) = 19.48, \quad \text{normality} = 0.867$$

Despite the question mark over homogeneity, all the diagnostics, including the Box-Ljung Q-statistic, indicate that the model is satisfactory. Estimating the effect of the intervention using data for 1983 to 1984 gave:

$$\tilde{\lambda} = \underset{(0.0511)}{-0.2782}$$

Thus the percentage reduction in drivers KSI is estimated to be slightly higher at 24.3%. The reduction in variance associated with the use of the control group is 6.8%, which is close to the 7.5% reduction predicted on the basis of the bivariate model. This is not as great as one might have hoped. Clearly HGVs are not the ideal control group for cars, possibly because the nature of HGV accidents tends to be rather different.

8.7 Missing observations, delayed observations and contemporaneous aggregation

Missing observations can be handled in a multivariate model by adopting the methods set out in sub-section 3.4.7. Estimates of the missing observations are then produced by a smoothing algorithm. If observations have been contemporaneously aggregated, the smoothing algorithm distributes the aggregated observations amongst the various series. Temporal aggregation can be handled by extending the procedures to include the cumulator variable device introduced in section 6.3.

This section examines three issues which arise when data irregularities are considered within a SUTSE framework. The first concerns the way in which related series can be used to estimate missing and temporally aggregated observations in the series of interest. The second is how related series can be used to obtain preliminary estimates of observations which have been delayed. The third concerns the consequences of working with a contemporaneously aggregated series rather than the individual series.

8.7.1 Estimation of missing observations using related series

The issues of interpolation and distribution were considered in section 6.3. In section 6.4, we looked at the related problems of temporal aggregation and missing observations. The methods for solving these problems can all be extended very easily to models which include an explanatory variable, or variables. Thus, the measurement equation becomes

$$y_t = \mathbf{z}_t'\boldsymbol{\alpha}_t + \mathbf{x}_t'\boldsymbol{\delta} + \varepsilon_t \tag{8.7.1}$$

The use of related variables to estimate values in the series of interest was considered by Chow and Lin (1971, 1976). They considered a standard regression model with stationary AR(1) disturbances. In a later paper, Fernandez (1981) argued the merits of having the disturbance term follow a random walk, while Litterman (1983) combined the two approaches by modelling the disturbance as an ARIMA (1, 1, 0) process. All of these models can be regarded as special cases of (8.7.1). However, in order for the proposed methods to be valid, $\mathbf{x}_t$ must be weakly exogenous. As will be shown below this is not an assumption which can necessarily be taken for granted.

In setting out a regression model, Chow and Lin, Fernandez and Litterman all assume that this represents the way the data are generated. However, this does not, in general, make sense in the present context because there is usually no behavioural relationship between the 'dependent' and 'explanatory' variables. Rather they are variables which tend to move together because they are measuring similar things and are affected by a similar environment. Thus, for example, Litterman (1983) quite sensibly uses the consumer price index, which is available on a monthly basis, as a related variable for estimating monthly values of the quarterly series on the personal consumption price deflator. But the personal consumption deflator obviously does not depend on the consumer price index in any behavioural way. Rather the two variables are jointly determined by the economic forces which underlie changes in the price level. The starting point should therefore not be a regression model, but a multivariate time series model, or, more specifically, a SUTSE model.

Suppose, without loss in generality, that y_{1t} is the series with missing or temporally aggregated observations and that we have available $N-1$ related series, $y_{2t}, \ldots, y_{Nt}$ with the full complement of observations. The full model can be estimated in the time domain and estimates of the missing or temporally aggregated observations made using a smoothing algorithm. This is, in principle, the optimal solution to the problem given that it is reasonable to regard the N series as being generated by a SUTSE model. The interesting question, however, concerns the circumstances in which the problem can be solved within a single equation framework.

Suppose, for simplicity, that $N=2$ and that these series can be modelled as a multivariate local level process, that is (8.2.1). Following the discussion in sub-section 8.6.1, we know that if the system is homogeneous, we can write

$$y_{1t}=\beta y_{2t}+\mu_t+\varepsilon_t \tag{8.7.2}$$

where β is as defined in (8.6.8) while $\eta_t=\eta_{1t}-\beta\eta_{2t}$ and $\varepsilon_t=\varepsilon_{1t}-\beta\varepsilon_{2t}$. This is a special case of (8.7.1) with y_{2t} being the explanatory variable. Given the signal–noise ratio, q, y_{2t} is weakly exogenous. Even if q is unknown, working with (8.7.2) is still perfectly valid, although there is a loss of efficiency in estimating q if the information in the equation for y_{2t}, (8.6.9b), is neglected. If the system is not homogeneous, and y_{2t} is used as a regressor in a model of the form (8.7.2), it will be correlated with the disturbance term. However, suppose that the disturbances in the trend component, η_{1t} and η_{2t}, are perfectly correlated. In this case we have a common trend model, (8.5.1), with $\boldsymbol{\theta}'=[1 \quad 1/\beta]$, and (8.7.1) becomes

$$y_{1t}=\beta y_{2t}+\bar{\mu}+\varepsilon_t \tag{8.7.3}$$

Because y_{1t} and y_{2t} are co-integrated, it follows from the general results in Stock (1987) that regressing y_{1t} on y_{2t} gives a consistent and asymptotically efficient estimator of β even though y_{2t} and ε_t are correlated.

Car front seat passengers The series on car drivers killed and seriously injured (KSI) introduced in sub-section 2.7.1 is closely related to the series on car front seat passengers KSI. The estimated parameters in the two models are roughly in the same proportion and this is a necessary condition for the series to be homogeneous. Thus if the passenger series were to contain missing observations, it might be reasonable to use the drivers to obtain better estimates of these observations. For illustrative purposes, it was supposed that the passenger

Table 8.7.1 *Estimates of missing observations on car front seat passenger KSI series*

	Dec. 73	May 74	June 74	May 77
Actual	992	910	883	742
Univariate	1079	862	850	777
Using drivers	1006	895	946	713

observations for December 1973, May and June 1974 and May 1977 were missing. This produced the following estimates for the period January 1969 to December 1982.

$$\tilde{\sigma}_\varepsilon^2 = 1.97 \times 10^{-3}, \quad \tilde{\sigma}_\eta^2 = 3.25 \times 10^{-7}, \quad \tilde{\sigma}_\zeta^2 = 1.55 \times 10^{-7}, \quad \tilde{\sigma}_\omega^2 = 0$$

Coefficient of car drivers = 0.946
(0.050)

These results are not consistent with the homogeneity hypothesis. Although the estimates of σ_ζ^2 and σ_ω^2 are both very close to zero in the individual and bivariate models, the estimate of σ_η^2 is also virtually equal to zero in the bivariate model while in the individual models it is of the order of one-tenth of σ_ε^2. However, the fact that the estimate of σ_η^2 is virtually zero indicates that estimating the missing observations by the bivariate model can be justified by an appeal to the properties of co-integrated variables. (The presence of deterministic trend and seasonal components in the bivariate model is a minor complication, but the trend coefficient is small and insignificant and so could be dropped from the model.) It also means that the estimation of the model could have been carried out by OLS. It is of some importance, though, that the more general technique is able to reduce to the simpler one when the latter is appropriate.

Table 8.7.1 compares the estimates of the 'missing values' computed using the related series with those obtained from a univariate model. The prediction error variances in the two models at the end of the series were 0.0024 and 0.0075 so some gain can be expected by using a related series. Both series were subject to shocks at the end of 1973 and the beginning of 1974 because of the oil crisis and so the information on a related variable should be particularly useful for the first three missing observations. This is apparent in the figures for December 1973 and May 1974, but not for June 1974.

8.7.2 Delayed observations

Statistical agencies are often faced with a situation in which the observations on some series typically become available somewhat later than the observations on related series. This is a special case of missing observations, and a SUTSE framework can be used to provide preliminary estimates of the current values of the series which have not been observed, by using the series which have been observed. However, because the observations are only missing temporarily, it is not necessary to employ a program which can handle missing observations. The appropriate expressions can be obtained explicitly.

To formalise matters, suppose that of N series, data on the first N_1 series are not available in the latest time period. Thus $\mathbf{y}_T = [\mathbf{y}'_{1T} \quad \mathbf{y}'_{2T}]'$ with $\mathbf{y}_{1T}$ and $\mathbf{y}_{2T}$ being $N_1 \times 1$ and $N_2 \times 1$ vectors respectively, and $\mathbf{y}_{2T}$ being observed. Information on $\mathbf{y}_{1T}$ will become available in due course, but the immediate problem is to find the best estimator of it based on the information which is available. This estimator is

$$\tilde{\mathbf{y}}_{1T} = \mathrm{E}(\mathbf{y}_{1T} | \mathbf{y}_{2T}, \mathbf{Y}_{T-1}) \tag{8.7.4}$$

For a general SUTSE model in the SSF of (8.2.11), the solution is given as follows. The measurement equation at time T is

$$\mathbf{y}_{2T} = (\mathbf{z}' \otimes \mathbf{W}_2)\boldsymbol{\alpha}_T + \boldsymbol{\varepsilon}_{2T} \tag{8.7.5}$$

where $\boldsymbol{\varepsilon}_{2T}$ comprises the last N_2 elements of $\boldsymbol{\varepsilon}_T$ and

$$\mathbf{W}_2 = [\mathbf{0} \quad \mathbf{I}_{N_2}]$$

At time T, it is possible to compute $\mathbf{a}_{T|T-1}$, the optimal estimator of the state vector at time T based on the full complement of observations on all N series up to, and including, $\mathbf{Y}_{T-1}$. In addition, the availability of $\mathbf{y}_{2T}$ means that partial updating of the estimator of the state vector is possible by setting $\mathbf{Z}_T = \mathbf{z}' \otimes \mathbf{W}_2$ in the Kalman filter updating equation. If $\tilde{\mathbf{a}}_T$ denotes the partially updated state vector then

$$\tilde{\mathbf{a}}_T = \mathbf{a}_{T|T-1} + \mathbf{P}_{T|T-1}(\mathbf{z} \otimes \mathbf{W}'_2)\mathbf{F}_T^{-1}(\mathbf{y}_{2T} - (\mathbf{z}' \otimes \mathbf{W}_2)\mathbf{a}_{T|T-1}) \tag{8.7.6}$$

where

$$\mathbf{F}_T = (\mathbf{z}' \otimes \mathbf{W}_2)\mathbf{P}_{T|T-1}(\mathbf{z} \otimes \mathbf{W}'_2) + \mathbf{H}_2$$

with $\mathbf{H}_2 = \mathrm{Var}(\boldsymbol{\varepsilon}_{2T})$. The optimal estimator of $\mathbf{y}_{1T}$, (8.7.4), is therefore

$$\tilde{\mathbf{y}}_{1T} = (\mathbf{z}' \otimes \mathbf{W}_1)\tilde{\mathbf{a}}_T \tag{8.7.7}$$

where $\mathbf{W}_1 = [\mathbf{I}_{N_1} \quad \mathbf{0}]$. Combining (8.7.6) and (8.7.7) gives the direct expression

$$\tilde{\mathbf{y}}_{1T} = \tilde{\mathbf{y}}_{1T|T-1} + (\mathbf{z}' \otimes \mathbf{W}_1)\mathbf{P}_{T|T-1}(\mathbf{z}' \otimes \mathbf{W}'_2)\mathbf{F}_T^{-1}(\mathbf{y}_{2T} - \tilde{\mathbf{y}}_{2T|T-1}) \tag{8.7.8}$$

The MSE of this estimator is

$$\mathrm{MSE}(\tilde{\mathbf{y}}_{1T}) = (\mathbf{z}' \otimes \mathbf{W}_1)\mathbf{P}_T(\mathbf{z} \otimes \mathbf{W}'_1) + \mathbf{H}_1 \tag{8.7.9}$$

where $\mathbf{H}_1 = \mathrm{Var}(\boldsymbol{\varepsilon}_{1T})$.

As might be expected, the above expressions simplify considerably in a homogeneous model. In a model of the form (8.3.19),

$$\mathbf{P}_{T|T-1} = \mathbf{P}^*_{T|T-1} \otimes \boldsymbol{\Sigma}_*$$

where $\sigma_*^2 \mathbf{P}_{T|T-1}^*$ is the MSE matrix appropriate to a univariate model. Partitioning $\mathbf{\Sigma}_*$ conformably with $\mathbf{y}_{1T}$ and $\mathbf{y}_{2T}$ and substituting for $\mathbf{P}_{T|T-1}$ in (8.7.8) gives

$$\begin{aligned}\tilde{\mathbf{y}}_{1T} &= \tilde{\mathbf{y}}_{1T|T-1} \\ &\quad + (\mathbf{z}'\mathbf{P}_{T|T-1}^*\mathbf{z} \otimes \mathbf{\Sigma}_{*,12})(\mathbf{z}'\mathbf{P}_{T|T-1}^*\mathbf{z} \otimes \mathbf{\Sigma}_{*,22} + h\mathbf{\Sigma}_{*,22})^{-1}(\mathbf{y}_{2T} - \tilde{\mathbf{y}}_{2T|T-1}) \\ &= \tilde{\mathbf{y}}_{1T|T-1} + [\mathbf{z}'\mathbf{P}_{T|T-1}^*\mathbf{z}/(\mathbf{z}'\mathbf{P}_{T|T-1}^*\mathbf{z} + h)]\mathbf{\Sigma}_{*,12}\mathbf{\Sigma}_{*,22}^{-1}(\mathbf{y}_{2T} - \tilde{\mathbf{y}}_{2T|T-1})\end{aligned}$$

Thus the extent to which the information in $\mathbf{y}_{2T}$ is used to get a better estimator of $\mathbf{y}_{1T}$ depends on the $N_1 \times N_2$ covariance matrix, $\mathbf{\Sigma}_{*,12}$. The MSE of $\mathbf{y}_{1T}$ can be evaluated in a similar way by first noting that

$$\mathbf{P}_T = \mathbf{P}_{T|T-1}^* \otimes \mathbf{\Sigma}_* - (\mathbf{P}_{T|T-1}\mathbf{z} \otimes \mathbf{\Sigma}_* \mathbf{W}_2')\mathbf{\Sigma}_{*,22}^{-1} f_T^{-1}(\mathbf{z}'\mathbf{P}_{T|T-1} \otimes \mathbf{W}_2 \mathbf{\Sigma}_*)$$

and so substituting in (8.7.9) gives

$$\text{MSE}(\tilde{\mathbf{y}}_{1T}) = f_T \mathbf{\Sigma}_{11} - [(\mathbf{z}'\mathbf{P}_{T|T-1}^*\mathbf{z})/f_T]^2 \mathbf{\Sigma}_{*,12}\mathbf{\Sigma}_{*,22}^{-1}\mathbf{\Sigma}_{*,21} \qquad (8.7.10)$$

The expression can be obtained by writing the error vector associated with (8.7.8) as

$$\mathbf{y}_{1T} - \tilde{\mathbf{y}}_{1T} = (\mathbf{y}_{1T} - \tilde{\mathbf{y}}_{1T|T-1}) - (\mathbf{z}'\mathbf{P}_{T|T-1}^*\mathbf{z}/f_T)\mathbf{\Sigma}_{*,12}\mathbf{\Sigma}_{*,22}^{-1}(\mathbf{y}_{2T} - \tilde{\mathbf{y}}_{2T|T-1})$$

and then evaluating its MSE matrix. Using the knowledge, from (8.3.14), that

$$\text{E}[(\mathbf{y}_{1T} - \tilde{\mathbf{y}}_{1T|T-1})(\mathbf{y}_{2T} - \tilde{\mathbf{y}}_{2T|T-1})'] = f_T \mathbf{\Sigma}_{*,12}$$

the first term in (8.7.10) is $\text{MSE}(\tilde{\mathbf{y}}_{1T|T-1})$. The second term is the reduction in MSE achieved by using the information in $\mathbf{y}_{2T}$. Thus

$$\text{MSE}(\tilde{\mathbf{y}}_{1T}) = \text{MSE}(\tilde{\mathbf{y}}_{1T|T-1})[\mathbf{I} - (1 - h/f_T)^2 \mathbf{\Sigma}_{*,12}\mathbf{\Sigma}_{*,22}^{-1}\mathbf{\Sigma}_{*,21}\mathbf{\Sigma}_{*,11}^{-1}] \qquad (8.7.11)$$

If $N_1 = 1$ and $h = 0$, the term in square brackets is $1 - \rho^2$, where ρ^2 is the coefficient of determination between the innovations in the first series and the innovations in the $N-1$ related series. A similar expression was obtained in the context of control groups in (8.6.7).

8.7.3 Contemporaneous aggregation

Suppose that it is possible to construct a SUTSE model for N series, $\mathbf{y}_t$, but that the ultimate goal is to forecast the weighted aggregate

$$y_{T+l}^a = \mathbf{w}'\mathbf{y}_{T+l}, \quad l = 1, 2, \ldots \qquad (8.7.12)$$

where $\mathbf{w}$ is an $N \times 1$ vector of weights. If the parameters in the SUTSE model are known, it follows from (8.2.4) that the parameters in the corresponding univariate model for y_t^a are also known. Given this information we wish to compare $\text{MSE}(\tilde{y}_{T+l|T}^a)$ with $\text{MSE}(\mathbf{w}'\tilde{\mathbf{y}}_{T+l|T})$.

If, in a homogeneous model, the parameters $h, q_1, \ldots, q_g$ are known, the forecasts for y_t^a are constructed using the same Kalman filter as is used for the individual series in $\mathbf{y}_t$. The forecast constructed from the individual series is therefore identical to the forecast constructed from the aggregate series, that is

$$y^a_{T+l|T} = \mathbf{w}'\tilde{\mathbf{y}}_{T+l|T} \tag{8.7.13}$$

Of course, if as is usually the case, the parameters h, $q_1, \ldots, q_g$ need to be estimated, there is a gain from using all the series to do so. This translates into a slight gain in the prediction MSE.

The result that forecasts are fully efficient holds under somewhat weaker conditions than homogeneity. In the multivariate local level model, (8.2.1), Fernández (1986) shows that if $\mathbf{\Sigma}_\eta$ and $\mathbf{\Sigma}_\varepsilon$ are known, a necessary and sufficient condition for (8.7.13) to hold is that the $N \times 1$ vector $\mathbf{\Sigma}_\eta \mathbf{w}$ be proportional to the $N \times 1$ vector $\mathbf{\Sigma}_\varepsilon \mathbf{w}$. Furthermore the factor of proportionality is the signal–noise ratio in the aggregate model, that is $q = \mathbf{w}'\mathbf{\Sigma}_\eta \mathbf{w}/\mathbf{w}'\mathbf{\Sigma}_\varepsilon \mathbf{w}$. Fernández also investigates the loss in forecasting efficiency in the random walk plus noise model when the above condition does not hold. He tabulates

$$\text{Eff}(l) = \frac{\text{MSE}(\mathbf{w}'\tilde{\mathbf{y}}_{T+l|T})}{\text{MSE}(y^a_{T+l|T})} = \frac{\mathbf{w}'\mathbf{P}_T\mathbf{w}' + r(l)}{p_T + r(l)} \tag{8.7.14}$$

where $\mathbf{P}_T$ is the MSE matrix of the estimator of the vector of levels, $\mathbf{m}_T$, in the multivariate model and p_T is the MSE of the estimator of m^a_T, the level in the aggregate model. The term

$$r(l) = l\mathbf{w}'\mathbf{\Sigma}_\eta \mathbf{w} + \mathbf{w}'\mathbf{\Sigma}_\varepsilon \mathbf{w}$$

appears in both the numerator and the denominator because of (8.7.14). As l increases, this term tends to dominate both the numerator and the denominator and as $l \to \infty$, $\text{Eff}(l) \to 1$.

8.8 Vector autoregressive models

A VAR(p) model was introduced in (8.1.2). Such models are very easy to estimate as it can be shown that OLS applied to each equation in turn is asymptotically efficient. The use of VARs in econometrics was advocated by Sims (1980, 1982), who argued that, in the absence of firm *a priori* theory concerning model specification, such models provided a practical method of forecasting. The main disadvantage of VARs is that they typically involve a large number of parameters, specifically N^2p excluding the parameters of the covariance matrix of the disturbance term.

A VAR with a low value of p, say one or two, can still yield a rich pattern of dynamics as the following example illustrates.

Example 8.8.1 The mink–muskrat data set was introduced in chapter 1 and was graphed in Figure 1.3.2. A preliminary analysis of the two series carried out by Chan and Wallis (1978) indicated that taking logarithms is appropriate, and that the mink series is stationary, while the muskrat series requires first-differencing.

In order not to distort the relationship between the two series, Chan and Wallis fitted various multivariate models after first detrending each series by regressing on t and t^2; see also Harvey (1981b, pp. 185–90). The model they eventually settled on for the detrended data was a VAR(1) process:

$$\hat{y}_{1t} = 0.79y_{1,t-1} - 0.68y_{2,t-1} \tag{8.8.1a}$$

$$\hat{y}_{2t} = 0.29y_{1,t-1} + 0.51y_{2,t-1} \tag{8.8.1b}$$

with

$$\hat{\boldsymbol{\Sigma}} = \begin{bmatrix} 0.061 & 0.022 \\ 0.022 & 0.058 \end{bmatrix}$$

The determinantal polynomial, defined implicitly by (8.1.10), is

$$|\boldsymbol{\Phi}(\mathrm{L})| = 1 - 1.30\mathrm{L} + 0.60\mathrm{L}^2 \tag{8.8.2}$$

This has complex roots and yields stochastic cycles similar to those observed in the data. Further analysis shows that the properties of the fitted VAR(1) process reveal that it reproduces a lead–lag structure consistent with the prey–predator relationship known to exist between minks and muskrats.

Fitting VARs to non-stationary series can lead to serious problems in small samples. Although prior detrending appears to work reasonably well in the mink–muskrat example, the discussion in sub-section 6.1.3 suggests that it may lead to considerable distortion. Remember that prior detrending is essentially the same as fitting a model of the form

$$\boldsymbol{\Phi}(\mathrm{L})\mathbf{y}_t = \boldsymbol{\alpha} + \boldsymbol{\beta}t + \boldsymbol{\varepsilon}_t \tag{8.8.3}$$

where $\boldsymbol{\alpha}$ and $\boldsymbol{\beta}$ are $n \times 1$ vectors of unknown parameters. Even if trends are allowed for in this way, allowance should still be made for the possibility that some roots in the AR polynomial may lie on the unit circle. The asymptotic properties of VARs estimated with and without detrending are discussed in Sims *et al.* (1987).

Differencing does not, in general, provide a satisfactory way of fitting VARs to non-stationary time series, since different series may have different orders of integration. This is illustrated in the mink–muskrat application where first-differencing of the mink series would lead to a strictly non-invertible MA component. Hence an autoregressive model would not provide a reasonable approximation. The same is true when the series are co-integrated.

Example 8.8.2 Consider the model

$$y_{1t} = y_{1,t-1} + \eta_t \tag{8.8.4a}$$

$$y_{2t} = \beta y_{1,t} + \varepsilon_t \tag{8.8.4b}$$

where η_t and ε_t are white-noise disturbances. Both series are $I(1)$ but the second equation immediately shows that they are co-integrated. Taking first differences gives the vector ARMA(1, 1) model

$$\begin{bmatrix}\Delta y_{1t}\\ \Delta y_{2t}\end{bmatrix}=\begin{bmatrix}0 & 0\\ \beta & 0\end{bmatrix}\begin{bmatrix}\Delta y_{1,t-1}\\ \Delta y_{2,t-1}\end{bmatrix}+\begin{bmatrix}1 & 0\\ \beta(1-\mathrm{L}) & (1-\mathrm{L})\end{bmatrix}\begin{bmatrix}\eta_t\\ \varepsilon_t\end{bmatrix} \tag{8.8.5}$$

The MA matrix polynomial has one root equal to unity and is therefore strictly non-invertible.

The only viable way of handling non-stationary vector autoregressions, in general, would appear to be to estimate them in levels. The main difficulty is that when the series are non-stationary, the need to have a high-order AR may be even stronger than in the stationary case. A structural model offers the possibility of a more parsimonious model. It also allows co-integration restrictions to be imposed.

8.8.1 *Vector autoregressions with stochastic trends*

There are a number of ways of incorporating stochastic trend components into vector autoregressions.

Additive The vector of observations may be regarded as being the sum of a vector of stochastic trends, $\boldsymbol{\mu}_t$, and a stationary VAR. Thus

$$\mathbf{y}_t=\boldsymbol{\mu}_t+\boldsymbol{\Phi}^{-1}(\mathrm{L})\boldsymbol{\varepsilon}_t \tag{8.8.6a}$$

$$\boldsymbol{\mu}_t=\boldsymbol{\mu}_{t-1}+\boldsymbol{\beta}+\boldsymbol{\eta}_t \tag{8.8.6b}$$

where $\boldsymbol{\Phi}(\mathrm{L})$ is an r-th order matrix polynomial of the form (8.1.3), in which the roots lie outside the unit circle. The trend component could be generalised by allowing the slope, $\boldsymbol{\beta}$, to follow a multivariate random walk. In addition other components, such as seasonals, could be added to (8.8.6a). However, the main points at issue can be conveyed by focussing attention on the model as it stands.

The model in (8.8.6) expresses the observations as the sum of a trend component and a short-term component. The latter may exhibit pseudo-cyclical behaviour due to the interactions between the variables induced by the form of $\boldsymbol{\Phi}(\mathrm{L})$; compare Example 8.8.1. The trend plus cycle model of (2.3.63) may provide a way of capturing the behaviour of a single equation in (8.8.6).

Vector autoregressive trends The cyclical trend model, (2.3.64), suggests a specification in which the VAR is incorporated within the trend component. Thus the model is:

$$\mathbf{y}_t=\boldsymbol{\mu}_t+\boldsymbol{\varepsilon}_t \tag{8.8.7a}$$

$$\boldsymbol{\mu}_t=\boldsymbol{\mu}_{t-1}+\boldsymbol{\beta}+\boldsymbol{\Phi}^{-1}(\mathrm{L})\boldsymbol{\eta}_t \tag{8.8.7b}$$

Dynamic The model in (8.8.6) is a generalisation of the univariate model in (2.3.72). In (2.3.73) an alternative autoregressive model was set up by directly including lagged values of y_t in the right-hand side of the equation. The multivariate generalisation of this model is:

$$\mathbf{\Phi}(L)\mathbf{y}_t = \boldsymbol{\mu}_t + \boldsymbol{\varepsilon}_t \tag{8.8.8a}$$

$$\boldsymbol{\mu}_t = \boldsymbol{\mu}_{t-1} + \boldsymbol{\beta} + \boldsymbol{\eta}_t \tag{8.8.8b}$$

where, as in the previous two multivariate models, the roots of $\mathbf{\Phi}(L)$ lie outside the unit circle. This formulation fits in somewhat more easily with the *multivariate autoregressive distributed lag* model,

$$\mathbf{\Phi}(L)\mathbf{y}_t = \mathbf{B}(L)\mathbf{x}_t + \boldsymbol{\xi}_t \tag{8.8.9}$$

where $\mathbf{x}_t$ is a $K \times 1$ vector of exogenous variables and $\mathbf{B}(L)$ is a matrix polynomial in the lag operator. In (8.8.9) the exogenous variables are able to account for the movement in the endogenous variables, $\mathbf{y}_t$, which in (8.8.8) are picked up by the vector of stochastic trends. There is an intermediate situation in which (8.8.8) would be extended to include some exogenous variables, but not enough to make the stochastic trends redundant.

The model in (8.8.8) includes VARs with deterministic trends, (8.8.3), as a special case. In fact some of the trends may be deterministic, while others remain stochastic. In the extreme case when $\mathbf{\Sigma}_\varepsilon = \mathbf{0}$, the model is a pure VAR in first differences, that is

$$\mathbf{\Phi}(L)\Delta\mathbf{y}_t = \boldsymbol{\beta} + \boldsymbol{\eta}_t \tag{8.8.10}$$

An attraction of working with (8.8.8) is that preliminary estimators may be obtained by estimating each of the N equations separately. The i-th equation is:

$$y_{it} = \sum_{j=1}^{N} \varphi_{ij}(L)y_{jt} + \mu_{it} + \varepsilon_{it}, \quad i = 1, \ldots, N \tag{8.8.11}$$

where $\varphi_{ij}(L)$ is the ij-th element in the matrix $\mathbf{I} - \mathbf{\Phi}(L)$. Estimation may be carried out in the time or the frequency domain. If, in the model as a whole, $\boldsymbol{\mu}_t$ and $\boldsymbol{\varepsilon}_t$ satisfy the homogeneity conditions, that is $\mathbf{\Sigma}_\eta = q\mathbf{\Sigma}_\varepsilon$, and q is known, then the estimators of the parameters in the $\varphi_{ij}(L)$'s will be asymptotically efficient in the absence of any known restrictions on them. When q is unknown, then it follows from section 8.3 that there is a gain in the efficiency of estimating it by pooling the equations. If $\mathbf{\Sigma}_\eta$ and $\mathbf{\Sigma}_\varepsilon$ are not proportional, single equation estimation at least provides a means of exploring possible specifications and gaining some idea of the appropriate length of lag to put on the autoregressive estimator. The estimators of $\boldsymbol{\varepsilon}_t$ and $\boldsymbol{\eta}_t$ obtained by smoothing each equation individually may perhaps be used to construct initial estimators of $\mathbf{\Sigma}_\eta$ and $\mathbf{\Sigma}_\varepsilon$.

Example 8.8.3 The mink–muskrat data was introduced earlier in Example 8.8.1.

The model presented there was fitted after prior detrending of the data. We now consider fitting a model of the form (8.8.8) without prior detrending. The first step is to fit univariate models as indicated by (8.8.11). For generality, the trend components were initially taken to be of the local linear trend form, even though the mink series shows no distinctive upward or downward movement.

If two lags on the variables are initially included in the mink equation, the result, using exact ML, is

$$y_{2t}=m_{2,t|T}+\underset{(0.15)}{0.51}y_{2,t-1}+\underset{(0.13)}{0.47}y_{1,t-1}+\underset{(0.17)}{0.15}y_{2,t-2}-\underset{(0.13)}{0.11}y_{1,t-2}+e_{2,t|T} \qquad (8.8.12)$$

with

$$\tilde{\sigma}_\eta^2=\underset{(0.0000018)}{0.0000012}, \quad \tilde{\sigma}_\zeta^2=0, \quad \tilde{\sigma}_\varepsilon^2=\underset{(0.0121)}{0.0644}$$

The diagnostics are acceptable. Clearly the second-order lags are insignificant and may be dropped. The variance of the slope is zero, while the variance of the level is close to zero. This suggests that a deterministic trend may be appropriate. Since the estimate of the slope had a t-value of -2.52, it would seem reasonable to keep this term in the equation. Estimating the simplified model gives

$$\hat{y}_{2t}=\underset{(0.075)}{0.087}-\underset{(0.0023)}{0.0070}t+\underset{(0.09)}{0.58}y_{2,t-1}+\underset{(0.08)}{0.35}y_{1,t-1} \qquad (8.8.13)$$

with

$$s=0.249, \quad N=5.46, \quad H(19)=0.52$$
$$Q(7)=2.59, \quad Q(14)=13.75$$

The model seems to give a good fit to the data.

As regards the muskrats, fitting the general model initially reported for the minks also showed second-order lags to be unnecessary. Furthermore σ_ζ^2 was estimated at zero. However, the estimate of σ_η^2 was not close to zero, suggesting a random walk plus drift specification. Estimating this model gave

$$y_{1t}=m_{1,t|T}+\underset{(0.10)}{0.61}y_{1,t-1}-\underset{(0.12)}{0.76}y_{2,t-1}+e_{1,t|T} \qquad (8.8.14)$$

and

$$\tilde{\sigma}_\eta^2=\underset{(0.013)}{0.032}, \quad \tilde{\sigma}_\varepsilon^2=\underset{(0.010)}{0.025}$$

with

$$s=0.272, \quad N=9.55, \quad H(19)=1.77$$
$$Q(7)=5.71, \quad Q(14)=14.55$$

Again this seems to give a reasonably good fit, except insofar as the normality test statistic is somewhat too high.

The specifications of the univariate models suggest fitting a multivariate model of the form (8.8.8) with $r=1$.

It is interesting to compare the coefficients of the lagged variables with the coefficients reported in Example 8.8.1. All four coefficients are relatively close in the two models. Hence the dynamic properties implied by (8.8.13) and (8.8.14) are similar to the Chan and Wallis model. However, it is possible to envisage situations in which the results from detrended data could be very different to the results obtained by modelling the trends as stochastic components.

8.8.2 Common trends and co-integration

Common trends may be introduced into the vector autoregressive models described in the previous sub-section in the same way as was done in section 8.5. Thus the dimension of the trend vector, $\boldsymbol{\mu}_t$, is reduced to $K \times 1$, and an $N \times K$ matrix, $\boldsymbol{\Theta}$, is introduced into the measurement equation.

As in the common factor models of section 8.5, the presence of common trends means that the N series are co-integrated. This follows immediately for models (8.8.6) and (8.8.7). In the case of model (8.8.8), it is perhaps easiest to re-express the system in terms of the level at time $t-1$ and an autoregression in differences. As a multivariate generalisation of what was done at the end of sub-section 7.1.2, first note that by rearranging terms, the autoregressive polynomial can be written as

$$\boldsymbol{\Phi}(\mathrm{L}) = \boldsymbol{\Phi}(1)\mathrm{L} + \boldsymbol{\Phi}^{\dagger}(\mathrm{L})\Delta \tag{8.8.15}$$

where $\boldsymbol{\Phi}^{\dagger}(\mathrm{L})$ is an $N \times N$ matrix polynomial of order $r-1$ with its leading term $\boldsymbol{\Phi}^{\dagger}(0)$ equal to the identity matrix. Using this result, (8.8.8) may be written as

$$\boldsymbol{\Phi}^{\dagger}(\mathrm{L})\Delta\mathbf{y}_t = -\boldsymbol{\Phi}(1)\mathbf{y}_{t-1} + \boldsymbol{\Theta}\boldsymbol{\mu}_t + \boldsymbol{\mu}_0 + \boldsymbol{\varepsilon}_t \tag{8.8.16}$$

Since, by assumption, all the roots of $\boldsymbol{\Phi}(\mathrm{L})$ lie outside the unit circle, $\boldsymbol{\Phi}(1)$ is of full rank, and so

$$\boldsymbol{\Phi}^{-1}(1)\boldsymbol{\Phi}^{\dagger}(\mathrm{L})\Delta\mathbf{y}_t = -\mathbf{y}_{t-1} + \boldsymbol{\Phi}^{-1}(1)\boldsymbol{\Theta}\boldsymbol{\mu}_t + \boldsymbol{\Phi}^{-1}(1)\boldsymbol{\mu}_0 + \boldsymbol{\Phi}^{-1}(1)\boldsymbol{\varepsilon}_t \tag{8.8.17}$$

The $(N-K) \times N$ matrix of co-integrating vectors, $\mathbf{A}$, must therefore have the property that

$$\mathbf{A}\boldsymbol{\Phi}^{-1}(1)\boldsymbol{\Theta} = \mathbf{0} \tag{8.8.18}$$

This being the case,

$$\mathbf{A}\mathbf{y}_{t-1} = -\mathbf{A}\boldsymbol{\Phi}^{-1}(1)\boldsymbol{\Phi}^{\dagger}(\mathrm{L})\Delta\mathbf{y}_t + \mathbf{A}\boldsymbol{\Phi}^{-1}(1)\boldsymbol{\mu}_0 + \mathbf{A}\boldsymbol{\Phi}^{-1}(1)\boldsymbol{\varepsilon}_t \tag{8.8.19}$$

Since $\mathbf{y}_t$ is $I(1)$, it follows that the right-hand side of (8.8.19) is stationary. Hence, for $K < N$, $\mathbf{y}_t$ is co-integrated of order (1, 1) with co-integrating rank $N-K$.

8.9 Simultaneous equation models

A dynamic simultaneous equation model takes the form

$$\boldsymbol{\Gamma}\mathbf{y}_t=\boldsymbol{\Phi}_1\mathbf{y}_{t-1}+\cdots+\boldsymbol{\Phi}_r\mathbf{y}_{t-r}+\mathbf{B}_0\mathbf{x}_t+\cdots+\mathbf{B}_s\mathbf{x}_{t-s}+\mathbf{u}_t \tag{8.9.1}$$

where $\boldsymbol{\Gamma}$ is an $N\times N$ matrix of unknown parameters, $\boldsymbol{\Phi}_1,\ldots,\boldsymbol{\Phi}_r$ are $N\times N$ matrices of autoregressive parameters, and $\mathbf{B}_0,\ldots,\mathbf{B}_s$ are $N\times K$ matrices of parameters associated with the $K\times 1$ vector of exogenous variables, $\mathbf{x}_t$, and their lagged values. If the disturbance term, $\mathbf{u}_t$, is NID($\mathbf{0},\boldsymbol{\Omega}$), the model can be handled by standard procedures described in the econometrics literature. It is the appearance of the matrix $\boldsymbol{\Gamma}$ which creates the simultaneity in the model and which leads to methods of estimation which are peculiar to econometrics. It also means that restrictions must be put on the model for it to be identifiable. These restrictions usually take the form of certain variables being excluded from certain equations on the basis of prior economic knowledge. Thus some of the elements of the parameter matrices are set equal to zero. In addition there are normalisation restrictions on $\boldsymbol{\Gamma}$; as a rule, one element in each row is set to unity.

The model in (8.9.1) is known as the *structural form.* Pre-multiplying through by $\boldsymbol{\Gamma}^{-1}$ leads to the *reduced form*

$$\mathbf{y}_t=\boldsymbol{\Pi}_1^{\dagger}\mathbf{y}_{t-1}+\cdots+\boldsymbol{\Pi}_r^{\dagger}\mathbf{y}_{t-r}+\boldsymbol{\Pi}_0\mathbf{x}_t+\cdots+\boldsymbol{\Pi}_s\mathbf{x}_{t-s}+\mathbf{v}_t \tag{8.9.2}$$

where the disturbance term, $\mathbf{v}_t$, has mean zero and covariance matrix $\boldsymbol{\Gamma}^{-1}\boldsymbol{\Omega}(\boldsymbol{\Gamma}^{-1})'$. The $N\times N$ matrices $\boldsymbol{\Pi}_1^{\dagger},\ldots,\boldsymbol{\Pi}_r^{\dagger}$ and the $N\times K$ matrices $\boldsymbol{\Pi}_0,\ldots,\boldsymbol{\Pi}_s$ contain the reduced form parameters and these are indirectly subject to the restrictions imposed on the structural form parameters. The predictions obtained from (8.9.1) and (8.9.2) will be identical. If the structural form restrictions are not imposed on (8.9.2), the system is the *unrestricted reduced form.* Ignoring the structural form restrictions will lead to inefficient estimators of the reduced form parameters and hence to inefficient predictions.

Now consider a model which contains unobserved time series components. Since the specification of (8.9.1) depends on economic theory, it will normally be the case that there is some rationale for the appearance of an unobserved component. In order to explore the implications of having unobserved components in the model, we will initially consider an otherwise static model in which a stochastic trend component appears in the first equation of the structural form. Thus

$$\boldsymbol{\Gamma}\mathbf{y}_t=\begin{bmatrix}1\\ \mathbf{0}_{N-1}\end{bmatrix}\mu_t+\mathbf{B}\mathbf{x}_t+\boldsymbol{\varepsilon}_t \tag{8.9.3}$$

where μ_t is a univariate stochastic trend and $\boldsymbol{\varepsilon}_t\sim$ NID($\mathbf{0},\boldsymbol{\Omega}_\varepsilon$). The reduced form is

$$\mathbf{y}_t=\boldsymbol{\theta}^*\mu_t+\boldsymbol{\Pi}\mathbf{x}_t+\mathbf{v}_t \tag{8.9.4}$$

where $\mathbf{\Pi}=\mathbf{\Gamma}^{-1}\mathbf{B}$, $\mathbf{v}_t=\mathbf{\Gamma}^{-1}\boldsymbol{\varepsilon}_t$ and $\boldsymbol{\theta}^*$ is the $N\times 1$ vector

$$\boldsymbol{\theta}^*=\mathbf{\Gamma}^{-1}\begin{bmatrix}1\\ \mathbf{0}\end{bmatrix} \tag{8.9.5}$$

Thus even though the stochastic trend only appears in the first equation in the structural form, it can be present in all the reduced form equations as a common trend.

More generally, we might have

$$\mathbf{\Gamma}\mathbf{y}_t=\mathbf{Z}_t\boldsymbol{\alpha}_t+\mathbf{B}\mathbf{x}_t+\boldsymbol{\varepsilon}_t \tag{8.9.6}$$

where the stochastic term $\mathbf{Z}_t\boldsymbol{\alpha}_t$ could incorporate trend and seasonal components, common trends and so on. In order to find the likelihood function of the observations, first let $\mathbf{y}_t^{\dagger}$ denote the stochastic part of the right-hand side of (8.9.6), that is

$$\mathbf{y}_t^{\dagger}=\mathbf{\Gamma}\mathbf{y}_t-\mathbf{B}\mathbf{x}_t=\mathbf{Z}_t\boldsymbol{\alpha}_t+\boldsymbol{\varepsilon}_t \tag{8.9.7}$$

The distribution of $\mathbf{y}_t^{\dagger}$, conditional on the information at time $t-1$, is multivariate normal with mean $\tilde{\mathbf{y}}_{t|t-1}^{\dagger}$ and covariance matrix, $\mathbf{F}_t$. Hence the distribution of $\mathbf{y}_t$, conditional on the same information set, is also multivariate normal with mean

$\mathbf{\Gamma}^{-1}\tilde{\mathbf{y}}_{t|t-1}^{\dagger}+\mathbf{\Gamma}^{-1}\mathbf{B}\mathbf{x}_t$ and covariance matrix $\mathbf{\Gamma}^{-1}\mathbf{F}_t(\mathbf{\Gamma}^{-1})'$

The likelihood function of the T sets of observations $\mathbf{y}=[\mathbf{y}_1' \quad \ldots \quad \mathbf{y}_T']'$ is therefore

$$\log L(\mathbf{y})=-\frac{TN}{2}\log 2\pi-\frac{1}{2}\sum_t \log|\mathbf{\Gamma}^{-1}\mathbf{F}_t(\mathbf{\Gamma}^{-1})'|-\frac{1}{2}\sum_t(\mathbf{y}_t-\mathbf{\Gamma}^{-1}\tilde{\mathbf{y}}_{t|t-1}^{\dagger}$$
$$-\mathbf{\Gamma}^{-1}\mathbf{B}\mathbf{x}_t)'[\mathbf{\Gamma}^{-1}\mathbf{F}_t(\mathbf{\Gamma}^{-1})']^{-1}(\mathbf{y}_t-\mathbf{\Gamma}^{-1}\tilde{\mathbf{y}}_{t|t-1}^{\dagger}-\mathbf{\Gamma}^{-1}\mathbf{B}\mathbf{x}_t)$$

This can be re-written as

$$\log L(\mathbf{y})=-\frac{TN}{2}\log 2\pi+T\log|\mathbf{\Gamma}|-\frac{1}{2}\sum\log|\mathbf{F}_t|-\frac{1}{2}\sum_t \mathbf{v}_t'\mathbf{F}_t^{-1}\mathbf{v}_t \tag{8.9.8}$$

where

$$\mathbf{v}_t=\mathbf{\Gamma}\mathbf{y}_t-\mathbf{B}\mathbf{x}_t-\tilde{\mathbf{y}}_{t|t-1}^{\dagger}$$

The $\mathbf{v}_t$'s are the innovations, and the $\mathbf{F}_t$'s the covariance matrices obtained by running the Kalman filter appropriate for the model for $\mathbf{y}_t^{\dagger}$ on the 'observations' $\mathbf{\Gamma}\mathbf{y}_t-\mathbf{B}\mathbf{x}_t$. Hence, conditional on all the parameters in the model, the likelihood function is straightforward to evaluate. Difficulties arise because, just as in the application of FIML to a static simultaneous equation system, the presence of the Jacobian term, $\log|\mathbf{\Gamma}|$, in the likelihood severely limits the number of parameters which can be concentrated out of the likelihood function. Thus the problem of estimating the model is really the practical one of having to carry out numerical optimisation with respect to a large number of unknown parameters.

If interest centres on a single equation, say the first, and there is not enough information to specify restrictions on the remaining equations, a limited information estimation procedure is appropriate. In a model of the form (8.9.1) where $\boldsymbol{\mu}_t$ is NID($\mathbf{0}, \boldsymbol{\Omega}$), the LIML estimator of the parameters in the first equation can be obtained by applying ML to a system consisting of the first (structural) equation and the reduced form for the endogenous variables appearing in that equation. Since the Jacobian of this system is unity, the estimator can be computed by iterating a feasible SURE estimator to convergence; see Hall and Pagan (1981).

Now consider the application of LIML in a system with stochastic trends. For simplicity, these will be assumed to be generated by a multivariate random walk. It will also be assumed that the system contains no lags, although the presence of lags in the exogenous variables does not alter anything. The system as a whole is

$$\boldsymbol{\Gamma}\mathbf{y}_t = \boldsymbol{\mu}_t + \mathbf{B}\mathbf{x}_t + \boldsymbol{\varepsilon}_t, \quad \text{Var}(\boldsymbol{\varepsilon}_t) = \boldsymbol{\Sigma}_\varepsilon \tag{8.9.9a}$$

$$\boldsymbol{\mu}_t = \boldsymbol{\mu}_{t-1} + \boldsymbol{\eta}_t, \quad \text{Var}(\boldsymbol{\eta}_t) = \boldsymbol{\Sigma}_\eta \tag{8.9.9b}$$

Hence the reduced form is

$$\mathbf{y}_t = \boldsymbol{\mu}_t^* + \boldsymbol{\Pi}\mathbf{x}_t + \boldsymbol{\upsilon}_t, \quad \text{Var}(\boldsymbol{\upsilon}_t) = \boldsymbol{\Sigma}_\upsilon = \boldsymbol{\Gamma}^{-1}\boldsymbol{\Sigma}_\varepsilon(\boldsymbol{\Gamma}^{-1})' \tag{8.9.10a}$$

$$\boldsymbol{\mu}_t^* = \boldsymbol{\mu}_{t-1}^* + \boldsymbol{\eta}_t^*, \quad \text{Var}(\boldsymbol{\eta}_t^*) = \boldsymbol{\Sigma}_\eta^* = \boldsymbol{\Gamma}^{-1}\boldsymbol{\Sigma}_\eta(\boldsymbol{\Gamma}^{-1})' \tag{8.9.10b}$$

where $\boldsymbol{\mu}_t^* = \boldsymbol{\Gamma}^{-1}\boldsymbol{\mu}_t$. The equation of interest, the first in (8.9.9), may be written as

$$y_{1t} = \mu_{1t} + \boldsymbol{\gamma}_1'\mathbf{y}_{2t} + \boldsymbol{\beta}_1'\mathbf{x}_{1t} + \varepsilon_{1t} \tag{8.9.11a}$$

$$\mu_{1t} = \mu_{1,t-1} + \eta_{1t} \tag{8.9.11b}$$

where $\mathbf{y}_{2t}$ and $\mathbf{x}_{1t}$ denote the vectors of included endogenous and exogenous variables respectively. The disturbances ε_{1t} and η_{1t} may be correlated with the corresponding disturbances in the other structural equations. Prior knowledge suggests the presence of a stochastic trend in (8.9.11), but there is no information on whether or not stochastic trends are present in the other structural equations in the system, and so they must be included for generality.

The reduced form for the endogenous variables included in (8.9.11) may be written as

$$\mathbf{y}_{2t} = \boldsymbol{\mu}_{2t}^* + \boldsymbol{\Pi}_2\mathbf{x}_t + \boldsymbol{\upsilon}_{2t} \tag{8.9.12a}$$

$$\boldsymbol{\mu}_{2t}^* = \boldsymbol{\mu}_{2,t-1}^* + \boldsymbol{\eta}_{2t}^* \tag{8.9.12b}$$

The LIML estimator is obtained by treating (8.9.11) and (8.9.12) as though they were the structural form of a system, and applying FIML. The complication of the Jacobian term in the likelihood is mercifully absent as

$$|\boldsymbol{\Gamma}| = \begin{vmatrix} 1 & -\boldsymbol{\gamma}_1' \\ \mathbf{0} & \mathbf{I} \end{vmatrix} = 1 \tag{8.9.13}$$

Estimation can therefore proceed by making use of the multivariate GLS algorithm of sub-section 3.4.2 in the same way as was suggested in sub-section 8.2.4. This requires writing $\boldsymbol{\Pi}_2 \mathbf{x}_t$ as $(\mathbf{I} \otimes \mathbf{x}_t')\boldsymbol{\pi}_2$ where $\boldsymbol{\pi}_2 = \text{vec}(\boldsymbol{\Pi}_2')$. If $\boldsymbol{\Sigma}_\eta = \mathbf{0}$, then the model reverts to a standard static SEM, and the iterative procedure can be set up within a SURE framework. The usual starting values for such a procedure are obtained by estimating the structural equation of interest by two-stage least squares (2SLS), while the reduced form equations for the included endogenous variables are estimated by OLS. In the case of (8.9.11) and (8.9.12), starting values for $\boldsymbol{\gamma}_1$, $\boldsymbol{\beta}_1$ and $\boldsymbol{\Pi}_2$ are given by applying 2SLS and OLS to the first-differences of y_{1t} and $\mathbf{y}_{2t}$ respectively. Finally it should be noted that the information matrix is not block diagonal with respect to the coefficients of the explanatory variables and the covariance matrices of $[\varepsilon_{1t} \quad \boldsymbol{\upsilon}_{2t}']'$ and $[\eta_{1t} \quad \boldsymbol{\eta}_{2t}']'$.

The LIML estimator in a simultaneous equation system with vector MA disturbances was derived by Hall and Pagan (1981). Although (8.9.9) has a vector MA representation when first-differences are taken, LIML estimation of (8.9.9) is considerably easier than LIML estimation of a model with unrestricted MA disturbances. As Hall and Pagan show, the presence of an unrestricted MA disturbance vector means that the reduced form for all endogenous variables in the system, apart from y_{1t}, must be used to form the LIML estimator for the first equation. Hence LIML is not a particularly attractive proposition. Furthermore the limited information set-up, in which all disturbances, apart from the one in the first equation, follow a vector MA does not seem to be a very natural one. On the other hand, the specification in (8.9.11) in which both ε_{1t} and η_{1t} may be correlated with the corresponding disturbances in the other structural equations seems very reasonable.

Looking at the model in terms of equations (8.9.11) and (8.9.12) provides further insight into the relative merits of the various IV estimators introduced in section 7.8. If the signal–noise ratio, q, was the same in each equation, and was known, the same transformation applied to all the endogenous variaoles in (8.9.11) and (8.9.12) would make the disturbances white noise. 2SLS could then be applied. This is the G2SLS estimator and it has the same asymptotic efficiency as LIML for known q.

EXERCISES

8.1 For the cycle model, (2.3.38), show that if the covariance matrix of $[\psi_t \quad \psi_t^*]'$ is a scalar matrix, it must satisfy (8.1.20). Hence find the variance and autocorrelation function of ψ_t.

8.2 Derive the fixed-interval smoother for the multivariate random walk plus noise model, (8.2.1), when the homogeneity restriction, (8.3.1), is imposed. Can the smoothed estimates be obtained by applying the same univariate smoother to each series in turn?

8.3 Determine an expression for the coherence between each pair of series in a homogeneous multivariate random walk plus noise model.

8.4 What is the objection to modelling the first-differences of the variables y_{1t} and y_{2t} by a vector autoregression when they are generated by the process:

$$y_{1t} = \varphi y_{1,t-1} + \beta y_{2,t-1} + \varepsilon_t$$
$$y_{2t} = \qquad\qquad y_{2,t-1} + \eta_t$$

where $|\varphi| < 1$ and ε_t and η_t are mutually independent normally distributed disturbances with mean zero and variances σ_ε^2 and σ_η^2 respectively?

8.5 In Exercise 7.1, are y_t and x_{t-2} co-integrated?

8.6 Construct a test for heteroscedasticity in a homogeneous structural time series model.

8.7 Is it possible for a particular multivariate random walk plus noise model to be both homogeneous and co-integrated?

8.8 It has sometimes been argued by time series analysts that the nature of the relationship between two series is best evaluated by differencing to achieve stationarity, and then examining the sample cross-correlation function. Discuss the usefulness of this approach by considering a common trend model, (8.5.5), in which the irregular components are mutually uncorrelated and their variances are much greater than the variance of the disturbance driving the common trend.

Chapter 9

Continuous time

A continuous time model is, in some ways, more fundamental than a discrete time model. For many variables, the process generating the observations can be regarded as a continuous one even though the observations themselves are only made at discrete intervals. Indeed a good deal of the theory in economics and other subjects is based on continuous time models. There is thus a strong argument for regarding the continuous time parameters as being the ones of interest. This point is argued very clearly in Bergstrom (1976, 1984).

There are also strong statistical arguments for working with a continuous time model. Although missing observations can be handled by a discrete time model, irregularly spaced observations cannot. Formulating the model in continuous time provides the solution. Furthermore, even if the observations are at regular intervals, a continuous time model has the attraction of not being tied to the time interval at which the observations happen to be made.

The aim of the present chapter is to set out the main structural time series models in continuous time. As with any model formulated at a timing interval smaller than the observation interval, it is important to make a distinction between stocks and flows; see section 6.3. Univariate structural models for stock variables are examined in section 9.2 and the relationship between these models and their discrete time counterparts is explored. An important result to emerge from this exercise is that the structure of the two sets of models is very similar. Thus from the forecasting point of view it makes virtually no difference whether a model is formulated in discrete or continuous time when regular observations are available. This is not the case with flow variables. As shown in section 9.3, differences do emerge between the two formulations, although, on the whole, the forecasts are unlikely to be dramatically different. Sections 9.2 and 9.3 also contain a discussion of how explanatory variables may be brought into continuous time models.

Section 9.4 provides a treatment of vector autoregressions in continuous time. The estimation procedures can allow for non-stationarity and mixed stocks and flows, as well as data irregularities such as missing observations, temporal aggregation and irregularly spaced observations. Univariate autoregressions emerge as a special case. The final sub-section incorporates vector autoregressions with trend components and includes the important special case of common trends.

9.1 Introduction

The first sub-section below is intended to give a flavour of continuous time models by describing the main features of the continuous time AR(1) process. More general concepts are described in section 9.1.2, while section 9.1.3 sets out the continuous time specification of the main structural components.

9.1.1 *Continuous time autoregressive models*

A continuous time white-noise process, $\xi(t)$, with mean zero and variance σ^2 is defined such that for $s>r$

$$\mathrm{E}\left[\int_r^s \xi(t)\,dt\right]=0 \tag{9.1.1a}$$

$$\mathrm{E}\left[\int_r^s \xi(t)\,dt\right]^2=(s-r)\sigma^2 \tag{9.1.1b}$$

and

$$\mathrm{E}\left[\int_r^s \xi(t)dt \int_p^q \xi(t)\,dt\right]=0, \quad r<s<p<q; \tag{9.1.1c}$$

see Priestley (1981, pp. 156–66), Jazwinski (1970) and Bergstrom (1984) for careful discussions of this concept. It follows that the unit integral of continuous time white noise satisfies the usual definition of a discrete time white noise process. It also has the further properties that if $f(t)$ and $g(t)$ are deterministic functions of time, then

$$\mathrm{E}\left[\int_r^s f(t)\xi(t)\,dt\right]=0 \tag{9.1.2a}$$

$$\mathrm{E}\left[\int_r^s f(t)\xi(t)\,dt\right]^2=\sigma^2\int_r^s f^2(t)\,dt \tag{9.1.2b}$$

and

$$\mathrm{E}\left[\int_r^s f(t)\xi(t)\,dt \int_r^s g(t)\xi(t)\,dt\right]=\sigma^2\int_r^s f(t)g(t)\,dt \tag{9.1.2c}$$

For non-overlapping intervals the expression in (9.1.2c) is zero.

Using the above definition of continuous time white noise, a first-order continuous time process can be represented as the stochastic differential equation

$$(d/dt)y(t)=\gamma+\alpha y(t)+\xi(t) \tag{9.1.3}$$

where α and γ are parameters. Strictly speaking, (9.1.3) is not valid as $\xi(t)$ does not exist, as such, and $y(t)$ is not mean-square differentiable. An alternative way of writing the equation is

$$dy(t)=[\gamma+\alpha y(t)]\,dt+dW(t) \tag{9.1.3$'$}$$

where $W(t)$ is a Wiener process and $dW(t)$ has mean zero, variance $\sigma^2 dt$ and is uncorrelated in different time periods. However, there is no objection to working with (9.1.3) provided its meaning is clearly understood, and it is probably more appealing pedagogically. In any case, (9.1.3) is to be interpreted as meaning that $y(t)$ satisfies the stochastic integral equation

$$y(t)-y(0)=\int_0^t [\gamma+\alpha y(r)]\,dr+\int_0^t \xi(r)\,dr \tag{9.1.4}$$

while (9.1.3)′ satisfies the same equation, but with $\xi(r)dr$ replaced by $dW(r)$ in the final integral. For any given value of $y(0)$, solving (9.1.4) yields

$$y(t)=[y(0)+\gamma/\alpha]e^{\alpha t}-(\gamma/\alpha)+\int_0^t e^{\alpha(t-r)}\xi(r)\,dr \tag{9.1.5}$$

and this satisfies the stochastic difference equation

$$y(t)=[(e^{\alpha}-1)\gamma/\alpha]+e^{\alpha}y(t-1)+\int_0^1 e^{\alpha(1-r)}\xi(r)\,dr \tag{9.1.6}$$

Suppose that $y(t)$ is observed at discrete time intervals one period apart. If the observation at time t is denoted by y_t, then, since $y_t=y(t)$, it follows from (9.1.6) that the observations satisfy the discrete time AR(1) process

$$y_t=\theta+\varphi y_{t-1}+\xi_t, \quad t=1,\dots T \tag{9.1.7}$$

where

$$\varphi=\exp(\alpha) \tag{9.1.8a}$$

$$\theta=(e^{\alpha}-1)\gamma/\alpha \tag{9.1.8b}$$

and ξ_t is white noise. It follows immediately from (9.1.2a) that the mean of ξ_t is zero, while the use of (9.1.2b) enables the variance to be evaluated as

$$\mathrm{Var}(\xi_t)=\sigma^2(e^{2\alpha}-1)/2\alpha \tag{9.1.8c}$$

The stationarity condition for the continuous time model is that α be negative; it is easy to see from (9.1.8a) that $\alpha<0$ corresponds to $\varphi<1$. Since $\alpha=-\infty$ corresponds to $\varphi=0$, negative values of φ are not permitted in the discrete time AR(1) process.

The assumption of a Gaussian distribution for integrals of $\xi(t)$ means that ξ_t also has a Gaussian distribution. This leads to the usual prediction error decomposition form of the likelihood function as in (3.4.7). The exact likelihood function is obtained by including the unconditional distribution of y_1. If the

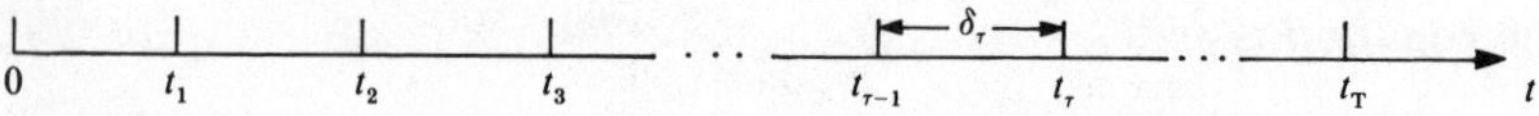

Fig. 9.1.1 Time scale for irregular observations.

initial value of $y(t)$ is taken to be $y(-\infty)$ rather than $y(0)$, equation (9.1.5) becomes

$$y(t)=-\gamma/\alpha+\int_{-\infty}^{t} e^{\alpha(t-r)}\xi(r)dr$$

and it follows that the mean of $y(t)$, and hence y_1, is $-\gamma/\alpha$. The unconditional variance of y_1 is obtained most easily from the above equation by setting $t=0$ and evaluating the expectation of the square of the integral to give $-\sigma^2/2\alpha$. If y_1 is treated as fixed, the discrete time parameters φ, θ and $\text{Var}(\xi_t)$ can be estimated by linear regression and the corresponding estimators of the continuous time parameters α, γ and σ^2 obtained from the three equations in (9.1.8).

Now suppose that observations are spaced at irregular intervals, but assume, for simplicity, that $\gamma=0$. Let the τ-th observation be denoted by y_τ for $\tau=1,\ldots,T$ and suppose that this observation is made at time t_τ. Let $t_\tau-t_{\tau-1}=\delta_\tau$ as indicated in Figure 9.1.1 and let $t_0=0$. Then equation (9.1.6) becomes

$$y(t_\tau)=\exp(\alpha\delta_\tau)y(t_{\tau-1})+\int_0^{\delta_\tau}\exp[\alpha(\delta_\tau-s)]\xi(t_{\tau-1}+s)ds \tag{9.1.9}$$

and so the discrete time model is

$$y_\tau=\varphi_\tau y_{\tau-1}+\xi_\tau \tag{9.1.10}$$

where the parameter φ_τ is given as

$$\varphi_\tau=\exp(\alpha\delta_\tau) \tag{9.1.11a}$$

and the error variance is

$$\text{Var}(\xi_\tau)=\sigma_\tau^2=\sigma^2(\varphi_\tau^2-1)/2\alpha\delta_\tau, \quad T=2,\ldots,T \tag{9.1.11b}$$

Thus the parameters φ_τ and σ_τ^2 in the discrete time model are time-varying according to the time between observations δ_τ. However, the likelihood function can still be expressed in the prediction error decomposition form, since the distribution of y_τ conditional on $y_{\tau-1}, y_{\tau-2},\ldots$ is $N(\varphi_\tau y_{\tau-1}, \sigma_\tau^2)$ for $\tau=2,\ldots,T$. Thus

$$\log L=-\frac{T}{2}\log 2\pi-\frac{1}{2}\sum_{\tau=1}^{T}\log\sigma_\tau^2-\frac{1}{2}\sum_{\tau=2}^{T}\frac{1}{\sigma_\tau^2}(y_\tau-\varphi_\tau y_{\tau-1})^2-\frac{1}{2\sigma_1^2}y_1^2 \tag{9.1.12}$$

where σ_τ^2 is given by (9.1.11b) for $\tau=2,\ldots,T$ and by $-\sigma^2/2\alpha$ for $\tau=1$. Maximisation of the likelihood function can be carried out directly with respect to σ^2 and α.

The treatment of higher-order models is less straightforward. A continuous time p-th order autoregressive process can be written as

$$D^p y(t) = \alpha_1 D^{p-1} y(t) + \cdots + \alpha_{p-1} Dy(t) + \alpha_p y(t) + \xi(t) \tag{9.1.13}$$

where D is the differential operator d/dt and $\alpha_1, \ldots, \alpha_p$ are parameters. With equally spaced observations, such a process becomes an ARMA($p, p-1$) process in discrete time, but the $2p-1$ ARMA parameters are complicated functions of the p continuous time parameters. Phadke and Wu (1974) give a discussion of the $p=2$ case, while Phillips (1959) derives the general result. The most satisfactory way to handle such models is to work in terms of the original continuous time models. This allows the extra flexibility of being able to handle irregularly spaced observations as in Jones (1981). However, solving the differential equations to obtain difference equations analogous to (9.1.6) or (9.1.9) is more difficult for higher-order models. The solution is given as a special case of the general method described in section 9.4.

9.1.2 *General form of continuous time models*

As with discrete time models the state space form provides a general framework within which estimation and prediction may be carried out. The continuous time analogue of the time-invariant discrete time transition equation in, say, (4.1.3) is

$$\frac{d}{dt}[\boldsymbol{\alpha}(t)] = \mathbf{A}\boldsymbol{\alpha}(t) + \mathbf{R}\boldsymbol{\eta}(t) \tag{9.1.14}$$

where the matrices $\mathbf{A}$ and $\mathbf{R}$ are $m \times m$ and $m \times g$ respectively, and may be functions of hyperparameters, and $\boldsymbol{\eta}(t)$ is a $g \times 1$ continuous time multivariate white-noise process with mean zero and covariance matrix $\mathbf{Q}$. The definition of a continuous time multivariate white-noise process is analogous to the univariate definition given in (9.1.1) with

$$\mathrm{E}\left[\int_r^s \boldsymbol{\eta}(t)\,dt\right]\left[\int_r^s \boldsymbol{\eta}(t)\,dt\right]' = (s-r)\mathbf{Q} \tag{9.1.15}$$

The condition for $\boldsymbol{\alpha}(t)$ to be stationary is that the characteristic roots of $\mathbf{A}$ should have negative real parts. The reason for this result will become clear in section 9.4.

The observations are at times $t = t_\tau$ for $\tau = 1, \ldots, T$. For a stock variable they are defined by

$$y_\tau = \mathbf{z}'\boldsymbol{\alpha}(t_\tau) + \varepsilon_\tau, \quad \tau = 1, \ldots, T \tag{9.1.16}$$

where ε_τ is a white-noise disturbance term with mean zero and variance σ_ε^2 which is uncorrelated with integrals of $\boldsymbol{\eta}(t)$ in all time periods; compare (6.3.8). For a flow

$$y_\tau = \int_0^{\delta_\tau} [\mathbf{z}'\boldsymbol{\alpha}(t_{\tau-1} + r) + \varepsilon(t_{\tau-1} + r)]dr \tag{9.1.17}$$

where $\varepsilon(t)$ is a continuous time white-noise process with mean zero and variance σ_ε^2, which is uncorrelated with $\boldsymbol{\eta}(t)$ in all time periods in the sense that

$$\mathrm{E}\left[\int_r^s \boldsymbol{\eta}(t)\,dt \int_p^q \varepsilon(t)\,dt\right] = \mathbf{0} \text{ for } r<s \text{ and } p<q$$

This is analogous to amalgamating equations (6.3.1a) and (6.3.3) in a discrete time model subject to temporal aggregation.

The above definitions can also be applied to a multivariate time series, although in this case there is the additional complication that the vector of observations may be a mixture of stocks and flows.

The treatment of continuous time models hinges on the solution to the differential equations in (9.1.14). The relationship between the state vector at time t_τ and time $t_{\tau-1}$ is given by

$$\boldsymbol{\alpha}(t_\tau) = e^{\mathbf{A}\delta_\tau}\boldsymbol{\alpha}(t_{\tau-1}) + \int_0^{\delta_\tau} e^{\mathbf{A}(\delta_\tau - s)}\mathbf{R}\boldsymbol{\eta}(t_{\tau-1}+s)ds \tag{9.1.18}$$

By defining $\boldsymbol{\alpha}_\tau$ as $\boldsymbol{\alpha}(t_\tau)$ for $\tau = 1, \ldots, T$, this expression may be written as a discrete time transition equation,

$$\boldsymbol{\alpha}_\tau = \mathbf{T}_\tau \boldsymbol{\alpha}_{\tau-1} + \boldsymbol{\eta}_\tau, \quad \tau = 1, \ldots, T \tag{9.1.19}$$

where

$$\mathbf{T}_\tau = \exp(\mathbf{A}\delta_\tau) \tag{9.1.20a}$$

and $\boldsymbol{\eta}_\tau$ is a multivariate white-noise disturbance term with zero and covariance matrix

$$\mathbf{Q}_\tau = \int_0^{\delta_\tau} e^{\mathbf{A}(\delta_\tau - s)}\mathbf{R}\mathbf{Q}\mathbf{R}' e^{\mathbf{A}'(\delta_\tau - s)} ds \tag{9.1.20b}$$

The evaluation of the transition matrix follows from the definition of a matrix exponential which is

$$\exp(\mathbf{A}) = \mathbf{I} + \mathbf{A} + \frac{1}{2!}\mathbf{A}^2 + \frac{1}{3!}\mathbf{A}^3 + \cdots \tag{9.1.21}$$

where $\mathbf{A}$ is an $N \times N$ matrix. This expression is straightforward to evaluate though, as Moler and van Loan (1978) point out, some care needs to be taken in performing the numerical computations. The more difficult task is to determine $\mathbf{Q}_\tau$ since this involves the integration of a matrix exponential. As will be seen in section 9.2, this turns out to be relatively easy for the principal structural time series models because $\mathbf{A}$ is block diagonal, and the form of the matrix exponentials in each block is relatively simple. This is not the case for many other models. In general it is necessary to diagonalise $\mathbf{A}$ in the manner described in section 9.4.

The condition for $\boldsymbol{\alpha}(t)$ in (9.1.14) to be stationary is that the real parts of the roots of $\mathbf{A}$ should be negative. This translates into the discrete time condition that the roots of $\mathbf{T}=\exp(\mathbf{A})$ should lie outside the unit circle. If $\boldsymbol{\alpha}(t)$ is stationary, then $\exp(\mathbf{A}s)\rightarrow\mathbf{0}$ as $s\rightarrow-\infty$. Hence it is possible to express $\boldsymbol{\alpha}(t)$ as

$$\boldsymbol{\alpha}(t)=\int_{-\infty}^{t} e^{\mathbf{A}(t-s)}\mathbf{R}\boldsymbol{\eta}(s)ds \tag{9.1.22}$$

It can be seen from (9.1.22) that the mean of $\boldsymbol{\alpha}(t)$ is zero. The covariance matrix is most easily evaluated by setting $t=0$ and is

$$\text{Var}[\boldsymbol{\alpha}(t)]=\int_{-\infty}^{0} e^{-\mathbf{A}s}\mathbf{RQR}'e^{\mathbf{A}'s}ds \tag{9.1.23}$$

When $\boldsymbol{\alpha}(t)$ is stationary, (9.1.22) provides the initial conditions for $\boldsymbol{\alpha}(t_0)$. In other words $\mathbf{a}_{1|0}=\mathbf{0}$ and $\mathbf{P}_{1|0}=\text{Var}[\boldsymbol{\alpha}(t)]$.

9.1.3 Structural components

The main structural components are formulated in continuous time in the following way.

Trend The local level trend component, $\mu(t)$, is a Wiener process, sometimes known as Brownian motion, and is simply

$$(d/dt)\mu(t)=\eta(t) \tag{9.1.24}$$

where $\eta(t)$ is continuous time white noise with variance σ_η^2.

The linear trend component is

$$\frac{d}{dt}\begin{bmatrix}\mu(t)\\ \beta(t)\end{bmatrix}=\begin{bmatrix}0 & 1\\ 0 & 0\end{bmatrix}\begin{bmatrix}\mu(t)\\ \beta(t)\end{bmatrix}+\begin{bmatrix}\eta(t)\\ \zeta(t)\end{bmatrix} \tag{9.1.25}$$

where $\eta(t)$ and $\zeta(t)$ are mutually uncorrelated continuous time white-noise processes with variances σ_η^2 and σ_ζ^2 respectively.

Cycle The continuous cycle is

$$\frac{d}{dt}\begin{bmatrix}\psi(t)\\ \psi^*(t)\end{bmatrix}=\begin{bmatrix}\log\rho & \lambda_c\\ -\lambda_c & \log\rho\end{bmatrix}\begin{bmatrix}\psi(t)\\ \psi^*(t)\end{bmatrix}+\begin{bmatrix}\kappa(t)\\ \kappa^*(t)\end{bmatrix} \tag{9.1.26}$$

where $\kappa(t)$ and $\kappa^*(t)$ are mutually uncorrelated continuous time white-noise processes with the same variance, σ_κ^2, and ρ and λ_c are parameters, the latter being the frequency of the cycle. The characteristic roots of the matrix containing these parameters are $\log\rho\pm i\lambda_c$. Since the general condition for stationarity of a model of the form (9.1.14) is that the characteristic roots must have negative real parts, the condition for $\psi(t)$ to be a stationary process is $\log \rho < 0$, and this corresponds to $\rho < 1$.

Seasonal The continuous time seasonal model is the sum of a suitable number of trigonometric components, $\gamma_j(t)$, generated by processes of the form (9.1.26) with ρ equal to unity and λ_c set equal to the appropriate seasonal frequency λ_j:

$$\frac{d}{dt}\begin{bmatrix}\gamma_j(t)\\ \gamma_j^*(t)\end{bmatrix}=\begin{bmatrix}0 & \lambda_j\\ -\lambda_j & 0\end{bmatrix}\begin{bmatrix}\gamma_j(t)\\ \gamma^*(t)\end{bmatrix}+\begin{bmatrix}\omega_j(t)\\ \omega_j^*(t)\end{bmatrix} \tag{9.1.27}$$

with the variances of $\omega_j(t)$ and $\omega_j^*(t)$ both equal to σ_ω^2 for $j=1,\ldots,[s/2]$.

Daily The continuous time daily model is

$$\frac{d}{dt}\boldsymbol{\theta}(t)=\boldsymbol{\chi}(t) \tag{9.1.28}$$

where $\boldsymbol{\theta}(t)$ and $\boldsymbol{\chi}(t)$ are $w\times 1$ vectors, the latter being a multivariate white-noise disturbance term with covariance matrix

$$\mathrm{Var}[\boldsymbol{\chi}(t)]=\sigma_\chi^2[\mathbf{I}-K^{-1}\mathbf{k}\mathbf{k}'] \tag{9.1.29}$$

where K and $\mathbf{k}$ are defined as for (4.1.17).

9.2 Stock variables

The discrete state space form for a stock variable generated by a continuous time process consists of the transition equation (9.1.19) together with the measurement equation (9.1.16) written in terms of $\boldsymbol{\alpha}_\tau$, i.e.

$$y_\tau=\mathbf{z}'\boldsymbol{\alpha}_\tau+\varepsilon_\tau,\quad \tau=1,\ldots,T \tag{9.1.16$'$}$$

The Kalman filter can therefore be applied in a standard way. The discrete time model is time-invariant for equally spaced observations, in which case it is usually convenient to set δ_τ equal to unity. Since the transition matrix is a matrix exponential, it is always p.d.

9.2.1 Structural models

The continuous time components defined in sub-section 9.1.3 can be combined to produce a continuous time structural model. As in the discrete case, the components are usually assumed to be mutually independent. Hence the **A** and **Q** matrices in (9.1.20) are block diagonal and so the discrete time components can be evaluated separately.

Trend For the local level model, (9.1.24), it follows almost immediately that

$$\mu_\tau=\mu_{\tau-1}+\eta_\tau \tag{9.2.1}$$

with $\mathrm{Var}(\eta_\tau)=\delta_\tau\sigma_\eta^2$. The discrete model is therefore a random walk for equally spaced observations. If the observation at time τ is

$$y_\tau=\mu(t_\tau)+\varepsilon_\tau, \quad \tau=1,\ldots,T \tag{9.2.2a}$$

where $\mathrm{Var}(\varepsilon_\tau)=\sigma_\varepsilon^2$, the discrete time measurement equation is

$$y_\tau=\mu_\tau+\varepsilon_\tau, \quad \tau=1,\ldots,T \tag{9.2.2b}$$

and the set-up corresponds exactly to the familiar random walk plus noise model.

For the local linear trend model, (9.1.25),

$$\exp\left[\delta_\tau\begin{pmatrix}0 & 1\\ 0 & 0\end{pmatrix}\right]=\mathbf{I}+\begin{bmatrix}0 & \delta_\tau\\ 0 & 0\end{bmatrix}=\begin{bmatrix}1 & \delta_\tau\\ 0 & 1\end{bmatrix}$$

Thus

$$\begin{bmatrix}\mu_\tau\\ \beta_\tau\end{bmatrix}=\begin{bmatrix}1 & \delta_\tau\\ 0 & 1\end{bmatrix}\begin{bmatrix}\mu_{\tau-1}\\ \beta_{\tau-1}\end{bmatrix}+\begin{bmatrix}\eta_\tau\\ \zeta_\tau\end{bmatrix} \tag{9.2.3}$$

In view of the simple structure of the matrix exponential, the evaluation of the covariance matrix of the discrete time disturbances can be carried out directly, yielding

$$\mathrm{Var}\begin{bmatrix}\eta_\tau\\ \zeta_\tau\end{bmatrix}=\delta_\tau\begin{bmatrix}\sigma_\eta^2+\frac{1}{3}\delta_\tau^2\sigma_\zeta^2 & \frac{1}{2}\delta_\tau\sigma_\zeta^2\\ \frac{1}{2}\delta_\tau\sigma_\zeta^2 & \sigma_\zeta^2\end{bmatrix} \tag{9.2.4}$$

When δ_τ is equal to unity, (9.2.3) reduces to the discrete time local linear trend (2.3.27). However, while in (2.3.27) the disturbances are independent, (9.2.4) shows that independence for the continuous time disturbances implies that the corresponding discrete time disturbances are correlated. However, this difference is unlikely to be of any great practical importance and for a measurement equation of the form (9.2.2) the continuous time local linear trend model can be regarded as being essentially the same as the discrete time model of (2.3.37); see also the discussion in sub-section 4.1.1.

Cycle For the cycle model, (9.1.26), use of the matrix exponential definition together with the power series expansions for the cosine and sine functions gives the discrete time model

$$\begin{bmatrix}\psi_\tau\\ \psi_\tau^*\end{bmatrix}=\rho^\delta\begin{bmatrix}\cos\lambda_c\delta_\tau & \sin\lambda_c\delta_\tau\\ -\sin\lambda_c\delta_\tau & \cos\lambda_c\delta_\tau\end{bmatrix}\begin{bmatrix}\psi_{\tau-1}\\ \psi_{\tau-1}^*\end{bmatrix}+\begin{bmatrix}\kappa_\tau\\ \kappa_\tau^*\end{bmatrix} \tag{9.2.5}$$

When δ_τ equals one, the transition matrix corresponds exactly to the transition matrix of the discrete time cyclical component (2.3.38). As regards the properties of the disturbances, specifying that $\kappa(t)$ and $\kappa^*(t)$ be independent of each other with equal variances means that, in the corresponding discrete time model, κ_τ and κ_τ^* will also be independent with the same variance for any δ_τ. In fact, the covariance matrix of $[\kappa_\tau \; \kappa_\tau^*]'$ is given by

$$\text{Var}\begin{bmatrix} \kappa_\tau \\ \kappa_\tau^* \end{bmatrix} = (\sigma_\kappa^2/\log \rho^{-2})(1-\rho^{2\delta_\tau})\mathbf{I} \tag{9.2.6}$$

As was noted in the discussion of the discrete time model, letting $\kappa(t)$ and $\kappa^*(t)$ be independent and making their variances equal amounts to one more restriction than is necessary for identifiability. However, having the specification of the discrete time model consistent with that of the continuous time model, and hence independent of the interval between observations, is clearly an attractive property.

Setting λ_c equal to zero in (9.2.5) means that it collapses to a continuous time AR(1) process exhibiting positive autocorrelation. When $\lambda_c \delta_\tau$ is equal to π, the corresponding discrete time model is an AR(1) process with negative autocorrelation; in terms of (9.1.8a), φ is equal to minus ρ.

A final point to note is that a pseudo-cyclical process is also obtained from a continuous time AR(2) or ARMA(2, 1) model since, as shown in Phadke and Wu (1974), the roots of the corresponding discrete time AR(2) polynomial are always complex. The attraction of working with the cycle model (9.2.5) is that it is easier to handle as well as being set up in terms of the parameters of interest.

Seasonal For a trigonometric seasonal component, (9.1.27), the discrete time specification is similar to (9.2.5) with ρ equal to unity. The covariance matrix of the disturbance is

$$\text{Var}\begin{bmatrix} \omega_\tau \\ \omega_\tau^* \end{bmatrix} = \sigma_\omega^2 \delta_\tau \mathbf{I} \tag{9.2.7}$$

when δ_τ is unity, the discrete time specification corresponds exactly to that given in sub-section 2.3.4.

Daily effects Since exp(**0**) is equal to the identity matrix it follows immediately that the discrete time specification of (9.1.28) is

$$\boldsymbol{\theta}_\tau = \boldsymbol{\theta}_{\tau-1} + \boldsymbol{\chi}_\tau \tag{9.2.8a}$$

with

$$\text{Var}(\boldsymbol{\chi}_\tau) = \sigma_\chi^2 \delta_\tau [\mathbf{I} - K^{-1}\mathbf{kk}'] \tag{9.2.8b}$$

This corresponds exactly to the discrete time model of sub-section 2.3.5 when δ_τ is equal to one.

As regards starting values for the Kalman filter for irregularly spaced observations, the considerations which arise are almost exactly the same as for a regular discrete time model. Thus, if the state vector contains d non-stationary components, d observations are needed before the elements of the state vector can be estimated with finite MSE. A diffuse prior can be used to initiate the non-stationary elements of the state vector. The starting values for the stationary components are provided by their respective unconditional distributions. Thus for the stationary cyclical component, (9.1.26), the unconditional mean of $[\psi(t) \quad \psi^*(t)]'$ is zero while the covariance matrix is obtained by evaluating (9.1.23). Since $\mathbf{RQR}'=\sigma_\kappa^2\mathbf{I}$,

$$\text{Var}(\boldsymbol{\alpha}_0)=\sigma_\kappa^2\int_{-\infty}^{0} e^{-(\mathbf{A}+\mathbf{A}')s}ds \tag{9.2.9}$$

However, $\mathbf{A}+\mathbf{A}'=2\log\rho\ \mathbf{I}$ and so evaluating the integral is easy. The result is

$$\text{Var}(\boldsymbol{\alpha}_0)=(-\sigma_\kappa^2/2\log\rho).\mathbf{I} \tag{9.2.10}$$

The net effect of the above results is that putting the various continuous time components together yields discrete time models which, for regularly spaced observations, are almost identical to the discrete time models set up in section 2.3. The only case where the implied discrete time model is different from the model originally formulated in section 2.3 is the local linear trend and there the difference is minor. These results are perhaps not surprising in view of the results obtained in sub-section 6.3.2. Thus for a stock variable the discrete time models we have been working with up to now are consistent with the corresponding continuous time models. The continuous time models are more general, however, in that they can handle irregularly spaced observations and interpolate at any point.

9.2.2 Prediction and interpolation

In the general model (9.1.14), the optimal predictor of the state vector for any positive lead time, l, is given by the forecast function

$$\mathbf{a}(t_T+l\,|\,T)=e^{\mathbf{A}l}\mathbf{a}_T \tag{9.2.11}$$

The state vector at lead time l is

$$\boldsymbol{\alpha}(t_T+l)=e^{\mathbf{A}l}\mathbf{a}_T+\mathbf{R}\int_0^l e^{\mathbf{A}(l-s)}\boldsymbol{\eta}(t_T+s)ds \tag{9.2.12}$$

and so the MSE matrix associated with $\mathbf{a}(T+l\,|\,T)$ is

$$\mathbf{P}(t_T+l\,|\,T)=\mathbf{T}_l\mathbf{P}_T\mathbf{T}_l'+\mathbf{RQ}_l\mathbf{R}', \quad l>0 \tag{9.2.13}$$

where $\mathbf{T}_l$ and $\mathbf{Q}_l$ are, respectively, (9.1.20a) and (9.1.20b) evaluated with δ_τ set equal to l.

The forecast function for the systematic part of the series,

$$\bar{y}(t)=\mathbf{z}'\boldsymbol{\alpha}(t) \tag{9.2.14}$$

can also be expressed as a continuous function of l, namely

$$\tilde{y}(t_T+l|T)=\mathbf{z}'e^{\mathbf{A}l}\mathbf{a}_T \tag{9.2.15a}$$

If we consider this to be the forecast of an observation made at time t_T+l, then we may write

$$\tilde{y}_{T+1|T}=\tilde{y}(t_T+l|T) \tag{9.2.15b}$$

where the observation to be forecast has been classified, arbitrarily, as the one indexed $\tau=T+1$. The MSE of this forecast is

$$\text{MSE}(\tilde{y}_{T+1|T})=\mathbf{z}'\mathbf{P}(t_T+l|T)\mathbf{z}+\sigma_\varepsilon^2$$

The evaluation of forecast functions for the various structural models is relatively straightforward. Thus the local level model, (9.1.24), with measurement equation, (9.2.2b), has a forecast function

$$\tilde{y}(t_T+l|T)=m(t_T+l|T)=m_T \tag{9.2.16}$$

This is simply a horizontal straight line passing through the final estimate of the trend. The MSE of the forecast of the $(T+1)$-th observation, at time t_T+l, is

$$\text{MSE}(\tilde{y}_{T+1|T})=p_T+l\sigma_\eta^2+\sigma_\varepsilon^2 \tag{9.2.17}$$

which is of exactly the same form as (3.6.8b). Introducing a slope component into the trend by (9.1.25) yields the straight-line forecast function

$$\tilde{y}(t_T+l|T)=m(t_T+l|T)=m_T+b_Tl \tag{9.2.18}$$

Both (9.2.16) and (9.2.18) are consistent with the idea of a trend as discussed in sub-section 6.1.1.

The forecast function for a cyclical component takes the form of a damped cosine wave

$$c(t_T+l|T)=\rho^l(c_T\cos\lambda_c l+c_T^*\sin\lambda_c l); \tag{9.2.19}$$

compare (2.3.39). The seasonal forecast function is a mixture of such components but without the damping factor. Finally, for the daily model, the forecast function is a level which is set at the particular day prevailing at lead time l.

Interpolation is the estimation of the series and/or its components at some point between observations. This may be carried out by defining the required points, constructing the appropriate transition equations and treating the corresponding observations as missing. Thus suppose interpolation is to be carried out at several points between $t_{\tau-1}$ and t_τ. Let these points be denoted by $t_{\tau-1}+r_1, t_{\tau-1}+r_2$, and so on where $0<r_1<r_2<\cdots<\delta_\tau$. All that is required is the definition of the discrete time transition equation, (9.1.19), at $t_{\tau-1}+r_1$, $t_{\tau-1}+r_2,\ldots$, and t_τ and the subsequent applications of the Kalman filter. The optimal estimators of $y(t)$ at these intermediate points are then obtained by applying a suitable smoothing algorithm. The estimators at time $t_{\tau-1}+r_j$ may be written as $\tilde{\bar{y}}(t_\tau + r_j|T)$ and this is equal to the optimal estimator of an observation at this point in time, that is

$$\tilde{y}_{\tau(j)|T} = \tilde{\bar{y}}(t_\tau + r_j|T) = \mathbf{z}'\mathbf{a}(t_\tau + r_j|T) \tag{9.2.20a}$$

The corresponding MSE is

$$\text{MSE}(\tilde{y}_{\tau(j)|T}) = \mathbf{z}'\mathbf{P}(t_{\tau-1} + r_j|T)\mathbf{z}' + \sigma_\varepsilon^2, \quad j = 1, 2, \ldots \tag{9.2.20b}$$

where $\mathbf{P}(t_{\tau-1} + r_j|T)$ is the MSE matrix of $\mathbf{a}(t_\tau + r_j|T)$, the smoothed estimator of the state vector at time $t_{\tau-1} + r_j$. A similar expression was given when interpolation for discrete time models was discussed in sub-section 6.3.2.

9.2.3 *Estimation and testing*

Estimation of Gaussian continuous time structural models poses no new problems when the observations are regularly spaced. The algorithms already developed can be applied directly with only a minor modification needed to handle the covariance matrix of the disturbances of the local linear trend model in (9.2.4) . On the other hand, when the observations are irregularly spaced, the time-domain estimation procedure must be adapted to account for the fact that the state space model is no longer time-invariant. Once this has been done, the construction of the likelihood function can proceed via the prediction error decomposition. Indeed any continuous time model may be handled in this way, and the log-likelihood function for a set of T multivariate observations may be written as

$$\log L = -\frac{(T-d)}{2}\log 2\pi - \frac{1}{2}\sum_{\tau=d+1}^{T}\log|\mathbf{F}_\tau| - \frac{1}{2}\sum_{\tau=d+1}^{T}\mathbf{v}_\tau'\mathbf{F}_\tau^{-1}\mathbf{v}_\tau \tag{9.2.21}$$

where the use of the τ, rather than the t, subscript stresses the point that the time interval between the observations may be irregular. Kitagawa (1984) gives some examples.

Since frequency-domain estimation procedures can no longer be applied when the observations are irregularly spaced, the information matrix must be obtained from the time-domain likelihood functions. This may be done numerically. It can also be done analytically, using the results set out in sub-sections 3.4.5 and 3.4.6. Having replaced t by τ as in (9.2.21), all the results in these sub-sections apply directly. In particular the information matrix as given in (3.4.69) depends only on first derivatives.

Given regularity conditions similar to those adopted in sub-section 3.4.1 the ML estimator of the hyperparameter vector, $\boldsymbol{\psi}$, based on irregularly spaced observations is asymptotically normal with mean zero and a covariance matrix given by the inverse of the information matrix. This result can be shown by using Martingale theory, as in Hall and Heyde (1980, chapter 6), Crowder (1976) and Pagan (1980). Since the usual asymptotic distributional theory goes through, asymptotic standard errors may be constructed from the information matrix and Wald tests carried out. Lagrange multiplier tests can be constructed in the way described in sub-section 5.2.1.

9.2.4 Explanatory variables

Explanatory variables can be introduced by assuming that the systematic part of the series, $\bar{y}(t)$, is generated by a continuous time model in which

$$\bar{y}(t)=\mathbf{z}'\mathbf{a}(t)+\mathbf{x}'(t)\boldsymbol{\delta} \tag{9.2.22}$$

where $\mathbf{x}(t)$ is a $k\times 1$ vector of continuous stock variables and $\boldsymbol{\delta}$ is a corresponding $k\times 1$ vector. If the elements of $\mathbf{x}(t)$ are measured at the same points in time as $y(t)$, or if continuous records of them are available, the measurement equation (9.1.16) can be modified to

$$y_\tau=\mathbf{z}'\boldsymbol{\alpha}_\tau+\mathbf{x}_\tau'\boldsymbol{\delta}+\varepsilon_\tau \tag{9.2.23}$$

where $\mathbf{x}_\tau=\mathbf{x}(t_\tau)$. No new issues are raised by the presence of the explanatory variables. Time-domain estimation can be carried out by augmenting the state vector by the elements of $\boldsymbol{\delta}$ or by the GLS transformation.

9.3 Flow variables

The treatment of flow variables in continuous time follows similar lines to the treatment of flow variables subject to temporal aggregation, as described in section 6.3.3. The key feature is the introduction of a cumulator variable, $y^f(t)$, into the state space model. The cumulator variable for the series at time t_τ is equal to the observation, y_τ, for $\tau=1,\ldots,T$. Since, from (9.1.18),

$$\boldsymbol{\alpha}(t_{\tau-1}+r)=e^{\mathbf{A}r}\boldsymbol{\alpha}(t_{\tau-1})+\int_0^r e^{\mathbf{A}(r-s)}\mathbf{R}\boldsymbol{\eta}(t_{\tau-1}+s)\,ds \tag{9.3.1}$$

for $0\leqslant r\leqslant\delta_\tau$, the cumulator variable at time t_τ

$$y^f(t_\tau)=\int_0^{\delta_\tau} y(t_{\tau-1}+r)\,dr=\mathbf{z}'\int_0^{\delta}\boldsymbol{\alpha}(t_{\tau-1}+r)\,dr+\int_0^{\delta}\varepsilon(t_{\tau-1}+r)\,dr$$

can be written as

$$\begin{aligned} y^f(t_\tau)&=\mathbf{z}'\left[\int_0^{\delta} e^{\mathbf{A}r}\,dr\right]\boldsymbol{\alpha}(t_{\tau-1})+\mathbf{z}'\int_0^{\delta}\int_0^{r} e^{\mathbf{A}(r-s)}\mathbf{R}\boldsymbol{\eta}(t_{\tau-1}+s)\,ds\,dr\\ &\quad+\int_0^{\delta}\varepsilon(t_{\tau-1}+r)\,dr\\ &=\mathbf{z}'\mathbf{W}(\delta)\boldsymbol{\alpha}(t_{\tau-1})+\mathbf{z}'\boldsymbol{\eta}^f(t_\tau)+\varepsilon^f(t_\tau) \end{aligned} \tag{9.3.2a}$$

where

$$\boldsymbol{\eta}^f(t_\tau)=\int_0^\delta \mathbf{W}(\delta-r)\mathbf{R}\boldsymbol{\eta}(t_{\tau-1}+r)\,dr \tag{9.3.2b}$$

$$\mathbf{W}(r)=\int_0^r e^{\mathbf{A}s}\,ds \tag{9.3.2c}$$

and

$$\varepsilon^f(t_\tau)=\int_0^\delta \varepsilon(t_{\tau-1}+s)\,ds \tag{9.3.2d}$$

Now letting $\boldsymbol{\eta}_\tau^f=\boldsymbol{\eta}^f(t_\tau)$, $\varepsilon_\tau^f=\varepsilon^f(t_\tau)$ and remembering that $y^f(t_\tau)=y_\tau$, we have, on combining (9.1.19) with (9.3.2a), the augmented state space form

$$\begin{bmatrix}\boldsymbol{\alpha}_\tau\\ y_\tau\end{bmatrix}=\begin{bmatrix}e^{\mathbf{A}\delta} & \mathbf{0}\\ \mathbf{z}'\mathbf{W}(\delta_\tau) & 0\end{bmatrix}\begin{bmatrix}\boldsymbol{\alpha}_{\tau-1}\\ y_{\tau-1}\end{bmatrix}+\begin{bmatrix}\mathbf{I} & \mathbf{0}\\ \mathbf{0}' & \mathbf{z}'\end{bmatrix}\begin{bmatrix}\boldsymbol{\eta}_\tau\\ \boldsymbol{\eta}_\tau^f\end{bmatrix}+\begin{bmatrix}\mathbf{0}\\ \varepsilon_\tau^f\end{bmatrix} \tag{9.3.3a}$$

$$y_\tau=[\mathbf{0}' \quad 1]\begin{bmatrix}\boldsymbol{\alpha}_\tau\\ y_\tau\end{bmatrix}, \quad \tau=1,\ldots,T \tag{9.3.3b}$$

with $\text{Var}(\varepsilon_\tau^f)=\delta_\tau\sigma_\varepsilon^2$ and

$$\text{Var}\begin{bmatrix}\boldsymbol{\eta}_\tau\\ \boldsymbol{\eta}_\tau^f\end{bmatrix}=\int_0^{\delta_\tau}\left[\begin{array}{c:c} e^{\mathbf{A}r}\mathbf{RQR}'e^{\mathbf{A}'r} & e^{\mathbf{A}r}\mathbf{RQR}'\mathbf{W}'(r)\\ \hdashline \mathbf{W}(r)\mathbf{RQR}'e^{\mathbf{A}'r} & \mathbf{W}(r)\mathbf{RQR}'\mathbf{W}'(r)\end{array}\right]dr \tag{9.3.4}$$

Maximum likelihood estimators of the hyperparameters can be constructed via the prediction error decomposition by running the Kalman filter on (9.3.3). No additional starting value problems are caused by bringing the cumulator variable into the state vector as $y^f(t_0)\equiv 0$.

The evaluation of the matrix integrals in(9.3.2c) and (9.3.4) is relatively easy for the trend and seasonal components in a structural model since exp(**A**) takes a very simple form. In other situations it may be necessary to diagonalise **A**; see sub-section 9.4.1.

As when the basic model is formulated in discrete time, the dimension of the vector is increased from m to $m+1$ in order to handle a flow variable with a standard Kalman filter. A modified but equivalent form of the Kalman filter in which the state vector remains of length m was derived in Harvey and Stock (1985). This was specialised to the basic structural model in Harvey (1983). The modified filter may be efficient computationally. The problem with it is that it does not easily lead to algorithms for smoothing and distribution. Another way of approaching the problem is not to augment the state vector, as such, but to treat the equation

$$y_\tau=\mathbf{z}'\mathbf{W}(\delta_\tau)\boldsymbol{\alpha}_{\tau-1}+\mathbf{z}'\boldsymbol{\eta}_\tau^f+\varepsilon_\tau^f \tag{9.3.5}$$

as a measurement equation as was done in sub-section 6.4.4. Redefining $\boldsymbol{\alpha}_{\tau-1}$ as $\boldsymbol{\alpha}_\tau^*$ enables (9.3.5) to be written as

$$y_\tau = \mathbf{z}_\tau'\boldsymbol{\alpha}_\tau^* + \varepsilon_\tau, \quad \tau = 1, \ldots, T \tag{9.3.6a}$$

where $\mathbf{z}_\tau' = \mathbf{z}'\mathbf{W}(\delta_\tau)$ and $\varepsilon_\tau = \mathbf{z}'\boldsymbol{\eta}_\tau^f + \varepsilon_\tau^f$. The corresponding transition equation is

$$\boldsymbol{\alpha}_{\tau+1}^* = \mathbf{T}_{\tau+1}\boldsymbol{\alpha}_\tau^* + \boldsymbol{\eta}_\tau, \quad \tau = 1, \ldots, T \tag{9.3.6b}$$

where $\mathbf{T}_{\tau+1} = \exp(\mathbf{A}\delta_\tau)$. Taken together the equations (9.3.6) are a system of the form (3.1.1a) and (3.1.10) with the measurement equation disturbance, ε_τ, and the transition equation disturbance, $\boldsymbol{\eta}_\tau$, correlated. If $\mathbf{Q}_\tau^\dagger$ denotes the covariance matrix in (9.3.4), the covariance matrix of $[\boldsymbol{\eta}_\tau' \quad \varepsilon_\tau]'$ is given by

$$\text{Var}\begin{bmatrix} \boldsymbol{\eta}_\tau \\ \varepsilon_\tau \end{bmatrix} = \begin{bmatrix} \mathbf{Q}_\tau & \mathbf{g}_\tau \\ \mathbf{g}_\tau' & h_\tau \end{bmatrix} = \begin{bmatrix} \mathbf{I} & \mathbf{0} \\ \mathbf{0}' & \mathbf{z}' \end{bmatrix} \mathbf{Q}_\tau^\dagger \begin{bmatrix} \mathbf{I} & \mathbf{0} \\ \mathbf{0} & \mathbf{z} \end{bmatrix} + \begin{bmatrix} \mathbf{0} & \mathbf{0} \\ \mathbf{0} & \delta\sigma_\varepsilon^2 \end{bmatrix} \tag{9.3.7}$$

The modified version of the Kalman filter needed to handle such systems is described in sub-section 3.2.4.

9.3.1 *Structural models*

The various matrix exponential expressions which need to be computed for the flow variable are relatively easy to evaluate for trend and seasonal components. The formulae for a stationary cyclical component are rather more tedious to derive and so will not be explicitly given here. The components in, say, a basic structural model are independent of each other and so the various blocks in (9.3.4) can be treated separately, as though there were only a single component in the model. Note that the top left-hand block in (9.3.4) is the same as the corresponding $\mathbf{Q}_\tau$ matrix evaluated for a stock variable in section 9.2.

Trend For the local linear trend component, (9.1.25)

$$\mathbf{W}(r) = \int_0^r \begin{bmatrix} 1 & s \\ 0 & 1 \end{bmatrix} ds = \begin{bmatrix} r & \frac{1}{2}r^2 \\ 0 & r \end{bmatrix} \tag{9.3.8}$$

Thus, in (9.3.4), the lower right-hand matrix is

$$\text{Var}(\boldsymbol{\eta}_\tau^f) = \int_0^\delta \mathbf{W}(r)\mathbf{R}\mathbf{Q}\mathbf{R}'\mathbf{W}'(r)dr$$

$$= \begin{bmatrix} \frac{1}{3}\delta_\tau^3\sigma_\eta^2 + \frac{1}{20}\delta_\tau^5\sigma_\zeta^2 & \frac{1}{8}\delta_\tau^4\sigma_\zeta^2 \\ \frac{1}{8}\delta_\tau^4\sigma_\zeta^2 & \frac{1}{3}\delta_\tau^3\sigma_\zeta^2 \end{bmatrix} \tag{9.3.9}$$

where in this case $\boldsymbol{\eta}_\tau^f$ is the 2×1 vector $[\eta_\tau^f \quad \zeta_\tau^f]'$.

The off-diagonal blocks are derived in a similar way. Thus

$$\mathrm{Cov}(\bar{\boldsymbol{\eta}}_\tau^f, \bar{\boldsymbol{\eta}}_\tau') = \int_0^\delta \mathbf{W}(r)\mathbf{RQR}'e^{\mathbf{A}'r}dr$$

$$= \begin{bmatrix} \frac{1}{2}\delta_\tau^2\sigma_\eta^2 + \frac{1}{8}\delta_\tau^4\sigma_\zeta^2 & \frac{1}{6}\delta_\tau^3\sigma_\zeta^2 \\ \frac{1}{3}\delta_\tau^3\sigma_\zeta^2 & \frac{1}{2}\delta_\tau^2\sigma_\zeta^2 \end{bmatrix} \tag{9.3.10}$$

The local level (9.1.24), is just a special case in which $\mathrm{Var}(\eta_\tau^f)$ and $\mathrm{Cov}(\eta_\tau^f, \eta_\tau)$ are scalars consisting of the top left-hand elements of (9.3.9) and (9.3.10) respectively with $\sigma_\zeta^2 = 0$.

Seasonal For a trigonometric component in a continuous time seasonal model, (9.1.23),

$$\mathbf{W}(r) = \int_0^r \begin{bmatrix} \cos\lambda s & \sin\lambda s \\ -\sin\lambda s & \cos\lambda s \end{bmatrix} ds = \frac{1}{\lambda}\begin{bmatrix} \sin\lambda r & 1-\cos\lambda r \\ \cos\lambda r - 1 & \sin\ \lambda r \end{bmatrix} \tag{9.3.11}$$

Thus, if $\boldsymbol{\eta}_\tau^f$ in (9.3.3) relates to the disturbances in a trigonometric term, we have

$$\mathrm{Var}(\boldsymbol{\eta}_\tau^f) = \frac{2\delta\sigma_\omega^2}{\lambda^2}\begin{bmatrix} 1-(1/\lambda\delta_\tau)\sin\lambda\delta & 0 \\ 0 & 1-(1/\lambda\delta_\tau)\sin\lambda\delta \end{bmatrix} \tag{9.3.12}$$

Similarly

$$\mathrm{Cov}(\boldsymbol{\eta}_\tau^f, \boldsymbol{\eta}_\tau') = \frac{\sigma^2}{\lambda^2}\begin{bmatrix} 1-\cos\lambda\delta_\tau & \sin\lambda\delta_\tau - \lambda\delta_\tau \\ \lambda\delta_\tau - \sin\lambda\delta_\tau & 1-\cos\lambda\delta_\tau \end{bmatrix} \tag{9.3.13}$$

The state space form with correlated measurement and transition equation, (9.3.6), gives more insight into the structure of the discrete time Kalman filter. If $\boldsymbol{\eta}_\tau$ and ε_τ were uncorrelated, these equations would yield a Kalman filter identical to the filter for the analogous model for a stock variable. Consider the continuous time local level model

$$y(t) = \mu(t) + \varepsilon(t) \tag{9.3.14}$$

with $\mu(t)$ given by (9.1.24). In terms of (9.3.6),

$$y_\tau = \delta\mu_\tau^* + \varepsilon_\tau \tag{9.3.15a}$$

$$\mu_{\tau+1}^* = \mu_\tau^* + \eta_\tau \tag{9.3.15b}$$

with

$$\mathrm{Var}\begin{bmatrix} \eta_\tau \\ \varepsilon_\tau \end{bmatrix} = \begin{bmatrix} \delta_\tau\sigma_\eta^2 & \frac{1}{2}\delta_\tau^2\sigma_\eta^2 \\ \frac{1}{2}\delta_\tau^2\sigma_\eta^2 & \frac{1}{3}\delta_\tau^3\sigma_\eta^2 + \delta_\tau\sigma_\varepsilon^2 \end{bmatrix} \tag{9.3.15c}$$

Applying the Kalman filter with the modification noted in (3.2.22) gives

$$m^*_{\tau+1} = (1-\lambda_\tau)m^*_\tau + \lambda_\tau y_\tau \tag{9.3.16a}$$

with

$$\lambda_\tau = \frac{(p_{\tau|\tau-1} + g_\tau)}{p_{\tau|\tau-1} + \mathrm{Var}(\varepsilon_\tau)} \tag{9.3.16b}$$

and $p_{\tau|\tau-1}$ updated according to (3.2.23). These equations are a generalisation of the EWMA recursion given in (4.1.25). If δ_τ is equal to unity for all τ, the filter has a steady-state solution. Setting $p_{\tau+1|\tau} = p_{\tau|\tau-1} = \bar{p}$ in (3.2.23) and rearranging gives

$$\bar{p}^2 + (2g - \sigma_\eta^2)\bar{p} + g^2 - \sigma_\eta^2 \, \mathrm{Var}(\varepsilon_\tau) = 0$$

The solution of this equation, bearing in mind that $\bar{p}$ must be non-negative and that $\mathrm{Var}(\varepsilon_\tau) = \frac{1}{3}\sigma_\eta^2 + \sigma_\varepsilon^2$ and $2g = \sigma_\eta^2$, is

$$\bar{p} = \sqrt{\sigma_\eta^2 \, \mathrm{Var}(\varepsilon_\tau) - g^2} = \sqrt{\tfrac{1}{12}\sigma_\eta^4 + \sigma_\eta^2 \sigma_\varepsilon^2} \tag{9.3.17}$$

Substituting in (9.3.16b) gives

$$\lambda_\tau = \lambda = \frac{\frac{1}{2}\sigma_\eta^2 + \sqrt{\frac{1}{12}\sigma_\eta^4 + \sigma_\eta^2\sigma_\varepsilon^2}}{\frac{1}{3}\sigma_\eta^2 + \sigma_\varepsilon^2 + \sqrt{\frac{1}{12}\sigma_\eta^4 + \sigma_\eta^2\sigma_\varepsilon^2}} \tag{9.3.18}$$

This expression may be rewritten in terms of the continuous time signal–noise ratio, $q = \sigma_\eta^2/\sigma_\varepsilon^2$, that is

$$\lambda = [\tfrac{1}{2}q + \sqrt{\tfrac{1}{12}q^2 + q}]/[\tfrac{1}{3}q + 1 + \sqrt{\tfrac{1}{12}q^2 + q}] \tag{9.3.19}$$

When q is equal to zero, λ is zero. The other extreme is not λ equal to unity, as is usually the case with the EWMA: setting σ_ε^2 equal to zero in (9.3.18) instead gives $\lambda = 1.27$. This corresponds to the result found earlier in section 6.3 for the aggregation of a random walk and it implies that the first-order autocorrelation of the first differences is 0.25. The value of λ equal to unity is obtained when q is equal to six. A useful subsidiary result to emerge is that the innovation variance is given by

$$\bar{f} = \bar{p} + \mathrm{Var}(\varepsilon_\tau) = \sqrt{\tfrac{1}{12}\sigma_\eta^4 + \sigma_\varepsilon^2\sigma_\eta^2} + \tfrac{1}{3}\sigma_\eta^2 + \sigma_\varepsilon^2 = \sigma_\varepsilon^2(\tfrac{1}{3}q + 1 + \sqrt{\tfrac{1}{12}q^2 + q})$$

US GNP The first-order autocorrelation in the logarithm of seasonally adjusted US GNP over the period 1953*Q*1 to 1984*Q*4 is 0.34. A pure Brownian motion model fits this data quite well; see Harvey and Stock (1988). The result noted above does not apply directly in this case because it is the integral of the level of GNP, rather than its logarithm, which is recorded. Nevertheless, this may be the explanation of why a continuous time Brownian motion model captures most of the dependence in the series, leaving a relatively small role for a stationary component.

A similar analysis could be carried out for more complicated models. The overall conclusion is that the structure of the discrete time model corresponding to a particular continuous time model is essentially the same for a flow as for a stock. The only difference is that for a flow variable, the implied discrete time model is slightly more flexible than for a stock.

9.3.2 Smoothing and distribution

Suppose that the observations are evenly spaced at intervals of δ and that we wish to estimate certain integrals of linear combinations of the state vector at evenly spaced intervals Δ time periods apart, where δ/Δ is a positive integer. The quantities to be estimated may be written in an $m^* \times 1$ vector as

$$\boldsymbol{\alpha}^f(t_i) = \boldsymbol{\alpha}_i^f = \int_0^{\Delta} \mathbf{Z}\boldsymbol{\alpha}(t_{i-1}+s)ds, \quad t_i, i=1,\ldots,(\delta/\Delta)T \tag{9.3.20}$$

where $\mathbf{Z}$ is an $m^* \times m$ selection matrix as in (6.3.24). In the continuous time basic structural model, the components of interest are normally the level of the trend, the slope and the seasonal. Thus $\boldsymbol{\alpha}^f(t) = [\mu(t) \quad \beta(t) \quad \gamma(t)]'$. In addition it may be desired to estimate the actual value of the series,

$$y(t_i) = y_i = \int_0^{\Delta} \mathbf{z}'\boldsymbol{\alpha}(t_{i-1}+s)ds + \int_0^{\Delta} \varepsilon(t_{i-1}+s)ds \tag{9.3.21}$$

The transition equation in the augmented discrete time SSF(i, Δ) is

$$\begin{bmatrix} \boldsymbol{\alpha}_i \\ y_i^f \\ \boldsymbol{\alpha}_i^f \\ y_i \end{bmatrix} = \begin{bmatrix} e^{\mathbf{A}\Delta} & 0 & 0 & \mathbf{0} \\ \mathbf{z}'\mathbf{W}(\Delta) & \psi_i & 0 & \mathbf{0}' \\ \mathbf{Z}\mathbf{W}(\Delta) & 0 & 0 & \mathbf{0} \\ \mathbf{z}'\mathbf{W}(\Delta) & 0 & 0 & \mathbf{0}' \end{bmatrix} \begin{bmatrix} \boldsymbol{\alpha}_{i-1} \\ y_{i-1}^f \\ \boldsymbol{\alpha}_{i-1}^f \\ y_{i-1} \end{bmatrix} + \begin{bmatrix} \mathbf{I} & \mathbf{0} \\ \mathbf{0}' & \mathbf{z}' \\ \mathbf{0} & \mathbf{Z} \\ \mathbf{0}' & \mathbf{z}' \end{bmatrix} \begin{bmatrix} \boldsymbol{\eta}_i \\ \boldsymbol{\eta}_i^f \end{bmatrix} + \begin{bmatrix} \mathbf{0} \\ 1 \\ \mathbf{0} \\ 1 \end{bmatrix} \varepsilon_i^f \tag{9.3.22}$$

with

$$\psi_i = \begin{cases} 0, & i = (\delta/\Delta)(\tau-1)+1, \quad \tau = 1,\ldots,T \\ 1, & \text{otherwise} \end{cases}$$

The covariance matrix of $[\boldsymbol{\eta}_i' \quad \boldsymbol{\eta}_i^{f\prime}]'$ is defined as in (9.3.4) with δ replaced by Δ, while $\text{Var}(\varepsilon_i^f) = \Delta\sigma_\varepsilon^2$. The matrix function $\mathbf{W}(\Delta)$ is as defined in (9.3.2c).

Setting $\Delta = \delta$ gives the special case in which smoothed estimates of elements of the state vector are required at the observation time. In this case the bottom line of the transition equation is unnecessary.

9.3.3 Prediction

In making predictions for a flow it is necessary to distinguish between the total accumulated effect from time t_τ to time $t_\tau + l$ and the amount of the flow in a single time period ending at time $t_\tau+l$. The latter concept corresponds to the usual idea of prediction in a discrete model. The cumulative prediction for a discrete time model was given special treatment in sub-section 4.6.3. Cumulative predictions are perhaps more natural in a continuous time model, particularly when the observations are observed at irregular intervals.

Cumulative predictions Predictions for the cumulative effect of $y(t)$ are obtained by noting that the quantity required is $y^f(t_\tau+l)$ which in terms of the state space model of (9.3.3) is y_{T+1} with δ_{T+1} set equal to l. The optimal predictor can therefore be obtained directly from the Kalman filter as can its MSE. Written out explicitly we have

$$\tilde{y}^f(t_T+l|T)=\tilde{y}_{T+1|T}=\mathbf{z}'\mathbf{W}(l)\mathbf{a}_T \tag{9.3.23}$$

and since the quantity to be estimated is

$$y^f(t_T+l)=\int_0^l y(t_\tau+r)\,dr=\mathbf{z}'\mathbf{W}(l)\boldsymbol{\alpha}_T+\mathbf{z}'\boldsymbol{\eta}_{T+1}^f+\varepsilon_{T+1}^f$$

the prediction MSE is

$$\text{MSE}[\tilde{y}^f(t_T+l|T)]=\mathbf{z}'\mathbf{W}(l)\mathbf{P}_T\mathbf{W}'(l)\mathbf{z}+\mathbf{z}'\text{Var}(\boldsymbol{\eta}_\tau^f)\mathbf{z}+\text{Var}(\varepsilon_{T+1}^f) \tag{9.3.24}$$

It is interesting to examine the form of the cumulative forecast function and its associated MSE for the principal structural models. For the local level model, (9.3.14),

$$\tilde{y}^f(t_T+l|T)=lm_T, \quad l\geqslant 0 \tag{9.3.25}$$

and

$$\text{MSE}[\tilde{y}^f(t_T+l|T)]=l^2p_T+\tfrac{1}{3}l^3\sigma_\eta^2+l\sigma_\varepsilon^2 \tag{9.3.26}$$

The corresponding expressions for the discrete time models were given in (4.6.15). The derivation of (9.3.25) is both simpler and more elegant.

As regards the local linear trend, (9.3.14) with $\mu(t)$ given by (9.1.25), evaluating $W(l)$ using (9.3.8) gives

$$\tilde{y}^f(t_T+l)=lm_T+\tfrac{1}{2}l^2b_T, \quad l\geqslant 0 \tag{9.3.27}$$

Because the forecasts from a linear trend are being cumulated, the result is a quadratic. From (9.3.24) and (9.3.9),

$$\text{MSE}[\tilde{y}^f(t_T+l|T)]=l^2p_T^{(1,1)}+l^3p_T^{(1,2)}+\tfrac{1}{4}l^4p_T^{(2,2)}+\tfrac{1}{3}l^3\sigma_\eta^2+\tfrac{1}{20}l^5\sigma_\zeta^2+l\sigma_\varepsilon^2 \tag{9.3.28}$$

where $p_T^{(i,j)}$ is the ij-th element of $\mathbf{P}_T$.

Predictions over the unit interval Predictions over the unit interval emerge quite naturally from the state space form, (9.3.3), as the predictions of y_{T+l}, $l=1, 2, \ldots$

with δ_{T+l} set equal to unity for all l. Thus

$$\tilde{y}_{T+l|T} = \mathbf{z}'\mathbf{W}(1)\mathbf{a}_{T+l-1|T}, \quad l=1,2,\ldots \tag{9.3.29a}$$

with

$$\mathbf{a}_{T+l-1|T} = e^{\mathbf{A}(l-1)}\mathbf{a}_T \tag{9.3.29b}$$

The forecast function for the state vector, (9.3.29b), is therefore of the same form as in the corresponding stock variable model. The presence of the term $\mathbf{W}(1)$ in (9.3.29a) leads to a slight modification when these forecasts are translated into a prediction for the series itself. Thus in the local linear trend model, (9.3.14) and (9.1.25)

$$\mathbf{a}'_{T+l-1|T} = [m_T + (l-1)b_T \quad b_T]$$

and so

$$\tilde{y}_{T+l|T} = m_T + (l - \tfrac{1}{2})b_T, \quad l=1,2,\ldots \tag{9.3.30}$$

The one-half in (9.3.30) arises because each observation is cumulated over the unit interval.

If predictions are required for the unobserved components in the model, as defined in (9.3.20), the transition equation (9.3.22) needs to be used. Thus in the local linear trend model, the prediction for the trend component is not $m_{T+l|T}$, as given from (9.3.29b), but

$$m^f_{T+l|T} = m_T + (l - \tfrac{1}{2})b_T \tag{9.3.31}$$

In terms of the estimators of the trend and slope, the forecast function for y_{T+l} is

$$\tilde{y}_{T+l|T} = m^f_T + b^f_T l, \quad l=1,2,\ldots \tag{9.3.32}$$

where $b^f_T = b_T$. The conditions linking trend estimation and prediction set out in sub-section 6.1.1 are therefore satisfied, since the forecast function passes through the estimator of the trend at time T.

9.3.4 *Cumulative predictions over a variable lead time*

In some applications, the lead time itself can be regarded as a random variable. This happens, for example, in inventory control problems where an order is put in to meet demand, but the delivery time is uncertain. In such situations it may be useful to determine the unconditional distribution of the cumulation of $y(t)$ from the current point in time, T. If this cumulative effect is denoted by y^f_T, its distribution is

$$p(y^f_T) = \int_0^\infty p(y^f_T | l)p(l)\,dl \tag{9.3.33}$$

where $p(l)$ is the p.d.f. of the lead time and $p(y^f_T|l)$ is the predictive distribution of

$y(t)$ at time $T+l$, that is the distribution of $y^f(t_T+l)$ conditional on the information at time T. In a Gaussian model, the mean of $y^f(t_{T+l})$ is given by (9.3.23), while its variance is the same as the expression for the MSE of $y^f(t_T+l)$ given in (9.3.24). Although it may be difficult to derive the full unconditional distribution of y_T^f, expressions for the mean and variance of this distribution may be obtained for the principal structural time series models. In the context of inventory control, the unconditional mean might be the demand expected in the period before a new delivery arrives. Such a quantity is clearly of some practical importance as is the measure of uncertainty provided by the variance. Further discussion can be found in Clark (1955). However, in this reference, as in nearly all the subsequent literature on this topic, the unconditional mean and variance are evaluated on the assumption that the observations are independently and identically distributed about a known mean. Such an assumption is virtually never true as it implies the absence of any trend or seasonal movements.

The mean of the unconditional distribution of y^f is

$$\mathrm{E}(y_T^f)=\mathrm{E}\{\mathrm{E}[y^f(t_T+l)]\}=\mathrm{E}[\tilde{y}^f(t_T+l|T)] \tag{9.3.34}$$

where the expectation outside the curly brackets is with respect to the distribution of the lead time; compare the derivation of (3.7.9). Similarly, the unconditional variance is

$$\mathrm{Var}(y_T^f)=\mathrm{E}\{\mathrm{E}[y^f(t_T+l)]^2\}-[\mathrm{E}(y_T^f)]^2 \tag{9.3.35}$$

where the second raw moment of y_T^f can be obtained as

$$\mathrm{E}[y^f(t_T+l)]^2=\mathrm{MSE}[y^f(t_T+l)]+[\tilde{y}^f(t_T+l|T)]^2 \tag{9.3.36}$$

As we shall see, the expressions for the mean and variance of y_T^f depend on the moments of the distribution of the lead time. In what follows the j-th raw moment of this distribution will be denoted by μ'_j, with the mean abbreviated to μ.

Local level model Using (9.3.25), the expected value of y_T^f in the local level model, (9.3.14), is seen to be

$$\mathrm{E}(y_T^f)=\mathrm{E}(lm_T)=\mathrm{E}(l)m_T=l\mu_T \tag{9.3.37}$$

From (9.3.26) and (9.3.36)

$$\mathrm{E}\{[y^f(t_T+l)]^2\}=\mu'_2 p_T+\tfrac{1}{3}\mu'_3\sigma_\eta^2+\mu\sigma_\varepsilon^2+\mu'_2 m_T^2$$

and so from (9.3.35) the unconditional variance of y_T^f is

$$\mathrm{Var}(y_T^f)=\ \mathrm{Var}(l).m_T^2+\mu\sigma_\varepsilon^2+\mu'_2 p_T+\tfrac{1}{3}\mu'_3\sigma_\eta^2 \tag{9.3.38}$$

The first two terms are the standard formulae found in the operational research literature, corresponding to a situation in which σ_η^2 is zero and the (constant) mean is known. The third term allows for the estimation of the mean, which now may or may not be constant, while the fourth term allows for the movements in the mean which take place beyond the current time period. Note that if $\sigma_\eta^2=0$, $p_T=\sigma_\varepsilon^2/T$ which is the standard expression for the variance of the sample mean.

Local linear trend model For the local linear trend model, (9.3.14) and (9.3.25), it follows from (9.3.27) and (9.3.28) that

$$E(y_T^f)=\mu m_T+\tfrac{1}{2}\mu_2' b_T \tag{9.3.39}$$

and

$$\begin{aligned}\mathrm{Var}(y_T^f)=&\mu_2' p_T^{(1,1)}+\mu_3' p_T^{(1,2)}+\tfrac{1}{4}\mu_4' p_T^{(2,2)}+\tfrac{1}{3}\mu_3'\sigma_\eta^2+\tfrac{1}{20}\mu_5'\sigma_\zeta^2+\mu\sigma_\varepsilon^2\\&+\mu_2' m_T^2+\mu_3' b_T m_T+\tfrac{1}{4}\mu_4' b_T^2-\mu^2 m_T^2-\mu\mu_2' m_T b_T-\tfrac{1}{4}(\mu_2')^2 b_T^2\end{aligned} \tag{9.3.40}$$

The unconditional distributions of y^f for other structural models can, in principle, be evaluated in a similar way. The extension to trigonometric seasonal components is dealt with in Harvey and Snyder (1989).

As regards the lead time distribution, it may be possible to estimate moments from past observations. Alternatively, a particular distribution may be fitted and the appropriate moments calculated for this distribution. Snyder (1984) argues that the gamma distribution has been found to work well in practice. Its p.d.f. is

$$p(l)=\frac{e^{-l\beta}l^{\alpha-1}}{\Gamma(\alpha)\beta^{-\alpha}},\quad l\geqslant 0 \tag{9.3.41}$$

and the parameters α and β may be estimated by the method of moments, for example. The higher-order raw moments are given by the formula

$$\mu_j'=\beta^{-r}\prod_{j=1}^{r}(\alpha+j-1),\quad j=1,2,\ldots \tag{9.3.42}$$

9.4 Multivariate models

We now consider models which generate a continuous $N\times 1$ vector which is observed at certain discrete points in time. The first sub-section examines SUTSE models, while sub-section 9.4.2 looks at continuous time autoregressive models. Continuous time autoregressive models can be regarded as analogues of discrete time vector autoregressions. However, the nature of these models changes once restrictions are put on certain parameters. The characteristics of the process generating the data are then much more akin to those of a simultaneous equations model. Hence the model is truly a structural one.

The final sub-section presents a continuous time version of the common trends model with an application to income and consumption in the USA.

9.4.1 *SUTSE models*

The treatment of a SUTSE model in continuous time follows in a relatively straightforward way from the treatment of the corresponding univariate model.

The only additional feature is that in some situations the elements of the vector $\mathbf{y}(t)$ may not all be observed at the same time. Consider the multivariate time local level model. The level components are generated by

$$(d/dt)\boldsymbol{\mu}(t)=\boldsymbol{\eta}(t) \tag{9.4.1}$$

where $\boldsymbol{\eta}(t)$ is multivariate continuous time white noise with mean zero and covariance matrix $\mathbf{Q}$. If observations are made at time t_τ, $\tau=1,\ldots,T$, the discrete time transition equation is

$$\boldsymbol{\mu}_\tau=\boldsymbol{\mu}_{\tau-1}+\boldsymbol{\eta}_\tau \tag{9.4.2}$$

with $\text{Var}(\boldsymbol{\eta}_\tau)=\delta_\tau\mathbf{Q}$. For stock variables the measurement equation is

$$\mathbf{y}_\tau=\mathbf{Z}_\tau\boldsymbol{\mu}_\tau+\boldsymbol{\varepsilon}_\tau, \quad \tau=1,\ldots,T \tag{9.4.3}$$

where $\mathbf{y}_\tau$ is an $N_\tau\times 1$ vector of variables which are actually observed at t_τ and $\mathbf{Z}_\tau$ is an $N_\tau\times N$ selection matrix which picks out the appropriate elements of $\boldsymbol{\mu}_\tau$. An application concerned with atomic clocks can be found in Jones (1984). The treatment of flow variables is by augmenting the state vector, as in section 9.3, though the details can become tedious to write down when not all the elements of $\mathbf{y}(t)$ are observed at the same time.

9.4.2 Autoregressive processes

A first-order continuous time multivariate autoregressive process for the $N\times 1$ vector $\mathbf{y}(t)$ can be written as

$$\mathbf{D}\mathbf{y}(t)=\boldsymbol{\gamma}+\mathbf{A}\mathbf{y}(t)+\boldsymbol{\xi}(t) \tag{9.4.4}$$

where $\boldsymbol{\xi}(t)$ is continuous time white noise with covariance matrix $\boldsymbol{\Sigma}$. This is a generalisation of (9.1.3) and it is to be interpreted in a similar fashion. The n parameters in the model, contained in a vector $\boldsymbol{\psi}$, enter into the model via the $N\times 1$ vector $\boldsymbol{\gamma}$ and the $N\times N$ matrix $\mathbf{A}$.

Solving (9.4.4) yields the vector autoregressive process

$$\mathbf{y}_t=\boldsymbol{\theta}+\boldsymbol{\Phi}\mathbf{y}_{t-1}+\boldsymbol{\xi}_t, \quad t=1,\ldots,T \tag{9.4.5}$$

where

$$\boldsymbol{\Phi}=\exp(\mathbf{A}) \tag{9.4.6a}$$

$$\boldsymbol{\theta}=(e^{\mathbf{A}}-\mathbf{I})\mathbf{A}^{-1}\boldsymbol{\gamma} \tag{9.4.6b}$$

and $\boldsymbol{\xi}_t$ is multivariate white noise with mean zero and covariance matrix

$$\text{Var}(\boldsymbol{\xi}_t)=\boldsymbol{\Omega}=\int_0^1 e^{r\mathbf{A}}\boldsymbol{\Sigma}e^{r\mathbf{A}'}\,dr; \tag{9.4.6c}$$

see Bergstrom (1984). The same solution was given for the transition equation of (9.1.14). However, for the structural models considered, the form of $\mathbf{A}$ made the evaluation of both the transition matrix and the covariance matrix very easy.

Equation (9.4.5) can be regarded as the reduced form of the continuous time model, (9.4.4). The continuous time model may incorporate restrictions on certain of its elements and can be interpreted as a system of causal relations. This is not true of (9.4.5), for each element in $\mathbf{\Phi}$ will reflect the interaction between the variables in the observation period. Even if the only *a priori* restrictions on $\mathbf{A}$ are that certain elements are zero, the elements of $\mathbf{\Phi}$ will be complicated transcendental functions of $\boldsymbol{\psi}$ and will, in general, be non-zero. Furthermore, even if $\mathbf{\Sigma}$ is diagonal, the elements of $\mathbf{\Omega}$ will, generally, depend on $\mathbf{A}$ and will all be non-zero. In a univariate continuous time AR(1) model, the parameters can be calculated from estimates of the parameters in the corresponding discrete time AR(1) model. As a rule, this is no longer possible in the multivariate case, even though the reduced form parameters in the VAR(1) model are estimated efficiently by least squares regression. Of course, once flow variables and higher-order systems are brought into the picture, the relationship between the structural and reduced forms becomes even more complicated. The method presented below is a very general one in which the model is put in state space form and the likelihood function evaluated in terms of the original structural parameters $\boldsymbol{\psi}$. The observations may be at equal intervals or irregularly spaced.

The continuous time vector AR(p) process is generated by the multivariate stochastic differential equations

$$\mathrm{D}^p\mathbf{y}(t)=\mathbf{A}_1\mathrm{D}^{p-1}\mathbf{y}(t)+\cdots+\mathbf{A}_{p-1}\mathrm{D}\mathbf{y}(t)+\mathbf{A}_p\mathbf{y}(t)+\boldsymbol{\xi}(t) \tag{9.4.7}$$

where $\boldsymbol{\xi}(t)$ is multivariate white noise with mean zero and covariance matrix $\mathbf{\Sigma}$. A vector of constants, $\boldsymbol{\gamma}$, could be included in (9.4.7), but the way in which it is treated should be apparent from the solution to (9.4.4).

The first step in the statistical treatment of (9.4.7) is to write it in continuous time state space form. The first-order differential equation, (9.1.14), is obtained by defining

$$\boldsymbol{\alpha}(t)=\begin{bmatrix}\mathbf{y}(t)\\ \mathrm{D}\mathbf{y}(t)\\ \vdots\\ \mathrm{D}^{p-1}\mathbf{y}(t)\end{bmatrix},\quad \mathbf{R}=\begin{bmatrix}\mathbf{0}\\ \mathbf{0}\\ \vdots\\ \mathbf{I}\end{bmatrix},\quad \text{and } \mathbf{A}=\left[\begin{array}{c|c}\mathbf{0} & \\ \mathbf{0} & \mathbf{I}\\ \vdots & \\ \mathbf{A}_p & \mathbf{A}_{p-1}\cdots\mathbf{A}_1\end{array}\right] \tag{9.4.8a}$$

while

$$\mathbf{y}(t)=\mathbf{Z}\boldsymbol{\alpha}(t) \tag{9.4.8b}$$

where $\mathbf{Z}$ is the $N\times Np$ matrix

$$\mathbf{Z}=[\mathbf{I}\quad \mathbf{0}\quad \ldots\quad \mathbf{0}] \tag{9.4.8c}$$

Although the corresponding discrete time transition equation is of the form

(9.1.19), the form of the **A** matrix in (9.4.8) makes it difficult, in general, to evaluate matrices such as $\mathbf{Q}_\tau$. The solution described below is to diagonalise **A**. Alternative techniques for computing matrix exponentials and integrals of matrix exponentials are given in van Loan (1978).

Assuming that **A** has distinct characteristic roots it can be diagonalised as

$$\mathbf{A}=\mathbf{G}\boldsymbol{\Lambda}\mathbf{G}^{-1} \tag{9.4.9}$$

where $\boldsymbol{\Lambda}$ is a diagonal matrix containing the roots, λ_i, $i=1,\ldots,Np$ of **A**, and **G** is an $Np\times Np$ matrix, the columns of which are the right characteristic vectors of **A**. Making the transformation

$$\boldsymbol{\alpha}^*(t)=\mathbf{G}^{-1}\boldsymbol{\alpha}(t) \tag{9.4.10}$$

enables (9.4.8) to be written in the more manageable form

$$\frac{d}{dt}[\boldsymbol{\alpha}^*(t)]=\boldsymbol{\Lambda}\boldsymbol{\alpha}^*(t)+\boldsymbol{\eta}^*(t) \tag{9.4.11}$$

where $\boldsymbol{\eta}^*(t)$ is a multivariate continuous time white-noise process, $\boldsymbol{\eta}^*(t)=\mathbf{G}^{-1}\mathbf{R}\boldsymbol{\eta}(t)$, with mean zero and covariance matrix

$$\mathbf{Q}^*=\mathbf{G}^{-1}\mathbf{R}\boldsymbol{\Sigma}\mathbf{R}'(\bar{\mathbf{G}}^{-1})' \tag{9.4.12}$$

Writing a 'bar' over a matrix indicates a matrix of complex conjugates.

Since $\boldsymbol{\Lambda}$ is diagonal, $\exp(\boldsymbol{\Lambda})$ is also diagonal and the conversion of (9.4.11) to a discrete time transition equation at t_τ, $\tau=1,\ldots,T$ is much easier. The only complication is that the state vector and associated quantities now consist of complex numbers. Thus in the transition equation corresponding to (9.1.19), $\boldsymbol{\alpha}_\tau$ is replaced by the complex vector $\boldsymbol{\alpha}_\tau^*$ while the covariance matrix of $\boldsymbol{\eta}_\tau^*$ has as its ij-th element

$$(Q_\tau^*)_{ij}=Q_{ij}^*v(\lambda_i+\bar{\lambda}_j;\,\delta) \tag{9.4.13}$$

the function being defined as

$$v(x;\delta)=\begin{cases}[\exp(\delta x)-1]/x, & x\neq 0\\ 0, & x=0\end{cases} \tag{9.4.14}$$

and Q_{ij}^* denoting the ij-th element of $\mathbf{Q}^*$.

If $\boldsymbol{\alpha}(t)$ is stationary, then the transformed process $\boldsymbol{\alpha}^*(t)$ is also stationary and, by analogy with (9.1.22),

$$\boldsymbol{\alpha}^*(t)=\int_{-\infty}^{t} e^{\boldsymbol{\Lambda}(t-s)}\boldsymbol{\eta}^*(s)ds \tag{9.4.15}$$

The unconditional mean of $\boldsymbol{\alpha}^*(t)$ is zero and its covariance matrix has as its ij-th element

$$\{\mathrm{Var}[\boldsymbol{\alpha}^*(t)]\}_{ij}=-q_{ij}^*/(\lambda_i+\bar{\lambda}_j),\quad i,j=1,\ldots,Np \tag{9.4.16}$$

Expression (9.4.16) therefore provides the initial values of $\mathbf{P}_{1|0}$ in the Kalman filter. Note that the condition for stationarity is that the real parts of the characteristic roots should be negative and so it is clear from (9.4.14) that the diagonal elements in $\text{Var}[\boldsymbol{\alpha}^*(t)]$ will be finite and positive.

If the elements of $\mathbf{y}(t)$ are stock variables, all of which are observed at time t_τ, $\tau=1,\ldots, T$, the full discrete time state space model is

$$\mathbf{y}_\tau=\mathbf{Z}^*\boldsymbol{\alpha}_\tau^* \tag{9.4.17a}$$

$$\boldsymbol{\alpha}_\tau^*=e^{\boldsymbol{\Lambda}\delta}\boldsymbol{\alpha}_{\tau-1}^*+\boldsymbol{\eta}_\tau^* \tag{9.4.17b}$$

where $\mathbf{Z}^*=\mathbf{ZG}$. The Kalman filter is applied to this system in the usual way, but noting that the state variables are complex and that $\mathbf{P}_{\tau|\tau-1}^*$ and $\mathbf{P}_\tau^*$ are Hermitian, that is $\mathbf{P}_\tau^*=\bar{\mathbf{P}}_\tau^{*\prime}$. When $\boldsymbol{\alpha}(t)$ is stationary, the starting values are $\mathbf{a}_{1|0}^*=\mathbf{0}$ and $\mathbf{P}_{1|0}^*=\text{Var}\,[\boldsymbol{\alpha}^*(t)]$. The likelihood function is evaluated from the prediction error decomposition in the usual way. A method of handling non-stationary series, based on Rosenberg's algorithm, is given in Harvey and Stock (1985, pp. 103–4).

If all the elements in $\mathbf{y}(t)$ are flows, the transformed state vector is augmented as in (9.3.3) with

$$\mathbf{y}_\tau=\mathbf{Z}^*\mathbf{W}^*(\delta_\tau)\boldsymbol{\alpha}_{\tau-1}^*+\mathbf{Z}^*\boldsymbol{\eta}_\tau^{*f} \tag{9.4.18a}$$

where

$$\boldsymbol{\eta}_\tau^{*f}=\int_0^\delta \mathbf{W}^*(\delta_\tau-r)\boldsymbol{\eta}^*(t_{\tau-1}+r)dr \tag{9.4.18b}$$

Mixtures of stocks and flows can also be handled, and are dealt with in the next sub-section. A general method for dealing with such mixtures as well as missing observations, temporal aggregation and data recorded at different frequencies is given in Harvey and Stock (1988).

As a final point, note that an irregular component may be added to $\mathbf{y}(t)$ as in (9.1.16) or (9.1.17). This is handled in essentially the same way as for a univariate model.

9.4.3 Vector autoregressions with common trends

The continuous time analogue of the model introduced in sub-section 8.7.3 is

$$\mathbf{y}(t)=\boldsymbol{\Theta}\boldsymbol{\mu}(t)+\bar{\boldsymbol{\mu}}+\mathbf{y}_p(t) \tag{9.4.19a}$$

where $\boldsymbol{\Theta}$ is an $N\times K$ matrix of factor loadings and $\boldsymbol{\mu}_0=[\mathbf{0}' \quad \bar{\boldsymbol{\mu}}]'$ as in (8.5.1), $\boldsymbol{\mu}(t)$ is a multivariate continuous time random walk (Brownian motion) as in (9.4.1) but with a drift vector, that is

$$(d/dt)\boldsymbol{\mu}(t)=\boldsymbol{\beta}+\boldsymbol{\eta}(t) \tag{9.4.19b}$$

and $\mathbf{y}_p(t)$ is a continuous time VAR(p) process as in (9.4.7). It will be assumed that the **A** matrix for $\mathbf{y}_p(t)$ can be diagonalised, and the transformed state vector will be denoted by $\boldsymbol{\alpha}^*(t)$ as in the previous sub-sections. Thus (9.4.19a) can be written as

$$\mathbf{y}(t)=\boldsymbol{\Theta}\boldsymbol{\mu}(t)+\boldsymbol{\mu}_0+\mathbf{Z}^*\boldsymbol{\alpha}^*(t) \tag{9.4.20}$$

Let $\mathbf{y}_\tau^s$ denote that part of the observable variable vector, $\mathbf{y}_\tau$, corresponding to stock variables and let $\mathbf{y}_\tau^f$ be the flows. Then

$$\mathbf{y}_\tau^s=\mathbf{Z}^s\mathbf{y}(t_\tau) \tag{9.4.21a}$$

and

$$\mathbf{y}_\tau^f=\mathbf{Z}^f\int_0^\delta \mathbf{y}(t_{\tau-1}+r)\,dr \tag{9.4.21b}$$

where $\mathbf{Z}^s$ and $\mathbf{Z}^f$ are respectively $N_s\times N$ selection matrices of ones and zeros. Suppose, for simplicity, that δ_τ is equal to unity for all τ. Using techniques similar to those adopted in sub-section 9.3.1 yields a discrete time state space based on an augmented state vector $\boldsymbol{\alpha}_\tau^\dagger=[\boldsymbol{\alpha}_\tau^{*\prime}\quad \boldsymbol{\mu}_\tau'\quad \mathbf{y}_\tau^{f\prime}]'$. The transition equation is most conveniently written in the following way:

$$\begin{bmatrix}\boldsymbol{\alpha}_\tau^*\\ \boldsymbol{\mu}_\tau\\ \mathbf{y}_\tau^f\end{bmatrix}=\begin{bmatrix}e^{\mathbf{\Lambda}} & \mathbf{0} & \mathbf{0}\\ \mathbf{0} & \mathbf{I} & \mathbf{0}\\ \mathbf{Z}^f\mathbf{Z}^*\mathbf{W} & \mathbf{Z}^f\boldsymbol{\Theta} & \mathbf{0}\end{bmatrix}\begin{bmatrix}\boldsymbol{\alpha}_{\tau-1}^*\\ \boldsymbol{\mu}_{\tau-1}\\ \mathbf{y}_{\tau-1}^f\end{bmatrix}+\begin{bmatrix}\mathbf{0}\\ \boldsymbol{\beta}\\ \mathbf{Z}^f(\bar{\boldsymbol{\mu}}+\tfrac{1}{2}\boldsymbol{\Theta}\boldsymbol{\beta})\end{bmatrix}$$

$$+\begin{bmatrix}\mathbf{I} & \mathbf{0} & \mathbf{0} & \mathbf{0}\\ \mathbf{0} & \mathbf{0} & \mathbf{I} & \mathbf{0}\\ \mathbf{Z}^f\mathbf{Z}^*\mathbf{\Lambda}^{-1} & -\mathbf{Z}^f\mathbf{Z}^*\mathbf{\Lambda}^{-1} & \mathbf{0} & \mathbf{Z}^f\boldsymbol{\Theta}\end{bmatrix}\begin{bmatrix}\mathbf{v}_{1\tau}\\ \mathbf{v}_{2\tau}\\ \mathbf{v}_{3\tau}\\ \mathbf{v}_{4\tau}\end{bmatrix} \tag{9.4.22}$$

where

$$\mathbf{v}_{1\tau}=\int_{\tau-1}^{\tau} e^{\mathbf{\Lambda}(\tau-r)}\boldsymbol{\eta}^*(r)\,dr,\quad \mathbf{v}_{2\tau}=\int_{\tau-1}^{\tau}\boldsymbol{\eta}^*(r)\,dr$$

$$\mathbf{v}_{3\tau}=\int_{\tau-1}^{\tau}\boldsymbol{\eta}(r)dr,\quad \mathbf{v}_{4\tau}=\int_{\tau-1}^{\tau}(\tau-r)\boldsymbol{\eta}(r)\,dr$$

and

$$\text{Var}\begin{bmatrix} \mathbf{v}_{1\tau} \\ \mathbf{v}_{2\tau} \\ \mathbf{v}_{3\tau} \\ \mathbf{v}_{4\tau} \end{bmatrix} = \begin{bmatrix} \mathbf{Q}_\tau^* & \mathbf{WQ}^* & \mathbf{0} & \mathbf{0} \\ \mathbf{Q}^*\mathbf{W}' & \mathbf{Q}^* & \mathbf{0} & \mathbf{0} \\ \mathbf{0} & \mathbf{0} & \mathbf{\Sigma}_\eta & \frac{1}{2}\mathbf{\Sigma}_\eta \\ \mathbf{0} & \mathbf{0} & \frac{1}{2}\mathbf{\Sigma}_\eta & \frac{1}{3}\mathbf{\Sigma}_\eta \end{bmatrix} \tag{9.4.23}$$

The matrices $\mathbf{Q}^*$ and $\mathbf{Q}_\tau^*$ are as defined in the previous sub-section while $\mathbf{W} = \mathbf{W}(1)$ in (9.3.2b) with $\mathbf{A}$ replaced by $\mathbf{\Lambda}$. The measurement equation is

$$\mathbf{y}_\tau = \mathbf{Z}^\dagger \boldsymbol{\alpha}_\tau^\dagger + \boldsymbol{\mu}_0^\dagger \tag{9.4.24}$$

where

$$\mathbf{Z}^\dagger = \begin{bmatrix} \mathbf{Z}^s\mathbf{Z}^* & \mathbf{Z}^s\mathbf{\Theta} & \mathbf{0} \\ \mathbf{0} & \mathbf{0} & \mathbf{I} \end{bmatrix} \text{ and } \bar{\boldsymbol{\mu}}_0^\dagger = \begin{bmatrix} \mathbf{Z}^s\boldsymbol{\mu}_0 \\ \mathbf{0} \end{bmatrix}$$

The continuous time decomposition presented above provides a framework that can be used for interpolation, distribution, and trend extraction when the variables are modelled as arising from continuous time processes with common trends. If the number of common trends is less than N, and if each row of $\mathbf{\Theta}$ has at least one non-zero element, then the continuous time process $\mathbf{y}(t)$ will be co-integrated; compare sub-section 8.8.2. That is, since $K < N$, there exist $N - K$ linearly independent co-integrating vectors such that for any one of these vectors, $\boldsymbol{\alpha}$, we have $\boldsymbol{\alpha}'\mathbf{\Theta} = \mathbf{0}$ and so, on examining (9.4.20) it is clear that $\boldsymbol{\alpha}'\mathbf{y}_t$ is a stationary continuous time process. As regards the corresponding discrete time process for the observed stocks and flows, we can assume, without loss of generality, that the variables can be ordered so that $\mathbf{Z}^s = [\mathbf{I}_s \quad \mathbf{0}]$ and $\mathbf{Z}^f = [\mathbf{0} \quad \mathbf{I}_f]$ where $\mathbf{I}_s$ and $\mathbf{I}_f$ are the $N_s \times N_s$ and $N_f \times N_f$ identity matrices. In order to stress that the observations are evenly spaced at unit intervals we write the observation vector with a t, rather than a τ subscript. Combining the transition equation and the measurement equation it follows that $\mathbf{y}_t$ has the representation

$$\mathbf{y}_t = \begin{bmatrix} \mathbf{Z}^s \\ \frac{1}{2}\mathbf{Z}^f \end{bmatrix} \mathbf{\Theta}\boldsymbol{\beta} + \mathbf{\Theta}\boldsymbol{\mu}_{t-1} + \mathbf{u}_t \tag{9.4.25}$$

where $\mathbf{u}_t$ is the N-dimensional stationary ARMA process implied by the autoregressive component, plus additional unit integrals of $\boldsymbol{\eta}(t)$ arising from the transition equation for $\boldsymbol{\mu}(t)$ and its integral. Since $\boldsymbol{\alpha}'\mathbf{\Theta} = \mathbf{0}$, $\boldsymbol{\alpha}'\mathbf{y}_t$ is evidently stationary, although it will, in general, have a non-zero mean.

US income and consumption Using quarterly seasonally adjusted data from the beginning of 1953 to the end of 1984, Harvey and Stock (1988) fitted a common trend model of the form (9.4.19) to the logarithms of US GNP and consumption. The order of the continuous time autoregression was two, and $\mathbf{\Theta}$ was set equal to $[1 \;\; 1]'$, thereby imposing the constraint that the underlying trends in the levels of income and consumption are proportional. The results were as follows, with income coming first in the vector $\mathbf{y}(t)$:

$$\tilde{\beta}=0.0045, \quad \tilde{\sigma}_\eta^2=0.612\times 10^{-4}$$

$$\tilde{\mathbf{A}}_1=\begin{bmatrix} -0.076 & -8.761 \\ 0.739 & -3.695 \end{bmatrix}$$

$$\tilde{\mathbf{A}}_2=\begin{bmatrix} 1.608 & -7.55 \\ 2.650 & -10.38 \end{bmatrix}$$

$$\tilde{\mathbf{\Sigma}}=\begin{bmatrix} 0.206 & 0.122 \\ 0.122 & 0.073 \end{bmatrix}\times 10^{-4}$$

The roots of the $\mathbf{A}$ matrix of (9.4.9a) are

$$-0.16, \quad -0.90\pm 3.30i, \quad -1.83$$

No attempt was made to put more structure on the model by imposing restrictions on $\mathbf{A}_1$ and $\mathbf{A}_2$. Restrictions of this kind could be imposed, but the case for doing so on *a priori* grounds is perhaps weakened by the fact that a structure is already present because of the common trend. The role of the autoregression is to pick up the dynamics of the series around the common trend and it is interesting to note that the complex roots of the $\mathbf{A}$ matrix suggest some kind of pseudo-cyclical behaviour. (There is an identifiability problem here, because an observationally equivalent model can be obtained by respectively adding and subtracting $2i\pi n$, where n is an integer, to the two elements in a pair of complex roots; see Bergstrom (1984, p. 1171). This does not pose computational problems but it does suggest that care needs to be taken if the estimates of $\mathbf{A}_1$ and $\mathbf{A}_2$ are to be given any structural interpretation.)

The trend for GNP obtained from the bivariate model is somewhat different from the trend obtained by fitting a univariate model. In the latter case, the stationary AR(2) component was found to play only a minor role, and so the trend is very similar to the series itself; see the discussion at the end of sub-section 9.3.1. In contrast, upon imposing the restriction that the trend in GNP is the same as that in consumption, the imperfect correlation between changes in GNP and changes in consumption means that changes in the common trend can only account for part of the movements in each series. Since consumption is much smoother than GNP, what effectively happens in the bivariate model is that the estimated trend for GNP is much closer to the actual consumption series than it is to GNP. To the extent that consumers' decisions incorporate forecasts of GNP over the longer run, the trend extracted from GNP may possibly be associated with some notion of 'permanent income'.

Appendix 1. Principal structural time series components and models

Model	Component	Specification
	1a *Random walk*	$\mu_t = \mu_{t-1} + \eta_t$
	1b *Random walk with drift*	$\mu_t = \mu_{t-1} + \beta + \eta_t$
A Local level/ random walk plus noise model		$y_t = \mu_t + \varepsilon_t$ with μ_t as in (1a)
	2 *Stochastic trend*	$\mu_t = \mu_{t-1} + \beta_{t-1} + \eta_t$ $\beta_t = \beta_{t-1} + \zeta_t$
B Local linear trend		$y_t = \mu_t + \varepsilon_t$ with μ_t as in (2)
	3 *Stochastic cycle*	$\begin{bmatrix} \psi_t \\ \psi_t^* \end{bmatrix} = \rho \begin{bmatrix} \cos \lambda_c & \sin \lambda_c \\ -\sin \lambda_c & \cos \lambda_c \end{bmatrix} \begin{bmatrix} \psi_{t-1} \\ \psi_{t-1}^* \end{bmatrix} + \begin{bmatrix} \kappa_t \\ \kappa_t^* \end{bmatrix}$ where ψ_t is cycle, $0 \leqslant \rho < 1$, and $0 \leqslant \lambda_c \leqslant \pi$
C Cycle plus noise model		$y_t = \mu + \psi_t + \varepsilon_t$, where $0 \leqslant \rho < 1$
D Trend plus cycle		$y_t = \mu_t + \psi_t + \varepsilon_t$ with μ_t as in (2)
E Cyclical trend		$y_t = \mu_t + \varepsilon_t$ $\mu_t = \mu_{t-1} + \psi_{t-1} + \beta_{t-1} + \eta_t$ with β_t as in (2)
	4 *Non-stationary cycle*	As (3) but $\rho = 1$
	5a *Dummy variable seasonality*	$\gamma_t = \sum_{j=1}^{s-1} \gamma_{t-j} + \omega_t$
	5b *Trigonometric seasonality*	$\gamma_t = \sum_{j=1}^{[s/2]} \gamma_{t,j}^{\dagger}$ where $\gamma_{t,j}^{\dagger}$ is a non-stationary cycle, (4), with $\lambda_c = \lambda_j = 2\pi j/s$, $j = 1, 2, \ldots, [s/2]$
F Basic structural model		$y_t = \mu_t + \gamma_t + \varepsilon_t$ where μ_t is as in (2) and γ_t is as in (5a) or (5b)

Stationarity operator, $\Delta(L)$	Reduced form	Comments
$\Delta = 1 - L$	—	—
Δ	—	—
Δ	ARIMA(0, 1, 1)	Forecast function is EWMA
Δ^2	—	Random walk with drift if $\sigma_\zeta^2 = 0$. Doubly integrated random walk if $\sigma_\eta^2 = 0$
	ARIMA(0, 2, 2)	Forecast function is non-seasonal Holt-Winters
1	ARMA(2,1)	Collapses to AR(1) if $\lambda_c = 0$ or π
1	Constant + ARMA(2, 2)	—
Δ^2	ARIMA(2, 2, 4)	—
Δ^2	ARIMA(2, 2, 4)	Gives the damped trend model if $\lambda_c = 0$ and β_t is removed
$1 - 2\cos\lambda_c + L^2$	$(1 - 2\cos\lambda_c + L^2)\psi_t \sim \text{MA}(1)$	—
$S(L) = 1 + L + L^2 + \cdots + L^{s-1}$	$S(L)\gamma_t \sim \text{WN}$	—
$S(L)$	$S(L)\gamma_t \sim \text{MA}(s-2)$	Evolves more smoothly than (5a)
$\Delta_s = (1 - L)(1 - L^s)$	$\Delta\Delta_s y_t \sim \text{MA}(s+1)$	(a) Forecasts from Holt-Winters are similar. (b) Close to 'airline model' for some series

Appendix 2. Data sets

A. *Energy demand of Other Final Users (millions of useful therms)*

Quarterly data 1960Q1–1986Q4

	Coal	Coal + other solid fuels	Gas	Electricity	Oil	Total
1960	303	245	100	177	313	1138
	169	163	81	141	208	763
	152	126	53	97	161	590
	257	208	75	148	266	954
1961	247	208	100	191	261	1007
	189	161	78	150	202	781
	146	121	53	116	152	588
	220	181	73	157	228	858
1962	248	227	106	218	306	1105
	195	183	88	179	248	893
	141	132	56	130	178	637
	235	191	77	175	257	934
1963	278	255	117	253	377	1280
	167	169	90	196	251	874
	150	139	58	140	206	692
	261	208	75	187	309	1040
1964	244	226	110	256	385	1220
	174	136	92	209	240	851
	104	96	56	148	167	570
	228	178	77	202	359	1042
1965	243	205	116	280	438	1282
	170	128	97	222	239	855
	113	107	62	166	193	642
	219	174	82	223	394	1092
1966	237	185	125	298	457	1302
	138	128	101	238	285	889
	114	92	64	172	193	633
	208	149	85	232	418	1092

	Coal	Coal + other solid fuels	Gas	Electricity	Oil	Total
1967	190	146	128	304	490	1257
	157	123	110	254	332	975
	93	96	70	185	196	639
	182	134	88	244	444	1091
1968	183	168	142	331	592	1417
	106	113	122	230	347	918
	86	95	72	198	235	686
	144	131	89	317	491	1171
1969	226	152	153	364	641	1537
	128	108	134	252	400	1021
	62	95	74	205	241	677
	130	103	96	337	549	1216
1970	169	128	153	379	701	1529
	94	83	135	262	424	997
	91	69	118	227	278	783
	188	81	89	350	571	1279
1971	148	64	188	395	715	1510
	114	45	123	277	431	989
	62	34	85	233	265	678
	139	36	167	356	582	1281
1972	104	54	198	380	717	1453
	99	29	144	285	483	1040
	76	40	95	255	293	757
	122	39	210	386	579	1335
1973	107	43	232	409	729	1520
	76	38	150	310	444	1018
	51	41	99	274	290	755
	111	48	222	417	629	1427
1974	95	41	281	326	601	1344
	71	40	179	291	389	971
	63	36	112	276	271	759
	107	36	252	409	573	1377
1975	65	35	307	391	595	1393
	62	27	201	294	420	1004
	39	35	111	255	261	700
	80	24	256	371	565	1296

	Coal	Coal + other solid fuels	Gas	Electricity	Oil	Total
1976	86	28	371	448	673	1607
	57	24	206	322	397	1006
	37	20	110	288	248	703
	79	19	302	379	576	1354
1977	83	28	365	445	683	1603
	59	20	247	347	452	1125
	42	25	117	311	292	787
	89	19	303	416	573	1399
1978	84	22	418	466	668	1658
	59	20	263	363	433	1138
	43	21	135	327	280	805
	73	21	318	445	532	1389
1979	90	23	517	519	739	1888
	56	25	292	383	426	1182
	40	19	131	340	278	807
	75	14	339	447	469	1343
1980	80	19	525	505	597	1726
	45	22	259	376	329	1031
	32	15	136	349	229	761
	73	18	419	469	461	1440
1981	72	16	530	490	515	1622
	46	18	273	386	319	1042
	38	17	131	353	238	775
	78	14	438	485	483	1498
1982	77	18	578	504	526	1703
	49	19	277	388	294	1027
	41	18	134	371	226	790
	77	11	427	477	413	1406
1983	78	16	573	518	488	1673
	49	19	322	428	309	1127
	34	20	140	391	220	805
	72	17	434	489	381	1393
1984	68	18	618	551	485	1740
	51	16	298	431	298	1094
	23	14	146	383	235	801
	42	17	456	483	376	1374

	Coal	Coal + other solid fuels	Gas	Electricity	Oil	Total
1985	72	24	679	583	498	1827
	49	23	332	460	263	1107
	39	22	170	441	228	884
	64	17	492	553	326	1426
1986	63	24	711	636	444	1878
	43	33	368	518	278	1240
	45	22	205	490	229	991
	56	15	503	586	299	1459

Source: Department of Energy, UK.

B. *US Real Gross National Product (GNP)*

Annual data 1910–70

1910	116.8	1941	227.2
1911	120.1	1942	263.7
1912	123.2	1943	297.8
1913	130.2	1944	337.1
1914	131.4	1945	361.3
1915	125.6	1946	355.2
1916	124.5	1947	312.6
1917	134.3	1948	309.9
1918	135.2	1949	323.7
1919	151.8	1950	324.1
1920	146.4	1951	355.3
1921	139.0	1952	383.4
1922	127.8	1953	395.1
1923	147.0	1954	412.8
1924	165.9	1955	406.0
1925	165.5	1956	438.0
1926	179.4	1957	446.1
1927	190.0	1958	452.5
1928	189.8	1959	447.3
1929	190.9	1960	475.9
1930	203.6	1961	487.7
1931	183.5	1962	497.2
1932	169.3	1963	529.8
1933	144.2	1964	551.0
1934	141.5	1965	581.1
1935	154.3	1966	617.8
1936	169.5	1967	658.1
1937	193.0	1968	675.2
1938	203.2	1969	706.6
1939	192.9	1970	724.7
1940	209.4		

C. *Purses snatched in Hyde Park area of Chicago*

28-day-period data from January 1968

10	26
15	21
10	17
10	19
12	13
10	20
7	24
17	12
10	6
14	14
8	6
17	12
14	9
18	11
3	17
9	12
11	8
10	14
6	14
12	12
14	5
10	8
25	10
29	3
33	16
33	8
12	8
19	7
16	12
19	6
19	10
12	8
34	10
15	5
36	7
29	

Source: McCleary and Hay (1980).

D. *Rainfall in Fortaleza, north-east Brazil (mm)*

Annual data 1849–1984

1849	2001	1894	2505	1939	1911
1850	852	1895	2491	1940	1447
1851	1806	1896	2144	1941	916
1852	1356	1897	1839	1942	780
1853	1233	1898	863	1943	1042
1854	1590	1899	2414	1944	1090
1855	1273	1900	940	1945	1750
1856	1770	1901	1545	1946	1724
1857	1734	1902	878	1947	1726
1858	1457	1903	789	1948	1384
1859	1357	1904	1136	1949	1881
1860	1716	1905	1189	1950	1114
1861	1445	1906	1430	1951	747
1862	1468	1907	697	1952	1378
1863	1452	1908	834	1953	1068
1864	1098	1909	1015	1954	1032
1865	1238	1910	2051	1955	1152
1866	2478	1911	1373	1956	806
1867	832	1912	2446	1957	1225
1868	1289	1913	1905	1958	504
1869	1470	1914	1512	1959	1493
1870	1628	1915	530	1960	1011
1871	1459	1916	1328	1961	1737
1872	2256	1917	2077	1962	1258
1873	2058	1918	1319	1963	2102
1874	1487	1919	656	1964	2428
1875	1581	1920	1847	1965	1630
1876	1569	1921	2496	1966	1288
1877	468	1922	1595	1967	1839
1878	503	1923	1513	1968	1385
1879	597	1924	1847	1969	1805
1880	1539	1925	1137	1970	1192
1881	1423	1926	1571	1971	2093
1882	1246	1927	1195	1972	1299
1883	1508	1928	995	1973	2331
1884	1047	1929	1230	1974	2512
1885	1307	1930	1107	1975	1778
1886	1399	1931	1133	1976	1417
1887	1320	1932	879	1977	1941
1888	736	1933	937	1978	1752
1889	784	1934	1888	1979	996
1890	1534	1935	1661	1980	1095
1891	1077	1936	820	1981	1100
1892	1211	1937	1313	1982	1004
1893	1430	1938	1586	1983	884
				1984	1981

E. *International airline passengers ('000s)*

Monthly data January 1949–December 1960

1949	112	1953	196	1957	315
	118		196		301
	132		236		356
	129		235		348
	121		229		355
	135		243		422
	148		264		465
	148		272		467
	136		237		404
	119		211		347
	104		180		305
	118		201		336
1950	115	1954	204	1958	340
	126		188		318
	141		235		362
	135		227		348
	125		234		363
	149		264		435
	170		302		491
	170		293		505
	158		259		404
	133		229		359
	114		203		310
	140		229		337
1951	145	1955	242	1959	360
	150		233		342
	178		267		406
	163		269		396
	172		270		420
	178		315		472
	199		364		548
	199		347		559
	184		312		463
	162		274		407
	146		237		362
	166		278		405
1952	171	1956	284	1960	417
	180		277		391
	193		317		419
	181		313		461
	183		318		472
	218		374		535
	230		413		622
	242		405		606
	209		355		508
	191		306		461
	172		271		390
	194		306		432

Source: Box and Jenkins (1976).

F. *Deaths and serious injuries in road accidents, Great Britain*

Monthly data January 1969–December 1984

	Car drivers killed	Car drivers killed and seriously injured	Light goods vehicle drivers killed
1969	107	1687	12
	97	1508	6
	102	1507	12
	87	1385	8
	119	1632	10
	106	1511	13
	110	1559	11
	106	1630	6
	107	1579	10
	134	1653	16
	147	2152	13
	180	2148	14
1970	125	1752	14
	134	1765	6
	110	1717	8
	102	1558	11
	103	1575	7
	111	1520	13
	120	1805	13
	129	1800	11
	122	1719	11
	183	2008	14
	169	2242	16
	190	2478	14
1971	134	2030	17
	108	1655	16
	104	1693	15
	117	1623	13
	157	1805	13
	148	1746	15
	130	1795	12
	140	1926	6
	136	1619	9
	140	1992	13
	187	2233	14
	150	2192	15
1972	159	2080	14
	143	1768	3
	114	1835	12
	127	1569	13
	159	1976	12

	Car drivers killed	Car drivers killed and seriously injured	Light goods vehicle drivers killed
1972	156	1853	8
	138	1965	8
	120	1689	15
	117	1778	8
	170	1976	5
	168	2397	17
	198	2654	14
1973	144	2097	13
	146	1963	5
	109	1677	8
	131	1941	5
	151	2003	12
	140	1813	11
	153	2012	13
	140	1912	15
	161	2084	11
	168	2080	11
	152	2118	10
	136	2150	13
1974	113	1608	8
	100	1503	6
	103	1548	8
	103	1382	14
	121	1731	12
	134	1798	14
	133	1779	13
	129	1887	9
	144	2004	4
	154	2077	13
	156	2092	6
	163	2051	15
1975	122	1577	12
	92	1356	16
	117	1652	7
	95	1382	12
	96	1519	10
	108	1421	9
	108	1442	9
	106	1543	6
	140	1656	7
	114	1561	13
	158	1905	14
	161	2199	13

	Car drivers killed	Car drivers killed and seriously injured	Light goods vehicle drivers killed
1976	102	1473	14
	127	1655	11
	101	1407	11
	125	1395	10
	97	1530	4
	112	1309	8
	112	1526	9
	113	1327	10
	108	1627	10
	128	1748	5
	154	1958	13
	162	2274	12
1977	112	1648	10
	79	1401	9
	82	1411	7
	127	1403	5
	108	1394	10
	110	1520	5
	123	1528	6
	103	1643	8
	97	1515	6
	140	1685	12
	165	2000	15
	183	2215	7
1978	148	1956	14
	111	1462	4
	116	1563	10
	115	1459	8
	100	1446	7
	106	1622	11
	134	1657	3
	125	1638	5
	117	1643	11
	122	1683	10
	153	2050	10
	178	2262	7
1979	114	1813	10
	94	1445	11
	128	1762	9
	119	1461	7
	111	1556	8
	110	1431	13
	114	1427	8

	Car drivers killed	Car drivers killed and seriously injured	Light goods vehicle drivers killed
1979	118	1554	5
	115	1645	8
	132	1653	7
	153	2016	12
	171	2207	10
1980	115	1665	7
	95	1361	4
	92	1506	10
	100	1360	4
	95	1453	8
	114	1522	8
	102	1460	7
	104	1552	10
	132	1548	8
	136	1827	14
	117	1737	8
	137	1941	9
1981	111	1474	8
	106	1458	6
	98	1542	7
	84	1404	6
	94	1522	5
	105	1385	4
	123	1641	5
	109	1510	10
	130	1681	7
	153	1938	10
	134	1868	12
	99	1726	7
1982	115	1456	4
	104	1445	5
	131	1456	6
	108	1365	4
	103	1487	4
	115	1558	8
	122	1488	8
	122	1684	3
	125	1594	7
	137	1850	12
	138	1998	2
	152	2079	7
1983	120	1494	8
	95	1057	3

	Car drivers killed	Car drivers killed and seriously injured	Light goods vehicle drivers killed
1983	100	1218	2
	89	1168	6
	82	1236	3
	89	1076	7
	60	1174	6
	84	1139	8
	113	1427	8
	126	1487	4
	122	1483	3
	118	1513	5
1984	92	1357	5
	86	1165	3
	81	1282	4
	84	1110	3
	87	1297	6
	90	1185	6
	79	1222	7
	96	1284	5
	122	1444	7
	120	1575	7
	137	1737	4
	154	1763	7

Source: HMSO: *Road Accidents in Great Britain 1984.*

G. *Tractors in Spain*

Annual data 1951–76

1951	13800	1964	130130
1952	15800	1965	147880
1953	19000	1966	169190
1954	21440	1967	180720
1955	26020	1968	204360
1956	29960	1969	234540
1957	34180	1970	259820
1958	40680	1971	282370
1959	47080	1972	306190
1960	56840	1973	330360
1961	71080	1974	355550
1962	92750	1975	379070
1963	114410	1976	400928

Source: Mar-Molinero (1980).

H. *Goals scored by England against Scotland in international football matches*

Annual data 1872–1987

1872	0	1911	1*	1950	1
1873	4*	1912	1	1951	2*
1874	1	1913	1*	1952	2
1875	2*	1914	1	1953	2*
1876	0	1915	—	1954	4
1877	1*	1916	—	1955	7*
1878	2	1917	—	1956	1
1879	5*	1918	—	1957	2*
1880	4	1919	—	1958	4
1881	1*	1920	5*	1959	1*
1882	1	1921	0	1960	1
1883	2*	1922	0*	1961	9*
1884	0	1923	2	1962	0
1885	1*	1924	1*	1963	1*
1886	1	1925	0	1964	0
1887	2*	1926	0*	1965	2*
1888	5	1927	2	1966	4
1889	2*	1928	1*	1967	2*
1890	1	1929	0	1968	1
1891	2*	1930	5*	1969	4*
1892	4	1931	0	1970	0
1893	5*	1932	3*	1971	3*
1894	2	1933	1	1972	1
1895	3*	1934	3*	1973	1*
1896	1	1935	0	1974	0
1897	1*	1936	1*	1975	5*
1898	3	1937	1	1976	1
1899	2*	1938	0*	1977	1*
1900	1	1939	2	1978	1
1901	2*	1940	—	1979	3*
1902	2	1941	—	1980	2
1903	1*	1942	—	1981	0*
1904	1	1943	—	1982	1
1905	1*	1944	—	1983	2*
1906	1	1945	—	1984	1
1907	1*	1946	—	1985	0
1908	1	1947	1*	1986	2*
1909	2*	1948	2	1987	0
1910	0	1949	1*		

* Matches played in England.
—No match played
Source: Football Association Yearbook.

I. *Employment ('000s) and output (1980 = 100) in UK manufacturing (seasonally adjusted)*

Quarterly data 1963Q1–1983Q3

	Employment	Output		Employment	Output
1963	8282	76.4	1973	7764	113.5
	8255	79.1		7784	113.5
	8248	81.8		7805	114.5
	8289	83.8		7832	114.8
1964	8323	86.6	1974	7818	109.0
	8371	86.6		7832	116.1
	8398	87.4		7839	115.2
	8439	89.8		7778	110.4
1965	8466	89.6	1975	7675	109.4
	8480	89.8		7525	104.0
	8500	89.6		7389	102.4
	8514	91.1		7300	103.7
1966	8521	92.6	1976	7246	105.0
	8514	92.1		7225	106.6
	8514	92.5		7232	106.4
	8418	89.5		7253	109.4
1967	8343	91.1	1977	7253	111.0
	8282	91.9		7273	108.6
	8221	92.1		7266	107.9
	8180	93.9		7253	108.2
1968	8173	97.8	1978	7253	107.9
	8180	98.8		7239	110.3
	8207	99.8		7225	110.0
	8227	100.6		7219	109.9
1969	8275	101.8	1979	7205	107.4
	8302	103.7		7198	112.1
	8302	103.2		7184	108.1
	8323	103.2		7137	110.1
1970	8316	102.5	1980	7055	106.8
	8309	103.4		6925	102.3
	8275	103.3		6741	97.4
	8234	104.0		6537	93.5
1971	8180	102.5	1981	6401	92.4
	8057	102.6		6249	92.7
	7968	102.0		6151	94.6
	7859	101.9		6080	94.9
1972	7784	99.1	1982	6030	94.3
	7757	104.2		5940	94.1
	7750	105.1		5856	93.5
	7737	109.3		5778	92.9
			1983	5715	94.5
				5673	94.1
				5641	96.2

Source: HMSO: *Economic Trends*, Annual Supplement.

J. *Mink and muskrat furs sold by Hudson's Bay Company*

Annual data 1848–1909

	Mink	Muskrat		Mink	Muskrat
1848	37123	224347			
1849	34712	179075			
1850	29619	175472			
1851	21151	194682	1881	36160	829034
1852	24859	292530	1882	45600	1029296
1853	25152	493952	1883	47508	1069183
1854	42375	512291	1884	52290	1083067
1855	50839	345626	1885	110824	817003
1856	61581	258806	1886	76503	347050
1857	61951	302267	1887	64303	380132
1858	76231	313502	1888	83023	344878
1859	63264	254246	1889	40748	223614
1860	44730	177291	1890	35396	322160
1861	31094	206020	1891	29479	574742
1862	49452	335385	1892	42264	806103
1863	43961	357060	1893	58171	934646
1864	61727	509769	1894	50815	648687
1865	60334	418370	1895	51285	674811
1866	51404	320824	1896	70229	813159
1867	58451	412164	1897	76365	551716
1868	73575	618081	1898	70407	568934
1869	74343	404173	1899	41839	701487
1870	27708	232251	1900	45978	767741
1871	31985	443999	1901	47813	928199
1872	39266	704789	1902	57620	1650214
1873	44740	767896	1903	66549	1488287
1874	60429	671982	1904	54673	924439
1875	72273	523802	1905	55996	1056253
1876	79214	583319	1906	60053	695070
1877	79060	437121	1907	39169	407472
1878	84244	486030	1908	21534	172418
1879	62590	499727	1909	17857	302195
1880	35072	478078			

Selected answers to exercises

2.2 See Nelson and Plosser (1982).

4.4 $\rho(1)=\sigma_\varepsilon^2/(2\sigma_\varepsilon^2+\sigma_1^2+\sigma_2^2)$.

4.8 See expression (6.1.9).

4.11 (i) Write $S(L)y_t=s\mu+\omega_t$, then

$$\tilde{\mu}=\frac{1}{(T-s-1)}\sum_{t=s}^{T}\sum_{j=0}^{s-1}\frac{y_{t-j}}{s}$$

i.e. the average of moving averages. Also

$$\tilde{\sigma}_\omega^2=\sum_t\left[\left(\sum_{j=0}^{s-1}y_{t-j}/s\right)-\tilde{\mu}\right]^2\Big/(T-s+1)$$

(ii) $\tilde{y}_{T+l|T}=-\sum_{j=l-s+1}^{l-1}\tilde{y}_{T+j|T}+s\tilde{\mu}$

Seasonal effects sum to zero over s consecutive seasons.

4.12 $\sigma_\eta^2 l[1+l(T-1)]$

6.3 $sg_T=\Delta_s y_T=\Delta_s\mu_T+\Delta_s\gamma_T+\Delta_s\varepsilon_T$

By repeated substitution

$$\mu_T=\mu_{T-s}+s\beta_{T-1}-\sum_{k=1}^{s-1}\sum_{j=1}^{k}\zeta_{T-j}+\sum_{j=0}^{s-1}\eta_{T-j}$$

Furthermore $\Delta_s\gamma_T=\Delta\omega_T$. Substituting for $\Delta_s\mu_T$ in the first equation gives an expression for $g_T-\beta_{T-1}$ in terms of disturbances. This has zero expectation and MSE as given in the question. If g_T is regarded as an estimator of β_T, the MSE is increased by σ_ζ^2. Recall from the discussion below (4.1.10) that this is also the difference between the MSE of b_T and b_{T-1}.

6.2 Since the coefficient of Δy_{t-2} is insignificant, the model is effectively an AR(2) process as fitted by McCleary and Hay (1980). However, although the roots of this AR are well inside the stationarity region, the unit root hypothesis cannot be rejected on a one-sided test at the 10% level of significance. For $T=50$ and $T=100$ the 10% critical values given by the Dickey–Fuller tables are -2.60 and -2.58 respectively.

6.10 MMSE is $\beta\varepsilon_T\varepsilon_{T-1}$. MMSLE is zero.

8.7 Not if Σ_η is p.d.

8.8. On taking first differences

$$\gamma_{12}(0)=\sigma_\eta^2/(\sigma_\eta^2+2\sigma_{\varepsilon 1}^2)^{\frac{1}{2}}(\sigma_\eta^2+2\sigma_{\varepsilon 2}^2)$$

and this will be close to zero if σ_η^2 is relatively small. For $\tau\neq 0$ we have $\gamma_{12}(\tau)=0$. Thus it may *appear* that there is no relationship between the series when there is quite a strong one. In the extreme case, when the common trend is deterministic, no evidence whatsoever of the relationship between the series appears in the cross-correlations.

References

Abraham, B., and G.E.P. Box (1978). Deterministic and forecast-adaptive time-dependent models. *Applied Statistics* 27: 120–30.

Abraham, B., and J. Ledolter (1983). *Statistical Methods for Forecasting.* New York: Wiley.

Adams, J.G.U. (1985). *Risk and Freedom: the Record of Road Safety Regulation.* Cardiff: Transport Publishing Projects.

Ahamad, B. (1967). An analysis of crimes by the method of principal components. *Applied Statistics* 16: 17–39.

Aitchison, J., and S.D. Silvey (1960). Maximum-likelihood estimation procedures and associated tests of significance. *Journal of the Royal Statistical Society, Series B* 22: 154–71.

Akaike, H. (1980). Seasonal adjustment by a Bayesian modeling. *Journal of Time Series Analysis* 1: 1–13.

Almon, S. (1965). The distributed lag between capital appropriations and expenditures. *Econometrica* 33: 178–96.

Amemiya, T. (1973). Regression analysis when the variance of the dependent variable is proportional to the square of its expectation. *Journal of the American Statistical Association* 68: 928–34.

Anderson, B.D.O., and J.B. Moore (1979). *Optimal Filtering.* Englewood Cliffs: Prentice-Hall.

Anderson, T.W. (1971). *The Statistical Analysis of Time Series.* New York: Wiley.

Anderson, T.W., and A. Takemura (1986). Why do noninvertible estimated moving averages occur? *Journal of Time Series Analysis* 7: 235–54.

Ansley, C.F., and R. Kohn (1982). A geometrical derivation of the fixed interval smoothing algorithm. *Biometrika* 69: 486–7.

(1985). Estimation, filtering and smoothing in state space models with incompletely specified initial conditions. *Annals of Statistics* 13: 1286–1316.

(1986). Prediction mean square error for state space models with estimated parameters. *Biometrika* 73: 467–74.

Ansley, C.F., and P. Newbold (1980). Finite sample properties of estimators for auto-regressive moving average processes. *Journal of Econometrics* 13: 159–84.

Ashenfelter, O., and P. Card (1982). Time series representations of economic variables and alternative models of the labour market. *Review of Economic Studies* 49: 761–82.

Ball, J., and E. St Cyr (1966). Short-term employment functions in British manufacturing. *Review of Economic Studies* 33: 179–207.

Bell, W.R. (1984). Signal extraction for nonstationary time series. *Annals of Statistics* 13: 646–64.

Bell, W.R., and S.C. Hillmer (1983). Modeling time series with calendar variation. *Journal of the American Statistical Association* 78: 526–34.

(1984). Issues involved with the seasonal adjustment of economic time series [with discussion]. *Journal of Business and Economic Statistics* 2: 292–349.

Berenblut I.I., and G.I. Webb (1973). A new test for autocorrelated errors in the linear regression model. *Journal of the Royal Statistical Society, Series B* 35: 33–50.

Bergstrom, A.R. (ed.) (1976). *Statistical Inference in Continuous Time Economic Models*. Amsterdam: North Holland.

Bergstrom, A.R. (1983). Gaussian estimation of structural parameters in higher order continuous time dynamic models. *Econometrica* 51: 117–52.

(1984). Continuous time stochastic models and issues of aggregation over time. In Z. Griliches and M. Intriligator (eds.) *Handbook of Econometrics*, vol. 2, pp. 1145–1212. Amsterdam: North Holland.

Beveridge, S., and C.R. Nelson (1981). A new approach to decomposition of economic time series into permanent and transitory components with particular attention to measurement of the 'Business cycle'. *Journal of Monetary Economics* 7: 151–74.

Bhattacharyya, M.N., and A.P. Layton (1979). Effectiveness of seat belt legislation on the Queensland road toll – an Australian case study in intervention analysis. *Journal of the American Statistical Association* 74: 596–603.

Bollerslev, T. (1986). Generalized autoregressive conditional heteroskedasticity. *Journal of Econometrics* 31: 307–27.

Bowden, R.J., and D.A. Turkington (1984). *Instrumental Variables*. Cambridge: Cambridge University Press.

Bowman, K.O., and L.R. Shenton (1975). Omnibus test contours for departures from normality based on $\sqrt{b_1}$ and b_2. *Biometrika* 62: 243–50.

Box, G.E.P., and G.M. Jenkins (1976). *Time Series Analysis: Forecasting and Control*, revised edn. San Francisco: Holden–Day.

Box, G.E.P., and G.C. Tiao (1975). Intervention analysis with applications to economic and environmental problems. *Journal of the American Statistical Association* 70: 70–79.

(1976). Comparison of forecast with actuality. *Applied Statistics* 25: 195–200.

(1977). A canonical analysis of multiple time series. *Biometrika* 64: 355–65.

Box, G.E.P., S.C. Hillmer and G.C. Tiao (1978). Analysis and modelling of seasonal time series. In A. Zellner (ed.) *Seasonal Analysis of Economic Time Series*, pp. 309–34. Washington, D.C: US Department of Commerce.

Box, G.E.P., D.A. Pierce and P. Newbold (1987). Estimating trend and growth rates in seasonal time series. *Journal of the American Statistical Association* 82: 276–82.

Boyles, R.A. (1983). On the convergence of the EM algorithm. *Journal of the Royal Statistical Society, Series B* 45: 47–50.

Brewer, K.R.W. (1973). Some consequences of temporal aggregation and systematic sampling for ARMA and ARMAX models. *Journal of Econometrics* 1: 133–54.

Brillinger, D.R. (1975). *Time Series: Data Analysis and Theory*. New York: Holt.

Brown, R.G. (1963). *Smoothing, Forecasting and Prediction*. Englewood Cliffs: Prentice Hall.

Brown, R.L., J. Durbin and J.M. Evans (1975). Techniques of testing the constancy of regression relationships over time. *Journal of the Royal Statistical Society, Series B* 37: 141–92.

Burman, J.P. (1980). Seasonal adjustment by signal extraction. *Journal of the Royal Statistical Society, Series A* 143: 321–37.

Burridge, P., and K.F. Wallis (1984). Unobserved-components models for seasonal adjustment filters. *Journal of Business and Economic Statistics* 2: 350–9.

Caines, P.E. and D.Q. Mayne (1970). On the discrete time matrix Riccati equation of optimal control. *International Journal of Control* 1: 785–94

Cairncross, A. (1971). *Essays in Economic Management*. London: Allen and Unwin.

Cameron, C.C., and P.K. Trivedi (1986). Econometric models based on count data:

comparisons and applications of some estimators and tests. *Journal of Applied Econometrics* 1: 29–53.

Campos, J. (1986). Instrumental variables estimation of dynamic simultaneous systems with ARMA errors. *Review of Economic Studies* 53: 125–38.

Chan, S.W., G.C. Goodwin and K.S. Sin (1984). Convergence properties of the Riccati difference equation in optimal filtering of nonstabilizable systems. *IEEE Transactions on Automatic Control* AC-29: 10–18.

Chan, W.Y.T., and K.F. Wallis (1978). Multiple time series modelling: another look at the mink–muskrat interaction. *Applied Statistics* 27: 168–75.

Chatfield, C. (1978). The Holt–Winters forecasting procedure. *Applied Statistics* 2: 264–79.

Chernoff, H. (1954). On the distribution of the likelihood ratio. *Annals of Mathematical Statistics* 25: 573–8.

Chitturi, R.V. (1974). Distribution of residual correlations in multiple autoregressive schemes. *Journal of the American Statistical Association* 69: 928–34.

Cholette, P.A. (1982). Prior information and ARIMA forecasting. *Journal of Forecasting* 1: 375–83.

Chow, G.C. (1984). Random and changing coefficient models. In Z. Griliches and M. Intriligator (eds.) *Handbook of Econometrics*, vol. 2, pp. 1213–45. Amsterdam: North Holland.

Chow, G.C., and A. Lin (1971). Best linear unbiased interpolation, distribution and extrapolation of time series by related series. *Review of Economics and Statistics* 53: 372–5.

(1976). Best linear unbiased estimation of missing observations in an economic time series. *Journal of the American Statistical Association* 71: 719–21.

Clark, C.E. (1955). Mathematical analysis of an inventory case. *Operations Research* 5: 627–43.

Cleveland, W.P. (1972). Analysis and forecasting of seasonal time series. Unpublished Ph.D. dissertation, Department of Statistics, University of Wisconsin–Madison.

Cleveland, W.P., and G.C. Tiao (1976). Decomposition of seasonal time series: a model for the X-11 program. *Journal of the American Statistical Association* 71: 581–7.

Cleveland, W.S., and S.J. Devlin (1980). Calendar effects in monthly time series: detection by spectrum analysis and graphical methods. *Journal of the American Statistical Association* 75: 487–96.

(1982). Calendar Effects in Monthly Time Series: Modelling and Adjustment *Journal of the American Statistical Association* 77: 520–528.

Cleveland, W.S., D.M. Dunn and I.J. Terpenning (1978). SABL: a resistant seasonal adjustment procedure with graphical methods for interpretation and diagnostics. In A. Zellner (ed.) *Seasonal Analysis of Economic Time Series*, pp. 201–31. Washington D.C.: Bureau of the Census.

Conrad, W., and C. Corrado (1979). Application of the Kalman filter to revisions in monthly sales estimates. *Journal of Economic Dynamics and Control* 1: 177–98.

Cooley T.F., B. Rosenberg and K.D. Wall (1977). A note on optimal smoothing for time-varying coefficient problems. *Annals of Economic and Social Measurement* 6: 453–6.

Cox, D.R., and D.V. Hinkley (1974). *Theoretical Statistics.* London: Chapman and Hall.

Cramér, H. (1946). *Mathematical Methods of Statistics.* Princeton: Princeton University Press.

Crowder, M.J. (1976). Maximum likelihood estimation of dependent observations. *Journal of the Royal Statistical Society, Series B* 38: 45–53.

Dagum, E.B. (1975). Seasonal factor forecasts from ARIMA models. *Bulletin of the International Statistical Institute* 46: 203–16.

Dagum, E.B., and B. Quenneville (1988). Deterministic and stochastic models for the estimation of trading-day variations. In *Bureau of the Census, Fourth Annual Research Conference*, pp. 569 – 90. Washington, D.C: US Department of Commerce.

Dahlhaus, R. (1988). Small sample effects in time series analysis: a new asymptotic theory and a new estimate. *Annals of Statistics* 16: 808–41.

Davidson, J., D.F. Hendry, F. Srba and S. Yeo (1978). Econometric modelling of the aggregate time-series relationship between consumers' expenditure and income in the United Kingdom. *Economic Journal* 88: 661–92.

de Jong, P. (1985). An asymptotically efficient estimator for variance component time series models. *Methods of Operations Research* 50: 275–86.

de Jong, P. (1987). Rational economic data revisions. *Journal of Business and Economic Statistics* 5: 539–48.

de Jong, P. (1988). The likelihood for a state space model. *Biometrika* 75: 165–9.

de Jong, P. (1989). The diffuse Kalman filter. Unpublished paper, University of British Columbia.

Dempster, A.P., N.M. Laird and D.B. Rubin (1977). Maximum likelihood from incomplete data via the EM algorithm. *Journal of the Royal Statistical Society, Series B* 39: 1–38.

Dickey, D.A., and W.A. Fuller (1979). Distribution of the estimators for autoregressive time series with a unit root. *Journal of the American Statistical Association* 74: 427–31.

Domowitz, I., and C.S. Hakkio (1985). Conditional variance and the risk premium in the foreign exchange market. *Journal of International Economics* 19: 47–66.

Duncan, D.B., and S.D. Horn (1972). Linear dynamic regression from the viewpoint of regression analysis. *Journal of the American Statistical Association* 67: 815–21.

Dunsmuir, W. (1979). A central limit theorem for parameter estimation in stationary vector time series and its applications to models for a signal observed with noise. *Annals of Statistics* 7: 490–506.

Durbin, J. (1969). Tests for serial correlation in regression analysis based on the periodogram of least-square residuals. *Biometrika* 56: 1–15.

(1975). Tests of model specification based on residuals. In J.N. Srivastava (ed.) *A Survey of Statistical Design and Linear Models*, pp. 129–43. Amsterdam: North Holland.

Durbin, J., and A.C. Harvey (1985). The effects of seat belt legislation on road casualties in Great Britain: report on assessment of statistical evidence. Annexe to *Compulsory Seat Belt Wearing Report by The Department of Transport*. London: HMSO.

Durbin, J., and M.J. Murphy (1975). Seasonal adjustment based on a mixed additive-multiplicative model. *Journal of the Royal Statistical Society, Series A* 138: 385–410.

Efron, B. (1982). Maximum likelihood and decision theory. *Annals of Statistics* 11: 95–103.

Ekern, S. (1981). Adaptive exponential smoothing revisited. *Journal of the Operational Research Society* 32: 775–82.

Engle, R.F. (1978). Estimating structural models of seasonality. In A. Zellner (ed.) *Seasonal Analysis of Economic Time Series*, pp. 281–308. Washington D.C: Bureau of the Census.

(1982a). Autoregressive conditional heteroscedasticity with estimates of the variance of UK inflation. *Econometrica* 50: 987–1007.

(1982b). A general approach to Lagrange multiplier model diagnostics. *Journal of Econometrics* 20: 83–104.

(1984). Wald, likelihood ratio and Lagrange multiplier tests in econometrics. In Z. Griliches and M.D. Intriligator (eds.) *Handbook of Econometrics*, vol. 2, pp. 775–826. Amsterdam: North Holland.

Engle, R.F., and C.W.J. Granger (1987). Co-integration and error correction: representation, estimation and testing. *Econometrica* 55: 251–76.

Engle, R.F., and M.W. Watson (1981). A one-factor multivariate time series model of

metropolitan wage rates. *Journal of the American Statistical Association* 76: 774–81.
Engle, R.F., D.F. Hendry and J.-F. Richard (1983). Exogeneity. *Econometrica* 51: 277–304.
Engle, R.F., D.M. Lilien and R.P. Robins (1987). Estimating time varying risk premia in the term structure: the ARCH-M model. *Econometrica* 55: 391–407.
Enns, P.G., J.A. Machak, W.A. Spivey and W.J. Wrobleski (1982). Forecasting applications of an adaptive multiple exponential smoothing model. *Management Science* 28: 1035–44.
Ericsson, N.R., and D.F. Hendry (1985). Conditional econometric modeling: an application to new house prices in the United Kingdom. In A.C. Atkinson and S.E. Fienberg (eds.) *A Celebration of Statistics.* New York: Springer-Verlag.
Fernández, F.J. (1986). Estimation and testing of multivariate structural time series models. Unpublished Ph.D. thesis, University of London.
Fernandez, R. (1981). A methodological note on the estimation of time series. *Review of Economics and Statistics* 63: 471–5.
Fishman, G.S. (1969). *Spectral Methods in Econometrics.* Cambridge, Mass: Harvard University Press.
Franzini, L., and A.C. Harvey (1983). Testing for deterministic trend and seasonal components in time series models. *Biometrika* 70: 673–82.
Frisch, R., and F.V. Waugh (1933). Partial time regressions as compared with individual trends. *Econometrica* 1: 387–401.
Fuller, W.A. (1976). *Introduction to Statistical Time Series.* New York: Wiley.
(1985). Nonstationary autoregressive time series. In E.J. Hannan, P.R. Krishnaiah and M.M. Rao (eds.) *Time Series in the Time Domain*, pp. 1–23. Amsterdam: North Holland.
Garbade, K. (1977). Two methods for examining the stability of regression coefficients. *Journal of the American Statistical Association* 72: 54–63.
Gardner, G., A.C. Harvey and G.D.A. Phillips (1980). An algorithm for exact maximum likelihood estimation of autoregressive-moving average models by means of Kalman filtering. *Applied Statistics* 29: 311–22.
Gersch, W., and G. Kitagawa (1983). The prediction of time series with trends and seasonalities. *Journal of Business and Economic Statistics* 1: 253–64.
Geweke J. (1977). The dynamic factor analysis of economic time series models. In D.J. Aigner and A.S. Goldberger (eds.) *Latent Variables in Socio-Economic Models.* New York: North Holland.
Geweke, J., and K. Singleton (1981). Maximum likelihood confirmatory factor analysis of economic time series. *International Economic Review* 2: 37–54.
Glass, G.V., V.L. Willson and J.M. Gottman (1975). *Design and Analysis of Time Series Experiments.* Boulder: Colorado Associated Universities Press.
Godolphin, E., and M. Stone (1980). On the structural representation for polynomial predictor models. *Journal of the Royal Statistical Society, Series B* 42: 35–45.
Gourieroux, C., A. Holly and A. Montfort (1980). Kuhn-Tucker likelihood ratio and Wald tests for nonlinear models with inequality constraints on the parameters. Discussion Paper 770, Department of Economics, Harvard University.
(1982). Likelihood ratio test, Wald test and Kuhn-Tucker test in linear models with inequality constraints on the regression parameters. *Econometrica* 50: 63–80.
Granger, C.W.J., and A.P. Andersen (1978). *An Introduction to Bilinear Time Series Models.* Grottingen: Vandenhoeck and Ruprecht.
Granger, C.W.J., and P. Newbold (1977). *Forecasting Economic Time Series.* New York: Academic Press.
Gregg, J.V., C.H. Hossell and J.T. Richardson (1964). *Mathematical Trend Curves: an Aid to Forecasting.* ICI Monograph No. 1. Edinburgh: Oliver & Boyd.

Hall, A.D., and A.R. Pagan (1981). The LIML and related estimators of an equation with moving average disturbances. *International Economic Review* 22: 719–30.

Hall, P. and C.C. Heyde (1980). *Martingale Limit Theory and Its Application.* New York: Academic Press.

Hannan, E.J. (1963). Regression for time series. In M. Rosenblatt (ed.) *Time Series Analysis,* pp. 14–37. New York: Wiley.

(1969). The identification of vector mixed autoregressive moving average systems. *Biometrika* 56, 223–5.

(1970). *Multiple time series.* New York: Wiley.

(1980). The estimation of the order of an ARMA process. *Annals of Statistics* 8: 1071–81.

Hannan, E.J. and D.F. Nicholls (1977). The estimation of the prediction error variance. *Journal of the American Statistical Association* 72: 834–40.

Hannan, E.J., R.D. Terrell and N. Tuckwell (1970). The seasonal adjustment of economic time series. *International Economic Review* 11: 24–52.

Harrison, P.J. (1967). Exponential smoothing and short-term sales forecasting. *Management Science* 13: 821–42.

Harrison, P.J., and M. Akram (1983). Generalised exponentially weighted regression and parsimonious dynamic linear modelling. In O.D. Anderson (ed.) *Time Series Analysis: Theory and Practice 3*, pp. 19–42. Amsterdam: North Holland.

Harrison, P.J., and C.F. Stevens (1971). A Bayesian approach to short-term forecasting. *Operational Research Quarterly* 22: 341–62.

(1976). Bayesian forecasting. *Journal of the Royal Statistical Society, Series B* 38: 205–47.

Harvey, A.C. (1981a). *The Econometric Analysis of Time Series.* Deddington, Oxford: Philip Allan; New York: Wiley.

(1981b). *Time Series Models.* Deddington, Oxford: Philip Allan; Atlantic Highlands, NJ: Humanities Press.

(1981c). Finite sample prediction and overdifferencing. *Journal of Time Series Analysis* 2: 221–32.

(1983). The formulation of structural time series models in discrete and continuous time. Invited paper at First Catalan International Symposium on Statistics, Barcelona, September 1983. *Questiió* 7: 563–75.

(1984). A unified view of statistical forecasting procedures [with discussion]. *Journal of Forecasting* 3: 245–83.

(1985). Trends and cycles in macroeconomic time series. *Journal of Business and Economic Statistics* 3: 216–27.

(1986). Analysis and generalization of a multivariate exponential smoothing model. *Management Science* 32: 374–80.

Harvey, A.C. and P. Collier (1977). Testing for functional misspecification in regressional analysis. *Journal of Econometrics* 6: 103–19.

Harvey, A.C., and J. Durbin (1986). The effects of seat belt legislation on British road casualties: a case study in structural time series modelling. *Journal of the Royal Statistical Society, Series A* 149: 187–227.

Harvey, A.C., and C. Fernandes (1989). Time series models for count data or qualitative observations. *Journal of Business and Economic Statistics* (to appear).

Harvey, A.C., and L.K. Hotta (1982). Specification tests for dynamic models with unobserved components. Unpublished paper, LSE.

Harvey, A.C., and C.R. McKenzie (1984). Missing observations in dynamic econometric models: a partial synthesis. In E. Parzen (ed.) *Time Series Analysis of Irregularly Observed Data*, pp. 108–33. Berlin: Springer-Verlag.

Harvey, A.C., and S. Peters (1984). Estimation procedures for structural time series models. LSE Econometrics Programme Discussion Paper A44.

Harvey, A.C., and G.D.A. Phillips (1979). The estimation of regression models with autoregressive-moving average disturbances. *Biometrika* 66: 49–58.

(1982). The estimation of regression models with time-varying parameters. In M. Deistler, E. Furst and G. Schwodiaur (eds.) *Games, Economic Dynamics and Time Series Analysis.* Würzburg and Cambridge, Mass: Physica-Verlag.

Harvey, A.C., and R.G. Pierse (1984). Estimating missing observations in economic time series. *Journal of the American Statistical Association* 79: 125–31.

Harvey, A.C., and R.D. Snyder (1989). Structural time series models in inventory control. *International Journal of Forecasting* (to appear).

Harvey, A.C., and R.C. Souza (1987). Assessing and modelling the cyclical behaviour of rainfall in north-east Brazil. *Journal of Climate and Applied Meteorology* 26: 1317–22.

Harvey, A.C. and J.H. Stock (1985). The estimation of higher order continuous time autoregressive models. *Econometric Theory* 1: 97–112.

(1986). Estimation, smoothing, interpolation and distribution for structural time series models in discrete and continuous Time. LSE/DEMEIC Econometrics Programme Discussion Paper A62.

(1988). Continuous time autoregressive models with common stochastic trends. *Journal of Economic Dynamics and Control* 12: 365–84.

Harvey, A.C., and P.H.J. Todd (1983). Forecasting economic time series with structural and Box-Jenkins models [with discussion]. *Journal of Business and Economic Statistics* 1: 299–315.

Harvey, A.C., B. Henry, S. Peters and S. Wren-Lewis (1986). Stochastic trends in dynamic regression models: an application to the employment-output equation. *Economic Journal* 96: 975–85.

Harvey, A.C., C.R. McKenzie, D. Blake and M.J. Desai (1983). Irregular data revisions. In A. Zellner (ed.) *Proceedings of the ASA-CENSUS-NBER Conference on Applied Time Series Analysis of Economic Data* pp. 329–47 Washington D.C.: Bureau of the Census.

Hatanaka, M. (1974). An efficient two-step estimator for the dynamic adjustment model with autoregressive errors. *Journal of Econometrics* 2: 199–220.

Hatanaka, M., and T.D. Wallace (1980). Multicollinearity and the estimation of low-order moments in stable lag distributions. In J. Kmenta and J.B. Ramsey (eds.) *Evaluation of Econometric Models* 323–38. New York: Academic Press.

Hausman, J.A., and M.W. Watson (1985). Errors in variables and seasonal adjustment procedures. *Journal of the American Statistical Association* 80: 541–52.

Hausman, J.A., B.H. Hall and Z. Griliches (1984). Econometric models for count data with an application to the patents–R & D relationship. *Econometrica* 52: 909–38.

Hendry, D.F., and J.-F. Richard (1983). The econometric analysis of economic time series. *International Statistical Review* 51: 111–64.

Hillmer, S.C. (1982). Forecasting time series with trading day variation. *Journal of Forecasting* 1: 385–95.

Hillmer, S.C., and G.C. Tiao (1982). An ARIMA-model-based approach to seasonal adjustment. *Journal of the American Statistical Association* 77: 63–70.

Holt, C.C. (1957). Forecasting seasonals and trends by exponentially weighted moving averages. ONR Research Memorandum 52, Carnegie Institute of Technology, Pittsburgh, Pennsylvania.

Hosking, J.R.M. (1980). The multivariate portmanteau statistic. *Journal of the American Statistical Association* 75: 602–7.

Hotta, L.K. (1983). Identification and testing of hypotheses in unobserved components models. Unpublished Ph.D. thesis, University of London.

Howrey, E.P. (1978). The use of preliminary data in econometric forecasting. *Review of Economics and Statistics* 60: 193–200.

(1984). Data revision, reconstruction, and prediction: an application to inventory investment. *Review of Economics and Statistics* 66: 386–93.

Imhof, J.P. (1961). Computing the distribution of quadratic forms in normal variables. *Biometrika* 48: 419–26.

Jacobs, R.L., and R.A. Jones (1980). Price expectations in the United States, 1947–75. *American Economic Review* 70: 267–77.

Jarque, C.M., and A.K. Bera (1980). Efficient tests for normality, homoscedasticity and serial independence of regression residuals. *Economics Letters* 6: 255–9.

Jazwinski, A.H. (1970). *Stochastic Processes and Filtering Theory*. New York: Academic Press.

Jeffreys, H. (1961). *The Theory of Probability*. Oxford: Oxford University Press.

Jenkins, G.M. (1982). Some practical aspects of forecasting in organisations. *Journal of Forecasting* 1:3–21.

Johnston, F.R., and P.J. Harrison (1986). The variance of lead time demand. *Journal of the Operational Research Society* 37: 303–8.

Jones, R.H. (1966). Exponential smoothing for multivariate time series. *Journal of the Royal Statistical Society, Series B* 28: 241–51.

(1976). Estimation of the innovation generalized variance of a multivariate stationary time series. *Journal of the American Statistical Association* 71: 386–8.

(1980). Maximum likelihood fitting of ARIMA models to time series with missing observations. *Technometrics* 22: 389–95.

(1981). Fitting a continuous time autoregression to discrete data. In D.F. Findley (ed.) *Applied Time Series Analysis II*, pp. 651–82. New York: Academic Press.

(1984). Fitting multivariate models to unequally spaced data. In E. Parzen (ed.) *Time Series Analysis of Irregular Observations*, pp. 158–88. New York: Springer-Verlag.

Jorgenson, D.W. (1966). Rational distributed lag functions. *Econometrica* 34: 135–49.

Kalbfleisch, J.D. and D.A. Sprott (1970). Application of likelihood methods to models involving large numbers of parameters [with discussion]. *Journal of the Royal Statistical Society, Series B* 32: 175–208.

Kalman, R.E. (1960). A new approach to linear filtering and prediction problems. *Journal of Basic Engineering, Transactions ASME. Series D* 82: 35–45.

Kalman, R.E., and R.S. Bucy (1961). New results in linear filtering and prediction theory, *Journal of Basic Engineering, Transactions ASME, Series D* 83: 95–108.

Kane, R.P. and N.B. Trivedi (1986). Are droughts predictable? *Climate Change* 8: 208–23.

Kendall, M.G. (1973). *Time Series*. London: Charles Griffin & Co.

King, M.L. (1981). The Durbin-Watson test for serial correlation: bounds for regressions with trend and/or seasonal dummy variables. *Econometrica* 49: 1571–81.

King, M.L. (1983). Testing for autoregressive against moving average errors in the linear regression model. *Journal of Econometrics* 21: 35–51.

(1985). A point optimal test for moving average regression disturbances. *Econometric Theory* 1: 211–22.

(1986). Towards a theory of point optimal tests. Mimeo, Monash University.

King, M.L., and M.A. Evans (1986). Locally optimal properties of the Durbin-Watson test. Unpublished paper, Monash University.

King, M.L., and G.H. Hillier (1985). Locally best invariant tests of the error covariance matrix in the linear regression model. *Journal of the Royal Statistical Society, Series B* 47: 98–102.

Kitagawa, G. (1981). A nonstationary time series model and its fitting by a recursive filter. *Journal of Time Series Analysis* 2: 103–16.

(1984). State space modelling of nonstationary time series and smoothing of unequally spaced data. In E. Parzen (ed.) *Time Series Analysis of Irregularly Observed Data*, pp. 189–210. New York: Springer-Verlag.

(1987). Non-Gaussian state space modeling of nonstationary time series [with discussion]. *Journal of the American Statistical Association* 82: 1032–63.

Kitagawa, G., and W. Gersch (1984). A smoothness priors-state space modeling of time series with trend and seasonality. *Journal of the American Statistical Association* 79: 378–89.

Kiviet, J.F. (1986). On the rigour of some misspecification tests for modelling dynamic relationships. *Review of Economic Studies* 53: 241–61.

Koenker, R. (1981). A note on Studentising a test for heteroscedasticity. *Journal of Econometrics* 17: 107–11.

Kohn, R. and C.F. Ansley (1983). Fixed interval estimation in state space models when some of the data are missing or aggregated. *Biometrika* 70: 683–8.

(1985). Efficient estimation and prediction in time series regression models. *Biometrika* 72: 694–7.

(1986). Estimation, prediction and interpolation for ARIMA models with missing data. *Journal of the American Statistical Association* 81: 751–61.

(1989). A fast algorithm for signal extraction, influence and cross-validation in state space models. *Biometrika* 76: 65–79.

La Motte, L.R., and A. McWhorter (1978). An exact test for the presence of random walk coefficients in a linear regression model. *Journal of the American Statistical Association* 73: 816–20.

Lehmann, E.L.(1959). *Testing Statistical Hypotheses.* New York: Wiley.

(1983). *Theory of Point Estimation.* New York: Wiley.

Levenbach, H., and B.E. Reuter (1976). Forecasting trending time series with relative growth rate models. *Technometrics* 18: 261–72.

Li, W.K. and A.I. McLeod (1981). Distribution of the residual autocorrelations in multivariate ARMA time series models. *Journal of the Royal Statistical Society, Series B*, 43: 231–39.

Liptser, R.S., and A.N. Shiryayev (1978). *Statistics of Random Processes II: Applications* (trans. A.B. Aries). New York: Springer-Verlag.

Litterman, R.B. (1983). A random walk Markov model for the distribution of time series. *Journal of Business and Economic Statistics* 1: 169–73.

Liu, L.M. (1980). Analysis of time series with calendar effects. *Management Science* 26: 106.

Ljung, G.M., and G.E.P. Box (1978). On a measure of lack of fit in time series models. *Biometrika* 66: 67–72.

Ljung, L., and P.E. Caines (1979). Asymptotic normality and prediction error estimators for approximate system models. *Stochastics* 3: 29–46.

Ljung, L., and T. Söderstrom (1983). *Theory and Practice of Recursive Identification.* Cambridge, Mass: MIT Press.

Lomnicki, Z.A. (1961). Tests for departure from normality in the case of linear stochastic processes. *Metrika* 4: 37–62.

Magnus, J.R., and H. Neudecker (1980). The elimination matrix: some lemmas and applications. *Journal on Algebraic and Discrete Methods* (Society for Industrial and Applied Mathematics) 1: 422–49.

Makridakis, S., A. Andersen, R. Carbone, R. Fildes, M. Hibon, R. Lewandowski, J. Newton, E. Parzen and R. Winkler (1982). The accuracy of extrapolation (time series) methods: results of a forecasting competition. *Journal of Forecasting* 1: 111–53.

Maravall, A. (1983). An application of nonlinear time series forecasting. *Journal of Business and Economic Statistics* 1: 66–74.

(1985). On structural time series models and the characterization of components. *Journal of Business and Economic Statistics* 3: 350–5.

Markham, C.G. (1974). Apparent periodicities in rainfall at Fortaleza, Ceará, Brazil. *Journal of Applied Meteorology* 13: 176–9.

Mar-Molinero, C. (1980). Tractors in Spain: a logistic analysis. *Journal of the Operational Research Society* 31: 141–52.
Martin, R.D., and V.J. Yohai (1985). Robustness in time series and estimating ARMA models. In E.J. Hannan, P.R. Krishnaiah and M.M. Rao (eds.) *Handbook of Statistics*, vol. 5, pp. 119–56. Amsterdam: North Holland.
Martin, R.D., A. Samarov and W. Vandaele (1983). Robust methods for ARIMA models. In A. Zellner (ed.) *Proceedings of the ASA-CENSUS-NBER Conference on Applied Time Series Analysis of Economic Data*, pp. 153–77. Washington, D.C: Bureau of the Census.
McCleary, R., and R.A. Hay, Jr (1980). *Applied Time Series Analysis for the Social Sciences.* Beverly Hills, Calif: Sage Publications.
McCullagh, P., and J.A. Nelder (1983). *Generalised Linear Models.* London: Chapman and Hall.
McKenzie, E. (1976). A comparison of some standard forecasting systems. *The Statistician* 25: 3–14.
McLeod, A.I. (1978). On the distribution of residual autocorrelations in Box-Jenkins models. *Journal of the Royal Statistical Society, Series B* 40: 296–302.
McLeod, A.I., and W.K. Li (1983). Diagnostic checking ARMA time series models using squared-residual autocorrelations. *Journal of Time Series Analysis* 4: 269–73.
Mizon, G.E. (1984). The encompassing approach in econometrics. In D.F. Hendry and K.F. Wallis (eds.) *Econometrics and Quantitative Economics*, pp. 135–72. Oxford: Blackwell.
Mizon, G.E., and J.-F. Richard (1986). The encompassing principle and its application to testing non-nested hypotheses. *Econometrica* 54: 657–78.
Moler, C., and C. van Loan (1978). Nineteen dubious ways to compute the exponential of a matrix. *SIAM Review* 20: 801–36.
Montgomery, D.C. and L.A. Johnson (1976). *Forecasting and Time Series Analysis.* New York: McGraw-Hill.
Morettin, P.A., A.R. Mesquita and J.G.C. Rocha (1985). Rainfall at Fortaleza in Brazil revisited. In O.D. Anderson, E.A. Robinson and K. Ord (eds.) *Time Series Analysis: Theory and Practice 6.* Amsterdam: North Holland.
Muth, J.F. (1960). Optimal properties of exponentially weighted forecasts. *Journal of the American Statistical Association* 55: 299–305.
Nabeya, S., and K. Tanaka (1988). Asymptotic theory of a test for the constancy of regression coefficients against the random walk alternative. *Annals of Statistics* 16: 218–35.
Nelson, C.R. (1976). Gains in efficiency from joint estimation of systems of autoregressive-moving average processes. *Journal of Econometrics* 4: 331–48.
Nelson, C.R., and H. Kang (1981). Spurious periodicity in inappropriately detrended series. *Econometrica* 49: 741–51.
(1984). Pitfalls in the use of time as an explanatory variable. *Journal of Business and Economic Statistics* 2: 73–82.
Nelson, C.R., and C.I. Plosser (1982). Trends and random walks in macroeconomic time series: some evidence and implications. *Journal of Monetary Economics* 10: 139–62.
Nerlove, M. and S. Wage (1964). On the optimality of adaptive forecasting. *Management Science* 10, 207–29.
Nerlove, M., D.M. Grether and J.L. Carvalho (1979). *Analysis of Economic Time Series.* New York: Academic Press.
Nicholls, D.F. (1976). The efficient estimation of vector linear time series models. *Biometrika* 63: 381–90.

Nicholls, D.F., and A.R. Pagan (1985). Varying coefficient regression. In E.J. Hannan, P.R. Krishnaiah and M.M. Rao (eds.) *Handbook of Statistics*, vol. 5, pp. 413–50. Amsterdam: North Holland.

Nickell, S. (1984). An investigation of the determinants of manufacturing employment in the United Kingdom. *Review of Economic Studies* 51: 529–59.

Nijman, T.E. (1985). *Missing Observations in Dynamic Macroeconomic Models*. Amsterdam: Free University Press.

Nyblom, J. (1986). Testing for deterministic linear trend in time series. *Journal of the American Statistical Association* 81: 545–9.

Pagan, A. (1980). Some identification and estimation results for regression models with stochastically varying parameters. *Journal of Econometrics* 13: 341–63.

Pagan, A.R., and A. Ullak (1986). The econometric analysis of models with risk terms. Discussion paper, Centre for Economic Policy Research (London).

Parzen, E. (1982). ARARMA models for time series analysis and forecasting. *Journal of Forecasting* 1: 67–82.

Pemberton, J., and H. Tong (1983). Threshold autoregression and some frequency domain characteristics. In D.R. Brillinger and P.R. Krishnaiah (eds.) *Handbook of Statistics*, vol. 3, pp. 249–73. Amsterdam: North Holland.

Phadke, M.S., and S.M. Wu (1974). Modelling of continuous stochastic processes from discrete observations with application to sunspots data. *Journal of the American Statistical Association* 69: 325–9.

Phillips, A.W.H. (1959). The estimation of parameters in systems of stochastic differential equations. *Biometrika* 46: 67–76.

Phillips, P.C.B. (1986). Understanding spurious regressions in econometrics. *Journal of Econometrics* 33: 311–40.

(1987). Time series regression with a unit root. *Econometrica* 55: 277–302.

Phillips, P.C.B., and S.N. Durlauf (1986). Multiple time series regression with integrated processes. *Review of Economic Studies* 53: 473–95.

Pierce, D.A. (1971). Least squares estimation in the regression model with autoregressive-moving average errors. *Biometrika* 58: 299–312.

(1977). Relationships – and the lack thereof – between economic time series, with special reference to money and interest rates. *Journal of the American Statistical Association* 72: 11–22.

(1978). Seasonal adjustment when both deterministic and stochastic seasonality are present. In A. Zellner (ed.) *Seasonal Analysis of Economic Time Series*, pp. 242–69. Washington, D.C: Bureau of the Census.

(1979). Signal extraction error in nonstationary time series. *Annals of Statistics* 7: 1303–20.

Pierce, D.A., M.R. Grupe and W.P. Cleveland (1984). Seasonal adjustment of the weekly monetary aggregate: a model-based approach. *Journal of Business and Economic Statistics* 2: 260–70.

Plosser, C.I. and G.W. Schwert (1977). Estimation of a non-invertible moving average process: the case of overdifferencing. *Journal of Econometrics* 6: 199–224.

Poskitt, D.S., and A.R. Tremayne (1981). A time series application of Monte Carlo methods to compare statistical tests. *Journal of Time Series Analysis* 2: 263–77.

Priestley, M.B. (1980). State-dependent models: a general approach to non-linear time series analysis. *Journal of Time Series Analysis* 1: 47–71.

(1981). *Spectral Analysis and Time Series*. London: Academic Press.

Prothero, D.L., and K.F. Wallis (1976). Modelling macroeconomic time series [with discussion]. *Journal of the Royal Statistical Society, Series A* 139: 468–500.

Pukkila, T. (1977). Fitting of autoregressive moving average models in the frequency domain. Report A-6, Department of Mathematical Sciences, University of Tampere, Finland.

(1979). The bias in periodogram ordinates and the estimation of ARMA models in the frequency domain. *Australian Journal of Statistics* 21: 121–8.

Reed, D. (1978). Whistlestop: a community alternative for crime prevention. Unpublished Ph.D. dissertation, Department of Sociology, Northwestern University.

Road Accidents in Great Britain 1984 (1985). London: Her Majesty's Stationery Office.

Robinson, P.M. (1980). The efficient estimation of a rational spectral density. In M. Kunt and F. de Coulon (eds.) *Signal Processing: Theories and Applications*, pp. 701–4. Amsterdam: North Holland.

(1985). Testing for serial correlation in regression with missing observations. *Journal of the Royal Statistical Society, Series B* 47: 429–37.

Rogers, A.J. (1986). Modified Lagrange multiplier tests for problems with one-sided alternatives. *Journal of Econometrics* 31: 341–61.

Rosenberg, B. (1973). Random coefficient models: the analysis of a cross-section of time series by stochastically convergent parameter regression. *Annals of Economic and Social Measurement* 2: 399–428.

Sargan, J.D. (1980). The consumer price equation in the post-war British economy: an exercise in equation specification analysis. *Review of Economic Studies* 47: 113–135.

Sargan, J.D., and A. Bhargava (1983). Maximum likelihood estimation of regression models with first order moving average errors when the root lies on the unit circle. *Econometrica* 51: 799–820.

Sargan, J.D., and E.G. Drettakis (1974). Missing data in an autoregressive model. *International Economic Review* 15: 39–58.

Schaefer, S., R. Brealey, S. Hodges and H. Thomas (1975). Alternative models of systematic risk. In E. Elton and M. Gruber (eds.) *International Capital Markets: An Inter and Intra Country Analysis*, pp. 150–61. Amsterdam: North Holland.

Schweppe, F. (1965). Evaluation of likelihood functions for Gaussian signals. *IEEE Transactions on Information Theory* 11: 61–70.

Schwert, G.W. (1987). Effects of model specification on tests for unit roots in macroeconomic data. *Journal of Monetary Economics* 20: 73–104.

Shephard, N.G., and A.C. Harvey (1989). On the probability of estimating a deterministic component in the local level model. Unpublished paper, LSE.

Shiskin, J., A.H. Young and J.C. Musgrave (1967). The X-11 variant of the census method II seasonal adjustment program. Technical Paper 15, Bureau of the Census, Washington D.C.

Silvey, S.D. (1970). *Statistical Inference*. London: Chapman and Hall.

Sims, C.A. (1980). Macroeconomics and reality. *Econometrica* 48: 1–48.

(1981). An autoregressive index model for the US, 1948–1975. In J. Kmenta and J.B. Ramsey (eds.) *Large Scale Macro-Econometric Models*, pp. 283–327. Amsterdam: North Holland.

(1982). Policy analysis with econometric models. *Brookings Papers on Economic Activity* 11: 107–64.

(1985). Comment on 'Issues involved with the seasonal adjustment of economic time series' by William R. Bell and Steven C. Hillmer. *Journal of Business and Economic Statistics* 3: 92–4.

Sims, C.A., J.H. Stock and M.W. Watson (1987). Inference in linear time series models with some unit roots. Working Paper in Economics E-87-1, Hoover Institution, Stanford University.

Smith, J.Q. (1979). A generalization of the Bayesian steady forecasting model. *Journal of the Royal Statistical Society, Series B* 41: 375–87.

(1981). The multiparameter steady model. *Journal of the Royal Statistical Society, Series B* 43: 256–60.

Smith, R.L., and J.E. Miller (1986). A non-Gaussian state space model and application to prediction of records. *Journal of the Royal Statistical Society, Series B* 48: 79–88.

Sneek, J.M. (1984). *Modelling Procedures for Economic Time Series.* Amsterdam: Free University Press.

Snyder, R.D. (1984). Inventory control with the gamma probability distribution. *European Journal of Operational Research* 17: 373–81.

Stock, J.H. (1987). Asymptotic properties of least squares estimators of co-integrating vectors. *Econometrica* 55: 1035–56.

Stock, J.H., and M.W. Watson (1988). Testing for common trends. *Journal of the American Statistical Association* 83: 1097–1107.

Stram, D.O., and W.W.S. Wei (1986). Temporal aggregation in the ARIMA process. *Journal of Time Series Analysis* 7: 279–92.

Tanaka, K. (1983). Non-normality of the Lagrange multiplier statistic for testing the constancy of regression coefficients. *Econometrica* 51: 1577–82.

Theil, H. (1961). *Economic Forecasts and Policy*, 2nd edn. Amsterdam: North Holland.

(1966). *Applied Economic Forecasting.* Amsterdam: North Holland.

Theil, H., and S. Wage (1964). Some observations on adaptive forecasting. *Management Science* 10: 198–206.

Thompson, H.E., and G.C. Tiao (1971). Analysis of telephone data: a case of forecasting seasonal time series. *The Bell System Journal of Economics and Management Science* 2: 515–41.

Tiao, G.C. (1972). Asymptotic behaviour of temporal aggregates of time series. *Biometrika* 59: 525–31.

Tiao, G.C., and S.C. Hillmer (1978). Some consideration of decomposition of a time series. *Biometrika* 65: 497–502.

Tong, H., and K.S. Lim (1980). Threshold autoregression, limit cycles and cyclical data. *Journal of the Royal Statistical Society, Series B* 42: 245–92.

Trigg, J.W., and A.G. Leach (1967). Exponential smoothing with an adaptive response rate. *Operational Research Quarterly* 18: 53–9.

van Loan, C.F. (1978). Computing integrals involving the matrix exponential. *IEEE Transactions on Automatic Control* AC-23: 395–404.

Varian, H.R. (1975). A Bayesian approach to real estate assessment. In S.E. Fienberg and A. Zellner (eds.) *Studies in Bayesian Econometrics and Statistics*, pp. 195–208. Amsterdam: North Holland.

Velu, R.P., G.C. Reinsel and D.W. Wichern (1986). Reduced rank models for multiple time series. *Biometrika* 73: 105–18.

Walker, A.M. (1964). Asymptotic properties of least squares estimates of the spectrum of a stationary non-deterministic time series. *Journal of the Australian Mathematical Society* 4: 363–84.

Wallis, K.F. (1987). Time series analysis of bounded economic variables. *Journal of Time Series Analysis* 8: 115–23.

Watson, M.W., and R.F. Engle (1983). Alternative algorithms for the estimation of dynamic factor, MIMIC and varying coefficient regression. *Journal of Econometrics* 23: 385–400.

Wecker, W.E., and C.F. Ansley (1983). The signal extraction approach to nonlinear regression and spline smoothing. *Journal of the American Statistical Association* 78: 81–9.

Weiss, A.A. (1985). The stability of the AR(1) process with an AR(1) coefficient. *Journal of Time Series Analysis* 6: 181–6.

West, M., and P.J. Harrison (1986). Monitoring and adaptation in Bayesian forecasting

models. *Journal of the American Statistical Association* 81: 741–50.
West M., P.J. Harrison and H.S. Migon (1985). Dynamic generalized linear models and Bayesian forecasting [with discussion]. *Journal of the American Statistical Association* 80: 73–97.
White, H. (1980). A heteroskedasticity-consistent covariance matrix estimator and a direct test for heteroskedasticity. *Econometrica* 48: 817–38.
(1982). Maximum likelihood estimation of misspecified models. *Econometrica* 50: 1–25.
(1984). *Asymptotic Theory for Econometricians.* Orlando, Fla: Academic Press.
Whittaker, E.T. (1923). On a new method of graduation. *Proceedings of the Edinburgh Mathematical Society* 41: 63–75.
Whittle, P. (1983). *Prediction and Regulation*, 2nd edn (revised). Oxford: Blackwell.
Wickens, M.R. (1969). The consistency and efficiency of generalized least squares in simultaneous equation systems with autocorrelated errors. *Econometrica* 37: 651–9.
Wilde, G.J.S. (1982). The theory of risk homeostasis: implications for safety and health. *Risk Analysis* 2: 209–25.
Winters, P.R. (1960). Forecasting sales by exponentially weighted moving averages. *Management Science* 6: 324–42.
Wold, H.O.A. (1938). *A Study in the Analysis of Stationary Time Series.* Uppsala: Almquist and Wiksell.
Working, H. (1960). Note on the correlations of first differences of a random chain. *Econometrica* 28: 916–18.
Wren-Lewis, S. (1984). The roles of output expectations and liquidity in explaining recent productivity movements. *National Institute Economic Review* 108.
Wu, C.F.J. (1983). On the convergence of the EM algorithm. *Annals of Statistics* 11: 95–103.
Young, P. (1984). *Recursive Estimation and Time-Series Analysis.* Berlin: Springer-Verlag.
(1985). Recursive indentification, estimation and control. In E.J. Hannan, P.R. Krishnaiah and M.M. Rao (eds.) *Time Series in the Time Domain*, pp. 213–55. Amsterdam: North Holland.
Zellner, A. (1963). Estimation for seemingly unrelated regression equations: some exact finite sample results. *Journal of the American Statistical Association* 58: 977–92.
(1986). Bayesian estimation and prediction using asymmetric loss functions. *Journal of the American Statistical Association* 81: 446–51.

Author index

Subject index